Bibliography of

BRITISH GARDENS

Catalogus plantarum . . . quae in hortis haud procul a Londino sitis . . . A catalogue of trees, shrubs, plants, and flowers . . . which are propagated for sale, in the gardens near London . . . By a Society of Gardeners, (London, 1730). Frontispiece etched by Henry Fletcher. An imaginary garden laid out on a formal plan fashionable in English gardens at the beginning of the eighteenth century.

Bibliography of
BRITISH GARDENS

Ray Desmond

St. Paul's Bibliographies

© 1988 Ray Desmond

All rights reserved. No part of this publication may be reproduced, stored in a retrieval system, or transmitted, in any form or by any means, electronic, mechanical, photocopying, recording or otherwise, without prior permission of St Paul's Bibliographies.

First published in 1984 by
St Paul's Bibliographies
West End House, 1 Step Terrace,
Winchester, Hampshire, SO22 5BW
Reprinted with corrections in 1988

British Library Cataloguing in publication data

Desmond, Ray
    Bibliography of British gardens.
    1. Gardens——Great Britain——Bibliography
    I. Title
    016.712′6′0941   Z5996.A1

ISBN 0-906795-15-X

Typeset by
Gem Publishing Company (Oxon) Ltd
Brightwell, Oxon

Printed in Great Britain by
Henry Ling Ltd, The Dorset Press,
Dorchester, Dorset.

Contents

Preface	vii
Introduction	1
Abbreviations	15
Bibliography of works consulted	17
Plates	39
Catalogue of gardens	41
County index	
England	283
Scotland	305
Wales	308
Channel Islands	309
Isle of Man	309
Ulster	309
Eire	309
Appendix	
Wedgwood dinner service	313

Preface

Gardening in Britain, as a subject of serious interest, has a history extending back for many centuries, but concern for the history of gardens hardly spans two: it was not until the time of John Claudius Loudon (1783–1843) that the development of horticulture as a study became self-conscious and articulate. Loudon himself pioneered the subject in his remarkable work of 1822, *An encyclopaedia of gardening*. The topographical survey of the gardens and country-residences of the British Isles which Loudon then compiled was the earliest body of information on what had already been achieved in gardening in these islands. Interspersed among the brief accounts of the chief gardens and grounds, county by county, is a great deal of strictly historical fact about individual properties. Nor did Loudon stand alone: at the same time Henry Phillips (1779–1840) was bringing out his *History of cultivated vegetables*, to be followed in the next year by *Sylva florifera* on ornamental trees and shrubs and their individual histories, and in 1824 by *Flora historica*, performing the same service for herbaceous and bulbous plants. Only five years afterwards George William Johnson (1802–1886) published the first *History of English gardening*.

The beginnings of a historical approach can be detected in the early volumes of the *Botanical Magazine*, published from 1787 by William Curtis (1746–1799), whose study of the early herbals and other sources ran parallel to that carried out by William Aiton (1731–1793) in his *Hortus Kewensis* of 1789, where dates of introduction were, as far as possible, given throughout, with the names of the persons to whom each introduction was due. In the twelfth volume of *Archaeologia* (1796) the Society of Antiquaries of London printed an account of the gardens and nurseries of London dating from 1691, and first-hand reminiscences of London horticulture of the eighteenth century, set down in old age by Peter Collinson (1694–1768), formed the subject of an article in the *Transactions of the Linnean Society* (vol. 10, 1811). History and biography were among the subjects covered by Loudon's pioneer *Gardener's Magazine* from the start in 1826, and were to take on major importance in the *Gardeners' Chronicle* from its foundation in 1841.

Detailed descriptions of individual gardens, which had long been included in manuscript journals of travel and in printed works on regional and local topography, appeared in ever-increasing numbers in the many periodicals devoted to gardening and its various aspects. Generally such descriptions had at least some historical content, but all of them were in themselves items of contemporary history of vital importance for future study. All through the long reign of Victoria, and on until 1914, gardens and gardening played an impressive role in British social history. At the time this was hardly realized, and it was not until 1965 that a body of enthusiasts founded the Garden History Society. In less than twenty years, mainly through the efforts of members of the Society, appreciation of historical horticulture has become general and has already yielded a rich harvest of serious studies, both amateur and academic.

The subject is not a simple one: the history of gardens crosses the boundary between the two worlds of science and art. On the one hand, garden design and landscape architecture are a part of the creative and graphic arts; yet on the other they interpenetrate the science of

Preface

botany, not merely at a superficial level, but are even profoundly affected by advancing knowledge of chromosome structure and consequent hybridizations. Strictly documentary history based on written and printed records goes hand in hand with archaeology, and this makes extensive use of aerial survey and of excavation. Lost sites of gardens, dating from the Roman period to the nineteenth century, are brought to light, and add to the immense number of British gardens worthy of serious historical study. In less than two hundred years the printed literature devoted to the significant gardens of the British Isles has burgeoned into a forest of many thousands of single items, from short notes to lengthy books. The information available, to change the metaphor, is now a mighty ocean; but it has hitherto remained uncharted.

In the present work Ray Desmond for the first time provides the garden historians of Britain with chart, compass and sailing directions. The fruit of many years of patient and very highly skilled study, it comprises many references, which are arranged topographically. The same meticulous attention to detail and the same flair for discovery which the author showed in his great *Dictionary of British and Irish botanists and horticulturists* (1977), can here be appreciated to the full. To the discerning eye of the serious research-worker, the list of works consulted will speak eloquently for itself. In the gigantic field of the printed word, little can remain for the gleaners after this bumper harvest.

A word may perhaps be added on the complementary study of unpublished archives. Few students of the history of gardens will be content to limit themselves to what has already appeared in print, and inevitably they will be drawn to original sources. Their entry into that world is here eased by the inclusion of entries of horticultural significance from the five volumes of *Architectural history* . . . issued by the National Register of Archives as an index to listed records; and also from the *Catalogue of drawings* . . . of the Royal Institute of British Architects. The next step may be to consult Professor Maurice Barley's *A Guide to British topographical collections*, issued in 1974 by the Council for British Archaeology; and after that to peruse the annual lists issued by H.M. Stationery Office of *Accessions to Repositories*, leading on to the search rooms of the National Register of Archives and of county and local record offices and libraries. Another generation will reap the harvest; but that the field has been reclaimed from the waste—the wilderness of unindexed matter—is due to the arduous and sustained efforts of the author of this remarkable book.

JOHN HARVEY

Introduction

As former Chief Librarian at the Royal Botanic Gardens, Kew and also as Honorary Librarian of the Garden History Society I have always been aware of the need for a guide to the literature on British gardens. Apart from obvious literary sources, it is often difficult and certainly time-consuming to unearth descriptions of individual gardens.

Since the last war there has been a remarkable burgeoning of interest in the evolution of garden design and a greater appreciation of its contribution to our cultural history. We have seen the formation of the Garden History Society in 1965, the creation of the National Council for the Conservation of Plants and Gardens in 1978, the highly successful exhibition celebrating one thousand years of British gardening staged at the Victoria and Albert Museum in 1979, the founding of the *Journal of Garden History* in 1981, the establishment of the Centre for the Conservation of Historic Parks and Gardens at the University of York in 1982, followed in 1983 by the National Heritage Act which provides for the compilation by the newly created Historic Buildings & Monuments Commission for England of an official register of historic gardens, the formation in some counties of very active trusts for the conservation of local gardens and, not least, the truly impressive number of people who visit gardens open to the public.

SCOPE

This *Bibliography of British gardens* does not claim to be comprehensive but it includes at least some of the principal references in horticultural literature, county histories, topographical works, diaries and letters. Inevitably the restricted size of the book and the personal limitations of time have influenced its scope. However if it proves to be a useful work there is no reason why a supplement should not take care of omissions and additional material.

The nucleus of the bibliography was formed as a by-product of my scanning of horticultural periodicals for the *Dictionary of British and Irish botanists and horticulturists* (1977). These references, recorded on cards, amounting to several thousand entries, set the pattern for all the subsequent references. I now regret that the presence of garden plans in some of the references is not indicated, and I also realise that the occasional annotation would have been useful, but it has not been possible to re-check all the references I had already accumulated for my *Dictionary*.

Just over 5,500 gardens in England, Scotland, Wales and, to a limited extent, in Ireland are listed. The *Bibliography* has a dual role: as a guide for the general reader who seeks some references on modern as well as historic gardens in popular and easily accessible books; and as an introduction to the literature on British gardens for the serious student and research worker. As many of the references describe the house as well as the garden, the *Bibliography* may also have some value for the architectural historian.

It was not possible to formulate absolute rules regarding the type of reference to be included. Many references by virtue of their length have automatically been noted; very short descriptions of gardens have been recorded only when they contained a vital piece of

Introduction

information such as the identity of the designer of a garden or a particularly succinct contemporary comment. No attempt has been made, for instance, to index all the fleeting references to gardens in Daniel Lysons's *Environs of London*. Richard Warner during the course of his energetic perambulations commented on many of the gardens he visited but many of his observations, in my opinion, lack sufficient substance to merit inclusion. Engravings, lithographs and photographs of gardens in books have been noted and also plates of country houses where some aspect of the garden is incorporated in the view.

There are a few references to cemeteries but no attempt has been made to collect them in a systematic way.

The 'List of works consulted' could have been greatly enlarged if all those books which yielded no references had been included. T. Cromwell's accounts of his excursions in Essex (1818–19), Kent (1820), Suffolk (1818–19), Surrey (1821) and Sussex (1822) are just one instance of this often fruitless search.

Unfortunately there was never time to locate and consult all editions of any one work to ascertain whether they varied in the information they provided on specific gardens. For example, there are some variations in the plans of gardens in the five editions of Thomas Mawson's *Art and craft of garden making* but only the third edition (1907) has been checked for this *Bibliography*.

Core journals such as *Cottage Gardener*, *Country Life*, *Garden History*, *Gardeners' Chronicle*, *Gardener's Magazine* and *Journal of Garden History* have been carefully scanned.

Gardens are frequently mentioned in county and regional histories, even those which are devoted primarily to antiquarian, architectural and genealogical matters. John Leland, who became the King's Antiquary in 1533, was one of the first to record his observations of the English countryside. County and town histories were a feature of eighteenth century publishing and in the nineteenth century most counties could boast a local historical or antiquarian society. The extension of the railway network which eased the difficulties of travel produced a rash of regional guidebooks which although they usually say something about well-known gardens have not been examined for this *Bibliography*. The early volumes of the Victoria County Histories seldom mention any gardens. The same lack of interest applies to the earliest of Pevsner's Buildings of England series; this deficiency was put right in the revised editions and later volumes.

General garden histories such as those by Lady Amherst and Eleanour Rohde include some useful contemporary descriptions of gardens. A popular work such as *The English garden* by L. Fleming and A. Gore is worth consulting for its good reproductions of pictures of gardens. David Jacques's *Georgian gardens* (1983) features quite a few contemporary plans of the gardens it discusses. Standard texts such as C. Hussey's *English gardens and landscapes, 1700–1750* (1967) and Sir Roy Strong's *The Renaissance garden in England* (1979) have been checked and indexed.

Gardens mentioned in monographic works on individual garden designers have also been indexed. Among them are G. Beard on Thomas H. Mawson, Jane Brown on Gertrude Jekyll, David Green on Henry Wise, John Harris on Sir William Chambers, Dorothy Stroud on Capability Brown and Humphry Repton, Laurence Whistler on Vanbrugh and Peter Willis on Charles Bridgeman.

ARRANGEMENT

The gardens are arranged alphabetically by their names or by locations if they have no distinctive names. Municipal parks and botanic gardens are listed under the towns in which they are located. Within each entry for a garden the references are arranged chronologically by date of publication. Titles of books and periodicals are abbreviated but given in full in the 'Bibliography of works consulted'. The names of gardens are classified under counties in the 'County Index' for the convenience of those readers who wish to survey them on a regional basis.

It is sometimes incredibly difficult to establish without much research the correct name of a country house. Abbey, Castle, Court, Hall, House, Lodge, Manor, Park, Place, Privy, etc. were often used with a wilful inconsistency. With the change of owner a 'Hall' could become a 'Park' and writers could also be careless in their use of these names, even getting the counties wrong as well. Occasionally one encounters two houses with the same name in the same county. To add to the confusion some writers perversely refer to a country house solely by the name of the place or the name of the owner. An estate could be known by different names: White Lodge in Richmond Park was also called Stone Lodge and New Lodge; just a few miles away stood Ormonde Lodge which became Richmond Lodge when the Prince of Wales acquired it in the eighteenth century but shortly afterwards it was generally referred to as Richmond Gardens. Variations and idiosyncracies in spelling add to the difficulty of correct identification: Broadgate (Bradgate), Clearwell (Clower Wall), Durhams (Derehams), Gobions (Gubbins), Hylands (Highlands), Hill (Hull), Risden (Rushden). All these nomenclatural problems prompt the caveat that it is conceivable that occasionally a particular garden may have been recorded in this *Bibliography* under different entries. My apologies if that has happened. John Harris's *A country house index* (1971) which lists the names of some two hundred houses has been a useful guide. *The survey gazetteer of the British Isles* Edition 9 (c. 1955) has proved invaluable in identifying and standardizing the spelling of a great many houses. Oliver Mason's *Bartholomew gazetteer of Britain* (1977) has been consulted for the changes in the county boundaries caused by the local government re-organisation in 1974–75. The nearest town cited in the heading for an entry is not necessarily in the same county as the garden; e.g. Bishop's Stortford in Hertfordshire is given as the nearest town to Down Hall just over the border in Essex.

ILLUSTRATIONS OF GARDENS

Engravings, lithographs and photographs which feature the garden, suggest its character or just give a glimpse of it around the house have been included. Unfortunately it has not been possible to add separate prints of gardens. The iconography of British gardens embracing oil paintings, watercolours, sketches, prints and old photographs would require extensive research, and deserves to be the theme of a separate project.

Works such as Knyff and Kip's *Britannia illustrata*, illustrated county and regional histories published mainly during the eighteenth and nineteenth centuries, and other obvious sources for garden views have been scanned. Reproductions of Kip's celebrated views in modern publications have also been noted since some readers may have difficulty in getting access to the original folios. For that reason M.E. Macartney's *English houses & gardens in the 17th and 18th centuries. A series of bird's eye views reproduced from contemporary engravings by Kip, Badeslade, Harris and others* (1908) is recommended as a substitute which it should be reasonably easy to borrow through one's college, society or public library. Excellent photographs of many of our gardens will be found in the pages of *Country Life*. Charles Holmes's three volumes on the *Gardens of England* (1907–11) is principally a

Introduction

photographic record. Gertrude Jekyll's *Garden ornament* (1918) is yet another example of a whole range of books whose value lies chiefly in their illustrations.

Windsor Castle, drawn in 1659 by Wenceslaus Hollar, has the distinction of being the first in this country of the bird's eye views of buildings and gardens which became so popular in the late seventeenth and early eighteenth centuries. Hollar whose six views of Albury Place in Surrey are well-known was the first artist to record the British landscape to any great extent. After the restoration the Prospect emerged as a distinctive form of landscape painting and Michael Rosenthal's *British landscape painting* (1982) provides a good introduction to the genre.

Leonard Knyff and Johannes Kip were the leading practitioners of the bird's eye view and much of their work is concentrated in *Britannia illustrata* (1707–15). The plates were reproduced in D. Mortier's *Nouveau théatre de la Grande Bretagne* (1715–16) which also incorporated Kip's plates from Sir Robert Atkyns's *The ancient and present state of Glostershire* (1712). The various printings of *the Britannia illustrata* is bibliographically extremely confusing and the reader is referred to Bernard Adams's *London illustrated 1604–1851* (1983) and John Harris's *The artist and the country house* (1979) for an elucidation of the complexities of its publication. For the purpose of this *Bibliography* the Society of Antiquaries's copy of *Britannia illustrata* was consulted.

Works such as *Britannia illustrata* or T. Badeslade's *Thirty six different views of noblemen and gentlemen's seats in the county of Kent* (1750s) reflect the opulent living of the immensely rich for whom grand houses and imposing estates were an essential status symbol. They willingly paid for the privilege of having an engraved plate of their property included in a book. Of particular interest to garden historians is the third volume of Colen Campbell's *Vitruvius Britannicus* (1715–25) which contains 'Geometrical Plans of the most considerable Gardens and Plantations'. Less magnificent books illustrating country seats rolled off the printing presses until well into the nineteenth century. Probably the most ambitious of all illustrated topographical works was John Britton and Edward Brayley's *Beauties of England and Wales* (1810–16) in 18 volumes. The value of such works to both architectural and garden historians has been recognized by the recent facsimile reprints of William Angus's *Seats of the nobility and gentry in Great Britain and Wales* (1787), William Watts's *Seats of the nobility and gentry in a collection of the most interesting and picturesque views* (1779) and Thomas Milton's *Seats and demesnes of the nobility and gentry in Ireland* (1783–93).

Views of British gardens even decorated snuff boxes and candlesticks; the ultimate extravagance was the dinner service of 952 pieces which Josiah Wedgwood specially designed for Empress Catherine of Russia with views of noblemen's seats (see Appendix).

The best account of the paintings of these seats is John Harris's *The artist and the country house: a history of country house and garden view painting in Britain 1540–1870* (1979). All its plates, in black and white and in colour, have been indexed in this *Bibliography*. Hugh Prince's booklet on *Parks in England* (1967) provides an alphabetical list of gardens illustrated by Knyff, Kip, Badeslade, Burghers, Drapentier and Harris.

The twentieth-century equivalent of the traditional bird's eye view is the aerial photograph which can reveal so clearly the structure and shape of long-vanished gardens. Marcus Binney and Anne Hills's *Elysian gardens* (1979) make effective use of some of these photographs. Some of the post-war volumes of the Royal Commission on Historical Monuments record the archaeological remains of gardens including the evidence of aerial photographs. Christopher Taylor's *The archaeology of gardens* (1983) is a useful if brief preamble to the subject.

Introduction

The unquestionable value of contemporary topographical drawings for the researcher has encouraged the printing of original sketches of houses and gardens such as those by Edmund Prideaux (*Architectural History* vol. 7 (1964)) and Samuel Buck (J. Hall *Samuel Buck's Yorkshire sketchbook* (1979)) and one hopes that other similar collections of drawings will be published in due course.

Some recommended books:

Russell, Ronald *Guide to British topographical prints*, Newton Abbot, 1979.
 A brief outline of their history; a description of the different graphic processes; a list of some of the books illustrated with prints.

Scenery of Great Britain and Ireland in aquatint and lithography 1770–1860 from the Library of J.R. Abbey: a bibliographical catalogue, London, 1952.
 A model bibliography of a rich and comprehensive collection which is now housed at Yale University. The entries are arranged under counties and towns. All the plates in the works described are listed with the names of artists and engravers when known. Some rare works like J.G. Wood's *Views in Kent* (1800) are in this collection. Sufficient details of each book are given to enable the researcher to decide whether he should examine the book itself.

Tooley, R.V. *English books with coloured plates, 1790 to 1860: a bibliographical account of the most important books illustrated by English artists in colour aquatint and colour lithography*, London, 1973.
 Like Abbey's *Scenery of Great Britain and Ireland* it lists plates and their artists and engravers. Most of the works have no particular interest for the garden historian but it does include the 40 volumes of R. Ackermann's *The repository of arts* (1809–28) and also his *Views of country seats* (1830), the plates of which were extracted from the former book.

Adams, Bernard *London illustrated 1604–1851: a survey and index of topographical books and their plates*, London, 1983.
 It lists more than 8,250 plates in 230 books and print sets some of which include views of gardens. An earlier work also devoted to London is Frederick Crace's *A catalogue of maps, plans and views of London, Westminster and Southwark*, London, 1878.

Libraries sometimes publish guides to local topographical prints, of which the following titles are good examples:
 Illustrated catalogue of prints, photographs and original drawings of places in Northamptonshire Northampton Public Library, 1925.
 Benedikz, Phyllis *Durham topographical prints up to 1800: an annotated bibliography* Durham University Library, 1968.
 Somers Cocks, J.V. *Devon topographical prints 1660–1870: a catalogue and guide* Devon Library Services, 1977.

One of the best collections of topographical prints in the United Kingdom is that formerly belonging to King George III, now kept in the Map Library of the British Library:
 British Museum *Catalogue of maps, prints, drawings, etc. forming the geographical and*

Introduction

topographical collection attached to the library of His Late Majesty King George the Third and presented by His Majesty King George the Fourth to the British Museum London, 1829. Its many prints of garden views have been noted in the *Bibliography*.

Harris, John *A catalogue of British drawings for architecture, decoration, sculpture and landscape gardening, 1550–1900 in American collections* New Jersey, 1971.
   The entries for gardens include, for example, locations for the Repton Red Books for Armley House, Brandesbury, Ferne Hall, Hatchlands Park, Moseley Hall, Royal Fort and Stonelands.

Barley, M.W. *A guide to British topographical collections* Council for British Archaeology, 1974.
   Covers topographical drawings, prints and photographs in public repositories and a few private collections.

In 1979 Bamber Gascoigne published *Images of Richmond* at his St. Helena Press. This comprehensive survey of topographical prints of Richmond, with reduced images of every print listed, has been followed by similar volumes on Twickenham, Chelsea, Brighton and Bath and further titles in the series are projected. As some of the prints are views of gardens the whole series is of value to the garden historian.

TRAVEL IN BRITAIN

In the eighteenth century owners of splendid estates were expected to open their property to public view from time to time. Horace Walpole once declined to visit a stately home because he happened to arrive there on the 'public day'. Daniel Defoe, engrossed as he was in economic and social affairs, could always pause to contemplate a house or a garden in his *Tour through the whole island of Great Britain* (1724–27). Even dedicated agronomists like William Pitt, Arthur Young and William Cobbett could not resist inspecting any grand house they passed on their travels. It has been aptly said of Arthur Young that in his reports he 'created a balance between agricultural statistics and Picturesque details'. And John Wesley's *Journal* reveals that his evangelical ardour did not diminish nor deflect his interest in such famous gardens as The Leasowes, Stourhead and Stowe. The reading public of the Georgian era was overwhelmed by a plethora of published journals and letters by earnest travellers who meticulously chronicled every country seat they visited. Their observations were on the whole predictably confined to a garden's well-known features but occasionally there is that fresh comment or insight that makes this body of literature worth the attention of the garden historian. The more lengthy and significant extracts to gardens in these journals, diaries and letters of the English Grand Tour have been noted. Passing references and slight descriptions, however, have been omitted in order to keep the *Bibliography* within prescribed limits.
   That paragon of travellers, the inquisitive and observant Peter Mundy, found time for a brief excursion to Southern England and Wales in between his visits to Europe and Asia. He seldom noticed gardens but on 10 September 1639 he visited two: Theobalds where he admired the 'Faire gardeine with spatious walks' and Hatfield whose garden he found 'somewhatt plaine, yet wondrous polite'. The indefatigable tourist, Celia Fiennes, covered some 3,000 miles, almost entirely on horseback, during 1685–1712. She had an insatiable appetite for houses and gardens. Grottoes, walks, flower-beds, topiary work were all

appraised, appreciated or dismissed and fountains and waterworks, especially those designed to drench the unsuspecting visitor, evoked cries of delight. Her favourite adjective was 'neat'. Her *Journeys* with illustrations of some of the houses she saw was reprinted in 1982. Did she ever meet the Duchess of Chandos who took to the English road about the same time, also diligently recording the country estates she saw? The naturalist, Thomas Pennant, whom Samuel Johnson declared to be 'the best traveller I ever read' revealed Scotland to the English traveller with his *Tour in Scotland* (1771) and did the same for Wales two years later with his *Tour of Wales*. Richard Warner was an English clergyman who eccentrically disdained the convenience of waggon or coach and resolutely tramped through the West Country, Wales and the Northern counties of England finding material for more than six books.

A reviewer in the *Gentleman's Magazine* for 1778 deplored the current fashion for 'excursion-making, touring, sketching, journeying, topographizing or whatever name belongs to this mode of writing'. Devotees of the Picturesque instinctively headed for Derbyshire, the Wye Valley, North Wales or the Lake District. Even Samuel Johnson who was not particularly susceptible to the charms of the countryside was thrilled by the 'striking scenes of terrifick terror' at Hawkstone and responded favourably to the 'grandeur tempered with softness' of Ilam. Publishers, never slow to spot a promising market, brought out attractively illustrated guide books, now so useful to the present-day historian and researcher. The extent of public interest in travel persuaded William Mavor in 1798 to risk the publication in six volumes of *The British tourist's or, traveller's pocket companion, through England, Wales, Scotland, and Ireland, comprehending the most celebrated modern tours in the British Isles and several originals*. In 1808 John Pinkerton produced another anthology of travel literature with *A general collection of the best and most interesting voyages and travels in all parts of the world*. It has not been possible to examine more than a few of all such tours published during the eighteenth century.

One of the first foreigners to discover England and to relate his experiences was Paul Hentzner whose *Itinerarium Germaniae, Galliae, Angliae, Italiae* was published in 1612. Horace Walpole thought sufficiently well of it to publish an English extract at his Strawberry Hill Press in 1757. Hentzner appears to have been more interested in the parks and gardens of the houses he visited than in their interiors. Like many other foreign visitors he relied heavily on writers like Camden and Chamberlayne for much of his information on this country. In his letters in 1726 to his family in Switzerland, César de Saussure especially approved of the close-cropped lawns in English gardens. He noted that 'English people like to have statues, ornamental ponds and fountains in their gardens, but you see very few beds of flowers'. Count Frederick Kielmansegge who came to England shortly after the accession of George III in 1760 expressed his surprise that many of the temples and pavilions in Princess Augusta's gardens at Kew 'consist of wood only, but are so cleverly covered with plaster, and painted in oil colours, that you would swear they were solid buildings of quarry stone, unless by knocking them you discovered the truth from the sound'. Most foreign visitors admired the work of Bridgeman, Kent and Brown and all made a pilgrimage to Stowe. While Thomas Jefferson was in England on a diplomatic mission in 1786 he seized the opportunity to explore some English gardens with Thomas Whately's *Observations on modern gardening* (1770) as his guide. Evidently a devotee of Whately—'his descriptions, in point of style, are models of perfect elegance and classical correctness, they are as remarkable for their exactness'—Jefferson was nevertheless delighted to discover at Wotton 'a Palladian bridge of which, I think, Whately does not speak'.

Introduction

Many of the early visitors to these islands never got much farther than the periphery of London, their itinerary taking in Greenwich, Theobalds, Hampton Court, Oatlands and Windsor. Much more adventurous later on, they explored more of the English countryside. When the Dutchman, Baron Johan Frederik Willem van Spaen van Biljoen came to England in 1791, he managed to see Richmond, Painshill, Wilton, Fonthill, Stourhead, Longleat, Blenheim, Stowe and Nuneham. His impressions remained unpublished until they were translated and appeared in the *Journal of Garden History* in 1982. There must be other contemporary accounts of gardens, languishing on the shelves of libraries and archives, awaiting discovery and subsequent publication.

Some recommended books:

Moir, Esther *The discovery of Britain: the English tourists, 1540 to 1840* London, 1964.
   Deals with the tourists of the seventeenth to the nineteenth centuries and assesses the contribution of the antiquaries and the Picturesque movement. A bibliography lists many of the important tours.

Cox, Edward Godfrey *A reference guide to the literature of travel, including tours, descriptions, towns, histories and antiquities, surveys, ancient and present state, gardening, etc.* vol. 3: *Great Britain* Seattle, 1949.
   Lists with copious annotations 'Tours by natives', 'Tours by foreigners', 'Views', 'Towns, Castles, Seats', 'Agriculture, Husbandry, Gardening', etc.'. An indispensable work for the serious student of English travel and topography.

Fussell, G.S. *The exploration of England: a select bibliography of travel and topography, 1570–1815* London, 1935.
   A chronological arrangement of 353 items with occasional annotations.

Mitchell, Sir Arthur *List of travels and tours in Scotland, 1296 to 1900* Edinburgh, 1902.
   A chronological arrangement of some 860 items with annotations.

DIARIES AND LETTERS

The development of our gardens, especially in the eighteenth century, has been influenced by the interaction of art and literature. The letters of writers like Horace Walpole, Gray, Pope, Shenstone and Mrs Delany express opinions on the aesthetics of garden design as well as on individual gardens. Alexander Pope's correspondence, as one would expect from a person who was also a competent gardener, has many allusions to gardening and gardens. He tells Martha Blount in a letter written in September 1728 that Rousham was 'the prettiest place for water-falls, jetts, ponds, enclosed with beautiful scenes of green and hanging wood, that ever I saw'. His letters to the Earl of Bathurst on the gardens at Cirencester and to Lord Burlington on those at Chiswick enlarge our knowledge and understanding of their creation.
   The volumes containing the meticulous index to the Yale edition of Horace Walpole's letters came out too late for this *Bibliography* but it must be consulted by students of Georgian gardens.

E.S. de Beer's edition of John Evelyn's *Diary* (1955) in six volumes is a model of impeccable scholarship. The exhaustive index lists all the gardens mentioned by Evelyn under two headings: 'subjects of important notices' and 'subjects of minor notices'.

GUIDE BOOKS

The popularity of country house visiting in the eighteenth century inevitably stimulated a demand for guide books. Stowe was one of the most frequently visited. Sarah Bridgeman produced *A general plan of the woods, parks and gardens of Stowe* in 1739. Guide books were frequently reprinted; the Northamptonshire edition of *A description of the house and gardens . . . at Stowe* was reissued six times between 1744 and 1749. Thirteen editions and reprints of *A walk round Mount Edgcumbe* appeared between 1808 and 1841. A selection of these guides is given in John Harris's *A country house index* (1971).

The guide book habit continues today with properties still in private ownership or in the custody of the National Trust and other bodies. As they are often reprinted or revised I have indicated their existence by the phrase 'Official Guide' in the *Bibliography* rather than attempt to list all the printings.

Another category of guide books containing information on specific gardens is county and regional guides. A & C Black began their series with Edinburgh and Glasgow in 1839; their rivals were John Murray who published the first of their county guides in 1851 reaching a total of 60 volumes before the series was closed in 1899. Ward, Lock & Co. began their well-known series in 1896. Any one interested in the general history and development of this special category of literature should consult J. Vaughan's *The English guide book, c.1780–1870: an illustrated history* Newton Abbot, 1974.

Nikolaus Pevsner's deservedly renowned Buildings of England series have been included in the *Bibliography* for their succinct descriptions of garden architecture.

ARCHIVES

All the references in the *Bibliography of British Gardens* have been culled from printed sources. No attempt has been made to list archives and original drawings in libraries, record offices and private collections except when such material appears in published catalogues and calendars. All the references to gardens, for instance, in *Architectural history & the fine & applied arts: sources in the National Register of Archives*, published by the Historical Manuscripts Commission in 5 volumes, 1969–74, have been taken up. Relevant material in the drawings collections of the Royal Institute of British Architect's *Catalogue of the drawings collections: A–S* (1968–76) and *Edwin Lutyens* (1973) have been indexed as have also those in John Harris's *A catalogue of British drawings for architecture, decoration, sculpture and landscape gardening, 1550–1900, in American collections* (1971).

Anyone seeking unpublished information on gardens should first confirm whether the National Register of Archives, Quality Court, Chancery Lane, London WC2 has any locations in its indexes. Public libraries and county record offices are an obvious source for enquiry and research. Some record offices have published calendars and lists of documents which are of interest to the garden historian. The West Sussex Record Office has listed the *Goodwood Estate archives* (F.W. Steer and J.E.A. Venables in 2 volumes, 1970–72) and also the *Petworth House archives* (F.W. Steer in 2 volumes, 1968–79), the latter having the contract between the 2nd Earl of Egremont and Capability Brown for the landscaping of Petworth in the 1750s.

On the whole the Victoria County Histories are disappointingly light on gardens, notwithstanding a greater awareness of their importance in the post-war volumes. They do, however, often give footnote references to archives on gardens in local record offices.

MAPS

Probably nothing gives a garden historian more satisfaction than an accurately drawn and detailed plan of the garden he is studying. The estate maps drawn by a local surveyor set a house in its parkland often with flower-beds, paths, lakes and other garden features carefully delineated. Auction catalogues of country properties sometimes include maps. The large-scale maps and atlases from about the middle of the eighteenth century are so detailed that practically every dwelling and garden can be discerned. The size, shape and design of local gardens can be established from such works as John Rocques' 2 inch to the mile atlases of Berkshire, Middlesex and Surrey and John Chapman and Peter André's Essex.

Several record offices have published guides to the estate maps in their possession, the most scholarly being F.G. Emmison's *Catalogue of maps in the Essex Record Office, 1566–1855* (1947–68). This and many others are listed in R.B. Down's *British library resources: a bibliographical guide* (American Library Association, 1973), 179–89. All the estate maps that appear to include the gardens in these published guides have been indexed in the *Bibliography*.

Some recommended books:

Rodger, Elizabeth M. *Large scale county maps of the British Isles, 1596–1850: a union list.* Edition 2. Bodleian Library, 1972.

Includes all printed county maps separately issued on the scale between ½ inch and 3 inches to a mile. Locations in 26 libraries are given.

Chubb, Thomas *The printed maps in the atlases of Great Britain and Ireland: a bibliography, 1579–1870* London, 1927.

The first comprehensive survey of British atlases now largely superseded by R.A. Skelton's *County atlases of the British Isles, 1579–1850: a bibliography* London, 1970.

PERIODICALS

The principal horticultural journals have been systematically scanned for references to gardens. J.C. Loudon's *Gardener's Magazine*, *Gardeners' Chronicle*, *Cottage Gardener*, William Robinson's *Garden* and *Journal of the Royal Horticultural Society* provide the best coverage of gardens including many of the less well-known ones. Their indexes are of variable quality and thoroughness; *Gardener's Magazine* is, as one would expect of any work edited by Loudon, well-indexed but the annual indexes to *Gardeners' Chronicle* and *Cottage Gardener* are merely passable or inadequate. *Journal of the Royal Horticultural Society* has cumulative indexes which assist retrospective searching but here again the level of indexing is not taken to any depth. (See my article on 'Victorian horticulture: a guide to the literature' *Garden History* v. 5 no. 3, 1971 for a list of the principal periodicals.)

Introduction

The garden articles which have always been a regular feature in *Country Life* have been indexed in the *Bibliography*. Those articles which discuss the house with little or no mention of the garden have been omitted. The cumulative indexes published from time to time by *Country Life* are useful but they do not include all that periodical's contributions on gardens.

The editorial policy of the *Architectural Review* has changed since the last war and it now seldom has any articles on gardens; during the same period *Apollo* and the *Connoisseur* have shown more interest in gardens.

The gardens reported in *Amateur Gardening* and *House & Garden* are not covered in the *Bibliography* nor are those which occasionally are discussed in local history and archaeological society journals except where they have come to my notice.

Two periodicals launched in recent years—*Garden History*, published by the Garden History Society, and *Journal of Garden History*—through their authoritative articles and book reviews are essential reading for the garden historian.

SOME BIBLIOGRAPHIES AND INDEXES

British local histories and topography:

Anderson, John P. *The book of English topography: a classified catalogue of the topographical works in the library of the British Museum, relating to Great Britain and Ireland* London, 1881.
  Alphabetical arrangement by towns within each county.

Humphreys, Arthur L. *A handbook to county bibliography: being a bibliography of bibliographies relating to the counties and towns of Great Britain and Ireland* London, 1917.
  A good coverage of standard county bibliographies; alphabetical arrangement by towns within each county.

Downs, Robert B. *British library resources: a bibliographical guide* American Library Association, 1973.
  Section on 'History', 197–223, lists catalogues and guides to local history collections relating to counties and towns.

Smith, Alfred Russell *A catalogue of ten thousand tracts and pamphlets and fifty thousand prints and drawings illustrating the topography and antiquities of England, Wales, Scotland and Ireland. Collected during the last thirty-five years by the late William Upcott and John Russell Smith. Now offered for sale for ready money by Alfred Russell Smith* London, 1878.
  A very substantial catalogue: alphabetical arrangement by towns within each county; brief notes on topographical prints including views of gardens.

Upcott, William *A bibliographical account of the principal works relating to English topography* London, 1818. 3 vols.
  Alphabetical arrangement of counties. Plate captions are given for the books it lists.

In addition there are guides and catalogues to the literature of individual counties. Typical of these is Walter Rye's *An index to Norfolk topography* (London, 1881) which has been large superseded by E. Darroch *and* B. Taylor's *Bibliography of Norfolk history*

Introduction

(University of East Anglia, 1975). L.R. Conisbee's *A Bedfordshire bibliography* (Bedfordshire Historical Record Society, 1962; 2nd Supplement, 1971) has references to gardens under the heading 'Architecture'.

Indexes to current literature:

The *Newsletter* of the Garden History Society regularly lists current books and periodical articles.

Journal of Garden History announced in vol. 2 no. 3, 1982, 293–96 its intention to publish an annual current bibliography of garden history. The first one covering 1981–82 appeared in vol. 3 no. 4, 1983, 347–81.

Landscape Design: Journal of the Landscape Institute 1971 to date; formerly *Journal of the Institute of Landscape Architects*.
   Bi-monthly. Its bibliography of current literature is a regular feature.

Art Index: a quarterly author & subject index to publications in the fields of archaeology, architecture, art history . . . Wilson, New York, 1929 to date.
   Quarterly with two or three-year cumulations. Indexes many fine art journals and museum bulletins with an emphasis on those published in the U.S.A. Has references on gardens.

Art Bibliographies Modern Clio Press, Oxford, 1969 to date.
   Twice yearly. Includes in its coverage journals that have articles on gardens: *Apollo, Country Life, Connoisseur, Journal of Garden History, Journal of Society of Architectural Historians, Royal Institute of British Architects Journal*, etc.

British Humanities Index Library Association, 1962 to date. Successor to *Subject Index to Periodicals*.
   Quarterly with annual cumulations. *Country Life* and *Journal of Garden History* are among the journals scanned.

Bibliography of Scotland National Library of Scotland, 1978 to date.
   Annual. Covers nearly a hundred periodicals; includes articles on gardens.

Bibliotheca Celtica: a register of publications relating to Wales and the Celtic peoples & languages, National Library of Wales, 1907 to date.
   Annual. Includes books and articles on gardens.

Guides to the literature of related subjects:

Two recent examples of guides which are useful to the garden historian are:

Kamen, Ruth H. *British and Irish architectural history. A bibliography and guide to sources of information*, London, 1981.

Introduction

Includes a section on 'Landscape architecture' and a useful directory of photograph and slide libraries.

Arntzen, Etta *and* Rainwater, Robert *Guide to the literature of art history*, American Library Association, 1981. Successor to Chamberlin's *Guide to art reference books*, 1959.

LIBRARIES

The copyright deposit libraries (British Library, Bodleian Library, Oxford, Cambridge University Library, National Library of Scotland, National Library of Wales, Trinity College Dublin) are obvious major repositories of information for the researcher. The Bodleian Library has also the Gough Collection of topographical prints.

People living in or near London have access to a wide range of libraries, a number of which I was fortunately able to use during the compilation of the *Bibliography of British gardens*.

British Library, Great Russell Street, London WC1.
On the open shelves in the General Reading Room are all the Victoria County Histories, many of the standard county histories and a good collection of county bibliographies. Its Map Library houses George III's collection of topographical prints and has all the published catalogues of estate maps in county record offices.

Royal Botanic Gardens, Kew, Richmond, Surrey
Has many of the standard texts on garden history. A very good coverage of nineteenth-century garden periodicals, conveniently housed on open shelves in the Main Library. Its equivalent in Scotland is the Royal Botanic Garden, Edinburgh and in Ireland the National Botanic Gardens, Glasnevin, Dublin.

Royal Horticultural Society, Vincent Square, London SW1
The most comprehensive horticultural library in the country. Has some periodicals which Kew lacks.

Royal Institute of British Architects, Portland Place, London W1
The National Library of Architecture. Sets of all the important journals including *Country Life* and those on landscape architecture are on the open shelves. Maintains an index of current periodical articles.

Guildhall Library, Aldermanbury, London EC2
Excellent collection of county and local histories including some not in the British Library. Has the most complete collection of topographical works and prints relating to London.

Society of Antiquaries, Burlington House, Piccadilly, London W1
Notable for its collection of British local history and sets of journals published by local historical and archaeological societies.

Introduction

Institute of Historical Research, University of London, Senate House, Malet Street, London WC1
  A very good collection of British local history arranged under counties on open shelves.

Fine Arts Library, Westminster Central References Library, Leicester Square, London WC2
  Sets of journals such as *Apollo, Art Index, Connoisseur*, etc. on the open shelves. A very good collection of current guides to country houses.

Victoria and Albert Museum, Department of Prints and Drawings & Photographs, Cromwell Road, London SW7
  Has a card index, arranged under towns, listing all the prints, drawings and water-colours of general topographical interest in the Department.

London Library, St. James' Square, London SW1
  Its rudimentary book classification works in a most pragmatic way. There are, for instance, several tiers of books labelled 'Foreign impressions of England' where will be found many of the tours listed in this *Bibliography*. The main attraction of this Library is that practically everything can be borrowed by its subscribing members.

Landscape Institute, Nash House, Carlton House Terrace, London SW1
  A small collection of books and periodicals.

National Monuments Record, Royal Commission on Historical Monuments (England), Savile Row, London, W1
  Has over 2,000,000 photographs, maps, plans and other documents of buildings and sites in England. A new series, *Photographic archives* published by HMSO and based upon these rich collections, includes two on gardens: Priscilla Boniface's *The garden room* 1982 and Alastair Forsyth's *Yesterday's gardens from early photographs* 1983.

All these libraries I know from personal use but obviously there are many others which can be of service to the garden historian, not least local public libraries many of which take great pride in their local history collections built up over the years and which are usually staffed by knowledgeable librarians. They are among the first places to consult for information on local gardens.

This Introduction does not claim in any way to be more than the briefest summary of some of the sources of information on the history of gardens. What garden historians urgently require is a bibliography and guide of the scope and depth of Ruth Kamen's *British and Irish architectural history*.

ACKNOWLEDGEMENTS

I have searched the literature and indexed myself most of the references in the *Bibliography of British gardens* but I am still indebted to friends and acquaintances who have sent me material. I would like to acknowledge in particular the help of Mrs M. Batey, Dr Brent Elliott, Mr Peter Goodchild, Dr John Harvey, Mr Peter Hayden, Mr David Jacques, Mr Matthew, Dr Charles Nelson, Mr John Sales and Miss Marion Waller.

Abbreviations

Beds	Bedfordshire
Berks	Berkshire
Bucks	Buckinghamshire
C.L.	*Country Life*
Cambs	Cambridgeshire
Central	Central Scotland
Co.	County
D.o.E.	Department of the Environment
E.	East
Ed.	Edition
G.C.	*Gardeners' Chronicle*
G.L.C.	Greater London Council
G.M.	*Gardener's Magazine* (edited by J.C. Loudon)
Gdn	Garden
Gdning	Gardening
Hants	Hampshire
Herts	Hertfordshire
Hort	Horticulture (al)
Hunts	Huntingdonshire
i (or ii)	Vol 1 (or 2) of each year's issue of the *Gardeners' Chronicle*
J.	Journal
L.C.C.	London County Council
Lancs	Lancashire
Leics	Leicestershire
Lincs	Lincolnshire
Mag.	Magazine
MSS	Manuscripts
N.	North
N.S.	New Series
no.	Number
Northants	Northamptonshire
Notts	Nottinghamshire
pl(s)	Plate(s)
Proc.	Proceedings
pt	Part
R.H.S.	Royal Horticultural Society
R.I.B.A.	Royal Institute of British Architects
S.	South
Soc.	Society
Staffs	Staffordshire

Abbreviations

Supplt	Supplement
Trans	Transactions
v.	Volume
V.C.H.	Victoria County History
W.	West
Wilts	Wiltshire
Worcs	Worcestershire
Yorks	Yorkshire

Bibliography of works consulted

PERIODICALS

Apollo   London, v. 1–114 (1925–81)

Architectural History: Journal of the Society of Architectural Historians of Great Britain   v. 1–25 (1958–82)

Architectural Review   London, v. 1–174 (1896–1983)

Connoisseur   London, v. 1–208 (1901–81)

Copper Plate Magazine, or monthly cabinet of picturesque prints consisting of sublime and interesting views in Great Britain and Ireland   London, v. 1–5 (1792–1802)

Cottage Gardener   London, v. 1–25 (1848–61); Cont'd as: *Journal of Horticulture, Cottage Gardener . . .*   v. 26–N.S. v. 71 (1861–1915)

Country Life   London, v. 1–174 (1897–1984)

Country Life Annual   London, 1938–52, 1954–66, 1968–70, 1972

Flora and Sylva   London, v. 1–3 (1903–05)

Florist   London, (1848–84)

Garden   London, v. 1–91 (1872–1927)

Garden Design   London, (1930–38)

Garden History   London, v. 1–12 (1972–84)

Gardeners' Chronicle   London, (1841–1983)

Gardener's Magazine   London, v. 1–19 (1826–44)

Gardening World   London, v. 1–15, 17–18 (1884–1902)

International Dendrology Society Year Book   (1970–81)

Irish Gardening   Dublin, v. 1–17 (1906–22)

Journal of Garden History   London, v. 1–4 (1981–84)

Journal of Royal Horticultural Society   London, v. 1–100 no. 5 (1846–1975); Cont'd as: *Garden*   v. 100 no. 6–108 (1975–83).

Landscape & Garden   London, v. 1–5 (1934–38); Cont'd as: *(Wartime) Journal of the Institute of Landscape Architects* no. 4–92 (1943–71); Cont'd as: *Landscape Design* no. 93–148 (1971–84)

Bibliography of works consulted

Landscape Planning   Amsterdam, v. 1–9 no. 2 (1974–82)

National Trust Year Book   London (1975–79); Cont'd as: *National Trust Studies*   (1980–81)

New Flora and Silva   London, v. 1–12 (1928–40)

Scottish Gardener   Edinburgh, v. 1–5 (1852–56)

Scottish Gardener and Northern Forester   Edinburgh, (1905–14)

BOOKS

— *Bibliotheca topographica Britannica*   London, 1780–95. 10 vols.

— *A companion to The Leasowes, Hagley, and Enville with a sketch of Fisherwick . . .*   London, 1789.

— *The delineator, a series of splendid engravings of remarkable edifices, places of antiquity, and views of celebrity in England, Wales, Scotland and Ireland*   London, 1831.

— *A general history of the county of Norfolk intended to convey all the information of a Norfolk tour . . .*   Norwich, 1829. 2 vols.

— *The history of Ripon: with descriptions of Studley Royal, Fountain's Abbey, Newby, Hackfall, etc. etc. . . .*   Ripon, 1806.

— *Jones's views of the seats, mansions, castles, etc. of noblemen and gentlemen in England, Wales, Scotland and Ireland and other picturesque scenery . . .*   London, 1829.

— *The journey-book of England: Berkshire (1840); Derbyshire (1841); Hampshire (1841); Kent (1842)*   London, 1840–42.

— *A new display of the beauties of England*   London, 1787. 2 vols.

— *Picturesque views of the principal seats of the nobility and gentry in England and Wales. By the most eminent British artists with a description of each seat*   London, 1788.

— *A peep into the principal seats and gardens in and about Twickenham . . .*   London, 1775.

— *Tombleson's Thames*   London, 1834.

— *The topographer . . . containing a variety of original articles illustrative of the local history and antiquities of England . . .*   London, 1789–91. 4 vols.

ACKERMANN, Rudolph   *The repository of arts, literature, commerce, manufactures, fashions and politics*   London, 1809–28. 40 vols.

ADAM, William   *The gem of the Peak; or, Matlock Bath and its vicinity . . .*   Edition 5.   London, 1851.

ADAMS, Ian H.   *Descriptive list of plans*   General Register House, Edinburgh, 1966–74. 3 vols.

ALLAN, Mea   *Fisons guide to gardens in England, Scotland, Ireland and Wales*   London, 1970.

ALLEN, Thomas   *The history of the county of Lincoln, from the earliest period to the present time*   London, 1834. 2 vols.

Bibliography of works consulted

ALLEN, Thomas *A new and complete history of the county of York* London, 1828–31. 3 vols.

ANGUS, William *Seats of the nobility and gentry in Great Britain and Wales, in a collection of select views . . .* London, 1787.

ANTHONY, John *Gardens of Britain, 6: Derbyshire, Leicestershire, Lincolnshire, Northamptonshire and Nottinghamshire* London, 1979.

ATKIN, J. *A description of the country from thirty to forty miles round Manchester . . .* London, 1795.

ATKYNS, Sir Robert *The ancient and present state of Glostershire* London, 1712.

AUNGIER, George James *The history and antiquities of Syon Monastery, the Parish of Isleworth and the Chapelry of Hounslow . . .* London, 1840.

BADESLADE, Thomas *Thirty six different views of noblemen and gentlemen's seats, in the county of Kent, all designed on the spot . . .* London, [1750s].

BADESLADE, Thomas *and* ROCQUE, J. *Vitruvius Brittanicus* vol. 4. London, 1739. (Reprinted 1967).

BAINES, Edward *History of the County Palatine and Duchy of Lancaster* London, 1836. 4 vols.

BATEY, Mavis *Oxford gardens* Oxford, 1982.

BEARD, Geoffrey *Thomas H. Mawson: a northern landscape architect* Lancaster, 1976.

BEEVERELL, James *Les delices de la Grande Bretagne, l'Irlande . . .* Leide, 1707. 8 vols.

BERRY, William *The history of the Island of Guernsey . . . from the remotest period of antiquity to the year 1814 . . .* London, 1815.

BIGLAND, Ralph *Historical, monumental and genealogical collections, relative to the county of Gloucester* London, 1791–92. 2 vols.

BINNEY, Marcus *and* HILLS, Anne *Elysian gardens* London, 1979.

BISGROVE, Richard *Gardens of Britain, 3: Berkshire, Oxfordshire, Buckinghamshire, Bedfordshire and Hertfordshire* London, 1978.

BORLASE, William *The natural history of Cornwall . . .* Oxford, 1758.

BOSWELL, Henry *Historical descriptions of new and elegant picturesque views of the antiquities of England and Wales . . .* London, 1800.

BOYDELL, John *A collection of views in England and Wales, drawn and engraved by John Boydell . . .* London, 1790.

BOYDELL, John *and* Josiah *An history of the River Thames* London, 1794. 2 vols.

BRADFORD ILLUSTRATED WEEKLY TELEGRAPH *A series of picturesque views of castles and country houses in Yorkshire.* 1885.

BRAY, William *Sketch of a tour into Derbyshire and Yorkshire, including part of Buckingham, Warwick, Leicester, Nottingham, Northampton, Bedford and Hertfordshire* Edition 2. London, 1783.

Bibliography of works consulted

BRAYBROOKE, Lord Richard *The history of Audley End* London, 1836.

BRAYLEY, Edward Wedlake *and* BRITTON, John *Topographical history of Surrey* London, 1841–48. 5 vols.

BREWER, James Norris *Delineations of Gloucestershire; being views of the principal seats of nobility & gentry* . . . London, [1825?].

BREWER, James Norris *The beauties of Ireland: being original delineations, topographical, historical, and biographical, of each county* . . . London, 1825–26. 2 vols.

BRITISH MUSEUM *Catalogue of maps, prints, drawings, etc. forming the geographical and topographical collection attached to the library of his late Majesty King George the Third* . . . London, 1829.

BRITTON, John *History and description with graphic illustrations, of Cassiobury Park, Hertfordshire* . . . London, 1837.

BRITTON, John *The beauties of Wiltshire* . . . *illustrated by views of the principal seats, etc* . . . London, 1801–25. 3 vols.

BRITTON, John *and* BRAYLEY, Edward Wedlake *Devonshire & Cornwall illustrated from original drawings* . . . London, 1832.

BROOKE, E. Adveno *The gardens of England* London, [c. 1857].

BROWN, Jane *Gardens of a golden afternoon. The story of a partnership: Edwin Lutyens & Gertrude Jekyll.* London, 1982.

BROWN, Jane *Miss Gertrude Jekyll, 1843–1932, gardener* London, 1981.

BROWNELL, Morris R. *Alexander Pope & the arts of Georgian England* Oxford, 1978.

BUCK, Samuel *and* Nathaniel *Buck's antiquities, or memorable remains of above four hundred castles, monasteries, palaces, etc. etc. in England and Wales* . . . London, 1774. 3 vols.

BURKE, John Bernard *A visitation of the seats and arms of the noblemen and gentlemen of Great Britain* London, 1852–55. 3 vols.

BURLINGTON, Charles *et al* *The modern universal and accurate tour through England, Wales and Scotland* . . . London, 1779.

BUTLER, Arthur Stanley *et al* *The architecture of Sir Edwin Lutyens. Vol 2: Gardens* [etc] London, 1950.

CALVERT, Frederick *Picturesque views and descriptions of cities, towns, castles, mansions and other objects of interesting features in Staffordshire & Shropshire* Birmingham, 1830–31.

CAMBRIDGE, Richard Owen *Works* . . . *By his son George Owen Cambridge* London, 1803.

CAMPBELL, Colen *Vitruvius Britannicus, or the British architect* . . . London, 1715–25 (reprinted in 1967).

CARTER, George, GOODE, Patrick *and* LAURIE, Kedrun *Humphry Repton, landscape gardener, 1752–1818* Norwich & London, 1982.

CARUS, Carl Gustav *The King of Saxony's journey through England and Scotland in the year 1844...* London, 1846.

CHADWICK, George F. *The park and the town: public landscape in the 19th and 20th centuries* London, 1966.

CHANCELLOR, Edwin Beresford *The pleasure haunts of London during four centuries* London, 1925.

CHAUNCY, Sir Henry *The historical antiquities of Hertfordshire* London, 1700.

CHERRY, Bridget *and* PEVSNER, Nikolaus *London 2: South* London, 1983. (Buildings of England).

CLARK, H. Frank *The English landscape garden* London, 1948.

CLARKE, Edward Daniel *A tour through the south of England, Wales and part of Ireland made during the summer of 1791* London, 1793.

CLUTTERBUCK, Robert *The history and antiquities of the county of Hertford...* London, 1815–27. 3 vols.

COATS, Peter *Great gardens of Britain* London, 1963.

COBBETT, William *Rural rides* London, 1853 (Everyman's library edition 1912).

COLE, Nathan *Royal parks and gardens of London...* London, 1877.

COLLINSON, John *History and antiquities of county of Somersetshire...* Bath, 1791. 3 vols.

COLVIN, Howard M. *The history of the King's Works* London, 1963–82. 6 vols.

COLVIN, Howard *and* HARRIS, John *The country seat: studies in the history of the British country house* London, 1970.

COMPTON, Thomas *The Northern Cambrian mountains, or a tour through North Wales...* London, 1817.

COOKE, William Bernard *and* OWEN, Samuel *The Thames; or, graphic illustrations of seats, villas, public buildings, and picturesque scenery on the banks of that noble river* London, 1811. 2 vols.

CRISP, Sir Frank *Mediaeval gardens, 'flowery medes' and other arrangements of herbs, flowers and shrubs grown in the Middle Ages...* London, 1924. 2 vols.

CRUTTWELL, Clement *A tour through the whole island of Great Britain; divided into journies...* London, 1801. 6 vols.

CUMBERLAND, George *An attempt to describe Hafod and the neighbouring scenes about the bridge over the Funack...* London, 1796.

CURL, James Stevens *A celebration of death* London, 1980.

CUSSANS, John Edwin *History of Hertfordshire...* London, 1870–81. 3 vols.

DALLAWAY, James *A history of the Western Division of the county of Sussex...* London, 1815–30. 2 vols.

Bibliography of works consulted

DAVY, Henry *Views of the seats of the noblemen and gentlemen in Suffolk* Southwold, 1827.

DEFOE, Daniel *A tour through the whole island of Great Britain, divided into circuits or journies* Edition 3. London, 1742; also 1778. 4 vols.

DELAMOTTE, William Alfred *Original views of Oxford, its colleges, chapels and gardens . . .* London, 1843.

DENNIS, Jonas *The landscape gardener, comprising the history and principles of tasteful horticulture* London, 1835.

DICKINSON, P.G.M. *Maps in the County Record Office, Huntingdon* Huntingdon, 1968.

DODSLEY, Robert *and* J. *London and its environs described . . .* London, 1761. 6 vols.

DRAPER, M.P.G. *Lambeth's open spaces: an historical account* Lambeth, 1979.

DUGDALE, *Sir* William *The antiquities of Warwickshire . . .* Edition 2. London, 1730. 2 vols.

ELMES, James *Metropolitan improvements, London in the nineteenth century . . .* London, 1828.

ELVEY, Elizabeth M. *Hand-list of Buckinghamshire estate maps* Buckingham, 1963.

EMMISON, Frederick George *Catalogue of maps in the Essex Record Office 1566–1855* Chelmsford, 1947; *Supplements 1–3*, 1952–68.

ERDBERG, Eleanor von *Chinese influence on European garden structures* Harvard, 1936.

EVANS, H. *The beautiful gardens of Britain* London, 1974.

EVANS, John *Letters written during a tour through South Wales in the year 1803 and at other times* London, 1804.

EVELYN, John *Diary.* Edited by E.S. de Beer Oxford, 1955. 6 vols.

FAUJAS DE SAINT FOND, B. *A journey through England and Scotland to the Hebrides in 1784* Glasgow, 1907. 2 vols.

FÈRET, Charles James *Fulham old and new: being an exhaustive history of the ancient parish of Fulham* London, 1900. 3 vols.

FERRAR, John *A view of ancient and modern Dublin . . . to which is added a tour to Bellevue in the county of Wicklow* Dublin, 1796.

FIELDING, Theodore Henry *A picturesque description of the River Wye, from the source to its junction with the Severn* London, 1841.

FIENNES, Celia *The journeys of Celia Fiennes, [c. 1685–1703].* Edited by C. Morris London, 1949 (reprinted 1982).

FISHER, Thomas *Collections, historical, genealogical and topographical for Bedfordshire* London, 1812–36.

FLEMING, Laurence *and* GORE, Alan *The English garden* London, 1979.

FOSBROKE, Thomas Dudley *Abstracts of records and manuscripts respecting the county of Gloucester* Gloucester, 1807. 2 vols.

FOSBROKE, Thomas Dudley *The Wye tour or Gilpin on the Wye, with picturesque additions from Wheatley, Price, etc. . . .* Edition 3. Ross, 1826.

GAGE, John *The history and antiquities of Suffolk: Thingoe Hundred* Bury St. Edmunds, 1838.

GENDALL, W.W.J. *Views of country seats of the royal family, nobility and gentry of England* London, 1830. 2 vols.

GIBSON, J. *Short account of several gardens near London, with remarks on some particulars wherein they excel, or are deficient, upon a view of them in December 1691 (Archaeologia v. 12, 1796, 181–92).*

GILBERT, Charles S. *An historical survey of the county of Cornwall . . .* Plymouth, 1817–20. 2 vols.

GILPIN, William *Observations relative chiefly to picturesque beauty, made in the year 1776, on several parts of Great Britain, particularly the Highlands of Scotland.* Edition 2. London, 1792. 2 vols.

GILPIN, William *Observations on the River Wye and several parts of South Wales, etc. relative chiefly to picturesque beauty, made in the summer of the year 1770.* Edition 5. London, 1800.

GILPIN, William *Observations on several parts of England, particularly the mountains and lakes of Cumberland and Westmoreland, relative chiefly to picturesque beauty, made in the year 1772.* Edition 3. London, 1808. 2 vols.

GILPIN, William *Observations on the Western parts of England, relative chiefly to picturesque beauty, to which are added a few remarks on the picturesque beauties of the Isle of Wight.* Edition 2. London, 1808.

GLOAG, M.R. *A book of English gardens . . .* London, 1906.

GLOVER, Stephen *The history and gazetteer of the county of Derby . . .* Derby, 1831–33. 2 vols.

GRAVES, John *The history of Cleveland in the North Riding of the county of York . . .* Carlisle, 1808.

GREEN, David *Gardener to Queen Anne: Henry Wise (1653–1738) and the formal garden* London, 1956.

GREENWOOD, C. *An epitome of county history . . . v.1: county of Kent* London, 1838.

GRIGOR, James *The Eastern arboretum, or register of remarkable trees, seats, gardens, etc. in the county of Norfolk* London, 1841.

GÜNTHER, Robert Theodore *Oxford gardens based upon Daubeny's popular guide to the Physick Garden of Oxford* Oxford, 1912.

HALL, Ivan *Samuel Buck's Yorkshire sketchbook* Wakefield, 1979.

HANWAY, Jonas *A journal of eight days journey from Portsmouth to Kingston upon Thames . . . with miscellaneous thoughts, moral and religious, in sixty-four letters, addressed to two ladies of the partie* London, 1757. 2 vols.

HARRIS, John *The history of Kent . . .* London, 1719.

HARRIS, John *The artist and the country house: a history of country house and garden view painting in Britain, 1540–1870.* London, 1979.

HARRIS, John *A catalogue of British drawings for architecture, decoration, sculpture and landscape gardening, 1550–1900, in American collections* New Jersey, 1971.

HARRIS, John *Gardens of delight: the Rococo English landscape of Thomas Robins the elder* London, 1978.

HARRIS, John *and* TAIT, A.A. *Catalogue of the drawings by Inigo Jones, John Webb and Isaac de Caus at Worcester College, Oxford* Oxford, 1979.

HASLAM, Richard *Powys* London, 1979 (Buildings of Wales)

HASSELL, John *Seats near London* London, 1804–05.

HASSELL, John *Tour of the Isle of Wight, 1790* In J. Pinkerton *General collection of the best and most interesting voyages and travels in all parts of the world* London, 1808. vol. 2.

HASSELL, John *Tour of the Grand Junction . . . with a historical and topographical description of . . . Middlesex, Hertfordshire, Buckinghamshire, Bedfordshire and Northamptonshire* London, 1819.

HASTED, Edward *The history and topographical survey of the county of Kent . . .* Canterbury, 1778–99. 4 vols. Part 1 revised, 1886.

HAVELL, Robert *and* Son *A series of picturesque views of noblemen's & gentlemen's seats with historical and descriptive accounts of each subject* London, 1823.

HEATH, Charles *Historical and descriptive accounts of the ancient and present state of the town and castle of Chepstow including the pleasurable regions of Persfield . . .* Monmouth, 1805.

HEELY, Joseph *A description of The Leasowes* London, 1777.

HEELY, Joseph *Letters on the beauties of Hagley, Envil and The Leasowes; with critical remarks, and observations on the modern taste in gardening* London, 1777. 2 vols.

HELLYER, Arthur *Gardens of genius* London, 1980.

HENTZNER, Paul *Travels in England during the reign of Queen Elizabeth, translated by Horace, late Earl of Orford* London, 1797.

HEWETSON, J. *Architectural and picturesque views of noble mansions in Hampshire* London, c. 1830.

HINDE, Thomas *Stately gardens of Britain* London, 1983.

HISTORICAL MANUSCRIPTS COMMISSION *Architectural history and the fine & applied arts: sources in the National Register of Archives* London, 1969–74. 5 vols.

HOARE, Sir Richard Colt *A collection of forty-eight views of noblemen's and gentlemen's seats, towns, castles, churches, monasteries and romantic places in North and South Wales* London, [1806].

HOARE, Sir Richard Colt *A description of the house and gardens at Stourhead* Bath, 1818.

HOARE, Sir Richard Colt *The modern history of South Wiltshire* London, 1822–44. 5 vols.

HODGSON, John *A history of Northumberland* Newcastle-upon-Tyne, 1820–58. 7 vols.

HOLME, Charles *The gardens of England in the Southern and Western counties* London, 1907.

HOLME, Charles *The gardens of England in the Midland and Eastern counties* London, 1908.

HOLME, Charles *The gardens of England in the Northern counties* London, 1911.

HORSFIELD, Thomas Walker *The history, antiquities and topography of the county of Sussex* Lewes, 1835. 2 vols.

HOUSMAN, John *Descriptive tour and guide to the lakes, caves, mountains and other natural curiosities in Cumberland, Westmorland, Lancashire and a part of the West Riding of Yorkshire* Edition 8. Carlisle, 1817.

HOWLETT, Bartholomew *A selection of views in the county of Lincoln . . .* London, 1805.

HULBERT, Charles *The stranger's friend, comprising a walk through Shrewsbury, an excursion to Hawkestone, a journey to Halton and Runcorn, and a trip to the Isle of Man* Shrewsbury, 1830.

HULL, F. *Catalogue of estate maps, 1590–1840, in the Kent County Archives Office* Maidstone, 1973.

HUNTER, Joseph *The history and topography of the parish of Sheffield in the county of York. New edition by Alfred Gatty* London, 1869.

HUSSEY, Christopher *English gardens and landscapes, 1700–1750.* London, 1967.

HUTCHINS, John *The history and antiquities of the county of Dorset* London, 1774. 2 vols. Edition 3. London, 1861–70. 4 vols.

HUTCHINSON, William *The history of the county of Cumberland and some places adjacent . . .* Carlisle, 1794. 2 vols.

HUTCHINSON, William *The history and antiquities of the County Palatine of Durham* Newcastle-upon-Tyne, 1785–95. 3 vols.

HUTCHINSON, William *A view of Northumberland with an excursion to the Abbey of Mailross in Scotland, anno 1776* Newcastle-upon-Tyne, 1778. 2 vols.

HYAMS, Edward *The English garden* London, 1964.

HYAMS, Edward *Great botanical gardens of the world* London, 1969.

HYAMS, Edward *Irish gardens* London, 1967.

IBBETSON, J.C., LAPORTE, J. *and* HASSELL, J. *A picturesque guide to Bath, Bristol Hot-*

Bibliography of works consulted

Wells, the River Avon, and the adjacent country; illustrated with a set of views, taken in the summer of 1792 London, 1793.

IRELAND, Samuel *Picturesque views on the River Medway, from the Nore to the vicinity of its sources in Sussex; with observations on the public buildings and other works of art in its neighbourhood* London, 1793.

IRELAND, Samuel *Picturesque views on the Upper or Warwickshire Avon from its source at Naseby to its junction with the Severn at Tewkesbury; with observations on the public buildings and other works of art in its vicinity* London, 1795.

IRELAND, Samuel William Henry *England's topographer, or a new and complete history of the county of Kent* London, 1828-30. 4 vols.

JACQUES, David *Georgian gardens: the reign of nature* London, 1983.

JARRETT, David *The English landscape garden* London, 1978.

JEFFERSON, Thomas *Garden book, 1766-1824* Philadelphia, 1944.

JEKYLL, Gertrude *Garden ornament* London, 1918.

JEKYLL, Gertrude *and* ELGOOD, Geroge S. *Some English gardens.* Edition 2. London, 1904.

JEKYLL, Gertrude *and* WEAVER, Lawrence *Gardens for small country houses* London, 1913.

JEWITT, Llewellyn *and* HALL, Samuel Carter *The stately homes of England* London, 1874. 2nd series London, 1877.

JOHNSON, Samuel *Complete works* London, 1787. 13 vols.

JONES, Barbara *Follies & grottoes.* Edition 2. London, 1974.

KALM, Pehr *Kalm's account of his visit to England on his way to America in 1748.* Translated by Joseph Lucas. London, 1892.

KEANE, William *The beauties of Middlesex; being a particular description of the principal seats of the nobility and gentry in the county of Middlesex* Chelsea, 1850.

KEANE, William *Beauties of Surrey; being a particular description of about one hundred and twenty seats of the nobility and gentry in the county of Surrey . . .* London [1849?]

KENNETT, White *Parochial antiquities attempted in the history of Ambrosden and Burcester and other parts in the counties of Oxford and Bucks* Oxford, 1695.

KIELMANSEGGE, *Count* Frederick *Diary of a journey to England in the years 1761-1762 . . .* Translated by Countess Kielmansegg. London, 1902.

KNYFF, Leonard *and* KIP, Johannes *Britannia illustrata or views of several of the Queen's Palaces and also of the principal seats of the nobility and gentry of Great Britain* London, 1714-15. 2 vols.

KNYFF, Leonard *and* KIP, Johannes, etc *Nouveau théâtre de la Grande Bretagne . . .* London, 1724-29. 4 vols. *Supplement.* London, 1728.

KNIGHT OF GLIN *and* BOWE, Patrick   *Gardens of outstanding historic interest in the Republic of Ireland*   Dublin, 1980.

LE ROUGE, George Louis   *Jardins Anglo-Chinois a la mode*   Paris, 1776–c.1787.

LEES-MILNE, Alvilde *and* VEREY, Rosemary   *The Englishwoman's garden*   London, 1980.

LEES-MILNE, Alvilde *and* VEREY, Rosemary   *The Englishman's garden*   London, 1982.

LEES-MILNE, James   *Earls of creation: five great patrons of eighteenth-century art*   London, 1962.

LEMMON, Kenneth   *Gardens of Britain, 5: Yorkshire and Humberside*   London, 1978.

LIPSCOMB, George   *A journey into Cornwall through the counties of Southampton, Wilts, Dorset, Somerset & Devon*   Warwick, 1799.

LIPSCOMB, George   *A journey into South Wales . . . in the year 1799*   London, 1802.

LIPSCOMB, George   *The history and antiquities of the county of Buckingham*   London, 1847–51. 4 vols.

LITTLE, G. Allan   *Scotland's gardens*   Edinburgh, 1981.

LOGGAN, David   *Cantabrigia illustrata . . .*   Cambridge, 1690.

LOGGAN, David   *Oxonia illustrata . . .*   Oxford, 1675.

LOUDON, John Claudius   *An encyclopaedia of gardening . . .*   London, 1822.

LOUDON, John Claudius   *Arboretum et fruticetum Britannicum; or the trees and shrubs of Britain . . .* Edition 2.   London, 1844. 8 vols.

LOUDON, John Claudius   *A treatise on forming, improving and managing country residences . . .*   London, 1806. 2 vols.

LOUDON, John Claudius   *The villa gardener . . .*   London, 1850.

LOVEDAY, John   *Diary of a tour in 1732 through parts of England, Wales Ireland and Scotland*   Edinburgh, 1890.

LYSONS, Daniel   *The environs of London; being an historical account of the towns, villages and hamlets, within twelve miles of that capital . . .*   London, 1792–96. 4 vols. Supplement. London, 1811.

LYSONS, Daniel   *An historical account of three parishes in the county of Middlesex which are not described in the Environs of London*   London, 1800.

MaCARTNEY, Mervyn   *English houses & gardens in the 17th and 18th centuries; a series of birds-eye views reproduced from contemporary engravings by Kip, Badeslade, Harris and others*   London, 1908.

MacGREGOR, Jessie   *Gardens of celebrities and celebrated gardens in and around London . . .*   London, 1918.

MacKENZIE, Eneas *and* ROSS, M.   *An historical, topographical, and descriptive view of the County Palatine of Durham*   Newcastle-upon-Tyne, 1834. 2 vols.

Bibliography of works consulted

McWILLIAM, Colin *Lothian except Edinburgh* London, 1978. (Buildings of Scotland).

MAGALOTTI, *Count* Lorenzo *Travels of Cosmo the Third, Grand Duke of Tuscany, through England during the reign of King Charles II* London, 1821.

MALINS, Edward *English landscaping and literature* London, 1966.

MALINS, Edward *Red books of Humphry Repton* [Antony House, Cornwall; Sheringham, Norfolk; Attingham, Shropshire] London, 1976. 4 vols.

MALINS, Edward *and* KNIGHT OF GLIN *Lost demesnes: Irish landscape gardening, 1660–1845* London, 1976.

MALINS, Edward *and* BOWE, Patrick *Irish gardens and demesnes from 1830* London, 1980.

MANNING, Owen *and* BRAY, W. *The history and antiquities of the county of Surrey* . . . London, 1804–14. 3 vols.

MARSHALL, William *On planting and rural ornament*. Edition 3. London, 1803. 2 vols.

MAVOR, William *The British tourist's or traveller's pocket companion through England, Wales, Scotland and Ireland. Comprehending the most celebrated modern tours in the British Isles and several originals* London, 1798–1809. 6 vols.

MAVOR, William *General view of the agriculture of Berkshire* . . . London, 1809.

MAWSON, Thomas H. *The art & craft of garden making*. Edition 3. London, 1907.

MAXWELL, *Sir* Herbert *Scottish gardens being a representative selection of different types, old and new* London, 1911.

MEISTER, Henry *Letters written during a residence in England* London, 1799.

MILTON, Thomas *The seats and demesnes of the nobility and gentry in Ireland* Dublin, 1783–93.

MORANT, Philip *The history and antiquities of the county of Essex* . . . London, 1768. 2 vols; 1816. 2 vols.

MORRIS, Francis Orpen *A series of picturesque views of seats of the noblemen and gentlemen of Great Britain and Ireland* London, 1866–80. 6 vols.

MORTON, John *The natural history of Northamptonshire* . . . London, 1712.

MUILMAN, Peter *A new and complete history of Essex* Chelmsford, 1771–72. 6 vols.

NAIRN, Ian *and* CHERRY, Bridget *Surrey*. Edition 2. London, 1971. (Buildings of England).

NAIRN, Ian *and* PEVSNER, Nikolaus *Sussex*. London, 1965. (Buildings of England).

NATTES, John Claude *Scotia depicta; or, the antiquities, castles, public buildings, noblemen and gentlemen's seats, cities, towns and picturesque scenery of Scotland* London, 1804.

NEALE, J.P. *An account of the Deep-dene in Surrey; the seat of Thomas Hope, Esq* . . . London, 1826.

NEALE, J.P. *Views of the seats of noblemen and gentlemen in England, Wales, Scotland and Ireland* London, 1818–23. 6 vols.

NEWMAN, John *North East and East Kent*. Edition 2. London, 1976. (Buildings of England).

NEWMAN, John *West Kent and the Weald*. Edition 2. London, 1976. (Buildings of England).

NEWMAN, John *and* PEVSNER, Nikolaus *Dorset*. London, 1972. (Buildings of England).

NEWTON, N.T. *Design on the land: the development of landscape architecture* Harvard, 1971.

NICHOLS, Harold *Local maps of Derbyshire to 1770: an inventory and introduction* Derbyshire Library Service, Matlock, 1980.

NICHOLS, John *The history and antiquites of the county of Leicester* London, 1795–1811. 4 vols.

NIGHTINGALE, Joseph *The beauties of England and Wales . . . vol. 13 pt 1: [Shropshire, Somersetshire]* London, 1813.

NIGHTINGALE, Joseph *A topographical and historical description of Staffordshire* London, 1810.

OPPÉ, Adolf Paul *The drawings of Paul and Thomas Sandby in the collection of His Majesty the King at Windsor Castle* London, 1947.

ORD, John Walker *The history and antiquities of Cleveland comprising the Wapentake of East and West Langburgh, North Riding, county Yorks* London, 1846.

ORMEROD, George *History of the County Palatine and city of Chester . . .* Edition 2. London, 1882. 3 vols.

OVERTON, Henry *and* HOOLE, J. *Britannia illustrata or views of all the King's Palaces, several seats of the nobility and gentry . . .* London, [c. 1724].

PAINE, Thomas *Plans, elevations, and sections of noblemen and gentlemen's houses, and also of stabling, bridges, public and private, temples, and other garden buildings, executed in . . . Derby, Durham, Middlesex, Northumberland, Nottingham and York* London, 1783. 2 vols.

PARREAUX, André *and* PLAISANT, M. *Jardins et paysages: le style Anglais* Lille, 1977.

PARSONS, M. *English house grounds: photographs* New York, 1924.

PARTINGTON, Charles Frederick *National history and views of London and its environs . . .* London, 1834. 2 vols.

PATERSON, Allen *Gardens of Britain, 2: Dorset, Hampshire and the Isle of Wight* London, 1978.

PENNANT, Thomas *The journey from Chester to London* London, 1782.

PENNANT, Thomas *A tour in Wales, 1773* London, 1778–81. 2 vols.

Bibliography of works consulted

PENNANT, Thomas *A tour from Downing to Alston-Moor* London, 1801.

PENNANT, Thomas *A journey from London to the Isle of Wight* London, 1801. 2 vols.

PENNANT, Thomas *A tour from Alston-Moor to Harrowgate and Brimham Crags* London, 1804.

PERRÉDÈS, P.E.F. *London botanic gardens* London, 1906.

PEVSNER, Nikolaus *Bedfordshire and the county of Huntingdon and Peterborough* London, 1968. (Buildings of England).

PEVSNER, Nikolaus *Berkshire* London, 1966. (Buildings of England).

PEVSNER, Nikolaus *Buckinghamshire* London, 1960. (Buildings of England).

PEVSNER, Nikolaus *Cambridgeshire* Edition 2. London, 1970. (Buildings of England).

PEVSNER, Nikolaus *Essex* Edition 2. London, 1965. (Buildings of England).

PEVSNER, Nikolaus *Herefordshire* London, 1963. (Buildings of England).

PEVSNER, Nikolaus *Hertfordshire* Edition 2. London, 1977. (Buildings of England).

PEVSNER, Nikolaus *Lancashire 1: the industrial and commercial south* London, 1969. (Buildings of England).

PEVSNER, Nikolaus *Lancashire 2: the rural north* London, 1969. (Buildings of England).

PEVSNER, Nikolaus *Leicestershire and Rutland* London, 1960. (Buildings of England).

PEVSNER, Nikolaus *London 1: the cities of London and Westminster* Edition 3. London, 1973. (Buildings of England).

PEVSNER, Nikolaus *London 2: except the cities of London and Westminster* London, 1952. (Buildings of England).

PEVSNER, Nikolaus *Middlesex* London, 1951. (Buildings of England).

PEVSNER, Nikolaus *North Devon* London, 1952. (Buildings of England).

PEVSNER, Nikolaus *North-East Norfolk and Norwich* London, 1962. (Buildings of England).

PEVSNER, Nikolaus *North Somerset and Bristol* London, 1958. (Buildings of England).

PEVSNER, Nikolaus *North-West and South Norfolk* London, 1962. (Buildings of England).

PEVSNER, Nikolaus *Northumberland* London, 1957. (Buildings of England).

PEVSNER, Nikolaus *Nottinghamshire* Edition 2. London, 1979. (Buildings of England).

PEVSNER, Nikolaus *Shropshire* London, 1959. (Buildings of England).

PEVSNER, Nikolaus *South and West Somerset* London, 1958. (Buildings of England).

PEVSNER, Nikolaus *Staffordshire* London, 1974. (Buildings of England).

PEVSNER, Nikolaus *Suffolk* Edition 2. London, 1974. (Buildings of England).

PEVSNER, Nikolaus *Wiltshire* Edition 2. London, 1975. (Buildings of England).

PEVSNER, Nikolaus *Worcestershire* London, 1968. (Buildings of England).

PEVSNER, Nikolaus *Yorkshire: the North Riding* London, 1966. (Buildings of England).

PEVSNER, Nikolaus *Yorkshire: West Riding* Edition 2. London, 1967. (Buildings of England).

PEVSNER, Nikolaus *Yorkshire: York and the East Riding* London, 1972. (Buildings of England).

PEVSNER, Nikolaus *and* HARRIS, John *Lincolnshire* London, 1964. (Buildings of England).

PEVSNER, Nikolaus *and* HUBBARD, Edward *Cheshire* London, 1971. (Buildings of England).

PEVSNER, Nikolaus *and* LLOYD, D. *Hampshire and the Isle of Wight* London, 1967. (Buildings of England).

PEVSNER, Nikolaus *and* WEDGEWOOD, Alexandra *Warwickshire* London, 1966. (Buildings of England).

PHELPS, William *The history and antiquities of Somersetshire; being a general and parochial survey of that interesting county* London, 1836–39. 2 vols.

PITT, William *General view of the agriculture of the county of Stafford* London, 1796.

PLOT, Robert *The natural history of Staffordshire* Oxford, 1685.

PLOT, Robert *The natural history of Oxfordshire* Edition 2. Oxford, 1705.

PLUMPTRE, G. *Royal gardens* London, 1981.

POCOCKE, Richard *Tours in Scotland, 1747, 1750, 1760* Edited by D.W. Kemp. Edinburgh, 1887.

POCOCKE, Richard *Travels through England . . . during 1750, 1751 and later years* London, 1888–89. 2 vols.

POLWHELE, Richard *The history of Devonshire* London, 1793–97. 3 vols.

POULSON, George *The history and antiquities of the Seigniory of Holderness in the East Riding of the county of York . . .* Hull, 1840–41. 2 vols.

PROSSER, George Frederick *Select illustrations of the county of Surrey comprising picturesque views of the seats of the nobility and gentry . . .* London, 1828.

PROSSER, George Frederick *Select illustrations of Hampshire comprising picturesque views of the seats of the nobility and gentry . . .* London, 1833.

PÜCKLER-MUSKAU, Herman Ludwig Heinrich von, Prince *Tour in England, Ireland and France in the years 1826, 1827, 1828 and 1829 . . .* Philadelphia, 1833.

PYNE, William Henry *The history of the royal residences of Windsor Castle, St. James's Palace, Carlton House, Kensington Palace, Hampton Court, Buckingham House and Frogmore . . .* London, 1819. 3 vols.

Bibliography of works consulted

QUINCY, Thomas *A short tour in the Midland counties of England; performed in the summer of 1772. Together with an account of a similar excursion undertaken, September 1774* London, 1775.

RAPHAEL, Sandra, THACKER, Christopher, BATEY, Mavis *and* WOOD, Dennis *Of Oxfordshire gardens* Oxford, 1982.

REPTON, Humphry *Sketches and hints on landscape gardening collected from designs and observations now in the possession of the different noblemen and gentlemen for whose use they were originally made . . .* London, 1794.

REPTON, Humphry *Observations on the theory and practice of landscape gardening* London, 1803.

REPTON, Humphry *Fragments on the theory and practice of landscape gardening, including some remarks on Grecian and Gothic architecture . . .* London, 1816.

(All three works were published in one volume in 1840 under the editorship of J.C. Loudon: *The landscape gardening and landscape architecture of the late Humphry Repton.* Reprinted 1969).

ROBERTSON, Archibald *A topographical survey of the Great Road from London to Bath and Bristol . . .* London, 1792. 2 vols.

ROBINSON, William *The English flower garden: style, position and arrangement . . .* London, 1883.

ROCKLEY, *Lady* Alicia Margaret *Historic gardens of England* London, 1938.

ROHDE, Eleanor Sinclair *Oxford's college gardens* London, 1932.

ROPER, Lanning *Royal gardens: Buckingham Palace, Windsor Castle, Sandringham House, the Palace of Holyroodhouse, Balmoral Castle* London, 1953.

RORSCHACH, Kimerly *The early Gerogian landscape garden* New Haven, Connecticut, 1983.

ROWAN, Alistair *North West Ulster: the counties of Londonderry, Donegal, Fermanagh and Tyrone* London, 1979. (Buildings of Ireland).

ROYAL COMMISSION ON HISTORICAL MONUMENTS, ENGLAND *An inventory of the historical monuments in . . . Northampton* vols. 3–4. London, 1981–82.

ROYAL COMMISSION ON HISTORICAL MONUMENTS OF SCOTLAND . . . *Peebleshire* vol. 2, 1967.

ROYAL COMMISSION ON HISTORICAL MONUMENTS IN WALES . . . *Glamorgan* vol. 4, 1981.

ROYAL INSTITUTE OF BRITISH ARCHITECTS *Catalogue of the drawings collection: A–S* London, 1968–76. 7 vols. *Edwin Lutyens* London, 1973.

RUDDER, Samuel *A new history of Gloucestershire . . .* Cirencester, 1779.

RUTLAND, J.H. Manners, *Duke of* *Journal of a tour round the southern coasts of England* London, 1805.

RUTLAND, J.H. Manners, *Duke of* *Journal of a tour through North and South Wales, the Isle of Man, etc, etc.* London, 1805.

RUTLAND, J.H. Manners, *Duke of* *Journal of a tour to the northern parts of Great Britain* London, 1813.

SALES, John *West Country gardens: the gardens of Gloucestershire, Avon, Somerset and Wiltshire* Gloucester, 1980.

SANDBY, Paul *A collection of one hundred and fifty select views in England, Scotland and Ireland* London, 1781. 2 vols.

SEXBY, John James *The municipal parks, gardens and open spaces of London: their history and associations* London, 1905.

SHAW, Stebbing *The history and antiquities of Staffordshire . . .* London, 1798–1801. 2 vols.

SHAW, Stebbing *A tour in 1787, from London, to the Western Highlands of Scotland . . .* London, 1788.

SHAW, Stebbing *Tour to West of England in 1788* In J. Pinkerton *General collection of the best and most interesting voyages and travels in all parts of the world* London, 1808. vol. 2.

SHENSTONE, William *The letters of William Shenstone* Edited by M. Williams Oxford, 1939.

SHERWOOD, Jennifer *and* PEVSNER, Nikolaus *Oxfordshire* London, 1974. (Buildings of England).

SHEWELL-COOPER, W.E. *The royal gardens, King George VI and his Queen* London, 1952.

SIDWELL, Ron *West Midland gardens* Gloucester, 1981.

[SIMOND, Louis] *Journal of a tour and residence in Great Britain during the years 1810 and 1811, by a French traveller . . .* Edinburgh, 1815. 2 vols.

SIREN, Osvald *China and gardens of Europe of the eighteenth century* New York, 1950.

SKELTON, Joseph *Oxonia antiqua restaurata containing upwards of one hundred and seventy engravings . . .* Oxford, 1823. 2 vols.

SKRINE, Henry *Two successive tours throughout the whole of Wales with several of the adjacent English counties . . .* Edition 2. London, 1812.

SKRINE, Henry *Three successive tours in the North of England to the Lakes, and great part of Scotland . . .* Edition 2. London, 1813.

SMITH, John Thomas *Antiquities of Westminster; the old Palace; St. Stephen's Chapel, . . .* London, 1807.

SOCIETY OF GENTLEMEN *England displayed: being a new . . . survey and description of . . . England and . . . Wales* London, 1769. 2 vols.

SPENCER, Nathaniel *The complete English traveller; or, a new survey and description of England and Wales* London, 1771.

Bibliography of works consulted

STORER, James *A description of Fonthill Abbey, Wiltshire* London, 1812.

STORER, James Sargant *Antiquarian and topographical cabinet, containing a series of elegant views of the most interesting objects of curiosity in Great Britain* London, 1807–11. 10 vols.

STRONG, Roy *The Renaissance garden in England* London, 1979.

STROUD, Dorothy *Capability Brown* Edition 2. London, 1975.

STROUD, Dorothy *Humphry Repton* London, 1962.

STUKELEY, William *Itinerarium curiosum; or, an account of the antiquities and remarkable curiosities in nature or art observed in travels through Great Britain* Edition 2. London, 1776. 2 vols.

STURDY, David *Twelve Oxford gardens* London, 1982.

SUCKLING, Alfred J. *The history and antiquities of the county of Suffolk* London, 1846–48. 2 vols.

SULIVAN, Richard Joseph *A tour through part of England, Scotland and Wales in 1778. In a series of letters* London, 1785. 2 vols.

SURTEES, Robert *The history and antiquities of the County Palatine of Durham* . . . London, 1816–40. 4 vols.

SWITZER, Stephen *Ichnographia rustica; or, the nobleman, gentleman and gardener's recreation* Edition 2. London, 1742. 3 vols.

SWITZER, Stephen *An introduction to a general system of hydrostaticks and hydraulicks* . . . London, 1729. 2 vols.

SYNGE, Patrick M. *Gardens of Britain, 1: Devon and Cornwall* London, 1977.

TAIT, A.A. *The landscape garden in Scotland, 1735–1835* Edinburgh, 1980.

TAYLOR, Christopher *The archaeology of gardens* Aylesbury, 1983.

TAYLOR, George *Old London gardens* London, 1953.

TEMPLE, *Sir* William *Works* London, 1814. 4 vols.

THOMAS, Graham S. *Gardens of the National Trust* London, 1979.

THORNTON, William *The new, complete and universal history, description and survey of the cities of London and Westminster, the borough of Southwark and the parts adjacent* London, 1786.

THOROTON, Robert *Thoroton's history of Nottinghamshire: republished, with large additions by John Throsby* London, 1797. 3 vols.

THROSBY, John *Select views in Leicestershire, from original engravings containing seats of the nobility and gentry, town views and ruins* . . . London, 1790. 2 vols.

THURSTON, H. *Royal parks for the people: London's ten* Newton Abbot, 1974.

TOD, George *Plans, elevations and sections of hot-houses, green-houses, an aquarium, conservatories, etc* . . . London, 1807.

TOOLEY, M. *and* R. *Gardens of Gertrude Jekyll in Northern England* Witton-le-Wear, 1982.

TORRINGTON, John Byng, Viscount *The Torrington diaries containing the tours through England and Wales . . . between the years 1781 and 1794* London, 1934–38. 4 vols.

TRIGGS, H. Inigo *Formal gardens in England and Scotland* London, 1902.

TYNE AND WEAR COUNTY COUNCIL MUSEUMS *and* NORTH EAST CHAPTER OF THE LANDSCAPE INSTITUTE *Capability Brown and the northern landscape* Newcastle-upon-Tyne, 1983.

UFFENBACH, Zacharias Conrad von *London in 1710 . . .* Translated and edited by W.H. Quarrell and Margaret Mare. London, 1934.

ULSTER ARCHITECTURAL HERITAGE SOCIETY *Northern gardens: gardens and parks of outstanding historic interest in Northern Ireland* Belfast, 1982.

URWIN, Alan C.B. *Railshead: the history of Lacy and St. Margaret's houses, Isleworth, Middlesex* Hounslow, 1974.

URWIN, Alan C.B. *Twicknam Parke* Hounslow, 1965.

VEREY, David *Gloucestershire 1: the Cotswolds* London, 1970. (Buildings of England).

VEREY, David *Gloucestershire 2: the Vale and the Forest of Dean* London, 1970. (Buildings of England).

VERNEY, Peter *The gardens of Scotland* London, 1976.

VICTORIA COUNTY HISTORIES :
    Berkshire v. 1–4. 1906–24.
    Bedford v. 1–3. 1904–12.
    Buckingham v. 1–4. 1905–27.
    Cambridge v. 1–8. 1938–82.
    Cheshire v. 2–3. 1979–80.
    Cornwall v. 1. 1906.
    Cumberland v. 1–2. 1901–05.
    Derby v. 1–2. 1905–07.
    Devon v. 1. 1906.
    Dorset v. 2–3. 1908–68.
    Durham v. 1–3. 1905–28.
    Essex v. 1–7. 1903–78.
    Gloucester v. 2, 6–8, 10, 11. 1907–76.
    Hampshire v. 1–5. 1900–12.
    Hertford v. 1–4. 1908–14.
    Huntingdon v. 1–3. 1926–36.
    Kent v. 1–3. 1908–32.
    Lancaster v. 1–8. 1906–14.
    Leicester v. 1–5. 1907–64.
    Middlesex v. 1–6. 1969–80.
    Norfolk v. 1–2. 1901–06.
    Northampton v. 1–4. 1902–37.

Bibliography of works consulted

Nottingham v. 1–2. 1906–10.
Oxford v. 1–11. 1939–83.
Rutland v. 1–2. 1908–35.
Shropshire v. 1–3, 8. 1908–68.
Somerset v. 1–4. 1906–78.
Stafford v. 1–6, 8, 17. 1908–76.
Suffolk v. 1–2. 1907–11.
Surrey v. 1–4. 1902–12.
Sussex v. 1–4, 6, 7, 9. 1905–80.
Warwick v. 1, 3–8. 1904–69.
Wiltshire v. 1–12. 1957–83.
Worcester v. 1–4. 1901–24.
York v. 1–3. 1907–13.
York. North Riding v. 1–2. 1914–23.
York. East Riding v. 1–4. 1969–79.

VIRTUE, G. *Picturesque beauties of Great Britain: Kent* 1829; *Essex* 1831. London.

WALPOLE, Horace *Essay on modern gardening* Twickenham, 1785.

WALPOLE, Horace *Horace Walpole's journals of visits to country seats, 1751–84.* Edited by Paget Toynbee. (Walpole Society v. 7, 1927/28, 9–80).

WALPOOLE, George Augustus *The new British traveller; or, a complete modern universal display of Great Britain and Ireland* London, 1784.

WARD, Cyril. *Royal gardens* London, 1912.

WARNER, Richard *A second walk through Wales in August and September 1798* Bath, 1799.

WARNER, Richard *Excursions from Bath* Bath, 1801.

WARNER, Richard *A tour through the northern counties of England, and the borders of Scotland* Bath, 1802. 2 vols.

WARNER, Richard *A tour through Cornwall in the autumn of 1808* London, 1809.

WATTS, William *The seats of the nobility and gentry in a collection of the most interesting & picturesque views* London, 1779.

WEAVER, Lawrence *Houses and gardens by E.L. Lutyens* London, 1913.

WEBB, Daniel Carless *Observations and remarks during four excursions made to various parts of Great Britain in . . . 1810 and 1811; I: from London to the Land's End in Cornwall; II: from London to Lancaster; III: from London to Edinburgh; IV: from London to Swansea* London, 1812.

WEBBER, Ronald *Percy Cane: garden designer* Edinburgh, 1975.

WESLEY, John *Journal [1735–1790]* London, 1903. 4 vols.

WHATELY, Thomas *Observations on modern gardening* Edition 3. London, 1771. New edition with notes by Horace Walpole and plates by W. Woollett. London, 1801.

WHISTLER, Laurence *The imagination of Vanbrugh and his fellow artists* London, 1954.

WHITAKER, Thomas Dunham *An history of Richmondshire in the North Riding of the county of York* London, 1823. 2 vols.

WHITAKER, Thomas Dunham *The history and antiquities of the Deanery of Craven in the county of York* Edition 3. Leeds, 1878.

WHITTOCK, Nathaniel *and* GASTINEAU, H. *Picturesque beauties of England and Wales in a series of views from original drawings* London, 1830.

WILKES, Lyall *John Dobson, architect & landscape gardener* Stocksfield, 1980.

WILLIAMS, David *The history of Monmouthshire* London, 1796.

WILLIAMS, Guy *The royal parks of London* London, 1978.

WILLIAMS, William *Oxonia depicta . . .* Oxford, 1732–33.

WILLIS, Peter *Charles Bridgeman and the English landscape garden* London, 1977.

WILLIS, Peter, *ed.* *Furor hortensis: essays on the history of the English landscape garden in memory of H.F. Clark* Edinburgh, 1974.

WOOLFE, John *and* GANDON, James *Vitruvius Britannicus* v. 4–5. London, 1767–71.

WORSLEY, *Sir* Richard *History of the Isle of Wight* London, 1781.

WRIGHT, Thomas *Arbours & grottos. A facsimile of the two parts of 'Universal architecture' (1755 and 1758) with a catalogue of Wright's works in architecture and garden design by Eileen Harris* London, 1979.

WRIGHT, Thomas *The history and topography of the county of Essex* London, 1836. 2 vols.

WRIGHT, Thomas *and* JONES. H.L. *Le Keux's memorials of Cambridge: a series of views of the colleges, halls and public buildings* London, 1841–42. 2 vols.

WRIGHT, Tom *Gardens of Britain, 4: Kent, East & West Sussex and Surrey* London, 1978.

WROTH, Warwick *The London pleasure gardens of the eighteenth century* London, 1896.

YOUNG, Arthur *A six weeks tour through the southern counties of England and Wales* London, 1768.

YOUNG, Arthur *A six months tour through the North of England* Edition 2. London, 1771. 4 vols.

YOUNG, Arthur *The farmer's tour through the East of England* London, 1771. 4 vols.

THE PLATES

Plate 1

Llanerch in Denbighshire, North Wales with St. Asaph's Cathedral in the distance. Oil painting by an unknown painter, 1662. One of the earliest bird's eye views of a British garden. *Yale Center for British Art, Paul Mellon Collection.*

Plate 2

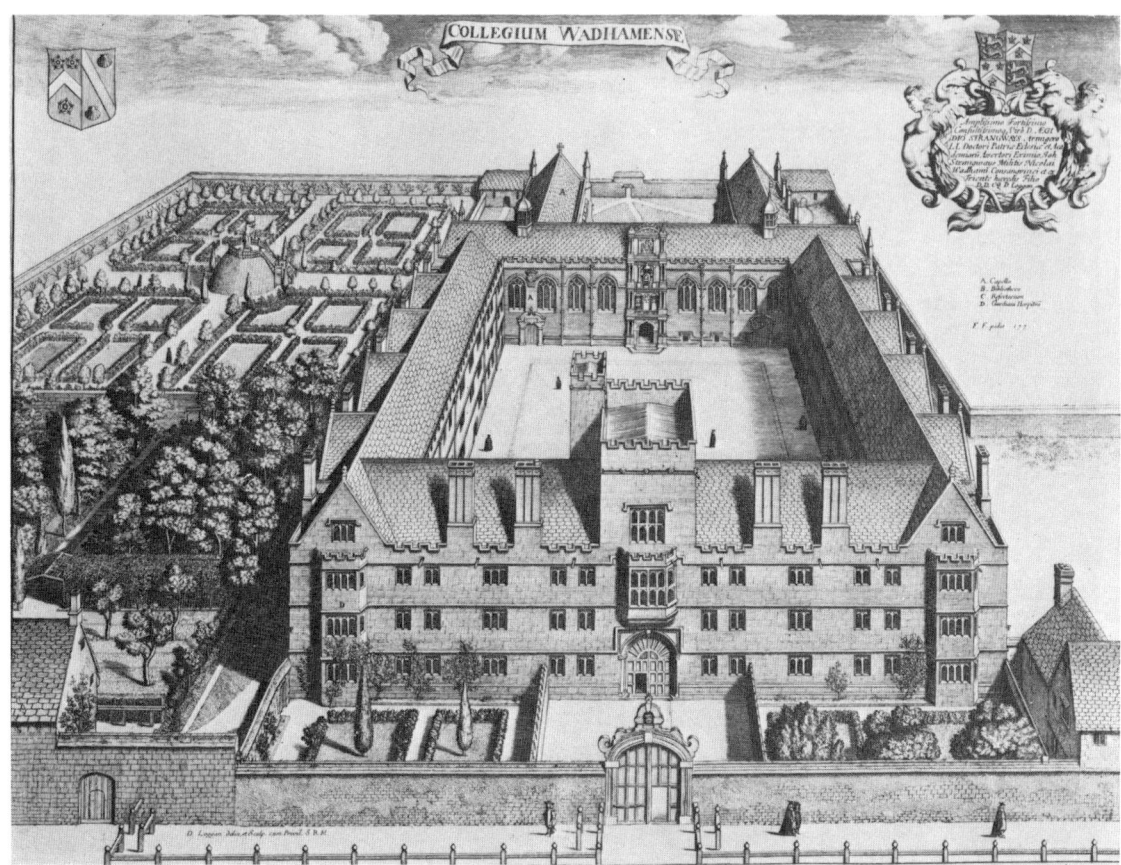

Wadham College, Oxford from *Oxonia illustrata* . . . by David Loggan (Oxford, 1675). Born in Danzig, Loggan was working as an artist and engraver in England by the 1650s. This book contains 37 engravings of public buildings, colleges and halls in Oxford, all executed in meticulous detail. He performed a similar service for Cambridge in his *Cantabrigia illustrata* . . . (Cambridge, 1690). It is interesting to compare this garden with the later version in Plate 3.

Plate 3

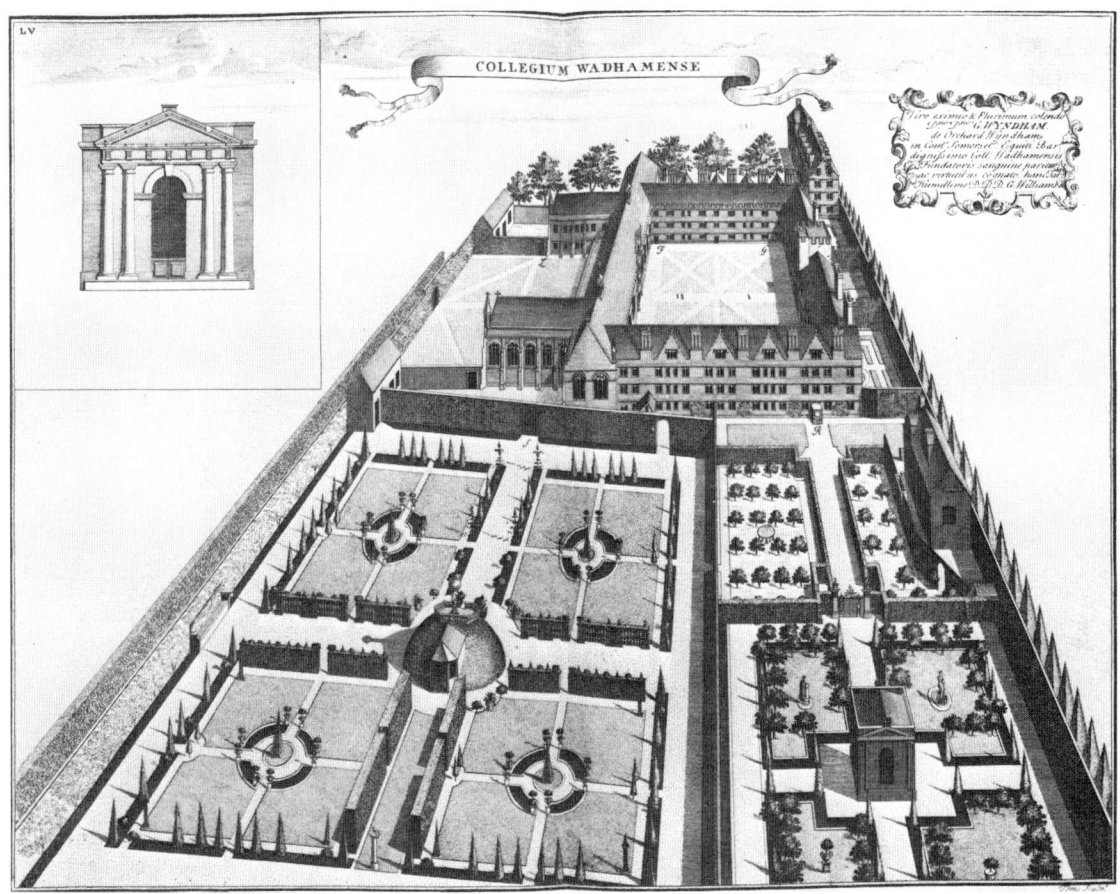

Wadham College, Oxford from *Oxonia depicta* . . . by William Williams, (Oxford, 1732–33). Engraved by Toms. The trees depicted in *Oxonia illustrata* . . . are now shaped and circular paths or beds in each quarter have appeared.

Plate 4

Robert Plot, the antiquary, proposed making a 'philosophical tour' through England and Wales but this ambitious project was limited to *The natural history of Oxfordshire* (Oxford, 1676; edition 2, 1705) and *The natural history of Staffordshire* (Oxford, 1685), both works including descriptions of gardens. *The natural history of Oxfordshire* describes in considerable detail the mechanism of the elaborate waterworks in the garden at Enstone. The jets of water were intended to be turned on suddenly to soak any unsuspecting passerby. This trick fountain would have delighted Celia Fiennes who, surprisingly, does not record having seen it.

Plate 5

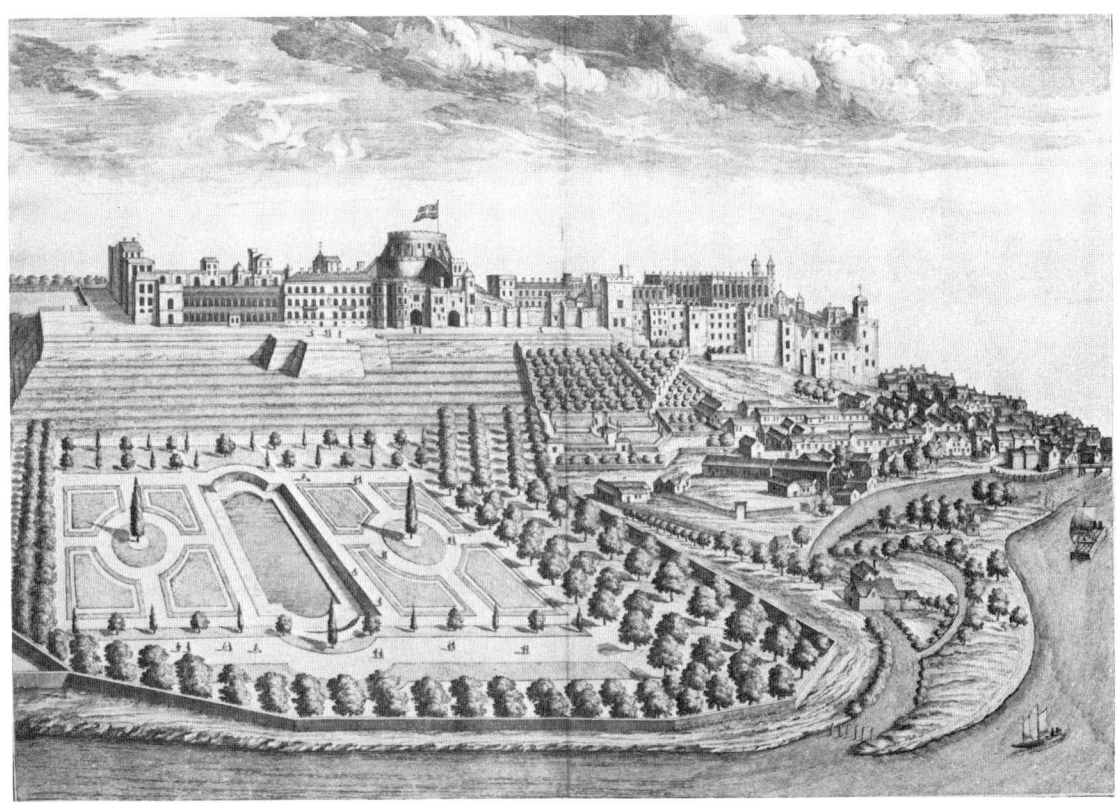

Windsor Castle and the town from *Britannia illustrata or views of several of the Queen's Palaces also of the principal seats of the nobility and gentry of Great Britain* vol. 1 (London, 1707). Leonard Knyff was the artist and Johannes Kip the engraver. Volume 2 which appeared in 1715 included Kip's own drawings from Sir Robert Atkyns's *Glostershire* (1712). The first aerial view of Windsor was drawn by Wencelaus Hollar in 1659 and engraved in E. Ashmole's *Institutions . . . of the . . . Order of the Garter* (1672).

Plate 6

Montagu House, Great Russell Street, Bloomsbury, London from *Nouveau théâtre de la Grande Bretagne* vol. 4 (London, 1729). This work is one of the subsequent versions of *Britannia illustrata* issued by various London booksellers. It was published in four volumes by Joseph Smith who was also co-publisher of Campbell's *Vitruvius Britannicus* (1717–25). The whole work is generally referred to as being by Kip but it also has engravings by other artists; this plate of Montagu House, for instance, was executed by James Simon.

Plate 7

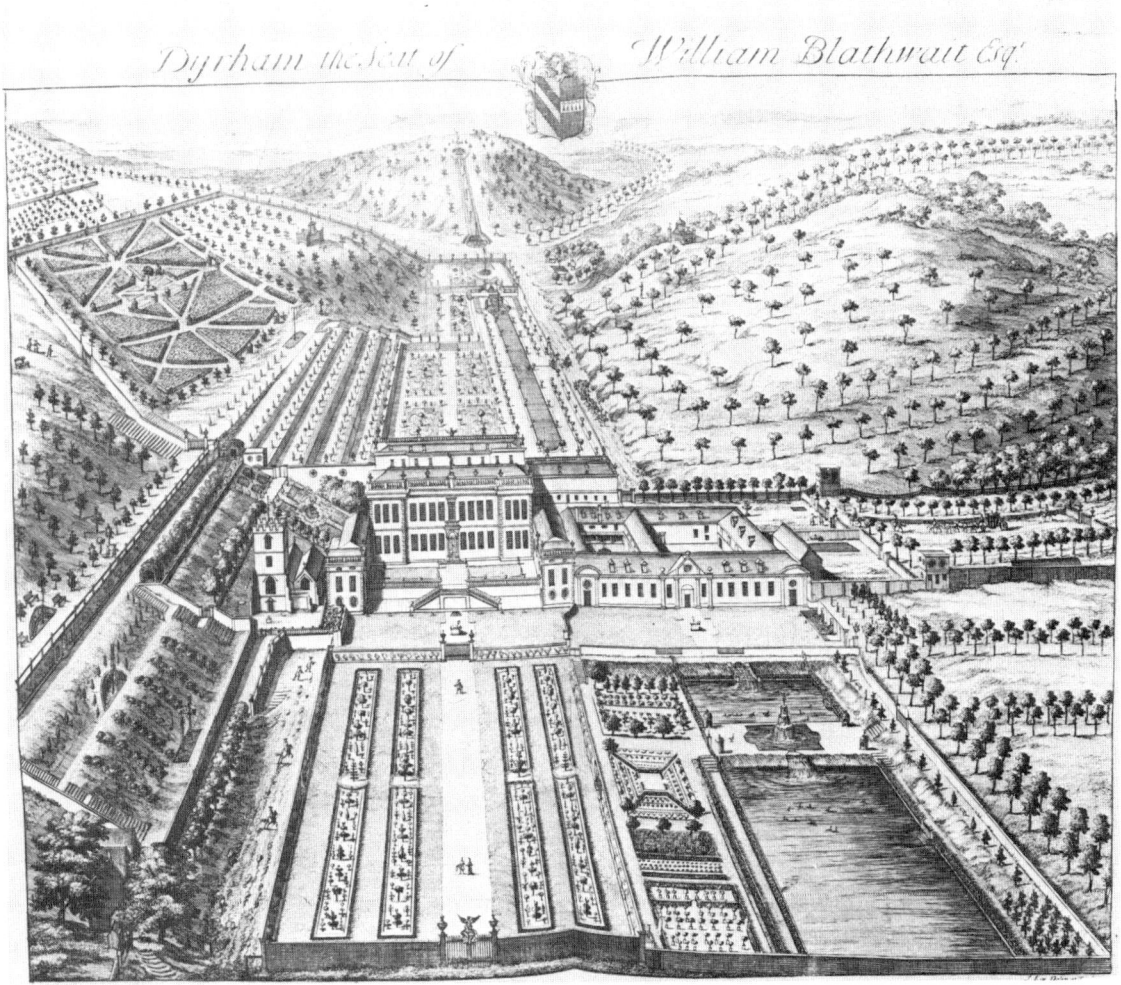

Dyrham, Avon from *Ancient and present state of Glostershire* by Sir Robert Atkyns (London, 1712). Kip drew and engraved all the plates. The survey of English counties began with William Lambarde's *Perambulation of Kent* (1570) which inspired the compilation of other county histories. They continued to be published and revised during the eighteenth and nineteenth centuries and the scholarly Victoria County Histories owe much to their pioneering research.

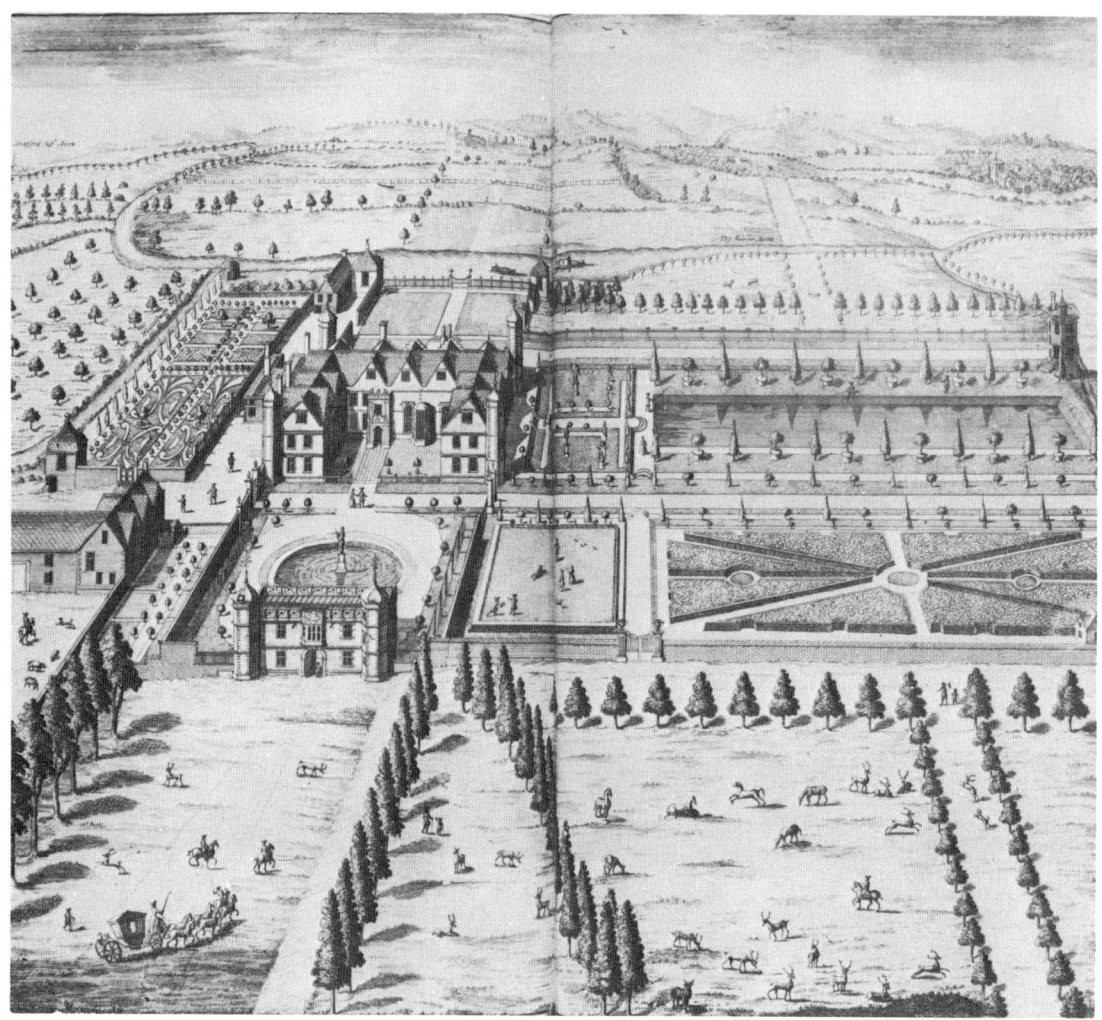

Charlecote Park, Warwickshire from *Antiquities of Warwickshire* by Sir William Dugdale, edition 2 (London, 1730). The second edition retains the etchings by Hollar of the original edition (1656) with additional plates. This one of Charlecote was drawn by H. Beighton in 1722 and engraved by E. Kirkall. All these impressive county histories— Sir Henry Chauncy's *Hertfordshire* (1700), John Harris's *Kent* (1719), P. Morant's *Essex* (1768), J. Hutchins's *Dorset* (1774), etc— are extremely useful to the garden historian.

Plate 9

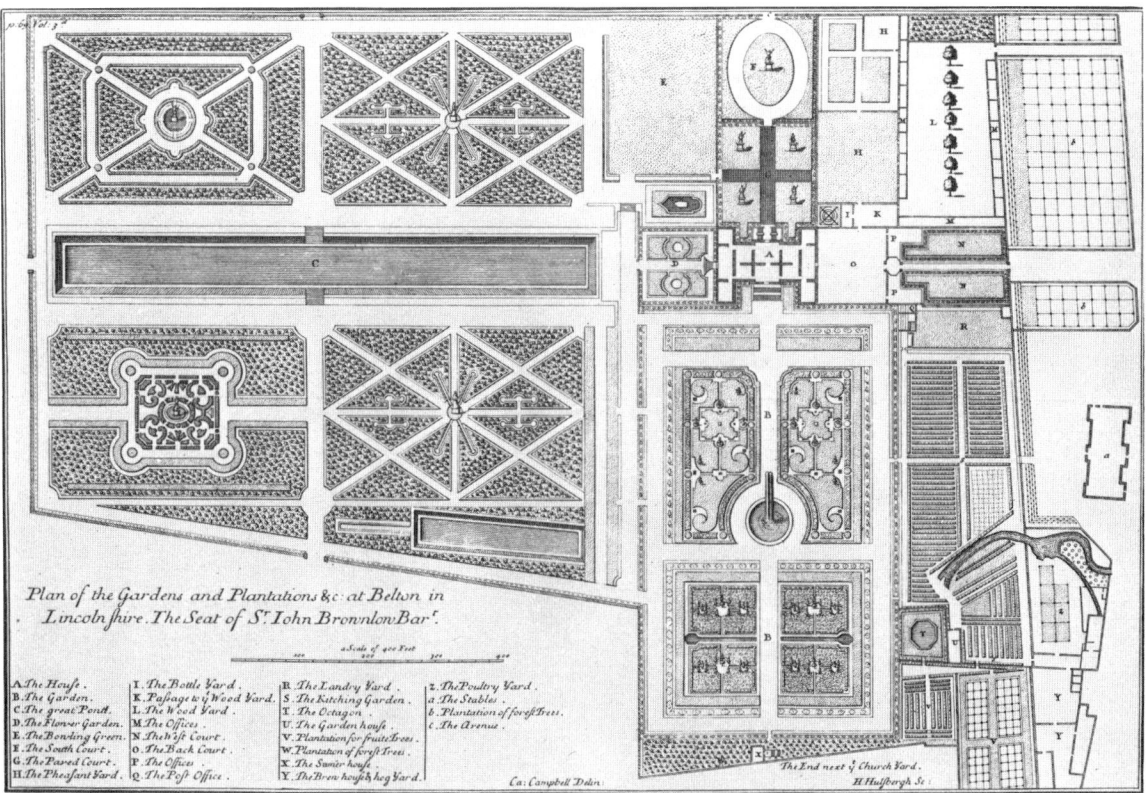

Belton House, Grantham, Lincolnshire from *Vitruvius Britannicus* . . . by Colen Campbell vol. 3 (London, 1725). Drawn by Campbell and engraved by Henry Hulsbergh. *Vitruvius Britannicus* (1715–25) was the first professional survey of British architecture. The number of country houses increases with the second and third volumes and the last volume has plans of fifteen different gardens.

Plate 10

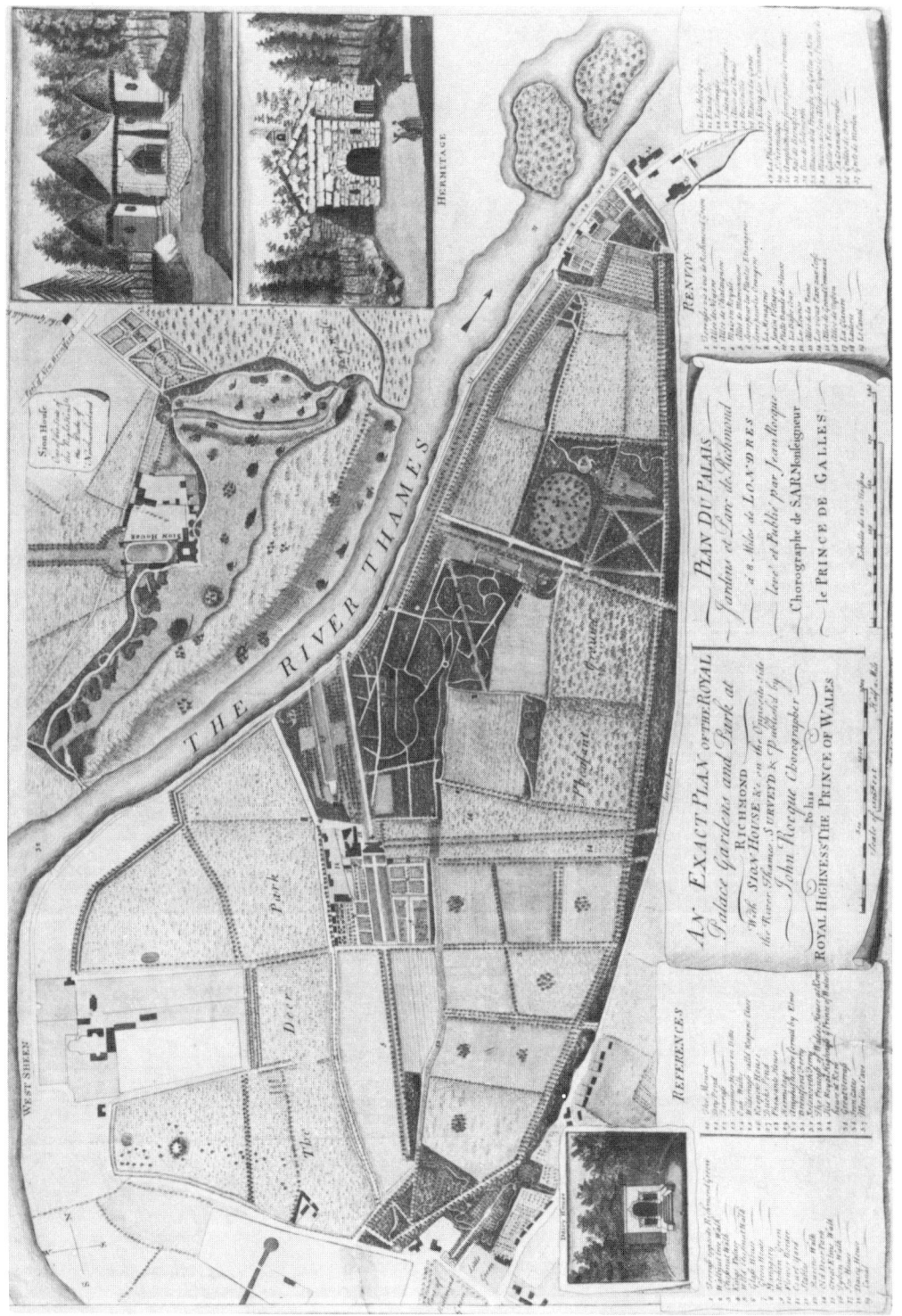

Richmond Gardens, Richmond, London by John Rocque. Rocque first surveyed this garden, designed by Charles Bridgeman and William Kent, in 1734. This is a much later plan, possibly 1754. Rocque started the fashion of adding small views of buildings in engraved garden plans. He surveyed other estates and with T. Badeslade published in 1739 a continuation of *Vitruvius Britannicus* by Colen Campbell: *Vitruvius Brittanicus Volume the Fourth* which illustrates four royal palaces and thirty seven country houses and their gardens.

Plate 11

The Doric Arch from *Stowe. A description of the house and gardens* . . . published by John Seeley, Buckingham, 1797. Engraved by Thomas Medland. The gardens of houses such as Hagley, The Leasowes, Mount Edgcumbe, Piercefield, Stourhead and Stowe were high on the list of the earnest eighteenth century tourist. The printed guides, which were often thoughtfully provided, recommended routes and viewpoints for the visitor. The first of a long series of guides to the house and garden at Stowe was published in 1744.

Plate 12

Esher Place, Surrey from *Observations on modern gardening* by Thomas Whately (London, 1801). Drawn by William Woollett and engraved by Walker. The author illustrates his principles of garden design by discussing contemporary gardens. First published in 1770 it went through six London editions and was translated into French and German. Extracts from Horace Walpole's *Essay on modern gardening* were added to the 1801 edition which was illustrated for the first time with coloured plates of some of the gardens described.

Plate 13

View of the gardens at Sezincote, Gloucestershire. One of ten aquatints drawn and etched by the artist, John Martin, and engraved by F.C. Lewis, c. 1817. Engraved views of the house and grounds were sometimes specially commissioned by the owner, in this particular instance, Sir Charles Cockerell, a retired Bengal civil servant, who built for himself this house in Indian style in the Cotswolds.

Plate 14

Above Whiteknights, Reading, Berkshire from *Descriptive account of the mansion and gardens of White-Knights, a seat of His Grace the Duke of Marlborough* by Mrs B. Hofland, (London, [1819]). Aquatint by T.C. Hofland. The Duke of Marlborough, who had commissioned the Hoflands to write and illustrate this book, encountered great financial difficulties, and left the Hoflands to pay the debts they had incurred in producing it. Many books have been written on stately homes and country seats; some notable ones include G. Cumberland's *Hafod* (1796), Sir Richard C. Hoare's *Stourhead* (1818), J.P. Neale's *Deep-dene* (1826), Lord Braybrooke's *Audley End* (1836) and J. Britton's *Cassiobury Park* (1837).

Right White Lodge, Richmond Park, London from *Fragments on the theory and practice of landscape gardening . . .* by Humphry Repton, (London, 1816). These two plates show the garden before and after the proposed improvement by the use of a moveable flap or overlay, a device Repton used in all his Red Books, so-called because all these slim, oblong volumes were bound in red leather. A Red Book embellished with delicate watercolour sketches was Repton's novel way of presenting his proposals to his client who did not necessarily accept or implement them. The excellent catalogue of the Repton exhibition in 1982/83 by G. Carter *et al.* records all the known Red Books under individual estates. Some additional Red Books discovered since the exhibition are listed in *The Garden* September 1983, 361–65.

Plate 15

Plate 16

at Drayton Green. 317

lawn to 29, we have the view *fig.* 59.; and, at 30, we have the fountain, surrounded by baskets of flowers, with the two garden nymphs *fig.* 62.

A page from an article in *The Gardener's Magazine* vol. 14, 1838, 317 describing Mrs Louisa Lawrence's garden at Drayton Green, Ealing, London. Its proprietor, John Claudius Loudon, edited it from its inception in 1826 until his death some eighteen years later. It reports, often in considerable detail, the frequent visits of Loudon and his contributors to British gardens. Loudon sometimes used these articles or their wood-engraved illustrations in his other publications. His *Encyclopaedia of gardening* (1822 and later editions) and *Arboretum et fruticetum Britannicum* 8 vols, (1844) are also worth consulting for their concise information on individual gardens.

Plate 17

The conservatory at Dalkeith Palace near Edinburgh from *The book of the garden* by Charles M'Intosh 2 vols, (London, 1853–55). The Victorian horticultural manual, in the main concerned with practical advice on gardening, sometimes includes, as does this book by M'Intosh, illustrations and useful comments on individual gardens.

Plate 18

Above Elvaston Castle from *The Gardener's Chronicle* vol. i, 1891, 523. *The Gardeners' Chronicle* was founded in January 1841 as a weekly periodical by Joseph Paxton and John Lindley, two of the most influential figures in Victorian horticulture. It was the most informative of all contemporary gardening journals and its pages, like those of one of its rivals, *The Cottage Gardener* (founded in 1848), abound in articles on or references to specific gardens. Unfortunately much of this information is inaccessible through inadequate indexing; all the important references, however, are now included in the *Bibliography of British gardens*. Wood engraving which was the process used to reproduce this drawing of Elvaston Castle was not superseded by photographs in books until the introduction of the half-tone block during the 1880s.

Top left The Colonnade at Alton Towers, Staffordshire from *The gardens of England* by E. Adveno Brooke (London, [c. 1857]). A folio that deserves to be better known for Brooke's boldly executed and richly coloured lithographs of some of the best of our Victorian gardens.

Bottom left Burton Agnes Hall, Humberside from *A series of picturesque views of seats of noblemen and gentlemen of Great Britain and Ireland* by F.O. Morris 6 vols, (London, 1866–80). Many of its 240 plates, superbly executed in colour woodblocks, incorporate a view of the surrounding gardens. Ten thousand copies were produced of this work which carried on the tradition of illustrated guides to country seats, so popular during the closing years of the eighteenth century and the beginning of the nineteenth century.

Plate 20

Belton House, Grantham, Lincolnshire from *Gardens old & new: the country house & its garden environment* 3 vols, (*Country Life*, London, [1900–09]). *Country Life* (founded 1897) was one of the first periodicals to exploit the published photograph. Articles on the design, history and development of individual gardens have always been a regular feature of this periodical; it is one of the first sources to check for a photograph of a specific garden.

CATALOGUE OF GARDENS

Abberley Hall near Stourport, Hereford and Worcester
J. Hort. Cottage Gdnr v. 15, 1887, 318–20. *G.C.* ii 1893, 713.

Abbey Dore Court, Abbey Dore, Hereford and Worcester
R. Sidwell *West Midland gardens* 1981, 18.

Abbey Gardens, Redditch, Hereford and Worcester
Garden v. 6, 1874, 484–85.

Abbey House, Barrow-in-Furness, Cumbria
J. Brown *Gardens of a golden afternoon* 1982, 172.

Abbey House, Waltham Abbey, Essex
P. Muilman *History of Essex* v. 4, 1770, 157.

Abbey House, Cirencester, Glos
J.N. Brewer *Delineations of Gloucestershire* 1825, 72.

Abbey House, Glastonbury, Somerset
W. Phelps *History . . . of Somersetshire* v. 1 no. 2, 1836, 541.

Abbey Leix, Co. Leix, Eire
G. Jekyll *and* G.S. Elgood *Some English gardens* 1904, 118–20. *Irish Gdning* v. 12, 1917, 147–48. Knight of Glin *and* P. Bowe *Gardens of outstanding historic interest in . . . Ireland* 1980. E. Malins *and* P. Bowe *Irish gardens and demesnes* 1980, 77–78.

Abbey St Bathans near Duns, Borders
G.A. Little *Scotland's gardens* 1981, 73.

Abbots Leigh near Bristol, Avon
D. Stroud *Humphry Repton* 1962, 165. G. Carter *et al. Humphry Repton* 1982, 161. *Garden* 1983, 365.

Abbots Ripton Hall, Abbots Ripton, Cambs
C.L. v. 155, 1974, 626–28. A. Lees-Milne *and* R. Verey *Englishman's garden* 1982, 48–51. *Garden* 1983, 44–48.

Abbotsbury Dorset
G.C. ii 1899, 142–44,147,153; ii 1912, 44–45. *C.L.* v. 2, 1899, 744–50. M.R. Gloag *Book of English gardens* 1906, 45–46. C. Holme *Gardens of England in Southern & Western counties* 1907, pls. 2–3. *Garden* 1918, 338. M. Allan *Fisons guide* 1970, 74–75. A. Paterson *Gardens of Britain* v. 2, 1978, 21–22.

Abbotsford near Melrose, Borders
F.O. Morris *Series of picturesque views* v. 5, 31. *G.C.* ii 1884, 583–84. A.A. Tait *Landscape garden in Scotland* 1980, passim. G.A. Little *Scotland's gardens* 1981, 73–75.

Abbotstone near Alresford, Hants
Hampshire Archaeology and Local History Newsletter v. 2 no. 2, 1971, 1–4.

Abbotswood near Stow-on-the-Wold, Glos
C.L. v. 33, 1913, 234–40,272–79; v. 54, 1924, 1007–09; v. 124, 1958, 768–69. L. Weaver *Houses and gardens by E.L. Lutyens* 1913, 67–74. G. Jekyll *Garden ornament* 1918, 410,412. *G.C.* i 1932, 85–86; ii 1938, 297. Lady Rockley *Historic gardens of England* 1938, 238–39. A.S. Butler *et al. Architecture of Sir Edwin Lutyens* v. 2, 1950, 12. *J. Royal Hort. Soc.* 1961, 383–92. P. Coats *Great gardens of Britain* 1967, 158–65. R.I.B.A. *Catalogue: Lutyens* 1973, 11. J. Sales *West Country gardens* 1980, 24–27. J. Brown *Gardens of a golden afternoon* 1982, 102,165.

Abercairny near Crieff, Tayside
J. Hort Cottage Gdnr N.S. v. 9, 1884, 572–74. *C.L.* v. 129, 1961, 506–09,584. M. Allan *Fisons guide* 1970, 314–15. A.A. Tait *Landscape garden in Scotland* 1980, passim. G.A. Little *Scotland's gardens* 1981, 115.

Aberdeen. Duthie Park, Grampian
Garden 1983, 9–11.

Aberdour Castle, Aberdour, Fife
Gdn History v. 11 no. 2, 1983, 93–111.

Aberuchill Castle near Comrie, Tayside
J.P. Neale *Views* v. 6, 1823. *Garden* 1917, 544–45. *G.C.* i 1930, 494–95; ii 1937, 135.

Aberystwyth University College, Dyfed
C.L. v. 162, 1977, 1026–29.

Abinger Hall, Abinger, Surrey
E.W. Brayley *and* J. Britton *Topographical history of Surrey* v. 5, 8.

Abington, Strathclyde
G.L. ii 1903, 381.

Abington Abbey near Northampton, Northants
J.P. Neale *Views* v. 3, 1820.

Abington Hall, Great Abington, Cambs
D. Stroud. *Humphry Repton* 1962, 165. G. Carter *et al. Humphry Repton* 1982, 149.

Abney Hall, Cheadle, Greater Manchester
Florist 1855, 365–68. *Cottage Gdnr* v. 19, 1857, 179–80. *J. Hort. Cottage Gdnr* v. 58, 1877, 272. Historical MSS Commission *Architectural history* v. 2, 1970, item 1245.

Abney Park Cemetery, Stoke Newington, London
G. Collinson *Cemetery interment* 1840, 314–408.
J.S. Curl *Celebration of death* 1980, 238–39.

Above Beck, Grasmere, Cumbria
G. Beard *Thomas H. Mawson* 1976, 42.

Aboyne Castle, Aboyne, Grampian
G. Beard *Thomas H. Mawson* 1976, 43.

Achamore House, Isle of Gigha, Strathclyde
Official guide. *Rhododendron & Camellia Yearbook* 1958, 25–31. E. Hyams *English garden* 1964, 217–18. *J. Royal Hort. Soc.* 1965, 236–45. M. Allan *Fisons guide* 1970, 290–92. *C.L.* v. 151, 1972, 679–82. A. Hellyer *Gardens of genius* 1980, 58–63. G.A. Little *Scotland's gardens* 1981, 213.

Achnacloich, Loch Etive, Strathclyde
G.C. ii 1963, 222–23. G.A. Little *Scotland's gardens* 1981, 214–17.

Acklam Hall near Middlesbrough, Cleveland
J. Beeverell *Les delices de la Grande Bretagne* v. 5, 1707, 872. L. Knyff *and* J. Kip *Britannia illustrata* v. 1, 1714. M. Macartney *English houses & gardens* 1908, pl. 43. *C.L.* v. 35, 1914, 342–49.

Acorn Bank, Temple Sowerby, Cumbria
G.S. Thomas *Gardens of National Trust* 1979, 93.

Acrise (Acryse) **Place**, Acrise, Kent
C.L. v. 122, 1957, 258–61,300.

Acton Burnell, Shropshire
J.P. Neale *Views* 2nd Series, v. 2, 1825. V.C.H. *Shropshire* v. 8, 1968, 3–4. B. Jones *Follies & grottoes* 1974, 169.

Acton Castle near Penzance, Cornwall
G.C. ii 1899, 237–38.

Adair Place, Englefield Green, Surrey
G.C. ii 1912, 363–65.

Adam and Eve Tea Gardens, Camden, London
W. Wroth *London pleasure gardens of the eighteenth century* 1896, 77–80,127–28. E.B. Chancellor *Pleasure haunts of London* 1925, 384.

Adare Manor, Adare, Co. Limerick, Eire
G.M. v. 12, 1836, 450–52. Countess *and* Earl of Dunraven *Memorials of Adare Manor* 1865. F.O. Morris *Series of picturesque views* v. 4, 39. *J. Hort. Cottage Gdnr* v. 48, 1872, 211–13,231–33,249. *G.C.* ii 1899, 393–94. Royal Hort. Soc. *Conifers in cultivation* 1932, 218. *C.L.* v. 145, 1969, 1230–31. E. Malins *and* Knight of Glin *Lost demesnes* 1976, 96–98. J. Harris *Artist and the country house* 1979, 298. Knight of Glin *and* P. Bowe *Gardens of outstanding historic interest in . . . Ireland* 1980.

Adcote, Shropshire
C.L. v. 26, 1909, 912–20. R. Sidwell *West Midland gardens* 1981, 97–99.

Adderbury, Oxfordshire
D. Stroud *Capability Brown* 1975, 214.

Addington near Winslow, Bucks
G.C. i 1908, 17–18.

Addington Park near Maidstone, Kent
J. Brown *Gardens of a golden afternoon* 1982, 172.

Addington Place, Croydon, London
W. Watts *Seats* 1779, pl. 19. G.A. Walpoole *New British traveller* 1784, 56. W. Thornton *New, complete and universal history* 1786, 506. G.F. Prosser *Select illustrations of Surrey* 1828. *G.C.* i 1902, 10. D. Stroud *Capability Brown* 1975, 214.

Addiscombe Farm, Croydon, London
W. Keane *Beauties of Surrey* 1849, 56–57.

Addiscombe Place, Croydon, London
W. Angus *Seats* 1787, pl. 58. J. Hassell *Seats near London* 1804–05.

Addison Lodge, Holland Park, London
C.L. v. 62, 1927, 706–08.

Addistoun House, Ratho, Lothian
G.A. Little *Scotland's gardens* 1981, 75.

Addlestone Lodge near Chertsey, Surrey
Garden v. 22, 1882, 112–13.

Adlestrop near Stow-on-the-Wold, Glos
J.P. Neale *Views* v. 2, 1819. D. Stroud *Humphry Repton* 1962, 165. V.C.H. *Gloucester* v. 6, 1965, 10. G. Carter *et al. Humphry Repton* 1982, 152.

Adlington Hall near Macclesfield, Cheshire
Official guide. J. Harris *Artist and the country house* 1979, 320–21.

Admington Hall, Shipston on Stour, Warwickshire
M. Allan *Fisons guide* 1970, 146–47. R. Sidwell *West Midland gardens* 1981, 185–87.

Adon Mount, Dulwich, London
G.C. ii 1891, 250–51.

Adwell House, Tetsworth, Oxfordshire
R. Bisgrove *Gardens of Britain* v. 3, 1978, 21.

Afton Lodge, Tarbolton, Strathclyde
Scottish Gdnr and Northern Forester v. 8, 1913, 549–50.

Agecroft Hall, Greater Manchester
Gdning World v. 1, 1885, 701. *C.L.* v. 12, 1902, 432–39.

Airds of Parton, Dumfries and Galloway
Scottish Gdnr and Northern Forester v. 8, 1913, 237–38.

Airlie Castle near Kirriemuir, Tayside
Scottish Gdnr v. 4, 1855, 208–10. *Scottish Gdnr and Northern Forester* v. 8, 1913, 441–42. M. Allan *Fisons guide* 1970, 334–35.

Airth Castle, Airth, Central
J.P. Neale *Views* 2nd Series v. 3, 1826.

Airthrey Castle near Stirling, Central
J.P. Neale *Views* v. 6, 1823. *G.M.* v. 18, 1842, 593–94. *Gdning World* v. 4, 1887, 23. *Scotland's Mag.* no. 70, 1974, 11–14. *G.C.* v. 179, 23 April 1976, 32–33.

Albert Park *see* Islington

Albourne Place near Brighton, E. Sussex
C.L. v. 56, 1924, 398–404.

Albro House Farm, Ilford, Redbridge, London
F.G. Emmison *Catalogue of maps in Essex Record Office* 2nd Supplt, 1964, 21.

Albury House near Guildford, Surrey
J. Harris *Artist and the country house* 1979, 329.

Albury Park near Guildford, Surrey
Official guide. J.P. Neale *Views* 2nd Series, v. 3, 1826. G.F. Prosser *Select illustrations of Surrey* 1828. *G.M.* v. 5, 1829, 10–11; v. 7, 1831, 364–65. N. Whittock and H. Gastineau *Picturesque beauties of England and Wales* 1830, 60. W. Keane *Beauties of Surrey* 1849, 138–42. *G.C.* ii 1879, 788; i 1892, 137,145,147. *C.L.* v. 2, 1897, 656–58; v. 61, 1927, 898–902,1016–20; v. 62, 1927, 374–77,534–37; v. 64, 1928, 496–500; v. 108, 1950, 598–602,764. M.R. Gloag *Book of English gardens* 1906, 59–68. W. Cobbett *Rural rides* v. 1, 1912, 151–52,154. A.B. Jackson *Albury Park trees and shrubs* 1914. Lady Rockley *Historic gardens of England* 1938, 148–49. J. Evelyn *Diary* v. 3, 1955, 154,496,561–62; v. 4, 111, 558. I. Nairn *and* B. Cherry *Surrey* 1971, 94. *Gdn History* v. 4, 1976, 10–14. *Landscape Design* no. 124, 1978, 36–38. J. Harris *Artist and the country house* 1979, 30–31. *J. Gdn History* v. 1, 1981, 37–54.

Albyns, Stapleford Abbots, Essex
P. Muilman *History of Essex* v. 4, 1770, 33. V.C.H. *Essex* v. 4, 1956, 226.

Aldborough, Yorks
I. Hall *Samuel Buck's Yorkshire sketchbook* 1979, 385.

Aldbury Place near Blackheath, London
J.C. Loudon *Encyclopaedia of gardening* 1822, 1228.

Aldby Park near York, N. Yorks
F.O. Morris *Series of picturesque views* v. 5, 47. *C.L.* v. 78, 1935, 486–90.

Aldenham House near Watford, Herts
J.E. Cussans *History of Hertfordshire* v. 3, 1881, 245. *G.C.* ii 1887, 593–94; ii 1889, 411–12; ii 1890, 360–61; ii 1891, 608–09; i 1896, 295–97; ii 1897, 266–67; ii 1909, 429; i 1910, 2–4,9,29; ii 1916, 155–56,157,163; ii 1922, 197, 304. *J. Hort. Cottage Gdnr* v. 33, 1896, 229–30; v. 37, 1898, 340–41; v. 41, 1900, 558–59; v. 54, 1907, 230–36. *Gdnrs Mag.* 1896, 498–500; 1903, 403–10. *C.L.* v. 1, 1901, 48–54, 80–86; v. 47, 1920, 103–05; v. 54, 1924, 282–90. *Garden* 1924, 320–22. *Estates Gazette* v. 152, 1948, 98–99,129.

Aldenham Park near Bridgnorth, Shropshire
F. Calvert *Picturesque views* 1831, 126. *C.L.* v. 161, 1977, 1734–37,1802–05; v. 162, 1977,18–21. J. Harris *Artist and the country house* 1979, 209,340.

Alderbrook Park, Cranleigh, Surrey
Gdn Design Autumn 1938, 72–76. R. Webber *Percy Cane* 1975, 183.

Alderley near Wotton-under-Edge, Glos
R. Atkyns *Ancient and present state of Glostershire* 1712, 208. L. Knyff *and* J. Kip *Britannia illustrata* v. 2, 1715. J.N. Brewer *Delineations of Gloucestershire* 1825, 174. *C.L.* v. 146, 1969, 882–84. J. Sales *West Country gardens* 1980, 27–29.

Alderley Grange, Alderley, Glos
C.L. v. 146, 1969, 882–84.

Aldermaston Court, Aldermaston, Berks
J.P. Neale *Views* 2nd Series, v. 4, 1828. *C.L.* v. 2, 1899, 240–44. *G.C.* ii 1902, 440,441–42; ii 1915, 345, 346,347. G. Jekyll *Garden ornament* 1918, 38.

Aldersbrook Manor, Newham, London
F.G. Emmison *Catalogue of maps in Essex Record Office* 1st Supplt, 1952, 12; 2nd Supplt, 1964, 7.

Aldersey Hall near Chester, Cheshire
Garden v. 65, 1904, 204–05.

Aldershaw near Lichfield, Staffs
G.M. v. 15, 1839, 457.

Alderton, Northants
C. Taylor *Archaeology of gardens* 1983, 22,24.

Aldestrop *see* Adlestrop

Aldingbourne House near Chichester, W. Sussex
Garden v. 35, 1889, 427.

Aldington West Court, Kent
J. Harris *History of Kent* 1719, 98. T. Badeslade *Thirty six different views of Kent* 1750s, pl. 1. J. Kip *Supplement du Nouveau theatre de la Grande Bretagne* 1728, pl. 20.

Aldwincle, Northants
Royal Commission on Historical Monuments *Inventory of historical monuments in . . . Northampton* v. 1, 1975, 6–7,8.

Aldworth, Haslemere, Surrey
G. Beard *Thomas H. Mawson* 1976, 43.

Alexandra College, Dublin, Eire
Irish Gdning v. 6, 1911, 145–49; v. 13, 1918, 7.

Alexandra Palace, Haringey, London
Garden v. 3, 1873, 386.

Alexandra Park *see* London

Alfreton Hall, Alfreton, Derbyshire
S. Glover *History of Derby* v. 2, 1833, 15. *J. Hort. Cottage Gdnr* v. 56, 1876, 468–70.

Alkerton Grange near Stroud, Glos
V.C.H. *Gloucester* v. 10, 1972, 125.

Allanbay Park, Binfield, Berks
R. Bisgrove *Gardens of Britain* v. 3, 1978, 21–22.

Allangate, Halifax, W. Yorks
Bradford Illustrated Weekly Telegraph *Series of picturesque views* 1885.

Allanton near Wishaw, Strathclyde
G.M. v. 13, 1837, 471–72; v. 14, 1838, 15–18; v. 18, 1842, 387–89. A.A. Tait *Landscape garden in Scotland* 1980, passim.

Allerton Beeches, Liverpool, Merseyside
G.C. ii, 1892, 432.

Allerton Tower, Liverpool, Merseyside
J.P. Neale *Views* 2nd Series, v. 1, 1824. *J. Hort. Cottage Gdnr* v. 25, 1892, 243.

Allington Castle near Maidstone, Kent
C.L. v. 63, 1928, 438–44.

Alloway, Strathclyde
J. Macky *Journey through Scotland* 1723, 182.

Alnwick Castle, Alnwick, Northumberland
Description of Alnwick Castle 1796; 1800. *Descriptive . . . view . . . of Alnwick Castle* 1822. *Garden* v. 5, 1874, 100–01,188; v. 20, 1881, 155–56. F.O. Morris *Series of picturesque views* v. 2, 1. L. Jewitt *and* S.C. Hall *Stately homes of England* 1874, 113–14. *G.C.* ii 1880, 523–24, 533,587–88; i 1902, 273–74,286–87. *J. Hort. Cottage Gdnr* v. 15, 1887, 296–98. *C.L.* v. 65, 1929, 890–98; v. 66, 1929, 16–22; v. 174, 1983, 275. N. Pevsner *Northumberland* 1957, 71–72. B. Jones *Follies & grottoes* 1974, 370–72. D. Stroud *Capability Brown* 1975, 103–04. *Gdn History* v. 9, 1981, 174–77. Tyne and Wear County Council Museums *Capability Brown and the northern landscape* 1983, 22–23,27,42.

Alresford Hall near Wivenoe, Essex
J. Harris *Artist and the country house* 1979, 356.

Alresford House near Winchester, Hants
C.L. v. 163, 1978, 18–21. D. Jacques *Georgian gardens* 1983, 83.

Alscott Park, Glos
J.P. Neale *Views* v. 2, 1819. Historical MSS Commission *Architectural history* v. 2, 1970, item 1326. R. Sidwell *West Midland Gardens* 1981, 187–88.

Althorne Lodge *see* Three Ash Farm

Althorp, Northants
Official guide. J. Beeverell *Les delices de la Grande Bretagne* v. 5, 1707, 872. L. Knyff *and* J. Kip *Britannia illustrata* v. 1, 1714. H. Overton *Britannia illustrata* c. 1724, pl. 13. D. Defoe *Tour* v. 2, 1778, 384–85. J.P. Neale *Views* v. 3, 1820. L. Magalotti *Travels of Cosmo the Third* 1821, 249. T.F. Dibdin *Aedes Althorpianae* 1822, 2 v. *Jones's views* 1829. *Cottage Gdnr* v. 13, 1854, 59–62,77–80,98–100. *C.L.* v. 49, 1921, 714–21, 792–97; v. 50, 1921, 14–20; v. 127, 1960, 1122–25; v. 170, 1981, 375–78. *Gdnrs Mag.* 1903, 494–96. *G.C.* ii 1909, 123–24. R. Dutton *English garden* 1937, pl. 90. J. Evelyn *Diary* v. 4, 1955, 70. D. Stroud *Capability Brown* 1975, 214–15. *Northamptonshire Past and Present* v. 5 no. 3, 1975, 219. J. Anthony *Gardens of Britain* v. 6, 1979, 17–27. J. Harris *Artist and the country house* 1979, 67. Royal Commission on Historical Monuments *Inventory of the historical monuments in . . . Northampton* v. 3, 1981, 1. D. Jacques *Georgian gardens* 1983, 141.

Altingham Hall near Shrewsbury, Shropshire
F. Calvert *Picturesque views* 1831, 127.

Alton Towers (Abbey) near Uttoxeter, Staffs
Official guide. *Jones's views* 1829. F. Calvert *Picturesque views* 1830, 28. J.P. Neale *Views* v. 4, 1821. *G.M.* v. 7, 1831, 390–95; v. 16, 1840, 280,580; v. 17, 1841, 41–42,368. J.C. Loudon *Encyclopaedia of cottage, farm and village architecture and furniture* 1842, figs. 1429, 1431. W. Adam *Gem of the Peaks* 1851, 222–41. E. Adveno Brooke *Gardens of England* 1857, pls. 12–14. F.O. Morris *Series of picturesque views* v. 1, 67. *J. Hort. Cottage Gdnr* v. 44, 1870, 287–90,307–10; v. 31, 1895, 60–62; v. 56, 1908, 217. *Garden* v. 2, 1872, 15,56–57. *G.C.* i 1887, 243–44,246–47; i 1889, 681; ii 1962, 331. L. Jewitt and S.C. Hall *Stately homes of England* 1874, 1–36. *C.L.* v. 3, 1898, 754–57, 788–91; v. 10, 1901, 838–39; v. 125, 1959, 368; v. 127, 1960, 1246–49,1305. C. Holme *Gardens of England in Midland & Eastern counties* 1908, pls. 2–5. E. von Erdberg *Chinese influence on European structures* 1936, 145–46. *Architectural Review* no. 87, 1940, 157–64. O. Siren *China and gardens of Europe* 1950, 86–88. R.I.B.A. *Catalogue* v. A, 1968, 15. M. Allan *Fisons guide* 1970, 212–13. *Landscape Design* no. 93, 1971, 8–10. H. Evans *Beautiful gardens of Britain* 1974, 95–96. N. Pevsner *Staffordshire* 1974, 57–59. B. Jones *Follies & grottoes* 1974, 235–37. L. Fleming and A. Gore *English garden* 1979, 179. A. Hellyer *Gardens of genius* 1980, 31–32. R. Sidwell *West Midland gardens* 1981, 161–64. *Landscape Research* v. 7 no. 1, 1981, 21.

Altrincham. Stamford Park, Greater Manchester
G.C. i 1881, 44–45.

Altyre, Forres, Grampian
G.A. Little *Scotland's gardens* 1981, 173.

Alva House, Alva, Central
G.M. v. 18, 1842, 592–93. J.B. Burke *Visitation* v. 1, 1852, 234.

Alvechurch. Bishop's Palace, Hereford and Worcester
Trans. Worcestershire Archaeological Soc. v. 3, 1970/72, 55–59.

Alveston near Stratford-on-Avon, Warwickshire
L. Knyff and J. Kip *Britannia illustrata* v. 2, 1715. R. Atkyns *Ancient and present state of Glostershire* 1712, 216. *C.L.* v. 97, 1945, 904–07,948–51.

Ambarrow Farm, Sandhurst, Berks
G. Beard *Thomas H. Mawson* 1976, 43.

Amberley near Stroud, Glos
B. Jones *Follies & grottoes* 1974, 326,327.

Ambrosden near Islip, Oxfordshire
W. Kennett *Parochial antiquities . . . in . . . Ambrosden and Burcester* 1695. M. Macartney *English houses & gardens* 1908, pl. 28.

Amesbury Abbey, Amesbury, Wilts
G.M. v. 8, 1832, 547–48. *C.L.* v. 11, 1902, 272–79. G. Jekyll *Garden ornament* 1918, 219,257,360. B. Jones *Follies & grottoes* 1974, 406. N. Pevsner *Wiltshire* 1975, 92–93. P. Willis *Charles Bridgeman* 1977, 177. *J. Gdn History* v. 2 no. 1, 1982, 47.

Amisfield House near Haddington, Lothian
C. McWilliam *Lothian* 1978, 77.

Ammerdown Park, Radstock, Avon
Description of the mansion c. 1818. C. Holme *Gardens of England in Southern & Western counties* 1907, pls. 5–8. A.S. Butler et al. *Architecture of Sir Edwin Lutyens* v. 2, 1950, 12. *C.L.* v. 65, 1929, 216–23,292–98,330–35. Lady Rockley *Historic gardens of England* 1938, 216–17. M. Allan *Fisons guide* 1970, 75–76. M. Binney and A. Hills *Elysian gardens* 1979, 19. J. Brown *Gardens of a golden afternoon* 1982, 78–81,166.

Amney (Ampney?), Glos
R. Atkyns *Ancient and present state of Glostershire* 1712, 218. L. Knyff and J. Kip *Britannia illustrata* v. 2, 1715.

Amport House near Andover, Hants
J.P. Neale *Views* v. 2, 1819. E.F. Prosser *Select illustrations of Hampshire* 1833. *C.L.* v. 25, 1909, 251. R.I.B.A. *Catalogue: Lutyens* 1973, 11. J. Brown *Gardens of a golden afternoon* 1982, 141–45,174.

Ampthill Park near Bedford, Beds
G. Tod *Plans, elevations and sections of hot-houses* 1817, 21, pl. 23. J.P. Neale *Views* v. 1, 1818. M.R. Gloag *Book of English gardens* 1906, 71–83. D. Stroud *Capability Brown* 1975, 215.

Ampton Hall, Ampton, Suffolk
T.K. Cromwell *Excusions in county of Suffolk* v. 1, 1818, 79–80. J.C. Loudon *Encyclopaedia of gardening* 1822, 1234–35.

Amwell House, Ware, Herts
C.L. v. 118, 1955, 90.

An Cala, Easdale, Strathclyde
G.C. ii 1963, 172–73, 176. M. Allan *Fisons guide* 1970, 293–94. *Scotts Mag.* v. 107 no. 2, 1977, 124–29. G.A. Little *Scotland's gardens* 1981, 217–18.

Anderson Manor, Anderson, Dorset
C.L. v. 37, 1915, 446–51. G. Jekyll *Garden ornament* 1918, 37.

Anderson's Place, Newcastle upon Tyne, Tyne and Wear
M. Macartney *English houses & gardens* 1908, pl. 8.

Angerton Hall, Morpeth, Northumberland
J. Brown *Gardens of a golden afternoon* 1982, 171. M. and R. Tooley *Gardens of Gertrude Jekyll in the North* 1982, 54.

Anglesey Abbey, Lode, Cambs
Official guide. *Connoisseur* v. 123, 1949, 88–93. *C.L.* v. 115, 1954, 770–73,860–63. L. Roper *Gardens of Anglesey Abbey* 1964. *G.C.* 23 August 1967, 11–13. P. Coats *Great gardens of Britain* 1967, 94–99. M. Allan *Fisons guide* 1970, 185–86. H. Evans *Beautiful gardens of Britain* 1974, 79–80. Royal Commission on Historical Monuments *Inventory of historical monuments in . . . Cambridge* v. 2, 1972, 78,80, pls. 118–20. L. Fleming and A. Gore *English garden* 1979, 216–17. G.S. Thomas *Gardens of National Trust* 1979, 93–95.

Annat, Tayside
G.M. v. 5, 1829, 28–30; v. 18, 1842, 155–57.

Anne's Grove, Castletownroche, Co. Cork, Eire
Garden Design 1933, 106–12. *J. Royal Hort. Soc.* 1950, 317–19; 1959, 460–62; 1966, 87–88. *C.L.* v. 142, 1967, 442–43. E. Hyams *Irish gardens* 1967, 42–50. *G.C.* v. 164 no. 4, 1968, 11–13. E. Malins and P. Bowe *Irish gardens and demesnes* 1980, 119–22. Knight of Glin and P. Bowe *Gardens of outstanding historic interest in . . . Ireland* 1980.

Annesley near Mansfield, Notts
R. Thoroton *Thoroton's history* v. 2, 1797, 270. *J. Hort. Cottage Gdnr* v. 55, 1876, 288–90.

Annfield, Tayside
J. Harris *Artist and the country house* 1979, 342.

Anstey Hall near Coventry, W. Midlands
J.B. Burke *Visitation* v. 1, 1852, 244.

Anstey Pastures near Leicester, Leics
Historical MSS Commission *Architectural history* v. 2, 1970, item 1048.

Antony House near Saltash, Cornwall
Official guide. W. Borlase *Natural history of Cornwall* 1758, pl. 9. H. Repton *Sketches* 1794, 53–55. H. Repton *Observations* 1803, 94. G.S. Gilbert *Historical survey of Cornwall* v. 2, 1820, 391–93. J.B. Burke *Visitation* 2nd Series, v. 1, 1855, 96–98. *C.L.* v. 74, 1933, 172–77; v. 134, 1963, 978–80. *G.C.* ii 1963, 244–45,248. D. Stroud *Humphry Repton* 1962, 70. *Architectural History* v. 7, 1964, 23,41–42. Historical MSS Commission *Architectural history* v. 2, 1970, item 2219. H. Evans *Beautiful gardens of Britain* 1974, 9–10. E. Malins *Red books of Humphry Repton* 1976, 14–21. P.M. Synge *Gardens of Britain* v. 1, 1977, 85–87. J. Harris *Artist and the country house* 1979, 134. G.S. Thomas *Gardens of National Trust* 1979, 95–96. G. Carter et al. *Humphry Repton* 1982, 150. D. Jacques *Georgian gardens* 1983, 138.

Antrim Castle, Co. Antrim, Ulster
J.P. Neale *Views* 2nd Series, v. 2, 1825. E. Malins and Knight of Glin *Lost demesnes* 1976, 13. E. Malins and P. Bowe *Irish gardens and demesnes* 1980, 34. Ulster Architectural Heritage Society *Northern gardens* 1982, 9,13.

Apethorne Hall near Wansford, Northants
J.P. Neale *Views* 2nd Series, v. 3, 1826. *Garden* v. 48, 1895, 495. *C.L.* v. 3, 1898, 560–62,592–94; v. 25, 1909, 414–23,450–59. V.C.H. *Northampton* v. 2, 1906, 545. G. Jekyll *Garden ornament* 1918, 190,214. M. Binney and A. Hills *Elysian fields* 1979, 20.

Apley Park near Bridgnorth, Shropshire
J.P. Neale *Views* 2nd Series, v. 3, 1826. *Jones's views* 1829. F.O. Morris *Series of picturesque views* v. 6. *C.L.* v. 21, 1907, 738–44. J. Harris *Gardens of delight* 1978, 28.

Appleby Castle near Penrith, Cumbria
F.O. Morris *Series of picturesque views* v. 4, 41. *C.L.* v. 87, 1940, 382–86.

Appleton Manor near Abingdon, Oxfordshire
C.L. v. 65, 1929, 670–77. R. Bisgrove *Gardens of Britain* v. 3, 1978, 22–23.

Appley House near Ryde, Isle of Wight
G.C. ii 1876, 838–39,843.

Appley Towers near Ryde, Isle of Wight
Scottish Gdnr v. 13, 1864, 316–18,341–45. *J. Hort. Cottage Gdnr* v. 60, 1878, 349–51. *G.C.* ii 1881, 494–95, 501; ii 1886, 181–82.

Apollo Gardens (Temple of Apollo), Lambeth, London
W. Wroth *London pleasure gardens of the eighteenth century* 1896, 268–70.

Appuldurcombe House near Ventnor, Isle of Wight
W. Watts *Seats* 1779, pl. 14. R. Worsley *History of the Isle of Wight* 1781, 218. J. Hassel *Tour of the Isle of Wight* In J. Pinkerton v. 2, 1808, 709. R. Ackermann *Repository* v. 8, 1826, pl. 2. W.W.J. Gendall *Views* v. 1, 1830, 91–93. *C.L.* v. 72, 1932, 568–72. D. Stroud *Capability*

Appuldurcombe House (*Cont.*)
Brown 1975, 215. *J. Gdn History* v. 2 no. 2, 1982, 46–47.

Apps Court near Walton-on-Thames, Surrey
M.R. Brownell *Alexander Pope & arts of Georgian England* 1978, 225.

Aqualate Hall near Newport, Staffs
R. Plot *Natural History of Staffordshire* 1685, 246. V.C.H. *Stafford* v. 4, 1958, 104.

Arabela near Tain, Highland
G.A. Little *Scotland's gardens* 1981, 173.

Aras an Auchtarain, Dublin, Eire
E. Malins *and* P. Bowe *Irish gardens and demesnes* 1980, 36.

Arbigland near Kirkbeam, Dumfries and Galloway
I.H. Adams *Descriptive list of plans* v. 3, 1974, 77. G.A. Little *Scotland's gardens* 1981, 241.

Arbury Hall near Nuneaton, Warwickshire
F.O. Morris *Series of picturesque views* v. 3, 41. *C.L.* v. 2, 1907, 522–29; v. 34, 1913, 356–64; v. 114, 1953, 1126–29. M. Allan *Fisons guide* 1970, 147–48. R. Sidwell *West Midland gardens* 1981, 189–93.

Arbuthnott House, Inverbervie, Grampian
J.P. Neale *Views* 2nd Series, v. 3, 1826. G.A. Little *Scotland's gardens* 1981, 174.

Archbishop's Park *see* Lambeth

Archerfield near N. Berwick, Lothian
Scottish Gdnr v. 10, 1861, 5–7,429–33. *J. Hort. Cottage Gdnr* v. 34, 1865, 399–401,425–26,446–49; v. 53, 1875, 8–10,29–32.

Arcleby Hall, Cumbria
W. Hutchinson *History of county of Cumberland* v. 2, 1794, 353.

Ard Cairn, Co. Cork, Eire
G.C. i 1893, 296,297.

Ardanaiseig, Taynuilt, Strathclyde
G.A. Little *Scotland's gardens* 1981, 218–19.

Ardanoir, Foynes, Co. Limerick, Eire
Irish Gdning v. 4, 1909, 1–2,17–18,36–37,49–51, 65–66, 82–83,104–06.

Ardbraccan, Co. Meath, Eire
G.M. v. 2, 1827, 150–51.

Ardchattan Priory, Loch Etive, Strathclyde
G.A. Little *Scotland's gardens* 1981, 219–20.

Ardchoille, Frinton-on-Sea, Essex
Garden Design 1937, 84–87. R. Webber *Percy Cane* 1975, 64,179.

Arddarroch near Garelochhead, Strathclyde
G.C. ii 1886, 615–16; i 1891, 611–12; ii 1899, 278. *Garden* v. 32, 1887, 481. *Gdning World* v. 6, 1890, 661.

Arden, Accrington, Lancs
J.B. Burke *Visitation* v. 2, 1853, 250.

Ardencraig near Rothesay, Strathclyde
R. Webber *Percy Cane* 1975, 154,187.

Ardenrun, Blindley Heath, Surrey
C.L. v. 29, 1911, 90–97.

Ardgowan House near Inverkip, Strathclyde
J.P. Neale *Views* v. 6, 1823. *G.M.* v. 9, 1833, 10. *G.C.* ii 1901, 304–05. H. Maxwell *Scottish gardens* 1908, 23–30.

Ardington House near Wantage, Oxfordshire
C.L. v. 170, 1981, 1282–85.

Ardkinglas near Inveraray, Strathclyde
C.L. v. 29, 1911, 746–54. H. Colvin *and* J. Harris *Country seat* 1970, 197. A.A. Tait *Landscape garden in Scotland* 1980, passim.

Ardleigh, Chigwell, Essex
R. Webber *Percy Cane* 1975, 167,179.

Ardleigh Park, Ardleigh, Essex
F.G. Emmison *Catalogue of maps in Essex Record Office* 2nd Supplt, 1964, 29.

Ardnagashel, Bantry Bay, Co. Cork, Eire
J. Royal Hort. Soc. 1959, 466–67. *Moorea* v. 3, 1984, 1–10.

Ardoch, Cardross, Strathclyde
G.A. Little *Scotland's gardens* 1981, 241–42.

Ardross Castle, Ardross, Highland
G.C. i 1875, 272–73.

Ardsallagh near Fethard, Co. Tipperary, Eire
J. Royal Hort. Soc. 1960, 482–85. E. Hyams *Irish gardens* 1967, 82–86. Knight of Glin *and* P. Bowe *Gardens of outstanding historic interest in . . . Ireland* 1980.

Ardtornish, Highland
G.A. Little *Scotland's gardens* 1981, 220.

Ardtully, Co. Kerry, Eire
F.O. Morris *Series of picturesque views* v. 2, 19.

Arduaine, Loch Melfort, Strathclyde
G.A. Little *Scotland's gardens* 1981, 220–23.

Ardvorlich House, Loch Earn, Tayside
Historical MSS Commission *Architectural history* v. 4, 1972, item 3694.

Ardwell House, Ardwell, Dumfries and Galloway
G.A. Little *Scotland's gardens* 1981, 242.

Argaty, Doune, Central
G.A. Little *Scotland's gardens* 1981, 115.

Argory near Verner's Bridge, Co. Armagh, Ulster
C.L. v. 174, 1983, 24.

Argyle House, Strathclyde
J. Kip *Nouveau theatre de la Grande Bretagne* v. 4, 1729, pl. 65. H. Boswell *Historical descriptions of new and picturesque views* 1800.

Arkley Manor, West Barnet, Herts
R. Bisgrove *Gardens of Britain* v. 3, 1978, 23.

Arle Court near Cheltenham, Glos
Scottish Gdnr and Northern Forester v. 8, 1859, 343–47. G.C. i 1896, 582–83.

Arlescote near Kineton, Warwickshire
C.L. v. 102, 1947, 478–81.

Arley Hall near Northwich, Cheshire
Official guide. H.I. Triggs *Formal gardens in England and Scotland* 1902, 24–25. C.L. v. 16, 1904, 942–50; v. 160, 1976, 950–52. G. Jekyll *and* G.S. Elgood *Some English gardens* 1904, 125–28. C. Holme *Gardens of England in the Midland & Eastern counties* 1908, pls. 6–7. G. Jekyll *Garden ornament* 1918, 420. M. Allan *Fisons guide* 1970, 214–15. A. Hellyer *Gardens of genius* 1980, 105–09. A. Lees-Milne *and* R. Verey *Englishman's garden* 1980, 26–30. *Garden* 1981, 183–90. T. Hinde *Stately gardens of Britain* 1983, 78–85.

Arley House near Kidderminster, Hereford and Worcester
R. Sidwell *West Midland gardens* 1981, 19–23.

Arlington Court, Arlington, Devon
Official guide. G.M. v. 14, 1838, 505–10. P.M. Synge *Gardens of Britain* v. 1, 1977, 21–23. G.S. Thomas *Gardens of National Trust* 1979, 96–97.

Armadale House, Skye, Highland
J.P. Neale *Views* 2nd Series, v. 1, 1824. Historical MSS Commission *Architectural history* v. 5, 1974, item 5529.

Armitage Park, Armitage, Staffs
J.P. Neale *Views* v. 4, 1821. F. Calvert *Picturesque views* 1830, 22. G.M. v. 12, 1836, 311. J.B. Burke *Visitation* v. 1, 1852, 211.

Armley (Gotts Park), Leeds, W. Yorks
J.P. Neale *Views* v. 5, 1822. *Jones's views* 1829, 41. D. Stroud *Humphry Repton* 1962, 165. J. Harris *Catalogue of British drawings . . . in American collections* 1971, 172, 174. Historical MSS Commission, v. 5, 1974, item 5103. *J. Historical Geography* v. 7, 1981, 379–96. G. Carter *et al. Humphry Repton* 1982, 164.

Armscote Manor, Ettington, Warwickshire
C.L. v. 53, 1923, 63–64. R. Sidwell *West Midland gardens* 1981, 193–94.

Armston, Hereford and Worcester
W. Angus *Seats* 1787, pl. 12.

Arncliffe Hall, Northallerton, N. Yorks
C.L. v. 48, 1920, 846–53.

Arngibbon near Port of Menteith, Central
Scottish Gdnr and Northern Forester v. 7, 1912, 381–82.

Arniston near Gorebridge, Lothian
R. Pococke *Tours in Scotland* 1887, 313. C.L. v. 58, 1925, 250–57. C. McWilliam *Lothian* 1978, 82. A.A. Tait *Landscape garden in Scotland* 1980, passim.

Arnos Castle near Bristol, Avon
B. Jones *Follies & grottoes* 1974, 63–65.

Arnos Grove, Southgate, London
W. Watts *Seats* 1779, pl. 63. J.C. Loudon *Encyclopaedia of gardening* 1822, 1225. G.M. v. 15, 1839, 510–11; v. 16, 1840, 584. W. Keane *Beauties of Middlesex* 1850, 93–95.

Arthington Hall, Arthington, W. Yorks
K. Lemmon *Gardens of Britain* v. 5, 1978, 153–55. C.L. v. 175, 1984, 1790–92.

Arthingworth, Northants
Royal Commission on historical monuments in . . . Northampton v. 3, 1981, 3.

Arundel Castle, Arundel, W. Sussex
C. Wright *History and description of Arundel Castle* 1817; 1818. G.M. v. 5, 1829, 585–88. R. Dally *Arundel Guide* 1830. F.O. Morris *Series of picturesque views* v. 4, 1. L. Jewitt *and* S.C. Hall *Stately homes of England* 1874,

Arundel Castle (*Cont.*)
153–71. *J. Hort. Cottage Gdnr* v. 51, 1874, 11–14; v. 11, 1885, 317–19. *G.C.* ii 1875, 10–11,39–40; 327–28,337; i 1886, 751–52. *Garden* v. 35, 1889, 25–26. *Gdnrs Mag.* 24 March 1900, Supplt i–viii. *C.L.* v. 36, 1914, 746–54, 782–90. Lady Rockley *Historic gardens of England* 1938, 72–73. J. Harris *Artist and the country house* 1979, 324–25.

Arundel House, Strand, London
J. Thane *Views of Arundel House in the Strand MDCXLVI* 1792. R. Strong *Renaissance garden in England* 1979, 169–74.

Ascog Hall, Isle of Bute, Strathclyde
G.C. ii 1879, 523–24,529.

Ascot House near Sunninghill, Berks
G.M. v. 5, 1829, 568–70. B. Jones *Follies & grottoes* 1974, 160–63.

Ascott, Leighton Buzzard, Bucks
Gdning World v. 1, 1885, 328–29; v. 13, 1897, 646. *G.C.* i 1891, 783–84; i 1893, 721–22; i 1896, 165–66,172. *J. Hort. Cottage Gdnr* v. 22, 1891, 105–06. *Gdnrs Mag.* 1905, 297–99,301. *C.L.* v. 2, 1897, 210–12; v. 8, 1900, 240–47; v. 108, 1950, 826–27; v. 150, 1971, 106; v. 159, 1976, 662–64. H. Evans *Beautiful gardens of Britain* 1974, 45–46. R. Bisgrove *Gardens of Britain* v. 3, 1978 24–25. M. Binney and A. Hills *Elysian gardens* 1979, 35. L. Fleming and A. Gore *English garden* 1979, 204. G.S. Thomas *Gardens of National Trust* 1979, 97–98. A. Hellyer *Gardens of genius* 1980, 114–20.

Ascreavie, Kingoldrum by Kirriemuir, Tayside
G.A. Little *Scotland's gardens* 1981, 174–75.

Asgill House, Richmond, London
W.B. Cooke and S. Owen *The Thames* v. 2, 1811. R. Ackermann *Repository* v. 4, 1824, pl. 13.

Ashbourne, Glounthane, Co. Cork, Eire
G.C. i 1909, 392–93; ii 1911, 315–17. *Gdnrs Mag.* 1909, 767–69. *New Flora & Silva* v. 1, 1929, 121.

Ashburne House, Newcastle upon Tyne, Tyne and Wear
J. Hort. Cottage Gdnr v. 60, 1878, 205–08; v. 15, 1887, 275.

Ashburnham Place near Battle, E. Sussex
W. Watts *Seats* 1779, pl. 61. R. Ackermann *Repository* v. 9, 1827, pl. 25. J.P. Neale *Views* 2nd Series, v. 4, 1828. W.W.J. Gendall *Views* v. 1, 1830, 60. *G.C.* i 1886, 783–84; ii 1912, 208–09. *C.L.* v. 39, 1916, 112–18, 144–51. *Architectural Review* v. 96, 1944, 159–62. D. Stroud *Capability Brown* 1975, 215.

Ashbury Manor, Ashbury, Oxfordshire
C.L. v. 140, 1966, 974–77,1084.

Ashby de la Zouch Manor House, Ashby de la Zouch, Leics
G.C. ii 1894, 161.

Ashby St Ledgers, Northants
C.L. v. 110, 1951,496–99. J. Brown *Gardens of a golden afternoon* 1982, 167.

Ashcombe, Devon
J. Harris *Artist and the country house* 1979, 176.

Ashcombe near Tisbury, Wilts
J. Britton *Beauties of Wiltshire* v. 1, 1801, 304–05.

Ashcombe Park near Leek, Staffs
F.O. Morris *Series of picturesque views* v. 4, 75.

Ashdown near East Grinstead, W. Sussex
J. Hort. Cottage Gdnr v. 60, 1878, 425–26.

Ashdown House, Lambourn, Oxfordshire
J. Beeverell *Les delices de la Grande Bretagne* v. 5, 1707, 872. L. Knyff and J. Kip *Britannia illustrata* v. 1, 1714. *C.L.* v. 33, 1913, 458–62. R. Bisgrove *Gardens of Britain* v. 3, 1978, 25–26. M. Binney and A. Hills *Elysian gardens* 1979, 52. G.S. Thomas *Gardens of National Trust* 1979, 98.

Ashe High House near Wickham Market, Suffolk
Gdn History v. 2 no. 3, 1974, 77–89.

Ashen Wilderness, Chiddingstone, Kent
F. Hull *Catalogue of estate maps 1590 to 1840 in the Kent County Archives Office* 1973, 47.

Ashfield House, Standish, Greater Manchester
G. Beard *Thomas H. Mawson* 1976, 43.

Ashford Chase, Petersfield, Hants
C.L. v. 48, 1920, 814–20. *Garden Design* 1935, 109–15. *Gdning Illustrated* v. 71, 1954, 216–18. A. Paterson *Gardens of Britain* v. 2, 1978, 50–51.

Ashford Court, Ashford Carbonel, Shropshire
R. Sidwell *West Midland gardens* 1981, 99.

Ashlands, Newchurch, Lancs
G.C. i. 1896, 520.

Ashley, Northants
Northamptonshire Past and Present v. 5 no. 3, 1975, 219.

Ashley Park, Walton-on-Thames, Surrey
J.P. Neale *Views* v. 4, 1821. W. Keane *Beauties of Surrey* 1849, 16–17.

Ashman's Hall near Beccles, Suffolk
J.P. Neale *Views* 2nd Series, v. 2, 1825.

Ashorne House, Ashorne, Warwickshire
R. Sidwell *West Midland gardens* 1981, 194–96.

Ashridge Park near Berkhampstead, Herts
H. Repton *Fragments* 1816, 137–44. J.C. Loudon *Encyclopaedia of gardening* 1822, 1233–34. R. Ackermann *Repository* v. 11, 1828, pl. 1. W.W.J. Gendall *Views* v. 2, 1830, 130. Prince Pückler-Muskau *Tour in England* 1833, 67–68. H.J. Todd *History of College of Bonhommes at Ashridge* 1833. *G.M.* v. 12, 1836, 289–92. *G.C.* ii 1885, 551–52; ii 1889, 468; i 1914, 127. *C.L.* v. 4, 1898, 560–63,592–96; v. 50, 1921, 160–66; v. 58, 1925, 687–89. H.I. Triggs *Formal gardens in England and Scotland* 1902, 29. M.R. Gloag *Book of English gardens* 1906, 87–115. C. Holme *Gardens of England in Southern & Western counties* 1907, pls. 9–13. J. Jekyll *Garden ornament* 1918, 351. D. Stroud *Humphry Repton* 1962, 160. H. Evans *Beautiful gardens of Britain* 1974, 49–50. D. Stroud *Capability Brown* 1975, 101–02. R. Bisgrove *Gardens of Britain* v. 3, 1978, 26–28. L. Fleming *and* A. Gore *English garden* 1979, 180. G. Carter *et al. Humphry Repton* 1982, 56,57,154. D. Watkin *English vision* 1982, 83. D. Jacques *Georgian gardens* 1983, 182.

Ashtead Park near Epsom, Surrey
J.P. Neale *Views* v. 4, 1821. *G.M.* v. 5, 1829, 595–97, 722. W. Keane *Beauties of Surrey* 1849, 104–07. *J. Hort. Cottage Gdnr* v. 40, 1900, 160–62. *G.C.* ii 1914, 274–75.

Ashton Cottage near Bishops Waltham, Hants
A. Paterson *Gardens of Britain* v. 2, 1978, 51–52.

Ashton Court, Long Ashton, Avon
J. Collinson *History . . . of . . . Somersetshire* v. 2, 1791, 294. H. Repton *Observations* 1803, 200–02. *G.C.* i 1882, 734; ii 1885, 295. *J. Hort. Cottage Gdnr* v. 7, 1883, 162–64; v. 43, 1901, 353–54; v. 54, 1907, 186–87,189. *Gdnrs Mag.* 1908, 376–78. D. Stroud *Humphry Repton* 1962, 122–23. G. Carter *et al. Humphry Repton* 1982, 161.

Ashton Hall near Lancaster, Lancs
E. Baines *History . . . of Lancaster* v. 4, 1836, 544.

Ashton Hall, N. Yorks
T.D. Whitaker *History of Richmondshire* v. 2, 1823, 475.

Ashurst House, Hornsey, London
V.C.H. *Middlesex* v. 6, 1980, 128. J. Harris *Artist and the country house* 1979, 170.

Ashurst Lodge, Ashurst, Kent
C. Greenwood *Epitome of county history . . . v. 1: Kent* 1838, 118.

Ashwell Bury House, Ashwell, Herts
G.M. v. 12, 1836, 97–99. *C.L.* v. 101, 1947, 810–13. J. Brown *Gardens of a golden afternoon* 1982, 174.

Ashwicke Hall near Marshfield, Avon
G.C. i 1902, 255–56,257,263.

Aske Hall near Richmond, N. Yorks
T.D. Whitaker *History of Richmondshire* v. 1, 1823, 115. F.O. Morris *Series of picturesque views* v. 5, 25. *Historical MSS Commission* v. 5, 1974, item 4839. B. Jones *Follies & grottoes* 1974, 366. D. Stroud *Capability Brown* 1975, 215–16. K. Lemmon *Gardens of Britain* v. 5, 1978, 53. J. Harris *Artist and the country house* 1979, 296.

Aspall Hall near Debenham, Suffolk
C.L. v. 4, 1898, 599–601.

Aspendon Hall near Buntingford, Herts
H. Chauncy *Historical antiquities of Hertfordshire* 1700, 124. J. Harris *Artist and the country house* 1979, 110.

Aspley Guise Gardens, Beds
R. Bisgrove *Gardens of Britain* v. 3, 1978, 28–30.

Aspley Wood near Woburn Abbey, Beds
H. Repton *Fragments* 1816, 13. D. Stroud *Humphry Repton* 1962, 149–50.

Astley Abbotts House near Bridgnorth, Shropshire
R. Sidwell *West Midland gardens* 1981, 101–02.

Astley Hall near Chorley, Lancs
F.O. Morris *Series of picturesque views* v. 5, 5. *C.L.* v. 52, 1922, 14–21. J. Harris *Artist and the country house* 1979, 142–43.

Aston Bury, Aston, Herts
C.L. v. 27, 1910, 450–58.

Aston Hall near Stone, Staffs
J. Nightingale *Topographical . . . description of Staffordshire* 1810, 938.

Aston Hall, Birmingham, W. Midlands
R. Ackermann *Repository* v. 7, 1826, pl. 13. W.W.J. Gendall *Views* v. 1, 1830, 103. *C.L.* v. 18, 1905, 306–16; v. 114, 1953, 552–55.

Aston Lodge near Derby, Derbyshire
G. Beard *Thomas H. Mawson* 1976, 44.

Aston Park near Nantwich, Cheshire
G. Carter *et al. Humphry Repton* 1982, 149.

Aston Rowant House, Aston Rowant, Oxfordshire
G.C. ii 1907, 196–97. *Gdnrs Mag.* 1907, 929–32.

Astrop, Northants
Garden v. 24, 1883, 289–90. D. Stroud *Capability Brown* 1975, 216.

Astrop House, Frankton, Warwickshire
R. Sidwell *West Midland gardens* 1981, 196–97.

Athelhampton near Dorchester, Dorset
Official guide. *Garden* v. 24, 1883, 39. *C.L.* v. 6, 1899, 272–78; v. 19, 1906, 786–94,906–12; v. 175, 1984, 1478–82. G. Jekyll *Garden ornament* 1918, 231,339,350. Lady Rockley *Historic gardens of England* 1938, 222–23. M. Allan *Fisons guide* 1970, 76–77. H. Evans *Beautiful gardens of Britain* 1974, 29–30. G. Beard *Thomas H. Mawson* 1976, 44. A. Paterson *Gardens of Britain* v. 2, 1978, 22–24.

Athenaeum *see* Brighton

Atherton Hall, Atherton, Greater Manchester
J. Harris *Artist and the country house* 1979, 216. *Gdn History* v. 1 no. 3, 1973, 16–18.

Attingham Park near Shrewsbury, Shropshire
Official guide. W. Angus *Seats* 1787, pl. 52.
H. Repton *Observations* 1803, 112–20. J.P. Neale *Views* 2nd Series, v. 3, 1826. *C.L.* v. 49, 1921, 158–66, 186–93. *J. Royal Hort. Soc.* 1971, 212–13. E. Malins *Red books of Humphry Repton* 1976, 21–27. G.S. Thomas *Gardens of National Trust* 1979, 99. G. Carter *et al. Humphry Repton* 1982, 39,46,53,160–61.

Auberies, Bulmer, Essex
P. Muilman *History of Essex* v. 2, 1769, 139.
F.G. Emmison *Catalogue of maps in Essex Record Ofice* 1947, 55.

Aucheneck House near Killearn, Central
Scottish Gdnr and Northern Forester v. 9, 1914, 37–38.

Auchincruive near Ayr, Strathclyde
G.M. v. 9, 1833, 9–10. G. Jekyll *and* G.S. Elgood *Some English gardens* 1904, 104–06. H. Maxwell *Scottish gardens* 1911, 96–100. *C.L.* v. 72, 1932, 690–95.

Auchinraith House near Bothwell, Strathclyde
Scottish Gdnr and Northern Forester v. 9, 1914, 13–14.

Auchmar, Drymen, Central
G.A. Little *Scotland's gardens* 1981, 115–17.

Auckland Castle, Bishop Auckland, Durham
C.L. v. 151, 1972, 198–202,266–70,462.

Audley End near Saffron Walden, Essex
Official guide. J. Kip *Supplement du Nouveau theatre de la Grande Bretagne* 1728. W. Watts *Seats* 1779, pl. 26.
J.P. Neale *Views* v. 1, 1818. Prince Pückler-Muskau *Tour in England* 1833, 31–32. Lord Braybrooke *History of Audley End* 1836, 134–37. T. Wright *History . . . of Essex* v. 2, 1836, 111. F.O. Morris *Series of picturesque views* v. 2, 55. L. Jewitt *and* S.C. Hall *Stately homes of England* 1877, 112–27. *Garden* v. 12, 1877, 57–58. *G.C.* ii 1884, 293–94. *C.L.* v. 59, 1926, 872–79,916; v. 60, 1926, 128–36. F.G. Emmison *Catalogue of maps in Essex Record Office* 1947, 46; 1st Supplt, 1952, 5,13,19, 22,29. W. Addison *Audley End* 1953. J. Evelyn *Diary* v. 3, 1955, 141. N. Pevsner *Essex* 1965, 65.
J.D. Williams *Audley End: restoration of 1762–1797* 1966, 42–48. M. Allan *Fisons guide* 1970, 187.
D. Stroud *Capability Brown* 1975, 113–14. P. Willis *Charles Bridgeman* 1977, 177. J. Harris *Artist and the country house* 1979, 101. Victoria and Albert Museum *The common chronicle* 1983, 29.

Aughentaine, Fivemiletown, Co. Tyrone, Ulster
R. Webber *Percy Cane* 1975, 86–89,187.

Avebury Manor, Avebury, Wilts
C.L. v. 49, 1921, 522–29,552. M. Allan *Fisons guide* 1970, 77–78.

Averham Park near Newark, Notts
T. Badeslade *and* J. Rocque *Vitruvius Brittanicus* 1739, pls. 51–52. J. Harris *Artist and the country house* 1979, 139.

Avery Hill, Kent
J. Hort. Cottage Gdnr v. 34, 1897, 406–07,413.

Aviary, Southall, London
C.L. v. 158, 1975, 1286–88.

Avington Park near Winchester, Hants
R. Ackermann *Repository* v. 6, 1825, pl. 31.
W.W.J. Gendall *Views* v. 1, 1830, 94. J. Hewetson *Architectural and picturesque views* 1830. E.F. Prosser *Select illustrations of Hampshire* 1833. *C.L.* v. 52, 1922, 882–89.

Avon Tyrell, Christchurch, Hants
C.L. v. 27, 1910, 846–52.

Avondale near Rathdrum, Co. Wicklow, Eire
Official guide. *Irish Gdning* v. 4, 1909, 100–02. Knight of Glin *and* P. Bowe *Gardens of outstanding historic interest in . . . Ireland* 1980.

Awbridge Danes Water near Romsey, Hants
R.I.B.A. *Catalogue* v. G-K, 1973, 12.

Axwell Park near Blaydon, Tyne and Wear
W. Watts *Seats* 1779 pl. 77. W. Hutchinson *History . . . of Durham* v. 2, 1787, 443. *Gdng World* v. 7, 1890, 38–39.

Aydon Castle, Aydon, Northumberland
C.L. v. 36, 1914, 518–26.

Aynhoe Park, Aynho, Northants
J.P. Neale *Views* v. 3, 1820. *C.L.* v. 114, 1953, 42–45. D. Stroud *Capability Brown* 1975, 106–07. J. Anthony *Gardens of Britain* v. 6, 1979, 22–24.

Ayscoughfee Hall, Lincs
C.L. v. 39, 1916, 730–35,772.

Ayton Castle, Ayton, Borders
G.C. i 1881, 170.

Babbacombe, Devon
G.M. v. 18, 1842, 534–35.

Baber (Bawburgh?) near Norwich, Norfolk
G. Carter *et al. Humphry Repton* 1982, 158.

Baberton near Edinburgh, Lothian
H. Maxwell *Scottish gardens* 1911, 52–53.

Babraham Hall near Cambridge, Cambs
G.C. ii 1891, 647,648.

Babworth, East Retford, Notts
N. Pevsner *Nottinghamshire* 1979, 63–64. G. Carter *et al. Humphry Repton* 1982, 160.

Bacton Hall, Bacton, Suffolk
J. Harris *Artist and the country house* 1979, 319.

Baddesley Clinton Hall, Baddesley Clinton, Warwickshire
C.L. v. 18, 1905, 942–53; v. 71, 1932, 408–14. C. Holme *Gardens of England in Midland & Eastern counties* 1908, pl. 8.

Badgers Cottage, Idlicote, Warwickshire
R. Sidwell *West Midland gardens* 1981, 197.

Badger's Rake near Hascombe, Surrey
C.L. v. 166, 1979, 2382–84.

Badminton Cottage, Badminton, Avon
C.L. v. 159, 1976, 1298–1300.

Badminton House, Badminton, Avon
J. Beeverell *Les delices de la Grande Bretagne* v. 5, 1707, 872. R. Atkyns *Ancient and present state of Glostershire* 1712, 242. L. Knyff *and* J. Kip *Britannia illustrata* v. 1, 1714; v. 2, 1715. S. Switzer *Ichnographia rustica* v. 1, 1742, 72–73. J.N. Brewer *Delineations of Gloucestershire* 1825, 19,30. J.P. Neale *Views* 2nd Series, v. 2, 1825. F.O. Morris *Series of picturesque views* v. 2, 75. *G.C.* i 1885, 405–06. *J. Hort. Cottage Gdnr* v. 44, 1902, 488–90. *C.L.* v. 22, 1907, 378–87; v. 86, 1939, 550–55, 574, 600–01; v. 143, 1968, 800–04; v. 150, 1971, 613; v. 173, 1983, 142–43. M. Macartney *English houses & gardens* 1908, pl. 30. R. Dutton *English garden* 1937, pl. 48. Historical MSS Commission *Architectural history* v. 2, 1970, item 1062; v. 3, 1971, item 2415. D. Verey *Gloucestershire* v. 1, 1970, 258. B. Jones *Follies & grottoes* 1974, 179–80. D. Stroud *Capability Brown* 1975, 216. L. Fleming *and* A. Gore *English garden* 1979, 65, 111, pl. 75. J. Harris *Artist and the country house* 1979, 125,315. T. Wright *Arbours & grottos* 1979. J. Johnson *Excellent Cassandra: the life and times of Duchess of Chandos* 1981, 66. D. Watkin *English vision* 1982, 35. G. Cottesloe *and* D. Hunt *Duchess of Beaufort's flowers* 1983. D. Jacques *Georgian gardens* 1983, 71.

Badsworth Hall near Pontefract, W. Yorks
Gdning World v. 10, 1894, 341.

Bagendon House near Cirencester, Glos
J. Sales *West Country gardens* 1980, 31.

Baggariff Hall, Leics
G.M. v. 7, 1831, 428.

Bagnigge Wells, Camden, London
W. Wroth *London pleasure gardens of the eighteenth century* 1896, 56–66. E.B. Chancellor *Pleasure haunts of London* 1925, 388–92.

Bagnor Manor near Newbury, Berks
C.L. v. 152, 1972, 274–77.

Bagshot Park near Ascot, Surrey
C. Burlington *Modern universal British traveller* 1779, 64. P. Sandby *Collection of one hundred and fifty select views* v. 1, 1781, pl. 66. G.A. Walpoole *New British traveller* 1784, 58. W. Thornton *New, complete and universal history* 1786, 502. *G.M.* v. 4, 1828, 433–37; v. 5, 1829, 382,570–71; v. 10, 1834, 332–34,532–37; v. 11, 1835, 360–61. G.F. Prosser *Select illustrations of . . . Surrey* 1828. J.C. Loudon *Villa gardener* 1850, 409. F.O. Morris *Series of picturesque views* v. 6, 1. *G.C.* ii 1902, 169–71. C. Ward *Royal gardens* 1912, 32–49.

Bailbrook House (Lodge) near Bath, Avon
J. Collinson *History . . . of Somersetshire* v. 1, 1791, 103. G. Carter *et al. Humphry Repton* 1982, 161.

Bailrigg House, Scotforth, Lancs
G. Beard *Thomas H. Mawson* 1976, 22,44.

Bake near St Germans, Cornwall
Architectural History v. 7, 1964, 23,43.

Bakers' Company *see* London

Balbirnie House, Markinch, Fife
J.P. Neale *Views* v. 6, 1823. *C.L.* v. 151, 1972, 1670–73. A.A. Tait *Landscape garden in Scotland* 1980, passim.

Balbithan House, Kintore, Grampian
C.L. v. 164, 1978, 1824–25. A. Lees-Milne *and* R. Verey *Englishwoman's garden* 1980, 84–85. G.A. Little *Scotland's gardens* 1981, 175.

Balcarres, Colinsburgh, Fife
G.M. v. 10, 1834, 530–31. *C.L.* v. 12, 1902, 176–85; v. 37, 1915, 120. H.I. Triggs *Formal gardens in England and Scotland* 1902, 45. H. Maxwell *Scottish gardens* 1911, 135–39. G. Jekyll *Garden ornament* 1918, 243, 252,280,409. M. Binney *and* A. Hills *Elysian gardens* 1979, 27.

Balcaskie near Pittenweem, Fife
G.M. v. 10, 1834, 529–30. *Garden* v. 36, 1889, 191. H.I. Triggs *Formal gardens in England and Scotland* 1902, 44–45. G. Jekyll *and* G.S. Elgood *Some English gardens* 1904, 39–41. M. Maxwell *Scottish gardens* 1911, 131–34. *C.L.* v. 31, 1912, 318–26. G. Jekyll *Garden ornament* 1918, 25,86,124,289. A.A. Tait *Landscape garden in Scotland* 1980, passim. G.A. Little *Scotland's gardens* 1981, 117–19.

Balcormo, Carnbee, Fife
I.H. Adams *Descriptive list of plans* v. 3, 1974, 56.

Baldersby Park near Ripon, N. Yorks
G.C. ii 1908, 113–14.

Baldon House near Oxford, Oxfordshire
G.M. v. 10, 1834, 98–99.

Bale's Mead near Porlock, Somerset
G.C. i 1960, 538–39,540.

Balfour House near Markinch, Fife
Garden v. 36, 1889, 593.

Balgray, Lockerbie, Dumfries and Galloway
G.A. Little *Scotland's gardens* 1981, 244.

Balkail House near Glenluce, Strathclyde
Scottish Gdnr and Northern Forester v. 7, 1912, 705–06.

Ball Haye, Staffs
J. Nightingale *Topographical . . . description of Staffordshire* 1810, 1021,1068.

Ballamodar, Patrick, Isle of Man
Proc. Isle of Man Natural History and Antiquarian Soc. v. 8 no. 3, 1976–78, 251–57,266–77.

Ballimore, Loch Fyne, Strathclyde
J. Hort. Cottage Gdnr v. 42, 1901, 304–05. T.H. Mawson *Art & craft of garden making* 1907, 262–68. G. Beard *Thomas H. Mawson* 1976, 44.

Ballinrobe, Co. Mayo, Eire
J. Harris *Artist and the country house* 1979, 305.

Balloch Castle, Balloch, Strathclyde
J.P. Neale *Views* v. 6, 1823.

Ballochmyle House near Pinwherry, Strathclyde
Scottish Gdnr and Northern Forester v. 8, 1913, 465–67.

Ball's Park near Hertford, Herts
H. Chauncy *Historical antiquities of Hertfordshire* 1700, 265. *C.L.* v. 31, 1912, 578–87. *G.C.* i 1914, 205–06. *Gdnrs Mag.* 1915, 118–19.

Ballyalolly House, Co. Down, Ulster
G.C. 5 April 1967, 16–17.

Ballyfinn, Co. Laois, Eire
J.P. Neale *Views* 2nd Series, v. 4, 1828. *C.L.* v. 154, 1973, 702–05,774–77. E. Malins *and* Knight of Glin *Lost demesnes* 1976, 96–97.

Ballyheigue Castle, Ballyheigue, Co. Cork, Eire
E. Malins *and* Knight of Glin *Lost demesnes* 1976, 114–15.

Ballynahinch near Clifden, Co. Galway, Eire
Irish Gdning v. 12, 1917, 114–15. E. Malins *and* Knight of Glin *Lost demesnes* 1976, 100.

Ballynastrach near Gorey, Co. Wexford, Eire
J.N. Brewer *Beauties of Ireland* v. 1, 1825, 387.

Ballysaggartmore near Lismore, Co. Waterford, Eire
B. Jones *Follies & grottoes* 1974, 224–25. E. Malins *and* Knight of Glin *Lost demesnes* 1976, 181.

Ballywalter Park, Co. Down, Ulster
C.L. v. 141, 1967, 456–60,516–20. *G.C.* v. 161 no. 13, 1967, 20–21. E. Malins *and* P. Bowe *Irish gardens and*

demesnes 1980, 78–79. Ulster Architectural Heritage Society *Northern gardens* 1982, 13.

Balmae, Dumfries and Galloway
G.C. ii 1906, 141.

Balmanno Castle, Dron, Tayside
C.L. v. 69, 1931, 344–49. *Gdn History* v. 5 no. 2, 1977, 35–38. *Garden* v. 104, 1979, 324. *Landscape* v. 24 no. 3, 1980, 24–26. G.A. Little *Scotland's gardens* 1981, 119–21.

Balmoral Castle near Braemar, Grampian
G.C. ii 1876, 519–20, 525; i 1897, 425; i 1937, 305. *J. Hort. Cottage Gdnr* v. 34, 1897, 565–66. L. Roper *Royal gardens* 1953, 86–91. C.L. v. 161, 1977, 1382–86. G.A. Little *Scotland's gardens* 1981, 175–76. G. Plumptre *Royal gardens* 1981, 180–95.

Balmuir House near Dundee, Tayside
G.A. Little *Scotland's gardens* 1981, 121.

Balrath near Duleek, Co. Meath, Eire
Cottage Gdnr v. 27, 1862, 478–81. G.C. i 1884, 476–77.

Balruddery House near Dundee, Tayside
Scottish Gdnr and Northern Forester v. 9, 1914, 49–50.

Balthayock near Perth, Tayside
Scottish Gdnr v. 4, 1855, 156–59.

Balygort near Balbriggan, Co. Dublin, Eire
G.M. v. 2, 1827, 147–48.

Bampton Manor, Bampton, Oxfordshire
C.L. v. 142, 1967, 510–12. R. Bisgrove *Gardens of Britain* v. 3, 1978, 30–31. *Architectural Digest* v.38, 1981, 90–95.

Bangors Park near Uxbridge, London
G.C. i 1913, 180.

Bank Farm *see* Point Pleasant

Bank Grove near Kingston, Surrey
W. Keane *Beauties of Surrey* 1849, 7–9.

Bank House, Warrington, Lancs
Architectural History v. 7, 1964, 38, 107.

Banks Hall near Barnsley(?), S. Yorks
I. Hall *Samuel Buck's Yorkshire sketchbook* 1979, 126.

Bankside, Four Oaks, Sutton Coldfield, W. Midlands
R. Webber *Percy Cane* 1975, 185.

Banner Cross, Sheffield, S. Yorks
J. Hunter *History . . . of . . . Sheffield* 1869, 352.

Bantaskin, Falkirk, Central
I.H. Adams *Descriptive list of plans* v. 1, 1966, 153.

Bantry House, Bantry, Co. Cork, Eire
E. Malins *and* Knight of Glin *Lost demesnes* 1976, 112.

Barford Hill, Warwickshire
J. Hort. Cottage Gdnr v. 27, 1893, 152–53. *Garden* v. 59, 1901, 298–300.

Barford House near Bridgwater, Somerset
C.L. v. 156, 1974, 1354–57.

Bargaly near Newton-Stewart, Dumfries and Galloway
G.M. v. 9, 1833, 13. J.C. Louden *Arboretum et Fruticetum Britannicum* v. 1, 1844, 95–99.

Bargany near Girvan, Strathclyde
G.M. v. 9, 1833, 9. C.L. v. 78, 1935, 64–70. A.A. Tait *Landscape garden in Scotland* 1980, *passim*. G.A. Little *Scotland's gardens* 1981, 244–45.

Barguillean, Taynuilt, Strathclyde
G.A. Little *Scotland's gardens* 1981, 223–24.

Barham, Bow of Fife, near Cupar, Fife
G.A. Little *Scotland's gardens* 1981, 121–23.

Barham Court near Canterbury, Kent
J. Hort. Cottage Gdnr v. 57, 1877, 48–50; N.S. v. 33, 1896, 223–24. C.L. v. 45, 1919, 142–47. J. Brown *Gardens of a golden afternoon* 1982, 172.

Barjarg Tower near Thornhill, Dumfries and Galloway
J.P. Neale *Views* 2nd Series, v. 1, 1824.

Barkby Hall, Barkby, Leics
G.M. v. 7, 1831, 428.

Barlaston Hall near Stone, Staffs
F. Calvert *Picturesque views . . . in Staffordshire & Shropshire* 1830, 37. *J. Hort. Cottage Gdnr* v. 37, 1867, 9–10.

Barlborough Hall near Chesterfield, Derbyshire
J.P. Neale *Views* v. 1, 1818. C.L. v. 8, 1900, 528–34. P. McArdle *Story of Balborough Hall* 1979. H. Nichols *Local maps of Derbyshire to 1770* 1980, 10.

Barley Mow Tea House and Gardens, Islington, London
W. Wroth *London pleasure gardens of the eighteenth century* 1896, 153.

Barley Wood, Wrington, Somerset
G. Beard *Thomas H. Mawson* 1976, 45.

Barleys near Lewes, E. Sussex
C.L. v. 92, 1942, 1178–81.

Barmston, Tyne and Wear
C. Fiennes *Journeys* 1949, 90–91.

Barn Elms, Barnes, London
E.W. Brayley *and* J. Britton *Topographical history of Surrey* v. 3, 438. *G.C.* i 1893, 391–92.

Barnbarroch near Wigtown, Dumfries and Galloway
J. Loudon *Treatise on forming, improving and managing country residences* v. 2, 1806, pl. 28. A.A. Tait *Landscape garden in Scotland* 1980, passim. D. Watkin *English vision* 1982, 87.

Barncluith near Hamilton, Strathclyde
G.M. v. 18, 1842, 342–43. *Scottish Gdnr* v. 3, 1854, 263–66. *Garden* v. 45, 1894, 545–46. *C.L.* v. 12, 1902, 302–06. H.I. Triggs *Formal gardens in England and Scotland* 1902, 46. H. Maxwell *Scottish gardens* 1911, 167–70.

Barne House near Clonmel, Co. Tipperary, Eire
J. Hort. Cottage Gdnr v. 63, 1880, 340–41.

Barnet (Mr Richardson), London
Archaeologia v. 12, 1796, 189–90.

Barnhill, Stamford, Lincs
C.L. v. 174, 1983, 1249.

Barnhourie Mill, Dumfries and Galloway
G.A. Little *Scotland's gardens* 1981, 245–46. *C.L.* v.172, 1982, 450–52.

Barningham Hall near Holt, Norfolk
G.M. v. 17, 1841, 30. J. Grigor *Eastern arboretum* 1841, 115–21. *C.L.* v. 27, 1910, 198–203. D. Stroud *Humphry Repton* 1962, 134. G. Carter *et al. Humphry Repton* 1982, 158.

Barns, Manor, Borders
I.H. Adams *Descriptive list of plans* v. 1, 1966, 127.

Barnsley House near Cirencester, Glos
C.L. v. 156, 1974, 840–42. *Garden* 1977, 281–88. A. Lees-Milne *and* R. Verey *English woman's garden* 1980, 139–43. *Architectural Digest* v. 39, 1982, 170–75.

Barnsley Park near Cirencester, Glos
J.N. Brewer *Delineations of Gloucestershire* 1825, 84. *C.L.* v. 116, 1954, 720–23, 806. Historical MSS Commission *Architectural history* v. 2, 1970, item 1080. L. Fleming *and* A. Gore *English garden* 1979, 175. J. Sales *West Country gardens* 1980, 35–36. V.C.H. *Gloucester* v. 7, 1981, 16.

Barnsley Locke Park, S. Yorks
G.C. i 1928, 425. B. Jones *Follies & grottoes* 1974, 386.

Barnwell Manor, Barnwell, Northants
C.L. v. 126, 1959, 238–41, 298–301. Royal Commission on Historical Monuments *Inventory of historical monuments in . . . Northampton* v. 1, 1975, 16, pl. 21. G. Plumptre *Royal gardens* 1981, 34–48. C. Taylor *Archaeology of gardens* 1983, 51–54.

Baron Hill, Anglesey, Gwynedd
W. Watts *Seats* 1779, pl. 11. *J. Hort. Cottage Gdnr* v. 50, 1873, 137–39, 176–78. *G.C.* i 1911, 122, 123.

Baronscourt near Newtown-Stewart, Co. Tyrone, Ulster
F.O. Morris *Series of picturesque views* v. 4, 51. Royal Hort. Soc. *Conifers in cultivation* 1932, 215–16. *G.C.* ii 1962, 166. *C.L.* v. 166, 1979, 162–65. A. Rowan *North West Ulster* 1979, 135–36. Ulster Architectural Heritage Society *Northern gardens* 1982, 13.

Barr Hall, Great Barr, W. Midlands
S. Shaw *History . . . of Staffordshire* v. 2, 1801, 106. J. Nightingale *Topographical . . . description of Staffordshire* 1810, 832–33. F. Calvert *Picturesque views . . . in Staffordshire & Shropshire* 1830, 49. *J. Hort. Cottage Gdnr* v. 30, 1863, 231–32.

Barra Castle near Old Meldrum, Grampian
C.L. v. 134, 1963, 424–27.

Barratt's Botanic Garden, St. John's, Wakefield, W. Yorks
G.M. v. 12, 1836, 312–14.

Barrels near Henley-in-Arden, Warwickshire
M. Williams *Letters of William Shenstone* 1939, passim. G. Carter *et al. Humphry Repton* 1982, 163.

Barrington near Burford, Glos
R. Atkyns *Ancient and present state of Glostershire* 1712, 250. L. Knyff *and* J. Kip *Britannia illustrata* v. 2, 1715. S. Rudder *New history of Gloucestershire* 1779, 262. P. Sandby *Collection of one hundred and fifty select views* v. 1, 1781, pl. 15. V.C.H. *Gloucester* v. 6, 1965, 18. D. Verey *Gloucestershire* v. 1, 1970, 260–61.

Barrington Court near Ilminster, Somerset
Official guide. *C.L.* v. 16, 1904, 414–17; v. 63, 1928, 370–77; v. 64, 1928, 332–38. M. Allan *Fisons guide* 1970, 79. V.C.H. *Somerset* v. 4, 1978, 115–16. G.S. Thomas *Gardens of National Trust* 1979, 100–01. J. Sales *West Country gardens* 1980, 133–37. J. Brown *Miss Gertrude Jekyll* 1981, 32–37. T. Hinde *Stately gardens of Britain* 1983, 134–39.

Barrington Hall, Hatfield Broad Oak, Essex
P. Muilman *History of Essex* v. 4, 1770, 113. P. Morant *History . . . of Essex* v. 2, 1816, 503. F.G. Emmison *Catalogue of maps in Essex Record Office* 2nd Supplt, 1964, 13.

Barrow Court, Flax Bourton, Bristol, Avon
J. Collinson *History . . . of Somersetshire* v. 2, 1791, 308. *C.L.* v. 11, 1902, 80–87. *Gdnrs Mag.* 1908, 375–76,377,378,379. G. Jekyll *Garden ornament* 1918, 229.

Barrowpoint Hill, Harrow, London
G.C. ii 1888, 415–17.

Barry's Close, Long Crendon, Bucks
R. Bisgrove *Gardens of Britain* v. 3, 1978, 31–32.

Barskimming near Mauchline, Strathclyde
Scottish Gdnr and Northern Forester v. 7, 1912, 317–18, 501–02. H. Maxwell *Scottish gardens* 1911, 101–07.

Barton Abbey, Steeple Aston, Oxfordshire
R. Bisgrove *Gardens of Britain* v. 3, 1978, 32.

Barton Hall near Bury St Edmunds, Suffolk
Garden v. 23, 1883, 511–12.

Barton Hartshorne Manor, Barton Hartshorne, Bucks
C.L. v. 34, 27 Sept. 1913 Supplt xxii–xxiii.

Barton House, Barton-on-the-Heath, Warwickshire
R. Sidwell *West Midland gardens* 1981, 200–01.

Barton St Mary, East Grinstead, W. Sussex
J. Brown *Gardens of a golden afternoon* 1982, 89–93, 169.

Barton Seagrave, Northants
G. Carter et al. *Humphry Repton* 1982, 159.

Barwell Court, Surbiton, London
G. Beard *Thomas H. Mawson* 1976, 45.

Barwick House near Fakenham, Norfolk
J. Grigor *Eastern arboretum* 1841, 302.

Barwick Park near Yeovil, Somerset
B. Jones *Follies & grottoes* 1974, 227–30.

Basford Hall near Leek, Staffs
B. Jones *Follies & grottoes* 1974, 389.

Basildon near Reading, Berks
Official guide. *Copper Plate Mag.* v. 2, pl. 60. W. Angus *Seats* 1787, pl. 49. J.P. Neale *Views* 2nd series, v. 2, 1825. *G.M.* v. 10, 1834, 3–4. N. Pevsner *Berkshire* 1966, 78. D. Stroud *Capability Brown* 1975, 216. *C.L.* v. 161, 1977, 1158–61,1298–1301.

Basing Park near Alton, Hants
E.F. Prosser *Select illustrations of Hampshire* 1833. *Scottish Gdnr* v. 6, 1857, 461–63. *G.C.* i 1886, 273–74; ii 1896, 588; ii 1904, 38.

Baskerville House, Birmingham, W. Midlands
J. Hort. Cottage Gdnr N.S. v. 35, 1897, 619,622,623, 625.

Basset Down House near Wootton Bassett, Wilts
G.C. ii 1897, 302–03.

Bassetsbury, High Wycombe, Bucks
C.L. v. 74, 1933, 338–42,362.

Bateman, James *see* Worthing

Bateman's, Burwash, E. Sussex
Official guide. *C.L.* v. 24, 1908, 224–33; v. 79, 1936, 90–95. *Architectural Review* v. 46, 1919, 30–34. *J. Royal Hort. Soc.* 1960, 344. M. Allan *Fisons guide* 1970, 33. G.S. Thomas *Gardens of National Trust* 1979, 101–02.

Bateman's House, Old Windsor, Berks
J. Harris *Gardens of delight* 1978, 12–14.

Bath. 18th century pleasure gardens, Avon
C.L. v. 106, 1949, 328–30.

Bath. Botanic Garden, Avon
Garden v. 59, 1901, 447–49. M. Allan *Fisons guide* 1970, 80. *G.C.* v. 192 no. 11, 1982, 28–29.

Bath. Royal Victoria Park, Avon
F. Hanham *Manual for the park* 1857. *G.C.* i 1902, 156–57,179. G. Chadwick *Park and the town* 1966, 28,34–35.

Bath. Sydney Gardens, Avon
G.C. ii 1886, 43–44.

Batheaston Villa near Bath, Avon
G.C. v. 160 no. 25, 1966, 14.

Batsford near Moreton-in-Marsh, Glos
R. Atkyns *Ancient and present state of Glostershire* 1712, 256. L. Knyff *and* J. Kip *Britannia illustrata* v. 2, 1715. J.P. Neale *Views* 2nd Series, v. 1, 1824. *C.L.* v. 14, 1903, 18–28. M. Macartney *English houses & gardens* 1908, pl. 15. *J. Hort. Home Farmer* N.S., v. 62, 1911, 78–79. *G.C.* i 1912, 163–64. *Gdnrs Mag.* 1914, 411–14. B. Jones *Follies & grottoes* 1974, 324–25. J. Sales *West Country gardens* 1980, 38–39.

Battersea Park *see* London

Battle Abbey, Battle, E. Sussex
J.P. Neale *Views* 2nd Series, v. 4, 1828. *G.M.* v. 18, 1842, 611–13. *J. Hort. Cottage Gdnr* v. 47, 1872, 193–96; N.S. v. 39, 1899, 102–03. *Garden* v. 8, 1875, 546–49. *G.C.* ii 1885, 423–24,433. *C.L.* v. 2, 1897, 496–98; v. 6, 1899, 496–501; v. 170, 1981, 2166–68.

Battlesden near Woburn, Beds
V.C.H. *Bedford* v. 3, 1912, 343. L. Fleming *and* A. Gore *English garden* 1979, pl. 107. G. Carter *et al. Humphry Repton* 1982, 147.

Bawburgh *see* Baber

Bawdsey, Suffolk
G.C. ii 1908, 406,407,409.

Baycliffe, Lymm, Cheshire
Garden v. 43, 1893, 385–86.

Bayfield Hall near Holt, Norfolk
G.M. v. 17, 1841, 272. J. Grigor *Eastern arboretum* 1841, 231–32.

Bayfordbury, Bayford, Herts
G.M. v. 16, 1840, 588–90. J.E. Cussans *History of Hertfordshire* v. 2, 1874, 142. *G.C.* ii 1885, 229–30; i 1909, 228–30. *Gdnrs Mag.* 1909, 969–70. *C.L.* v. 57, 1925, 92–99,124–33. Lady Rockley *Historic gardens of England* 1938, 178–79. *J. Royal Hort. Soc.* 1953, 441–48. Historical MSS Commission *Architectural history* v. 3, 1971, item 2443. N. Pevsner *Hertfordshire* 1977, 91.

Bayhall, Kent
J. Harris *Artist and the country house* 1979, 72, pl. 4.

Bayham Abbey near Lamberhurst, E. Sussex
H. Repton *Observations* 1803, 203–09. *Garden* v. 9, 1876, 128–30. *Gdning World* v. 13, 1896, 57–58. *G.C.* ii 1908, 170. *Architectural Review* v. 80, 1936, 195–200. *C.L.* v. 94, 1943, 640–43. D. Stroud *Humphry Repton* 1962, 124. G. Carter *et al. Humphry Repton* 1982, 155.

Baylis, Bucks
G. Tod *Plans, elevations and sections of hot houses* 1807, 18, pl. 17.

Baynard's Castle Palace, Blackfriars, London
Antiquaries J. v. 57, 1977, 31–66.

Bayon's Manor near Market Rasen, Lincs
J.B. Burke *Visitation* v. 1, 1852, 236.

Bayswater Tea Gardens, Lancaster Gate, Westminster, London
W. Wroth *London pleasure gardens of the eighteenth century* 1896, 117–19.

Beach House, Worthing, W. Sussex
C.L. v. 49, 1921, 126–33.

Beachborough near Hythe, Kent
J. Harris *History of Kent* 1719, 216. T. Badeslade *Thirty six different views . . . of Kent* 1750s, pl. 2. C. Greenwood *Epitome of county history . . . v. 1: Kent* 1838, 305. J. Harris *Artist and the country house* 1979, 220.

Beacon Hill near Harwich, Essex
C.L. v. 57, 1925, 692–98.

Beaconsfield Place *see* Wilton Park

Beaminster Manor, Beaminster, Dorset
B. Jones *Follies & grottoes* 1974, 316.

Beamish near Albrighton, Shropshire
J. Royal Hort. Soc. 1954, 348–56.

Bear Forest, Co. Cork, Eire
J.P. Neale *Views* v. 6, 1823.

Bear Park, Wensleydale, N. Yorks
G.C. ii 1893, 8–10,13.

Bear Place near Maidenhead, Berks
Copper Plate Mag. v. 3, pl. 110.

Bearwood near Wokingham, Berks
G.M. v. 9, 1833, 679–83; v. 11, 1835, 502. F.O. Morris *Series of picturesque views* v. 6, 29. *Garden* v. 16, 1879, 53–54. *G.C.* i 1885, 797,798–99; i 1891, 667–68; ii 1894, 137–38. *C.L.* v. 11, 1902, 336–43; v. 144, 1968, 964–67.

Beau-Séjour, Guernsey, Channel Islands
W. Berry *History of Island of Guernsey*, 1815, 158.

Beaucastle near Bewdley, Hereford and Worcester
R. Sidwell *West Midland gardens* 1981, 24–27.

Beauchief, Sheffield, S. Yorks
H. Nichols *Local maps of Derbyshire to 1770* 1980, 13.

Beaudesert near Lichfield, Staffs
R. Plot *Natural history of Staffordshire* 1685, 126.
S. Shaw *History . . . of Staffordshire* v. 1, 1798, 222.
J. Nightingale *Topographical . . . description of Staffordshire* 1810, 785. H. Repton *Fragments* 1816, 40–48.
F. Calvert *Picturesque views . . . in Staffordshire & Shropshire* 1830, 67. *G.M.* v. 12, 1836, 311–12.
F.O. Morris *Series of picturesque views* v. 2, 3. *J. Hort. Cottage Gdnr* v. 47, 1872, 387–89. *G.C.* ii 1884, 748–49; i 1893, 164–65. D. Stroud *Humphry Repton* 1962, 166. Historical MSS Commission *Architectural history* v. 3, 1971, item 2446. D. Stroud *Capability Brown* 1975, 217. G. Carter *et al. Humphry Repton* 1982, 53,54,59,161.

Beaufort near Beauly, Highland
G.M. v. 11, 1835, 553–54.

Beaufort House, Chelsea, London
L. Knyff *and* J. Kip *Britannia illustrata* v. 1, 1714.
M. Macartney *English houses & gardens* 1908, pl. 3.
E.S. Rohde *Story of the garden* 1932, 78–80. *History Today* v. 26, 1976, 118–24.

Beaufront Castle near Hexham, Northumberland
C.L. v. 159, 1976, 286–89,342–45. J. Harris *Artist and the country house* 1979, 358–59.

Beauhurst Hall, Staffs
F. Calvert *Picturesque views . . . in Staffordshire & Shropshire* 1830, 152.

Beaulieu near Drogheda, Co. Louth, Eire
C.L. v. 125, 1959, 106–09.

Beaulieu, Guernsey, Channel Islands
W. Berry *History of Island of Guernsey* 1815, 157.

Beaulieu Abbey, Beaulieu, Hants
C. Holme *Gardens of England in Southern & Western counties* 1907 pl. 14. *Landscape & Gdn* v. 3 no. 2, 1936, 80–82.

Beaumanor near Loughborough, Leics
J. Throsby *Select views in Leicestershire* v. 1, 1790, 227.
J. Nichols *History . . . of county of Leicester* v. 3, 1804, 1128. J.B. Burke *Visitation* v. 1, 1852, 4. *Gdning World* v. 7, 1890, 74–75. Victoria and Albert Museum *The common chronicle* 1983, 29.

Beaumont Lodge, Berks
J.P. Neale *Views* v. 1, 1818. R. Ackermann *Repository* v. 2, 1823, pl. 33. W.W.J. Gendall *Views* v. 2, 1830, 45.

Beauparc near Navan, Co. Meath, Eire
G.M. v. 2, 1827, 150. E. Malins *and* Knight of Glin *Lost demesnes* 1976, 89–90.

Beauport near Battle, E. Sussex
G.M. v. 18, 1842, 613–15.

Beauvale, Basford, Notts
R.I.B.A. *Catalogue* v. G-K, 1973, 27.

Beaver Hall, Southgate, Enfield, London
J. Hassell *Seats near London* 1804–05.

Beckbury Hall near Shifnal, Shropshire
R. Sidwell *West Midland gardens* 1981, 103.

Beckenham, Bromley, London
E. Hasted *History . . . of . . . Kent* v. 1, 1778, 82.
J.P. Neale *Views* v. 2, 1819. D. Stroud *Humphry Repton* 1962, 54. G. Carter *et al. Humphry Repton* 1982, 155.

Beckett near Shrivenham, Oxfordshire
J. Hort. Cottage Gdnr v. 50, 1873, 120–22; v. 5, 1882, 521–22. *C.L.* v. 8, 1900, 592–97. *Archaeologia* v. 58, 1903, 571–73. M.R. Gloag *Book of English gardens* 1906, 119–34. T. Wright *Arbours & grottos* 1979.

Beckford Hall, Beckford, Hereford and Worcester
J.P. Neale *Views* v. 2, 1819. *G.C.* ii 1894, 751–52; i 1906, 400–01.

Beckford House, Southampton, Hants
R.I.B.A. *Catalogue* v. O-R, 1976, 117.

Beddington, Sutton, London
D. Lyons *Environs of London* v. 1, 1792, 56–58; *Supplement* 1811, 6. *Archaeologia* v. 12, 1796, 182–83.
J.C. Loudon *Encyclopaedia of gardening* 1822, 1229.
G.F. Prosser *Select illustrations of . . . Surrey* 1828.
N. Whittock *and* H. Gastineau *Picturesque beauties of England and Wales* 1830, 38–39. E.W. Brayley *and* J. Britton *Topographical history of Surrey* v. 4, 1848, 66,69. W. Keane *Beauties of Surrey* 1849, 86–89.
J.B. Burke *Visitation* 2nd Series, v. 1, 1855, 37–38.
Gdning World v. 3, 1886, 4–6. V.C.H. *Surrey* v. 4, 1912, 171,172. E.S. Rohde *Story of the garden* 1932, 149–50.
J. Evelyn *Diary* v. 1, 1955, 9; v. 2, 11; v. 3, 221; v. 5, 427. *J. Gdn History* v. 3 no. 2, 1983, 113–20.

Bedford Lodge, Campden Hill, London
W. Keane *Beauties of Middlesex* 1850, 135–37. *G.M.* v. 14, 1838, 401–11, 561. J.C. Loudon *Villa gardener* 1850, 246–55.

Bedford Priory, Beds
S. *and* N. Buck *Buck's antiquities* v. 1, 1774, pl. 1.

Bedfords, Havering atte Bower, Essex
J.P. Neale *Views* v. 1, 1818.

Bedgebury, Kent
W.H. Ireland *History . . . of Kent* v. 3, 1829, 210.
G. Virtue *Picturesque beauties of Great Britain: Kent* 1829, 114.

Bedgebury Pinetum near Goudhurst, Kent
Official guide. *J. Hort. Cottage Gdnr* v. 38, 1867, 253–55. *Quarterly J. Forestry* 1946, 1–16. *C.L.* v. 110, 1951, 1144–45; v. 117, 1955, 1108–09. *G.C.* ii 1963, 64–65; ii 1965, 38–39; v. 154, 1973, 2094–96. M. Allan *Fisons guide* 1970, 34–35. T. Wright *Gardens of Britain* v. 4, 1978, 23–26. *Garden* 1980, 357–62.

Bedwell Park, Essendon, Herts
H. Chauncy *Historical antiquities of Hertfordshire* 1700, 276. G. Carter et al. *Humphry Repton* 1982, 154.

Bedwellty Park near Tredegar, Gwent
B. Jones *Follies & grottoes* 1974, 415.

Beech Hill Park near Potters Bar, Herts
W. Keane *Beauties of Middlesex* 1850, 16–17.

Beech Lawn, Leamington, Warwickshire
G.M. v. 16, 1840, 585.

Beechwood near Markyate, Herts
J.P. Neale *Views* v. 2, 1819. *C.L.* v. 84, 1938, 474–78. D. Stroud *Capability Brown* 1975, 70–71.

Beechwood, Highgate, London
C.L. v. 111, 1952, 652–55.

Beechwood, Lavington, W. Sussex
C.L. v. 106, 1949, 538–41; v. 160, 1976, 1644–46,1758.

Beechworth Castle *see* Betchworth Castle

Beedingwood, Beeding, W. Sussex
Garden v. 61, 1902, 158–59.

Beeleigh Abbey, Maldon, Essex
C.L. v. 52, 1922, 406–12.

Beeston, Norfolk
W. Watts *Seats* 1779, pl. 36. J.P. Neale *Views* v. 3, 1820. *G.M.* v. 17, 1841, 272. J. Grigor *Eastern arboretum* 1841, 225–27. *C.L.* v. 173, 1983, 270–71.

Beeston Leasowes near Sandy, Beds
D. Stroud *Humphry Repton* 1962, 166. G. Carter et al. *Humphry Repton* 1982, 147.

Belan near Athy, Co. Kildare, Eire
T. Milton *Seats* 1783–93, 11. *Delineator* 1831, 67. J. Loveday *Diary* 1890, 28–29. E. Malins *and* Knight of Glin *Lost demesnes* 1976, 68–69. J. Harris *Artist and the country house* 1979, 302–03.

Belchamp Hall, Belchamp Walter, Essex
C.L. v. 126, 1959, 1206–09,1258.

Belchester House, Eccles, Borders
I.H. Adams *Descriptive list of plans* v. 3, 1974, 32.

Belcombe Court near Bradford-on-Avon, Wilts
C.L. v. 108, 1950, 2146–50.

Belfast Botanic Garden, Ulster
Scottish Gdnr v. 3, 1854, 207–11. *G.C.* i 1875, 817–18, 821; i 1898, 50–52,53,57; ii 1904, 417–18. *Garden* v. 66, 1904, 172. E. McCracken *Palm House and Botanic Garden, Belfast* 1971.

Belford, Northumberland
G.M. v. 16, 1840, 583.

Belgrave Hall near Leicester, Leics
Official guide. M. Allan *Fisons guide* 1970, 217. J. Anthony *Gardens of Britain* v. 6, 1979, 24–25.

Belgrove near Cobh, Co. Cork, Eire
Garden v. 59, 1901, 61–64. *G.C.* ii 1904, 1–2. *Moorea* v. 2, 1983, 23–24.

Belhaven, Dunbar, Lothian
G.A. Little *Scotland's gardens* 1981, 75–76.

Belhus (Bellhouse) near Aveley, Essex
P. Morant *History . . . of Essex* v. 1 pt 2, 1768, 78. J.P. Neale *Views* v. 1, 1818. R. Ackermann *Repository* v. 7, 1826, pl. 8. W.W.J. Gendall *Views* v. 1, 1830, 78. G. Virtue *Picturesque beauties of Great Britain: Essex* 1831, 42. T. Wright *History . . . of Essex* v. 2, 1836, 512. *C.L.* v. 47, 1920, 656–62. F.G. Emmison *Catalogue of maps in Essex Record Office* 1947, 42. D. Stroud *Capability Brown* 1975, 72–74.

Bell Hall, Naburn, N. Yorks
Historical MSS Commission *Architectural history* v. 4, 1972, item 4400.

Belladrum near Beauly, Highland
G.M. v. 11, 1835, 555.

Bellamour House, Staffs
F. Calvert *Picturesque views . . . in Staffordshire & Shropshire* 1830, 144.

Bellarena near Londonderry, Ulster
A. Rowan *North West Ulster* 1979, 141.

Belleisle near Enniskillen, Co. Fermanagh, Ulster
E. Malins *and* Knight of Glin *Lost demesnes* 1976, 77–78. T. Wright *Arbours & grottos* 1979.

Bellenden near Aberdeen, Grampian
Leopard no. 53, 1979, 31–32.

Bellevue, Halifax, W. Yorks
Bradford Illustrated Weekly Telegraph *Series of picturesque views* 1885.

Bellevue near Greystones, Co. Wicklow, Eire
J. Ferrar *View of ancient and modern Dublin* 1796, 98,103–12. E. Malins *and* Knight of Glin *Lost demesnes* 1976, 168–69.

Bellhouse *see* Belhus

Bellinter near Navan, Co. Meath, Eire
J.P. Neale *Views* v. 6, 1823.

Bell's Castle near Kemerton, Hereford and Worcester
R. Sidwell *West Midland gardens* 1981, 27–28.

Belmont, Devonport, Devon
R. Ackermann *Repository* v. 12, 1828, pl. 1.
W.W.J. Gendall *Views* v. 2, 1830, 123.

Belmont, Clehonger, Hereford and Worcester
G. Carter *et al. Humphry Repton* 1982, 153.

Belmont, Staffs
W. Pitt *General view of agriculture of . . . Stafford* 1796, 203. J. Nightingale *Topographical . . . description of Staffordshire* 1810, 1024. J.C. Loudon *Encyclopaedia of gardening* 1822, 1239.

Belmont *see* Warnford

Belmont Castle, Tayside
G.C. i 1903, 113,115.

Belmont Lodge, Guernsey, Channel Islands
W. Berry *History of Island of Guernsey* 1815, 164.

Belmont Park, Throwley, Kent
C.L. v. 117, 1955, 246–49,318–21. Historical MSS Commission *Architectural history* v. 3, 1971, item 3521.

Belmount, Mill Hill, London
W. Keane *Beauties of Middlesex* 1850, 262–63.

Belrath *see* Balrath

Belsay (Belso) **Castle** near Morpeth, Northumberland
Society of Gentlemen *England displayed* v. 2, 1769, 178.
S. *and* N. Buck *Buck's antiquities* v. 1, 1774, pl. 215.
J.P. Neale *Views* v. 3, 1820. C.L. v. 88, 1940, 324–28, 346–47. L. Fleming *and* A. Gore *English garden* 1979, 169. Victoria and Albert Museum *The common chronicle* 1983, 29.

Belsize Court, Hampstead, Camden, London
G.C. ii 1905, 389–90.

Belsize House, Hampstead, Camden, London
W. Wroth *London pleasure gardens of the eighteenth century* 1896, 189–93.

Belton House, Grantham, Lincs
Official guide. C. Campbell *Vitruvius Britannicus* v. 3, 1725, pl. 69. T. Badeslade *and* J. Rocque *Vitruvius Brittanicus* 1739, pls. 86–89. G.L. le Rouge *Jardins Anglo-Chinois a la mode* 6^e cahier, 1777, pl. 6.
W. Angus *Seats* 1787, pl. 39. J.P. Neale *Views* v. 2, 1819. British Museum *Catalogue of maps, prints, drawings* 1829, 27. G.M. v. 16, 1840, 571–72. G.C. ii 1888, 506; i 1895, 710; v. 188 no. 2, 1980, 29–31. C.L. v. 4, 1898, 368–71,400–03; v. 30, 1911, 308–16; v. 136, 1964, 562–65,620,700–03. H.I. Triggs *Formal gardens in England and Scotland* 1902, 25–26. M Macartney *English houses & gardens* 1908, pls. 36–37. E. Cecil *History of gardening in England* 1910, 228. *Garden* 1916, 421. G. Jekyll *Garden ornament* 1918, 43,191,262.
N. Pevsner *and* J. Harris *Lincolnshire* 1964, 454.
H. Evans *Beautiful gardens of Britain* 1974, 101–02.
J. Anthony *Gardens of Britain* v. 6, 1979, 25–30.
J. Harris *Artist and the country house* 1979, 269.

Belvedere, Harrogate, N. Yorks
Garden v. 60, 1901, 16.

Belvedere near Mullingar, Co. Westmeath, Eire
G.C. ii 1901, 448–49. C.L. v. 129, 1961, 1480–83, 1538–41; v. 150, 1971, 615. B. Jones *Follies & grottoes* 1974, 222–23. E. Malins *and* Knight of Glin *Lost demesnes* 1976, 85–87. T. Wright *Arbours & grottos* 1979. Knight of Glin *and* P. Bowe *Gardens of outstanding historic interest in . . . Ireland* 1980.

Belvedere House, Erith, Bexley, London
R. *and* J. Dodsley *London and its environs described* v. 1, 1761, 271. E. Hasted *History . . . of . . . Kent* v. 1, 1778, 198. G.M. v. 16, 1840, 583. *Copper Plate Mag.* v. 2, pl. 56.

Belvedere House, Lambeth, London
W. Wroth *London pleasure gardens of the eighteenth century* 1896, 261–62.

Belvedere Tea Gardens, Islington, London
W. Wroth *London pleasure gardens of the eighteenth century* 1896, 145–46.

Belvoir Castle, Belvoir, Leics
T. Badeslade and J. Rocque *Vitruvius Brittanicus* 1739, pls. 47–50. Society of Gentlemen *England displayed* v. 1, 1769, 377. S. and N. Buck *Buck's antiquities* v. 1, 1774, pls. 158–59. *Bibliotheca topographica Britannica* v. 8 no. 51, 1790, 1251. J. Throsby *Select views in Leicestershire* v. 1, 1790, 104. J. Nichols *History . . . of county of Leicester* v. 2, 1795, 22. J.P. Neale *Views* v. 2, 1819. *Jones's views* 1829. *G.M.* v. 7, 1831, 421–22. I. Eller *History of Belvoir Castle* 1841. *Garden* v. 3, 1873, 378–81; v. 61, 1902, 340–41. *J. Hort. Cottage Gdnr* v. 54, 1875, 9–11,29–31,272–74; v. 55, 1876, 404–05, 429–30; N.S. v. 16, 1888, 425–28; N.S. v.48, 1904, 447–48; N.S. v. 69, 1914, 174–76. *G.C.* i 1903, 121, 154–55,186,209–10,216; ii 1910, 102; i 1911, 184,185; i 1914, 296–98. F.O. Morris *Series of picturesque views* v. 2, 5. L. Jewitt and S.C. Hall *Stately homes of England* 1877, 23–29. *C.L.* v. 4, 1898, 240–43,272–75; v. 120, 1936, 1284–90,1402–05,1500. W.H. Divers *Catalogue of the trees, shrubs and plants* 1904. *Gdnrs Mag.* 1905, 165–68. C. Holme *Gardens of England in Midland & Eastern counties* 1908, pls. 9–10. W.H. Divers *Spring flowers at Belvoir Castle* 1909. B. Jones *Follies & grottoes* 1974, 355. D. Stroud *Capability Brown* 1975, 217. J. Harris *Artist and the country house* 1979, 167–196.

Bemersyde near St Boswells, Borders
G.A. Little *Scotland's gardens* 1981, 76.

Bemerton Rectory, Bemerton, Wilts
G.C. ii 1881, 116–17. *C.L.* v. 11, 1902, 300–02.

Ben Lawers, Tayside
C.L. v. 163, 1978, 552–55.

Benacre Hall near Southwold, Suffolk
H. Davy *Views* 1827.

Benacre Manor near Melksham, Wilts
C.L. v. 82, 1937, 578–80.

Benendon School, Kent
G.C. ii 1965, 474–75.

Benhall Lodge near Saxmundham, Suffolk
H. Davy *Views* 1827.

Benham near Newbury, Berks
A. Robertson *Topographical survey of the Great Road* 1792, pt 1, 152–53. *Copper Plate Mag.* v. 5, 1802, pl. 118. *G.M.* v. 10, 1834, 114–15. *J. Hort. Cottage Gdnr* N.S., v. 33, 1896, 630–32. D. Stroud *Capability Brown* 1975, 170–71.

Beningbrough Hall near York, N. Yorks
Florist 1855, 107–08. F.O. Morris *Series of picturesque views* v. 5, 7. *C.L.* v. 62, 1927, 772–80. K. Lemmon *Gardens of Britain* v. 5, 1978, 53–56. J. Harris *Artist and the country house* 1979, 317. *G.C.* v. 185 no. 21, 1979, 34. I. Hall *Samuel Buck's Yorkshire sketchbook* 1979, 234.

Benington Lordship, Benington, Herts
B. Jones *Follies & grottoes* 1974, 343. R. Bisgrove *Gardens of Britain* v. 3, 1978, 33. *Hertfordshire Countryside Mag.* v. 36 no. 264, 1981, 49–50. *C.L.* v. 171, 1982, 1346–48.

Benmore (Younger Botanic Garden), Dunoon, Strathclyde
Official guide. M. Allan *Fisons guide* 1970, 295–96. *C.L.* v. 164, 1978, 366–67. A. Hellyer *Gardens of genius* 1980, 68–73. G.A. Little *Scotland's gardens* 1981, 238.

Bennett, William *see* Whitechapel Botanical Garden

Benthall Hall near Broseley, Shropshire
Official guide. *Garden* v. 1, 1872, 625–26. *G.C.* i 1881, 205–06,208–09. *C.L.* v. 41, 1917, 664–69. G.S. Thomas *Gardens of National Trust* 1979, 102–03. *National Trust Studies* 1980, 10–20. R. Sidwell *West Midland gardens* 1981, 103–05.

Bentley near Halland, E. Sussex
C.L. v. 153, 1973, 524–25.

Bentley Hall, Staffs
R. Plot *Natural history of Staffordshire* 1685, 308.

Bentley Priory, Stanmore, London
W. Keane *Beauties of Middlesex* 1850, 113–18. *J. Hort. Cottage Gdnr* v. 40, 1868, 133,186–87,361–64. *G.C.* i 1885, 788–89. *Gdning World* v. 1, 1885, 279.

Benton End, Hadleigh, Suffolk
C.L. v. 165, 1979, 1532–34.

Bentworth Lodge, Bentworth, Hants
A. Paterson *Gardens of Britain* v. 2, 1978, 52.

Benwell Hall, Newcastle-upon-Tyne, Tyne and Wear
Historical MSS Commission *Architectural history* v. 2, 1970, item 1109.

Benwell Tower, Newcastle-upon-Tyne, Tyne and Wear
D. Stroud *Capability Brown* 1975, 42.

Berden Priory, Berden, Essex
F.G. Emmison *Catalogue of maps in Essex Record Office* 2nd Supplt, 1964, 2.

Berkeley Castle, Berkeley, Glos
Official guide. L. Knyff *and* J. Kip *Britannia illustrata* v. 2, 1715. R. Atkyns *Ancient and present state of Glostershire* 1712, 260. Society of Gentlemen *England displayed* v. 2, 1769, 26. S. *and* N. Buck *Buck's antiquities* v. 1, 1774, pl. 97. S. Rudder *New history of Gloucestershire* 1779, 270. T.D. Fosbrooke *Abstracts of . . . county of Gloucester* v. 1, 1807, 462. *J. Hort. Cottage Gdnr* N.S., v. 17, 1888, 307. *Garden* v. 35, 1889, 525. *C.L.* v. 16, 1904, 126–35,955; v. 40, 1916, 126–32, 154–60; v. 71, 1932, 626–33; v. 118, 1955, 1430–33. G. Jekyll *and* G.S. Elgood *Some English gardens* 1905, 23–25. Lady Rockley *Historic gardens of England* 1938, 74–75. T. Wright *Arbours & grottos* 1979. J. Sales *West Country gardens* 1980, 40–41.

Bermerside, Halifax, W. Yorks
Bradford Illustrated Weekly Telegraph *Series of picturesque views* 1885.

Bermondsey Spa Gardens, Southwark, London
W. Wroth *London pleasure gardens of the eighteenth century* 1896, 231–37. E.B. Chancellor *Pleasure haunts of London* 1925, 357–58.

Berrington Hall near Leominster, Hereford and Worcester
C.L. v. 116, 1954, 1952–56,2102. D. Stroud *Capability Brown* 1975, 189. G.S. Thomas *Gardens of National Trust* 1979, 103–04. R. Sidwell *West Midland gardens* 1981, 28–29.

Berry Hill near Mansfield, Notts
J.B. Burke *Visitation* 2nd Series, v. 1, 1855, 245.

Berry Pomeroy Castle near Totnes, Devon
G.M. v. 18, 1842, 536–37.

Berrydowne Court, Ashe, Overton, Hants
J. Brown *Gardens of a golden afternoon* 1982, 162.

Berwick near Shrewsbury, Shropshire
G.C. ii 1890, 387–88.

Berwick St John (Mr Foot), Wilts
Gdn History v. 8 no. 3, 1980, 81–83.

Bescot Hall, Walsall, W. Midlands
S. Shaw *History . . . of Staffordshire* v. 2, 1801, 82. J. Nightingale *Topographical . . . description of Staffordshire* 1810, 838.

Bessacre Manor, Bessacarr, S. Yorks
D. Stroud *Humphry Repton* 1962, 166. G. Carter *et al. Humphry Repton* 1982, 164.

Bessborough near Carrick, Co. Kilkenny, Eire
J.P. Neale *Views* v. 6, 1823. *G.C.* i 1904, 324–25. *Delineator* 1831, 69.

Bestwood Lodge near Nottingham, Notts
F.O. Morris *Series of picturesque views* v. 3, 61.

Beswick near Beverley(?), Humberside
I. Hall *Samuel Buck's Yorkshire sketchbook* 1979, 16.

Betchworth Castle near Reigate, Surrey
S. *and* N. Buck *Buck's antiquities* v. 2, 1774, pl. 277. G.F. Prosser *Select illustrations of . . . Surrey* 1828. E.W. Brayley *and* J. Britton *Topographical history of Surrey* v. 5, 1848, 79.

Betchworth House near Reigate, Surrey
G.F. Prosser *Select illustrations of . . . Surrey* 1828. W. Keane *Beauties of Surrey* 1849, 160. D. Stroud *Humphry Repton* 1962, 110. J. Harris *Artist and the country house* 1979, 197. G. Carter *et al. Humphry Repton* 1982, 162.

Betteshanger near Deal, Kent
G.C. ii 1897, 286–87; ii 1905, 172–73.

Bettisfield, Clwyd
I. Elstob *Garden book of Sir Thomas Hanmer* 1933. *C.L.* v. 164, 1978, 1752–55; v. 165, 1979, 1196.

Beverston Castle near Tetbury, Glos
J. Sales *West Country gardens* 1980, 42–43.

Bevis Mount, Southampton, Hants
M.R. Brownell *Alexander Pope & arts of Georgian England* 1978, 216–19.

Bewerley House near Pateley Bridge, N. Yorks
K. Lemmon *Gardens of Britain* v. 5, 1978, 57–59.

Bibury, Glos
S. Rudder *New history of Gloucestershire* 1779, 284. *C.L.* v. 32, 1912, 324–29.

Bicester House, Oxon
J. Harris *Artist and the country house* 1979, 106.

Bickleigh Castle near Exeter, Devon
C.L. v. 85, 1939, 416–20, 442–46.

Bickley, Bromley, London
J.P. Neale *Views* v. 2, 1819.

Bickmarsh Hall near Bidford-on-Avon, Warwickshire
R. Sidwell *West Midland gardens* 1981, 29–30.

Bicton, East Budleigh, Devon
Official guide. *Copper Plate Mag.* v. 5, 1802, pl. 110.
R. Ackermann *Repository* v. 5, 1825, pl. 1.
W.W.J. Gendall *Views* v. 2, 1830, 63. *G.M.* v. 14, 1838, 510–12; v. 18, 1842, 552,555,617–21; v. 19, 1843, 20–23,46–52,111–13,138–39,164–66,234–38,301–06, 367–68,419–26,495–97,539–40,601–05,606–07, 653–57. *Florist* 1857, 144–47,173–75. *Cottage Gdnr* v. 21, 1858, 49–51,65–68. *J. Hort. Cottage Gdnr* v. 46, 1871, 201–03, 221–23. *G.C.* ii 1894, 529–30; ii 1898, 153–54,177–78, 183,190–91; i 1963, 237; v. 188 no. 5, 1980, 18–19. *Gdning World* v. 15, 1899, 393–94,444. *C.L.* v. 14, 1903, 854–62. G. Jekyll *Garden ornament* 1918, 343–44, 346. *Landscape and Garden* v. 2 no. 3, 1935, 89–90. Lady Rockley *Historic gardens of England* 1938, 154–55. N.D.G. James *Trees of Bicton* 1969. H. Evans *Beautiful gardens of Britain* 1974, 17–18. P.M. Synge *Gardens of Britain* v. 1, 1977, 23–29. B. Jones *Follies & grottoes* 1974, 311–12. M. Allan *Fisons guide* 1970, 118–19.

Biddesden House near Ludgershall, Wilts
C.L. v. 45, 1919, 782–90; v. 83, 1938, 352–56.
N. Pevsner *Wiltshire* 1975, 110.

Biddestone Manor near Chippenham, Wilts
C.L. v. 17, 1905, 666–68.

Biddick Hall, Chester-le-Street, Co. Durham
C.L. v. 139, 1966, 1016–19. A. Lees-Milne *and* R. Verey *Englishman's garden* 1982, 80–83.

Biddlesden Park, Biddlesden, Bucks
E.M. Elvey *Handlist of Buckinghamshire estate maps* 1963, 12.

Biddulph Grange, Biddulph, Staffs
Scottish Gdnr v. 6, 1857, 232–33. *G.C.* 1862, 478–80, 527–28,575–76,670–72,719–20; i 1960, 48–49. *C.L.* v. 17, 1905, 18–29. G. Jekyll *Garden ornament* 1918, 284,419,450. B. Jones *Follies & grottoes* 1974, 119–20. *Garden* 1977, 193–96. *Gdn History* v. 6 no. 1, 1978, 25–45A. M. Binney *and* A. Hills *Elysian gardens* 1979, 64–65. L. Fleming *and* A. Gore *English garden* 1979, 182–84. *World of Interiors* March 1983, 110–17.

Bidston Priory, Birkenhead, Merseyside
G. Beard *Thomas H. Mawson* 1976, 25,45.

Biel, Prestonkirk, Lothian
C.L. v. 12, 1902, 272–79. G.A. Little *Scotland's gardens* 1981, 76–79.

Bierley Hall, Oakenshaw, W. Yorks
C.L. v. 120, 1956, 1126. B. Jones *Follies & grottoes* 1974, 405.

Bifrons near Canterbury, Kent
J. Harris *Artist and the country house* 1979, 76, pl. 6.

Biggar, Strathclyde
G.M. v. 18, 1842, 437–38.

Biggin Hall near Oundle, Northants
C.L. v. 116, 1954, 1758–61,1852–55.
Northamptonshire Past and Present v. 5 no. 3, 1975, 219.

Bigland Hall near Cartmel, Cumbria
E. Baines *History . . . of Lancaster* v. 4, 1836, 734.

Bignor Park near Petworth, W. Sussex
C.L. v. 119, 1956, 860–63.

Billesley Manor, Alcester, Warwickshire
C.L. v. 62, 1927, 56–62. *G.C.* ii 1936, 135.

Billingbear House, Binfield, Berks
R. Havell *Series of picturesque views* 1823, pl. 5.
R. Bisgrove *Gardens of Britain* v. 3, 1978, 34.

Bilsdons Farm, Bobbingworth, Essex
F.G. Emmison *Catalogue of maps in Essex Record Office* 2nd Supplt, 1964, 11.

Bilton Hall near Rugby, Warwickshire
S. Ireland *Picturesque views on the Upper, or Warwickshire Avon* 1795, 69–71.

Bingham's Melcombe, Dorset
G.A. Jellicoe *Gardens of Europe* 1937, 8–9. Lady Rockley *Historic gardens of England* 1938, 88–89. *C.L.* v. 102, 1947, 778–81,826. J. Newman *and* N. Pevsner *Dorset* 1972, 281.

Binns near Linlithgow, Lothian
Scottish Gdnr and Northern Forester v. 8, 1913, 637–38.

Binstead near Ryde, Isle of Wight
E.A. Brooke *Gardens of England* 1857, pl. 37.
A. Paterson *Gardens of Britain* v. 2, 1978, 53.

Birch Grove House, Haywards Heath, W. Sussex
G. Beard *Thomas H. Mawson* 1976, 45.

Birch Hall, Bolton, Greater Manchester
E. Baines *History . . . of Lancaster* v. 2, 1836, 355.

Birchanger, Essex
Gdn History v. 6 no. 3, 1978, 40–43.

Birchleaves near Weymouth, Dorset
G.C. ii 1892, 440–41.

Birdsall, N. Yorks
J. Hort. Cottage Gdnr v. 61, 1879, 326–28. Historical MSS Commission *Architectural history* v. 3, 1971, 2466.

Birken Shaw, Borders
G.C. i 1966, 500–01.

Birkenhead. Public Park, Merseyside
Garden v. 10, 1876, 550–51. *J. Institute of Landscape Architects* no. 71, 1965, 11–14. G. Chadwick *Park and the town* 1966, passim. N.T. Newton *Design on the land* 1971, 230. N. Pevsner *and* E. Hubbard *Cheshire* 1971, 91–92.

Birkhall near Ballater, Grampian
G. Plumptre *Royal gardens* 1981, 196–207.

Birkhill, Balmerino, Fife
G.A. Little *Scotland's gardens* 1981, 123–24.

Birmingham Botanical Garden, W. Midlands
G.M. v. 15, 1839, 456–57. G.C. 1872, 1291,1293; ii 1893, 723–24. *J. Hort. Cottage Gdnr* N.S. v. 10, 1885, 420–22. *Gdning World* v. 2, 1885, 121–22. *Garden* v. 59, 1901, 268. *Gdnrs Mag.* 1909, 201–02. M. Hadfield *et al. British gardeners* 1980, 58. *Gdn History* v. 8 no. 2, 1980, 66–74. R. Sidwell *West Midland gardens* 1981, 201–03. P. Ballard *An oasis of delight* 1983.

Birnam near Dunkeld, Tayside
G.C. ii 1890, 651–52.

Birr Castle, Birr, Co. Offaly, Eire
Official guide. J.N. Brewer *Beauties of Ireland* v. 2, 1826, 155. F.O. Morris *Series of picturesque views* v. 3, 39. *J. Royal Hort. Soc.* 1958, 459–62; 1964, 446–57, 489–94. C.L. v. 136, 1964, 1024–26,1154–57; v. 137, 1965, 410–14,468,526–29. E. Hyams *Irish gardens* 1967, 98–114. G.C. v. 163 no. 14, 1968, 12–14. M. Allan *Fisons guide* 1970, 354–55. E. Malins *and* Knight of Glin *Lost demesnes* 1976, 98–99. Knight of Glin *and* P. Bowe *Gardens of outstanding historic interest in . . . Ireland* 1980. E. Malins *and* P. Bowe *Irish gardens and demesnes* 1980, 163–66.

Birtsmorton Court near Tewkesbury, Hereford and Worcester
C.L. v. 11, 1902, 560–65. R. Sidwell *West Midland gardens* 1981, 30–31.

Bisham Abbey, Bisham, Berks
C.L. v. 1, 1897, 212–13; v. 17, 1905, 906–15.

Bishop Auckland Palace, Bishop Auckland, Co. Durham
S. *and* N. Buck *Buck's antiquities* v. 1, 1774, pl. 80. C. Holme *Gardens of England in Northern counties* 1911, pl. 2. B. Jones *Follies & grottoes* 1974, 217–18. *Gdn History* v. 8 no. 2, 1980, 47,49,51.

Bishop Burton Hall, Bishop Burton, Humberside
I. Hall *Samuel Buck's Yorkshire sketchbook* 1979, 15.

Bishop's Court near Exeter, Devon
R. Ackermann *Repository* v. 11, 1828, pl. 13. W.W.J. Gendall *Views* v. 2, 1830, 119.

Bishop's Court near Naas, Co. Kildare, Eire
F.O. Morris *Series of picturesque views* v. 4, 19.

Bishop's Palace, Salisbury, Wilts
C.L. v. 3, 1898, 432–34.

Bishop's Park *see* Fulham

Bishopsbarns, York, N. Yorks
M. *and* R. Tooley *Gardens of G. Jekyll in Northern England* 1982, 44–46,54.

Bishopscourt, Isle of Man
Proc. Isle of Man Natural History and Antiquarian Soc. v. 8 no. 3, 1976–78, 248–49,257–61.

Bishopstoke Vicarage, Bishopstoke, Hants
G.M. v. 10, 1834, 124–31.

Bishopstone House, Bishopstone, Wilts
C.L. v. 126, 1959, 838–41.

Bishopstowe near Torquay, Devon
J. Hort. Cottage Gdnr v. 56, 1876, 98–99,115.

Bishopthorpe, York, N. Yorks
M. *and* R. Tooley *Gardens of G. Jekyll in Northern England* 1982, 54.

Bishton Hall near Rugeley, Staffs
J.P. Neale *Views* v. 4, 1821. F. Calvert *Picturesque views . . . in Staffordshire & Shropshire* 1830, 27.

Bitton Vicarage, Bitton, Avon
J. Hort. Cottage Gdnr v. 62, 1879, 208–09. G.C. ii 1884, 775–76. H.N. Ellacombe *In a Gloucestershire garden* 1895. A.W. Hill *Henry Nicholson Ellacombe* 1919, 133–53. C.L. v. 39, 1916, 253–54; v. 130, 1961, 546–47; v. 166, 1979, 1792–95.

Bixley Park near Norwich, Norfolk
J. Grigor *Eastern arboretum* 1841, 269–70.

Black Queen Coffee-House and Tea Gardens, Shacklewell, Hackney, London
W. Wroth *London pleasure gardens of the eighteenth century* 1896, 173.

Blackadder House near Chirnside, Borders
G.C. ii 1880, 622. R.I.B.A. *Catalogue* v. G-K, 1973, 25.

Blackdown House near Haslemere, W. Sussex
G.M. v. 5, 1829, 579–81.

Blackett, Sir William *see* Newcastle upon Tyne

Blackfriars, Oxford, Oxfordshire
Oxoniensia v. 41, 1976, 168–231.

Blackheath *see* London

Blackhills near Elgin, Grampian
M. Allan *Fisons guide* 1970, 335–36.

Blackhurst, Tonbridge, Kent
C. Greenwood *Epitome of county history . . . v. 1: Kent* 1838, 124.

Blackmoor House near Petersfield, Hants
G.C. i 1893, 328–29.

Blackwell, Windermere, Cumbria
G. Beard *Thomas H. Mawson* 1976, 46.

Bladon, Newton Solney, Derbyshire
B. Jones *Follies & grottoes* 1974, 68, 70.

Blagdon, Seaton Burn, Northumberland
Garden v. 49, 1896, 112–13. C. Holme *Gardens of England in Northern counties* 1911, pls. 3–7. *C.L.* v. 112, 1952, 188–91, 396–99. R.I.B.A. *Catalogue: Lutyens* 1973, 13. J. Harris *Artist and the country house* 1979, 126. *Gdn History* v. 8 no. 3, 1980, 44, 46–57. J. Brown *Gardens of a golden afternoon* 1982, 48–59, 151, 175. M. and R. Tooley *Gardens of G. Jekyll in Northern England* 1982, 28–40, 55.

Blair Castle, Blair Atholl, Tayside
G.C. i 1877, 683–84, 720. B. Jones *Follies & grottoes* 1974, 98. J. Harris *Artist and the country house* 1979, 285. A.A. Tait *Landscape garden in Scotland* 1980, passim. *Publications of Bedfordshire Historical Record Soc.* v. 47, 1968, 156.

Blair Drummond near Doune, Central
G.M. v. 13, 1837, 59; v. 17, 1841, 505–08; v. 18, 1842, 594–96. J.B. Burke *Visitation* v. 2, 1853, 77. *Scottish Gdnr* v. 5, 1856, 213–16. Historical MSS Commission *Architectural history* v. 3, 1971, item 2479.

Blairadam near Kinross, Tayside
G.M. v. 18, 1842, 357–65, 587. A.A. Tait *Landscape garden in Scotland* 1980, passim.

Blairhill, Scotland
G.M. v. 18, 1842, 588. *Scottish Gdnr and Northern Forester* v. 7, 1912, 97–98.

Blairhoyle, Thornhill, Central
Scottish Gdnr and Northern Forester v. 9, 1914, 177–78. G.A. Little *Scotland's gardens* 1981, 124–26.

Blairquhan, Straiton, Strathclyde
J.P. Neale *Views* 2nd Series, v. 3, 1826. *G.M.* v. 9, 1833, 8. A.A. Tait *Landscape garden in Scotland* 1980, passim. G.A. Little *Scotland's gardens* 1981, 246.

Blaise Castle near Bristol, Avon
H. Repton *Observations* 1803, 145, 155. J.P. Neale *Views* v. 2, 1819. J.N. Brewer *Delineations of Gloucestershire* 1825, 103. G.C. ii 1879, 724, 725; i 1880, 48, 49, 80, 81. *C.L.* v. 7, 1900, 400–04. *Gdnrs Mag.* 1908, 945–47. G. Jekyll *Garden ornament* 1918, 256. *Architectural Review* v. 83, 1938, 249–51. D. Stroud *Humphry Repton* 1962, 98. R.I.B.A. *Catalogue* v. L-N, 1973, 106. J.D. Hunt and P. Willis *Genius of the place* 1975, 359–65. G. Carter *et al. Humphry Repton* 1982, 152.

Blaise Hamlet near Bristol, Avon
Views of Blaise Hamlet, Henbury, etc. c.1840. *C.L.* v. 86, 1939, 396–97; v. 158, 1975, 1218–19. *Architectural Review* v. 160, 1976, 96–100. N. Temple *John Nash and the village picturesque* 1979.

Blakesley Hall, Woodend, Northants
Northamptonshire Past and Present v. 5 no. 3, 1975, 220. Royal Commission on Historical Monuments *Inventory of the historical monuments in . . . Northampton* v. 4, 1982, 173.

Blandsfort near Abbeyleix, Co. Laois, Eire
Royal Hort. Soc. *Conifers in cultivation* 1932, 216.

Blatherwycke, Northants
Northamptonshire Past and Present v. 5 no. 3, 1975, 220.

Bleby House, Winchcomb, Glos
B. Jones *Follies & grottoes* 1974, 327.

Blendon Hall, Bexley, London
H. Repton *Fragments* 1816, 23–28. D. Stroud *Humphry Repton* 1962. G. Carter *et al. Humphry Repton* 1982, 155.

Blenheim Palace, Woodstock, Oxfordshire
Official guide (from 1787 onwards). C. Campbell *Vitruvius Britannicus* v. 3, 1725, pls. 71–72. T. Whately *Observations on modern gardening* 1771, 78–81. S. Shaw *Tour to West of England in 1788* In J. Pinkerton, v. 2, 1808, 193, 194–95. J. Boydell *Collection of views in England and Wales* 1790, pls. 44–47. E.D. Clarke *Tour*

Blenheim Palace *(Cont.)*

through South of England 1793, 393–97. W. Mavor *New description of Blenheim* 1793. J. and J. Boydell *History of River Thames* v. 1, 1794, 88–91. W. Gilpin *Observations on several parts of England* v. 1, 1808, 28–31. J. Hodgson *and* F.C. Laird *Beauties of England and Wales* v. 12, pt 2, 1813, 412–17. L. Simond *Journal of a tour . . . in . . . 1810 and 1811* v. 2, 1815, 604–06. J.P. Neale *Views* v. 3, 1820. R. Havell *Series of picturesque views* 1823, pls. 14–15. J.P. Neale *Six views of Blenheim . . . with historical description* 1823. British Museum *Catalogue of maps, prints* 1829, 33. *G.M.* v. 9, 1833, 515; v. 10, 1834, 99–104. Prince Pückler-Muskau *Tour in England, Ireland and France* 1833, 85–86. F.O. Morris *Series of picturesque views* v. 1, 79. *Garden* v. 3, 1873, 478–80. *J. Hort. Cottage Gdnr* v. 51, 1874, 275–77,293,333–34, 344–45,363–64,419–20; N.S., v. 38, 1894, 192–94. *G.C.* i 1900, 10; i 1964, 249–50. *C.L.* v. 5, 1899, 688–92; v. 25, 1909, 786–97,834–43; v. 103, 1948, 81; v. 110, 1951, 268–69. *C.L. Annual* 1966, 22–24. C. Holme *Gardens of England in Southern & Western counties* 1907, pls. 15–19. T. Jefferson *Garden book 1766–1824* 1944, 114. D. Green *Blenheim Palace* 1951. L. Whistler *Imagination of Vanbrugh and his fellow artists* 1954, 115–23. D. Green *Gardener to Queen Anne* 1956, passim. P. Coats *Great gardens of Britain* 1967, 28–35. Historical MSS Commission *Architectural history* v. 3, 1971, item 3642. H. Evans *Beautiful gardens of Britain* 1974, 83–84. J. Sherwood *and* N. Pevsner *Oxfordshire* 1974, 472–75. D. Stroud *Capability Brown* 1975, 129–32,218. B. Willis *Charles Bridgeman* 1977, 177. R. Bisgrove *Gardens of Britain* v. 3, 1978, 35–37. D. Jarrett *English landscape garden* 1978, 69–75. L. Fleming *and* A. Gore *English garden* 1979, 71,122, 124. *Arboricultural J.* v. 5, 1981, 201–09. *Quarterly J. Forestry* v. 75, 1981, 207–14. *J. Gdn History* v. 2, 1982, 52–53. *Garden* 1983, 432–37. D. Jacques *Georgian gardens* 1983, 79. *Landscape Design* no. 146, 1983, 9–12.

Blessington near Maas, Co. Wicklow, Eire
E. Malins *and* Knight of Glin *Lost demesnes* 1976, 126–27.

Bletchley Park, Bucks
G.C. ii 1893, 529,534; ii 1900, 434–35; ii 1914, 289–90, 291,295; i 1919, 24. *Garden* 1914, 329.

Bletsoe Castle, Beds
R. Bisgrove *Gardens of Britain* v. 3, 1978, 38.

Blickling Hall, Aylsham, Norfolk
Official guide. A. Young *Farmer's tour through East of England* v. 2, 1771, 63–64. D. Defoe *Tour* v. 1, 1778, 61. W. Angus *Seats* 1787, pl. 54. J.P. Neale *Views* v. 3, 1820. *G.M.* v. 17, 1841, 29–30. J. Grigor *Eastern arboretum* 1841, 96–101. *General history of county of Norfolk* v. 1, 1829, 190–91. *J. Hort. Cottage Gdnr* v. 49, 1873, 166–67. *G.C.* ii 1894, 533–34; i 1912, 156,157; i 1961, 180–81,185. *C.L.* v. 3, 1898, 112–15,144–47; v. 18, 1905, 822–32; v. 27, 1910, 673–77; v. 67, 1930, 814–21, 902,936. *Gdning World* v. 4, 1887, 36–38. *Garden* v. 64, 1903, 267–69. C. Holme *Gardens of England in Midland & Eastern counties* 1908, pls. 11–13. G. Jekyll *Garden ornament* 1918, 91,255,277. *J. Royal Hort. Soc.* 1960, 345. D. Stroud *Humphry Repton* 1962, 81. N. Pevsner *North–East Norfolk and Norwich* 1962, 98–99. *Architectural History* v. 7, 1964, 24,44–45. M. Allan *Fisons guide* 1970, 188–89. M. Binney *and* A. Hills *Elysian gardens* 1979, 31. G.S. Thomas *Gardens of National Trust* 1979, 104–05. T. Wright *Arbours & grottos* 1979. J.L. Phibbs *Blickling Hall* National Trust, 1981..

Blithe Hall, Warwickshire
W. Dugdale *Antiquities of Warwickshire* v. 2, 1730, 1050.

Blithfield Hall near Abbots Bromley, Staffs
Official guide. R. Plot *Natural history of Staffordshire* 1685, 225. W. Pitt *General view of agriculture of . . . Stafford* 1796, 92. J. Nightingale *Topographical . . . description of Staffordshire* 1810, 733,877. *G.C.* ii 1892, 487–88. *C.L.* v. 116, 1954, 1488–92,1576; v. 154, 1973, 2008. M. Allan *Fisons guide* 1970, 264–65.

Blochairn, Glasgow, Strathclyde
I.H. Adams *Descriptive list of plans* v. 3, 1974, 62.

Bloomsbury Square *see* London

Bloxholm Hall, Kesteven, Lincs
J. Hort. Cottage Gdnr v. 55, 1876, 352–54.

Blundells, Broadwell, Glos
A. Lees-Milne *and* R. Verey *Englishman's garden* 1982, 60–63.

Blyborough, Lindsey, Lincs
G. Jekyll *and* G.S. Elgood *Some English gardens* 1904, 5–7.

Blyth near Worksop, Notts
G.C. i 1928, 111. C. Fiennes *Journeys* 1949, 75. Historical MSS Commission *Architectural history* v. 5, 1974, item 4884.

Blythswood near Renfrew, Strathclyde
J.P. Neale *Views* 2nd Series, v. 3, 1826. *Scottish Gdnr* v. 11, 1862, 365–70; v. 12, 1863, 88. *G.C.* ii 1888, 233–34.

Boarn Hill Cottage, Cadland, Hants
Landscape Design no. 144, 1983, 23–24.

Boarstall Tower, Boarstall, Bucks
W. Kennett *Parochial antiquities . . . in . . . Ambrosden and Burcester* 1695, pl. 7. M. Macartney *English houses & gardens* 1908, pl. 4. D. Stroud *Capability Brown* 1975, 218. J. Harris *Artist and the countryside* 1979, 105.

Bocking Hall, Bocking, Essex
F.G. Emmison *Catalogue of maps in Essex Record Office* 2nd Supplt, 1964, 26.

Bocking Place, Bocking, Essex
G.C. ii 1890, 382–83; i 1891, 240,241.

Boconnoc near Lostwithiel, Cornwall
G.S. Gilbert *Historical survey of . . . Cornwall* v. 2, 1820, 908–12. G.M. v. 13, 1837, 121. *Architectural Review* v. 73, 1933, 156–58.

Bodelwyddan Castle near St Asaph, Clwyd
G. Beard *Thomas H. Mawson* 1976, 46.

Bodens Ride, Swinley Forest, Ascot, Berks
Gdn Design no. 2, 1930, 52–61.

Bodnant, Talycafn, Colwyn Bay, Gwynedd
Official guide. G.C. i 1884, 207,209,212; ii 1892, 331–32; i 1928, 156–58,203; ii 1936, 37; ii 1940, 85,89. *Garden* v. 34, 1888, 551–52; 1915, 583. C.L. v. 48, 1920, 84–90; v. 70, 1931, 330–36; v. 106, 1949, 1732–35; v. 108, 1950, 613–16; v. 130, 1961, 554–56. *Landscape Architecture* April 1937, 151–57. *J. Royal Hort. Soc.* 1940, 71–74; 1950, 261–69. Lady Rockley *Historic gardens of England* 1938, 232–33. *Gdning Illustrated* 1952, 132–35. P. Coats *Great gardens* 1963, 210–17. E. Hyams *English gardens* 1964, 205–12. M. Allan *Fisons guide* 1970, 265–68. H. Evans *Beautiful gardens of Britain* 1974, 117–18. H.T. Milliken *Road to Bodnant* 1975. G.S. Thomas *Gardens of National Trust* 1979, 107–09. *Architectural Digest* v. 37, 1980, 142–49. A. Hellyer *Gardens of genius* 1980, 200–04. T. Hinde *Stately gardens of Britain* 1983, 110–17.

Bodorgan, Anglesey, Gwynedd
Cottage Gdnr v. 11, 1854, 320–22. G.C. ii 1882, 331; i 1892, 75–76.

Bodrhyddan near Rhuddlan, Clwyd
C.L. v. 164, 1978, 158–61, 226.

Bodysgallan near Llandudno, Gwynedd
C.L. v. 164, 1978, 2066–69.

Bohemia Park, Hastings, E. Sussex
G.M. v. 17, 1841, 593–95.

Bohunt Manor near Liphook, Hants
A. Paterson *Gardens of Britain* v. 2, 1978, 54–55.

Bold Hall, Lancs
E. Baines *History . . . of Lancaster* v. 3, 1836, 716.

Bolehyde Manor near Chippenham, Wilts
C.L. v. 104, 1948, 528–31,578–81.

Bolfracks, Aberfeldy, Tayside
G.A. Little *Scotland's gardens* 1981, 126.

Bolsover Castle, Bolsover, Derbyshire
Official guide. J. Beeverell *Les delices de la Grande Bretagne* v. 5, 1707, 872. L. Knyff and J. Kip *Britannia illustrata* v. 1, 1714. S. Glover *History . . . of . . . Derby* v. 2, 1833, 137. C.L. v. 16, 1904, 198–207; v. 42, 1917, 132–39,156–63. R.I.B.A. *Catalogue* v. S, 1976, 97.

Bolton Abbey near Ilkley, N. Yorks
British Museum *Catalogue of maps, prints* 1829, 35. G.C. ii 1890, 209–10.

Bolton Royd, Bradford, W. Yorks
Bradford Illustrated Weekly Telegraph *Series of picturesque views* 1885.

Bolwick Hall, Aylsham, Norfolk
G. Carter *et al. Humphry Repton* 1982, 158.

Bonnington near Stanstead Abbots, Herts
J. Harris *Artist and the country house* 1979, 82.

Bonnytoun House near Linlithgow, Lothian
C. McWilliam *Lothian* 1978, 116.

Bonskeid near Pitlochry, Tayside
G.C. i 1886, 205–06.

Booth's Hall near Knutsford, Cheshire
J. Aikin *Description of the country . . . round Manchester* 1795, 424.

Booton Hall near Aylsham, Norfolk
G.M. v. 17, 1841, 31–32. J. Grigor *Eastern arboretum* 1841, 142–43.

Borde Hill near Cuckfield, W. Sussex
C.L. v. 12, 1902, 840–45; v. 165, 1979, 702–04. A.B. Jackson *Catalogue of trees and shrubs* 1935. M. Allan *Fisons guide* 1970, 36–37. H. Evans *Beautiful gardens of Britain* 1974, 65–66. T. Wright *Gardens of Britain* v. 4, 1978, 121–24.

Bore Place, Chiddingstone, Kent
J. Kip *Nouveau theatre de la Grande Bretagne* v. 2, 1724. T. Badeslade *Thirty six different views . . . in Kent* 1750s, pl. 31.

Boreham near Chelmsford, Essex
P. Muilman *History of Essex* v. 1, 1771, 133. P. Morant *History . . . of Essex* v. 2, 1816, 15. G. Virtue *Picturesque beauties of Great Britain: Essex* 1831, 28. T. Wright *History . . . of Essex* v. 1, 1836, 108. *C.L.* v. 36, 1914, 54–60. F.G. Emmison *Catalogue of maps in Essex Record Office* 1947, 54.

Boringdon, Plympton St Mary, Devon
C.L. v. 35, 1914, 918–19.

Borlases, Waltham St Lawrence, Berks
R. Bisgrove *Gardens of Britain* v. 3, 1978, 39.

Borris, Co. Carlow, Eire
J.P. Neale *Views* v. 6, 1823.

Borthwick Castle, Borthwick, Lothian
Scottish Gdnr v. 4, 1855, 346–48.

Borwick Hall near Carnforth, Lancs
V.C.H. *Lancaster* v. 8, 1914, 174. *C.L.* v. 29, 1911, 710–16; v. 78, 1935, 142–48. Lady Rockley *Historic gardens of England* 1938, 96–97.

Bosahan near Helford, Cornwall
G.C. ii 1895, 214; i 1896, 364.

Boscobel House near Shifnal, Shropshire
Official guide. E. Cecil *History of gardening in England* 1910, 102.

Boston Manor, Brentford, London
W. Keane *Beauties of Middlesex* 1850, 245–48. *Gdning World* 1893, 98.

Boswells, Wendover, Bucks
R. Bisgrove *Gardens of Britain* v. 3, 1978, 39–40.

Bosworth Hall, Market Bosworth, Leics
J. Throsby *Select views in Leicestershire* v. 1, 1740, 197.

Botleys, Chertsey, Surrey
G.F. Prosser *Select illustrations of . . . Surrey* 1828. E.W. Brayley *and* J. Britton *Topographical history of Surrey* v. 2, 1841, 220. W. Keane *Beauties of Surrey* 1849, 43–44.

Bottisham Park, Bottisham, Cambs
Royal Commission on Historical Monuments *Inventory of historical monuments in . . . Cambridge* v. 2, 1972, 13–15.

Bothwell Castle, Uddingston, Strathclyde
G.M. v. 18, 1842, 195–97. *Scottish Gdnr* v. 8, 1859, 389–94. *J. Hort. Cottage Gdnr* v. 62, 1879, 482–83. *Gdning World* v. 17, 1901, 689–90.

Boughton (Monchelsea Place) near Maidstone, Kent
J. Harris *History of Kent* 1719, 49. J. Kip *Supplement du Nouveau theatre de la Grande Bretagne* 1728, pl. 14. T. Badeslade *Thirty six different views . . . of Kent* 1750s, pl. 3. *C.L.* v. 133, 1962, 1488–93.

Boughton near Kettering, Northants
Official guide. J. Morton *Natural history of Northamptonshire* 1712, 491–92. C. Campbell *Vitruvius Britannicus* v. 3, 1725, 73–74. T. Badeslade *and* J. Rocque *Vitruvius Brittanicus* 1739, pls. 36–37. J.P. Neale *Views* 2nd Series, v. 1, 1824. *C.L.* v. 25, 1909, 162–70, 198–205; v. 72, 1932, 596–601; v. 149, 1971, 420–23, 476–80, 536–39. *Northamptonshire Past and Present* v. 5 no. 3, 1975, 220; v. 5 no. 5, 1977, 20–23, 402–05. B. Jones *Follies & grottoes* 1974, 368. P. Willis *Charles Bridgeman* 1977, 177. J. Anthony *Gardens of Britain* v. 6, 1979, 30–35. Royal Commission on Historical Monuments *Inventory of historical monuments in . . . Northampton* v. 2, 1979, 156–62, pls. 23–25. J. Johnson *Excellent Cassandra: the life and times of Duchess of Chandos* 1981, 67. C. Taylor *Archaeology of gardens* 1983, 19, 48–51, 54–55, 64.

Boughton. Dower House, Kettering, Northants
A. Lees-Milne *and* R. Verey *Englishman's garden* 1982, 124–27.

Boultibrook near Presteigne, Powys
G.M. v. 16, 1840, 379–80.

Bourn Hall near Caxton, Cambs
J.P. Neale *Views* v. 1, 1818. G. Carter *et al. Humphry Repton* 1982, 149.

Bourne Park near Bishopsbourne, Kent
C. Greenwood *Epitome of county history . . . v. 1: Kent* 1838, 399. *C.L.* v. 51, 1922, 602–09; v. 96, 1944, 816–19.

Bourne Vincent Park, Co. Kerry, Eire
Knight of Glin *and* P. Bowe *Gardens of outstanding historic interest in . . . Ireland* 1980.

Bourton House, Bourton-on-the-Hill, Glos
J. Sales *West Country gardens* 1980, 44–46.

Boveridge Park, Cranborne, Dorset
G. Beard *Thomas H. Mawson* 1976, 46.

Bovey House, Beer, Devon
C.L. v. 32, 1912, 674–79.

Bowden Hall, Upton St Leonards, Glos
J.N. Brewer *Delineations of Gloucestershire* 1825, 92.

Bowden Hill, Lacock, Wilts
G. Beard *Thomas H. Mawson* 1976, 46. J. Sales *West Country gardens* 1980, 191–92.

Bower Hall, Steeple Bumpstead, Essex
P. Muilman *History of Essex* v. 2, 1769, 236.
F.G. Emmison *Catalogue of maps in Essex Record Office* 2nd Supplt, 1964, 15. J. Harris *Artist and the country house* 1979, 176.

Bower House, Havering, London
C.L. v. 95, 1944, 464–67,508.

Bowes Manor, Southgate, London
W. Keane *Beauties of Middlesex* 1850, 118–20.

Bowes Museum, Barnard Castle, Co. Durham
G.C. ii 1911, 368.

Bowhill near Chichester, W. Sussex
R. Webber *Percy Cane* 1975, 164.

Bowhill near Selkirk, Borders
C.L. v. 157, 1975, 1448–51. A.A. Tait *Landscape garden in Scotland* 1980, passim. G.A. Little *Scotland's gardens* 1981, 79.

Bowling Hall near Bradford, W. Yorks
J.P. Neale *Views* v. 5, 1822. *Jones's views* 1829, 44.

Bowood near Calne, Wilts
Official guide. A. Robertson *Topographical survey of the Great Road* pt. 2, 1792, 51–54. J. Britton *Beauties of Wiltshire* v. 2, 1801, 213–15,216,221–27. R. Warner *Excursions from Bath* 1801, 209–12. J.P. Neale *Views* 2nd Series, v. 2, 1825. British Museum *Catalogue of maps, prints* 1829, 37. G.M. v. 14, 1838, 326–28; v. 19, 1843, 677. *Florist* 1852, 213–14; 1854, 155–56. J.B. Burke *Visitation* 2nd Series, v. 1, 1855, 92. E.A. Brooke *Gardens of England* 1857 pls. 9–11. F.O. Morris *Series of picturesque views* v. 5, 3. *J. Hort. Cottage Gdnr* v. 38, 1867, 345–46,364–65; v. 46, 1871, 509–11; v. 47, 1872, 32–33; v. 48, 1904, 474–76. G.C. ii 1891, 125–26; i 1903, 40,56,251; ii 1909, 293,298–99. C.L. v. 7, 1900, 432–36; v. 17, 1905, 126–36; v. 34, 1913, 324–31; v. 151, 1972, 1448–51,1610–13; v. 152, 1972, 546–49. H.I. Triggs *Formal gardens in England and Scotland* 1902, 16–17. C. Holme *Gardens of England in Southern & Western counties* 1907, pls. 21–22. G. Jekyll *Garden ornament* 1918, 57,186. Lady Rockley *Historic gardens of Britain* 1938, 198–99. N. Pevsner *Wiltshire* 1975, 122–23. D. Stroud *Capability Brown* 1975, 90–92,218. L. Fleming *and* A. Gore *English garden* 1979, 119. C. Thacker *History of gardens* 1979, 226–27. J. Sales *West Country gardens* 1980, 193–94. G. Carter *et al. Humphry Repton* 1982, 163. D. Jacques *Georgian gardens* 1983, pl. 6.

Bowringsleigh near Kingsbridge, Devon
C.L. v. 37, 1915, 304–08.

Boxwell Court, Boxwell, Glos
J.N. Brewer *Delineations of Gloucestershire* 1825, 171.

Boyle Farm, Thames Ditton, Surrey
W. Keane *Beauties of Surrey* 1849, 9–10.

Boynton Hall, Carnaby, Humberside
C.L. v. 116, 1954, 280–83,356–59. B. Jones *Follies & grottoes* 1974, 346.

Boyton House near Heytesbury, Wilts
C.L. v. 28, 1910, 262–68.

Brabourne near Ashford, Kent
E. Hasted *History . . . of . . .Kent* v. 1, 1778, 350; v. 2, 1782, 214. W. Angus *Seats* 1787, pl. 46. C.L. v. 44, 1918, 152–57; v. 141, 1967, 774–77.

Bracebridge Court, Lincoln, Lincs
G. Beard *Thomas H. Mawson* 1976, 46.

Bracken Hill, Platt, Kent
A. Lees-Milne *and* R. Verey *Englishman's garden* 1982, 100–03.

Brackenbrough, Calthwaite, Cumbria
B. Jones *Follies & grottoes* 1974, 357. *Gdn History* v. 8 no. 3, 1980, 30. M. *and* R. Tooley *Gardens of G. Jekyll in Northern England* 1982, 4–5,54.

Brackla House, Cawdor, Highland
G.A. Little *Scotland's gardens* 1981, 176–77.

Brackley near Ballater, Grampian
G. Beard *Thomas H. Mawson* 1976, 46–47.

Braco Castle, Tayside
G.A. Little *Scotland's gardens* 1981, 126–28.

Bracondale Lodge, Norwich, Norfolk
D. Stroud *Humphry Repton* 1962, 66–67. G. Carter *et al. Humphry Repton* 1982, 103,158.

Bradbourne near Sevenoaks, Kent
C. Greenwood *Epitome of county history . . . v. 1: Kent* 1838, 94.

Bradden House, Bradden, Northants
Royal Commission on Historical Monuments *Inventory of the historical monuments in . . . Northampton* v. 4, 1982, 24.

Bradenham near High Wycombe, Bucks
G.C. ii 1882, 551–52. C.L. v. 72, 1932, 154–59. Lady Rockley *Historic gardens of England* 1938, 134–35.

Bradeston Brook House, Shalford, Surrey
E.W. Brayley and J. Britton *Topographical history of Surrey* v. 5, 1848, 146.

Bradfield near Collumpton, Devon
Gdning World v. 15, 1899, 613. C.L. v. 15, 1904, 18–28. G. Jekyll *Garden ornament* 1918, 279.

Bradford. Lister Park, W. Yorks
K. Lemmon *Gardens of Britain* v. 5, 1978, 179–80.

Bradford. Oakworth Park, W. Yorks
K. Lemmon *Gardens of Britain* v. 5, 1978, 186–87.

Bradgate Park near Leicester, Leics
L. Knyff and J. Kip *Britannia illustrata* v. 1, 1714. J. Throsby *Select views in Leicestershire* v. 1, 1790, 118. B. Jones *Follies & grottoes* 1974, 356.

Bradiford House near Barnstaple, Devon
G.C. ii 1882, 180.

Bradley, Grimsby, Humberside
M. and R. Tooley *Gardens of G. Jekyll in Northern England* 1982, 41–43, 55.

Bradley Court near Wotton-under-Edge, Glos
R. Atkyns *Ancient and present state of Glostershire* 1712, 854. L. Knyff and J. Kip *Britannia illustrata* v. 2, 1715. J. Sales *West Country gardens* 1980, 46–47.

Bradley House, Leamington, Warwickshire
G.M. v. 16, 1840, 585.

Bradwell Lodge, Bradwell-on-Sea, Essex
W. Angus *Seats* 1787, pl. 35.

Brahan, Conon Bridge, Highland
I.H. Adams *Descriptive list of plans* v. 2, 1970, 127. G.A. Little *Scotland's gardens* 1981, 224.

Brairstrie House, Hatfield, Herts
G. Beard *Thomas H. Mawson* 1976, 47.

Bramblebury, Plumstead, Greenwich, London
C. Greenwood *Epitome of county history . . . v. 1: Kent* 1838, 43.

Brambletye, East Grinstead, W. Sussex
J. Hort. Cottage Gdnr v. 55, 1876, 512–13. J. Brown *Miss Gertrude Jekyll* 1981, 40–43.

Bramall Hall near Stockport, Greater Manchester
F.O. Morris *Series of picturesque views* v. 5, 19.

Bramdean House near Winchester, Hants
C.L. v. 107, 1950, 1714–17; v. 135, 1964, 1384–86. M. Allan *Fisons guide* 1970, 112. A. Paterson *Gardens of Britain* v. 2, 1978, 56–59. A. Lees-Milne and R. Verey *Englishwoman's garden* 1980, 144–45.

Bramham Park, Wetherby, W. Yorks
Official guide. J. Paine *Plans, elevations and sections of noblemen and gentlemen's houses* v. 1, 1783, pl. 73. J.P. Neale *Views* v. 5, 1822. *Jones's views* 1829, 33. British Museum *Catalogue of maps, prints* 1829, 38. *Florist* 1857, 26–29. R. Pococke *Travels through England* v. 1, 1888, 61. *J. Hort. Cottage Gdnr* N.S., v. 37, 1898, 88–89. C.L. v. 16, 1904, 450–58; v. 50, 1921, 416–23, 448–55; v. 123, 1958, 350–53, 1294–97, 1368–71; v. 124, 1958, 190. G. Jekyll and G.S. Elgood *Some English gardens* 1904, 15–17. E. Cecil *History of gardening in England* 1910, 223–24. C. Holme *Gardens of England in Northern counties* 1911, pls. 8–14. *Architectural Review* v. 32, 1912, 189–91. Lady Rockley *Historic gardens of England* 1938, 144–45. C. Hussey *English gardens and landscapes* 1967, 70–77. N. Pevsner *Yorkshire: West Riding* 1967, 142–43. M. Allan *Fisons guide* 1970, 240–41. N.T. Newton *Design on the land* 1971, 200–01. H. Evans *Beautiful gardens of Britain* 1974, 105–06. K. Lemmon *Gardens of Britain* v. 5, 1978, 156–59. A. Hellyer *Gardens of genius* 1980, 15–17.

Bramley Grange near Ripon, N. Yorks
I. Hall *Samuel Buck's Yorkshire sketchbook* 1979, 78.

Bramley Hall, Yorks
I. Hall *Samuel Buck's Yorkshire sketchbook* 1979, 77.

Brampton Bryan, Hereford and Worcester
S. and N. Buck *Buck's antiquities* v. 1, 1774, pl. 114. P. Willis *Charles Bridgeman* 1977, 177.

Brampton Hall, Brampton, Suffolk
H. Davy *Views* 1827.

Brampton Park near Huntingdon, Cambs
V.C.H. *Huntingdon* v. 3, 1936, 12. P.G.M. Dickinson *Maps in the County Record Office, Huntingdon* 1968, 6–9.

Bramshill Park near Winchfield, Hants
G.C. ii 1882, 391–92. C.L. v. 5, 1899, 432–35, 464–67; v. 53, 1923, 758–68, 818–25. G. Jekyll *Garden ornament* 1918, 172–73.

Brancepeth Castle, Brancepeth, Co. Durham
S. and N. Buck *Buck's antiquities* v. 1, 1774, pl. 81.

Brancepeth Castle (*Cont.*)
F.O. Morris *Series of picturesque views* v. 6, 3. *J. Hort. Cottage Gdnr* v. 62, 1879, 509–10. *G.C.* ii 1880, 231–32. C. Holme *Gardens of England in Northern counties* 1911, pls. 15–16. D. Jacques *Georgian gardens* 1983, 116.

Branches Park near Newmarket, Suffolk
D. Stroud *Capability Brown* 1975, 114.

Brandsbury *see* Brondesbury

Branklyn, Perth, Tayside
Official guide. *G.C.* ii 1938, 322–23; ii 1959, 6–8. *C.L.* v. 139, 1966, 1380–82; v. 143, 1968, 346; v. 160, 1976, 406–07. M. Allan *Fisons guide* 1970, 316–17. *J. Scottish Rock Gdn Club* v. 15 no. 1, 1976, 60–62. P. Verney *Gardens of Scotland* 1976, 106–15. G.A. Little *Scotland's gardens* 1981, 128–29.

Branksome Tower, Great Canford, Dorset
J. Hutchins *History . . . of Dorset* v. 3, 1868, 303.

Brannockstown near Kilcudden, Co. Kildare, Eire
Irish Gdning v. 6, 1911, 109,183.

Brantingham Thorpe near Brough, Humberside
F.O. Morris *Series of picturesque views* v. 3, 19. *Garden* v. 6, 1874, 294–96. *G.C.* ii 1878, 464–65,468–69. *C.L.* v. 17, 1905, 342–46. G. Jekyll *Garden ornament* 1918, 121.

Braunstone Hall, Leicester, Leics
J. Throsby *Select views in Leicestershire* v. 1, 1790, 257. J. Nichols *History . . . of county of Leicester* v. 4, 1811, 620.

Braxted Lodge near Witham, Essex
G. Virtue *Picturesque beauties of Great Britain: Essex* 1831, 18. F.G. Emmison *Catalogue of maps in Essex Record Office* 1947, 55; 3rd Supplt, 1968, 3,12,14.

Brayton Hall, Brayton, Cumbria
G.C. ii 1879, 11–13. *J. Hort. Cottage Gdnr* N.S. v. 42, 1901, 522.

Breadsall Priory, Derby, Derbyshire
G. Beard *Thomas H. Mawson* 1976, 47.

Breamore House near Fordingbridge, Hants
E.F. Prosser *Select illustrations of Hampshire* 1833. *G.C.* ii 1890, 466–67. *C.L.* v. 121, 1957, 1198–1201,1320.

Breccles Hall, Breckles, Norfolk
C.L. v. 26, 1909, 670–78,706–13; v. 83, 1938, 194–99. G. Jekyll *Garden ornament* 1918, 33. Lady Rockley *Historic gardens of England* 1938, 226–27.

Brechin Castle, Brechin, Tayside
J.P. Neale *Views* v. 6, 1823. F.O. Morris *Series of picturesque views* v. 6, 25. *C.L.* v. 150, 1971, 436–40. G.A. Little *Scotland's gardens* 1981, 177.

Breckdenstown, Co. Dublin, Eire
E. Malins *and* Knight of Glin *Lost demesnes* 1976, 15–17,18.

Bredon Spring, Paris near Ashton under Hill, Hereford and Worcester
R. Sidwell *West Midland gardens* 1981, 32.

Brent Pelham Hall near Buntingford, Herts
H. Chauncy *Historical antiquities of Hertfordshire* 1700, 142.

Brentry Hill, Bristol, Avon
D. Stroud *Humphry Repton* 1962, 123. G. Carter *et al.* *Humphry Repton* 1982, 80,152.

Brereton Hall, Brereton, Cheshire
C.L. v. 26, 1909, 388–94.

Bressingham Hall near Diss, Norfolk
Jardins de France no. 1, 1933, 19–33. *G.C.* i 1962, 8–10. M. Allan *Fisons guide*, 1970, 189–90.

Bretby near Burton-on-Trent, Derbyshire
J. Beeverell *Les delices de la Grande Bretagne* v. 5, 1707, 872. L. Knyff *and* J. Kip *Britannia illustrata* v. 1, 1714. *Topographer* v. 2, 1790, 162. S. Glover *History and gazetteer of . . . Derby* v. 2, 1833, 183. *G.M.* v. 15, 1839, 449. M. Macartney *English houses & gardens* 1908, pl. 31. C. Fiennes *Journeys* 1949, 170–73. J. Johnson *Excellent Cassandra: life and times of Duchess of Chandos* 1981, 69.

Breteton Hall *see* Brereton Hall

Bretton Hall, West Bretton, W. Yorks
J.P. Neale *Views* v. 5, 1822. *Jones's views* 1829, 42. *G.M.* v. 5, 1829, 680–84; v. 8, 1832, 361,607–08. *C.L.* v. 83, 1938, 530,35. N. Pevsner *Yorkshire: West Riding* 1967, 146.

Briar Cottage, Horsell, Surrey
A. Lees-Milne *and* R. Verey *Englishman's garden* 1982, 140–43.

Brickendonbury, Hertford, Herts
Gdnrs Mag. 1909, 949–51.

Bricklehampton Hall, Bricklehampton, Hereford and Worcester
G.C. ii 1893, 802.

Brickwall, Northiam, E. Sussex
C.L. v. 8, 1900, 400–06. H.I. Triggs *Formal gardens in England and Scotland* 1902, 29–30. G. Jekyll *and* G.S. Elgood *Some English gardens* 1904, 87–89. G. Jekyll *Garden ornament* 1918, 274,290. *Architectural Review* v. 35, 1914, pl. 1. *Landscape Design* no. 137, 1982, 32.

Bridehead House near Dorchester, Dorset
Gdning World v. 5, 1889, 324–25.

Bridge End, Saffron Walden, Essex
H.I. Triggs *Formal gardens in England and Scotland* 1902, 24. *C.L.* v. 33, 1913, 58–61. G. Jekyll *and* L. Weaver *Gardens for small country houses* 1913, xxxiii–xxxvi.

Bridge Hill, Belper, Derbyshire
J. Hort. Cottage Gdnr v. 31, 1864, 40–41.

Bridge House, Weybridge, Surrey
G.C. ii 1903, 249–50. *C.L.* v. 24, 1908, 558–66; v. 39, 1916, 422–28. *Architectural Review* v. 33, 1913, 55, pls. 1–3. G. Jekyll *Garden ornament* 1918, 310, 330–32.

Bridge House, Chilton Foliat, Wilts
C.L. v. 135, 1964, 1048–51.

Bridge House near Sheffield, S. Yorks
I. Hall *Samuel Buck's Yorkshire sketchbook* 1979, 102.

Bridge Place, Kent
J. Harris *Artist and the country house* 1979, 77 pl. 7.

Bridgelands, Selkirk, Borders
G.A. Little *Scotland's gardens* 1981, 80.

Bridwell near Tiverton, Devon
R. Polwhele *History of Devonshire* v. 2, 1793. *C.L.* v. 169, 1981, 710–14.

Briery Close, Windermere, Cumbria
M. Allan *Fisons guide* 1970, 242.

Brightling near Battle, E. Sussex
I. Nairn *and* N. Pevsner *Sussex* 1965, 425. R.I.B.A. *Catalogue* v. S, 1976, 64. J. Harris *Artist and the country house* 1979, 352. G. Carter *et al. Humphry Repton* 1982, 163.

Brightlingsea Hall, Brightlingsea, Essex
G.C. ii 1963, 370–71,376.

Brighton. Public Parks, E. Sussex
Apollo Jan. 1975, 44–51.

Brighton. Athenaeum and Oriental Gardens, E. Sussex
J. Taylor *Royal Brighton guide* 1826, 13–16. *Bruce's history of Brighton and stranger's guide* 1827, 29–31. A. Dale *Fashionable Brighton 1820–1860* 1947, 171–74, pl. 86. J. and J. Ford *Images of Brighton* 1981, 118–19. C. Musgrave *Life in Brighton from the earliest times to the present* 1981, 187–88.

Brighton. Brown's Gardens, E. Sussex
F. Coghlan *Brighton and its environs* 1838, 59.

Brighton. German Spa, E. Sussex
J. and J. Ford *Images of Brighton* 1981, 77. C. Musgrave *Life in Brighton from the earliest times to the present* 1981, 224–26.

Brighton. Hollingbury Park, E. Sussex
W.H. Attwick *Jubilee of the Brighton Corporation* 1904, 110.

Brighton. Ireland's Royal Brighton Gardens, E. Sussex
J. Taylor *Royal Brighton guide* 1826, 9–11. J. Ackerson Erredge *History of Brighthelmston* 1862, 301–04. J. and J. Ford *Images of Brighton* 1981, 86,88. C. Musgrave *Life in Brighton from the earliest times to the present* 1981, 222–24.

Brighton. Kemp Town Gardens, E. Sussex
A. Dale *History of the Kemp Town Gardens, Brighton* 1964.

Brighton. Preston Park, E. Sussex
Norman May's guide to Brighton [1885], 74–75. W.H. Attwick *Jubilee of the Brighton Corporation* 1904, 106–08. Brighton Parks and Recreation Department *Preston Park centenary* 1983.

Brighton. Promenade Grove, E. Sussex
Description of Brighthelmstone and the adjacent country [1794], 22–23. J.G. Bishop *'A peep into the past': Brighton in the olden time* 1892, 67–80.

Brighton. Queen's Park, E. Sussex
F. Coghlan *Brighton and its environs* 1838, 58. W.H. Attwick *Jubilee of the Brighton Corporation* 1904, 108–09. J. and J. Ford *Images of Brighton* 1981, 114. C. Musgrave *Life in Brighton from the earliest times to the present* 1981, 247–48, 315.

Brighton. Royal Pavilion, E. Sussex
H. Repton *Designs for the Pavillon at Brighton* 1808. C. Wright *Brighton ambulator* 1818, 37–40. *Sickelmore's descriptive views of Brighton* 1824, p 1.1,32–33. J. Nash *Views of the Royal Pavilion* 1826. *Bruce's history of Brighton and stranger's guide* 1827, 15. *Descriptive guide to the Palace and gardens of the Royal Pavilion at Brighton*

Brighton. Royal Pavilion (*Cont.*)

1850, 31,36–38. J. Ackerson Erredge *History of Brighthelmston* 1862, 253–55,268–69. H.D. Roberts *History of the Royal Pavilion Brighton* 1939. C. Musgrave *Royal Pavilion* 1959. D. Stroud *Humphry Repton* 1962, 105. L. Fleming *and* A. Gore *English garden* 1979, pls. 95–96. P. Conner *Oriental architecture in the West* 1979, 136–41. *Gdn History* v. 8 no. 1, 1980, 50–54. J. *and* J. Ford *Images of Brighton* 1981, passim. C. Musgrave *Life in Brighton from the earliest times to the present* 1981, 136–37,141–43,378. G. Carter *et al. Humphry Repton* 1982, 57,69,163. *Sussex Archaeological Collections* v. 120, 1982, 171–84. *C.L.* v. 175, 1984, 1152–54,1564.

Brighton. Steine, E. Sussex
W.H. Mason's *fashionable handbook for visitors to Brighton* [1841], 11–12. *Illustrated hand-book of Brighton and its environs* 1847, 26–32. J. Sawyer *Brighton handbook and guide to the town* 1890, 27–31. J. Ackerson Erredge *History of Brighthelmston* 1862, 187–89. E. Hepple Hall *Page's handbook to Brighton and its vicinity* 1871, 58–62. *Norman May's guide to Brighton* [1885], 73–74. J. *and* J. Ford *Images of Brighton* 1981, passim.

Brighton. Victoria Gardens, E. Sussex
W.H. Attwick *Jubilee of the Brighton Corporation* 1904, 110.

Brightwell near Ipswich, Suffolk
J. Beeverell *Les delices de la Grande Bretagne* v. 5, 1707, 872. L. Knyff *and* J. Kip *Britannia illustrata* v. 1, 1714.

Brigstock, Northants
Northamptonshire Past and Present v. 5 no. 3, 1975, 220.

Brigton near Forfar, Tayside
G.A. Little *Scotland's gardens* 1981, 177–78.

Brington near Kimbolton, Cambs
J. Evelyn *Diary* v. 4, 1955, 593.

Brinsop Court, Brinsop, Hereford and Worcester
C.L. v. 25, 1909, 738–46; v. 36, 1914, 614–22,646–52. G. Jekyll *Garden ornament* 1918, 151.

Bristol House, Roehampton, London
Garden v. 38, 1890, 315–16,319.

Bristol Zoo, Bristol, Avon
G.C. v. 154 no. 6, 1963, 104–05.

Brittens, Hornchurch, Havering, London
F.G. Emmison *Catalogue of maps in Essex Record Office* 1st Supplt, 1952, 2.

Britwell Salome, Oxfordshire
C.L. v. 152, 1972, 810–14.

Brixworth Hall near Northampton, Northants
J.P. Neale *Views* v. 3, 1820.

Brizes, Kelvedon Hatch, Essex
F.G. Emmison *Catalogue of maps in Essex Record Office* 1st Supplt, 1952, 19, pl. 4. V.C.H. *Essex* v. 4, 1956, 64.

Broad Oak, Accrington, Lancs
T.H. Mawson *Art & craft of garden making* 1907, 258–61. G. Beard *Thomas H. Mawson* 1976, 47.

Broadfield Court near Bodenham, Hereford and Worcester
R. Sidwell *West Midland gardens* 1981, 33–34.

Broadfield Grange, Broadfield, Herts
H. Chauncy *Historical antiquities of Hertfordshire* 1700, 72.

Broadgate near Barnstaple, Devon
G.C. ii 1882, 167.

Broadgate *see* Bradgate Park

Broadhatch House, Bentley, Hants
A. Paterson *Gardens of Britain* v. 2, 1978, 59.

Broadlands near Romsey, Hants
W. Angus *Seats* 1787, pl. 1. J.P. Neale *Views* v. 2, 1819. R. Ackermann *Repository* v. 6, 1825, pl. 14. *Jones's views* 1829. W.W.J. Gendall *Views* v. 2, 1830, 22. J. Hewetson *Architectural and picturesque views . . . in Hampshire* 1830. E.F. Prosser *Select illustrations of Hampshire* 1833. F.O. Morris *Series of picturesque views* v. 1, 69. *G.C.* ii 1884, 391–92. *Gdning World* v. 1, 1885, 327. *Garden* v. 32, 1887, 507–08. C. Holme *Gardens of England in Southern & Western counties* 1907, pls. 25–26. *C.L.* v. 53, 1923, 434–41; v. 168, 1980, 2246–50,2334–37. *Gdnrs Yearbook* 1928, 45–51. C. Fiennes *Journeys* 1949, 55–57. D. Stroud *Capability Brown* 1975, 137–38, 218. A. Paterson *Gardens of Britain* v. 2, 1978, 60–61. *J. Gdn History* v. 2, 1982, 47.

Broadlane House, Hawarden, Clwyd
Historical MSS Commission *Architectural history* v. 5, 1974, item 5164.

Broadleas, Potterne, Wilts
A. Lees-Milne *and* R. Verey *Englishwoman's garden* 1980, 52–54. J. Sales *West Country gardens* 1980, 196–98.

Broadwell, Glos
R. Atkyns *Ancient and present state of Glostershire* 1712, 300. L. Knyff *and* J. Kip *Britannia illustrata* v. 2, 1715.

Brockenhurst near Lymington, Hants
P. Sandby *Collection of one hundred and fifty select views* v. 1, 1781, pl. 20. *C.L.* v. 10, 1901, 656–61,688–93. G. Jekyll *and* G.S. Ellgood *Some English gardens* 1904, 1–4. C. Holme *Gardens of England in Southern & Western counties* 1907, pls. 27–30. G. Jekyll *Garden ornament* 1918, 288. M. Binney *and* A. Hills *Elysian gardens* 1979, 66. A. Paterson *Gardens of Britain* v. 2, 1978, 61–62.

Brocket Hall near Hatfield, Herts
W. Angus *Seats* 1787, pl. 2. *Copper Plate Mag.* v. 2, pl. 76. *C.L.* v. 58, 1925, 16–22,96–103. *G.C.* ii 1926, 321–22. Lady Rockley *Historic gardens of England* 1938, 228–29. N. Pevsner *Hertfordshire* 1977, 112. P. Willis *Charles Bridgeman* 1977, 177. J. Harris *Artist and the country house* 1979, 294.

Brockhall near Daventry, Northants
C.L. v. 136, 1964, 1428–32. J. Harris *Artist and the country house* 1979, 231.

Brockhole, Windermere, Cumbria
C. Holme *Gardens of England in Northern counties* 1911, pls. 18–19. G. Beard *Thomas H. Mawson* 1976, 47.

Brockhurst, East Grinstead, W. Sussex
G.C. ii 1912, 259–60,262,263. *C.L.* v. 54, 1923, 148–54. *Garden* 1924, 82–86. Lady Rockley *Historic gardens of England* 1938, 254–55.

Brockhurst, Didsbury, Greater Manchester
J. Hort. Cottage Gdnr N.S., v. 1, 1880, 73–74. *G.C.* i 1883, 624–25.

Brocklesby Park, Brocklesby, Lincs
B. Howlett *Selection of views in county of Lincoln* 1805. T. Allen *History of county of Lincoln* v. 2, 1834, 229–30. *G.C.* ii 1891, 38–40. *J. Hort. Cottage Gdnr* N.S., v. 31, 1895, 151. *C.L.* v. 75, 1934, 192–98,218–24. D. Stroud *Humphry Repton* 1962, 166. N. Pevsner *and* J. Harris *Lincolnshire* 1964, 200,201. Historical MSS Commission *Architectural history* v. 3, 1971, item 2523. B. Jones *Follies & grottoes* 1974, 358. D. Stroud *Capability Brown* 1975, 160–61,218. G. Carter *et al. Humphry Repton* 1982, 156.

Brockley Hall near Bristol, Avon
F.O. Morris *Series of picturesque views* v. 6, 75.

Brockley Park, Co. Laois, Eire
T. Milton *Seats . . . in Ireland* 1783–93,19.

Brockwell Park *see* Lambeth

Brodick Castle, Isle of Arran, Strathclyde
Official guide. *C.L.* v. 89, 1941, 188–91. *J. Royal Hort. Soc.* 1961, 356–59; 1965, 500–01. *G.C.* i 1965, 427–28. M. Allan *Fisons guide* 1970, 297–98. H. Evans *Beautiful gardens of Britain* 1974, 121–22. P. Verney *Gardens of Scotland* 1976, 95–105. G.A. Little *Scotland's gardens* 1981, 225.

Brodie Castle near Forres, Grampian
C.L. v. 168, 1980, 554–57.

Brodsworth Hall near Doncaster, S. Yorks
C.L. v. 134, 1963, 804–07.

Broke Hall near Ipswich, Suffolk
J.P. Neale *Views* v. 4, 1821.

Bromborough Hall, Bebington, Merseyside
C. Holme *Gardens of England in Northern counties* 1911, pls. 20–21.

Brome Hall near Eye, Suffolk
J. Beeverell *Les delices de la Grande Bretagne* v. 5, 1707, 872. L. Knyff *and* J. Kip *Britannia illustrata* v. 1, 1714. *C.L.* v. 3, 1898, 656–58,688–90. C. Holme *Gardens of England in Midland & Eastern counties* 1908, pls. 14–17.

Bromley College, Bromley, London
T. Badeslade *Thirty six different views of . . . Kent* 1750s. T. Philipott *Villare Cantianum* 1776, frontispiece.

Bromley Place near Rochester, Kent
J. Hassell *Seats near London* 1804–05.

Brompton Botanic Garden, Kensington, London
W. Salisbury *A short address to the public relative to a new botanical establishment at Cadogan Place* 1807.

Brompton Cemetery, Kensington, London
J.S. Curl *Celebration of death* 1980, 242–43.

Bron-y-De, Churt, Surrey
C.L. v. 52, 1922, 578–84.

Broncroft Castle, Craven Arms, Shropshire
R. Sidwell *West Midland gardens* 1981, 105–06.

Brondesbury (Brandsbury), Willesden, London
H. Repton *Sketches* 1794, 2–3. D. Stroud *Humphry Repton* 1962, 39. J. Harris *Catalogue of British drawings . . . in American collections* 1971, 172,174. G. Carter *et al. Humphry Repton* 1982, 65,157.

Brook Cottage, Alkerton, Oxfordshire
R. Bisgrove *Gardens of Britain* v. 3, 1978, 40–42. *Garden* 1979, 86–93.

Brook House near Colwall, Hereford and Worcester
R. Sidwell *West Midland gardens* 1981, 34–37.

Brooke Hall near Loddon, Norfolk
G.M. v. 17, 1841, 273. J. Grigor *Eastern arboretum* 1841, 241–42.

Brooke House, Isle of Wight
J. Hort. Cottage Gdnr N.S., v. 54, 1907, 484–86.

Brooke House near Loddon, Norfolk
G.M. v. 17, 1841, 273. J. Grigor *Eastern arboretum* 1841, 243–45.

Brookland, Charminster, Dorset
J. Hort. Cottage Gdnr v. 46, 1871, 65–66.

Brooklands, Crocketford, Dumfries and Galloway
C.L. v. 168, 1980, 2139–42. G.A. Little *Scotland's gardens* 1981, 246.

Brookmans, North Minns, Herts
D. Stroud *Humphry Repton* 1962, 166. B. Jones *Follies & grottoes* 1974, 345. G. Carter *et al. Humphry Repton* 1982, 154.

Brookwood Park, Hinton Ampner, Hants
J.P. Neale *Views* 2nd Series, v. 1, 1824.

Broom House, Fulham, London
G.C. ii 1887, 305–06; ii 1898, 348–49; i 1900, 366. *C.L.* v. 9, 1901, 552–55.

Broome Park, Barham, Kent
J. Harris *History of Kent* 1719, 35. T. Badeslade *Thirty six different views . . . of Kent* 1750s, pl. 5. W. Angus *Seats* 1787, pl. 18. C. Greenwood *Epitome of county history . . . v. 1: Kent* 1838, 402. *C.L.* v. 22, 1907, 18–25; v. 86, 1939, 494–98. M. Macartney *English houses & gardens* 1908, pl. 17.

Broomfield, Chelmsford, Essex
G.C. i 1882, 768.

Broomhill, Tunbridge Wells, Kent
G.C. i 1891, 435-36.

Broomholm, Langholm, Dumfries and Galloway
G.A. Little *Scotland's gardens* 1981, 246–48.

Brough Hall near Richmond, N. Yorks
W. Angus *Seats* 1787, pl. 22. *G.M.* v. 12, 1836, 167–69. *C.L.* v. 142, 1967, 894,948.

Brougham Hall near Penrith, Cumbria
W. Hutchinson *History of county of Cumberland* v. 1, 1794, 305–08. J. Housman *Descriptive tour and guide to the Lakes* 1817, 83–84. *G.C.* ii 1880, 713–14; ii 1885, 69–70; ii 1896, 329. *J. Hort. Cottage Gdnr* N.S., v. 43, 1901, 490–91. C. Holme *Gardens of England in Northern counties* 1911, pls. 22–23.

Broughton Castle near Banbury, Oxfordshire
F.O. Morris *Series of picturesque views* v. 3, 25. *Garden* v. 48, 1895, 97. *G.C.* i 1908, 146–47,295. *C.L.* v. 4, 1898, 756–62; v. 9, 1901, 112–19; v. 67, 1930, 50–57, 84–91,126; v. 160, 1976, 1636–39. *Architectural Review* v. 34, 1913, 122–24, pls. 1–4. Lady Rockley *Historic gardens of England* 1938, 86–87. R. Bisgrove *Gardens of Britain* v. 3, 1978, 42–43.

Broughton Hall near Eccleshall, Staffs
W. Pitt *General view of agriculture of . . . Stafford* 1796, 96. J. Nightingale *Topographical . . . description of Staffordshire* 1810, 924. *C.L.* v. 28, 1910, 126–33.

Broughton Hall near Skipton, N. Yorks
C.L. v. 107, 1950, 876–79,1034; v. 169, 1981, 270–72. L. Fleming *and* A. Gore *English garden* 1979, 192. *Garden* 1982, 119.

Broughton House, Broughton, Northants
C.L. v. 25, 1909, 162–70,198–205.

Broughton House, Kirkcudbright, Dumfries and Galloway
G.A. Little *Scotland's gardens* 1981, 248–49.

Broughton Place, Broughton, Borders
G.A. Little *Scotland's gardens* 1981, 80.

Broughton Tower, Lancs
W. Watts *Seats* 1779, pl. 80.

Brown's Gardens *see* Brighton

Brownshill, Painswick, Glos
J.N. Brewer *Delineations of Gloucestershire* 1825, 199.

Brownsea Castle, Brownsea Island, Dorset
J.P. Neale *Views* v. 1, 1818. M.R. Gloag *Book of English gardens* 1906, 137–54. *C.L.* v. 49, 1921, 430–36.

Broxbourne, Herts
G.C. ii 1884, 211–12; ii 1886, 711–12,713,717.

Broxholme Hall, Yorks
I. Hall *Samuel Buck's Yorkshire sketchbook* 1979, 175.

Broxmouth Park, Dunbar, Lothian
G.C. ii 1880, 714–15. *Scottish Gdnr and Northern Forester* v. 7, 1912, 49.

Bruce Castle, Tottenham, London
Copper Plate Mag. v. 2, pl. 82.

Bruern Abbey, Churchill, Oxfordshire
R. Bisgrove *Gardens of Britain* v. 3, 1978, 46–47.

Bruton Abbey, Bruton, Somerset
Gentleman's Mag. v. 59, 1789, 800–01. P. Couzens *Bruton in Selwood* 1972, 49–50.

Bryanston House near Blandford Forum, Dorset
J. Beeverell *Les delices de la Grande Bretagne* v. 5, 1707, 872. L. Knyff and J. Kip *Britannia illustrata* v. 1, 1714. J. Hutchins *History . . . of Dorset* v. 1, 1774, 87. W. Watts *Seats* 1779, pl. 83. J.P. Neale *Views* v. 1, 1818. *G.M.* v. 11 1835, 333–34. *J. Hort. Cottage Gdnr* v. 38, 1867, 79–80. *G.C.* ii 1898, 429–30.

Bryerswood, Sawrey, Cumbria
G. Beard *Thomas H. Mawson* 1976, 48.

Brympton D'Evercy, Yeovil, Somerset
Official guide. J. Beeverell *Les delices de la Grande Bretagne* v. 5, 1707, 872. L. Knyff and J. Kip *Britannia illustrata* v. 1, 1714. J. Collinson *History . . . of . . . Somersetshire* v. 3, 1791, 215. *C.L.* v. 4, 1898, 656–59; v. 22, 1907, 774–80; v. 61, 1927, 718–26,762–69. G. Jekyll and G.S. Elgood *Some English gardens* 1904, 36–38. C. Holme *Gardens of England in Southern & Western counties* 1907, pls. 31–32. G. Jekyll *Garden ornament* 1918, 58. B. Jones *Follies & grottoes* 1974, 382.

Bryn Bras Castle, Llanrug, Gwynedd
R.D. Gray-Williams *Guide to the garden* 1973.

Bryn Glas, Newport, Gwent
J. Hort. Cottage Gdnr N.S., v. 11, 1885, 472–74.

Bryn-y-Neuadd, Llanfairfechan, Gwynedd
J. Hort. Cottage Gdnr v. 32, 1864, 294. *Gdn History* v. 5 no. 3, 1977, 68–72.

Bryngwyn, Hereford and Worcester
G.C. i 1892, 103–04.

Brynhyfryd, Powys
C.L. v. 170, 1981, 938–40.

Brynkinalt near Chirk, Clwyd
J. Hort. Cottage Gdnr v. 62, 1879, 489–90.

Buccleuch House, Richmond, London
Tombleson's Thames 1834.

Buchanan Castle near Drymen, Central
A.A. Tait *Landscape garden in Scotland* 1980, passim.

Buckden Palace, Buckden, Cambs
C.L. v. 26, 1909, 162–66. V.C.H. *Huntingdon* v. 2, 1932, 260.

Buckenham House, Buckenham Tofts, Norfolk
D. Stroud *Humphry Repton* 1962, 166. G. Carter *et al. Humphry Repton* 1982, 158.

Buckhurst Park, Withyham, E. Sussex
C.L. v. 31, 1912, 686–95,722–29. G. Jekyll *Garden ornament* 1918, 158,307. J. Brown *Gardens of a golden afternoon* 1982, 166.

Buckingham House, St James's Park, London
L. Knyff and J. Kip *Britannia illustrata* v. 2, 1715. H. Overton *Britannia illustrata* c.1724, pl. 16. R. Havell *Series of picturesque views* 1823, pl. 11. *C.L.* v. 126, 1959, 253; v. 132, 1962, 86–88.

Buckingham Palace, London
J. Dennis *Landscape gardener* 1835, 103–06. W.H.L. Gruner *Decorations of garden pavilion in grounds of Buckingham Palace* 1846. W. Keane *Beauties of Middlesex* 1850, 1–8. *Garden* v. 4, 1873, 530–32. *J. Hort. Cottage Gdnr* v. 56, 1876, 533–34; N.S., v. 14, 1887, 507,510–11; N.S., v. 34, 1897, 562–63; N.S., v. 60, 1910, 422–23. N. Cole *Royal parks and gardens of London* 1877, 1–6. *G.C.* i 1897, 396,402; i 1900, 265; i 1937, 302,303. H.I. Triggs *Formal gardens in England and Scotland* 1902, 41–42. B. Graeme *Story of Buckingham Palace* 1928. L. Roper *Royal gardens* 1953, 20–27. G. Taylor *Old London gardens* 1953, 161–68. R.I.B.A. *Catalogue* v. L-N, 1973, 112–13. P. Coats *Gardens of Buckingham Palace* 1978. G. Plumptre *Royal gardens* 1981, 158–78.

Buckland near Reigate, Surrey
Garden v. 1, 1871, 28–30.

Buckland Abbey, Tavistock, Devon
S. and N. Buck *Buck's antiquities* v. 1, 1774, pl. 60. *G.M.* v. 18, 1842, 550–51. *Garden* v. 44, 431–32. G.S. Thomas *Gardens of National Trust* 1979, 109–110.

Buckland Filleigh near Hatherleigh, Devon
J.P. Neale *Views* 2nd Series, v. 1, 1824. R. Ackermann *Repository* v. 10, 1827, pl. 26. *Jones's Views* 1829. W.W.J. Gendall *Views* v. 2, 1830, 85,88–89. *Architectural History* v. 7, 1964, 24–25,48.

Buckland House, Faringdon, Oxfordshire
Architectural Review v. 25, 1909, 290–91. *C.L.* v. 37, 1915, 652–69,698–705. G. Jekyll *Garden ornament* 1918, 119. B. Jones *Follies & grottoes* 1974, 376–77. R. Bisgrove *Gardens of Britain* v. 3, 1978, 47.

Buckland Monachorum near Tavistock, Devon
C.L. v. 135, 1964, 921–24. P.M. Synge *Gardens of Britain* v. 1, 1977, 48–52.

Bucklebury. Old Vicarage, Berks
C.L. v. 146, 1969, 146–48.

Bucklebury Place, Woolhampton, Berks
Gdning World v. 17, 1900, 89–90; v. 18, 1902, 654–55. *J. Hort. Cottage Gdnr* N.S., v. 45, 1902, 178–79,183.

Buckminster, Leics
D. Stroud *Humphry Repton* 1962, 64–65. G. Carter *et al. Humphry Repton* 1982, 156.

Bucknowle House near Corfe Castle, Dorset
J. Harris *Artist and the country house* 1979, 132.

Budbrooke House, Warwick, Warwickshire
G. Beard *Thomas H. Mawson* 1976, 48.

Bughtrig near Coldstream, Borders
G.C. v. 160 no. 15, 1966, 18–19. G.A. Little *Scotland's gardens* 1981, 80–81.

Bulbridge House, Wilton, Wilts
C.L. v. 133, 1963, 420–23,472; v. 138, 1965, 86–88.

Bulcote Manor, Bulcote, Notts
C.L. v. 52, 1922, 385.

Bulgaden, Kilmallock, Co. Limerick, Eire
G. Carter *et al. Humphry Repton* 1982, 164.

Bulmershe Court near Reading, Berks
J. Harris *Catalogue of British drawings . . . in American collections* 1971, 134. D. Jacques *Georgian gardens* 1983, 201.

Bulstrode Park near Beaconsfield, Bucks
T. Badeslade *and* J. Rocque *Vitruvius Brittanicus* 1739, pl. 40–44. *Picturesque views of the principal seats* 1788. W. Gilpin *Observations relative chiefly to picturesque beauty* v. 2, 1792, 187–88. *Copper Plate Mag.* v. 2, pl. 54. H. Repton *Observations* 1803, 67–72. British Museum *Catalogue of maps, prints* 1829, 47. *G.M.* v. 9, 1833, 648. R. Pococke *Travels through England* v. 2, 1889, 259–60. *Gdnrs Mag.* 1914, 194–96. C.L. v. 68, 1930, 624–26. D. Stroud *Humphry Repton* 1962, 40. E.M. Elvey *Hand-list of Buckinghamshire estate maps* 1963, 27. Historical MSS Commission *Architectural history* v. 2, 1970, item 1191. J. Harris *Artist and the country house* 1979, 168. G. Carter *et al. Humphry Repton* 1982, 148. D. Jacques *Georgian gardens* 1983, 137.

Bulwell Hall, Bulwell, Notts
F.O. Morris *Series of picturesque views* v. 4, 17. *Gdning World* v. 2, 1886, 426–27.

Bulwick Hall near Oundle, Northants
Garden v. 47, 1895, 195–96,197,206. C.L. v. 6, 1899, 48–53. G. Jekyll *and* G.S. Elgood *Some English gardens* 1904, 11–14. G. Jekyll *Garden ornament* 1918, 416.

Bunny Hall, Bunny, Notts
R. Ackermann *Repository* v. 5, 1825, pl. 2. W.W.J. Gendall *Views* v. 1, 1830, 61.

Buntingsdale near Market Drayton, Shropshire
C.L. v. 42, 1917, 420–25.

Burbage near Hinckley, Leics
J. Nichols *History . . . of county of Leicester* v. 4, 1811, 461.

Burford House, Tenbury Wells, Shropshire
C.L. v. 102, 1947, 1313; v. 154, 1973, 602–05. G.C. v. 160 no. 7, 1966, 20–21; v. 185 no. 29, 1979, 35–36, 38. M. Allan *Fisons guide* 1970, 269–70. H. Evans *Beautiful gardens of Britain* 1974, 91–92. A. Hellyer *Gardens of genius* 1980, 161–65. R. Sidwell *West Midland gardens* 1981, 106–09. A. Lees-Milne *and* R. Verey *Englishman's garden* 1982, 144–47.

Burford Lodge near Dorking, Surrey
E.W. Brayley *and* J. Britton *Topographical history of Surrey* v. 4, 459. G.C. ii 1884, 107–08; ii 1885, 165–66; ii 1894, 134–35; ii 1897, 75; ii 1898, 87–88; i 1899, 273–74,275; ii 1906, 87–88. *J. Hort. Cottage Gdnr* v. 62, 1879, 61–62. C.L. v. 6, 1899, 432–36.

Burford Priory, Burford, Oxfordshire
R. Ackermann *Repository* v. 9, 1827, pl. 19. W.W.J. Gendall *Views* v. 1, 1830, 66. C.L. v. 29, 1911, 306–15; v. 85, 1939, 586–91,616–17. G. Jekyll *Garden ornament* 1918, 152. Lady Rockley *Historic gardens of England* 1938, 132–33.

Burgate Court, Burgate, Hants
A. Paterson *Gardens of Britain* v. 2, 1978, 62–63.

Burghley House near Stamford, Cambs
P. Sandby *Collection of one hundred and fifty select views* v. 1, 1781, pl. 29. W. Watts *Seats* 1779, pls. 21,41. J. Horn *History or description . . . of Burghley House* 1797. H. Repton *Observations* 1803, 129–33. J. Blore *Guide to Burghley House* 1815, 1816. R. Havell *Series of picturesque views* 1819, pl. 17. J.P. Neale *Views* v. 3, 1823. R. Ackermann *Repository* v. 5, 1825, pl. 19. *G.M.* v. 5, 1829, 673. W.W.J. Gendall *Views* v. 2, 1830, 99. F.O. Morris *Series of picturesque views* v. 1, 65. *J. Hort. Cottage Gdnr* v. 47, 1872, 11–14. *Garden* v. 6,

Burghley House (*Cont.*)

1874, 27–28. *G.C.* ii 1881, 400–02,405; i 1892, 105–06. L. Jewitt *and* S.C. Hall *Stately homes of England* 1877, 128–46. V.C.H. *Northampton* v. 2, 1906, 525. C. Fiennes *Journeys* 1949, 68. *C.L.* v. 114, 1953, 2164–67; v. 158, 1975, 982–85. J. Evelyn *Diary* v. 4, 1955, 350–51. Historical MSS Commission *Architectural history* v. 2, 1970, item 1180. D. Stroud *Capability Brown* 1975, 74–79,218. L. Fleming *and* A. Gore *English garden* 1979, 121.

Burley Grange, Burley, Hants
A. Paterson *Gardens of Britain* v. 2, 1978, 63–64.

Burley on the Hill, Burley, Leics
J. Hort. Cottage Gdnr v. 51, 1874, 468–69. *C.L.* v. 7, 1900, 240–44. E. Cecil *History of gardening in England* 1910, 258–61. N. Pevsner *Leicestershire and Rutland* 1960, 290. D. Stroud *Humphry Repton* 1962, 106–07. J. Harris *Artist and the country house* 1979, 233. G. Carter *et al. Humphry Repton* 1982, 160.

Burlingham Hall, Acle, Norfolk
G. Carter *et al. Humphry Repton* 1982, 158.

Burlington House, Piccadilly, London
J. Beeverell *Les delices de la Grand Bretagne* v. 5, 1707, 872. L. Knyff *and* J. Kip *Britannia illustrata* v. 1, 1714.

Burloes, Royston, Herts
R. Bisgrove *Gardens of Britain* v. 3, 1978, 48.

Burnby Hall, Pocklington, Humberside
M. Allan *Fisons guide* 1970, 243–44. *C.L.* v. 163, 1978, 530–31. K. Lemmon *Gardens of Britain* v. 5, 1978, 33–34.

Burnt Norton near Chipping Campden, Glos
Gdn History v. 7 no. 1, 1979, 78–85. J. Sales *West Country gardens* 1980, 48–49.

Burrow Hall near Kirkby Lonsdale, Cumbria
C.L. v. 127, 1960, 806–09,864.

Burstwick, Humberside
H.M. Colvin *History of the King's Works* v. 2, 1963, 904,905.

Burton, Burton on the Wolds, Leics
G.M. v. 7, 1831, 427.

Burton Agnes Hall near Bridlington, Humberside
Official guide. F.O. Morris *Series of picturesque views* v. 1, 89. *C.L.* v. 33, 1913, 880–86; v. 113, 1953, 1804–07,1972–75. K. Lemmon *Gardens of Britain* v. 5, 1978, 34–35. I. Hall *Samuel Buck's Yorkshire sketchbook* 1979, 279.

Burton Constable near Hull, Humberside
J. Beeverell *Les delices de la Grande Bretagne* v. 5, 1707, 872. W. Watts *Seats* 1779, pl. 12. G. Poulson *History . . . of Seigniory of Holderness* v. 2, 1841, 242. F.O. Morris *Series of picturesque views* v. 1, 45. *C.L.* v. 21, 1907, 126–33; v. 72, 1932, 238–43; v. 171, 1982, 1198–1200,1278. N. Pevsner *Yorkshire: York and the East Riding* 1972, 211–12. D. Stroud *Capability Brown* 1975, 173,218. K. Lemmon *Gardens of Britain* v. 5, 1978, 36. J. Harris *Artist and the country house* 1979, 83,287.

Burton House, Co. Cork, Eire
E. Malins *and* Knight of Glin *Lost demesnes* 1976, 76.

Burton Manor, Weston, Cheshire
C.L. v. 32, 1912, 490–97. G. Beard *Thomas H. Mawson* 1976, 48. R.I.B.A. *Catalogue* v. O-R, 1976, 59.

Burton Park near Petworth, W. Sussex
J.P. Neale *Views* 2nd Series, v. 1, 1824. *C.L.* v. 80, 1936, 38–43. Lady Rockley *Historic gardens of England* 1938, 260–61.

Burton Pynsent near Langport, Somerset
J. Collinson *History . . . of Somersetshire* v. 1, 1791, 24. G. Lipscomb *Journey into Cornwall* 1799, 134–35. *C.L.* v. 76, 1934, 360–66. Lady Rockley *Historic gardens of England* 1938, 172–73. B. Jones *Follies & grottoes* 1974, 383. D. Stroud *Capability Brown* 1975, 135–36,219.

Burton upon Trent Abbey, Staffs
J. Nightingale *Topographical . . . description of Staffordshire* 1810, 757.

Burwarton House near Ditton Priors, Shropshire
R. Sidwell *West Midland gardens* 1981, 109.

Burwood House near Cobham, Surrey
W. Keane *Beauties of Surrey* 1849, 31–32.

Burwood Park near Walton, Surrey
W. Keane *Beauties of Surrey* 1849, 21–22.

Bury, St Paul's Walden, Herts
N. Pevsner *Hertfordshire* 1977, 330.

Bury Hill, Dorking, Surrey
O. Manning *and* W. Bray *History . . . of Surrey* v. 1, 1804, 578. R. Ackermann *Repository* v. 2, 1823, pl. 14. J.P. Neale *Views* 2nd Series, v. 1, 1824. *G.M.* v. 5, 1829, 593–95. W.W.J. Gendall *Views of country seats* v. 1, 1830, 48–50. W. Keane *Beauties of Surrey* 1849, 148–51. E.W. Brayley *and* J. Britton *Topographical history of Surrey* v. 5, 108. *J. Hort. Cottage Gdnr* v. 33, 1865, 7–9.

Bury St Edmunds Abbey, Suffolk
Garden v. 5, 1874, 140–41. Historical MSS Commission *Architectural History* v. 3, 1971, item 2543.

Busbridge near Godalming, Surrey
W. Angus *Seats* 1787, pl. 6. J.P. Neale *Views* 2nd Series, v. 1, 1824. G.F. Prosser *Select illustrations of . . . Surrey* 1828. *G.M.* v. 9, 1833, 481. E.W. Brayley and J. Britton *Topographical history of Surrey* v. 5, 218. W. Keane *Beauties of Surrey* 1849, 133–37. *G.C.* 1862, 1126–28. B. Jones *Follies & grottoes* 1974, 394–95. *Surrey Archaeological Collections* v. 70, 1975, 154.

Busbridge Wood, Hascombe, Surrey
R. Webber *Percy Cane* 1975, 181,183–84. T. Wright *Gardens of Britain* v. 4, 1978, 210.

Buscot Park near Faringdon, Oxfordshire
W. Mavor *General view . . . of Berkshire* 1809, 44–45. *G.C.* i 1901, 119–20,21. *Architectural Review* v. 33, 1913, 74–75, pls. 4–6. *C.L.* v. 40, 1916, 490–97; v. 87, 1940, 502–07. G. Jekyll *Garden ornament* 1918, 340–41, 352,372. H. Evans *Beautiful gardens of Britain* 1974, 39–40. R. Bisgrove *Gardens of Britain* v. 3, 1978, 49–50. G.S. Thomas *Gardens of National Trust* 1979, 110–11.

Bush, Antrim, Co. Antrim, Ulster
Irish Gdning v. 10, 1915, 114–15; v. 11, 1916, 33; v. 14, 1919, 100–01; v. 15, 1920, 97–99. *G.C.* i 1929, 10–12.

Bush Hill Park, Edmonton, London
Copper Plate Mag. v. 2, pl. 58. J. Hassell *Seats near London* 1804–05. *V.C.H. Middlesex* v. 5, 1976, 161.

Bushey Hall, Bushey, Herts
H. Chauncy *Historical antiquities of Hertfordshire* 1700, 540.

Bushey House, Bushey, Herts
G.C. ii 1907, 261–62.

Bushey Park *see* Hampton

Bushey Villa, Teddington, London
W. Keane *Beauties of Middlesex* 1850, 103–05.

Busketts near Southampton, Hants
G.C. ii 1890, 652,653.

Bussock Mayne, Snelsmore Common, Berks
R. Bisgrove *Gardens of Britain* v. 3, 1978, 50–51.

Butleigh Court, Butleigh, Somerset
R.I.B.A. *Catalogue* v. L-N, 1973, 9.

Butley Priory, Butley, Suffolk
C.L. v. 73, 1933, 308–14.

Buxted Park, Buxted, E. Sussex
J. Hort. Cottage Gdnr v. 62, 1879, 284–85. *C.L.* v. 75, 1934, 404–09.

Buxton. Pavilion Gardens, Derbyshire
Landscape Design no. 108, 1974, 10–12. J. Anthony *Gardens of Britain* v. 6, 1979, 36–37.

Byers Green Lodge near Bishop Auckland, Co. Durham
T. Wright *Arbours & grottos* 1979.

Byfleet (Joseph Spence), Surrey
Gdn History v. 6 no. 3, 1978, 38–64; v. 7 no. 3, 1979, 29–48; v. 8 no. 2, 1980, 44–65; v. 8 no. 3, 1980, 77–114. *J. Gdn History* v. 3 no. 2, 1983, 121–29.

Byram Hall near Ferrybridge, W. Yorks
J. Hort. Cottage Gdnr v. 37, 1898, 168,169. C. Holme *Gardens of England in Northern counties* 1911, pls. 26–27. D. Stroud *Capability Brown* 1975, 219.

Bystock near Exmouth, Devon
G.C. i 1881, 471,474–75; ii 1903, 292. *Gdning World* v. 12, 1896, 321–22.

Caches, Guernsey, Channel Islands
W. Berry *History of Island of Guernsey* 1815, 138.

Cadbury House, Somerset
W. Phelps *History . . . of Somersetshire* v. 1 pt. 2, 1836, 396.

Cadbury Manor, Cadbury, Somerset
G. Beard *Thomas H. Mawson* 1976, 48.

Cadland, Fawley, Hants
W. Watts *Seats* 1779, pl. 24. J.B. Burke *Visitation* 2nd Series, v. 1, 1855, 56. *Florist* 1859, 309–11. D. Stroud *Capability Brown* 1975, 177,219. Historical MSS Commission *Architectural history* v. 3, 1971, items 2778, 3585.

Cadogan Place, Chelsea, London
G. Carter *et al. Humphry Repton* 1982, 156–57.

Cadzow Castle, Cadzow, Strathclyde
G.M. v. 18, 1842, 341–42.

Caen Wood Towers, Highgate, London
J. Hort. Cottage Gdnr N.S., v. 32, 1896, 508–10. *G.C.* ii 1928, 307,309,310–11.

Caerhays Castle near Tregony, Cornwall
C.S. Gilbert *Historical survey of . . . Cornwall* v. 2, 1820, 845–47. *G.C.* i 1956, 364–65. D. Stroud *Humphry Repton* 1962, 77. E. Hyams *English gardens* 1964, 212–14. *J. Royal Hort. Soc.* 1966, 279–86. *J. Scottish Rock Garden* v. 13 no. 3, 1973, 175–79. P.M. Synge *Gardens of Britain* v. 1, 1977, 88–90.

Cainham Court near Ludlow, Shropshire
F. Calvert *Picturesque views . . . in Shropshire* 1831, 134.

Caldrees Manor, Ickleton, Cambs
V.C.H. *Cambridge* v. 6, 1978, 234.

Caledon, Co. Tyrone, Ulster
F.O. Morris *Series of picturesque views* v. 4, 79. *C.L.* v. 81, 1937, 224–29. B. Jones *Follies & grottoes* 1974, 438. E. Malins *and* Knight of Glin *Lost demesnes* 1976, 44–46. A. Rowan *North West Ulster* 1979, 163–64. Ulster Architectural Heritage Society *Northern gardens* 1982, 4,14. M. McGarvie *Home is house and garden* 1984, 18–37.

Calke Abbey, Calke, Derbyshire
G. Glover *History and gazetteer of . . . Derby* v. 2, 1833, 218. J.B. Burke *Visitation* v. 1, 1852, 107. *C.L.* v. 174, 1983, 1062–65,1162–65.

Callaly Castle, Callaly, Northumberland
C.L. v. 125, 1959, 304–07.

Callander Lodge, Callander, Central
Scottish Gdnr and Northern Forester v. 6, 1911, 689–90.

Cally near Gatehouse of Fleet, Dumfries and Galloway
G.M. v. 9, 1833, 7–8. A.A. Tait *Landscape garden in Scotland* 1980, passim.

Calverley Park, Tunbridge Wells, Kent
C.L. v. 145, 1969, 1080–83, 1166–69.

Camberwell (John Coakley Lettsom), Southwark, London
Cottage Gdnr v. 5, 1850, 79; v. 57, 1877, 385–86. R.H. Fox *Dr John Fothergill and his friends* 1919, 99–117. M. Hadfield *et al. British gardeners* 1980, 180.

Camden Place, Chislehurst, London
Copper Plate Mag. v. 2, pl. 62.

Camfield Place near Hatfield, Herts
H. Chauncy *Historical antiquities of Hertfordshire* 1700, 276.

Cambo near Crail, Fife
G.M. v. 10, 1834, 526–27.

Cambridge. Botanic Garden, Cambs
Official guide. *Short account of the late donation of a botanic garden to the University of Cambridge* 1763. T. Martyn *Catalogus horti botanici Cantabrigiensis* 1771. J. Donn *Hortus Cantabrigiensis* 1796 and subsequent editions to 1845. R. Harraden *Views of Cambridge* 1800, pl. 24. R. Ackermann *History of the University of Cambridge* 1815. T. Wright *and* H.L. Jones *Le Keux's memorials of Cambridge* v. 2, 1842, 3–7. *G.C.* ii 1882, 585,587–90,593; i 1899, 329–30; ii 1958, 280–81; v. 160 no. 6, 1966, 4. *Garden* v. 59, 1901, 109–10. *J. Royal Hort. Soc.* 1940, 171–81; 1955, 205–14. H. Gilbert-Carter *Guide to the University Garden* 1947. V.C.H. *Cambridge* v. 3, 1959, 324–25. *Orchid Review* v. 81, 1973, 76–78. *Gdn History* v. 7 no. 3, 1979, 49–52. *Garden* 1981, 456–58. P.F. Yeo *and* C.J. King *Catalogue of plants in Cambridge Botanic Garden* 1981.

Cambridge. Christ's College, Cambs
D. Loggan *Cantabrigia illustrata* 1690. J. Beeverell *Les delices de la Grande Bretagne* v. 1, 1707, 122. T. Wright *and* H.L. Jones *Le Keux's memorials of Cambridge* v. 1, 1841, 9–10. *C.L.* v. 40, 1916, 406–12.

Cambridge. Clare College, Cambs
D. Loggan *Cantabrigia illustrata* 1690. J. Beeverell *Les delices de la Grande Bretagne* v. 1, 1707, 110. *J. Royal Hort. Soc.* 1958, 388–91. *Architectural History* v. 7, 1964, 26,55. *C.L.* v. 150, 1971, 552–53.

Cambridge. Corpus Christi College, Cambs
D. Loggan *Cantabrigia illustrata* 1690.

Cambridge. Emmanuel College, Cambs
D. Loggan *Cantabrigia illustrata* 1690. M. Macartney *English houses & gardens* 1908, pl. 61.

Cambridge. Gonville College Cambs
D. Loggan *Cantabrigia illustrata* 1690. J. Beeverell *Les delices de la Grande Bretagne* v. 1, 1707, 112.

Cambridge. Jesus College, Cambs
D. Loggan *Cantabrigia illustrata* 1690. J. Beeverell *Les delices de la Grande Bretagne* v. 1, 1707, 121.

Cambridge. King's College, Cambs
D. Loggan *Cantabrigia illustrata* 1690.

Cambridge. Magdalene College, Cambs
D. Loggan *Cantabrigia illustrata* 1690. J. Beeverell *Les delices de la Grande Bretagne* v. 1, 1707, 119.

Cambridge. Pembroke College, Cambs
D. Loggan *Cantabrigia illustrata* 1690. J. Beeverell *Les delices de la Grande Bretagne* v. 1, 1707, 105. M. Macartney *English houses & gardens* 1908, pl. 60.

Cambridge. Queens' College, Cambs
J. Beeverell *Les delices de la Grande Bretagne* v. 1, 1707, 107.

Cambridge. St John's College, Cambs
D. Loggan *Cantabrigia illustrata* 1690. J. Beeverell *Les delices de la Grande Bretagne* v. 1, 1707, 117,118. D. Stroud *Capability Brown* 1975, 171–72.

Cambridge. Sidney Sussex College, Cambs
D. Loggan *Cantabrigia illustrata* 1690. J. Beeverell *Les delices de la Grande Bretagne* v. 1, 1707, 120.

Cambridge. Trinity College, Cambs
D. Loggan *Cantabrigia illustrata* 1690. J. Beeverell *Les delices de la Grande Bretagne* v. 1, 1707, 113. T. Wright and H.L. Jones *Le Keux's memorials of Cambridge* v. 1, 1841, 65–66. G.C. i 1889, 752. C.L. v. 18, 1905, 635–41. F. Crisp *Mediaeval gardens* v. 2, 1924, figs. 20,29. L. Fleming and A. Gore *English garden* 1979, 56–57.

Cambridge. Trinity Hall, Cambs
J. Beeverell *Les delices de la Grande Bretagne* v. 1, 1707, 116.

Cambridge House, Twickenham, London
R.O. Cambridge *Works* 1803, xxxviii. *G.M.* v. 13, 1837, 12–13. W. Keane *Beauties of Middlesex* 1850, 162–65.

Came, Winterborne Came, Dorset
J. Hutchins *History . . . of Dorset* v. 1, 1774, 345; 3rd ed. v. 2, 1863, 289.

Cameron, Loch Lomond, Strathclyde
G.A. Little *Scotland's gardens* 1981, 249.

Camerton Court, Camerton, Avon
J. Collinson *History . . . of . . . Somersetshire* v. 3, 1791, 331.

Camis Eskan, Helensburgh, Strathclyde
Scottish Gdnr and Northern Forester v. 8, 1913, 1–2.

Camp Hill, Woolton, Liverpool, Merseyside
J. Hort. Cottage Gdnr N.S., v. 44, 1902, 82–83.

Campden House, Chipping Campden, Glos
C.L. v. 40, 1916, 602–08.

Campsbourne Lodge, Hornsey, London
W. Keane *Beauties of Middlesex* 1850, 254–55.

Campsea Ash, Suffolk
G. Jekyll and G.S. Elgood *Some English gardens* 1904, 67–69. *C.L.* v. 18, 1905, 54–62. *Garden* 1914, 443–44. *G.C.* i 1933, 269; ii 1933, 135. Lady Rockley *Historic gardens of England* 1938, 122–23. *Gdn History* v. 3 no. 3, 1975, 62–75.

Cams Hall near Fareham, Hants
G.C. ii 1935, 26.

Candacraig, Strathdon, Grampian
G.A. Little *Scottish gardens* 1981, 178–79.

Candie Gardens, Guernsey, Channel Islands
G.C. ii 1963, 160.

Canford Manor, Canford Magna, Dorset
J. Hort. Cottage Gdnr N.S., v. 21, 1890, 182–83. C. Holme *Gardens of England in Southern & Western counties* 1907, pls. 33–34.

Cann House, Plymouth, Devon
G.C. ii 1906, 4.

Cannizaro Park, Wimbledon, London
Garden 1981, 7–12.

Cannon Hall near Barnsley, S. Yorks
J.P. Neale *Views* v. 5, 1822. *Jones's views* 1829, 14–16. *Trans. Hunter Archaeological Soc.* v. 8, 1963, 303–06. K. Lemmon *Gardens of Britain* v. 5, 1978, 135–36.

Cannongate House, Edinburgh, Lothian
Historical MSS Commission *Architectural history* v. 5, 1974, item 5034.

Canonbury House Tea Gardens, Islington, London
W. Wroth *London pleasure gardens of the eighteenth century* 1896, 154–55.

Canonmills Cottage, Edinburgh, Lothian
G.M. v. 12, 1836, 333–41.

Canons Ashby, Northants
H.I. Triggs *Formal gardens in England and Scotland* 1902, 12. *C.L.* v. 16, 1904, 978–87; v. 49, 1921, 246–52, 278–84; v. 169, 1981, 930–33,1026–29. C. Holme *Gardens of England in Midland & Eastern counties* 1908, 19–21. E. Cecil *History of gardening in England* 1910, 206. G. Jekyll *Garden ornament* 1918, 29. Lady Rockley *Historic gardens of England* 1938, 106–07. Royal Commission on Historical Monuments *Inventory of the historical monuments in . . . Northampton* v. 3, 1981, 36–37. C. Taylor *Archaeology of gardens* 1983, 41–42.

Canons Park, Edgware, London
J. Macky *Journey through England* v. 2, 1722, 9–10. W. Watts *Seats* 1779. J.C. Loudon *Encyclopaedia of gardening* 1822, 1225–26. *G.M.* v. 5, 1829, 557–58; v. 12, 1836, 278–79. W. Keane *Beauties of Middlesex* 1850, 257–60. *C.L.* v. 40, 1916, 518–26. *G.C.* ii 1916,

208,209,211. H. Walpole *Correspondence*; edited by W.S. Lewis and R.A. Smith, v. 30, 1961, 60–61. V.C.H. *Middlesex* v. 5, 1976, 115,117. J. Johnson *Excellent Cassandra: life and times of Duchess of Chandos* 1981, 89–90. G. Carter *et al. Humphry Repton* 1982, 157.

Canterbury. Christchurch, Kent
E. Cecil *History of gardening in England* 1910, 8. J. Harvey *Mediaeval gardens* 1981, pl. 37.

Canterbury. Public Park, Kent
B. Jones *Follies & grottoes* 1974, 348.

Canwell Hall near Tamworth, Staffs
S. Shaw *History . . . of Staffordshire* v. 2, 1801, 22.

Capel, Sir Henry *see* Kew

Capel Manor, Waltham Cross, Herts
R. Bisgrove *Gardens of Britain* v. 3, 1978, 51–53.

Capernwray Hall near Carnforth, Lancs
F.O. Morris *Series of picturesque views* v. 4, 15. G. Beard *Thomas H. Mawson* 1976, 13, 48.

Capesthorne near Macclesfield, Cheshire
Official guide. F.O. Morris *Series of picturesque views* v. 3, 29. M. Allan *Fisons guide* 1970, 218. C.L. v. 162, 1977, 607–10. J. Harris *Artist and the country house* 1979, 135.

Capheaton, Northumberland
J.P. Neale *Views* v. 3, 1820. B. Jones *Follies & grottoes* 1974, 374. J. Harris *Artist and the country house* 1979, 79. Tyne and Wear County Council Museums *Capability Brown and the northern landscape* 1983, 16.

Caprington Castle near Kilmarnock, Strathclyde
G.M. v. 9, 1833, 10.

Carberry Tower near Musselburgh, Lothian
G.C. i 1885, 473–74,477; ii 1905, 194; ii 1938, 388–89. C.L. v. 91, 1942, 398–401.

Carbrook Hall (Carhouse), Sheffield, S. Yorks
J. Kip *Nouveau theatre de la Grande Bretagne* v. 4, 1729. J. Harris *Artist and the country house* 1979, 148.

Carclew near Penryn, Cornwall
W. Borlase *Natural history of Cornwall* 1758, pl. 11. G.S. Gilbert *Historical survey of . . . Cornwall* v. 2, 1820, 802–03. *J. Hort. Cottage Gdnr* v. 52, 1874, 383–85,403–06. C.L. v. 39, 1916, 590–94; v. 75, 1934, 378–82; v. 132, 1962, 774. P.M. Synge *Gardens of Britain* v. 1, 1977, 91–92.

Cardiff. Public Parks, S. Glamorgan
G.C. ii 1894, 11–12; i 1911, 234; i 1923, 118–19.

Cardiff Castle, S. Glamorgan
J. Hort. Cottage Gdnr v. 58, 1877, 252–54; N.S., v. 31, 1895, 280–81; N.S., v. 41, 1900, 224–25. G.C. ii 1882, 10–11; ii 1893, 295–97,305; i 1908, 349. *Gdnrs Mag.* 1899, 655–60. D. Stroud *Capability Brown* 1975, 179–80.

Cardigan House, Richmond, London
J.H. Pye *A peep into the principal seats and gardens in and about Twickenham* 1775, 8.

Carham Hall, Carham, Northumberland
J.P. Neale *Views* v. 3, 1820.

Carhouse Hall *see* Carbrook Hall

Carie, Fortingall, Perth, Tayside
I.H. Adams *Descriptive list of plans* v. 3, 1974, 109.

Carleton Hall, Carleton, Cumbria
W. Hutchinson *History of county of Cumberland* v. 1, 1794, 341–43.

Carlowrie near Kirkliston, Lothian
C. McWilliam *Lothian* 1978, 133.

Carlton Curlieu, Leics
J. Throsby *Select views in Leicestershire* v. 1, 1790, 192. J. Nichols *History . . . of county of Leicester* v. 2, 1798, 543. J.P. Neale *Views* 2nd Series, v. 3, 1826. G.M. v. 7, 1831, 424.

Carlton Hall, Ealing, London
G.M. v. 6, 1830, 669–70; v. 7, 1831, 551.

Carlton Hall, Leics
J. Nichols *History . . . of county of Leicester* v. 3, 1804, 1125.

Carlton House, East Carlton, Northants
J.P. Neale *Views* v. 3, 1820.

Carlton House, St James, Westminster, London
G.L. le Rouge *Jardins Anglo-Chinois a la mode* 6[e] cahier, 1777, pl. 30, W. Marshall *Planting and ornamental gardening* 1785, 576. T. Whately *Observations on modern gardening* 1801, pl. 3. British Museum *Catalogue of maps, prints* 1829, 203. G. Carter *et al. Humphry Repton* 1982, 157. K. Rorschach *Early Georgian landscape garden* 1983, 18–19,24–25.

Carlton Towers, Carlton, N. Yorks
Architectural History v. 22, 1979, 116–24. D. Jacques *Georgian gardens* 1983, 86,87.

Carlyle House, Chelsea, London
J. MacGregor *Gardens of celebrities and celebrated gardens in and around London* 1918, 255–70.

Carnanton near St Colomb, Cornwall
G.S. Gilbert *Historical survey of . . . Cornwall* v. 2, 1820, 661. F.O. Morris *Series of picturesque views* v. 4, 25.

Carne near Penzance, Cornwall
G.C. i 1898, 298.

Carnell, Hurlford, Strathclyde
Scottish Gdnr and Northern Forester v. 6, 1911, 633–34; v. 8, 1913, 480–81. G.A. Little *Scotland's gardens* 1981, 249–52. *Garden* 1982, 127–32.

Carnock near Stirling, Central
H. Maxwell *Scottish gardens* 1911, 140–43.

Carpenders Park, Watford, Herts
J.E. Cussans *History of Hertfordshire* v. 3, 1881, 183.

Carr Head near Skipton, N. Yorks
Florist 1858, 120–22. *Cottage Gdnr* v. 22, 1859, 359–60. *J. Hort. Cottage Gdnr* v. 32, 1864, 128–29.

Carrablagh, Portsalon, Co. Donegal, Eire
E. Malins *and* P. Bowe *Irish gardens and demesnes* 1980, 133.

Carrhouse Grange, Yorks
I. Hall *Samuel Buck's Yorkshire sketchbook* 1979, 114.

Carrog near Aberystwyth, Dyfed
C.L. v. 166, 1979, 1058–60.

Carron House, Central
J. Hort. Cottage Gdnr N.S., v. 13, 1886, 202–04.

Carrow Abbey, Carrow, Norfolk
C. Holme *Gardens of England in Midland & Eastern counties* 1908, pl. 22.

Carrow House, Carrow, Norfolk
C. Holme *Gardens of England in Midland & Eastern counties* 1908, pls. 23–24.

Carshalton House, Sutton, London
W. Watts *Seats* 1779, pl. 60. C.L. v. 105, 1949, 480–83, 1254–55. I. Nairn *and* B. Cherry *Surrey* 1971, 135. B. Jones *Follies & grottoes* 1974, 328. B. Cherry *and* N. Pevsner *London 2: South* 1983, 648.

Carshalton Park, Sutton, London
J. Hassell *Picturesque rides and walks* v. 1, 1817, 99–101.

C.L. v. 4, 1898, 549–50. *Architectural Review* v. 19, 1906, 3–15. B. Jones *Follies & grottoes* 1974, 328.

Carstairs near Lanark, Strathclyde
J.P. Neale *Views* 2nd Series, v. 1, 1824.

Carton near Maynooth, Co. Kildare, Eire
J.P. Neale *Views* 2nd Series, v. 2, 1825. J.N. Brewer *Beauties of Ireland* v. 2, 1826, 69,71–72. *J. Hort. Cottage Gdnr* v. 29, 1863, 115–18,130–32; v. 47, 1872, 405–07, 419–22; N.S., v. 32, 1896, 126–27; v. 33, 1896, 278–79. G.C. ii 1899, 181–82. *Gdnrs Mag.* 1909, 491–92. C.L. v. 80, 1936, 488–93. E. Malins *and* Knight of Glin *Lost demesnes* 1976, 9–10,56–60,66. J. Harris *Artist and the country house* 1979, 151,301. *Landscape Design* no. 131, 1980, 33–36. Knight of Glin *and* P. Bowe *Gardens of outstanding historic interest in . . . Ireland* 1980.

Casa di Sole, Salcombe, Devon
J. Royal Hort. Soc. 1968, 173–78.

Casewick near Stamford, Lincs
C.L. v. 136, 1964, 1762–66,1808–12.

Casina, Dulwich, Southwark, London
J. Hassell *Seats near London* 1804–05. D. Stroud *Humphry Repton* 1962, 105. G. Carter *et al. Humphry Repton* 1982, 162.

Cassiobury Park, Watford, Herts
J. Beeverell *Les delices de la Grand Bretagne* v. 5, 1707, 872. L. Knyff *and* J. Kip *Britannia illustrata* v. 1, 1714. S. Switzer *Ichnographia rustica* v. 1, 1742, 62. R. Havell *Series of picturesque views* 1816, pl. 10. J.P. Neale *Views* v. 2, 1819. J. Hassell *Tour of the Grand Junction* 1819, 19–25. Prince Pückler-Muskau *Tour in England, Ireland and France* 1833, 65–66. G.M. v. 12, 1836, 279–89. J. Britton *History . . . of Cassiobury Park* 1837, 26–27. J.C. Loudon *Arboretum et Fruticetum Britannicum* v. 1, 1844, 59. F.O. Morris *Series of picturesque views* v. 2, 73. L. Jewitt *and* S.C. Hall *Stately homes of England* 1874, 308–21. G.C. i 1886, 679–80. C.L. v. 28, 1910, 392–400. G. Jekyll *Garden ornament* 1918, 191. J. Evelyn *Diary* v. 4, 1955, 200. D. Stroud *Humphry Repton* 1962, 122–23. T. Wright *Arbours & grottos* 1979. M. Hadfield *et al. British gardeners* 1980, 78. G. Carter *et al. Humphry Repton* 1982, 154.

Castle, Castle Bellingham, Co. Louth, Eire
J.B. Burke *Visitation* 2nd Series, v. 1, 1855, 134.

Castle Ashby, Northants
Official guide. T. Pennant *Journey from Chester to London* 1782, pl. 17. J.P. Neale *Views* v. 3, 1820. G.C. 1871, 1324; ii 1889, 465; ii 1909, 49–50,51. *Garden* v. 19, 1881, 7–8. *Gdnrs Mag.* 4 June 1898 Suppl., i–x. C.L. v. 3, 1898, 16–19,48–50; v. 16, 1904, 666–75,702–11;

Castle Ashby (*Cont.*)

v. 60, 1926, 422–31. C. Holme *Gardens of England in Midland & Eastern counties* 1908, pls. 25–28. G. Jekyll *Garden ornament* 1918, 241,244. V.C.H. *Northampton* v. 4, 1937, 232. Lady Rockley *Historic gardens of England* 1938, 180–81. J. Evelyn *Diary* v. 4, 1955, 593–94. M. Allan *Fisons guide* 1970, 152–53. B. Jones *Follies & grottoes* 1974, 190,192. D. Stroud *Capability Brown* 1975, 107–09,219. J. Anthony *Gardens of Britain* v. 6, 1979, 38–43. M. Binney *and* A. Hills *Elysian gardens* 1979, 15,37.

Castle Blayney, Co. Monaghan, Ulster
E. Malins *and* P. Bowe *Irish gardens and demesnes* 1980, 23.

Castle Bromwich Hall near Birmingham, W. Midlands
W. Dugdale *Antiquities of Warwickshire* v. 2, 1730, 887. C.L. v. 8, 1900, 144–51; v. 32, 1912, 228–35; v. 111, 1952, 1408–11.

Castle Caldwell near Belleek, Co. Fermanagh, Ulster
E. Malins *and* Knight of Glin *Lost demesnes* 1976, 79.

Castle Combe, Wilts
E.A. Brooke *Gardens of England* 1857, pl. 42. *Florist* 1857, 291–93. C.L. v. 7, 1900, 560–64.

Castle Coole near Enniskillen, Co. Fermanagh, Ulster
G.M. v. 12, 1836, 109–11. F.O. Morris *Series of picturesque views* v. 4, 45. C.L. v. 80, 1936, 654–57,682. E. Malins *and* Knight of Glin *Lost demesnes* 1976, 79–80. *National Trust Studies* 1981, 10–11. Ulster Architectural Heritage Society *Northern gardens* 1982, 14.

Castle Dobbs near Carrickfergus, Co. Antrim, Ulster
Ulster Architectural Heritage Society *Northern gardens* 1982, 15.

Castle Drogo, Drewsteignton, Devon
Garden 1975, 426–29. P.M. Synge *Gardens of Britain* v. 1, 1977, 29–30. G.S. Thomas *Gardens of National Trust* 1979, 111–12. G.C. v. 192 no. 10, 1982, 21–25. J. Brown *Gardens of a golden afternoon* 1982, 171.

Castle Eden, Co. Durham
C. Holme *Gardens of England in Northern counties* 1911, pls. 30–31.

Castle Farm, Ilchester, Somerset
B. Jones *Follies & grottoes* 1974, 385.

Castle Forbes near Whitehouse, Grampian
F.O. Morris *Series of picturesque views* v. 5, 61.

Castle Forbes near Longford, Co. Longford, Eire
Bulletin of Royal Hort. & Arboricultural Soc. of Ireland no. 22, 1945, 346–48.

Castle Fraser near Monymusk, Grampian
C.L. v. 164, 1978, 442–45.

Castle Freke near Clonakilty, Co. Cork, Eire
J.P. Neale *Views* v. 6, 1823.

Castle Grant near Grantown, Highland
A.A. Tait *Landscape garden in Scotland* 1980, passim.

Castle Hill near South Molton, Devon
W. Watts *Seats* 1779, pl. 74. J. Britton *and* E.W. Brayley *Devonshire & Cornwall* 1832, 80. F.O. Morris *Series of picturesque views* v. 6, 35. G.C. ii 1884, 651–52. C.L. v. 75, 1934, 272–77; v. 84, 1938, 426–30; v. 165, 1979, 18–21. Lady Rockley *Historic gardens of England* 1938, 168–69. N. Pevsner *North Devon* 1952, 68. P.M. Synge *Gardens of Britain* v. 1, 1977, 31–33. J. Harris *Artist and the country house* 1979, 180–81,230.

Castle Hill, Duntish, Dorset
J. Hutchins *History . . . of Dorset* v. 3, 1868, 708.

Castle Hill, Ealing, London
H. Repton *Sketches* 1794, 39–40. D. Stroud *Humphry Repton* 1962, 166. G. Carter *et al. Humphry Repton* 1982, 157.

Castle Hill, Englefield Green, Surrey
G.C. ii 1891, 191–92.

Castle Hill (Dunimarle) near Culross Abbey, Fife
G.M. v. 18, 1842, 592.

Castle House, Deddington, Oxfordshire
C.L. v. 23, 1908, 906–14.

Castle Howard near Malton, N. Yorks
Official guide. C. Campbell *Vitruvius Britannicus* v. 3, 1725, 5–6. Society of Gentlemen *England displayed* v. 2, 1769, 144,147. N. Spencer *Complete English traveller* 1771, 520. A. Young *Six months tour through North of England* v. 2, 1771, 60–62. C. Burlington *Modern universal British traveller* 1779, 574. W. Angus *Seats* 1787, pl. 3. *Copper Plate Mag.* v. 5, pl. 135. Duke of Rutland *Journal of a tour to the northern parts of Great Britain* 1813, 101–07. *Jones's views* 1829, 3–5. British Museum *Catalogue of maps, prints* 1829, 62. G.M. v. 11, 1835, 17–19. E.A. Brooke *Gardens of England* 1857, pls. 33–34. H. Smithson *Illustrated handbook to Castle Howard* 1857. *J. Hort. Cottage Gdnr* v. 44, 1870, 352–54, 372–73. F.O. Morris *Series of picturesque views* v. 1, 11. L. Jewitt *and* S.C. Hall *Stately homes of England* 1877,

Castle Howard (*Cont.*)

74–92. G.C. ii 1890, 321–22. C.L. v. 16, 1904, 486–95; v. 20, 1906, 492–94; v. 61, 1927, 884–93, 1022–30; v. 62, 1927, 200–08, 230–37; v. 156, 1974, 694; v. 173, 1983, 636. C. Holme *Gardens of England in Northern counties* 1911, pls. 32–35. G. Jekyll *Garden ornament* 1918, 121. H. Walpole *Visits to country seats. Walpole Society* v. 7, 1927–28, 72, 73. H.F. Clark *English landscape garden* 1948, 39–40. L. Whistler *Imagination of Vanbrugh and his fellow artists* 1954, 28–31, 62–82. N. Pevsner *Yorkshire: the North Riding* 1966, 114–18. C. Hussey *English gardens and landscapes* 1967, 114–31. *Publications of Bedfordshire Historical Record Soc.* v. 47, 1968, 130–31. M. Allan *Fisons guide* 1970, 245–46. H. Evans *Beautiful gardens of Britain* 1947, 111–12. B. Jones *Follies & grottoes* 1974, 26–29. K. Lemmon *Gardens of Britain* v. 5, 1978, 59–64. L. Fleming *and* A. Gore *English garden* 1979, 87, 89, 90, 91. J. Harris *Artist and the country house* 1979, 288, 338. *Landscape Research* v. 7 no. 1, 1982, 19.

Castle Howard near Rathdrum, Co. Wicklow, Eire
J.P. Neale *Views* v. 6, 1823. E. Malins *and* Knight of Glin *Lost demesnes* 1976, 172, 174, 175.

Castle Huntly near Dundee, Tayside
J.P. Neale *Views* v. 6, 1823.

Castle Inn Tea Gardens, Islington, London
W. Wroth *London pleasure gardens of the eighteenth century* 1896, 147.

Castle Kennedy near Stranraer, Dumfries and Galloway
Scottish Gdnr v. 13, 1864, 55–56. G.C. 1873, 327–28, 329; i 1883, 14, 15; ii 1922, 298; v. 189 no. 4, 1981, 16–17, 20. *J. Hort. Cottage Gdnr* v. 56, 1876, 122–24, 163–64. H. Maxwell *Scottish gardens* 1911, 65–72. C.L. v. 150, 1971, 384–86. A. Hellyer *Gardens of genius* 1980, 195–96. A.A. Tait *Landscape garden in Scotland* 1980, passim. G.A. Little *Scotland's gardens* 1981, 261–62.

Castle Levan near Gourock, Strathclyde
G.C. ii 1892, 467, 468.

Castle MacGarrett near Claremorris, Co. Mayo, Eire
F.O. Morris *Series of picturesque views* v. 6, 71.

Castle Menzies near Aberfeldy, Tayside
J.P. Neale *Views* 2nd Series, v. 2, 1825.

Castle of Mey near Thurso, Highland
G.A. Little *Scotland's gardens* 1981, 225–28.
G. Plumptre *Royal gardens* 1981, 208–20.

Castle Mona, Douglas, Isle of Man
Proc. Isle of Man Natural History and Antiquarian Soc. v. 8 no. 3, 1976–78, 261–64.

Castle Richard near Lismore, Co. Waterford, Eire
J.P. Neale *Views* v. 6, 1823.

Castle Semple near Lochwinnoch, Strathclyde
G.M. v. 6, 1830, 702–04; v. 9, 1833, 11.

Castle Stewart near Newton Stewart, Dumfries and Galloway
G.M. v. 15, 1839, 628.

Castle Toward near Rothesay, Strathclyde
J.P. Neale *Views* v. 6, 1823. *Scottish Gdnr* v. 3, 1854, 362–64.

Castle Ward, Downpatrick, Co. Down, Ulster
J.C. Loudon *Arboretum et fruticetum Britannicum* v. 1, 1844, 112–13. J. Stevenson *Two centuries of life in Down* 1920, 447–49. C.L. v. 130, 1961, 1260–63. E. Malins *and* Knight of Glin *Lost demesnes* 1976, 111, 112. J. Harris *Artist and the country house* 1979, 302–05. G.S. Thomas *Gardens of National Trust* 1979, 112–13. Ulster Architectural Heritage Society *Northern gardens* 1982, 10, 15.

Castleboro near Enniscorthy, Co. Wexford, Eire
G.C. ii 1894, 65–66. *Gdning World* v. 15, 1899, 297. E. Malins *and* P. Bowe *Irish gardens and demesnes* 1980, 27.

Castlecor near Mallow, Co. Cork, Eire
J.P. Neale *Views* v. 6, 1823.

Castledykes near Dumfries, Dumfries and Galloway
G.M. v. 9, 1833, 11–12.

Castlegar near Galway, Co. Galway, Eire
J.P. Neale *Views* v. 6, 1823.

Castlehill, Kirkmahoe, Dumfries and Galloway
G.A. Little *Scotland's gardens* 1981, 252.

Castlemilk near Lockerbie, Dumfries and Galloway
Scottish Gdnr and Northern Forester v. 7, 1912, 417–18. *J. Hort. Home Farmer* N.S., v. 67, 1913, 556–58. C.L. v. 162, 1977, 350–53.

Castleroy, Broughty Ferry, Tayside
G.C. i 1897, 315–16.

Castletown (Lord's Gardens), Isle of Man
Proc. Isle of Man Natural History and Antiquarian Society v. 8 no. 3, 1976–78, 249–51, 264–65.

Castletown, Celbridge, Co. Kildare, Eire
C.L. v. 80, 1936, 170–75; v. 145, 1969, 798–802,882–85. B. Jones *Follies & grottoes* 1974, 220. E. Malins *and* Knight of Glin *Lost demesnes* 1976, 53–60. J. Harris *Artist and the country house* 1979, 284. Knight of Glin *and* P. Bowe *Gardens of outstanding historic interest in . . . Ireland* 1980.

Castletown near Carrick on Suir, Co. Kilkenny, Eire
C.L. v. 44, 1918, 190–95,214.

Castlewellan near Newcastle, Co. Down, Ulster
List of plants hardy in the garden 1890 etc. *G.C.* i 1891, 639–40,641,647; ii 1896, 683–85,720–22; i 1902, 46; i 1917, 17; ii 1962, 131. *Garden* v. 48, 1895, 257–58,268. *C.L.* v. 7, 1900, 272–76. Earl Annesley *Beautiful and rare trees & plants* 1903. *Flora and Sylva* v. 2, 1904, 210–14. *Irish Gdning* v. 1, 1906, 148–49,168–69,187; v. 2, 1907, 101,121; v. 7, 1912, 113–17. Royal Hort. Soc. *Conifers in cultivation* 1932, 214. *J. Royal Hort. Soc.* 1961, 201–11. E. Hyams *Irish gardens* 1967, 135–43. M. Allan *Fisons guide* 1970, 352–53. *Plant list of trees and shrubs* c.1975. E. Malins *and* P. Bowe *Irish gardens and demesnes* 1980, 64–69. Ulster Architectural Heritage Society *Northern gardens* 1982, 17.

Catchfrench near Liskeard, Cornwall
D. Stroud *Humphry Repton* 1962, 77. G. Carter *et al. Humphry Repton* 1982, 150.

Catesby, Northants
Royal Commission on Historical Monuments *Inventory of the historical monuments in . . . Northampton* 1981, 40–41.

Catton Hall, Norwich, Norfolk
C.L. v. 127, 1960, 566–69,624. D. Stroud *Humphry Repton* 1962, 36. G. Carter *et al. Humphry Repton* 1982, 15,101,158.

Cauldhame, Dunblane, Central
G.A. Little *Scotland's gardens* 1981, 129.

Caunton Manor, Caunton, Notts
C.L. v. 6, 1899, 491–93,618–20.

Cave, Humberside
A. Young *Six months tour through North of England* v. 1, 1771, 150–51.

Caversham Court, Reading, Berks
T. Jefferson *Garden book 1766–1824* 1944, 112. *Gdn History* v. 4 no. 2, 1976, 10–13.

Caversham Park, Reading, Berks
C. Campbell *Vitruvius Britannicus* v. 3, 1725, 96–97. *Copper Plate Mag.* v. 1, 1792, pl. 29. W. Woollett *Observations on modern gardening* 1801, 78–80. J.P. Neale *Views* 2nd Series, v. 1, 1824. *G.M.* v. 10, 1834, 1–3. D. Stroud *Capability Brown* 1975, 132–33, 219.

Caverswall Castle, Staffs
R. Plot *Natural History of Staffordshire* 1685, 448. *C.L.* v. 29, 1911, 886–95.

Cawdor Castle, Nairn, Highland
G.M. v. 15, 1839, 628. *Garden* v. 50, 1896, 5. *C.L.* v. 20, 1906, 942–50; v. 97, 1945, 863. H. Maxwell *Scottish gardens* 1911, 108–15. G.A. Little *Scotland's gardens* 1981, 180.

Cawkeld, Kilnwick, Humberside
K. Lemmon *Gardens of Britain* v. 5, 1978, 37.

Cedar Lodge, Puckpool, Isle of Wight
A. Paterson *Gardens of Britain* v. 2, 1978, 160–61. *C.L.* v. 175, 1984, 462–63.

Cedar Mount, Dundrum, Co. Dublin, Eire
Bulletin of Royal Hort. & Arboricultural Soc. of Ireland no. 8, 1938, 130.

Cedars, Harrow Weald, Harrow, London
G.C. ii 1890, 136–37; ii 1892, 105; ii 1896, 186–87.

Cedars, Isleworth, London
W. Keane *Beauties of Middlesex* 1850, 92–93.

Cedars, Lee, Lewisham, London
E. Hasted *History . . . of Kent* part 1 revised 1886, 225.

Cefn Mabley near Cardiff, S. Glamorgan
C.L. v. 24, 1908, 738–44.

Cefn-On, Cardiff, S. Glamorgan
G.C. v. 160 no. 13, 1966, 10–11.

Cefnaes Hall, Rhayader, Powys
G. Beard *Thomas H. Mawson* 1976, 48.

Cerney House, North Cerney, Glos
J.N. Brewer *Delineations of Gloucestershire* 1825, 97.

Chaddlewood near Plymouth, Devon
G.C. i 1901, 70–71,73,81; ii 1902, 458–59. C. Holme *Gardens of England in Southern & Western counties* 1907, pls. 36–37.

Chadderton Hall, Chadderton, Greater Manchester
J. Aikin *Description of the country . . . round Manchester* 1795, 241.

Chalfont House, Chalfont St Peter, Bucks
W. Angus *Seats* 1787, pl. 34. J.C. Loudon *Encyclopaedia of gardening* 1822, 1233. *G.C.* ii 1882, 714,721; i 1883, 116,117. *Gdning World* v. 2, 1896, 824–25. G. Carter *et al. Humphry Repton* 1982, 148.

Chalford House *see* Shalford House

Champfleurie House, Linlithgow, Lothian
I.H. Adams *Descriptive list of plans* v. 3, 1974, 135.

Champions Manor, Woodham Ferrers, Essex
F.G. Emmison *Catalogue of maps in Essex Record Office* 1947, 20.

Chandos Lodge, Eye, Suffolk
A. Lees-Milne *and* R. Verey *Englishmen's garden* 1982, 20–24.

Chantmarle near Cattistock, Dorset
C.L. v. 21, 1907, 344–48; v. 107, 1950, 1966–71.

Chantry, Whatley, Somerset
C.L. v. 129, 1961, 1266–67.

Chantry. 100 Acres, Hants
A. Paterson *Gardens of Britain* v. 2, 1978, 66–67.

Chantry Sproughton *see* Sproughton Chantry

Chapel, Kingskettle, Fife
Scottish Gdnr and Northern Forester v. 6, 1911, 729–31.

Chapel Allerton (Richard Anthony Salisbury) near Leeds, W. Yorks
R.A. Salisbury *Chapel Allerton* 1796.

Chapel Farm, Amersham, Bucks
C.L. v. 57, 1925, 908–15.

Charborough Park, Morden, Dorset
J.B. Burke *visitation* v. 2, 1853, 166. J. Hutchins *History . . . of Dorset* v. 3, 1868, 497. *C.L.* v. 77, 1935, 322–27. Royal Commission on Historical Monuments *Inventory of historical monuments in . . . Dorset* v. 1, 1970, 164. J. Newman *and* N. Pevsner *Dorset* 1972, 140–41. B. Jones *Follies & grottoes* 1974, 317. J. Harris *Artist and the country house* 1979, 210.

Charlecote Park near Stratford-on-Avon, Warwickshire
Official guide. W. Dugdale *Antiquities of Warwickshire* v. 1, 1730, 507. J.P. Neale *Views* v. 4, 1821. F.O. Morris *Series of picturesque views* v. 1, 61. *J. Hort. Cottage Gdnr* v. 50, 1873, 355–57. *C.L.* v. 1, 1897, 46–47,78–79; v. 35, 1914, 126–35; v. 111, 1952, 1080–83,1328–31. Historical MSS Commission *Architectural history* v. 2, 1970, items 1179,1241,1351. H. Evans *Beautiful gardens of Britain* 1974, 85–86. D. Stroud *Capability Brown* 1975, 56–57. M. Binney *and* A. Hills *Elysian gardens* 1979, 36. J. Harris *Artist and the country house* 1979, 144. G.S. Thomas *Gardens of National Trust* 1979, 113–14. R. Sidwell *West Midland gardens* 1981, 205–06.

Charles Hill Court, Tilford, Surrey
C.L. v. 123, 1958, 164–65.

Charleston Manor, Seaford, E. Sussex
C.L. v. 131, 1962, 1286–88; v. 160, 1976, 350–53. M. Allan *Fisons guide* 1970, 37–38. T. Wright *Gardens of Britain* v. 4, 1978, 124–30.

Charleville Forest, Co. Offaly, Eire
E. Malins *and* Knight of Glin *Lost demesnes* 1976, 87–89.

Charlton House, Greenwich, London
P. Sandby *Collection of one hundred and fifty select views* v. 1, 1781, pl. 25. T. Pennant *Journey from London to Isle of Wight* v. 1, 1801, 35. J.P. Neale *Views* 2nd Series, v. 4, 1828. C. Greenwood *Epitome of county history . . . v. 1: Kent* 1838, 17. *G.M.* v. 16, 1840, 582–83. *J. Hort. Cottage Gdnr* N.S., v. 10, 1885, 10–12. *C.L.* v. 1, 1897, 323–25; v. 25, 1909, 630–38,676. G. Jekyll *Garden ornament* 1918, 210.

Charlton Kings, Cheltenham, Glos
R. Bigland *Historical . . . collections . . . of Gloucester* v. 1, 1791, 300.

Charlton Park, Cheltenham, Glos
J. Harris *Gardens of delight* 1978, 8–9.

Charlton Park near Malmesbury, Wilts
W. Watts *Seats* 1779, pl. 45. *C.L.* v. 74, 1933, 388–94. D. Stroud *Capability Brown* 1975, 95–96. J. Harris *Artist and the country house* 1979, 339.

Charlwood House, Huyton, Liverpool, Merseyside
J. Hort. Cottage Gdnr N.S., v. 1, 1880, 526.

Chart Sutton near Maidstone, Kent
J. Harris *History of Kent* 1719, 69. J. Kip *Supplement du Nouveau theatre de la Grande Bretagne* 1728, pl. 15. T. Badeslade *Thirty six different views . . . of Kent* 1750s, pl. 6.

Charterhouse, Finsbury, London
C.L. v. 166, 1979, 746–48.

Charterhouse Square *see* London

Chartley near Stafford, Staffs
R. Plot *Natural history of Staffordshire* 1685, 93.

Chartwell, Westerham, Kent
C.L. v. 137, 1965, 169–72. *G.C.* v. 60 no. 2, 1966, 18–19. M. Allen *Fisons guide* 1970, 38–39. H. Evans *Beautiful gardens of Britain* 1974, 75–76. T. Wright *Gardens of Britain* v. 4, 1978, 26–28. G.S. Thomas *Gardens of National Trust* 1979, 114.

Chase Side, Enfield, London
W. Keane *Beauties of Middlesex* 1850, 185–86.

Chastleton House near Chipping Norton, Oxfordshire
C.L. v. 12, 1902, 80–89; v. 45, 1919, 90–96,116–23. H.I. Triggs *Formal gardens in England and Scotland* 1902, 17. G. Jekyll *Garden ornament* 1918, 231,279. Lady Rockley *Historic gardens of England* 1938, 230–31. R. Bisgrove *Gardens of Britain* v. 3, 1978, 55.

Chatelherault, Hamilton, Strathclyde
A.A. Tait *Landscape garden in Scotland* 1980, passim.

Chatsworth near Bakewell, Derbyshire
Official guide. J. Beeverell *Les delices de la Grande Bretagne* v. 5, 1707, 872. L. Knyff *and* J. Kip *Britannia illustrata* v. 1, 1714. N. Spenser *Complete English traveller* 1771, 499. W. Stukeley *Itinerarium curiosum* v. 1, 1776, 55–56. D. Defoe *Tour* v. 2, 1778, 582–84. C. Burlington *Modern universal British traveller* 1779, 107. W. Watts *Seats* 1779, pl. 81. P. Sandby *Collection of one hundred and fifty select views* v. 1, 1781, pl. 11. W. Bray *Sketch of a tour* 1783, 169–73. R.J. Sulivan *Tour* v. 2, 1785, 91–92. S. Shaw *Tour* 1788, 35. L. Simond *Journal* v. 2, 1815, 84–85. D. *and* S. Lysons *Magna Britannia v. 5: Derbyshire* 1817, 154. J.P. Neale *Views* v. 1, 1818. *G.M.* v. 7, 1831, 395–97, 404; v. 11, 1835, 385–95; v. 15, 1839, 450–53; v. 16, 1840, 103,229–30,275,572–79; v. 17, 1841, 40–41,42,45, 92,333–34; v. 18, 1842, 331. S. Glover *History and gazetteer of . . . Derby* v. 2, 1833, 272. *Journey-book of England* 1841, 96–98. Duke of Devonshire *Handbook of Chatsworth and Hardwick* 1844. C.G. Carus *King of Saxony's journey through England and Scotland* 1846, 162–63. W. Adam *Gem of the Peak* 1851, 165–84. J.B. Burke *Visitation* 2nd Series, v. 1, 1855, 9–10. *Cottage Gdnr* v. 17, 1857, 426–27; v. 18, 1857, 5–6, 25–26. *G.C.* 1873, 1175–76,1238–41; i 1875, 816–17,26 June 1875 8p.; ii 1883, 176,177; ii 1887, 251,253–54; ii 1891, 759; i 1908, 205; i 1920, 119; ii 1933, 3,6,7,8–10, 11; i 1937, 136; ii 1964, 400–01. *J. Hort. Cottage Gdnr* v. 34, 1865, 377–78; v. 44, 1870, 432–34; v. 51, 1874, 125–26,148–50; N.S., v. 27, 1893, 80–82; N.S., v. 58, 1909, 185–91. *Garden* v. 5, 1874, 5–7,26–27; v. 59, 1901, 65–67; 1913, 610–11. F.O. Morris *Series of picturesque views* v. 1, 49. L. Jewitt *and* S.C. Hall *Stately homes of England* 1874, 322–96. *Gdning World* v. 2, 1886, 1822. *C.L.* v. 7, 1900, 800–05,832–38; v. 43, 1918, 12–20, 60–66; v. 111, 1952, 914–15; v. 143, 1968, 890–93,958, 1113; v. 144, 1968, 146–49,220–23,552–55; v. 154, 1973, 1250–52; v. 166, 1979, 2151. *Gdnrs Mag.* 1901, 804–08. C. Holme *Gardens of England in Midland & Eastern counties* 1908, pls. 29–34. M. Macartney *English houses & gardens* 1908, pl. 34. H. Walpole *Visits to country seats. Walpole Society* v. 7, 1927–28, 28,65. Viscount Torrington *Diaries* v. 2, 37–39. V. Markham *Paxton and the batchelor Duke* 1935. Lady Rockley *Historic gardens of England* 1938, 146–47. C. Fiennes *Journeys* 1949, 97–98. F. Thompson *Chatsworth* 1951, 108–24. D. Green *Gardener to Queen Anne* 1956, 33–38. *Architectural History* v. 4, 1961, 77–91; v. 6, 1963, 106–09. G.F. Chadwick *Works of Sir Joseph Paxton* 1961, 22–43. P. Coats *Great gardens* 1963, 126–35. *Park Administration* May 1965, 51–55. *Morris Arboretum Bulletin* v. 19 no. 1, 1968, 8–13. M. Allan *Fisons guide* 1970, 219–20. Historical MSS Commission *Architectural history* v. 3, 1971, item 3268. *Apollo* v. 100, 1974, 127,133. H. Evans *Beautiful gardens of Britain* 1974, 97–98. B. Jones *Follies & grottoes* 1974, 308. D. Stroud *Capability Brown* 1975, 104–05,219. D. Jarrett *English landscape garden* 1978, 80–89. N. Pevsner *Derbyshire* 1978, 138–39. J. Anthony *Gardens of Britain* v. 6, 1979, 44–55. L. Fleming *and* A. Gore *English garden* 1979, 193–94. J. Harris *Artist and the country house* 1979, 75,268. M. Hadfield *et al. British gardeners* 1980, 100–01. A. Hellyer *Gardens of genius* 1980, 181–85. H. Nichols *Local maps of Derbyshire to 1770* 1980, 39. *Landscape Research* v. 7 no. 1, 1982, 24–26. T. Hinde *Stately gardens of Britain* 1983, 70–77. *Garden* 1983, 471–74. *Landscape Design* no. 146, 1983, 8.

Chatt House, Burton Pidsea, Humberside
K. Lemmon *Gardens of Britain* v. 5, 1978, 38–39.

Chavenage (Chevenage) **House** near Tetbury, Glos
J.N. Brewer *Delineations of Gloucestershire* 1825, 157. *C.L.* v. 29, 1911, 524–31.

Chawton House, Alton, Hants
E.F. Prosser *Select illustrations of Hampshire* 1833. *C.L.* v. 13, 1903, 874–81; v. 97, 1945, 244–47.

Cheadle. Bruntwood Park, Greater Manchester
G. Chadwick *Park and the town* 1966, 326–28.

Cheam, Sutton, London
W. Keane *Beauties of Surrey* 1849, 92–93.

Checkendon Court, Checkendon, Oxfordshire
C.L. v. 50, 1921, 754–56. *Garden* 1921, 576–78. R. Bisgrove *Gardens of Britain* v. 3, 1978, 55–56.

Cheddington Court near Beaminster, Dorset
A. Paterson *Gardens of Britain* v. 2, 1978, 25.

Cheesburn Grange near Newcastle upon Tyne, Tyne and Wear
L. Wilkes *John Dobson* 1980, passim. D. Jacques *Georgian gardens* 1983, 172.

Chelsea. Physic Garden, London
P. Miller *Catalogus plantarum officinalium* 1730. I. Rand *Index plantarum officinalium* 1730. D. Lysons *Environs* v. 2, 1795, 166–68. J.L. Wheeler *Catalogus rationalis plantarum medicinalium* 1830. *Cottage Gdnr* v. 5, 1850, 158–59. W. Keane *Beauties of Middlesex* 1850, 233–36. H. Field *Memoirs of the Botanic Garden at Chelsea* 1878. *G.C.* ii 1886, 336–37; ii 1890, 67,71,74; ii 1900, 147,150; ii 1910, 243–44,245; i 1912, 327–29; i 1964, 574–75. *Garden* v. 62, 79–80; 1924, 516–17. P.E.F. Perrédès *London botanic gardens* 1906, 48–99. G.L.C. *Survey of London v. 2: Chelsea* pt. 1, 1909, 15–22. *Gdnrs Mag.* 1913, 597–99,600. J. MacGregor *Gardens of celebrities . . . in and around London* 1918, 114–38. F.D. Drewitt *Romance of the Apothecaries' Garden at Chelsea* Ed. 3, 1928. *J. Royal Hort. Soc.* 1940, 8–12; 1975, 234–37. *Connoisseur* v. 111, 1943, 96–101. G. Taylor *Old London gardens* 1953, 127–36. J. Evelyn *Diary* 1955, v. 3, 217; v. 4, 462. *C.L.* v. 122, 1957, 1372–73; v. 163, 1978, 14–15. *Medical History* v. 5 no. 2, 1961, 154–56. Earl of Morton *Chelsea Physic Garden* 1965. *Trans. Botanical Soc. of Edinburgh* v. 41, 1972, 293–307. *Parks and Recreation* August 1973, 32–34. *Bulletin University of London* no. 29, 1975, 1–4. *Gdn History* v. 3 no. 2, 1975, 68–73; v. 9 no. 1, 1981, 55–56.

Chelsea. Royal Hospital, London
J. Beeverell *Les delices de la Grande Bretagne* v. 4, 1707, 853. H. Overton *Britannia illustrata* c.1724, pls. 31–32. *G.C.* i 1911, 154–55. *Gdnrs Mag.* 1911, 591; 1912 18 May, Supplement, 6–8. C.G.T. Dean *Royal Hospital, Chelsea* 1950. G. Taylor *Old London gardens* 1953, 122–27. *C.L.* v. 172, 1982, 1477.

Chelsea House, London
J. Beeverell *Les delices de la Grande Bretagne* v. 5, 1707, 872.

Chelsfield Rectory, Chelsfield, Kent
C. Greenwood *Epitome of county history . . . v. 1: Kent* 1838, 61.

Chelvey Court near Clevedon, Avon
C.L. v. 27, 1910, 738–44.

Chelwood Manor, E. Sussex
G. Beard *Thomas H. Mawson* 1976, 49.

Chequers, Boxford, Suffolk
J. Royal Hort. Soc. 1968, 376–84. A. Lees-Milne *and* R. Verey *Englishwoman's garden* 1980, 113–15.

Chequers Court near Princes Risborough, Bucks
G.C. ii 1906, 285–86. *C.L.* v. 28, 1910, 970–81; v. 42, 1917, 324–33,372–79. B. Jones *Follies & grottoes* 1974, 293.

Cherkley Court, Leatherhead, Surrey
G.C. i 1885, 755–56,757,765. *C.L.* v. 7, 1900, 528–31.

Chertsey Abbey, Chertsey, Surrey
E.W. Brayley *and* J. Britton *Topographical history of Surrey* v. 2, 1841, 184.

Chesfield, Hampton Wick, London
G.C. i 1905, 396–97.

Cheshunt Cottage, Cheshunt, Herts
G.M. v. 15, 1839, 633–74.

Chester-le-Street. Deanery Garden, Co. Durham
Historical MSS Commission *Architectural history* v. 4, 1972, item 3861.

Chesterford Park, Little Chesterford, Essex
F.G. Emmison *Catalogue of maps in Essex Record Office* 2nd Supplt, 1964, 33.

Chesterholme Cottage, Northumberland
G.M. v. 13, 1837, 161–66.

Chesters, Humshaugh, Northumberland
C.L. v. 31, 1912, 244–48.

Chestham Park near Henfield, W. Sussex
R. Webber *Percy Cane* 1975, 103–05,185.

Chestnut Wilderness, Chiddingstone, Kent
F. Hull *Catalogue of estate maps 1590 to 1840 in the Kent County Archives Office* 1973, 73.

Chestnuts, Denmark Hill, Camberwell, London
G.C. ii 1889, 687–88.

Chettle House near Farnham, Dorset
C.L. v. 64, 1928, 466–72.

Cheveley Park near Newmarket, Cambs
L. Fleming *and* A. Gore *English garden* 1979, pl. 23. J. Harris *Artist and the country house* 1979, 70–71.

Chevenage *see* Chavenage

Chevening near Sevenoaks, Kent
J. Harris *History of Kent* 1719, 74. J. Kip *Supplement du*

Chevening (*Cont.*)

Nouveau theatre de la Grande Bretagne 1728, pl. 1.
T. Badeslade *Thirty-six different views . . . of Kent* 1750s, pl. 8. R. Ackermann *Repository* v. 12, 1828, pl. 31. G. Virtue *Picturesque beauties of Great Britain: Kent* 1829, 103. W.W.J. Gendall *Views* v. 1, 1830, 123. W.H. Ireland *History . . . of Kent* v. 4, 1830, 579. G.C. ii 1880, 390–91. M. Macartney *English houses & gardens* 1908, pl. 18. C.L. v. 47, 1920, 512–20,586–93; v. 143, 1968, 102–04; v. 166, 1979, 850–52. R. Dutton *English garden* 1937, pl. 52. F. Hull *Catalogue of estate maps, 1590 to 1840 in the Kent County Archives Office* 1973, 85. M. Binney *and* A. Hills *Elysian gardens* 1979, 19.

Chevet Park near Wakefield, W. Yorks
C. Holme *Gardens of England in Northern counties* 1911, pl. 36.

Chevithorne Barton, Devon
G.C. i 1956, 716–17. C.L. v. 127, 1960, 757–61. *J. Royal Hort. Soc.* 1965, 344–53.

Chew Court, Chew Magna, Avon
J. Leland *Itinerary* 1964, v. 1, 294; v. 5, 103.

Chewton Glen, Hants
J. Hort N.S., v. 68, 1914, 559–62.

Chicheley Hall, Newport Pagnell, Bucks
J.B. Burke *Visitation* v. 1, 1852, 94. C.L. v. 17, 1905, 594–602; v. 79, 1936, 482–88,508; v. 157, 1975, 434–37. R. Bisgrove *Gardens of Britain* v. 3, 1978, 56–57.

Chicksands Priory near Ampthill, Beds
S. *and* N. Buck *Buck's antiquities* v. 1, 1774, pl. 2. W. Watts *Seats* 1779, pl. 25.

Chidmere House, Chidham, W. Sussex
Sussex Life v. 4 no. 6, 1968, 28–29. C.L. v. 168, 1980, 1400–04.

Chiefswood, Melrose, Borders
G.A. Little *Scotland's gardens* 1981, 81.

Childwall Hall, Liverpool, Merseyside
J.P. Neale *Views* 2nd Series, v. 2, 1825.

Chilham Castle near Canterbury, Kent
Official guide. W. Watts *Seats* 1779, pl. 72. E. Hasted *History . . . of Kent* v. 3, 1790, 131. J.P. Neale *Views* 2nd Series, v. 2, 1825. C. Greenwood *Epitome of county history . . . v. 1: Kent* 1838, 300. G.C. i 1894, 525–26; ii 1964, 121–22. C.L. v. 5, 1899, 368–71; v. 32, 1912, 126–33; v. 54, 1924, 812–18. Lady Rockley *Historic gardens of England* 1938, 102–03. M. Allan *Fisons guide* 1970, 39–40. H. Evans *Beautiful gardens of Britain* 1974, 73–74. D. Stroud *Capability Brown* 1975, 219–20. T. Wright *Gardens of Britain* v. 4, 1978, 28–30.

Chipstead Place

Chilland near Winchester, Hants
A. Paterson *Gardens of Britain* v. 2, 1978, 68–69. C.L. v. 172, 1982, 26–28.

Chillingham Castle, Chillingham, Northumberland
Garden v. 2, 1872, 462; v. 48, 1895, 335–36. F.O. Morris *Series of picturesque views* v. 6, 33. *J. Hort. Cottage Gdnr* N.S., v. 17, 1888, 314–16; N.S., v. 35, 1897, 403. C.L. v. 33, 1913, 346–55.

Chillington Hall near Wolverhampton, W. Midlands
W. Pitt *General view of agriculture of . . . Stafford* 1796, 93. F. Calvert *Picturesque views* 1830, 112. V.C.H. *Stafford* v. 5, 1959, 29. C.L. v. 103, 1948, 326–29,426. Historical MSS Commission *Architectural history* v. 3, 1971, item 2604. N. Pevsner *Staffordshire* 1974, 103. D. Stroud *Capability Brown* 1975, 147–48. R. Sidwell *West Midland gardens* 1981, 164–65.

Chilston Park, Boughton Malherbe, Kent
J. Harris *History of Kent* 1719, 48. T. Badeslade *Thirty six different views . . . in Kent* 1750s, pl. 9. E. Hasted *History . . . of Kent* v. 2, 1782, 435. C. Greenwood *Epitome of county history . . . v. 1: Kent* 1838, 156. C.L. v. 112, 1952, 2030–33; v. 155, 1974, 1680. F. Hull *Catalogue of estate maps 1590 to 1840 in the Kent County Archives Office* 1973, 171.

Chilton House near Thame, Bucks
C.L. v. 35, 1914, 702–08.

Chilton Lodge, Berks
G. Carter *et al. Humphry Repton* 1982, 147.

Chilworth Manor, Chilworth, Hants
J. Hort. Cottage Gdnr N.S., v. 47, 1903, 354,355. N. Pevsner *and* D. Lloyd *Hampshire and the Isle of Wight* 1967, 166–67. A. Paterson *Gardens of Britain* v. 2, 1978, 70.

Chilworth Manor near Guildford, Surrey
C.L. v. 118, 1955, 1078–81,1138–41. T. Wright *Gardens of Britain* v. 4, 1978, 211–13. A. Lees-Milne *and* R. Verey *Englishwoman's garden* 1980, 61–62.

Chinthurst Hill, Bramley, Surrey
J. Brown *Miss Gertrude Jekyll* 1981, 15. J. Brown *Gardens of a golden afternoon* 1981, 161.

Chipchase Castle near Bellingham, Northumberland
C.L. v. 119, 1956, 1292–95,1362.

Chippenham Park near Newmarket, Cambs
J.C. Loudon *Encyclopaedia of gardening* 1822, 1234.

Chipstead Place, Sevenoaks, Kent
J. Harris *History of Kent* 1719, 75. T. Badeslade *Thirty*

six different views . . . of Kent 1750s, pl. 7. C. Greenwood *Epitome of county history . . . v. 1: Kent* 1838, 89. J.B. Burke *Visitation* v. 2, 1853, 203.

Chirk Castle, Wrexham, Clwyd
Society of Gentlemen *England displayed* v. 2, 1769, 252. S. *and* N. Buck *Buck's antiquities* v. 2, 1774, pl. 379. T. Pennant *Tour in Wales* v. 1, 1778, pl. 22. *C.L.* v. 9, 1901, 656–62; v. 110, 1951, 896–99, 980, 1148–51, 1469; v. 172, 1982, 810–12; v. 173, 1983, 524. M. Allan *Fisons guide* 1970, 271. J. Harris *Artist and the country house* 1979, 232. G.S. Thomas *Gardens of National Trust* 1979, 114–15. Manpower Services Commission *Chirk Castle* 1981.

Chisenbury Priory, Chisenbury, Wilts
J. Sales *West Country gardens* 1980, 198–99.

Chislehampton House near Abingdon, Oxfordshire
C.L. v. 115, 1954, 216–19. *V.C.H. Oxford* v. 7, 1962, 8. L. Fleming *and* A. Gore *English garden* 1979, 174.

Chiswick *see* Royal Horticultural Society, Chiswick

Chiswick House, Hounslow, London
Official guide. J. Beeverell *Les delices de la Grande Bretagne* v. 5, 1707. L. Knyff *and* J. Kip *Britannia illustrata* v. 1, 1714. C. Campbell *Vitruvius Britannicus* v. 3, 1725, 26. T. Badeslade *and* J. Rocque *Vitruvius Brittanicus* 1739, pls. 82–83. D. Defoe *Tour* v. 3, 1742, 287–90. W. Thornton *New, complete and universal history* 1786, 478. C. Burlington *Modern universal British traveller* 1779, 330. W. Watts *Seats* 1779, pls. 30, 50. G.A. Walpoole *New British traveller* 1784, 282. *New display of the beauties of England* v. 2, 1787, 69–71. L. Simond *Journal* v. 2, 1815, 119–20. R. Ackermann *Repository* v. 1, 1823, pls. 19–20. R. Havell *Series of picturesque views* 1823, pl. 19. British Museum *Catalogue of maps, prints* 1829, 70. W.W.J. Gendall *Views* v. 1, 1830, 37, 41. Prince Pückler-Muskau *Tour* 1833, 19. *G.M.* v. 19, 1843, 453–54. W. Keane *Beauties of Middlesex* 1850, 216–23. *Cottage Gdnr* v. 15, 1855, 69–70, 108–09. *J. Hort. Cottage Gdnr* v. 51, 1874, 386–88; N.S., v. 14, 1887, 327–29. *Gdning World* v. 1, 1885, 504–05; v. 3, 1887, 568–70, 792. *Gdnrs Mag.* 17 December 1898, 836–38. *C.L.* v. 4, 1898, 464–67; v. 9, 1901, 520–21; v. 14, 1903, 336–40; v. 43, 1918, 130–37, 160–65; v. 66, 1929, 181–83; v. 124, 1958, 228–31; v. 163, 1978, 624–25; v. 174, 1983, 570–71. Count F. Kielmansegge *Diary* 1902, 156–57. H.I. Triggs *Formal gardens in England and Scotland* 1902, 36–37. G. Jekyll *Garden ornament* 1918, passim. J. MacGregor *Gardens of celebrities . . . in and around London* 1918, 154–87. H. Walpole *Visits to country seats. Walpole Society* v. 7, 1927–28, 22–23. *Architectural Review* May 1944, 125–29; April 1953, 269–70. H.F. Clark *English landscape garden* 1948, 37–39. O. Siren *China and gardens of Europe* 1950, 25–26. N. Pevsner *Middlesex* 1951, 34–35. G. Taylor *Old London gardens* 1953, 153–60. *British Museum Quarterly* February 1960, 40–43. J. Lees-Milne *Earls of creation* 1962, 140–47. M. Allan *Fisons guide* 1970, 14–15. R.I.B.A. *Catalogue* v. B, 1972, 99–100. *Gdn History* v. 1 no. 3, 1973, 23–30; v. 10 no. 1, 1982, 36–39. *Apollo* v. 100, 1974, 126–37. A. Parreaux *and* M. Plaissant *Jardins et paysages: le style Anglais* 1977, 71–79. L. Fleming *and* A. Gore *English garden* 1979, pls. 57–59. J. Harris *Artist and the country house* 1979, 182–85, 261, pl. 19. *J. Gdn History* v. 2 no. 2, 1982, 133–42. D. Watkin *English vision* 1982, 6–7. K. Rorschach *Early Geogian landscape garden* 1983, 16–18, 21–24.

Chithurst, W. Sussex
G.C. i 1885, 825, 826.

Chobham Place, Chobham, Surrey
T. Wright *Gardens of Britain* v. 4, 1978, 214.

Cholmondeley Castle, Cholmondeley, Cheshire
Official guide. C. Campbell *Vitruvius Britannicus* v. 3, 1725, 79–80. F.O. Morris *Series of picturesque views* v. 2, 33. *G.C.* i 1894, 589. *Gdnrs Mag.* 1906, 845–48. *C.L.* v. 154, 1973, 154–57, 226–30; v. 166, 1979, 2000–02. *Apollo* v. 101, 1975, 22–25.

Christchurch Manor, Ipswich, Suffolk
C. Fiennes *Journeys* 1949, 144.

Church Town Botanical Gardens, Southport, Merseyside
Gdning World v. 1, 1885, 823. *G.C.* ii 1891, 363–64.

Chussex, Walton Heath, Surrey
J. Brown *Garden of a golden afternoon* 1982, 170.

Chute Lodge, Chute Forest, Wilts
D. Stroud *Capability Brown* 1975, 220.

Chyverton near Truro, Cornwall
P.M. Synge *Gardens of Britain* v. 1, 1977, 93–95.

Cill-Alaithe, Co. Mayo, Eire
C.L. v. 12, 1902, 604–05.

Cintra Lodge, Whitley, Berks
C.L. v. 3, 1898, 821–25.

Cirencester Abbey, Cirencester, Glos
R. Atkyns *Ancient and present state of Glostershire* 1712, 346. L. Knyff *and* J. Kip *Britannia illustrata* v. 2, 1715. Historical MSS Commission *Architectural history* v. 5, 1974, item 4958.

Cirencester House, Cirencester, Glos
S. Rudder *New history of Gloucestershire* 1779, 355.
R.J. Sulivan *Tour* v. 1, 1785, 273–74. W. Angus *Seats* 1787, pl. 41. J. and J. Boydell *History of River Thames* v. 1, 1794, 31–35. S. Shaw *Tour to West of England* In J. Pinkerton, v. 2, 1808, 239–40,241. J.N. Brewer *Delineations of Gloucestershire* 1825, 61,68–71.
J.P. Neale *Views* 2nd Series, v. 2, 1825. *C.L.* v. 24, 1908, 192–99; v. 107, 1950, 1796–1801,1880–84; v. 169, 1981, 1329. *J. Hort. Home Farmer* N.S., v. 62, 1911, 185–90. W.St.C. Baddeley *History of Cirencester* 1924, 266–77. Viscount Torrington *Diaries* v. 1, 1934, 259–60. J. Lees-Milne *Earls of creation* 1962, 37–56.
C. Hussey *English gardens and landscapes* 1967, 78–83. D. Verey *Gloucestershire* v. 1, 1970, 185–87. B. Jones *Follies & grottoes* 1974, 31–33. *Gdn History* v. 4 no. 1, 1976, 37. M.R. Brownell *Alexander Pope & the arts of Georgian England* 1978, 188–95. J. Harris *Gardens of delight* 1978, 49. L. Fleming and A. Gore *English garden* 1979, 110. J. Sales *West Country gardens* 1980, 49–51.
K. Rorschach *Early Georgian landscape garden* 1983, 34–37.

Clandeboye near Belfast, Co. Down, Ulster
Royal Hort. Soc. *Conifers in cultivation* 1932, 215.
Ulster Architectural Heritage Society *Northern gardens* 1982, 16,17.

Clandon Park near Guildford, Surrey
Copper Plate Mag. v. 1, 1792, pl. 24. J.P. Neale *Views* 2nd Series, v. 3, 1826. R. Ackermann *Repository* v. 11, 1828, pl. 14. G.F. Prosser *Select illustrations of . . . Surrey* 1828. W.W.J. Gendall *Views* v. 2, 1830, 106.
W. Keane *Beauties of Surrey* 1849, 119–20. *G.C.* ii 1885, 711–12; ii 1910, 112–14,115,116,123,394. *Gdnrs Mag.* 1911, 341–42. *C.L.* v. 62, 1927, 366–72,434–40. I. Nairn and B. Cherry *Surrey* 1971, 510. B. Jones *Follies & grottoes* 1974, 397. D. Stroud *Capability Brown* 1975, 220. J. Harris *Artist and the country house* 1979, 118.
G.S. Thomas *Gardens of National Trust* 1979, 115–16.

Clapham Common *see* London

Clapton Court near Crewkerne, Somerset
G.C. v. 189 no. 19, 1981, 12–13,15.

Clare House near West Malling, Kent
C.L. v. 106, 1949, 826–29.

Clare Lawn, East Sheen, London
Gdning World v. 4, 1887, 217; v. 12, 1896, 562–63.

Clare Priory, Clare, Suffolk
C.L. v. 60, 1926, 208–15.

Claremont, Esher, Surrey
Official guide. C. Campbell *Vitruvius Britannicus* v. 3, 1725, pls. 77–78. S. Switzer *Hydrostaticks and hydraulicks* v. 2, 1729, 405, pl. 37. T. Badeslade and J. Rocque *Vitruvius Brittanicus* 1739, pls. 9–23. R. and J. Dodsley *London and its environs described* v. 2, 1761, 139. *Short account of the principal seats and gardens in and about Richmond and Kew* [1760s?] 13–14. T. Whately *Observations on modern gardening* 1771, 48–50. G.L. le Rouge *Jardins Anglo-Chinois a la mode* 2^e cahier, 1776, pls. 8–9. W. Watts *Seats* 1779, pl. 6. *New display of the beauties of England* v. 2, 1787, 293–94. H. Gouldsmith [*Four views of Claremont*] 1819. P. Neale *Views* v. 4, 1821. J.C. Loudon *Encyclopaedia of gardening* 1822, 1229. G.F. Prosser *Select illustrations of . . . Surrey* 1828. British Museum *Catalogue of maps, prints* 1829, 71. *G.M.* v. 5, 1829, 381; v. 9, 1833, 478–79; v. 10, 1834, 325–30. N. Whittock and H. Gastineau *Picturesque beauties of England and Wales* 1830, 40–41.
E.W. Brayley and J. Britton *Topographical history of Surrey* v. 2, 1841, 446–50. W. Keane *Beauties of Surrey* 1849, 25–30. J.B. Burke *Visitation* 2nd Series, v. 1, 1855, 21–22. *G.C.* i 1882, 555–57; i 1897, 413–14; ii 1916, 181,182,184,185; i 1921, 207; i 1922, 188; v. 187 no. 25, 1980, 35–36. *C.L.* v. 2, 1897, 688–90; v. 10, 1901, 776–81; v. 37, 1915, 769; v. 40, 1916, 177; v. 63, 1928, 80–88; v. 111, 1952, 364; v. 125, 1959, 471; v. 160, 1976, 532; v. 165, 1979, 1547–50. C. Ward *Royal gardens* 1912, 105–20. T. Jefferson *Garden book* 1944, 112. H.F. Clarke *English landscape garden* 1948, 54–55.
L. Whistler *Imagination of Vanbrugh and his fellow artists* 1954, 151–55. *Surrey Archaeological Collections* v. 65, 1968, 92–95. I. Nairn and B. Cherry *Surrey* 1971, 161–62. D. Stroud *Capability Brown* 1975, 142–44,220.
National Trust Year Book 1975-76, 32–37. P. Willis *Charles Bridgeman* 1977, 178. *Garden* 1979, 181–85.
L. Fleming and A. Gore *English garden* 1979, pls. 53–54. J. Harris *Artist and the country house* 1979, 186. G.S. Thomas *Gardens of National Trust* 1979, 116–18. D. Watkin *English vision* 1982, 11–13. K. Rorschach *Early Georgian landscape garden* 1983, 52–54, 56–57. D. Jacques *Georgian gardens* 1983, 36, pl. 1.

Clarendon Park near Salisbury, Wilts
G.C. ii 1880, 779–80. H.M. Colvin *History of the King's Works* v. 2, 1963, 912.

Claverton Manor near Bath, Avon
G.C. ii 1903, 34; ii 1962, 25; ii 1964, 49. *C.L.* v. 147, 1970, 682–84. M. Allan *Fisons guide* 1970, 81–82.
J. Sales *West Country gardens* 1980, 139–40.

Claybury, Woodford, Essex
D. Stroud *Humphry Repton* 1962, 169. G. Carter et al. *Humphry Repton* 1982, 51,151.

Claydon House near Winslow, Bucks
Official guide. *C.L.* v. 9, 1901, 617–20. *G.C.* i 1907, 49–50.

Claylands, Kennington, London
E.W. Brayley and J. Britton *Topographical history of Surrey* v. 3, 362.

Clearwell (Clower Wall), Glos
R. Atkyns *Ancient and present state of Glostershire* 1712, 574. L. Knyff and J. Kip *Britannia illustrata* v. 2, 1715.

Cleddans near Airdrie, Strathclyde
Scottish Gdnr and Northern Forester v. 9, 1914, 61–62.

Cleeve Prior near Evesham, Hereford and Worcester
C.L. v. 7, 1900, 656–59, 736–41. *Garden* v. 58, 1900, 248–49, 252. G. Jekyll and G.S. Elgood *Some English gardens* 1904, 70–73. C. Holme *Gardens of England in Midland & Eastern counties* 1908, pl. 36. G. Jekyll *Garden ornament* 1918, 14, 232, 277.

Clent Hall near Stourbridge, W. Midlands
R. Sidwell *West Midland gardens* 1981, 37–38.

Cleuchhead House, Minto, Borders
G.A. Little *Scotland's gardens* 1981, 81–83.

Cleve Hill near Bristol, Avon
R. Atkyns *Ancient and present state of Glostershire* 1712, 547. L. Knyff and J. Kip *Britannia illustrata* v. 2, 1715. J.N. Brewer *Delineations of Gloucestershire* 1825, 168. *J. Hort. Cottage Gdnr* N.S., v. 50, 1905, 54. T. Wright *Arbours & grottos* 1979.

Cleve House, Windermere, Cumbria
G. Beard *Thomas H. Mawson* 1976, 49.

Clevedon Court, Clevedon, Avon
Official guide. *C.L.* v. 6, 1899, 692–99; v. 117, 1955, 1672–75; v. 118, 1955, 16–19. C. Holme *Gardens of England in Southern & Western counties* 1907, pls. 38–40. G. Jekyll *Garden ornament* 1918, 434. M. Allan *Fisons guide* 1970, 82. *J. Royal Hort. Soc.* 1971, 221. J. Harris *Artist and the country house* 1979, 117. G.S. Thomas *Gardens of National Trust* 1979, 119–20. J. Sales *West Country gardens* 1980, 140–43.

Cleveland House, Clapham, London
J. Hort. Cottage Gdnr v. 54, 1875, 205–08, 226–28.

Cleveley, Allerton, Merseyside
Gdning World v. 3, 1887, 312–13. *G.C.* i 1889, 46. *J. Hort. Cottage Gdnr* N.S., v. 21, 1890, 272–73. C. Holme *Gardens of England in Northern counties* 1911, pl. 37.

Cliddesdon Down House, Cliddesdon, Hants
A. Paterson *Gardens of Britain* v. 2, 1978, 71–72.

Cliff near Tamworth, Warwickshire
G. Beard *Thomas H. Mawson* 1976, 49.

Cliffe Castle, Keighley, W. Yorks
Bradford Illustrated Weekly Telegraph *Series of picturesque views* 1885. *Gdning World* v. 4, 1887, 88–89.

Clifford Manor, Clifford Chambers, Warwickshire
C. Holme *Gardens of England in Midland & Eastern counties* 1908, pl. 37. *C.L.* v. 64, 1928, 168–75.

Clifton Hall near Nottingham, Notts
F.O. Morris *Series of picturesque views* v. 2, 39. *J. Hort. Cottage Gdnr* v. 55, 1876, 510–11. *C.L.* v. 7, 1900, 592–98; v. 54, 1923, 246–54. G. Jekyll *Garden ornament* 1918, 63, 68. N. Pevsner *Nottinghamshire* 1979, 272.

Clint Hall, N. Yorks
I. Hall *Samuel Buck's Yorkshire sketchbook* 1979, 375.

Clipstone Park, Clipstone, Notts
Historical MSS Commission *Architectural history* v. 3, 1971, item 2616.

Clissold Park *see* London

Clive House, Esher, Surrey
G.C. ii 1882, 496, 497, 499.

Cliveden, Maidenhead, Bucks
Official guide. C. Burlington *Modern universal British traveller* 1779, 224. A. Robertson *Topographical survey of the Great Road* pt. 1, 1792, 85–86. *G.M.* v. 9, 1833, 645–46; v. 13, 1837, 5–6. *Tombleson's Thames* 1834. F.O. Morris *Series of picturesque views* v. 6, 13. *J. Hort. Cottage Gdnr* v. 28, 1862, 336–37; v. 31, 1864, 416–17. *Garden* v. 2, 1872, 234–35; v. 16, 1879, 572–73, 574. *G.C.* ii 1877, 69–71, 73, 76, 77, 81, 84; i 1889, 554; i 1893, 541–42; i 1895, 765–66; ii 1898, 1; 1913, 65–66, 67, 82–83, 84. L. Jewitt and S.C. Hall *Stately homes of England* 1877, 265–79. *C.L.* v. 32, 1912, 808–18; v. 68, 1930, 800–01; v. 70, 1931, 38–44, 68–74, 165; v. 161, 1977, 438–41, 498–501. *Gdnrs Mag.* 1914, 10–12, 13. G. Jekyll *Garden ornament* 1918, 93, 95, 217, 382. Lady Rockley *Historic gardens of England* 1938, 170–71. J. Evelyn *Diary* v. 4, 1955, 177. N. Pevsner *Buckinghamshire* 1960, 99. *Park Administration* September 1965, 49–51. M. Allan *Fisons guide* 1970, 6–7. *J. Royal Hort. Soc.* 1971, 210–11. H. Evans *Beautiful gardens of Britain* 1974, 43–44. B. Jones *Follies & grottoes* 1974, 117. D. Stroud *Capability Brown* 1975, 182. *Architectural History* v. 19, 1976, 5–16. *Garden* 1977, 91–96. *National Trust Year Book* 1976–77, 100–17; 1979, 91–98. R. Bisgrove *Gardens of Britain* v. 3, 1978, 58–61. G.S. Thomas *Gardens of National Trust* 1979, 120–23. Manpower Services Commission *Cliveden* 1980.

Cliveden, Shenfield, Essex
G.C. i 1924, 50,51,53.

Clontra, Dublin, Eire
C.L. v. 157, 1975, 1390–93.

Clopton House, Stratford-upon-Avon, Warwickshire
J.P. Neale *Views* v. 4, 1821.

Cloquhat, Bridge of Cally, Tayside
G.A. Little *Scotland's gardens* 1981, 129.

Closeburn Hall, Closeburn, Dumfries and Galloway
G.M. v. 9, 1833, 5–6.

Clouds, Salisbury, Wilts
C.L. v. 16, 1904, 738–48.

Clovelley Hall near Whitchurch, Shropshire
J. Hort. Cottage Gdnr v. 61, 1879, 10–12.

Clowance, Crowan, Cornwall
W. Borlase *Natural history of Cornwall* 1758, pl. 22.
R. Ackermann *Repository* v. 9, 1827, pl. 2.
W.W.J. Gendall *Views* v. 2, 1830, 72. G.M. v. 13, 1837, 121.

Clower Wall *see* Clearwell

Clumber Park, Worksop, Notts
Official guide. W. Watts *Seats* 1779, pl. 29.
R. Thoroton *History of Nottinghamshire* v. 3, 1797, 405–06. J.P. Neale *Views* v. 3, 1820. R. Ackermann *Repository* v. 7, 1826, pl. 7. W.W.J. Gendall *Views* v. 1, 1830, 75. *Garden* v. 3, 1873, 263. L. Jewitt *and* S.C. Hall *Stately homes of England* 1877, 317–26. W. Robinson *English flower garden* 1883, xiv–xv. G.C. ii 1889, 182. C.L. v. 24, 1908, 384–90. C. Holme *Gardens of England in Midland & Eastern counties* 1908, pls. 38–41. *Gdnrs Mag.* 1910, 469–71. J. Anthony *Gardens of Britain* v. 6, 1979, 55–61. N. Pevsner *Nottinghamshire* 1979, 102. M. Binney *and* A. Hills *Elysian gardens* 1979, 13. G.S. Thomas *Gardens of National Trust* 1979, 124.

Cluniemore near Pitlochry, Tayside
G.A. Little *Scotland's gardens* 1981, 131.

Cluny House near Aberfeldy, Tayside
G.A. Little *Scotland's gardens* 1981, 131–33.

Clyffe Hall, Market Lavington, Wilts
G.C. ii 1882, 820–21.

Clytha Park near Abergavenny, Gwent
B. Jones *Follies & grottoes* 1974, 67–69. C.L. v. 162, 1977, 1718–21.

Coach House, Little Haseley, Oxfordshire
A. Lees-Milne *and* R. Verey *Englishwoman's garden* 1980, 80.

Coalstoun near Haddington, Lothian
Historical MSS Commission *Architectural history* v. 4, 1972, item 4100.

Coates Manor, Fittleworth, W. Sussex
C.L. v. 154, 1973, 1715–18. T. Wright *Gardens of Britain* v. 4, 1978, 130–33. A. Lees-Milne *and* R. Verey *Englishwoman's garden* 1980, 131–33.

Cobblers near Crowborough, E. Sussex
T. Wright *Gardens of Britain* v. 4, 1978, 133–34. C.L. v. 170, 1981, 1304,1308–09.

Coberley near Cheltenham, Glos
R. Atkyns *Ancient and present state of Glostershire* 1712, 376. L. Knyff *and* J. Kip *Britannia illustrata* v. 2, 1715. V.C.H. *Gloucester* v. 7, 1981, 177.

Cobham (Mr Bridges), Surrey
Society of Gentlemen *England displayed* v. 1, 1769, 224.

Cobham Hall, Cobham, Kent
Official guide. E. Hasted *History . . . of . . . Kent* v. 1, 1778, 497. S. Ireland *Picturesque views on the River Medway* 1793, 76–77. H. Repton *Sketches* 1794, 49–50. H. Repton *Fragments* 1816, 10–12. J.P. Neale *Views* v. 2, 1819. W.W.J. Gendall *Views* v. 1, 1830, 55–57. C. Greenwood *Epitome of county history . . . v. 1: Kent* 1838, 215. *Florist* 1859, 282–83. J. Hort. Cottage Gdnr v. 41, 1869, 222–24. F.O. Morris *Series of picturesque views* v. 2, 25. L. Jewitt *and* S.C. Hall *Stately homes of England* 1874, 37–53. *Garden* v. 21, 1882, 19–20,143. G.C. ii 1884, 261–62. C.L. v. 15, 1904, 906–13; v. 75, 1934, 619; v. 119, 1956, 212; v. 173, 1983, 450. *Landscape & Garden* v. 3 no. 4, 1936, 218–20. Lady Rockley *Historic gardens of England* 1938, 212–13. D. Stroud *Humphry Repton* 1962, 52–53. F. Hull *Catalogue of estate maps 1590 to 1840 in the Kent County Archives Offices* 1973, 86. P. Hunt *Garden lover's companion* 1974, 95–104. J. Newman *West Kent and the Weald* 1976, 236. T. Wright *Gardens of Britain* v. 4, 1978, 30–33. M. Binney *and* A. Hills *Elysian gardens* 1979, 51. G. Carter *et al. Humphry Repton* 1982, 155. *Garden* 1983, 365.

Cobham Park, Cobham, Surrey
G.C. i 1905, 74–75.

Cocken Hall near Durham, Co. Durham
J. Kip *Nouveau theatre de la Grande Bretagne* v. 2, 1724. Society of Gentlemen *England displayed* v. 2, 1769, 169. A. Young *Six months tour through the North of England*

Cocken Hall (*Cont.*)
v. 3, 1771, 1–5. E. Mackenzie *and* M. Ross *Historical . . . view of . . . Durham* v. 1, 1834, 366.

Cockenzie House, Cockenzie, Lothian
C. McWilliam *Lothian* 1978, 139.

Cockermouth Castle, Cockermouth, Cumbria
C.L. v. 156, 1974, 210–13.

Cockfield Hall, Cockfield, Suffolk
H. Davy *Views* 1827. *C.L.* v. 54, 1924, 532–38.

Codford Manor, Wilts
G. Beard *Thomas H. Mawson* 1976, 49.

Cogges Manor Farm, Cogges, Oxfordshire
J. Harris *Artist and the country house* 1979, 364.

Coghill near Harrogate, N. Yorks
W. Angus *Seats* 1787, pl. 11.

Cokenach, Barkway, Herts
H. Chauncy *Historical antiquities of Hertfordshire* 1700, 102. R. Bisgrove *Gardens of Britain* v. 3, 1978, 62.

Coker Court, East Coker, Somerset
C.L. v. 25, 1909, 18–25.

Coke's House *see* Cooke's House

Cokethorpe Park near Witney, Oxfordshire
T. May *Excursion to Cockthorpe Park* 1769. J.P. Neale *Views* v. 3, 1820; 2nd Series, v. 1, 1824.

Cold Ashton Manor near Bath, Avon
C.L. v. 18, 1905, 738–43; v. 57, 1925, 240–46.

Cold Hayes near Petersfield, Hants
A. Paterson *Gardens of Britain* v. 2, 1978, 72–73.

Cold Overton Hall, Cold Overton, Leics
C.L. v. 67, 1930, 386–93.

Coldham Hall near Bury St Edmunds, Suffolk
Garden v. 46, 1894, 333.

Cole Green near Hertingfordbury, Herts
D. Stroud *Capability Brown* 1975, 220–21. *Architectural History* v. 24, 1981, 53–58.

Cole Park, Malmesbury, Wilts
C.L. v. 135, 1964, 985–89.

Coleby Hall near Scunthorpe, Lincs
B. Howlett *Selection of views* 1805.

Colehill Cottage, Fulham, Hammersmith, London
C.J. Fèret *Fulham old and new* v. 3, 1900, 48,50.

Colehill House, Fulham, Hammersmith, London
C.J. Fèret *Fulham old and new* v. 3, 1900, 44,46.

Coleorton Hall near Ashby-de-la-Zouch, Leics
J.P. Neale *Views* v. 2, 1819. R. Ackermann *Repository* v. 7, 1826, pl. 2. *Jones's views* 1829. W.W.J. Gendall *Views* v. 1, 1830, 76. *J. Hort. Cottage Gdnr* v. 54, 1875, 446–47,558–60. *C.L.* v. 136, 1964, 772–73.

Coleraine (Guy L. Wilson's Daffodil Garden), Co. Londonderry, Ulster
Official guide. Ulster Architectural Heritage Society *Northern gardens* 1982, 17.

Coles near Petersfield, Hants
C.L. v. 133, 1963, 460–63.

Colesbourne, Glos
J.N. Brewer *Delineations* 1825, 107. *V.C.H. Gloucester* v. 7, 1981, 183–84.

Coleshill, Oxfordshire
J. Britton *and* E.W. Brayley *Beauties of England and Wales* v. 1, 1801, 132. J.P. Neale *Views* v. 1, 1818. R. Pococke *Travels through England* v. 2, 1889, 249–50. W. Cobbett *Rural rides* v. 2, 1912, 86. *C.L.* v. 46, 1919, 108–16. C. Fiennes *Journeys* 1949, 24. Historical MSS Commission *Architectural history* v. 2, 1970, item 1270.

Coleton Fishacre, Devon
C.L. v. 67, 1930, 782–89.

Coley Park near Reading, Berks
J. Beeverell *Les delices de la Grande Bretagne* v. 5, 1707, 872. L. Knyff *and* J. Kip *Britannia illustrata* v. 1, 1714.

Colinton House, Edinburgh, Lothian
H. Maxwell *Scottish gardens* 1911, 80–82.

Collacombe Barton near Tavistock, Devon
C.L. v. 35, 1914, 914–18.

College, Kirkoswald, Strathclyde
C.L. v. 64, 1928, 700–07.

Collinson, Peter *see* Peckham; Ridgeway House

Collipriest House, Tiverton, Devon
J.P. Neale *Views* v. 1, 1818.

Collyweston, Northants
V.C.H. Northampton v. 2, 1906, 550. *Northamptonshire Past and Present* v. 5 no. 3, 1975, 220–21. Royal Commission on Historical Monuments *Inventory of*

Collyweston (*Cont.*)

historical monuments in . . . Northampton v. 1, 1975, 30–31. C. Taylor *Archaeology of gardens* 1983, 38,39.

Colney Hall, Colney, Norfolk
J. Grigor *Eastern arboretum* 1841, 304.

Colney Hatch, Barnet, London
W. Keane *Beauties of Middlesex* 1850, 160–62.

Colney House, Shenley, Herts
J.C. Loudon *Encyclopaedia of gardening* 1822, 1233. J.P. Neale *Views* 2nd Series, v. 2, 1825.

Colonsay House, Colonsay, Strathclyde
G.C. ii 1964, 550–51.

Colosseum, Regent's Park, London
R. Ackermann *publisher.* [*Colisseum, Regent's Park*] 1829. *Gdnrs Mag.* v. 5, 1829, 222–23.

Coltness, Wishaw, Strathclyde
Gdning World v. 4, 1887, 100–01; v. 7, 1890, 53–54.

Colwick Hall, Colwick, Notts
J. Throsby *New Copper Plate Mag.* 1792. R. Thoroton *History of Nottinghamshire* v. 3, 1797, 7–8.

Colworth House, Sharnbrook, Beds
Historical MSS Commission *Architectural history* v. 1, 1969, item 810.

Colzium near Kilsyth, Strathclyde
Scottish Gdnr and Northern Forester v. 8, 1913, 601–03.

Combe near Gittisham, Devon
C.L. v. 117, 1955, 1486–89,1556–59.

Combe (Coombe) **Abbey** near Coventry, W. Midlands
J. Beeverell *Les delices de la Grande Bretagne* v. 5, 1707, 872. L. Knyff *and* J. Kip *Britannia illustrata* v. 1, 1714. S. *and* N. Buck *Buck's antiquities* v. 2, 1774, pl. 298. *J. Hort. Cottage Gdnr* v. 33, 1865, 441–42; v. 42, 1869, 126–27; v. 50, 1873, 420–22. *Scottish Gdnr* v. 15, 1866, 246–48,288–92,370–74. *Garden* v. 1, 1872, 559–60. G.C. ii 1898, 229–31. C. Holme *Gardens of England in Midland & Eastern counties* 1908, pls. 45–46. C.L. v. 26, 1909, 794–805,840–49. D. Stroud *Capability Brown* 1975, 169–70. M. Binney *and* A. Hills *Elysian gardens* 1979, 11. R. Sidwell *West Midland gardens* 1981, 206–08.

Combe Bank near Brasted, Kent
W. Angus *Seats* 1787, pl. 4. R. Pococke *Travels through England* v. 2, 1889, 74.

Combe-down-Side near Croydon, London
J. Hassell *Seats near London* 1804–05.

Combe Royal near Kingsbridge, Devon
J. Hort. Cottage Gdnr v. 46, 1871, 162–64. G.C. i 1904, 1–3.

Combend Manor, Elkstone, Glos
J. Brown *Miss Gertrude Jekyll* 1981, 45–46.

Combermere Abbey near Nantwich, Cheshire
F.O. Morris *Series of picturesque views* v. 2, 43. G. Ormerod *History of . . . Chester* v. 3, 1882, 416. G.C. ii 1892, 363–64. N. Pevsner *and* E. Hubbard *Cheshire* 1971, 181–82. J. Harris *Artist and the country house* 1979, 132–33.

Comlongon Castle near Ruthwell, Dumfries and Galloway
Scottish Gdnr and Northern Forester v. 8, 1913, 370.

Compton Acres, Poole, Dorset
Official guide. G.C. v. 162 no. 1, 1967, 12. H. Evans *Beautiful gardens of Britain* 1974, 27–28. M. Allan *Fisons guide* 1970, 83–84.

Compton Beauchamp, Oxfordshire
C.L. v. 5, 1899, 784–89; v. 44, 1918, 484–91. R. Bisgrove *Gardens of Britain* v. 3, 1978, 62–63.

Comptons Brow near Horsham, W. Sussex
C.L. v. 68, 1930, 118–21.

Compton End near Winchester, Hants
C.L. v. 46, 1919, 240–48.

Compton House, Over Compton, Dorset
J. Hutchins *History . . . of Dorset* v. 4, 1870, 168.

Compton Park, Compton Chamberlayne, Wilts
J.B. Burke *Visitation* v. 2, 1853, 1. C.L. v. 28, 1910, 228–35.

Compton Place, Eastbourne, E. Sussex
G.C. i 1894, 232; i 1908, 202,300. C.L. v. 40, 1916, 266–73,294–303; v. 77, 1935, 144–50; v. 113, 1953, 734–37.

Compton Verney, Warwickshire
J.P. Neale *Views* v. 4, 1821. *Jones's views* 1829. F.O. Morris *Series of picturesque views* v. 3, 3. C.L. v. 34, 1913, 528–35. G. Jekyll *Garden ornament* 1918, 88. *Warwickshire History* v. 1, 1969, 18–24. D. Stroud *Capability Brown* 1975, 141–42,221.

Compton Wynyates, Tysoe, Warwickshire
Garden v. 45, 1894, 63. C.L. v. 10, 1901, 144–52; v. 38, 1915, 584–91. G. Jekyll *and* G.S. Elgood *Some English gardens* 1904, 96–98. C. Holme *Gardens of England in the Midland & Eastern counties* 1908, pls. 42–44.

G. Jekyll *Garden ornament* 1918, 408,410. M. Allan *Fisons guide* 1970, 155. H. Evans *Beautiful gardens of Britain* 1974, 87–88. D. Stroud *Capability Brown* 1975, 109,111,221.

Conderton Manor near Tewkesbury, Hereford and Worcester
R. Sidwell *West Midland gardens* 1981, 38–40.

Condover Hall, Condover, Shropshire
Garden v. 50, 1896, 159. *C.L.* v. 3, 1898, 368–70,400–02; v. 43, 1918, 508–13,530–36. G. Jekyll *and* G.S. Elgood *Some English gardens* 1904, 74–75. G. Jekyll *Garden ornament* 1918, 289. Lady Rockley *Historic gardens of England* 1938, 190–91. M. Binney *and* A. Hills *Elysian gardens* 1979, 24.

Conington Castle, Conington, Cambs
J.P. Neale *Views* v. 2, 1819.

Conock Manor, Conock, Wilts
C.L. v. 109, 1951, 2040–44. J. Sales *West Country gardens* 1980, 200.

Constable Burton Hall, Leyburn, N. Yorks
L. Knyff *and* J. Kip *Britannia illustrata* v. 1, 1714. *C.L.* v. 144, 1968, 1396–1400. K. Lemmon *Gardens of Britain* v. 5, 1978, 64–65. I. Hall *Samuel Buck's Yorkshire sketchbook* 1979, 390.

Cooke's House (Coke's), West Burton, W. Sussex
C.L. v. 25, 1909, 942–47; v. 102, 1947, 878–81,926. T. Wright *Gardens of Britain* v. 4, 1978, 134–35.

Cooksbridge, Fernhurst, Surrey
T. Wright *Gardens of Britain* v. 4, 1978, 215.

Coolayna near Carbury, Co. Kildare, Eire
J. Hort. Cottage Gdnr v. 47, 1872, 368–70.

Coole Park, Co. Galway, Eire
E. Malins *and* Knight of Glin *Lost demesnes* 1976, 182–83. E. Malins *and* P. Bowe *Irish gardens and demesnes* 1980, 141–45.

Coolhurst, Horsham, W. Sussex
T.W. Horsfield *History . . . of Sussex* v. 2, 1835, 265. *Garden* v. 31, 1887, 21–22,25. *Gdning World* v. 3, 1887, 793–94.

Coollatin Park, Co. Wicklow, Eire
Gdning World v. 6, 1890, 790–91.

Coolmore near Carrigaline, Co. Cork, Eire
J.P. Neale *Views* 2nd Series, v. 3, 1826. Mrs Alder *Coolmore* 1839.

Coombe Court, Kingston upon Thames, London
Gdnrs Mag. 1914, 74–76.

Coombe House, Croydon, London
G.C. ii 1922, 151,153.

Coombe Lodge near Pangbourne, Berks
H. Repton *Observations* 1803, 54–57. D. Stroud *Humphry Repton* 1962, 80. G. Carter *et al. Humphry Repton* 1982, 147.

Coombe Warren, Kingston upon Thames, London
J. Hort. Cottage Gdnr v. 58, 1877, 34–36. *Garden* v. 30, 1886, 284,285. *G.C.* i 1887, 39–40,41,73,76,77. *Gdning World* v. 5, 1888, 87; v. 7, 1890, 72–73. *Architectural Review* v. 21, 1907, 25–29,74.

Cooper's Hill, Englefield Green, Surrey
W. Keane *Beauties of Surrey* 1849, 51–54. *Florist* 1854, 118–22.

Coopersale, Theydon Garnon, Essex
P. Muilman *History of Essex* v. 3, 1770, 404. P. Morant *History . . . of Essex* v. 1, 1816, 160. V.C.H. *Essex* v. 4, 1956, 269. D. Stroud *Capability Brown* 1975, 221.

Coote Hill, Co. Cavan, Eire
M. Delany *Autobiography and correspondence* v. 1, 1861, 376–77.

Copenhagen House, Islington, London
W. Wroth *London pleasure gardens of the eighteenth century* 1896, 156–60. E.B. Chancellor *Pleasure haunts of London* 1925, 378–80.

Copford Hall, Copford, Essex
F.G. Emmisson *Catalogue of maps in Essex Record Office* 2nd Supplt, 1964, 17.

Copped (Copt) **Hall** near Epping, Essex
W. Watts *Seats* 1779, pl. 27. *G.C.* ii 1887, 73; i 1917, 194; i 1921, 209. *Gdnrs Mag.* 1916, 4–6,58. *C.L.* v. 28, 1910, 610–17,646–54; v. 34, 1913, 688. V.C.H. *Essex* v. 5, 1966, 123,124. D. Stroud *Capability Brown* 1975, 221. M. Binney *and* A. Hills *Elysian gardens* 1979, 46–47. J. Harris *Artist and the country house* 1979, 264.

Copped Hall, Totteridge, Barnet, London
T. Badeslade *and* J. Rocque *Vitruvius Brittanicus* 1739, pls. 98–99.

Coppins, Iver, Bucks
C.L. v. 84, 1938, 300–04.

Copse Hill, Wimbledon, London
G.M. v. 13, 1837, 114–15.

Copt Hall *see* Copped Hall

Copt Hewick, N. Yorks
K. Lemmon *Gardens of Britain* v. 5, 1978, 65–67.

Corbels, Windermere, Cumbria
G. Beard *Thomas H. Mawson* 1976, 49.

Corby Castle, Great Corby, Cumbria
W. Gilpin *Observations on several parts of England* v. 2, 1808, 104–06. J.C. Loudon *Encyclopaedia of gardening* 1822, 1244. J. Loveday *Diary* 1890, 107. *C.L.* v. 115, 1954, 32–35,92. *G.C.* ii 1880, 389–90. B. Jones *Follies & grottoes* 1974, 213–15.

Corehouse, Lanark, Strathclyde
G.M. v. 18, 1842, 433–37.

Cork. Botanical Garden, Co. Cork, Eire
Gdn History v. 8 no. 1, 1980, 41–45.

Cornbury Park, Charlbury, Oxfordshire
R. Plot *Natural history of Oxfordshire* 1705, 175,194,266. G. Jekyll *Garden ornament* 1918, 317.

Cornwell Manor, Kingham, Oxfordshire
C.L. v. 89, 1941, 454–57,476. J. Sherwood *and* N. Pevsner *Oxfordshire* 1974, 557. R. Bisgrove *Gardens of Britain* v. 3, 1978, 63–64.

Corridor House, Tottenham, London
G. Carter *et al. Humphry Repton* 1982, 157.

Corrour, Highland
H. Maxwell *Scottish gardens* 1911, 85–90.

Corsewall, Dumfries and Galloway
Scottish Gdnr and Northern Forester v. 7, 1912, 453–54. *C.L.* v. 76, 1934, 70–72.

Corsham Court, Corsham, Wilts
Official guide. W. Watts *Seats* 1779, pl. 32.
A. Robertson *Topographical survey of the Great Road* pt. 2, 1792, 66. J. Britton *Beauties of Wiltshire* v. 2, 1801, 285. H. Repton *Observations* 1803, 187–89.
J. Britton *Historical account of Corsham House* 1806.
R. Havell *Series of picturesque views* 1816, pl. 9.
J.P. Neale *Views* 2nd Series, v. 2, 1825. *Jones's views* 1829. *Florist* 1861, 326–27. F.O. Morris *Series of picturesque views* v. 2, 69. *C.L.* v. 8, 1900, 272–78; v. 12, 1902, 94–95; v. 82, 1937, 516–21; v. 142, 1967, 437. C. Holme *Gardens of England in Southern & Western counties* 1907, pls. 41–43. *Landscape & Garden* v. 3 no. 3, 1936, 149–52.
D. Stroud *Humphry Repton* 1962, 95–97. B. Jones *Follies & grottoes* 1974, 407. D. Stroud *Capability Brown* 1975, 86–90, 221. F.J. Ladd *Architects at Corsham Court* 1979. J. Sales *West Country gardens* 1980, 201–04.

Landscape Design no. 133, 1981, 28–32. G. Carter *et al. Humphry Repton* 1982, 163.

Corsley House, Corsley, Wilts
Architectural Review v. 55, 1924, 20–25.

Cortachy Castle, Cortachy, Tayside
J.P. Neale *Views* v. 6, 1823.

Coryton near Tavistock, Devon
J.P. Neale *Views* v. 1, 1818.

Costessey (Cossey) **Park**, Costessey, Norfolk
J.P. Neale *Views* 2nd Series, v. 1, 1824. *G.M.* v. 16, 1840, 601. J. Grigor *Eastern arboretum* 1841, 31–36.

Cote (Cotham) **Bank** near Bristol, Avon
D. Stroud *Humphry Repton* 1962, 169. G. Carter *et al. Humphry Repton* 1982, 152.

Cote House, Westbury on Trym, Avon
J.N. Brewer *Delineations of Gloucestershire* 1825, 110. *Gdnrs Mag.* 1908, 393–94,395.

Cotehele, Calstock, Cornwall
Official guide. C.S. Gilbert *Historical survey of . . . Cornwall* v. 2, 1820, 449–51. F.V.J. Arundell *Cothele* c.1840. L. Jewitt *and* S.C. Hall *Stately homes of England* 1874, 76–77. *Garden* v. 44, 1893, 21,117; v. 62, 1902, 44–45,46. *C.L.* v. 11, 1902, 485–88; v. 17, 1905, 822–33; v. 56, 1924, 324–31. *J. Royal Hort. Soc.* 1960, 345–46. *G.C.* ii 1961, 102–04. M. Allan *Fisons guide* 1970, 119–20. H. Evans *Beautiful gardens of Britain* 1974, 11–12. B. Jones *Follies & grottoes* 1974, 298. P.M. Synge *Gardens of Britain* v. 1, 1977, 96–97. G.S. Thomas *Gardens of National Trust* 1979, 124–26. Manpower Services Commission *Cotehele* 1982.

Cotgrave Hall, Yorks
I. Hall *Samuel Buck's Yorkshire sketchbook* 1979, 245.

Cothay Manor, Greenham, Somerset
C.L. v. 62, 1927, 596. *G.C.* ii 1964, 71–72. M. Allan *Fisons guide* 1970, 121.

Cothelstone, Taunton, Somerset
J.P. Neale *Views* 2nd Series, v. 4, 1828. *Jones's views* 1829. *C.L.* v. 23, 1908, 54–61.

Coton Manor, Coton, Northants
J. Anthony *Gardens of Britain* v. 6, 1979, 61–63.

Cotswold House, North Cerney, Glos
J.N. Brewer *Delineations of Gloucestershire* 1825, 99.

Cottage, Badminton, Avon
C.L. v. 159, 1976, 1298–1300.

Cottage Farm, Little Blakenham, Suffolk
A. Lees-Milne *and* R. Verey *Englishman's garden* 1982, 40–43.

Cottered, Herts
L. Fleming *and* A. Gore *English garden* 1979, pl. 131.

Cotterstock Hall near Oundle, Northants
J. Anthony *Gardens of Britain* v. 6, 1979, 64.

Cottesbrooke Hall, Brixworth, Northants
C.L. v. 79, 1936, 168–73, 194; v. 117, 1955, 736–39, 806; v. 147, 1970, 434–37. Royal Commission on Historical Monuments *Inventory of the historical monuments in . . . Northampton* v. 3, 1981, 57. C. Taylor *Archaeology of gardens* 1983, 17, 20.

Cottingham near Hull, Humberside
A. Young *Six months tour through North of England* v. 1, 1771, 152–55.

Coughton Court near Alcester, Warwickshire
J.P. Neale *Views* v. 4, 1821. F.O. Morris *Series of picturesque views* v. 3, 45. *C.L.* v. 43, 1918, 319–24. Historical MSS Commission *Architectural history* v. 2, 1970, item 1290.

Coulmony House, Ardclach, Grampian
I.H. Adams *Descriptive list of plans* v. 2, 1970, 115.

Coupland Castle near Wooler, Northumberland
M. Binney *and* A. Hills *Elysian gardens* 1979, 17.

Court Farm, Little Haseley, Oxfordshire
R. Bisgrove *Gardens of Britain* v. 3, 1978, 64–65.

Court Hall, East Meon, Hants
A. Paterson *Gardens of Britain* v. 2, 1978, 73–74.

Court House, Painswick, Glos
C.L. v. 37, 1915, 523. G. Jekyll *Garden ornament* 1918, 74.

Court House, Shipton Moyne, Glos
M. Allan *Fisons guide* 1970, 156–57.

Court House, Somerset
J. Collinson *History . . . of Somersetshire* v. 3, 1791, 454.

Court House near Birmingham, W. Midlands
R. Sidwell *West Midland gardens* 1981, 42–43.

Court Lodge, Lamberhurst, Kent
C. Greenwood *Epitome of country history . . . v. 1: Kent* 1838, 132.

Court Lodge, Groombridge, E. Sussex
C.L. v. 47, 1920, 891–92.

Court of Hill near Tenbury, Shropshire
C.L. v. 100, 1946, 716–19.

Courteenhall near Northampton, Northants
Cottage Gdnr v. 25, 1860, 49–51. *C.L.* v. 86, 1939, 144–48. D. Stroud *Humphry Repton* 1962, 64. G. Carter *et al. Humphry Repton* 1982, 159–60, col. pl. 3. *Garden* 1983, 361.

Courtlands, Exmouth, Devon
G.C. i 1898, 363–64.

Courts, Holt, Wilts
C.L. v. 93, 1943, 26–29. *G.C.* i 1964, 361–62. M. Allan *Fisons guide* 1970, 86–87. G.S. Thomas *Gardens of National Trust* 1979, 126–27. J. Sales *West Country gardens* 1980, 204–07.

Coventry. London Road Cemetery, W. Midlands
Garden v. 1, 1872, 594.

Coverwood, Ewhurst, Surrey
C.L. v. 68, 1930, 51–54; v. 72, 1932, 5–8; v. 162, 1977, 640.

Cowane's Hospital, Stirling, Central
H.I. Triggs *Formal gardens in England and Scotland* 1902, 49.

Cowdray Park, Midhurst, W. Sussex
F.O. Morris *Series of picturesque views* v. 5, 51. *J. Hort. Cottage Gdnr* v. 38, 1867, 138–39. *Garden* v. 34, 1888, 433–34. G. Jekyll *Garden ornament* 1918, 358.

Cowhill Tower, Holywood, Dumfries and Galloway
G.A. Little *Scotland's gardens* 1981, 252.

Cowley House, Oxford
D. Sturdy *Twelve Oxford gardens* 1982.

Cowley Manor near Cheltenham, Glos
C.L. v. 20, 1906, 162–72. G. Jekyll *Garden ornament* 1918, 387. V.C.H. *Gloucester* v. 7, 1981, 195.

Cowling, York
I. Hall *Samuel Buck's Yorkshire sketchbook* 1979, 392.

Coworth Park, Sunningdale, Berks
J. Brown *Miss Gertrude Jekyll* 1981, 26–27.

Cowper, William *see* Olney

Cragside, Rothbury, Northumberland
G.C. ii 1880, 325–26; i 1882, 436, 437. *C.L.* v. 7, 1900,

Cragside (*Cont.*)

464–68. *Garden* v. 58, 1900, 271–72; v. 59, 1901, 31.
C. Holme *Gardens of England in Northern counties* 1911, pls. 38–39. M. Allan *Fisons guide* 1970, 317–18.
G.S. Thomas *Gardens of National Trust* 1979, 127–28.

Craig-y-Nos Castle, Brecon, Powys
G.C. i 1882, 464–65,469. *J. Hort. Cottage Gdnr* N.S., v. 9, 1884, 198; v. 31, 1895, 108,109.

Craigantaggart, Dunkeld, Tayside
G.A. Little *Scotland's gardens* 1981, 133.

Craigdarroch, Moniaive, Dumfries and Galloway
G.A. Little *Scotland's gardens* 1981, 252–53.

Craigie Hall, Craigie, Lothian
British Museum *Catalogue of maps, prints* 1829, 78.

Craigievar Castle, Lumphanan, Grampian
C.L. v. 19, 1906, 162–67.

Craigston Castle near Turriff, Grampian
J.P. Neale *Views* 2nd Series, v. 3, 1826. *C.L.* v. 134, 1963, 1050–53. Historical MSS Commission *Architectural history* v. 2, 1970, item 1301. *Gdn History* v. 11 no. 1, 1983, 37–56.

Crailing Hall near Jedburgh, Borders
G.A. Little *Scotland's gardens* 1981, 83.

Cranborne Manor, Cranborne, Dorset
C.L. v. 10, 1901, 732–41; v. 55, 1924, 910–18,964–72; v. 153, 1973, 1218–22,1350–53. G. Jekyll *Garden ornament* 1918, 93,168–70,175. P. Coats *Great gardens of Britain* 1967, 146–51. M. Allan *Fisons guide* 1970, 87–88. *J. Royal Hort. Soc.* 1975, 111–16. A. Paterson *Gardens of Britain* v. 2, 1978, 26–28. A. Hellyer *Gardens of genius* 1980, 155–61. T. Hinde *Stately gardens of Britain* 1983, 12–19.

Cranbourne (Cranburn) **Lodge** near Ascot, Berks
W.W.J. Gendall *Views* v. 1, 1830, 11–13. R. Ackermann *Repository* v. 1, 1823, pls. 7–8.

Cranbury Park near Winchester, Hants
F.O. Morris *Series of picturesque views* v. 1, 81. *C.L.* v. 120, 1956, 944–47,1058,1116. N. Pevsner and D. Lloyd *Hampshire and Isle of Wight* 1967, 184–85. B. Jones *Follies & grottoes* 1974, 336. A. Paterson *Gardens of Britain* v. 2, 1978, 75–76.

Cranford, Aughton, Lancs
M. Allan *Fisons guide* 1970, 221–22.

Cranford Park, Hounslow, London
W. Keane *Beauties of Middlesex* 1850, 204–07.

Cranmore (Orange Grove), Malone, Belfast, Co. Antrim, Ulster
Trans. Royal Irish Academy v. 8, 1802, 111–29.
J.C. Loudon *Arboretum et fruticetum Britannicum* v. 1, 1844, 111–12.

Cranmore Hall near Wells, Somerset
C.L. v. 5, 1899, 752–56.

Crarae, Loch Fyne, Strathclyde
Rhododendron & Camellia Year Book 1959, 25–32. *G.C.* ii 1962, 264–65. E. Hyams *English garden* 1964, 216–17. *J. Royal Hort. Soc.* 1966, 325–34. G.A. Little *Scotland's gardens* 1981, 228–30. *Scottish Field* v. 127 no. 953, 1981, 32–33. *C.L.* v. 174, 1983, 328–30.

Crathes Castle near Banchory, Grampian
Official guide. J.P. Neale *Views* v. 6, 1823. G. Jekyll and G.S. Elgood *Some English gardens* 1904, 42–46. *C.L.* v. 33, 1913, 598–603; v. 82, 1937, 272–76,322–27. G. Jekyll *Garden ornament* 1918, 281. *J. Royal Hort. Soc.* 1953, 240–42; 1961, 446–52. *G.C.* v. 160 no. 8, 1966, 14–15. M. Allan *Fisons guide* 1970, 337–38. H. Evans *Beautiful gardens of Britain* 1974, 123–24. P. Verney *Gardens of Scotland* 1976, 84–94. *Garden* 1977, 338–40. A. Hellyer *Gardens of genius* 1980, 171–75. G.A. Little *Scotland's gardens* 1981, 180–81.

Crathorne Hall near Yarm, N. Yorks
C.L. v. 29, 1911, 598–604. K. Lemmon *Gardens of Britain* v. 5, 1978, 68.

Craven Cottage, Fulham, London
T.C. Croker *Walk from London to Fulham* 1860, 190–91.
C.J. Féret *Fulham old and new* v. 3, 1900, 91–92.

Craycombe House near Evesham, Hereford and Worcester
C.L. v. 88, 1940, 10–14.

Crayford Workhouse, Bexley, London
G. Carter et al. *Humphry Repton* 1982, 155.

Creech Grange near Corfe Castle, Dorset
P. Pouncy *Dorset photographically illustrated* 1857.
J. Hutchins *History . . . of Dorset* v. 1, 1861, 605. *C.L.* v. 70, 1931, 252–58,278–82. Lady Rockley *Historic gardens of England* 1938, 156–57. M. Allan *Fisons guide* 1970, 89. J. Newman and N. Pevsner *Dorset* 1972, 175. M. Paterson *Gardens of Britain* v. 2, 1978, 28.

Cressbrook, Miller's Dale, Derbyshire
L. Fleming and A. Gore *English garden* 1979, 201.

Cresswell House, Northumberland
J. Hodgson *History of Northumberland* pt. 2, v. 2, 1832, 206; pt. 3, v. 3, 1835.

Cresswells Manor House (Philiberds), Berks
J. Harris *Artist and the country house* 1979, 58, pl. 8.

Cremorne, Chelsea, London
E.B. Chancellor *Pleasure haunts of London* 1925, 396–406.

Crete Hall, Northfleet, Kent
R. Ackermann *Repository* v. 8, 1826, pl. 26.
W.W.J. Gendall *Views* v. 1, 1830, 502. C. Greenwood *Epitome of county history . . . v. 1: Kent* 1838, 228.

Crewe. Queen's Park, Cheshire
N. Pevsner and E. Hubbard *Cheshire* 1971, 190.

Crewe Hall, Crewe, Cheshire
H. Repton *Sketches* 1794, 7–8. H. Vyse *Views of Crewe Hall* c.1840. G.C. 1863, 124; i 1885, 75–76; ii 1892, 737, 740–41. G. Ormerod *History of . . . Chester* v. 3, 1882, 310. C.L. v. 11, 1902, 400–08; v. 33, 1913, 634–40. D. Stroud *Humphry Repton* 1962, 78. D. Stroud *Capability Brown* 1975, 222. J. Harris *Artist and the country house* 1979, 142. G. Carter et al. *Humphry Repton* 1982, 149.

Crichel House near Wimborne Minster, Dorset
A. Young *Farmer's tour through East of England* v. 3, 1771, 259–60. J. Hutchins *History . . . of Dorset* v. 2, 1774, 49. J.P. Neale *Views* v. 1, 1818. P. Pouncy *Dorsetshire photographically illustrated* 1857. G.C. ii 1880, 8–10; i 1893, 508–10. C.L. v. 23, 1908, 90–96; v. 57, 1925, 766–74,874–81. G. Jekyll *Garden ornament* 1918, 257. J. Harris *Artist and the country house* 1979, 138.

Crimplesham Hall near Downham Market, Norfolk
B. Jones *Follies & grottoes* 1974, 360.

Cringlemere, Troutbeck, Cumbria
G. Beard *Thomas H. Mawson* 1976, 49.

Cripland Court, Sussex
G. Beard *Thomas H. Mawson* 1976, 69.

Crittenden House, Matfield, Kent
J. Royal Hort. Soc. 1960, 77–91. C.L. v. 135, 1964, 556–58; v. 157, 1975, 890–92. M. Allan *Fisons guide* 1970, 40–41. T. Wright *Gardens of Britain* v. 4, 1978, 33–36.

Croft Cappanach near Pitlochry, Tayside
G.A. Little *Scotland's gardens* 1981, 133–34.

Croft Castle near Leominster, Hereford and Worcester
Official guide. C.L. v. 122, 1957, 1255. G.C. v. 162 no. 20, 1967, 13. M. Hadfield *Hortus Croftensis*. G.S. Thomas *Gardens of National Trust* 1979, 128–29. R. Sidwell *West Midland gardens* 1981, 43–44.

Croft House, Ashton-under-Lyne, Greater Manchester
J.B. Burke *Visitation* v. 1, 1852, 123.

Crom Castle near Lisnaskea, Co. Fermanagh, Ulster
Florist 1859, 269–71. *Irish Gdning* v. 3, 1908, 186–87. A. Rowan *North West Ulster* 1979, 223–24. E. Malins and P. Bowe *Irish gardens and demesnes* 1980, 24. Ulster Architectural Heritage Society *Northern gardens* 1982, 17–18.

Cromer Hall, Cromer, Norfolk
J. Grigor *Eastern arboretum* 1841, 130–31.

Cromford House near Matlock, Derbyshire
Copper Plate Mag. v. 4, pl. 172.

Cromwell's Gardens (Florida Gardens), Brompton, Kensington, London
W. Wroth *London pleasure gardens of the eighteenth century* 1896, 225–28. E.B. Chancellor *Pleasure haunts of London* 1925, 368–69.

Crondon, Stock, Essex
F.G. Emmison *Catalogue of maps in Essex Record Office* 1947, 1,7,39, pl. 7; 2nd Supplt, 1964, 34.

Crooksbury House near Farnham, Surrey
C.L. v. 8, 1900, 336–43; v. 96, 1944, 596–99,640–43. L. Weaver *Houses and gardens by E.L. Lutyens* 1913, 1–5. J. Brown *Gardens of a golden afternoon* 1982, 160.

Croome Court, Croome D'Abitot, Hereford and Worcester
R.J. Sulivan *Tour . . . in 1778*, v. 1, 1785, 296–300. G. Tod *Plans, elevations and sections of hot-houses* 1807, 16, pl. 13. J.P. Neale *Views* v. 5, 1822. W. Dean *Historical and descriptive account of Croome D'Abitot . . . to which is annexed an Hortus Croomensis* 1824. *Gdning World* v. 3, 1887, 409–10. C.L. v. 13, 1903, 536–42; v. 37, 1915, 482–89. G. Jekyll *Garden ornament* 1918, 188. N. Pevsner *Worcestershire* 1968, 127–28. J. Harris *Catalogue of British drawings . . . in American collections* 1971, 4–5. D. Stroud *Capability Brown* 1975, 57–60,221. *Landscape Design* no. 116, 1976, 20–22. Worcestershire Archaeological Society *Trans.* v. 5, 1976, 41–49. J. Harris *Artist and the country house* 1979, 271. M. Hadfield et al. *British gardeners* 1980, 82.

Crosbie Tower, Strathclyde
Scottish Gdnr and Northern Forester v. 7, 1912, 369–70.

Cross O'Cliff, Lincoln, Lincs
G. Beard *Thomas H. Mawson* 1976, 50.

Crosslee Cottage, Strathclyde
G.M. v. 9, 1833, 14.

Crowcombe Court near Watchet, Somerset
J. Collinson *History . . . of Somersetshire* v. 3, 1791, 516. C.L. v. 73, 1933, 414–19.

Crowcombe Rectory, Watchet, Somerset
G.C. i 1961, 456–57.

Crowe Hall, Bath, Avon
J. *Hort. Cottage Gdnr* N.S., v. 53, 1906, 342–43. J. Sales *West Country gardens* 1980, 143–46.

Crowfield, Needham Market, Suffolk
D. Stroud *Humphry Repton* 1962, 169. G. Carter *et al. Humphry Repton* 1982, 161.

Crowhurst near Battle, E. Sussex
G. Jekyll *Garden ornament* 1918, 337, 353–54, 395, 417.

Crowhurst Place near Edenbridge, Surrey
C.L. v. 46, 1919, 12–19, 76–83. G.C. v. 164 no. 9, 1968, 15–17.

Crown East Court, Martley, Hereford and Worcester
J. *Hort. Cottage Gdnr* v. 33, 1865, 321.

Crow's Hall, Debenham, Suffolk
C.L. v. 5, 1899, 20–23.

Crowsley Park, Rotherfield, Oxfordshire
B. Jones *Follies & grottoes* 1974, 378.

Croxdale Hall, Croxdale, Co. Durham
C.L. v. 86, 1939, 202–06.

Croxteth near Prescot, Merseyside
J.P. Neale *Views* 2nd Series, v. 1, 1824. E. Baines *History . . . of Lancaster* v. 4, 1836, 28. J. *Hort. Cottage Gdnr* v. 62, 1879, 368–70; N.S., v. 12, 1886, 510, 511. G.C. ii 1891, 545–46. C. Holme *Gardens of England in Northern counties* 1911, pls. 40–42.

Croxton Park, Croxton, Cambs
Royal Commission on Historical Monuments *Inventory of historical monuments in . . . Cambridge* v. 1, 1968, pl. 67.

Crystal Palace *see* London

Cuckfield Park, Cuckfield, W. Sussex
J. *Hort. Cottage Gdnr* N.S., v. 50, 1905, 320–21. C.L. v. 45, 1919, 278–85.

Cuckfield Place, Cuckfield, W. Sussex
Garden v. 35, 1889, 355–56.

Cuerdon Hall near Chorley, Lancs
G.C. ii 1883, 362–63. T.H. Mawson *Art & craft of garden making* 1907, 254, 255–59. G. Beard *Thomas H. Mawson* 1976, 50.

Cuffnells near Lyndhurst, Hants
J. Hewetson *Architectural and picturesque views of noble mansions in Hampshire* c.1830. E.F. Prosser *Select illustrations of Hampshire* 1833. G.M. v. 11, 1835, 329–30. D. Stroud *Capability Brown* 1975, 221–22.

Culbuie, Buchlyvie, Central
G.A. Little *Scotland's gardens* 1981, 135.

Culdees Castle near Crieff, Tayside
J.P. Neale *Views* v. 6, 1823.

Culeaze, near Wareham, Dorset
A. Paterson *Gardens of Britain* v. 2, 1978, 29.

Culford near Bury St Edmunds, Suffolk
H. Repton *Sketches* 1794, 7. J.P. Neale *Views* v. 4, 1821. J. *Hort. Cottage Gdnr* v. 53, 1875, 164–66. D. Stroud *Humphry Repton* 1962, 67–68. M. Binney and A. Hills *Elysian gardens* 1979, 25. T. Wright *Arbors & grottos* 1979. G. Carter *et al. Humphry Repton* 1982, 161–62.

Culham Court, Aston, Berks
R. Bisgrove *Gardens of Britain* v. 3, 1978, 65–66.

Culham Manor, Culham, Oxfordshire
C.L. v. 108, 1950, 130–34.

Cullen House, Cullen, Grampian
C.L. v. 20, 1906, 378–83. A.A. Tait *Landscape garden in Scotland* 1980, passim.

Culloden House, Inverness, Highland
I.H. Adams *Descriptive list of plans* v. 3, 1974, 66.

Culross Abbey, Culross, Fife
J. Kip *Nouveau theatre de la Grande Bretagne* v. 4, 1729. G.M. v. 18, 1842, 591–92. C.L. v. 121, 1957, 981–83. G.A. Little *Scotland's gardens* 1981, 135–36.

Culverthorpe near Sleaford, Lincs
C.L. v. 54, 1923, 350–56, 386–91. Historical MSS Commission *Architectural history* v. 5, 1974, item 4995.

Culzean Castle near Maybole, Strathclyde
Official guide. J.P. Neale *Views* v. 6, 1823. G.M. v. 9, 1833, 8–9. *Scottish Gdnr and Northern Forester* v. 9, 1914, 25–26. J. *Hort. Cottage Gdnr* N.S., v. 5, 1882, 389–91. *Gdnrs Mag.* 1901, 139–40, 141. H. Maxwell *Scottish gardens* 1911, 149–57. C.L. v. 38, 1915, 328–35. G. Jekyll *Garden ornament* 1918, 263. P. Verney

Culzean Castle (*Cont.*)

Gardens of Scotland 1976, 38–49. *J. Royal Hort. Soc.* 1953, 238–39; 1961, 359–60. M. Allan *Fisons guide* 1970, 300–01. A.A. Tait *Landscape garden in Scotland* 1980, passim. G.A. Little *Scotland's gardens* 1981, 253–56.

Cumberland Tea Gardens, Vauxhall, Lambeth, London
W. Wroth *London pleasure gardens of the eighteenth century* 1896, 283–85.

Cumbernauld House, Cumbernauld, Strathclyde
Scottish Gdnr and Northern Forester v. 9, 1914, 285–86.

Cumnor Place, Cumnor, Oxfordshire
A.D. Bartlett *Historical and descriptive account of Cumnor Place, Berks* 1850, 23–24.

Cunnoquhie, Monimail, Fife
G.M. v. 7, 1831, 22–23. I.H. Adams *Descriptive list of plans* v. 3, 1974, 60.

Cuper's Gardens, Lambeth, London
W. Wroth *London pleasure gardens of the eighteenth century* 1896, 247–57. E.B. Chancellor *Pleasure haunts of London* 1925, 358–64.

Curragh Grange, Co. Kildare, Eire
Irish Gdning v. 11, 1916, 37,51,53.

Curraghmore near Portlaw, Co. Waterford, Eire
Royal Hort. Soc. *Conifers in cultivation* 1932, 218. *C.L.* v. 133, 1963, 256–60,308–11,368–71. M. Allan *Fisons guide* 1970, 355–56. B. Jones *Follies & grottoes* 1974, 166–68. E. Malins *and* Knight of Glin *Lost demesnes* 1976, 93–94. Knight of Glin *and* P. Bowe *Gardens of outstanding historic interest in . . . Ireland* 1980. E. Malins *and* P. Bowe *Irish gardens and demesnes* 1980, 35.

Curtis, William *see* London Botanic Garden

Cusworth Hall near Doncaster, S. Yorks
Official guide. W. Angus *Seats* 1787, pl. 16. J.P. Neale *Views* v. 5, 1822. *Jones's views* 1829, 37. *Trans. Hunter Archaeological Soc.* v. 8, 1963, 298–303.

Dagnams, Noak Hill, Havering, London
P. Muilman *History of Essex* v. 4, 1771, 291. P. Morant *History . . . of Essex* v. 1, 1816, 62. F.G. Emmison *Catalogue of maps in Essex Record Office* 1947, 16. D. Stroud *Humphry Repton* 1962, 169. *V.C.H. Essex* v. 5, 1966, 200. G. Carter *et al*. *Humphry Repton* 1982, 151.

Dairy House, Ludstone, Shropshire
R. Sidwell *West Midland gardens* 1981, 110–12.

Dalawoodie, Dumfries and Galloway
Scottish Gdnr and Northern Forester v. 7, 1912, 173–74.

Dalby Hall near Spilsby, Lincs
Copper Plate Mag. v. 5, 1802, pl. 120.

Dale Park, Arundel, W. Sussex
Garden v. 38, 1890, 75.

Dalemain, Penrith, Cumbria
Official guide. *C.L.* v. 111, 1952, 736–39,820–24,908. S.M. McCosh *Between two gardens: diary of two Border gardens* 1982.

Dalgairn House, Cupar, Fife
Scots Mag. N.S., v. 113, 1980, 245–51. G.A. Little *Scotland's gardens* 1981, 136.

Dalguise near Dunkeld, Tayside
J.P. Neale *Views* v. 6, 1823.

Dalham Hall near Higham, Suffolk
T.H. Mawson *Art & craft of garden making* 1907, 24,60. *C.L.* v. 54, 1923, 280–85. R.I.B.A. *Catalogue* v. G-K, 1973, 55. G. Beard *Thomas H. Mawson* 1976, 50.

Dalhousie Castle near Edinburgh, Lothian
G.M. v. 18, 1842, 585–86. J. Harris *Artist and the country house* 1979, 341. A.A. Tait *Landscape garden in Scotland* 1980, passim.

Dalkeith Palace near Edinburgh, Lothian
J.P. Neale *Views* 2nd Series, v. 4, 1828. C. McIntosh *Book of the garden* 1853–55, pls. 4,12,15. *Cottage Gdnr* v. 17, 1856, 35–37. *J. Hort. Cottage Gdnr* v. 44, 1870, 329–32; v. 53, 1875, 181–83,203–04. *G.C.* i 1902, 81–83; i 1906, 33–34. *J. Hort. Home Farmer* N.S., v. 64, 1912, 14–17. F.O. Morris *Series of picturesque views* v. 5, 49. C. McWilliam *Lothian* 1978, 161. A.A. Tait *Landscape garden in Scotland* 1980, passim.

Dallam Tower, Milnthorpe, Cumbria
G.C. i 1875, 108–10. *C.L.* v. 172, 1982, 1578–80.

Dallington House near Northampton, Northants
J.P. Neale *Views* v. 3, 1820.

Dalmahoy near Ratho, Lothian
J.C. Loudon *Arboretum et fruticetum Britannicum* v. 1, 1844, 101–02.

Dalmeny near Edinburgh, Lothian
J.P. Neale *Views* v. 6, 1823. *Scottish Gdnr and Northern Forester* v. 7, 1912, 717–18. *G.C.* ii 1892, 787–89.

Dalmore, Helensburgh, Strathclyde
Scottish Gdnr and Northern Forester v. 6, 1911, 753–54.

Dalquharran Castle, Dailly, Strathclyde
Scottish Gdnr and Northern Forester v. 7, 1912, 645–46.

Dalswinton House, Dalswinton, Dumfries and Galloway
Copper Plate Mag. v. 3, pl. 108. G.A. Little *Scotland's gardens* 1981, 256.

Dalton Hall near Beverley, Humberside
F.O. Morris *Series of picturesque views* v. 6, 55. *G.C.* ii 1907, 141–42.

Dalvey House near Forres, Grampian
G.M. v. 19, 1843, 416–18.

Dalzell House, Dalziel, Strathclyde
C.L. v. 9, 1901, 176–81. H. Maxwell *Scottish gardens* 1911, 161–66. G. Jekyll *Garden ornament* 1918, 247.

Danbury near Chelmsford, Essex
T. Wright *History . . . of Essex* v. 1, 1836, 128.
F.O. Morris *Series of picturesque views* v. 2, 77.
F.G. Emmison *Catalogue of maps in Essex Record Office* 3rd Supplt, 1968, 3.

Danby Hall near Middleham, N. Yorks
C.L. v. 9, 1901, 804–09.

Dane Court, Tilmanstone, Kent
C. Greenwood *Epitome of county history . . . v. 1: Kent* 1838, 420.

Dane Park, Margate, Kent
G.C. ii 1898, 71.

Danes Cottage, Oxshott, Surrey
C.L. v. 174, 1983, 1072–74.

Danesbury Park, Welwyn, Herts
Garden v. 20, 1881, 417–18.

Danesfield near Great Marlow, Bucks
F.O. Morris *Series of picturesque views* v. 5, 77. *Gdning World* v. 11, 1895, 597; v. 15, 1899, 581–82, 603–04.

Daneshill, Basingstoke, Hants
L. Weaver *Houses and gardens by E.L. Lutyens* 1913, 119–22. J. Brown *Gardens of a golden afternoon* 1982, 167.

Danett's Hall, Leics
J. Throsby *Select views in Leicestershire* v. 1, 1790, 262.
J. Nichols *History . . . of county of Leicester* v. 4, 1811, 571.

Dangstein near Petersfield, Hants
J. Hort. Cottage Gdnr v. 31, 1864, 9–10; v. 48, 1872, 515–18; v. 49, 1873, 33–34.

Danny, Hurstpierpoint, W. Sussex
T.W. Horsfield *History . . . of Sussex* v. 1, 1835, 244.
C.L. v. 33, 1913, 418–24. Historical MSS Commission *Architectural history* v. 4, 1972, item 4164.

Danson, Bexley, London
Copper Plate Mag. v. 2, pl. 52. D. Stroud *Capability Brown* 1975, 222. D. Jacques *Georgian gardens* 1983, 84.

Danvers House, Chelsea, London
Architectural Review v. 29, 1911, 275.

Darfield Rectory, Darfield, S. Yorks
J. Gdn History v. 2 no. 1, 1982, 5–9.

Dargle Cottage, Enniskerry, Co. Wicklow, Eire
C.L. v. 157, 1975, 1332–33. Knight of Glin and P. Bowe *Gardens of outstanding historic interest in . . . Ireland* 1980. E. Malins and P. Bowe *Irish gardens and demesnes* 1980, 135–36. *Moorea* no. 1, 1982, 21–36.

Darlaston Hall, Darlaston, Staffs
F. Calvert *Picturesque views . . . in Staffordshire & Shropshire* 1830, 43.

Darley Hall, Darley, Derbyshire
N. Nichols *Local maps of Derbyshire to 1770* 1980, 63.

Darnaway Castle near Forres, Grampian
Historical MSS Commission *Architectural history* v. 5, 1974, item 5026.

Darrington, W. Yorks
I. Hall *Samuel Buck's Yorkshire sketchbook* 1979, 59.

Dartington Hall near Totnes, Devon
Official guide. J. Britton and E.W. Brayley *Devonshire & Cornwall* 1832, 70. *C.L.* v. 84, 1938, 204–09, 232; v. 145, 1969, 232–35; v. 152, 1972, 6–9. *J. Royal Hort. Soc.* 1954, 246–56. *G.C.* ii 1962, 404–05. E. Hyams *English garden* 1964, 242–47. *Illustrated London News* v. 247, 1965, 32. M. Allan *Fisons guide* 1970, 122–23. H. Evans *Beautiful gardens of Britain* 1974, 13–14. R. Webber *Percy Cane* 1945, 94–99, 179. P.M. Synge *Gardens of Britain* v. 1, 1977, 33–39.

Dartmoor Prison near Princetown, Devon
G.C. v. 160 no. 11, 1966, 18–19.

Dartrey near Cootehill, Co. Monaghan, Ulster
Florist 1860, 240–42. F.O. Morris *Series of picturesque views* v. 3, 57.

Davenham Bank, Malvern, Hereford and Worcester
Gdning World v. 1, 1884, 247; v. 2, 1886, 820. *G.C.* ii 1899, 162.

Davenport House near Bridgnorth, Shropshire
Harrison and Co. *Picturesque views of the principal seats . . . in England and Wales* c.1788. F. Calvert *Picturesque views . . . in Shropshire* 1831, 124. *C.L.* v. 111, 1952, 1996–99; v. 112, 1952, 40. J. Harris *Gardens of delight* 1978, 24–27. D. Watkin *English vision* 1982, 32.

Davids, Northfield, W. Midlands
R. Sidwell *West Midland gardens* 1981, 209–10.

Dawley, Uxbridge, London
J. Beeverell *Les delices de la Grande Bretagne* v. 5, 1707, 872. L. Knyff *and* J. Kip *Britannia illustrata* v. 1, 1714. H.I. Triggs *Formal gardens in England and Scotland* 1902, 40. M. Macartney *English houses & gardens* 1908, pl. 26. V.C.H. *Middlesex* v. 3, 1962, 265. *Gdn History* v. 4 no. 1, 1976, 45,50. M.R. Brownell *Alexander Pope & the arts of Georgian England* 1978, 225–29.

Dawpool, Thurstaston, Merseyside
C.L. v. 29, 1911, 234–41.

Daws Hill, High Wycombe, Bucks
C. Holme *Gardens of England in the Southern & Western counties* 1907, pls. 44–45. M. Binney *and* A. Hills *Elysian gardens* 1979, 40.

Dawson's Grove, Co. Monaghan, Ulster
E. Malins *and* Knight of Glin *Lost demesnes* 1976, 84–85.

Dawyck, Stobo, Borders
C.L. v. 74, 1933, 156–58. *J. Royal Hort. Soc.* 1947, 5–12. M. Allan *Fisons guide* 1970, 319–20. P. Verney *Gardens of Scotland* 1976, 50–62. G.A. Little *Scotland's gardens* 1981, 83–84.

Daylesford near Stow-on-the-Wold, Glos
J.P. Neale *Views* v. 5, 1822. *Field* 7 April 1977, 566–68. L. Fleming *and* A. Gore *English garden* 1979, 200.

Deane, Barham, Kent
J. Harris *History of Kent* 1719, 335. J. Kip *Nouveau theatre de la Grande Bretagne* v. 4, 1729. T. Badeslade *Thirty six different views . . . in Kent* 1750s, pl. 10. J.P. Neale *Views* 2nd Series, v. 2, 1825. M. Macartney *English houses & gardens* 1908, pl. 12. J. Harris *Artist and the country house* 1979, 138.

Deanery, Sonning, Berks
L. Weaver *Houses and gardens by E.L. Lutyens* 1913, 53–63. G. Jekyll *Garden ornament* 1918, passim.

A.S. Butler *et al. Architecture of Sir Edwin Lutyens* v. 2, 1950, 11. R.I.B.A. *Catalogue: Lutyens* 1973, 47. J. Brown *Gardens of a golden afternoon* 1982, 66–69,165.

Deanery, Rochester, Kent
G. Jekyll *and* G.S. Elgood *Some English gardens* 1904, 93–95.

Debden Hall, Debden, Essex
J.P. Neale *Views* v. 1, 1818. T. Wright *History . . . of Essex* v. 2, 1836, 139. F.G. Emmison *Catalogue of maps in Essex Record Office* 1st Supplt, 1952, 31.

Decker, Sir Matthew *see* Richmond

Deene Park near Rockingham, Northants
Official guide. J.P. Neale *Views* 2nd Series, v. 1, 1824. F.O. Morris *Series of picturesque views* v. 4, 37. *Garden* v. 46, 1894, 241–42. *C.L.* v. 25, 1909, 234–44; v. 159, 1976, 610–13,750–53,810–13. J. Anthony *Gardens of Britain* v. 6, 1979, 65–68. A. Lees-Milne *and* R. Verey *Englishwoman's garden* 1980, 45–46.

Deepdene near Dorking, Surrey
Topographer v. 1, 1789, 11–12. J.C. Loudon *Encyclopaedia of gardening* 1822, 1228. R. Ackermann *Repository* v. 1, 1823, pls. 31–32. J.P. Neale *Views* 2nd Series, v. 3, 1826. J.P. Neale *Account of Deep-dene* 1826. G.F. Prosser *Select illustrations of . . . Surrey* 1828. *G.M.* v. 5, 1829, 589–93. W.W.J. Gendall *Views* v. 2, 1830, 23–27. N.W. Wittock *and* H. Gastineau *Picturesque beauties of England and Wales* 1830, 55–58. E.W. Brayley *and* J. Britton *Topographical history of Surrey* v. 5, 1848, 89–90. W. Keane *Beauties of Surrey* 1849, 152–57. J.B. Burke *Visitation* 2nd Series, v. 1, 1855, 218–19. *J. Hort. Cottage Gdnr* v. 55, 1876, 252–54. *Gdning World* v. 2, 1886, 776–78. *C.L.* v. 5, 1899, 624–29. *G.C.* i 1900, 42–43. J. Evelyn *Diary* v. 3, 1955, 154,561. D. Watkin *Thomas Hope* 1968, 158–92,250–54. R.I.B.A. *Catalogue* v. B, 1972, 108. B. Jones *Follies & grottoes* 1974, 16–17. J. Harris *Artist and the country house* 1979, 326.

Delaford Park near Colnbrook, Bucks
R. Ackermann *Repository* v. 3, 1824, pl. 26. W.W.J. Gendall *Views* v. 2, 1830, 84. G. Lipscombe *History . . . of Buckingham* v. 4, 1847, 529.

Delapré Abbey, Northampton, Northants
J.P. Neale *Views* v. 3, 1820. *C.L.* v. 127, 1960, 218–21. J. Anthony *Gardens of Britain* v. 6, 1979, 68–69.

Dell, Egham, Surrey
G.C. i 1884, 764–66; i 1888, 714; ii 1891, 244–45; i 1908, 377–78. *Garden* v. 29, 1886, 516,517,521. *Gdning World* v. 3, 1886, 72. *J. Hort. Cottage Gdnr* N.S., v. 12, 1886, 513–14.

Delrow near Watford, Herts
G.C. ii 1892, 430.

Delville, Glasnevin, Co. Dublin, Eire
J.N. Brewer *Beauties of Ireland* v. 1, 1825, 219–20.
E. Malins *and* Knight of Glin *Lost demesnes* 1976, 36–39.

Den, Cropthorne, Hereford and Worcester
Studio v. 34, 1905, 292–97.

Denbies near Dorking, Surrey
New display of the beauties of England v. 2, 1787, 302–03. *Gentleman's Magazine* 1781, 123–24. J. Hassell *Picturesque rides and walks* v. 1, 1817. J.P. Neale *Views* 2nd Series, v. 3, 1826. G.F. Prosser *Select illustrations of . . . Surrey* 1828. E.W. Brayley *and* J. Britton *Topographical history of Surrey* v. 5, 1848, 90. W. Keane *Beauties of Surrey* 1849, 157–59. *J. Hort. Cottage Gdnr* v. 37, 1867, 143; v. 55, 1876, 234–36. G.C. ii 1886, 261–62. *Gdning World* v. 2, 1886, 694. *Gdn History* v. 3 no. 3, 1975, 58–61. *J. Gdn History* v. 1 no. 23, 1981, 215–38.

Denbrae near St Andrews, Fife
G.M. v. 7, 1831, 681.

Denbry House near Haslemere, Surrey
G.M. v. 5, 1829, 576.

Denby Grange, Kirkheaton, W. Yorks
J.P. Neale *Views* v. 5, 1822.

Denford near Hungerford, Berks
G.M. v. 7, 1831, 136.

Denham Place near Uxbridge, Bucks
C.L. v. 18, 1905, 702–09; v. 57, 1925, 602–09. D. Stroud *Capability Brown* 1975, 222. J. Harris *Artist and the country house* 1979, 123 pl. 14.

Denmans near Chichester, W. Sussex
T. Wright *Gardens of Britain* v. 4, 1978, 137–40. *Garden* 1981, 47–51.

Denne Hill near Barham, Kent
C. Greenwood *Epitome of county history . . . v. 1: Kent* 1838, 404.

Denne Park near Horsham, W. Sussex
Garden v. 35, 1889, 401–02.

Denton House, Denton, Lincs
B. Howlett *Selection of views in . . . Lincoln* 1885. J.P. Neale *Views* v. 2, 1819. *Jones's views* 1829. B. Jones *Follies & grottoes* 1974, 358.

Denton House, Denton, Norfolk
B. Jones *Follies & grottoes* 1974, 360.

Denton Park, Denton, N. Yorks
J.P. Neale *Views* v. 5, 1822. *Jones's views* 1829. F.O. Morris *Series of picturesque views* v. 5, 33. Historical MSS Commission *Architectural history* v. 3, 1971, item 2680.

Deoran, Stirling, Central
G. Beard *Thomas H. Mawson* 1976, 50.

Deptford Park *see* London

Derby (Mr Chambers), Derbyshire
S. and N. Buck *Buck's antiquities* v. 3, 1774, pl. 20.

Derby Arboretum, Derbyshire
G.M. v. 16, 1840, 59–63, 520–45. J.C. Loudon *Derby Arboretum* 1840. *Journey-book of England: Derbyshire* 1841, 49–53. W. Adam *Gem of the Peak* 1851, 3–5. G. Chadwick *Park and the town* 1966, passim. C.L. v. 160, 1976, 1582–84. J. Anthony *Gardens of Britain* v. 6, 1979, 69–70.

Dereham, Norfolk
J. Grigor *Eastern arboretum* 1841, 37–39.

Derehams (Durhams) **Manor**, South Mimms, Herts
V.C.H. *Middlesex* v. 5, 1976, 284.

Derncleugh near Dawlish, Devon
G.C. i 1882, 826–27.

Derreen near Kenmare, Co. Kerry, Eire
New Flora & Silva v. 1, 1929, 121. *J. Royal Hort. Soc.* 1966, 14–16. C.L. v. 162, 1977, 84–85. A. Hellyer *Gardens of genius* 1980, 56–57. Knight of Glin *and* P. Bowe *Gardens of outstanding historic interest in . . . Ireland* 1980. E. Malins *and* P. Bowe *Irish gardens and demesnes* 1980, 108–11.

Derrymore near Bessbrook, Co. Armagh, Ulster
National Trust Studies 1981, 12–15.

Derry's Wood, Wonersh, Surrey
C.L. v. 48, 1920, 144–51.

Derwent Hall, Derwent, Derbyshire
C.L. v. 21, 1907, 198–205. Historical MSS Commission *Architectural history* v. 1, 1969, item 275.

Detling Hall near Maidstone, Kent
G. Beard *Thomas H. Mawson* 1976, 50.

Devizes Castle, Devizes, Wilts
G.C. ii 1878, 240–42, 245; ii 1887, 196.

Devonhall, Ochil Hills, Tayside
C.L. v. 76, 1934, 640–45. G.C. ii 1938, 214–15.

Devonhurst, Chiswick, London
G.C. ii 1888, 726.

Devonshire House, Piccadilly, London
C.L. v. 36, 1914, 266–67.

Dews Hall, Lambourne, Essex
J.P. Neale *Views* 2nd Series, v. 1, 1824.

Diddington, Cambs
J. Hort. Cottage Gdnr N.S., v. 9, 1884, 121,163–64.

Didlington Hall, Northwold, Norfolk
B. Jones *Follies & grottoes* 1974, 362.

Dilmarton near Tetbury, Glos
R. Atkyns *Ancient and present state of Glostershire* 1712, 390. L. Knyff and J. Kip *Britannia illustrata* v. 2, 1715.

Didsbury Lodge, Greater Manchester
Cottage Gdnr v. 23, 1860, 320–23.

Digswell near Hatfield, Herts
D. Stroud *Capability Brown* 1975, 222.

Dillington House, Ilminster, Somerset
J.P. Neale *Views* 2nd Series, v. 4, 1828.

Dilston Castle, Dilston, Northumberland
G.C. ii 1880, 555–56.

Dimland Castle (Dimlands), Cowbridge, S. Glamorgan
J.B. Burke *Visitation* v. 2, 1853, 213.

Dingley Hall near Market Harborough, Northants
C.L. v. 13, 1903, 208–16; v. 49, 1921, 462–69,494. G. Jekyll *Garden ornament* 1918, 171.

Dinmore Manor, Hope under Dinmore, Hereford and Worcester
M. Allan *Fisons guide* 1970, 272–73. B. Jones *Follies & grottoes* 1974, 272–73. R. Sidwell *West Midland gardens* 1981, 45.

Dinorben House near Tunbridge Wells, Kent
J. Hort. Cottage Gdnr v. 32, 1864, 435–36.

Dinton, Wilts
J. Britton *Beauties of Wiltshire* v. 3, 1825, 326. C.L. v. 94, 1943, 1080–83.

Ditchingham Hall, Ditchingham, Norfolk
R. Webber *Percy Cane* 1975, 91–93.

Ditchingham House, Ditchingham, Norfolk
G.M. v. 17, 1841, 273. J. Grigor *Eastern arboretum* 1841, 253–55.

Ditchley Park near Woodstock, Oxfordshire
Society of Gentlemen *England displayed* v. 1, 1769, 268. C. Burlington *Modern universal British traveller* 1779, 237. J.P. Neale *Views* v. 3, 1820. C.L. v. 16, 1904, 594–602; v. 75, 1934, 590–95. Historical MSS Commission *Architectural history* v. 3, 1971, items 2692, 2992. J. Sherwood and N. Pevsner *Oxfordshire* 1974, 576. D. Stroud *Capability Brown* 1975, 222. R. Bisgrove *Gardens of Britain* v. 3, 1978, 67–68. L. Fleming and A. Gore *English garden* 1979, 226. *Royal Soc. of Arts J.* v. 128, 1980, 284–94. *Gdn History* v. 10 no. 1, 1982, 80–91.

Ditton House near Slough, Berks
E.M. Elvey *Hand-list of Buckinghamshire estate maps* 1963, 36.

Ditton Park near Slough, Berks
R. Ackermann *Repository* v. 2, 1823, pl. 7. W.W.J. Gendall *Views* v. 2, 1830, 27–28. G.M. v. 9, 1833, 650–51; v. 13, 1837, 1–2. G.C. ii 1913, 176. E.M. Elvey *Hand-list of Buckinghamshire estate maps* 1963, 36. D. Stroud *Capability Brown* 1975, 222–23.

Ditton Place, Balcombe, W. Sussex
C.L. v. 30, 1911, 18–25.

Dixton Manor near Winchcombe, Glos
C.L. v. 99, 1946, 762–65, 808. J. Harris *Artist and the country house* 1979, 270, pl. 24.

Dobney's Bowling Green, Islington, London
W. Wroth *London pleasure gardens of the eighteenth century* 1896, 141–44.

Docking, Norfolk
A. Young *Six weeks tour through the southern counties of England and Wales* 1768, 39–40.

Doddinghurst Place, Doddinghurst, Essex
F.G. Emmison *Catalogue of maps in Essex Record Office* 2nd Supplt, 1964, 16.

Doddington Hall, Doddington, Cheshire
C.L. v. 113, 1953, 344–47,414. D. Stroud *Capability Brown* 1975, 223.

Doddington Hall, Doddington, Lincs
J. Beeverell *Les delices de la Grande Bretagne* v. 5, 1707, 872. L. Knyff and J. Kip *Britannia illustrata* v. 1, 1714. *J. Hort. Cottage Gdnr* v. 57, 1877, 312–14; N.S., v. 39, 1899, 452–53. C.L. v. 10, 1901, 176–82; v. 80, 1936, 356–61. M. Macartney *English houses & gardens* 1908,

Doddington Hall (*Cont.*)
pl. 14. R. Dutton *English garden* 1937, pl. 51.
J. Anthony *Gardens of Britain* v. 6, 1979, 71–73.

Dodford, Northants
Northamptonshire Past & Present v. 5 no. 3, 1975, 221.

Dodington House, Dodington, Avon
J.N. Brewer *Delineations of Gloucestershire* 1825, 31.
C.L. v. 54, 1924, 170–75; v. 120, 1956, 1176–79.
Architectural Review v. 71, 1932, 95–99, pls. 4–7.
D. Verey *Gloucestershire* v. 1, 1970, 214. B. Jones *Follies & grottoes* 1974, 284. D. Stroud *Capability Brown* 1975, 134. L. Fleming *and* A. Gore *English garden* 1979, 119–20. J. Sales *West Country gardens* 1980, 52–54.

Dodpits House, Newbridge, Isle of Wight
A. Paterson *Gardens of Britain* v. 2, 1978, 161–62.

Dodsley, Robert *see* Richmond

Dogmersfield Park near Odiham, Hants
J.P. Neale *Views* v. 2, 1819. E.F. Prosser *Select illustrations of Hampshire* 1833. J.B. Burke *Visitation* 2nd Series, v. 1, 1855, 243. *G.C.* ii 1883, 463. *J. Hort. Cottage Gdnr* N.S., v. 19, 1889, 246–48. R. Pococke *Travels through England* v. 2, 1889, 161–62. *C.L.* v. 9, 1901, 528–33; v. 135, 1964, 20–23. G. Jekyll *Garden ornament* 1918, 121, 211. J. Harris *Artist and the country house* 1979, 175, 240.

Dollarbeg near Dollar, Central
Scottish Gdnr and Northern Forester v. 7, 1912, 333–34.

Domaine des Vaux, Jersey, Channel Islands
C.L. v. 160, 1976, 28–30.

Donaghadee, Co. Down, Ulster
B. Jones *Follies & grottoes* 1974, 74–75.

Doneraile, Co. Cork, Eire
J. Hort. Cottage Gdnr N.S., v. 13, 1886, 523–24. Knight of Glin *and* P. Bowe *Gardens of outstanding historic interest in . . . Ireland* 1980.

Donibristle, Fife
J.P. Neale *Views* 2nd Series, v. 4, 1828. Historical MSS Commission *Architectural history* v. 5, 1974, item 4999.

Donington near Castle Donington, Leics
A. Young *Farmer's tour through East of England* v. 4, 1771, 45–46. J. Throsby *Select views in Leicestershire* v. 1, 1790, 166. J. Nichols *History . . . of county of Leicester* v. 3, 1804, 778. J.P. Neale *Views* v. 2, 1819. F.O. Morris *Series of picturesque views* v. 5, 9. *G.C.* ii 1880, 687–88. D. Stroud *Humphrey Repton* 1962, 51. G. Carter *et al. Humphry Repton* 1982, 156.

Donnington Castle House, Newbury, Berks
R. Bisgrove *Gardens of Britain* v. 3, 1978, 68.

Donnington Grove near Speen, Berks
A. Robertson *Topographical survey of the Great Road* v. 1, 1792, 148–49.

Dorfold Hall near Nantwich, Cheshire
S.C. Hall *Baronial halls and picturesque edifices of England* 1848. *C.L.* v. 24, 1908, 594–606.

Dormey House, Walton Heath, Surrey
G. Jekyll *and* L. Weaver *Gardens for small country houses* 1913, xxxvii–xl. J. Brown *Gardens of a golden afternoon* 1982, 169.

Dorney Court, Dorney, Bucks
G. Lipscombe *History . . . of Buckingham* v. 4, 1847, 273. B. Jones *Follies & grottoes* 1974, 293.

Dorneywood, Burnham Beeches, Bucks
C.L. v. 110, 1951, 1892–96, 2024. G.S. Thomas *Gardens of National Trust* 1979, 129.

Dornford, Oxfordshire
D. Stroud *Capability Brown* 1975, 223.

Dorton House, Dorton, Bucks
G. Lipscomb *History . . . of Buckingham* v. 1, 1847, 243.

Doughton Manor House near Tetbury, Glos
C.L. v. 17, 1905, 668–69.

Doune, Central
P. Verney *Gardens of Scotland* 1976, 129–39.

Douneside House, Tarland, Grampian
G.A. Little *Scotland's gardens* 1981, 181.

Dove Cottage, Grasmere, Cumbria
Gdnrs Yearbook 1930, 33–37. *Gdn History* v. 2 no. 2, 1974, 45–50.

Dover House, Roehampton, London
G.C. ii 1892, 557–58; ii 1899, 125; i 1910, 225–26, 227. *Garden* v. 59, 1901, 133–34.

Doveridge House near Uttoxeter, Derbyshire
J.P. Neale *Views* v. 1, 1818. *Jones's views* 1829.

Dowdeswell Court, Dowdeswell, Glos
J.B. Burke *Visitation* v. 1, 1852, 247. *G.C.* ii 1921, 249.

Dower House, Badminton, Avon
A. Lees-Milne *and* R. Verey *Englishwoman's garden*

Dower House, Dogmersfield, Hants
A. Paterson *Gardens of Britain* v. 2, 1978, 76–77.

Dower House, Northampton, Northants
C.L. v. 160, 1976, 166–67.

Dowley Court near Uxbridge, London
W. Keane *Beauties of Middlesex* 1850, 110–12.

Down Hall near Bishop's Stortford, Essex
J.P. Neale *Views* v.1, 1818. P. Willis *Charles Bridgeman* 1977, 178.

Down House near Blandford, Dorset
F.O. Morris *Series of picturesque views* v. 5, 55. G.C. i 1899, 316.

Down House, Downe, Kent
G.C. i 1888, 359–60.

Down Lodge, Epsom, Surrey
Garden v. 28, 1885, 629–30.

Downes, Hayle, Cornwall
G.C. i 1898, 217, 219–20.

Downes, Crediton, Devon
R. Polwhele *History of Devonshire* v. 2, 1793, 89. G.C. ii 1882, 172–73.

Downhill near Coleraine, Co. Londonderry, Ulster
J.P. Neale *Views* v. 6, 1823. C.L. v. 150, 1971, 154–57. E. Malins *and* Knight of Glin *Lost demesnes* 1976, 145–53. A. Rowan *North West Ulster* 1979, 247. Ulster Architectural Heritage Society *Northern gardens* 1982, 18.

Downhills, Hornsey, London
W. Keane *Beauties of Middlesex* 1850, 142–43.

Downing near Holywell, Clwyd
R.C. Hoare *Collection of forty-eight views* 1806, pl. 2.

Downshire House, Roehampton, London
G.C. ii 1886, 389–90.

Downside near Leatherhead, Surrey
G.C. i 1882, 631–32; ii 1902, 398. C.L. v. 4, 1898, 336–39.

Downton Castle, Downton on the Rock, Hereford and Worcester
H. Skrine *Two successive tours throughout . . . Wales* 1812, 260–61. J.C. Loudon *Encyclopaedia of gardening* 1822, 1238. J.P. Neale *Views* 2nd Series, v. 3, 1826. G.M. v. 9, 1833, 17–18; v. 14, 1838, 209–12. *Cottage Gdnr* v. 28, 1862, 177–78. G.C. ii 1884, 679–80; i 1892, 747–48. C.L. v. 42, 1917, 36–42, 60–66. N. Pevsner *Herefordshire* 1963, 118. B. Jones *Follies & grottoes* 1974, 380. M. Clarke *and* N. Penny *Arrogant connoisseur: Richard Payne Wright* 1982.

Downton Hall near Ludlow, Shropshire
F. Calvert *Picturesque views . . . in Shropshire* 1831, 129. F.O. Morris *Series of picturesque views* v. 5, 71.

Drakelow Hall near Burton on Trent, Derbyshire
F.O. Morris *Series of picturesque views* v. 2, 51. C.L. v. 11, 1902, 368–75; v. 21, 1907, 378–84. C. Holme *Gardens of England in Midland & Eastern counties* 1908 pls. 47–51. G. Jekyll *Garden ornament* 1918, 161. G. Carter *et al. Humphry Repton* 1982, 150.

Drapers' Company *see* London

Draycot House near Chippenham, Wilts
A. Robertson *Topographical survey of the Great Road* 1792, pt. 2, 63–64. *J. Hort. Cottage Gdnr* v. 50, 1873, 489–91; N.S., v. 43, 1901, 220.

Drayton Green (Mrs L. Lawrence), Ealing, London
G.M. v. 9, 1833, 517–18; v. 14, 1838, 305–22. C.G. Carns *King of Saxony's journey through England and Scotland* 1846, 117. J.C. Loudon *Villa gardener* 1850, 270–75. *J. Royal Hort. Soc.* 1955, 423–28. C.L. v. 154, 1973, 580–81. L. Fleming *and* A. Gore *English garden* 1979, 177.

Drayton House near Uxbridge, London
W. Keane *Beauties of Middlesex* 1850, 81–83.

Drayton House, Kettering, Northants
Official guide. J. Morton *Natural history of Northamptonshire* 1712, 493–94. Society of Gentlemen *England displayed* v. 1, 1769, 366. S. *and* N. Buck *Buck's antiquities* v. 1, 1774, pl. 209. J.P. Neale *Views* 2nd Series, v. 4, 1828. *Jones's views* 1829. H.I. Triggs *Formal gardens in England and Scotland* 1902, 19–20. C.L. v. 25, 1909, 528–29; v. 31, 1912, 898–908, 934–44; v. 137, 1965, 1146–50, 1216–19, 1286. G. Jekyll *Garden ornament* 1918, 51, 85, 91, 210, 314. H. Walpole *Visits to country seats*. Walpole Society v. 7, 1927–28, 57. Lady Rockley *Historic gardens of England* 1938, 110–11. *Northamptonshire Past & Present* v. 5 no. 3, 1975, 221, 222–23. Royal Commission on Historical Monuments *Inventory of historical monuments in . . . Northampton* v. 1, 1975, 63, pl. 11. M. Binney *and* A. Hills *Elysian gardens* 1979, 14. J. Harris *Artist and the country house* 1979, 136–37.

Drayton Manor, Drayton Bassett, Staffs
G.M. v. 15, 1839, 457–58. G.C. 1868, 766–68. C.L. v. 23, 1908, 450–55.

Drenagh near Limavady, Co. Londonderry, Ulster
A. Rowan *North West Ulster* 1979, 250. *Gdn History* v. 8 no. 1, 1980, 17–24. Ulster Architectural Heritage Society *Northern gardens* 1982, 19.

Drinstone Park near Stowmarket, Suffolk
G.C. i 1884, 339.

Dromana near Cappoquin, Co. Waterford, Eire
E. Malins *and* Knight of Glin *Lost demesnes* 1976, 99.

Dromoland near Newmarket, Co. Clare, Eire
F.O. Morris *Series of picturesque views* v. 4, 27. E. Malins *and* Knight of Glin *Lost demesnes* 1976, 22,23. B. Jones *Follies & grottoes* 1974, 427. Knight of Glin *and* P. Bowe *Gardens of outstanding historic interest in . . . Ireland* 1980.

Dromore, Co. Down, Ulster
E. Malins *and* Knight of Glin *Lost demesnes* 1976, 132–33.

Dropmore near Beaconsfield, Bucks
J.P. Neale *Views* v. 1, 1818. R. Ackermann *Repository* v. 2, 1823, pls. 31–32. G.M. v. 3, 1828, 257–69; v. 5, 1829, 383,727–28; v. 9, 1833, 559–61,643–45; v. 13, 1837, 4–5. W.W.J. Gendall *Views* v. 2, 1830, 90 pls.92–93. *Florist* 1852, 195–97. *Cottage Gdnr* v. 11, 1854, 101–02. G.C. ii 1884, 165–66; ii 1886, 325–26; i 1890, 789–90; i 1895, 550; i 1899, 138,139; ii 1957, 86–87. *Gdning World* v. 7, 1891, 671. *J. Hort. Cottage Gdnr* N.S., v. 52, 1906, 207–11. C. Holme *Gardens of England in Southern & Western counties* 1907, pls. 46–48. C.L. v. 120, 1956, 772–75,834–37. B. Jones *Follies & grottoes* 1974, 292. L. Fleming *and* A. Gore *English garden* 1979, 173. D. Jacques *Georgian gardens* 1983, 193.

Drum near Aberdeen, Grampian
J.P. Neale *Views* 2nd Series, v. 1, 1824.

Drum Manor near Cookstown, Co. Tyrone, Ulster
Ulster Commentary no. 351, 1975, 4.

Drum-na-Vullin near Lochgilphead, Strathclyde
R. Webber *Percy Cane* 1975, 92–93,96,187.

Drumdevan House, Inverness, Highland
I.H. Adams *Descriptive list of plans* v. 3, 1974, 66.

Drumkilbo, Meigle, Tayside
C.L. v. 138, 1965, 608–10. G.A. Little *Scotland's gardens* 1981, 184.

Drumlanrig Castle near Thornhill, Dumfries and Galloway
T. Badeslade *and* J. Rocque *Vitruvius Brittanicus* 1739, pls. 45–46. W. Watts *Seats* 1779, pl. 9. P. Sandby *Collection of one hundred and fifty select views* v. 2, 1781, pl. 12. British Museum *Catalogue of maps, prints* 1829, 90. G.M. v. 9, 1833, 1–4. *Cottage Gdnr* v. 28, 1862, 571–73. *Garden* v. 3, 1873, 123–24. *J. Hort. Cottage Gdnr* v. 58, 1877, 195–98; N.S., v. 6, 1883, 157–60; N.S. v. 45, 1902, 336–37. F.O. Morris *Series of picturesque views* v. 4, 23. R. Pococke *Tours in Scotland* 1887, 9. R. Pococke *Travels through England* v. 1, 1888, 25. J. Loveday *Diary* 1890, 112–13. C.L. v. 12, 1902, 240–48; v. 33, 1913, 382–90; v. 78, 1935, 246–51; v. 128, 1960, 378–81,491. H.I. Triggs *Formal gardens in England and Scotland* 1902, 48. G. Jekyll *Garden ornament* 1918, 240. R.I.B.A. *Catalogue* v. B, 1972, 22. M. Binney *and* A. Hills *Elysian gardens* 1979, 27. A.A. Tait *Landscape garden in Scotland* 1980, passim. G.A. Little *Scotland's gardens* 1981, 256–57.

Drummond Castle near Crieff, Tayside
J.B. Burke *Visitation* v. 2, 1853, 240. *Florist* 1854, 361–65. *Scottish Gdnr* v. 8, 1859, 268–69. *Garden* v. 5, 1874, 442–44. G.C. i 1877, 657,660–61,663,688,689; i 1933, 181; ii 1935, 433. *J. Hort. Cottage Gdnr* N.S., v. 9, 1884, 528–30. C.L. v. 12, 1902, 112–22,144–53; v. 152, 1972, 338–40. H.I. Triggs *Formal gardens in England and Scotland* 1902, 50–51. G. Jekyll *Garden ornament* 1918, 261. P. Coats *Great gardens of Britain* 1967, 36–41. M. Allan *Fisons guide* 1970, 320–21. M. Binney *and* A. Hills *Elysian gardens* 1979, 32. A. Hellyer *Gardens of genius* 1980, 96–100. A.A. Tait *Landscape garden in Scotland* 1980, passim. G.A. Little *Scotland's gardens* 1981, 136–39. T. Hinde *Stately gardens of Britain* 1983, 62–69.

Drummonie House, Bridge of Farn, Tayside
G.A. Little *Scotland's gardens* 1981, 139.

Drumpark near Dunscore, Dumfries and Galloway
Scottish Gdnr and Northern Forester v. 7, 1912, 405–06.

Drumpellier House, Coatbridge, Strathclyde
Scottish Gdnr and Northern Forester v. 9, 1914, 189–90.

Dry Grange near Liverpool, Merseyside
J. Hort. N.S., v. 68, 1914, 338–40.

Dryburgh Abbey near Melrose, Borders
G.M. v. 18, 1842, 578.

Drynham, Oatlands Chase, Walton, Surrey
Gdnrs Mag. 1914, 134–36. G.C. i 1920, 257–58.

Dublin. National Botanic Gardens, Glasnevin, Co. Dublin, Eire
Official guide. W. Wade *Catalogue of plants . . . in the*

Society's Botanic Garden, Glasnevin 1800. J. Warburton et al. *History of the City of Dublin* 1818, 1279–1304. J.C. Loudon *Encyclopaedia of gardening* 1822, 1258–59. J.N. Brewer *Beauties of Ireland* v. 1, 1825, 222–25. *Irish Farmer's Gdnrs Mag.* v. 1, 1834, 406–08, 569–70. N. Niven *Visitor's companion* 1838. D. Moore *Handbook for the Botanic Gardens* 1850. *Cottage Gdnr* v. 27, 1862, 372–74. G.C. 1864, 988–89, 1011, 1035–36, 1083–84, 1131; ii 1883, 389–90, 619–20; ii 1884, 487–88, 497, 525–26, 529; ii 1892, 33–35, 43; ii 1896, 89–90, 93, 96, 97, 100, 103; i 1899, 241–42, 243; ii 1927, 239; v. 175 no. 14, 1975, 24–25, 27. *J. Hort. Cottage Gdnr* v. 34, 1865, 270–71; N.S., v. 33, 1896, 302–03. *Garden* v. 2, 1872, 10–12; v. 63, 1903, 227–29. *Gdning World* v. 4, 1888, 361. *Gdnrs Mag.* 1909, 494, 495. Royal Hort. Soc. *Conifers in cultivation* 1932, 216. *C.L.* v. 79, 1936, 148–50; v. 148, 1970, 313–14; v 168, 1980, 192–94. *J. Royal Hort. Soc.* 1940, 349–53; 1958, 368–69. E. Hyams *Irish gardens* 1967, 144–52. *Quarterly J. of Forestry* v. 63, 1969, 242–53. E. Hyams *Great botanical gardens of the world* 1969, 54–58. *Glasra* no. 4, 1980, 13–16; no. 5, 1981, 1–20, 45–50. E. Malins *and* P. Bowe *Irish gardens and demesnes* 1980, 37.

Dublin. Phoenix Park, Co. Dublin, Eire
G.C. ii 1892, 152. *Irish Gdning* v. 10, 1915, 100–01, 109. E. Malins *and* Knight of Glin *Irish demesnes* 1976, 195–96. Knight of Glin *and* P. Bowe *Gardens of outstanding historic interest in . . . Ireland* 1980. J. O'Connor *and* K. Wilson *Survey of the trees in the Zoological Gardens, Phoenix Park* 1980.

Dublin. Physic Garden, Dublin Philosophical Society, Co. Dublin, Eire
Huntia v. 4, 1982, 134.

Dublin. Trinity College, Co. Dublin, Eire
H. Nicholson *Methodus plantarum in horto medico, Collegii Dublinensis* 1712. *J. Hort. Cottage Gdnr* v. 34, 1865, 311–12. G.C. ii 1901, 385. *Irish Gdning* v. 15, 1920, 162–64. *Gdn History* v. 7 no. 1, 1979, 86–90. *Huntia* v. 4 no. 2, 1982, 133–45.

Duchray Castle near Aberfoyle, Central
G.A. Little *Scotland's gardens* 1981, 139–49.

Duckswich House, Upton upon Severn, Hereford and Worcester
R. Sidwell *West Midland gardens* 1981, 45–49.

Duckyls, East Grinstead, W. Sussex
C.L. Annual 1964, 92–95.

Duddingston House, Edinburgh, Lothian
J.C. Loudon *Encyclopaedia of gardening* 1822, 1250. *C.L.* v. 126, 1959, 358–61. A.A. Tait *Landscape garden in Scotland* 1980, passim.

Dudley Lodge, Harrow on the Hill, London
G.C. ii 1896, 365–66.

Dudmaston near Bridgnorth, Shropshire
Official guide. W. Angus *Seats* 1787, pl. 7. Harrison and Co. *Picturesque views of principal seats . . . in England and Wales* c.1788. *Copper Plate Mag.* v. 1, 1792, pl. 18. *C.L.* v. 165, 1979, 634–37, 714, 818–21. G.S. Thomas *Gardens of National Trust* 1979, 129–30. R. Sidwell *West Midland gardens* 1981, 112–13.

Duff House near Banff, Grampian
Copper Plate Mag. v. 3, pl. 124. P. Sandby *Collection of one hundred and fifty select views* v. 2, 1781, pl. 13. J.P. Neale *Views* v. 6, 1823. A.A. Tait *Landscape garden in Scotland* 1980, passim.

Duffryn near Cardiff, S. Glamorgan
G.C. ii 1914, 379–80, 381, 387; ii 1920, 5, 7–8. G. Beard *Thomas H. Mawson* 1976, 51.

Dukeld, Blair Atholl, Tayside
R. Pococke *Tours in Scotland* 1887, 229–31.

Dulany Cottage, Patching, W. Sussex
T.W. Horsfield *History . . . of Sussex* v. 2, 1835, 219.

Dullingham, Cambs
D. Stroud *Humphry Repton* 1962, 123–24. V.C.H. *Cambridge* v. 6, 1978, 161. G. Carter *et al. Humphry Repton* 1982, 149.

Dulwich House, Cardiff, S. Glamorgan
J. Hort. Cottage Gdnr N.S., v. 3, 1881, 409–10.

Dulwich Park *see* London

Dumbleton near Winchcombe, Glos
R. Atkyns *Ancient and present state of Glostershire* 1712, 406. L. Knyff *and* J. Kip *Britannia illustrata* v. 2, 1715.

Dunbarney near Perth, Tayside
G.A. Little *Scotland's gardens* 1981, 140–41.

Duncan House, Torquay, Devon
G.C. ii 1903, 329.

Dunchurch Lodge near Rugby, Warwickshire
G. Jekyll *Garden ornament* 1918, 318. G. Beard *Thomas H. Mawson* 1976, 51.

Duncombe Park near Hemsley, N. Yorks
Official guide. Society of Gentlemen *England displayed* v. 2, 1769, 149–51. A. Young *Six months tour through North of England* v. 2, 1771, 79–87. R.J. Sulivan *Tour . . . in 1778* v. 2, 1785, 19–20. *New display of the beauties of England* v. 2, 1787, 425–29. *Copper Plate Mag.* v. 1,

Duncombe Park (*Cont.*)
1792, pl. 22. *Description of Duncombe Park and Rivalx attempted* 1812. J.P. Neale *Views* 2nd Series, v. 1, 1824. *Jones's views* 1829, 31. T. Allen *New . . . history of . . . York* v. 3, 1831, 472. *C.L.* v. 17, 1905, 270–78; v. 122, 1957, 1198–1202,1328–31; v. 173, 1983, 914. G. Jekyll *Garden ornament* 1918, 204,253. N. Pevsner *Yorkshire: the North Riding* 1966, 141–42. C. Hussey *English gardens and landscapes* 1967, 140–46. K. Lemmon *Gardens of Britain* v. 5, 1978, 69–70.
See also Rievaulx Terrace

Duncow near Dumfries, Dumfries and Galloway
Scottish Gdnr and Northern Forester v. 7, 1912, 149–50.

Dundalk Archepiscopal Palace, Co. Lough, Eire
C.L. Falkiner *Illustrations of Irish history and topography* 1904, 368–69.

Dundalk House, Co. Louth, Eire
T. Wright *Arbours & grottos* 1979.

Dundas Castle near Queensferry, Lothian
J.P. Neale *Views* 2nd Series, v. 2, 1825.

Dundonnell House near Ullapool, Highland
J. Royal Hort. Soc. 1971, 290–302.

Dunecht House, Dunecht, Grampian
G.A. Little *Scotland's gardens* 1981, 184.

Dunedin, Streatham, London
Gdning World v. 2, 1886, 648–49; v. 8, 1892, 594.

Duneevan near Walton-on-Thames, Surrey
J. Hort. Cottage Gdnr v. 54, 1875, 294–97.

Dunfermline. Pittencrieff Park and Glen, Fife
Scottish Gdnr and Northern Forester v. 8, 1913, 189–90.

Dunganstown Castle near Wicklow, Co. Wicklow, Eire
Bulletin Royal Hort. & Arboricultural Soc. of Ireland no. 15, 1941, 248–50.

Dungarth, Honley, Huddersfield, W. Yorks
M. and R. Tooley *Gardens of Gertrude Jekyll in Northern England* 1982, 55.

Dunglass near Cockburnspath, Lothian
J.P. Neale *Views* v. 6, 1823, *C.L.* v. 58, 1925, 396–403. Historical MSS Commission *Architectural history* v. 3, 1971, item 2706. A.A. Tait *Landscape garden in Scotland* 1980, passim.

Dunham Massey Hall near Altrincham, Greater Manchester
J. Beeverell *Les delices de la Grande Bretagne* v. 5, 1707, 872. L. Knyff *and* J. Kip *Britannia illustrata* v. 1, 1714. J. Aikin *Description of the country . . . round Manchester* 1795, 426. *G.C.* i 1888, 108,109. M. Macartney *English houses & gardens* 1908, pl. 23. *Trans. Lancashire & Cheshire Antiquarian Soc.* v. 42, 1925, 53–78. R. Dutton *English garden* 1937, pl. 50. N. Pevsner *and* E. Hubbard *Cheshire* 1971, 205. *Apollo* July 1978, 4–11. L. Fleming *and* A. Gore *English garden* 1979, pls. 26, 52. J. Harris *Artist and the country house* 1979, 146, 172–73, pls. 17–18. *C.L.* v. 169, 1981, 1664–68; v. 170, 1981, 18.

Dunira near Comrie, Tayside
C.L. v. 69, 1931, 379–82. *G.C.* ii 1934, 347. G. Beard *Thomas H. Mawson* 1976, 51. A.A. Tait *Landscape garden in Scotland* 1980, passim.

Dunkeld House, Dunkeld, Tayside
W. Gilpin *Observations relative chiefly to picturesque beauty* v. 1, 1792, 113–14,119–24. Duke of Rutland *Journal of a tour to the northern parts of Great Britain* 1813, 207–10. J.C. Loudon *Arboretum et fruticetum Britannicum* v. 1, 1844, 99–101. *G.C.* ii 1880, 651–52. *Garden.* v. 27, 1885, 389–90,397,401,404. *Gdning World* v. 17, 1900, 53–54. *J. Hort. Cottage Gdnr* N.S., v. 42, 1901, 156–57. *Gdnrs Mag.* 1908, 493–94,495. *Publications of Bedfordshire Historical Record Soc.* v. 47, 1968, 157. B. Jones *Follies & grottoes* 1974, 423. A.A. Tait *Landscape garden in Scotland* 1980, passim.

Dunley Hall near Stourport-on-Severn, Hereford and Worcester
R. Sidwell *West Midland gardens* 1981, 49–50.

Dunmore, Stirling, Central
J.P. Neale *Views* 2nd Series, v. 3, 1826. F.O. Morris *Series of picturesque views* v. 5, 11. B. Jones *Follies & grottoes* 1974, 96–97. M. Binney *and* A. Hills *Elysian gardens* 1979, 50.

Dunninald, Tayside
C.L. v. 146, 1969, 384–87,444–45.

Dunorland, Tunbridge Wells, Kent
J. Hort. Cottage Gdnr v. 54, 1875, 364–66. *G.C.* ii 1881, 526–27,532,533.

Dunraven Castle near Cowbridge, S. Glamorgan
J.P. Neale *Views* v. 5, 1822.

Dunrobin Castle, Dunrobin, Highland
F.O. Morris *Series of picturesque views* v. 2, 49. H. Maxwell *Scottish gardens* 1911, 171–80. *G.C.* ii 1874, 324–26. *Garden* 1921, 452–53. *C.L.* v. 50, 1921, 284–91, 318. M. Binney *and* A. Hills *Elysian gardens* 1979, 26.

Duns Castle, Duns, Borders
J.P. Neale *Views* v. 6, 1823. *G.C.* i 1899, 49,57,68.
A.A. Tait *Landscape garden in Scotland* 1980, passim.

Dunsany Castle, Dunsany, Co. Meath, Eire
Knight of Glin and P. Bowe *Gardens of outstanding historic interest in . . . Ireland* 1980.

Dunsland House, Devon
Architectural History v. 7, 1964, 26,56.

Dunstall near Croome, Hereford and Worcester
B. Jones *Follies & grottoes* 1974, 66–67.

Dunster Castle, Dunster, Somerset
S. and N. Buck *Buck's antiquities* v. 2, 1774, pl. 257. P. Collinson *History . . . of Somersetshire* v. 2, 1791, 13. *G.M.* v. 18, 1842, 489. F.O. Morris *Series of picturesque views* v. 6, 43. *C.L.* v. 14, 1903, 686–95. M. Allan *Fisons guide* 1970, 123–24. B. Jones *Follies & grottoes* 1974, 384. *National Trust Year Book* 1976–77,88–99. G.S. Thomas *Gardens of National Trust* 1979, 130–31. J. Sales *West Country gardens* 1980, 146–48.

Dunsyre, Strathclyde
Architectural Review v. 163, 1978, 88–89.

Duntisbourne Abbots near Cirencester, Glos
J.N. Brewer *Delineations of Gloucestershire* 1825, 155.

Dunton Hall, Lincs
J. Harris *Artist and the country house* 1979, 260.

Duntreath Castle near Strathblane, Central
Gdning World v. 13, 1896, 105–06.

Dunval Hall, Bridgnorth, Shropshire
R. Sidwell *West Midland gardens* 1981, 113–14.

Dunvegan Castle, Isle of Skye, Highland
G.A. Little *Scotland's gardens* 1981, 230.

Dupplin Castle near Perth, Tayside
Scottish Gdr v. 13, 1864, 209–11. *G.C.* i 1877, 240–42, 245; i 1884, 745; ii 1892, 525–26. *Garden* v. 23, 1883, 239–41. *J. Hort. Cottage Gdnr* N.S., v. 10, 1885, 50–52.

Durdans near Epsom, Surrey
J. Hassell *Picturesque rides and walks* v. 1, 1817. C. Fiennes *Journeys* 1949, 342–44. J. Harris *Artist and the country house* 1979, 61–62. *C.L.* v. 174, 1983, 628–29.

Durham. College Court, Co. Durham
Gdn History v. 8 no. 2, 1980, 56,58.

Durhams *see* Derehams

Durmast House, Burley, Hants
A. Paterson *Gardens of Britain* v. 2, 1978, 78–79.

Durrington House, Sheering, Essex
P. Muilman *History of Essex* v. 4, 1770, 106. P. Morant *History . . . of Essex* v. 2, 1816, 500.

Duthie Park *see* Aberdeen

Dutton Homestalls, East Grinstead, W. Sussex
Gdn Design 1937, 6–11.

Dyffryn Aled near Denbigh, Clwyd
W. Angus *Seats* 1787, pl. 48. R.C. Hoare *Collection of forty-eight views* 1806, pl. 10.

Dyke Nook Lodge, Accrington, Lancs
Gdn History v. 8 no. 3, 1980, 28–31,33. M. and R. Tooley *Gardens of Gertrude Jekyll in Northern England* 1982, 6–9,54.

Dynes Hall near Halstead, Essex
P. Muilman *History of Essex* v. 2, 1769, 83. *New display of the beauties of England* v. 1, 1776. P. Morant *History . . . of Essex* v. 2, 1816, 277.

Dynevor Castle near Llandeilo, Dyfed
J.P. Neale *Views* v. 5, 1822. *G.C.* i 1909, 165–66. D. Stroud *Capability Brown* 1975, 180. J. Harris *Artist and the country house* 1979, 80–81.

Dyrham Park near Barnet, London
W. Keane *Beauties of Middlesex* 1850, 146–48. *Cottage Gdnr* v. 18, 1857, 232–33.

Dyrham Park near Chippenham, Avon
Official guide. L. Knyff and J. Kip *Britannia illustrata* v. 2, 1715. S. Switzer *Ichnographia rustica* v. 3, 1718, 113–27. R. Atkyns *Ancient and present state of Glostershire* 1712, 414. R. Bigland *Historical . . . collections . . . of Gloucester* v. 1, 1791, 533. *C.L.* v. 14, 1903, 434–41; v. 40, 1916, 546–52; v. 131, 1962, 335–39, 396–99. *C.L. Annual* 1963, 92–95. G. Jekyll *Garden ornament* 1918, 96. *Connoisseur* v. 149, 1962, 139–44. D. Stroud *Humphry Repton* 1962, 169. M. Allan *Fisons guide* 1970, 90–91. D. Verey *Gloucestershire* v. 1, 1970, 232. Historical MSS Commission *Architectural history* v. 3, 1971, items 2713,2846,2887,3174,3186,3309,3339, 3383,3627. *National Trust Year Book* 1977–78, 83–108. G.S. Thomas *Gardens of National Trust* 1979, 131. J. Sales *West Country gardens* 1980, 58–60. G. Carter *et al. Humphry Repton* 1982, 153.

Eagle House, Clapham Common, London
W. Keane *Beauties of Surrey* 1849, 75–76.

Eagle Tavern, Islington, London
W. Wroth *London pleasure gardens of the eighteenth century* 1896, 86–87. E.B. Chancellor *Pleasure haunts of London* 1925, 406–10.

Eaglehurst near Fawley, Hants
N. Pevsner *and* D. Lloyd *Hampshire and the Isle of Wight* 1967, 196–97. M. Binney *and* A. Hills *Elysian gardens* 1979, 59.

Ealing Park, Ealing, London
H. Repton *Fragments* 1816, 80–83. W. Keane *Beauties of Middlesex* 1850, 25–30. *Scottish Gdnr* v. 3, 1854, 54–55. *G.C.* i 1884, 704–05,709. D. Stroud *Humphry Repton* 1962, 169. *C.L.* v. 154, 1973, 580–81. G. Carter *et al. Humphry Repton* 1982, 157–58.

Ealing Place, Ealing(?), London
D. Stroud *Capability Brown* 1975, 223–24.

Earlham Hall, Norwich, Norfolk
Garden 1917, 114–15. *C.L.* v. 49, 1921, 628–29. *Architectural History* v. 7, 1964, 26,57.

Earlshall near Leuchars, Fife
Architectural Review v. 12, 1902, 73,76; v. 46, 1919, 14–18. H.I. Triggs *Formal gardens in England and Scotland* 1902, 49–50. *C.L.* v. 17, 1905, 942–52. G. Jekyll *Garden ornament* 1918, 418. P. Coats *Great gardens* 1963, 32–37. *Gdn History* v. 5 no. 2, 1977, 34,36. *Garden* 1979, 320–24. *Landscape* v. 24 no. 3, 1980, 21–23. G.A. Little *Scotland's gardens* 1981, 144.

Earlstoke Park *see* Erlestoke Park

Earnshill near Langport, Somerset
C.L. v. 128, 1960, 800–03, 858.

Earnock near Hamilton, Strathclyde
Gdning World v. 13, 1896, 184–85.

Earsham near Bungay, Norfolk
G.M. v. 17, 1841, 273. J. Grigor *Eastern arboretum* 1841, 256–58.

Eartham House near Chichester, W. Sussex
J. Brown *Gardens of a golden afternoon* 1982, 169.

Easby Hall, Easby, N. Yorks
J. Harris *Artist and the country house* 1979, 296.

Eashing Park, Godalming, Surrey
C.L. v. 6, 1899, 840–45.

Easneye, Ware, Herts
R. Bisgrove *Gardens of Britain* v. 3, 1978, 69–70.

East Bergholt Place, East Bergholt, Suffolk
International Dendrological Society Year Book 1972, 30–39.

East Burnham Park, East Burnham, Bucks
Garden v. 59, 1901, 469. *Gdnrs Mag.* 1907, 727–30. *G.C.* ii 1910, 407,408–09,413.

East Combe, Blackheath, London
G. Virtue *Picturesque beauties of Great Britain: Kent* 1829, 2. W.H. Ireland *History . . . of Kent* v. 4, 1830, 679. *G.M.* v. 16, 1840, 581–82.

East Cowes Castle, Cowes, Isle of Wight
R. Ackermann *Repository* v. 7, 1826, pl. 25. W.W.J. Gendall *Views* v. 1, 1830, 15–16.

East End House, Fulham, Hammersmith, London
C.J. Fèret *Fulham old and new* v. 2, 1900, 96–97.

East Haddon Hall, East Haddon, Northants
Gdnrs Mag. 1915, 186–87. R.I.B.A. *Catalogue: Lutyens* 1973, 19.

East Horndon Manor, East Horndon, Essex
F.G. Emmison *Catalogue of maps in Essex Record Office* 1947, 2.

East Horsley Towers, East Horsley, Surrey
G.C. i 1886, 39–40.

East Lambrook Manor, East Lambrook, Somerset
Official guide. M. Allan *Fisons guide* 1970, 91–92. H. Evans *Beautiful gardens of Britain* 1974, 25–26. J. Sales *West Country gardens* 1980, 149–51. T. Hinde *Stately gardens of Britain* 1983, 176–81.

East Lodge, Lamberhurst, Kent
G. Beard *Thomas H. Mawson* 1976, 51.

East Riddlesden Hall, Keighley, W. Yorks
K. Lemmon *Gardens of Britain* v. 5, 1978, 161–63. G.S. Thomas *Gardens of National Trust* 1979, 132.

East Sutton Place, East Sutton, Kent
C. Greenwood *Epitome of county history . . . v. 1: Kent* 1838, 153. *Cottage Gdnr* v. 28, 1862, 392–94. *C.L.* v. 19, 1906, 666–73. F. Hull *Catalogue of estate maps 1590 to 1840 in the Kent County Archive Office* 1973, 82.

East Thorpe, Reading, Berks
G.C. ii 1899, 340–41.

East Wickham House, East Wickham, Kent
C. Greenwood *Epitome of county history . . . v. 1: Kent* 1838, 43.

Eastbury near Blandford, Dorset
C. Campbell *Vitruvius Britannicus* v. 3, 1725, pls. 15, 18–19. D. Defoe *Tour* v. 3, 1742, 298–99. *C.L.* v. 62, 1927, 330–37. L. Whistler *Imagination of Vanbrugh and his fellow artists* 1954, 164–71, 177. J. Newman *and* N. Pevsner *Dorset* 1972, 193. P. Willis *Charles Bridgeman* 1977, 178. J. Harris *Artist and the country house* 1979, 206. C. Taylor *Archaeology of gardens* 1983, 12,14,55–56.

Easter Duddingston Lodge near Edinburgh, Lothian
Gdning World v. 5, 1888, 263–64. C. Jenner *Catalogue of plants in garden at Easter Duddingston Lodge* 1894.

Easter Weens, Bonchester Bridge, Borders
G.A. Little *Scotland's gardens* 1981, 84.

Easthampstead Park, Easthampstead, Berks
G.M. v. 19, 1843, 690–92. Historical MSS Commission *Architectural history* v. 3, 1971, items 2719,2952.

Eastington near Stroud, Glos
R. Atkyns *Ancient and present state of Glostershire* 1712, 418. L. Knyff *and* J. Kip *Britannia illustrata* v. 2, 1715. J.N. Brewer *Delineations of Gloucestershire* 1825, 197.

Eastleigh near Teignmouth, Devon
G.C. i 1882, 829–30.

Eastnor Castle near Ledbury, Hereford and Worcester
J.P. Neale *Views* v. 2, 1819. F.O. Morris *Series of picturesque views* v. 4, 33. G.E.F. Morgan *Eastnor Castle guide* c.1889. *G.C.* i 1878, 76–78,80,107–08,109,113, 170–71; ii 1903, 155. *Gdning World* v. 1, 1884, 93. *Garden* v. 33, 1888, 357–58. C. Holme *Gardens of England in Midland & Eastern counties* 1908 pls. 43–44. *C.L.* v. 143, 1968, 524–27,668,1708–11. R. Sidwell *West Midland gardens* 1981, 51–52.

Easton-on-the-Hill, Northants
Northamptonshire Past and Present v. 5 no. 3, 1975, 221.

Easton Grey House, Easton Grey, Wilts
J. Sales *West Country gardens* 1980, 208–09.

Easton Hall, Easton, Lincs
F.O. Morris *Series of picturesque views* v. 3, 73. *G.C.* i 1881, 80,81,83; i 1889, 177,178. *C.L.* v. 11, 1902, 112–19. M. Binney *and* A. Hills *Elysian gardens* 1978, 48–49.

Easton Lodge near Dunmow, Essex
P. Morant *History . . . of Essex* v. 2, 1768, 431. G. Virtue *Picturesque beauties of Great Britain: Essex* 1831, 37. T. Wright *History . . . of Essex* v. 2, 1836, 227. *J. Hort. Cottage Gdnr* N.S., v. 13, 1886, 231,232; N.S., v. 29, 1894, 154–56. *Gdnrs Mag.* 1907, 132–39.
Countess of Warwick *An old English garden* 1898. *C.L.* v. 22, 1907, 738–48; v. 25, 1909, 639–41. C. Holme *Gardens of England in Midland & Eastern counties* 1908, pls. 45–60. *G.C.* ii 1913, 222–23. G. Jekyll *Garden ornament* 1918, 90,311–12,333. F.G. Emmison *Catalogue of maps in Essex Record Office* 1947, 56. R. Webber *Percy Cane* 1975, 16–18. M. Binney *and* A. Hills *Elysian gardens* 1979, 41.

Easton Lodge, Norfolk
J. Grigor *Eastern arboretum* 1841, 309–13.

Easton Maudit, Northants
Royal Commission on Historical Monuments *Inventory of historical monuments in . . . Northampton* v. 2, 1979, 45–46.

Easton Neston near Towcester, Northants
J. Morton *Natural history of Northamptonshire* 1712, 493. W. Stukeley *Itinerarium curiosum* v. 1, 1776, 38–40. *C.L.* v. 24, 1908, 630–38; v. 62, 1927, 262–69. G. Jekyll *Garden ornament* 1918, 114. P. Coats *Great gardens of Britain* 1967, 240–45. *Northamptonshire Past and Present* v. 5 no. 3, 1975, 224. M. Binney *and* A. Hills *Elysian gardens* 1979, 3.

Easton Park, Easton, Suffolk
J. Harris *Artist and the country house* 1979, 319.

Eastwell Park near Ashford, Kent
J.P. Neale *Views* 2nd Series, v. 2, 1825. W.H. Ireland *History . . . of Kent* v. 2, 1829, 426. G. Virtue *Picturesque beauties of Great Britain: Kent* 1829, 41. F.O. Morris *Series of picturesque views* v. 6, 45. *G.C.* ii 1874, 645,648; ii 1896, 777–78,781; ii 1907, 337–39. *C.L.* v. 1, 1897, 379–81. *J. Hort. Cottage Gdnr* N.S., v. 66, 1913, 219–22,223,224,225,226. Historical MSS Commission *Architectural history* v. 5, 1974, item 5028. J. Harris *Artist and the country house* 1979, 234.

Eastwick Park near Leatherhead, Surrey
E.W. Brayley *and* J. Britton *Topographical history of Surrey* v. 4, 470. W. Keane *Beauties of Surrey* 1849, 110–11.

Eastwood, Northants
Northamptonshire Past and Present v. 5 no. 3, 1975, 224.

Eaton Hall, Eaton, Cheshire
J. Beeverell *Les delices de la Grande Bretagne* v. 5, 1707, 872. L. Knyff *and* J. Kip *Britannia illustrata* v. 1, 1714. R. Ackermann *Repository* v. 2, 1823, pls. 19–21. J. Seacombe *Eaton tourist* 1825. J. *and* J.C. Buckler *Views of Eaton Hall in Cheshire* 1826. British Museum *Catalogue of maps, prints* 1829, 95. W.W.J. Gendall *Views* v. 1, 1830, 23,29,31. *G.M.* v. 7, 1831, 547–48. J. Bartlett *Selections from views of residences and country*

Eaton Hall (*Cont.*)

seats of nobility and gentry 1851. J.B. Burke *Visitation* v. 1, 1852, 169. E.A. Brooke *Gardens of England* 1857 pls. 26–28. F.O. Morris *Series of picturesque views* v. 1, 31. *G.C.* 1871, 13–15; ii 1884, 743–44; i 1886, 647–48; ii 1886, 7–8; i 1896, 71–72; ii 408–09; ii 1913, 68,256. *J. Hort. Cottage Gdnr* v. 56, 1876, 30–32; N.S., v. 56, 1908, 256–64. *Gdning World* v. 9, 1893, 757–58. *C.L.* v. 2, 1897, 182–84; v. 9, 1901, 496–503; v. 32, Supplt to 26 October 1912, xx–xxvii; v. 47, 1920, 724–31; v. 149, 1971, 304–07. *Gdnrs Mag.* 1904, 21–24. C. Holme *Gardens of England in Midland & Eastern counties* 1908, pls. 61–64. M. Macartney *English houses & gardens* 1908, pls. 44–45. Lady Rockley *Historic gardens of England* 1938, 206–07. N. Pevsner and E. Hubbard *Cheshire* 1971, 210–11. R.I.B.A. *Catalogue* v. L-N, 1973, 59; *Lutyens* 1973, 19. D. Stroud *Capability Brown* 1975, 224. M. Binney *and* A. Hills *Elysian gardens* 1979, 4. J. Brown *Gardens of a golden afternoon* 1982, 160. *Gdn History* v. 12 no. 1, 1984, 39–57.

Ebberston Hall, Ebberston, N. Yorks
Architectural Review v. 26, 1909, 231–44. *C.L.* v. 116, 1954, 1158–61,1254. C. Hussey *English gardens and landscapes* 1967, 65–69. K. Lemmon *Gardens of Britain* v. 5, 1978, 72–73. L. Fleming *and* A. Gore *English garden* 1979, 86. J. Harris *Artist and the country house* 1979, 190–91.

Eccleshall Castle, Eccleshall, Staffs
J. Nightingale *Topographical . . . description of Staffordshire* 1810, 922.

Eccleston Hall near St Helens, Merseyside
Cottage Gdnr v. 13, 1855, 7–8.

Ecton Hall, Ecton, Northants
C.L. v. 115, 1954, 600.

Eden Hall, Edenhall, Cumbria
F.O. Morris *Series of picturesque views* v. 2, 63. *G.C.* ii 1879, 75–78; ii 1897, 380–82,385. *Garden* v. 49, 1896, 227. *J. Hort. Cottage Gdnr* N.S., v. 37, 1898, 29–30; N.S., v. 42, 1901, 414–15.

Eden House, Ednam, Borders
G.A. Little *Scotland's gardens* 1981, 85.

Eden Park, Beckenham, Bromley, London
C. Greenwood *Epitome of county history . . . v. 1: Kent* 1838, 32.

Edgbaston, Birmingham, W. Midlands
W. Dugdale *Antiquities of Warwickshire* v. 2, 1730, 896. D. Stroud *Capability Brown* 1975, 224.

Edgcote, Northants
C.L. v. 47, 1920, 46–54.

Edge Hall near Malpas, Cheshire
G.C. ii 1882, 455–56; i 1884, 606,613; ii 1884, 332–34, 366; ii 1892, 395–96. *Garden* v. 42, 1892, 555–56.

Edgehill, Warwickshire
B. Jones *Follies & grottoes* 1974, 54–55.

Edgeworthstown, Co. Longford, Eire
J.N. Brewer *Beauties of Ireland* v. 2, 1826, 263.

Edinburgh. Horticultural Society, Lothian
I.H. Adams *Descriptive list of plans* v. 3, 1974, 52.

Edinburgh. Princes Street Gardens, Lothian
H. Maxwell *Scottish gardens* 1908, 54–58. Historical MSS Commission *Architectural history* v. 3, 1971, item 2729.

Edinburgh. Royal Botanic Garden, Lothian
Official guide. *G.C.* 18 September 1875, 1–8; ii 1938, 449; i 1959, 22–23,30. *Garden* 1901, 316–17; 1924, 600–01; 1925, 500–01. *C.L.* v. 53, 1923, 290–91; v. 74, 1933, 306–11; v. 155, 1974, 422–24. *Notes from Royal Botanic Garden, Edinburgh* v. 19 no. 91, 1933, 1–62. *J. Royal Hort. Soc.* 1940, 77–83; 1970, 251–66,431–32. T. Jefferson *Garden book* 1944, 492. *Building* v. 213, December 1967, 85–86. E. Hyams *Great botanical gardens of the world* 1969, 44–53. H. Fletcher *and* W.H. Brown *Royal Botanic Garden, Edinburgh, 1670–1970* 1970. Historical MSS Commission *Architectural history* v. 3, 1971, item 2730. *J. Scottish Rock Gdn Club* v. 13 no. 3, 1973, 212–15. *Scots Mag.* N.S., 113, 1980, 618–27. *Garden* 1981, 407–11.

Edmondsham House, Edmondsham, Dorset
C.L. v. 142, 1967, 1058–62. A. Paterson *Gardens of Britain* v. 2, 1978, 29–30.

Edmondthorpe Hall, Edmondthorpe, Leics
J. Throsby *Select views in Leicestershire* v. 1, 1790, 266.

Ednaston Lodge, Ednaston, Derbyshire
F.O. Morris *Series of picturesque views* v. 4, 63.

Ednaston Manor, Ednaston, Derbyshire
Official guide. *C.L.* v. 53, 1923, 398–405; v. 166, 1979, 24–25. *Garden* 1979, 271–76. J. Anthony *Gardens of Britain* v. 6, 1979, 74–76. A. Lees-Milne *and* R. Verey *Englishwoman's garden* 1980, 101–05. J. Brown *Gardens of a golden afternoon* 1982, 172.

Edwinstowe Hall, Edwinstowe, Notts
J. Harris *Artist and the country house* 1979, 214.

Edzell Castle, Edzell, Tayside
Official guide. *C.L.* v. 32, 1912, 859–62; v. 148, 1970, 402–04. M. Allan *Fisons guide* 1970, 339. R.I.B.A.

Edzell Castle (*Cont.*)
Catalogue v. G-K, 1973, 162. P. Verney *Gardens of Scotland* 1976, 33–37. A. Hellyer *Gardens of genius* 1980, 11–13. G.A. Little *Scotland's gardens* 1981, 184–87.

Effingham House, Leatherhead, Surrey
G.C. ii 1890, 470,471.

Eggesford House, Eggesford, Devon
F.O. Morris *Series of picturesque views* v. 6, 17.

Eglingham Hall, Eglingham, Northumberland
C.L. v. 158, 1975, 1458–61.

Eglinton Castle near Irvine, Strathclyde
J.C. Nattes *Scotia depicta* 1804, pl. 22. G.M. v. 9, 1833, 10. I.H. Adams *Descriptive list of plans* v. 1, 1966, 35.

Eilean Aigas, Aigas, Highland
Scottish Gdnr v. 4, 1855, 302–04.

Eilean Darach, Dundonnell, Highland
G.A. Little *Scotland's gardens* 1981, 230–32.

Elbridge House, Littlebourne, Kent
C. Greenwood *Epitome of county history . . . v. 1: Kent* 1838, 353.

Elcot Park near Newbury, Berks
G.M. v. 10, 1834, 301–02. R. Bisgrove *Gardens of Britain* v. 3, 1978, 71.

Elford Hall, Elford, Staffs
G.M. v. 12, 1836, 312,562–63. *J. Hort. Cottage Gdnr* N.S., v. 15, 1887, 141–42.

Elleron Lodge near Pickering, N. Yorks
Bradford Illustrated Weekly Telegraph *Series of picturesque views* 1885.

Ellicombe, Williton, Somerset
G.C. i 1957, 556–57.

Ellon Castle, Ellon, Grampian
Scottish Forestry v. 11, 1957, 77–78.

Elmbank, Dumfries, Dumfries and Galloway
Scottish Gdnr and Northern Forester v. 9, 1914, 549–50.

Elmcourt, Harrogate, N. Yorks
G. Beard *Thomas H. Mawson* 1976, 51.

Elmer Lodge, Beckenham, Bromley, London
C. Greenwood *Epitome of county history . . . v. 1: Kent* 1838, 32.

Elmet Hall, Leeds, W. Yorks
G.C. i 1894, 533,568–69; ii 1895, 40.

Elmham Park, Elmham, Norfolk
J. Grigor *Eastern arboretum* 1841, 169–74.

Elmhurst Hall near Congleton, Staffs
R. Plot *Natural history of Staffordshire* 1685, 30. G.M. v. 12, 1836, 563.

Elmore Court, Elmore, Glos
C.L. v. 36, 1914, 846–52.

Elmwood, Isle of Thanet, Kent
G.C. ii 1909, 196–97,199.

Elsenham Hall, Elsenham, Essex
Florist and Pomologist 1864, 201–03. F.G. Emmison *Catalogue of maps in Essex Record Office* 3rd Supplt, 1968, 12.

Elsfield House, Maidstone, Kent
G.C. i 1896, 609,611.

Elsham House, Elsham, Humberside
J. Hort. Cottage Gdnr v. 44, 1870, 510–11; v. 52, 1874, 34–35.

Eltham (James Sherard), Woolwich, London
J.J. Dillenius *Hortus Elthamensis* 1732. D. Lyson *Environs of London* v. 4, 1790, 403.

Eltham Palace, Woolwich, London
C.L. v. 81, 1937, 568–73,594; v. 168, 1980, 1842–44. H.M. Colvin *History of the King's Works* v. 2, 1963, 931,933,934.

Elton Hall, Elton, Cambs
F.O. Morris *Series of picturesque views* v. 4, 31. C.L. v. 121, 1957, 334–37,426,818–21. V.C.H. *Huntingdon* v. 3, 1936, 154.

Elvaston Castle, Elvaston, Derbyshire
Official guide. J.P. Neale *Views* v. 1, 1818. G.M. v. 15, 1839, 458–60. W. Barron *British winter garden* 1852, passim. *Florist* 1852, 60,77; 1854, 134–36. E.A. Brooke *Gardens of England* 1857, pls. 15–17. *Cottage Gdnr* v. 21, 1859, 211–12. F.O. Morris *Series of picturesque views* v. 2, 21. *J. Hort. Cottage Gdnr* v. 54, 1875, 229; N.S., v. 42, 1901, 13,15. G.C. ii 1876, 807,838; i 1891, 523,525. J. Veitch *Manual of the coniferae* 1881, 300. C.L. v. 5, 1899, 48–52,80–83. N. Pevsner *Derbyshire* 1978, 210. J. Anthony *Gardens of Britain* v. 6, 1979, 76–80.

Elvedon near Thetford, Suffolk
D. Stroud *Capability Brown* 1975, 224.

Elvetham Park, Winchfield, Hants
Garden v. 36, 1889, 95–96. *Gdning World* v. 11, 1894, 40–41.

Elvills, Englefield Green, Surrey
R. Ackermann *Repository* v. 9, 1827, pl. 14.
W.W.J. Gendall *Views* v. 2, 1830, 104.

Elvingston, Gladsmuir, Lothian
G.A. Little *Scotland's gardens* 1981, 85–86.

Ely Court, Cardiff, S. Glamorgan
G.C. i 1882, 680–81.

Ely Place, Holborn, London
G. Taylor *Old London gardens* 1953, 23–25.

Ember Court, Thames Ditton, Surrey
P. Sandby *Collection of one hundred and fifty select views* v. 1, 1781, pl. 63. *Copper Plate Mag.* v. 3, pl. 114.
W. Keane *Beauties of Surrey* 1849, 11–13.

Embley Park near Romsey, Hants
C. Holme *Gardens of England in Southern & Western counties* 1907, pls. 51–53. *C.L.* v. 78, 1935, 5–7. Lady Rockley *Historic gardens of England* 1938, 236–37.

Emmetts, Ide Hill, Kent
M. Allan *Fisons guide* 1970, 42. T. Wright *Gardens of Britain* v. 4, 1978, 37–39. G.S. Thomas *Gardens of National Trust* 1979, 132–33. *C.L.* v. 174, 1983, 1896–98.

Emo Court near Portarlington, Co. Laois, Eire
C.L. v. 155, 1974, 1346–49.

Emral Hall near Bangor, Gwynedd
C.L. v. 27, 1910, 270–79.

Encombe near Corfe Castle, Dorset
J. Hutchins *History . . . of Dorset* v. 1, 1774, 187; ed. 3, v. 1, 1861, 520. J.P. Neale *Views* 2nd Series, v. 4, 1828. *Jones's views* 1829. *C.L.* v. 133, 1963, 164–67,214.
J. Newman *and* N. Pevsner *Dorset* 1972, 201.

Encombe, Shorncliffe, Sandgate, Kent
C.L. v. 56, 1924, 992–99.

Endcliffe Hall, Sheffield, S. Yorks
J. Hunter *History . . . of . . . Sheffield* 1869, 379. *G.C.* ii 1875, 205,207–09. *J. Hort. Cottage Gdnr* v. 62, 1879, 343–44.

Enderby Hall, Enderby, Leics
J. Throsby *Select views in Leicestershire* v. 1, 1790, 270.
C. Holme *Gardens of England in Midland & Eastern counties* 1908, 65.

Endsleigh near Tavistock, Devon
H. Repton *Fragments* 1816, 213–26. J.P. Neale *Views* v. 1, 1818. R. Ackermann *Repository* v. 12, 1828, pl. 2. W.W.J. Gendall *Views* v. 1, 1830, 135. *G.M.* v. 18, 1842, 549–50. *Garden* v. 20, 1881, 131–32. *C.L.* v. 130, 1961, 246–49,296–99. D. Stroud *Humphry Repton* 1962, 149–50. *International Dendrology Soc. Yearbook* 1974, 19–27. B. Jones *Follies & grottoes* 1974, 315. P.M. Synge *Gardens of Britain* v. 1, 1977, 39–44. M. Hadfield *et al. British gardeners* 1980, 240. G. Carter *et al. Humphry Repton* 1982, 76,150, col.pls. 1–2,4.

Enfield (J. Mellish), Enfield, London
C. Burlington *Modern universal British traveller* 1779, 336.

Enfield Hall, Staffs
R. Plot *Natural History of Staffordshire* 1685, 121.
R. Pococke *Travels through England* v. 2, 1889, 231.

Enfield Mills, Enfield, London
W. Keane *Beauties of Middlesex* 1850, 76–78.

Enfield Palace, Enfield, London
D. Lysons *Environs of London* v. 2, 1795, 285; *Supplement* 1811, 138–39. *Archaeologia* v. 12, 1796, 188.
J.C. Loudon *Arboretum et fruticetum Britannicum* v. 1, 1844, 47–48,61. J. Thorne *Handbook to the environs of London* 1876, 175–76.

Engaynes *see* Gaynes

Englefield House, Theale, Berks
H. Boswell *Historical descriptions of new and picturesque views* 1800. J.P. Neale *Views* 2nd Series, v. 4, 1828. *G.M.* v. 9, 1833, 670–73. V.C.H. *Berkshire* v. 3, 1923, 409. *G.C.* ii 1962, 62–63. R. Bisgrove *Gardens of Britain* v. 3, 1978, 72–73. J. Harris *Artist and the country house* 1979, 356. *C.L.* v. 170, 1981, 642–45.

English Grotto, Clerkenwell, Islington, London
W. Wroth *London pleasure gardens of the eighteenth century* 1896, 37–39. E.B. Chancellor *Pleasure haunts of London* 1925, 382.

Enmore Castle near Bridgwater, Somerset
W. Watts *Seats* 1779, pl. 54. R. Ackerman *Repository* v. 7, 1826, pl.26. J.C. Loudon *Encyclopaedia of gardening* 1822, 1246. W.W.J. Gendall *Views* v. 1, 1830, 16.

Enstone, Oxfordshire
R. Plot *Natural history of Oxfordshire* 1705, 241–44.
S. Raphael *et al. Of Oxfordshire gardens* 1982, 27–48.

Enton Lodge, Witley, Surrey
J. Brown *Miss Gertrude Jekyll* 1981, 19.

Enville Hall, Enville, Staffs
J. Heeley *Letters on the beauties of Hagley, Envil and The Leasowes* v. 2, 1777, 23–90. R.J. Sulivan *Tour . . . in 1778* v. 2, 1785, 10–13. *Companion to The Leasowes, Hagley and Enville* 1789, 91–108. W. Gilpin *Observations, relative chiefly to picturesque beauty* v. 2, 1792, 185–87. W. Pitt *General view of agriculture of . . . Stafford* 1796, 95. *Description of Hagley, Envil and The Leasowes* c.1800. W. Marshall *On planting and rural ornament* v. 1, 1803, 327–34. J. Nightingale *Topographical . . . description of Staffordshire* 1810, 853–54. H. Skrine *Two successive tours throughout . . . Wales* 1812, 165–66. *G.M.* v. 16, 1840, 514. *Cottage Gdnr* v. 11, 1854, 263–64. *Florist* 1855, 325–29. E.A. Brooke *Gardens of England* 1857, pls. 6–8. *J. Hort. Cottage Gdnr* v. 32, 1864, 353–56, 372–76, 393–96. E. Burritt *Walks in the Black Country and its green borderland* 1868, 302–08. *G.C.* ii 1884, 330; ii 1887, 551–52; i 1896, 199–200. *Gdning World* v. 7, 1891, 313. *C.L.* v. 9, 1901, 336–42; v. 171, 1982, 1900; v. 172, 1982, 260. O. Siren *China and gardens of Europe of eighteenth century* 1950, 42. B. Jones *Follies & grottoes* 1974, 388–89. N. Pevsner *Staffordshire* 1974, 130. D. Stroud *Capability Brown* 1975, 224. M. Binney and A. Hills *Elysian gardens* 1979, 42, 45, 70. *J. Gdn History* v. 8 no. 2, 1982, 134–43. *Landscape research* v. 7 no. 1, 1982, 21.

Enys, St Gluvias, Cornwall
W. Borlase *Natural history of Cornwall* 1758, pl. 7. *G.C.* ii 1889, 756; i 1901, 417. Historical MSS Commission *Architectural history* v. 5, 1974, 5234, 5489.

Epsom, Surrey
Brief description of house and garden of Josiah Diston Esq at Epsom in Surrey 1726.

Epsom. New Inn Lane, Surrey
C. Fiennes *Journeys* 1949, 344–47.

Epwell Mill, Banbury, Oxfordshire
R. Bisgrove *Gardens of Britain* v. 3, 1978, 73–74.

Erddig, Wrexham, Clwyd
Official guide. *Copper Plate Mag.* v. 1, 1792, pl. 8. *C.L.* v. 26, 1909, 742–51; v. 68, 1930, 206–12; v. 162, 1977, 750–51; v. 163, 1978, 906–09, 1070; v. 164, 1978, 1034–36, 1331–32. *J. Hort. Cottage Gdnr* N.S., v. 58, 1909, 98, 99. *Gdn History* v. 3 no. 4, 1975, 56, 57, 65; v. 5 no. 3, 1977, 7. M. Binney and A. Hills *Elysian gardens* 1979, 58. G.S. Thomas *Gardens of National Trust* 1979, 133–34.

Ericht Bank, Kirn, Strathclyde
G.C. ii 1894, 473.

Eridge Castle (Park), Frant, E. Sussex
R. Ackermann *Repository* v. 9, 1827, pl. 26.

W.W.J. Gendall *Views* v. 1, 1830, 107. T.W. Horsfield *History . . . of Sussex* v. 1, 1835, 402. *G.M.* v. 18, 1842, 615–16. *J. Hort. Cottage Gdnr* v. 48, 1872, 250–52. C. Holme *Gardens of England in Southern & Western counties* 1907, pls. 55–56. *C.L.* v. 138, 1965, 750–53, 818.

Erlestoke Park near Devizes, Wilts
J.P. Neale *Views* v. 5, 1822. J. Britton *Beauties of Wiltshire* v. 3, 1825, 357–58. *G.C.* ii 1882, 235. D. Jacques *Georgian gardens* 1983, 115.

Errol Park, Errol, Tayside
R. Pococke *Tours in Scotland* 1887, 259. *Gdning World* v. 4, 1888, 294; v. 15, 1899, 291–92.

Erskine House, Hampstead, London
G. Carter *et al. Humphry Repton* 1982, 157.

Erskine House, Erskine, Strathclyde
G.M. v. 8, 1832, 670–72.

Erwarton Hall, Erwarton, Suffolk
C.L. v. 65, 1929, 157–59.

Escourt Grange near Tetbury, Glos
J. Sales *West Country gardens* 1980, 61–62.

Escrick Park, Escrick, N. Yorks
T. Allen *New . . . history of . . . York* v. 2, 1831, 350. *J. Hort. Cottage Gdnr* N.S., v. 41, 1900, 178–79.

Esher Place, Esher, Surrey
J. Beeverell *Les delices de la Grande Bretagne* v. 5, 1707, 872. L. Knyff and J. Kip *Britannia illustrata* v. 1, 1714. T. Badeslade and J. Rocque *Vitruvius Brittanicus* 1739, pls. 110–11. R. and J. Dodsley *London and its environs described* v. 2, 1761, 277. Society of Gentlemen *England displayed* v. 1, 1769, 223, 224. *Short account of the principal seats and gardens in and about Richmond and Kew* [1760s?] 12. T. Whately *Observations on modern gardening* 1771, 50–51; 1801, pl. 2. *Picturesque views of the principal seats* 1788. G.L. le Rouge *Jardins Anglo-Chinois a la mode* 2^e cahier, 1776, pl. 11. *Copper Plate Mag.* v. 1, 1792, pl. 2. G.F. Prosser *Select illustrations of . . . Surrey* 1828. British Museum *Catalogue of maps, prints* 1829, 105. E.W. Brayley and J. Britton *Topographical history of Surrey* v. 2, 1841, 438–40. W. Keane *Beauties of Surrey* 1849, 22–24. *C.L.* v. 7, 1900, 16–22; v. 125, 1959, 1076–78. *Garden* v. 60, 1901, 213–14. T. Jefferson *Garden book 1766–1824* 1944, 111. J. Harris *Artist and the country house* 1979, 187. J. Brown *Gardens of a golden afternoon* 1982, 168. K. Rorschach *Early Georgian landscape garden* 1983, 54–56, 57.

Esholt Hall, Esholt, W. Yorks
J.P. Neale *Views* v. 5, 1822. *Jones's views* 1829, 38.

Esholt Hall *(Cont.)*

G.M. v. 17, 1841, 610–13. J.C. Loudon *Villa gardener* 1850, 411–14.

Eshton Hall, Eshton, N. Yorks
F.O. Morris *Series of picturesque views* v. 3, 35.
T.D. Whitaker *History and antiquities of the Deanery of Craven* 1878, 239.

Eslington Hall near Whittingham, Northumberland
Garden v. 49, 1896, 200–01.

Essex House, Badminton, Avon
C.L. v. 172, 1982, 252–53. *Garden* 1983, 5–8.

Essex House, Strand, Westminster, London
J.T. Smith *Antiquities of Westminster* 1807.

Esslemont, Ellon, Grampian
G.A. Little *Scotland's gardens* 1981, 187–88.

Etal Manor, Etal, Northumberland
C.L. v. 134, 1963, 68–70.

Eton College, Eton, Berks
D. Loggan *Cantabrigia illustrata* 1690. R. Bisgrove *Gardens of Britain* v. 3, 1978, 115.

Etruria, Stoke-on-Trent, Staffs
W. Pitt *General view of agriculture of . . . Stafford* 1796, 202.

Ettington Park, Ettington, Warwickshire
J. Hort. Cottage Gdnr N.S., v. 64, 1912, 122–23.

Euston Hall, Euston, Suffolk
E.W. Brayley *Views in Suffolk, Norfolk and Northamptonshire illustrative of the works of Robert Bloomfield* 1818, 23–25. J.P. Neale *Views* v. 4, 1821. J.C. Loudon *Encyclopaedia of gardening* 1822, 1235. F.O. Morris *Series of picturesque views* v. 3, 47. C. Fiennes *Journeys* 1949, 151. J. Evelyn *Diary* 1955, v. 3, 591; v. 4, 116–17. C.L. v. 121, 1957, 58–61,148–51. *Architectural History* v. 7, 1964, 26–27,58–62. *Connoisseur* v. 163, 1966, 142–47. C. Hussey *English gardens and landscapes* 1967, 154–57. *Publications of Bedfordshire Historical Record Soc.* v. 47, 1968, 140–41. N. Pevsner *Suffolk* 1974, 203–04. D. Stroud *Capability Brown* 1975, 224–25. L. Fleming and A. Gore *English garden* 1979, 97. M. Hadfield et al. *British gardeners* 1980, 136. D. Watkin *English vision* 1982, 27.

Everingham Park, Everingham, Humberside
G.M. v. 12, 1836, 347–52. F.O. Morris *Series of picturesque views* v. 1, 25.

Eversley Rectory, Eversley, Hants
Garden v. 11, 1877, 95. W. Robinson *English flower garden* 1883, xxvii–xxx.

Ewell Castle, Ewell, Surrey
G.F. Prosser *Select illustrations of . . . Surrey* 1828. W. Keane *Beauties of Surrey* 1849, 99–100. *J. Hort. Cottage Gdnr* v. 57, 1877, 367–68.

Ewell Grove, Ewell, Surrey
W. Keane *Beauties of Surrey* 1849, 100–01.

Ewelme Down, Ewelme, Oxfordshire
C.L. v. 31, 1912, 430–36.

Ewhurst, Hants
C.L. v. 28, 1910, 898–905. G. Jekyll *Garden ornament* 1918, 148.

Exbury House, Exbury, Hants
J. Royal Hort. Soc. 1940, 111–14. C.L. v. 91, 1942, 296–99. P. Coats *Great gardens of Britain* 1967, 194–99. M. Allan *Fisons guide* 1970, 92–93. C.E.L. Phillips and P.N. Barber *Rothschild rhododendrons: a record of the gardens at Exbury* 1979. A. Paterson *Gardens of Britain* v. 2, 1978, 79–84.

Exeter. University, Devon
C.L. v. 125, 1959, 1002–03; v. 158, 1975, 1748–49; v. 159, 1976, 1045. G.C. v. 160 no. 9, 1966, 14–15. *Grounds and gardens of University of Exeter* 1969. *International Dendrology Soc. Year Book* 1971, 8–13; 1972, 13–17; 1973, 52–56.

Exton Park, Exton, Leics
T. Badeslade *and* J. Rocque *Vitruvius Brittanicus* 1739, pls. 59–62. British Museum *Catalogue of maps, prints* 1829, 109. G.M. v. 5, 1829, 673–74. F.O. Morris *Series of picturesque views* v. 4, 5. *J. Hort. Cottage Gdnr* v. 47, 1872, 311–14,330–32. V.C.H. *Rutland* v. 2, 1935, 128. B. Jones *Follies & grottoes* 1974, 18–19. M. Binney *and* A. Hills *Elysian gardens* 1978, 47. J. Harris *Artist and the country house* 1979, 168.

Eyam Hall, Eyam, Derbyshire
C.L. v. 8, 1900, 16–21. G. Jekyll *Garden ornament* 1918, 60,69,75.

Eydon Hall, Eydon, Northants
C.L. v. 10, 1901, 304–10. G. Jekyll *Garden ornament* 1918, 190.

Eyebury, Northants
Northamptonshire Past and Present v. 5 no. 3, 1975, 224.

Eyford near Stow-on-the-Wold, Glos
Architectural Review v. 46, 1919, 11–13, pl. 3. V.C.H.
Gloucester v. 6, 1965, 73–74.

Eyhorne House, Hollingbourne, Kent
C. Greenwood *Epitome of county history . . . v. 1: Kent*
1838, 162.

Eynsham Hall, Eynsham, Oxfordshire
Garden v. 49, 1896, 57.

Eyot House, Weybridge, Surrey
C.L. v. 51, 1922, 323.

Eyre's Folly, Whiteparish, Wilts
B. Jones *Follies & grottoes* 1974, 409.

Eythrope near Aylesbury, Bucks
R. Pococke *Travels through England* v. 1, 1888, 112.
J. Hort. Cottage Gdnr N.S., v. 20, 1890, 529–32.

Eyton on Severn near Much Wenlock, Shropshire
C.L. v. 47, 1920, 236–40.

Eywood near Kington, Hereford and Worcester
G.M. v. 16, 1840, 377–79. D. Stroud *Capability Brown*
1975, 225.

Fairfield near Bridgwater, Somerset
J. Collinson *History . . . of Somersetshire* v. 1, 1791, 254.

Fairfield House, Hambledon, Hants
A. Paterson *Gardens of Britain* v. 2, 1978, 84–85. *C.L.*
v. 165, 1979, 1510–12.

Fairford Park, Fairford, Glos
R. Atkyns *Ancient and present state of Glostershire* 1712,
431. J. Knyff *and* J. Kip *Britannia illustrata* v. 2, 1715.
Scottish Gdnr v. 6, 1857, 513–15. H.I. Triggs *Formal
gardens in England and Scotland* 1902, 40–41.
M. Macartney *English houses & gardens* 1908, 41.
D. Verey *Gloucestershire* v. 1, 1970, 248. V.C.H.
Gloucester v. 7, 1981, 69,75.

Fairlawn near Sevenoaks, Kent
J. Beeverell *Les delices de la Grande Bretagne* v. 5, 1707,
872. J. Knyff *and* J. Kip *Britannia illustrata* v. 1, 1714.
H. Overton *Britannia illustrata* c.1724, pl. 12.
J.P. Neale *Views* v. 2, 1819. W.H. Ireland *History . . .
of Kent* v. 3, 1829, 534. G. Virtue *Picturesque beauties of
Great Britain: Kent* 1829, 123. C. Greenwood *Epitome of
county history . . . v. 1: Kent* 1838, 135. *J. Hort. Cottage
Gdnr* v. 31, 1864, 432–33,453. *G.C.* ii 1899, 265–66,273.
C.L. v. 44, 1918, 50–56,72–77; v. 124, 1958, 998–1001,
1050–53.

Fairlawn, Wimbledon, London
G.C. i 1893, 268.

Fairlee near Newport, Isle of Wight
R. Worsley *History of Isle of Wight* 1781.

Falkland Palace, Falkland, Fife
Official guide. *C.L.* v. 126, 1959, 118–21,178; v. 154,
1973, 364–66; v. 161, 1977, 1382–86. *G.C.* v. 162 no. 3,
1967, 19–21. M. Allan *Fisons guide* 1970, 324–25.
R. Webber *Percy Cane* 1975, 75–78,187. P. Verney
Gardens of Scotland 1976, 16–27. A. Hellyer *Gardens of
genius* 1980, 150–55. G.A. Little *Scotland's gardens*
1981, 144–47. T. Hinde *Stately gardens of Britain* 1983,
182–87.

Falkland Park, Norwood, London
Gdning World v. 7, 1891, 296–97; v. 8, 1892, 437–38;
v. 13, 1897, 281; v. 15, 1898, 200–01. *G.C.* i 1896,
39–40,49,73–74; ii 1900, 32–34.

Fanhams Hall, Ware, Herts
Architectural Review v. 18, 1905, 269–77; v. 35, 1914,
pl. 14. R. Bisgrove *Gardens of Britain* v. 3, 1978, 74–75.

Farfield Hall, Bolton Abbey, N. Yorks
C. Holme *Gardens of England in Northern counties* 1911,
pl. 44. *C.L.* v. 37, 1915, 240–44. G. Beard *Thomas H.
Mawson* 1976, 51.

Faringdon House, Faringdon, Oxfordshire
C.L. v. 139, 1966, 1184–87,1246. R. Bisgrove *Gardens
of Britain* v. 3, 1978, 75–76.

Farleigh House, Farleigh, Avon
Garden 1920, 454–55.

Farley near Wokingham, Berks
C.L. v. 93, 1943, 1056–59. P. Willis *Charles Bridgeman*
1977, 178.

Farm Hall, Godmanchester, Cambs
C.L. v. 130, 1961, 1134–37.

Farmingwoods near Oundle, Northants
J.P. Neale *Views* 2nd Series, v. 3, 1826.

Farnborough Hall, Farnborough, Warwickshire
C.L. v. 115, 1954, 354–57,430; v. 174, 1983, 1856–57.
J. Royal Hort. Soc. 1971, 212. G.S. Thomas *Gardens of
National Trust* 1979, 134–36. R. Sidwell *West Midland
gardens* 1981, 210–11.

Farnham Castle, Farnham, Surrey
J.P. Neale *Views* v. 4, 1821. *G.M.* v. 11, 1835,503–05.
E.W. Brayley *and* J. Britton *Topographical history of
Surrey* v. 5, 270. W. Keane *Beauties of Surrey* 1849,

Farnham Castle (*Cont.*)
130–31. *J. Hort. Cottage Gdnr* v. 30, 1863, 127–28. *Garden* v. 51, 1897, 75. C. Holme *Gardens of England in Southern & Western counties* 1907, pl. 57.

Farnham House near Cavan, Co. Cavan, Eire
Florist 1859, 178–80. F.O. Morris *Series of picturesque views* v. 1, 39.

Farnley Hall, Farnley, N. Yorks
J. Loudon *Treatise on forming, improving and managing country residences* v. 2, 1806, pls. 22–23. J.P. Neale *Views* v. 5, 1822. *Jones's views* 1829, 50. *C.L.* v. 115, 1954, 1808. I. Hall *Samuel Buck's Yorkshire sketchbook* 1979, 200.

Farrer, Reginald *see* Ingleborough

Farringford, Isle of Wight
G.C. ii 1892, 461, 463.

Fasque near Fettercairn, Grampian
C.L. v. 166, 1979, 386–89.

Fatherwell House, Ryarsh, Kent
C. Greenwood *Epitome of county history . . . v. 1: Kent* 1838, 191.

Faulkbourne Hall, Faulkbourne, Essex
G. Virtue *Picturesque beauties of Great Britain: Essex* 1831, 2. T. Wright *History . . . of Essex* v. 1, 1836, 230. *C.L.* v. 16, 1904, 630–39; v. 66, 1929, 718–26. G. Jekyll *Garden ornament* 1918, 127.

Fawley Court, Fawley, Bucks
W.B. Cooke *and* S. Owen *The Thames* v. 1, 1811, 23. J.P. Neale *Views* 2nd Series, v. 3, 1826. *Tombleson's Thames* 1834. B. Jones *Follies & grottoes* 1974, 293. D. Stroud *Capability Brown* 1975, 225.

Fawley Court near Ross-on-Wye, Hereford and Worcester
R. Sidwell *West Midland gardens* 1981, 52–53.

Fawsley Dower House, Fawsley, Northants
Royal Commission on Historical Monuments *Inventory of the historical monuments in . . . Northampton* v. 3, 1981, 90.

Fawsley Hall, Fawsley, Northants
Cottage Gdnr v. 15, 1855, 21–22, 54–55. *J. Hort. Cottage Gdnr* v. 30, 1863, 124–25. *C.L.* v. 24, 1908, 18–27. D. Stroud *Capability Brown* 1975, 225.

Feathercombe, Hambledon, Surrey
Field 7 April 1977, 569–70. T. Wright *Gardens of Britain* v. 4, 1978, 216.

Featherstone Castle, Featherstone, Northumberland
C.L. v. 154, 1973, 1246–49.

Felbridge Place, East Grinstead, W. Sussex
J. Brown *Gardens of a golden afternoon* 1982, 173.

Felbrigg Hall near Cromer, Norfolk
Official guide. *Copper Plate Mag.* v. 1, 1792, pl. 40. *G.M.* v. 17, 1841, 31. J. Grigor *Eastern arboretum* 1841, 122–29. R.W. Ketton-Cremer *Felbrigg* 1962. D. Stroud *Humphry Repton* 1962, 146. G.S. Thomas *Gardens of National Trust* 1979, 136. G. Carter *et al. Humphry Repton* 1982, 113, 158.

Felix Hall near Coggeshall, Essex
P. Muilman *History of Essex* v. 1, 1769, 386. T. Wright *History . . . of Essex* v. 1, 1836, 261. J. Harris *Artist and the country house* 1979, 288–89. G. Carter *et al. Humphry Repton* 1982, 151.

Felthorpe Park, Felthorpe, Norfolk
G.M. v. 17, 1841, 31. J. Grigor *Eastern arboretum* 1841, 137–41.

Fen Ditton Hall, Fen Ditton, Cambs
C.L. v. 136, 1964, 764–67, 834–35.

Fenagh, Co. Carlow, Eire
R.H.S. *Conifers in cultivation* 1932, 218, 220. E. Malins *and* P. Bowe *Irish gardens and demesnes* 1980, 76–77.

Ferguslie House, Paisley, Strathclyde
Scottish Gdnr v. 10, 1861, 146–47.

Fern Hill, Co. Dublin, Eire
E. Malins *and* P. Bowe *Irish gardens and demesnes* 1980, 123.

Ferney (Ferne) **Hall** near Ludlow, Shropshire
D. Stroud *Humphry Repton* 1962, 42. J. Harris *Catalogue of British drawings . . . in American collections* 1971, 172, 175–76. G. Carter *et al. Humphry Repton* 1982, 161.

Fernie Castle near Cupar, Fife
G.M. v. 7, 1831, 23.

Ferniehurst near Shipley, W. Yorks
J. Hort. Cottage Gdnr N.S., v. 1, 1880, 434–35.

Fernwood near Birmingham, W. Midlands
J. Hort. Cottage Gdnr N.S., v. 43, 1901, 400–01.

Ferry House, Isleworth, Hounslow, London
C.L. v. 152, 1972, 1272–74.

Festival Gardens *see* London

Fetcham Park, Fetcham, Surrey
C. Fiennes *Journeys* 1949, 352–53.

Fethard, Co. Tipperary, Eire
Moorea v. 3, 1984, 23–30.

Fettercairn House, Fettercairn, Grampian
G.A. Little *Scotland's gardens* 1981, 188.

Fiddlers Copse, Plaistow, W. Sussex
C.L. v. 136, 1964, 1640–42.

Field Place near Horsham, W. Sussex
C.L. v. 118, 1955, 724–27,788. *G.C.* ii 1960, 192–93, 206.

Fillingham Castle, Fillingham, Lincs
Garden v. 51, 1897, 239.

Finborough Hall, Great Finborough, Suffolk
H. Davy *Views* 1827.

Finchcocks near Goudhurst, Kent
W.H. Ireland *History . . . of Kent* v. 3, 1829, 208. G. Virtue *Picturesque beauties of Great Britain: Kent* 1829, 114. C. Greenwood *Epitome of county history . . . v. 1: Kent* 1838, 230. *C.L.* v. 50, 1921, 132–37; v. 99, 1946, 670–73.

Finches, Lindfield, W. Sussex
G.C. i 1893, 625–26,629.

Finch's Grotto Gardens, Southwark, London
W. Wroth *London pleasure gardens of the eighteenth century* 1896, 241–46.

Finedon Hall, Finedon, Northants
H. Repton *Sketches and hints* 1794, 42–43. *C.L.* v. 10, 1901, 48–54. D. Stroud *Humphry Repton* 1962, 169. G. Carter *et al. Humphry Repton* 1982, 160. *Garden* 1983, 365.

Fingask Castle near Errol, Tayside
J.P. Neale *Views* 2nd Series, v. 4, 1828. *Scottish Gdnr* v. 3, 1854, 9–12. *C.L.* v. 80, 1936, 62–63. G.A. Little *Scotland's gardens* 1981, 147–48.

Finlaystone, Langbank, Strathclyde
G.A. Little *Scotland's gardens* 1981, 257. *G.C.* v. 193 no. 23, 1982, 25–27.

Finmere Rectory, Finmere, Oxfordshire
D. Stroud *Capability Brown* 1975, 53–54.

Finnart near Arddarroch, Strathclyde
Gdning World v. 6, 1890, 661–62.

Finsbury Park *see* London

Fir Grange, Weybridge, Surrey
G.C. i 1903, 186–87; ii 1907, 217.

Firbeck Hall, Firbeck, S. Yorks
J. Hort. Cottage Gdnr N.S., v. 21, 1890, 246–47.

Firle Place, West Firle, E. Sussex
C.L. v. 47, 1920, 78–85; v. 117, 1955, 480–84,564,620. Historical MSS Commission *Architectural history* v. 2, 1970, item 1410.

Firle Vicarage, West Firle, E. Sussex
C.L. v. 158, 1975, 762–64.

Firs, Lee, Lewisham, London
E. Hasted *History . . . of . . . Kent* part 1, 1886, 224. *Garden* v. 23, 1883, 583–84.

Firs, Warwick, Warwickshire
G.C. ii 1892, 613.

Fishbourne near Chichester, W. Sussex
G.C. v. 163 no. 25, 1968, 21–25. B. Cunliffe *A Roman palace and its garden* 1971. B. Cunliffe *Excavations at Fishbourne* v. 1, 1971, 120–34. Dumbarton Oaks *Ancient Roman gardens* 1981, 101–08. C. Taylor *Archaeology of gardens* 1983, 30–31.

Fishers Farm, Wakes Colne, Essex
F.G. Emmison *Catalogue of maps in Essex Record Office* 1st Supplt, 1952, 28.

Fisher's Hill, Hook Heath, Woking, Surrey
J. Brown *Gardens of a golden afternoon* 1982, 164.

Fisherwick, Staffs
R. Plot *Natural history of Staffordshire* 1685, 209. *Companion to The Leasowes, Hagley and Enville* 1789, 111–30. W. Pitt *General view of agriculture of . . . Stafford* 1796, 95,185. S. Shaw *History . . . of Staffordshire* v. 1, 1798, 368. W. Marshall *On planting and rural ornament* v. 1, 1803, 305–13. J. Nightingale *Topographical . . . description of Staffordshire* 1810, 819. *Archaeological J.* v. 120, 1963, 264. D. Stroud *Capability Brown* 1975, 151–53,225. *Geographical Mag.* v. 54, 1982, 341–46. *C.L.* v. 174, 1983, 250–51.

Fitzroy Farm, Highgate, London
G. Carter *et al. Humphry Repton* 1982, 157.

Fixby Hall near Huddersfield, W. Yorks
Cottage Gdnr v. 19, 1857, 213–15.

Flagstaff, Colwyn Bay, Clwyd
T.H. Mawson *Art & craft of garden making* 1907, 120.
G. Beard *Thomas H. Mawson* 1976, 52.

Flambards (Flamberts), Harrow, London
W. Keane *Beauties of Middlesex* 1850, 211–12.
D. Stroud *Capability Brown* 1975, 225–26.

Flaxley Abbey, Flaxley, Glos
R. Atkyns *Ancient and present state of Glostershire* 1712, 437. J. Knyff *and* J. Kip *Britannia illustrata* v. 2, 1715. J.N. Brewer *Delineations of Gloucestershire* 1825, 119. *C.L.* v. 153, 1973, 842–45, 908, 980–84.

Fleet House, Fleet, Dorset
J. Hutchins *History . . . of Dorset* v. 1, 1774, 545; v. 2, 1863, 744.

Flesk Castle near Killarney, Co. Kerry, Eire
J.P. Neale *Views* 2nd Series, v. 1, 1824.

Flete near Ivybridge, Devon
C.L. v. 38, 1915, 680–88. *Landscape and Garden* v. 2 no. 3, 1935, 90. P.M. Synge *Gardens of Britain* v. 1, 1977, 45–48.

Fleurs Castle *see* Floors Castle

Flintham Hall near Newark, Notts
C.L. v. 167, 1980, 18–21.

Flitwick Manor, Flitwick, Beds
G.M. v. 5, 1829, 559–60. J.B. Burke *Visitation* v. 1, 1852, 8–9. B. Jones *Follies & grottoes* 1974, 286.

Flixton Hall, Flixton, Suffolk
J.C. Loudon *Encyclopaedia of gardening* 1822, 1235. A. Suckling *History . . . of Suffolk* v. 1, 1846, 200. *J. Hort. Cottage Gdnr* v. 42, 1869, 306–07. *G.C.* ii 1896, 401, 403–04.

Floors (Fleurs) **Castle**, Kelso, Borders
J.P. Neale *Views* v. 6, 1823. *Scottish Gdnr* v. 7, 1858, 249–53. *J. Hort. Cottage Gdnr* v. 39, 1868, 113–15. *G.C.* ii 1874, 712–13. F.O. Morris *Series of picturesque views* v. 1, 35. *C.L.* v. 68, 1930, 761–64; v. 163, 1978, 1298–1301. I.H. Adams *Descriptive list of plans* v. 3, 1974, 125. J. Harris *Artist and the country house* 1979, 343. G.A. Little *Scotland's gardens* 1981, 86.

Flora Tea Gardens (Mount Gardens), Lambeth, London
W. Wroth *London pleasure gardens of the eighteenth century* 1896, 265.

Flore House, Flore, Northants
G.C. ii 1883, 330–31; ii 1884, 587–88. G. Beard *Thomas H. Mawson* 1976, 69.

Florence Court near Enniskillen, Co. Fermanagh, Ulster
Official guide. T. Milton *Seats . . . in Ireland* 1783, 29. *Delineator* 1831, 51. *Irish Gdning* v. 3, 1908, 172–73. E. Malins *and* Knight of Glin *Lost demesnes* 1976, 80. G.S. Thomas *Gardens of National Trust* 1979, 136–37. T. Wright *Arbours & grottos* 1979. *Glasra* v. 5, 1981, 33–44. *National Trust Studies* 1981, 8–9. Ulster Architectural Heritage Society *Northern gardens* 1982, 19.

Florida Gardens *see* Cromwell's Gardens

Foaty Island *see* Fota Island

Foldsdown, Thursley, Surrey
G.C. ii 1916, 112, 113.

Folkestone. Winter Garden, Kent
Gdning World v. 1, 1885, 649.

Folkington, E. Sussex
J. Beeverell *Les delices de la Grande Bretagne* v. 5, 1707, 872. J. Knyff *and* J. Kip *Britannia illustrata* v. 1, 1714. *C.L.* v. 175, 1984, 280–81.

Follaton House near Totnes, Devon
R. Ackermann *Repository* v. 10, 1827, pl. 7. W.W.J. Gendall *Views* v. 1, 1830, 63. J. Britton *and* E.W. Brayley *Devonshire & Cornwall* 1832, 70.

Folly Farm, Sulhamstead, Berks
L. Weaver *Houses and gardens by E.L. Lutyens* 1913, 275–83. *C.L.* v. 51, 1922, 112–19, 146–53; v. 130, 1961, 6–8; v. 157, 1975, 1230–32. R. Bisgrove *Gardens of Britain* v. 3, 1978, 77–78. J. Brown *Gardens of a golden afternoon* 1982, 93–95, 165.

Fonmon Castle, Fonmon, S. Glamorgan
C.L. v. 105, 1949, 606–09, 734.

Fonthill Abbey, Fonthill Gifford, Wilts
H. Meister *Letters* 1799, 300, 303–06. J. Britton *Beauties of Wiltshire* v. 1, 1801, 240–49; v. 3, 1825, 328. J. Storer *Description of Fonthill Abbey, Wiltshire* 1812, 2–6. J.C. Loudon *Encyclopaedia of gardening* 1822, 1246. J. Rutter *Description of Fonthill Abbey and demesne* 1822. G. *and* W.B. Whittaker *New guide to Fonthill Abbey* 1822. R. Ackermann *Repository* v. 2, 1823, pl. 9. J. Britton *Graphical and literary illustrations of Fonthill Abbey, Wiltshire* 1823. R. Havell *Series of picturesque views* 1823. pl. 20. J. Rutter *Delineations of Fonthill and its abbey* 1823. J.P. Neale *Views* 2nd Series, v. 1, 1824. R.C. Hoare *Modern history of South Wiltshire* v. 4, 1829,

Fonthill Abbey (*Cont.*)

24,28. *G.M.* v. 11, 1835, 441–49. J.C. Loudon *Arboretum et fruticetum Britannicum* v. 1, 1844, 128. *J. Hort. Cottage Gdnr* N.S., v. 17, 1888, 69–70. *G.C.* i 1893, 40; ii 1893, 551–52. *C.L.* v. 10, 1901, 840–46; v. 121, 1957, 157; v. 140, 1966, 1370–73. H.A.N. Brockman *Caliph of Fonthill* 1956. *Gazette des Beaux-arts* v. 80, 1972, 335–56. B. Jones *Follies & grottoes* 1974, 407. N. Pevsner *Wiltshire* 1975, 248–49. *J. Gdn History* v. 2 no. 1, 1982, 48–49. D. Jacques *Georgian gardens* 1983, pl. 10.

Fonthill House, Fonthill Gifford, Wilts
R.J. Sulivan *Tour . . . in 1778* v. 1, 1785, 129. W. Angus *Seats* 1787, pl. 50. J. Harris *Artist and the country house* 1979, 262.

Fontmell Parva near Child Okeford, Dorset
J. Hutchins *History . . . of Dorset* v. 4, 1870, 80.

Foots Cray Place, Foots Cray, Bexley, London
Society of Gentlemen *England displayed* v. 1, 1769, 144. G.A. Walpoole *New British traveller* 1784, pl. after p. 22. H. Boswell *Historical descriptions of new and picturesque views* 1800. J.P. Neale *Views* 2nd Series, v. 4, 1828. G. Virtue *Picturesque beauties of Great Britain: Kent* 1829, 2. W.H. Ireland *History . . . of Kent* v. 4, 1830, 524. T.H. Mawson *Art & craft of garden making* 1907 passim. *Architectural Review* v. 27, 1910, 102–04. G. Beard *Thomas H. Mawson* 1976, 52.

Forcett Park, Forcett, N. Yorks
C.L. v. 155, 1974, 194. J. Harris *Artist and the country house* 1979, 297.

Ford Castle, Ford, Northumberland
C. Holme *Gardens of England in Northern counties* 1911, pls. 45–46. *C.L.* v. 89, 1941, 32–35,56–60,78–82. M. Binney *and* A. Hills *Elysian gardens* 1979, 17. J. Harris *Artist and the country house* 1979, 205.

Forde Abbey, Chard, Dorset
Official guide. S. *and* N. Buck *Buck's antiquities* v. 1, 1774, pl. 63. J. Hutchins *History . . . of Dorset* v. 4, 1870, 528. *G.C.* ii 1897, 322–24; ii 1907, 245–46; ii 1956, 290–91; ii 1964, 12; v. 192 no. 5, 1982, 28–29. *Garden* v. 59, 1901, 398–99. *C.L.* v. 7, 1900, 368–74; v. 26, 1909, 18–26; v. 131, 1962, 587; v. 133, 1963, 540–43,595–99,656,714–17; v. 134, 1963, 588–90. J. Roper *Forde Abbey* 1962. *Architectural History* v. 7, 1964, 28,64–68. M. Allan *Fisons guide* 1970, 93–94. A. Paterson *Gardens of Britain* v. 2, 1978, 30–31.

Fordell, Inverkeithing, Fife
G.C. i 1887, 834–35,837. H.I. Triggs *Formal gardens in England and Scotland* 1902, 43. G.A. Little *Scotland's gardens* 1981, 148–49.

Foremark near Derby, Derbyshire
A. Young *Farmer's tour through East of England* v. 1, 1771, 180–82. D. Defoe *Tour* 1778, 76–77. J. Britton *and* E.W. Brayley *Beauties of England and Wales* v. 3, 1802, 399–400. *G.M.* v. 15, 1839, 450. *C.L.* v. 54, 1923, 214–20. Lady Rockley *Historic gardens of England* 1938, 218–19.

Forest Lodge, Hythe, Hants
B. Jones *Follies & grottoes* 1974, 336. N. Pevsner *and* D. Lloyd *Hampshire and the Isle of Wight* 1967, 304.

Formakin near Bishopton, Strathclyde
C.L. v. 34 Supplt to 27 Sept. 1913, xxiv–xxviii. G. Jekyll *Garden ornament* 1918, 262,352. *G.C.* ii 1921, 111,113–14.

Fornham near Bury St Edmunds, Suffolk
H. Davy *Views* 1827. *Garden* v. 24, 1883, 444–45.

Fort *see* Royal Fort

Fort Belvedere near Virginia Water, Surrey
C.L. v. 126, 1959, 898–901,960–63.

Fort Hill, Enniskillen, Co. Fermanagh, Ulster
Ulster Architectural Heritage Society *Northern gardens* 1982, 19,23.

Fortis Green, Muswell Hill, London
G.M. v. 16, 1840, 49–58. J.C. Loudon *Villa gardener* 1850, 276–85.

Fota Island, Cobh, Co. Cork, Eire
J.P. Neale *Views* 2nd Series, v. 4, 1828. *List of trees and shrubs growing in the open at Fota* 1912. *Irish Gdning* v. 9, 1913, 38–40; v. 12, 1917, 139–40. *J. Royal Hort. Soc.* 1960, 477–80; 1966, 86–87. *G.C.* ii 1962, 206–07. E. Hyams *Irish gardens* 1967, 76–81. B. Jones *Follies & grottoes* 1974, 428. *Trees, shrubs and other plants of Fota gardens* 1978. Knight of Glin *and* P. Bowe *Gardens of outstanding historic interest in . . . Ireland* 1980. E. Malins *and* P. Bowe *Irish gardens and demesnes* 1980, 69–73.

Fothergill, John *see* Upton House

Fotheringhay, Northants
Northamptonshire Past and Present v. 5 no. 3, 1975, 224.

Four Oaks near Sutton Coldfield, W. Midlands
T. Badeslade *and* J. Rocque *Vitruvius Brittanicus* 1739, pls. 75–76. J.P. Neale *Views* v. 4, 1821.

Fowlers, Hawkhurst, Kent
F. Hull *Catalogue of estate maps 1590 to 1840 in the Kent County Archives Office* 1973, 230.

Fox Hill near Chertsey, Surrey
W. Keane *Beauties of Surrey* 1849, 44–45.

Foxbury, Chislehurst, Bromley, London
J. Hort. Cottage Gdnr N.S., v. 33, 1896, 36–37.

Foxcote near Shipston on Stour, Warwickshire
J.P. Neale *Views* v. 4, 1821.

Foxhill, Reading, Berks
G.C. i 1910, 186.

Foxlease near Lyndhurst, Hants
E.F. Prosser *Select illustrations of Hampshire* 1833.

Foxley near Hereford, Hereford and Worcester
G.M. v. 14, 1838, 217–18. Dumbarton Oaks *Picturesque garden and its influence outside the British Isles* 1974, 71–76.

Fragnall *see* Frognal

Frampton Court, Frampton, Dorset
J. Hutchins *History . . . of Dorset* v. 2, 1863, 297.

Frampton Court, Frampton on Severn, Glos
J.N. Brewer *Delineations of Gloucestershire* 1825, 87. *C.L.* v. 62, 1927, 506–12,538. J. Sales *West Country gardens* 1980, 64–65. D. Verey *Gloucestershire* v. 2, 1970, 192.

Frankleigh near Bradford-on-Avon, Wilts
C.L. v. 8, 1900, 48–53.

Franks near Farningham, Kent
F.O. Morris *Series of picturesque views* v. 1, 47. *C.L.* v. 1, 1897, 295–98; v. 34, 1913, 126–33.

Freeford near Lichfield, Staffs
W. Pitt *General view of agriculture of . . . Stafford* 1796, 18. S. Shaw *History . . . of Staffordshire* v. 1, 1798, 360.

Freemantle, Southampton, Hants
E.F. Prosser *Select illustrations of Hampshire* 1833.

Friar Park, Henley-on-Thames, Oxfordshire
Official guide. *Gdnrs Mag.* 1899, 442–44,754–55; 1911, 641–43. *G.C.* ii 1899, 321–24,325,338; ii 1900, 292; i 1901, 368; ii 1909, 281. *Garden* v. 64, 1903, 111; 1907, 5–6,16,505; 1912, 541. *Alphabetical list of plants* 1907. *C.L.* v. 18, 1905, 162–66; v. 33, 1913, 641–44; v. 46, 1919, 174–76. *Irish Gdning* 1915, 49–51. B. Jones *Follies & grottoes* 1974, 377–78. C. Aslet *Lost country houses* 1982, 297–99.

Friars Carse, Dumfries, Dumfries and Galloway
Scottish Gdnr and Northern Forester v. 9, 1914, 237–38.

Friar's House, Barry, S. Glamorgan
G.C. ii 1912, 127.

Friars Well, Aynho, Northants
C.L. v. 167, 1980, 1088–90.

Frocester Court, Frocester, Glos
C.L. v. 17, 1905, 702–04. *J. Roman Studies* v. 58, 1968, 198. *Proc. Cotteswold Naturalists Field Club* v. 35 no. 3, 1968–69, 154–55. *Britannia* v. 2, 1971, 243–88.

Frogmore *see* Windsor

Frognal, Chislehurst, Bromley, London
J. Harris *History of Kent* 1719, 72. J. Kip *Nouveau theatre de la Grande Bretagne* v. 2, 1724. T. Badeslade *Thirty six different views of . . . Kent* 1750s. G. Virtue *Picturesque beauties of Great Britain: Kent* 1829, 41. *G.M.* v. 6, 1830, 653–54. W.H. Ireland *History . . . of Kent* v. 4, 1830, 481. *Garden* v. 25, 1884, 79. M. Macartney *English houses & gardens* 1908, pl. 24.

Frog's Island, Walton Heath, Surrey
J. Brown *Gardens of a golden afternoon* 1982, 172.

Frome Billet (House) *see* Stafford House

Froyle House near Alton, Hants
E.F. Prosser *Select illustrations of Hampshire* 1833.

Froyle Mill near Alton, Hants
A. Paterson *Gardens of Britain* v. 2, 1978, 86–87.

Fryars, Aylesford, Kent
G. Virtue *Picturesque beauties of Great Britain: Kent* 1829, 32.

Frythe, Welwyn, Herts
J.E. Cussans *History of Hertfordshire* v. 2, 1874, 214.

Fulbeck Hall, Fulbeck, Lincs
C.L. v. 151, 1972, 394–98.

Fulbrook House, Elstead, Surrey
C.L. v. 13, 1903, 144–52. L. Weaver *Houses and gardens by E.L. Lutyens* 1913, 19–22. J. Brown *Gardens of a golden afternoon* 1982, 162.

Fulford Hall, Fulford, N. Yorks
C.L. v. 16, 1904, 417–19. C. Holme *Gardens of England in Northern counties* 1911, pl. 47. Lady Rockley *Historic gardens of England* 1938, 104–05.

Fulford House, Dunsford, Devon
W.R. Ackermann *Repository* v. 8, 1826, pl. 20. W.W.J. Gendall *Views* v. 1, 1830, 77.

Fulham. Bishop's Park, London
C.J. Fèret *Fulham old and new* v. 3, 1900, 209–13.

Fulham Palace, Fulham, London
S. Switzer *Ichnographia rustica* v. 1, 1742, 70–71. *Philosophical Trans. Royal Soc.* 1751, 241. W. Thornton *New, complete and universal history* 1786, 480. D. Lysons *Environs of London* v. 2, 1795, 350–53; *Supplement* 1811, 146,432–33. J.C. Loudon *Arboretum et fruticetum Britannicum* v. 1, 1844, 41–44. *Garden* v. 4, 1873, 61–62. *G.C.* ii 1877, 234; i 1879, 112,113,145; ii 1888, 5–6. C.J. Fèret *Fulham old and new* v. 3, 1900, 128–46. J. MacGregor *Gardens of celebrities . . . in and around London* 1918, 62–93. E.S. Rohde *Story of the garden* 1932, 166–67. G. Taylor *Old London gardens* 1953, 60–64. J. Evelyn *Diary* v. 4, 1955, 258. *Gdn History* v. 4 no. 3, 1976, 14–20; v. 9 no. 1, 1981, 57–58. *C.L.* v. 162, 1977, 1712–13.

Fuller, Thomas *see* Sevenoaks

Furzey, Minstead, Hants
Gdning Illustrated 1951, 325–27. *J. Royal Hort. Soc.* 1955, 258–64. A. Paterson *Gardens of Britain* v. 2, 1978, 87–89.

Fyfield Manor near Pewsey, Wilts
C.L. v. 68, 1930, 260–65; v. 130, 1961, 626–29.

Fyvie Castle near Turriff, Grampian
J.P. Neale *Views* 2nd Series, v. 1, 1824. *Scottish Gdnr* v. 4, 1855, 472–74. *C.L.* v. 32, 1912, 388–94.

Gaddesden Place, Great Gaddesden, Herts
J.E. Cussans *History of Hertfordshire* v. 3, 1881, 118.

Galloway House near Garliestown, Dumfries and Galloway
F.O. Morris *Series of picturesque views* v. 4, 35. *Gdnrs Mag.* 1903, 55–58. *G.C.* ii 1930, 10–11. G.A. Little *Scotland's gardens* 1981, 258.

Gamlingay, Cambs
Royal Commission on Historical Monuments *Inventory of historical monuments in . . . Cambridge* v. 1, 1968, 110–12, pls. 3, 28. C. Taylor *Archaeology of gardens* 1983, 14,15.

Garbally near Ballinasloe, Co. Galway, Eire
G.M. v. 7, 1831, 23–26.

Garden House, Buckland Monachorum, Devon
A. Lees-Milne and R. Verey *Englishman's garden* 1982, 64–67.

Garden House, Cottered, Herts
R. Bisgrove *Gardens of Britain* v. 3, 1978, 80.

Garendon near Loughborough, Leics
J. Throsby *Select views in Leicestershire* v. 1, 1790, 274. J. Nichols *History . . . of county of Leicester* v. 3, 1804, 802. *G.M.* v. 7, 1831, 427–28.

Gargunnock House, Gargunnock, Central
G.A. Little *Scotland's gardens* 1981, 149.

Garinish Island (Ilnacullin), Glengariff, Co. Cork, Eire
Official guide. *Inventory of plants, shrubs, etc.* 1915. *G.C.* ii 1956, 523; ii 1964, 250–51; v. 190 no. 22, 1981, 16–19. *C.L.* v. 137, 1965, 512–14. *J. Royal Hort. Soc.* 1966, 16–18. E. Hyams *Irish gardens* 1967, 58–66. M. Allan *Fisons guide* 1970, 359–60. E. Malins and P. Bowe *Irish gardens and demesnes* 1980, 94–100. A. Hellyer *Gardens of genius* 1980, 165–70. Knight of Glin *and* P. Bowe *Gardens of outstanding historic interest in . . . Ireland* 1980.

Garinish Island, Parknasilla, Co.Kerry, Eire
E. Malins and P. Bowe *Irish gardens and demesnes* 1980, 115–17.

Garnkirk House near Glasgow, Strathclyde
Scottish Gdnr and Northern Forester v. 7, 1912, 429–30.

Garnons, Mansell Gamage, Hereford and Worcester
J.P. Neale *Views* 2nd Series, v. 4, 1828. *G.M.* v. 14, 1838, 218–20. D. Stroud *Capability Brown* 1962, 65. L. Fleming and A. Gore *English garden* 1979, pls. 93–94. R. Sidwell *West Midland gardens* 1981, 53–54. G. Carter *et al. Humphry Repton* 1982, 73,153.

Garnstone near Weobley, Hereford and Worcester
J.P. Neale *Views* 2nd Series, v. 4, 1828. *G.M.* v. 14, 1838, 215–17. F.O. Morris *Series of picturesque views* v. 1, 57.

Garrick's Villa, Hampton, Richmond, London
Short account of the principal seats and gardens in and about Richmond and Kew [1760s?] 17. C. Burlington *Modern universal British traveller* 1779, 332. D. Defoe *Tour* v. 1, 1778, 237–38. W. Watts *Seats* 1779, pl. 68. G.A. Walpoole *New British traveller* 1784, 58. W. Thornton *New, complete and universal history* 1786, 502. *Picturesque views of the principal seats* 1788. J. and J. Boydell *History of the River Thames* v. 1, 1794, 306. W.B. Cooke and S. Owen *The Thames* v. 1, 1811. J.N. Brewer *Histrionic topography* 1818. R. Ackermann *Repository* v. 4, 1824, pl. 7. W.W.J. Gendall *Views* v. 2, 1830. *Tombleson's Thames* 1834. G. Jekyll *Garden ornament* 1918, 221. *C.L.* v. 52, 1922, 792. D. Stroud *Capability Brown* 1975, 81–82. J. Harris *Artist and the country house* 1979, 280. Tyne and Wear County Council Museums *Capability Brown and the northern landscape* 1983, 36–37,43.

Garrowby Hall near Pocklington, Humberside
C.L. v. 106, 1949, 394–97,466.

Garscube near Maryhill, Strathclyde
G.M. v. 18, 1842, 144–49.

Garsington Manor, Garsington, Oxfordshire
C.L. v. 171, 1982, 690–92.

Garthewin, Llanfair Talhaiarn, Clwyd
C.L. v. 123, 1958, 298–301.

Gartincaber near Doune, Central
H. Maxwell *Scottish gardens* 1911, 40–46.

Gartshore near Kirkintilloch, Strathclyde
Scottish Gdnr and Northern Forester v. 9, 1914, 121–23.

Garvald House, Dolphinton, Strathclyde
Gdnrs Mag. 1900, 396–99.

Gask near Perth, Tayside
J.P. Neale *Views* v. 6, 1823.

Gatacre, Six Ashes, Shropshire
F. Calvert *Picturesque views . . . in Shropshire* 1831, 132. R. Sidwell *West Midland gardens* 1981, 115–16.

Gatcombe House, Gatcombe, Isle of Wight
R. Worsley *History of Isle of Wight* 1781.

Gatcombe Park near Tetbury, Glos
J.N. Brewer *Delineations of Gloucestershire* 1825, 42.

Gateside, Drymen, Central
G.C. ii 1897, 427–28.

Gatley Park, Leinthall Earls, Hereford and Worcester
R. Sidwell *West Midland gardens* 1981, 54–55.

Gatton Park near Reigate, Surrey
E.W. Brayley *and* J. Britton *Topographical history of Surrey* v. 4, 310. G.F. Prosser *Select illustrations of . . . Surrey* 1828. W. Keane *Beauties of Surrey* 1849, 70–72. G.C. ii 1896, 37–38; ii 1897, 341,342,343,347; ii 1908, 225–26,231; ii 1915, 161–62,163,165,168; i 1916, 299. *Gdnrs Mag.* 1904, 299–300,301,303,304. *J. Hort. Cottage Gdnr* N.S., v. 52, 1906, 478–80. *J. Hort. Home Farmer* N.S. v. 67, 1913, 451–53. D. Stroud *Capability Brown* 1975, 226.

Gaulden Manor near Tolland, Somerset
J. Sales *West Country gardens* 1980, 152–53.

Gaunts House near Wimborne Minster, Dorset
J.P. Neale *Views* v. 1, 1818.

Gawthorpe near Leeds, W. Yorks
J. Kip *Nouveau theatre de la Grande Bretagne* v. 4, 1729.
J. Harris *Artist and the country house* 1979, 148.

Gawthorpe Hall, Padiham, Lancs
C.L. v. 33, 1913, 670–74. *Gdn History* v. 1 no. 3, 1973, 13. J. Harris *Artist and the country house* 1979, 214. G.S. Thomas *Gardens of National Trust* 1979, 137.

Gayhurst (Gothurst), Bucks
T. Pennant *Journey from Chester to London* 1782, pl. 20. G.A. Walpoole *New British traveller* 1784, after 186. J.P. Neale *Views* v. 1, 1818. C.L. v. 13, 1903, 80–86. G. Jekyll *Garden ornament* 1918, 105,275. D. Stroud *Humphry Repton* 1962, 81. D. Stroud *Capability Brown* 1975, 227. G. Carter et al. *Humphry Repton* 1982, 148.

Gaynes, Upminster, Havering, London
V.C.H. *Essex* v. 7, 1978, 150.

Gayton, Northants
Northamptonshire Past and Present v. 5 no. 3, 1975, 224.

Geanies, Fearn, Highland
G.A. Little *Scotland's gardens* 1981, 232.

Geddington, Northants
Northamptonshire Past and Present v. 5 no 3, 1975, 225.

Germains, Chesham, Bucks
Gdn Design 1933, 43–47.

German Spa *see* Brighton

Ghyll Manor, Rusper, W. Sussex
Sussex Life v. 1 no.5, 1965, 58–59.

Gibberd, Sir Frederick *see* House

Gibliston, Colinsburgh, Fife
G.A. Little *Scotland's gardens* 1981, 150.

Gibside, Rowlands Gill, Tyne and Wear
R. Surtees *History . . . of County . . . of Durham* v. 2, 1820, 254. G.M. v. 10, 1834, 364. C.L. v. 111, 1952, 354–57; v. 166, 1979, 2460–61. B. Jones *Follies & grottoes* 1974, 398. D. Stroud *Capability Brown* 1975, 227.

Gidea Hall, Romford, Havering, London
Copper Plate Mag. v. 2, pl. 66. F.G. Emmison *Catalogue of maps in Essex Record Office* 1947, 30; 1st Supplt, 1952, 2. Historical MSS Commission *Architectural history* v. 3, 1971, item 2819. V.C.H. *Essex* v. 7, 1978, 69.

Giffords Hall near Nayland, Suffolk
C.L. v. 14, 1903, 578–86; v. 45, 1919, 552–57; v. 54, 1923, 524–31.

Gilfach, Tyn-y-Groes, Conway, Gwynedd
M. Allan *Fisons guide* 1970, 273–74.

Gillibrand Hall near Chorley, Lancs
E. Baines *History . . . of Lancaster* v. 3, 1836, 423.

Gilling Castle, East Gilling, N. Yorks
A. Young *Six months tour through North of England* v. 2, 1771, 458. *C.L.* v. 24, 1908, 416–26. G. Jekyll *Garden ornament* 1918, 435. K. Lemmon *Gardens of Britain* v. 5, 1978, 73–74.

Gillingham Hall, Gillingham, Norfolk
G.M. v. 17, 1841, 273–74. J. Grigor *Eastern arboretum* 1841, 259–61.

Gipping Hall, Stowmarket, Suffolk
H. Davy *Views* 1827.

Gisburn Park, Gisburn, Lancs
T.D. Whitaker *History and antiquities of the Deanery of Craven* 1878, 54. J. Harris *Artist and the country house* 1979, 218.

Glamis Castle near Forfar, Tayside
Official guide. W. Watts *Seats* 1779 pl. 42. J.P. Neale *Views* v. 6, 1823. F.O. Morris *Series of picturesque views* v. 5, 21. *J. Hort. Cottage Gdnr* v. 42, 1869, 414–15,78–79,519–20. *C.L.* v. 20, 1906, 234–40; v. 36, 1914, 196–204. *Gdnrs Yearbook* 1928, 52–60. *G.C.* ii 1930, 145; i 1937, 417. *Park Administration* January 1966, 23–25. *Archives* 14, 1980, 143–44. A.A. Tait *Landscape garden in Scotland* 1980, passim. G.A. Little *Scotland's gardens* 1981, 189.

Glan-y-Mawddach, Barmouth, Gwynedd
M. Allan *Fisons guide* 1970, 274–75. *C.L.* v. 158, 1975, 704–06.

Glanbran near Llandovery, Dyfed
J.P. Neale *Views* v. 5, 1822.

Glanleam, Valentia Island, Co. Kerry, Eire
New Flora & Silva v. 1, 1929, 121. *Moorea* v. 2, 1983, 7–12.

Glanusk near Crickhowell, Powys
J.B. Burke *Visitation* v. 1, 1852, 210. F.O. Morris *Series of picturesque views* v. 1, 87. *G.C.* i 1876, 301–02; i 1892, 521–22. *J. Hort. Cottage Gdnr* N.S., v. 24, 1892, 278–80.

Glasgow. Botanic Garden, Strathclyde
Official guide. J.C. Loudon *Encyclopaedia of gardening* 1822, 1253–54. W.J. Hooker *Catalogue of plants* 1825. *G.C.* ii 1875, 326–27; i 1884, 269–70,271,275,279; ii 1887, 241–42; ii 1889, 209–10; i 1903, 129; v. 162 no. 26, 16–17; v. 178 no. 20, 1975, 21–23. E.W. Curtis *Glasgow Botanic Garden* 1971. G.A. Little *Scotland's gardens* 1981, 258–59.

Glasgow. Cemetery, Strathclyde
G.M. v. 18, 1842, 51–55. J.S. Curl *Celebration of death* 1980, 209–11.

Glasgow. Queen's Park, Strathclyde
Historical MSS Commission *Architectural history* v. 1, 1969, item 393.

Glasgow. Tollcross Park, Strathclyde
G.C. ii 1899, 147–48.

Glasnevin see Dublin

Glastonbury. Abbot's Lodgings, Glastonbury, Somerset
W. Stukeley *Itinerarium curiosum* v. 1, 1776, pl. 37.

Glastonbury Abbey, Glastonbury, Somerset
Proc. Somerset Archaeological and Natural History Soc. v. 103, 1958/59, 96–101; v. 104, 1960, 99–101.

Gledhow Hall, Leeds, W. Yorks
C. Holme *Gardens of England in Northern counties* 1911, pl. 48.

Gledstone Hall near Skipton, N. Yorks
T.D. Whitaker *History and antiquities of the Deanery of Craven* 1878, 94. *C.L.* v. 77, 1935, 374–79,400–05; v. 170, 1981, 2292–94. *Gdn History* v. 8 no. 3, 1980, 40–43,45,48. J. Brown *Gardens of a golden afternoon* 1982, 138–39. M. and R. Tooley *Gardens of Gertrude Jekyll in Northern England* 1982, 20–27,55.

Glemham Hall, Little Glemham, Suffolk
C.L. v. 27, 1910, 18–26. G. Jekyll *Garden ornament* 1918, 129, 259. J. Harris *Artist and the country house* 1979, 203. G. Carter *et al. Humphry Repton* 1982, 162. *Gdn History* v. 8 no. 2, 1980, 55.

Glen, Innerleithen, Borders
G.C. ii 1899, 6–8,11,33.

Glen Eyre, Southampton, Hants
G.C. i 1877, 752–53,757.

Glen Tana, Aboyne, Grampian
G. Beard *Thomas H. Mawson* 1976, 52.

Glenapp Castle, Ballantrae, Strathclyde
M. Allan *Fisons guide* 1970, 301–02.

Glenarm Castle, Glenarm, Co. Antrim, Ulster
T. Milton *Seats . . . in Ireland* 1783, pl. 21. E. Malins *and* Knight of Glin *Lost demesnes* 1976, 109–10.

Glenarn, Rhu, Strathclyde
E. Hyams *English gardens* 1964, 214–16. *J. Royal Hort. Soc.* 1967, 341–47. M. Allan *Fisons guide* 1970, 302–03. G.A. Little *Scotland's gardens* 1981, 259.

Glenart Castle near Arklow, Co. Wicklow, Eire
Gdning World v. 6, 1890, 806–07.

Glenbervie, Drumlithie, Grampian
Gdning World v. 4, 1888, 405; v. 5, 1889, 322. G.A. Little *Scotland's gardens* 1981, 189–90.

Glenburn Hall, Jedburgh, Borders
G.A. Litle *Scotland's gardens* 1981, 86–87.

Glencormac, Co. Wicklow, Eire
G.C. i 1884, 510–11,517. *Irish Landscape J.* v. 1 no. 2, 1979, 39–40.

Glendoick House, Glendoick, Tayside
Scottish Gdnr v. 4, 1855, 107–10. *G.C.* i 1939, 232.

Glendon Hall near Kettering, Northants
J.P. Neale *Views* 2nd Series, v. 4, 1828. *C.L.* v. 52, 1922, 676–81.

Glendurgan, Falmouth, Cornwall
Official guide. *J. Royal Hort. Soc.* 1963, 197–99; 1971, 220. *G.C.* i 1963, 404–05. M. Allan *Fisons guide* 1970, 125–26. H. Evans *Beautiful gardens of Britain* 1974, 7–8. P.M. Synge *Gardens of Britain* v. 1, 1977, 99–101. G.S. Thomas *Gardens of National Trust* 1979, 138–39. Manpower Services Commission *Glendurgan* 1982.

Glenearn, Bridge of Earn, Tayside
Scottish Gdnr and Northern Forester v. 7, 1912, 205–06.

Glenfeochan near Oban, Strathclyde
Historical MSS Commission *Architectural history* v. 4, 1972, item 4068.

Glenfinart near Helensburgh, Strathclyde
Gdning World v. 5, 1889, 403.

Glenhurst, Esher, Surrey
Gdning World v. 2, 1886, 808–10.

Glenoick, Glencarse, Tayside
G.A. Little *Scotlands gardens* 1981, 150–52.

Glenoran, Helensburgh, Strathclyde
Scottish Gdnr and Northern Forester v. 7, 1912, 561–63.

Glenrothes, Rothes, Grampian
Concrete quarterly no. 101, 1974, 12–16.

Glenstal Castle near Limerick, Co. Limerick, Eire
Gdning World v. 3, 1886, 26–27. *J. Hort. Cottage Gdnr* N.S., v. 16, 1888, 515–16. *C.L.* v. 156, 1974, 934–37.

Glentanar, Aboyne, Grampian
G.A. Little *Scotland's gardens* 1981, 190.

Glenveagh Castle, Co. Donegal, Eire
G.C. ii 1962, 166–67. E. Hyams *Irish gardens* 1967, 51–57. M. Allan *Fisons guide* 1970, 356–57. *C.L.* v. 153, 1973, 1468–70. A. Rowan *North West Ulster* 1979, 310. Knight of Glin *and* P. Bowe *Gardens of outstanding historic interest in . . . Ireland* 1980. E. Malins *and* P. Bowe *Irish gardens and demesnes* 1980, 168–71.

Glevering Hall, Easton, Suffolk
H. Davy *Views* 1827. D. Stroud *Humphry Repton* 1962, 169. G. Carter *et al. Humphry Repton* 1982, 162. *Garden* 1983, 365.

Glin Castle, Glin, Co. Limerick, Eire
C.L. v. 135, 1964, 446–50,502–05. B. Jones *Follies & grottoes* 1974, 434. E. Malins *and* Knight of Glin *Lost demesnes* 1976, 116–17.

Gloddaeth near Conway, Gwynedd
R.C. Hoare *Collection of forty-eight views* 1806, pl. 12.

Gloster near Recess, Co. Offaly, Eire
B. Jones *Follies & grottoes* 1974, 436. E. Malins *and* Knight of Glin *Lost demesnes* 1976, 28.

Glympton Park, Glympton, Oxfordshire
J. Sherwood *and* N. Pevsner *Oxfordshire* 1974, 613.

Glynde Place, Glynde, E. Sussex
F.O. Morris *Series of picturesque views* v. 5, 37. *G.C.* ii 1886, 37–38. *C.L.* v. 22, 1907, 342–51; v. 117, 1955, 978–81,1040,1104–07.

Glyndebourne, Glynde, E. Sussex
C.L. v. 85, 1939, 554–59; v. 175, 1984, 1466–68. *G.C.* ii 1957, 288–89; v. 163 no. 24, 1968, 12–14. A. Scott-James *and* C. Lloyd *Glyndebourne: the gardens* 1983.

Glynn near Bodmin, Cornwall
Architectural History v. 7, 1964, 28,69.

Gnoll, Neath, W. Glamorgan
J.P. Neale *Views* v. 5, 1822. *Archaeologia Cambrensis*

v. 128, 1979, 160–62. *Trans. Neath Antiquarian Soc.* 1979, 120–24. *C.L.* v. 169, 1981, 579–80.

Goathurst near Enmore, Somerset
J.C. Loudon *Encyclopaedia of gardening* 1822, 1246.

Gobions (Gubbins), Brookmans Park, Herts
H. Boswell *Historical descriptions of new and picturesque views* 1800. J.P. Neale *Views* v. 2, 1819.

Goddards, Abinger Common, Surrey
C.L. v. 15, 1904, 162–68. L. Weaver *Houses and gardens* 1913, 35–41. J. Brown *Gardens of a golden afternoon* 1982, 14.

Godden Green, Sevenoaks, Kent
G.C. ii 1895, 453–54.

Godinton near Ashford, Kent
J.P. Neale *Views* 2nd Series, v. 3, 1826. *C.L.* v. 21, 1907, 666–73; v. 132, 1962, 1396,1546,1600. T. Wright *Gardens of Britain* v. 4, 1978, 40–43.

Godmersham Park, Godmersham, Kent
W. Watts *Seats* 1779, pl. 67. E. Hasted *History . . . of Kent* 1790, 158. J.P. Neale *Views* 2nd Series, v. 3, 1826. C. Greenwood *Epitome of county history . . . v. 1: Kent* 1838, 298. *C.L.* v. 48, 1920, 596–603; v. 97, 1945, 288–91. T. Wright *Gardens of Britain* v. 4, 1978, 44–45.

Godolphin House, Godolphin, Cornwall
W. Borlase *Natural history of Cornwall* 1758, pl. 12. *C.L.* v. 38, 1915, 868–74.

Gogerddan near Aberystwyth, Dyfed
J.P. Neale *Views* v. 5, 1822.

Gola House, Monaghan, Co. Monaghan, Ulster
J.B. Burke *Visitation* 2nd Series, v. 1, 1855, 121.

Golden Acre Park near Leeds, W. Yorks
K. Lemmon *Gardens of Britain* v. 5, 1978, 163–64.

Golden Square *see* London

Golders Hill, Hampstead, London
W. Keane *Beauties of Middlesex* 1850, 174–76. *Garden* v. 16, 1879, 530–33; v. 18, 1880, 105. G. Carter *et al.* *Humphry Repton* 1982, 157.

Golding Manor near Shrewsbury, Shropshire
R. Sidwell *West Midland gardens* 1981, 117–18.

Goldings near Hertford, Herts
J. Hort. Cottage Gdnr v. 62, 1879, 213.

Goldney House, Clifton, Avon
Official guide. J. Wesley *Journal* v. 4, 1903, 420. *C.L.* v. 104, 1948, 218–81,328–31,635. N. Pevsner *North Somerset and Bristol* 1958, 447. P.K. Stembridge *Goldney: a house and a family* 1969. B. Jones *Follies & grottoes* 1974, 152. L. Fleming *and* A. Gore *English garden* 1979, 113–16.

Goldsborough Hall, Goldsborough, N. Yorks
C.L. v. 16, 1904, 558–60.

Goldsmiths' Company *see* London

Goodnestone Park near Faversham, Kent
J. Harris *History of Kent* 1719, 132. J. Kip *Supplement du Nouveau theatre de la Grande Bretagne* 1728, pl. 10. T. Badeslade *Thirty six different views . . . in Kent* 1750s, pl. 11. E. Hasted *History . . . of Kent* v. 3, 1790, 705. J.P. Neale *Views* 2nd Series, v. 2, 1825. C. Greenwood *Epitome of county history . . . v. 1: Kent* 1838, 348. T. Wright *Gardens of Britain* v. 4, 1978, 46–48.

Goodrich Court, Goodrich, Hereford and Worcester
J. Hort. Cottage Gdnr N.S., v. 21, 1890, 542–43; N.S., v. 26, 1893, 52–53; N.S., v. 49, 1904, 240–41. *G.C.* i 1911, 257–58,259.

Goodwood near Chichester, W. Sussex
Official guide. C. Campbell *Vitruvius Britannicus* v. 3, 1725, pls. 51–52. D. Jacques *A visit to Goodwood* 1822. J.C. Loudon *Encyclopaedia of gardening* 1822, 1230. *G.M.* v. 5, 1829, 583–85; v. 15, 1839, 523–24. T.W. Horsfield *History . . . of Sussex* v. 2, 1835, 61. W.H. Mason *Goodwood; its house, park and grounds* 1839. J.C. Loudon *Arboretum et fruticetum Britannicum* v. 1, 1844, 59. *Garden* v. 18, 1880, 507–09. W. Robinson *English flower garden* 1883, xv. R. Pococke *Travels through England* v. 2, 1889, 111. *Trees of interest at Goodwood* 1912. *C.L.* v. 61, 1927, 472–75,574–76; v. 72, 1932, 38–44,66–71. I. Nairn *and* N. Pevsner *Sussex* 1965, 228–29. F.W. Steer *and* J.E.A. Venables *Goodwood estate archives* 1970–72, 2 vols, passim. B. Jones *Follies & grottoes* 1974, 154–55. *Sussex Archaeological Collections* v. 117, 1979, 185–93.

Goosewells, Belford, Northumberland
C.L. v. 171, 1982, 416–18.

Gopsall Hall near Market Bosworth, Leics
J. Paine *Plans, elevations and sections of noblemen and gentlemen's houses* v. 1, 1783, pl. 74. J. Throsby *Select views in Leicestershire* v. 1, 1790, 280. F.O. Morris *Series of picturesque views* v. 2, 47. R.I.B.A. *Catalogue* v. G–K, 1973, 131–32; v. O–R, 1976, 12. J. Harris *Artist and the country house* 1979, 238–39.

Gordon Castle near Fochabars, Grampian
J.P. Neale *Views* v. 6, 1823. *Gdnrs Mag.* 1903, 562–64.
I.H. Adams *Descriptive list of plans* v. 2, 1970, 104.
A.A. Tait *Landscape garden in Scotland* 1980, passim.
G.A. Little *Scotland's gardens* 1981, 192.

Gordon House (Seaton House, Railshead), Isleworth, London
G.J. Aungier *History and antiquities of Syon Monastery* 1840, 232. A.C.B. Urwin *Railshead* 1974, 12,13.

Gore Court, Tunstall, Kent
C. Greenwood *Epitome of county history . . . v. 1: Kent* 1838, 274.

Gorhambury near St Albans, Herts
C. Grimston *History of Gorhambury* c.1821. *Cottage Gdnr* v. 20, 1858, 159–61. *J. Hort. Cottage Gdnr* v. 46, 1871, 397–400,419–21. *C.L.* v. 74, 1933, 556–57,649. N. Pevsner *Hertfordshire* 1977, 148.

Gormanstown Castle, Gormanstown, Co. Meath, Eire
J.P. Neale *Views* v. 6, 1823. *G.M.* v. 2, 1827, 148.

Gosfield Hall, Gosfield, Essex
P. Muilman *History of Essex* v. 2, 1769, 34. P. Morant *History of Essex* v. 2, 1816, 378. G. Virtue *Picturesque beauties of Great Britain: Essex* 1831, 33. *G.C.* i 1881, 103–04. F.G. Emmison *Catalogue of maps in Essex Record Office* 2nd Supplt, 1964, 14; 3rd Supplt, 1968, 19.

Gosford near Aberlady, Lothian
G.C. ii 1898, 181,182. *C.L.* v. 150, 1971, 1200–02.

Gough Park, Enfield, London
W. Keane *Beauties of Middlesex* 1850, 151–53.

Government House, Guernsey, Channel Islands
W. Berry *History of Island of Guernsey* 1815, 146.

Gowran Castle near Kilkenny, Co. Kilkenny, Eire
J.P. Neale *Views* 2nd Series, v. 3, 1826.

Gracefield Lodge near Athy, Co. Laois, Eire
J.P. Neale *Views* v. 6, 1823.

Grafton Manor near Bromsgrove, Hereford and Worcester
V.C.H. *Worcester* v. 3, 1913, 125.

Grafton Regis, Northants
Northamptonshire Past and Present v. 5 no. 3, 1975, 225.
Royal Commission on Historical Monuments *Inventory of the historical monuments in . . . Northampton* v. 4, 1982, 62–63, pl. 3.

Grafton Underwood, Northants
Northamptonshire Past and Present v. 5 no. 3, 1975, 225.

Graigueconna, Bray, Co. Wicklow, Eire
L.B. Meredith *Rock gardens, how to make and maintain them* 1910.

Grandtully Castle near Aberfeldy, Tayside
J.P. Neale *Views* v. 6, 1823. *Gdning World* v. 17, 1900, 200–02.

Grange, Charlcombe, Avon
G.C. i 1894, 782.

Grange, Wraysbury, Berks
T.H. Mawson *Art & craft of garden making* 1907, 48,59,61,67. G. Beard *Thomas H. Mawson* 1976, 52.

Grange, Broadhembury, Devon
J.P. Neale *Views* 2nd Series, v. 3, 1826.

Grange near Northington, Hants
R. Ackermann *Repository* v. 6, 1825, pl. 26.
W.W.J. Gendall *Views* v. 2, 1830, 127. J. Hewetson *Architectural and picturesque views of . . . Hampshire* 1830. E.F. Prosser *Select illustrations of Hampshire* 1833. *G.M.* v. 1, 1826, 105–12; v. 2, 1827, 170–71; v. 11, 1835, 57–59. *Garden* v. 4, 1873, 360–61. *G.C.* ii 1884, 229–30. *C.L.* v. 157, 1975, 795–96,1242–45.

Grange, Hartley Wintney, Hants
Garden v. 36, 1889, 333–34.

Grange, Bishop's Stortford, Herts
J. Hort. Cottage Gdnr N.S., v. 44, 1902, 360–61.

Grange, Benenden, Kent
T. Wright *Gardens of Britain* v. 4, 1978, 48–50.

Grange near Maidstone, Kent
J. Harris *History of Kent* 1719, 172. J. Kip *Supplement du Nouveau theatre de la Grande Bretagne* 1728, pl. 23. T. Badeslade *Thirty six different views . . . in Kent* 1750s, pl. 12.

Grange, Highbury, London
G.C. i 1903, 3–4.

Grange, Southgate, London
Gdning World v. 12, 1896, 674–75.

Grange, Sutton, London
Gdning World v. 3, 1886, 57–58; v. 3, 1887, 628–29.

Grange, Farnham, Surrey
C.L. v. 76, 1934, 90–95.

Grange, Rottingdean, E. Sussex
C.L. v. 62, 1927, 698–704.

Grange, Swansea, W. Glamorgan
G.C. i 1883, 473,475–76.

Grange, Lamancha, Borders
A.A. Tait *Landscape garden in Scotland* 1980, 10–13.

Grange, Co. Limerick, Eire
G.C. ii 1887, 219.

Grangemuir near Pittenweem, Fife
G.M. v. 10, 1834, 528–29.

Grantham (William Stukeley), Lincs
C.L. v. 174, 1983, 1248–49.

Granton House, Edinburgh, Lothian
Scottish Gdnr and Northern Forester v. 9, 1914, 465–66.

Gravetye Manor near East Grinstead, W. Sussex
W. Robinson *Gravetye Manor* 1911. *C.L.* v. 32, 1912, 409–10; v. 33, 1913, 606–07; v. 34, 1913, 452–53; v. 37, 1915, 669–72; v. 57, 1925, 650–53. *Architectural Review* v. 35, 1914, 75–77, pls. 7–8; v. 37, 1915, 120–22; v. 43, 1918, 294–301. W. Robinson *Home landscapes* ed. 2, 1920. *Garden* 1916, 560–61. G. Jekyll *Garden ornament* 1918, 160,305. *G.C.* i 1920, 157; i 1964, 594; ii 1964, 530. *Landscape & Garden* v. 1 no. 1, 1934, 49–50. Lady Rockley *Historic gardens of England* 1938, 244–45. *J. Royal Hort. Soc.* 1957, 173–78. *Gdn History* v. 6 no. 1, 1978, 71–80. L. Fleming *and* A. Gore *English garden* 1979, 202. M. Allan *William Robinson* 1982. *Garden* 1983, 69–72.

Gray's Inn *see* London

Grayswood Hill, Haslemere, Surrey
C.L. v. 80, 1936, 326–32; v. 126, 1959, 6–8. M. Allan *Fisons guide* 1970, 44–45.

Graythwaite Hall near Ulverston, Cumbria
J.B. Burke *Visitation* 2nd Series, v. 1, 1855, 227. *G.C.* ii 1890, 624–25. T.H. Mawson *Art & craft of garden making* 1907, 48,78,282–91. G. Beard *Thomas H. Mawson* 1976, 52–53. *C.L.* v. 172, 1982, 2016–18.

Great Bardfield Lodge near Finchingfield, Essex
F.G. Emmison *Catalogue of maps in Essex Record Office* 1st Supplt, 1952, 25; 2nd Supplt, 1964, 22.

Great Bentley Lodge, Great Bentley, Essex
F.G. Emmison *Catalogue of maps in Essex Record Office* 2nd Supplt, 1964, 33.

Great Chalfield Manor, Great Chalfield, Wilts
C.L. v. 36, 1914, 230–37,294–301.

Great Comp near Maidstone, Kent
T. Wright *Gardens of Britain* v. 4, 1978, 51–55.
R. Cameron *Great Comp and its garden* 1981. *Garden* 1981, 89–96.

Great Culverden, Tunbridge Wells, Kent
C. Greenwood *Epitome of county history . . . v. 1: Kent* 1838, 124.

Great Dixter, Northiam, E. Sussex
C.L. v. 33, 1913, 18–26. *G.C.* i 1963, 390–91.
E. Hyams *English garden* 1964, 161–63. P. Coats *Great gardens of Britain* 1967, 266–71. M. Allan *Fisons guide* 1970, 45–46. T. Wright *Gardens of Britain* v. 4, 1978, 144–50. *Architectural Digest* 39, 1982, 90–95. J. Brown *Gardens of a golden afternoon* 1982, 171. A. Lees-Milne *and* R. Verey *Englishman's garden* 1982, 92–95.
T. Hinde *Stately gardens of Britain* 1983, 126–33.

Great Doddington, Northants
Northamptonshire Past and Present v. 5 no. 3, 1975, 225.

Great Fosters, Egham, Surrey
C.L. v. 52, 1922, 610–16. *Landscape & Garden* v. 1 no. 4, 1934, 14–16. M. Binney *and* A. Hills *Elysian gardens* 1979, 31.

Great Fulford, Dunsford, Devon
C.L. v. 36, 1914, 160–68.

Great Horton House, Bradford, W. Yorks
Bradfield Illustrated Weekly Telegraph *Series of picturesque views* 1885.

Great House, Cheltenham, Glos
J. Harris *Gardens of delight* 1978, 20–21.

Great Maytham, Rolvenden, Kent
C.L. v. 32, 1912, 746–53. L. Weaver *Houses and gardens by E.L. Lutyens* 1913, 247–56. J. Brown *Gardens of a golden afternoon* 1982, 170.

Great More House *see* Beaufort House, Chelsea

Great Oakley Hall near Kettering, Northants
J.P. Neale *Views* 2nd Series, v. 3, 1826.

Great Purston, Newbottle, Northants
Royal Commission on Historical Monuments *Inventory of the historical monuments in . . . Northampton* v. 4, 1982, 106.

Great Rissington Manor, Great Rissington, Glos
J. Sales *West Country gardens* 1980, 65–67.

Great Surries, Ashurstwood, W. Sussex
C.L. v. 125, 1958, 164–65.

Great Tangley Manor near Guildford, Surrey
C.L. v. 4, 1898, 109–12; v. 17, 1905, 90–100; v. 20, 1906, 418–21. G. Jekyll *and* G.S. Elgood *Some English gardens* 1905, 8–10. C. Holme *Gardens of England in Southern & Western counties* 1907, pls. 58–59. *Architectural Review* v. 28, 1910, 157–60.

Great Tew (Village and Park), Oxfordshire
J.C. Loudon *Designs for laying out farms and farm buildings* 1811. *C.L.* v. 106, 1949, 254–57. D. Stroud *Humphry Repton* 1962, 125. J. Sherwood *and* N. Pevsner *Oxfordshire* 1974, 626–27. *J. Gdn History* v. 2 no. 2, 1982, 178–79. G. Carter *et al. Humphry Repton* 1982, 160. V.C.H. *Oxford* v. 11, 1983, 33, 227–28, 233, 239.

Great Wigsell near Robertsbridge, E. Sussex
C.L. v. 44, 1918, 32–37.

Greatford Hall, Greatford, Lincs
Architectural Review v. 67, 1930, 1–6.

Greatham Mill, Liss, Hants
A. Paterson *Gardens of Britain* v. 2, 1978, 90–91.

Greatness, Sevenoaks, Kent
F. Hull *Catalogue of estate maps 1590 to 1840 in the Kent County Archives Office* 1973, 165.

Greatworth, Northants
Northamptonshire Past and Present v. 5 no. 4, 1976, 311–14. Royal Commission on Historical Monuments *Inventory of the historical monuments in . . . Northampton* v. 4, 1982, 65.

Green, Eckington, Renishaw, Derbyshire
J. Brown *Gardens of a golden afternoon* 1982, 172–73.

Green Park *see* London

Greenbank, Glasgow, Strathclyde
C.L. v. 159, 1976, 694. G.A. Little *Scotland's gardens* 1981, 260.

Greenfield Hall near Holywell, Clwyd
R.C. Hoare *Collection of forty-eight views* 1806, pl. 16.

Greenfields, Co. Tipperary, Eire
Irish Gdning v. 15, 1920, 6–9; v. 16, 1921, 104.

Greenham Common, Newbury, Berks
Architectural Review v. 34, 1913, 101–02, pls. 11–12.

Greenlands, Henley-on-Thames, Oxfordshire
W. Robinson *English flower garden* 1883, xiii–xv. *G.C.* i 1880, 806–07, 812–13; i 1897, 364–65. *Gdning World* v. 15, 1899, 659–60.

Greens Norton, Northants
Royal Commission on Historical Monuments *Inventory of the historical monuments in . . . Northampton* v. 4, 1982, 72.

Greensted Hall, Greensted, Essex
P. Muilman *History of Essex* v. 3, 1770, 378.

Greenthorne, Edgeworth, Bolton, Greater Manchester
G. Beard *Thomas H. Mawson* 1976, 53.

Greenway House near Dartmouth, Devon
G.C. i 1901, 169–70. C. Holme *Gardens of England in Southern & Western counties* 1907, pls. 60–61.

Greenwich Hospital, Greenwich, London
J. Beeverell *Les delices de la Grande Bretagne* v. 4, 1707, 750. H. Overton *Britannia illustrata* c.1724, pl. 30.

Greenwich Palace, Greenwich, London
H.M. Colvin *History of the King's Works* v. 4, 1982, 107, 110, 111, 113.

Greenwich Park *see* London

Greenwoods, Stock, Essex
G. Beard *Thomas H. Mawson* 1976, 53.

Gregories near Beaconsfield, Bucks
Copper Plate Mag. v. 1, 1792, pl. 34.

Gregynog near Newtown, Powys
G.C. i 1913, 232–33. R. Haslam *Powys* 1979, 203–04.

Gresford Cottage near Denbigh, Clwyd
Copper Plate Mag. v. 1, 1792, pl. 28.

Greville, Charles, Gloucester, Glos
Bristol and Gloucestershire Archaeological Soc. Trans. v. 99, 1981, 125–26.

Grey Abbey House, Grey Abbey, Co. Down, Ulster
B. Jones *Follies & grottoes* 1974, 429.

Grey Friars, Dunwich, Suffolk
A. Suckling *History . . . of Suffolk* v. 2, 1848, 262.

Grey Towers, Nunthorpe, Cleveland
G.C. ii 1904, 49.

Grey Walls, Gullane, Lothian
C.L. v. 30, 1911, 374–81. L. Weaver *Houses and gardens by E.L. Lutyens* 1913, 94–102. J. Brown *Gardens of a golden afternoon* 1982, 165.

Greys Court, Henley-on-Thames, Oxfordshire
Official guide. C.L. v. 95, 1944, 1080–83, 1124–27. R. Bisgrove *Gardens of Britain* v. 3, 1978, 82–83. G.S. Thomas *Gardens of National Trust* 1979, 139.

Greystoke Castle, Greystoke, Cumbria
G.C. ii 1884, 647–48. *Garden* v. 33, 503. B. Jones *Follies & grottoes* 1974, 303–04.

Greywell Hill near Basingstoke, Hants
G.C. ii 1907, 212.

Grimshaw Hall near Knowle, W. Midlands
C.L. v. 74, 1933, 280–84.

Grimsthorpe Castle, Grimsthorpe, Lincs
J. Beeverell *Les delices de la Grande Bretagne* v. 5, 1707, 872. J. Knyff *and* J. Kip *Britannia illustrata* v. 1, 1714. B. Howlett *Selection of views in county of Lincoln* 1805. J.P. Neale *Views* v. 2, 1819. C.L. v. 54, 1924, 572–79. N. Pevsner *and* J. Harris *Lincolnshire* 1964, 558. Historical MSS Commission *Architectural history* v. 2, 1970, item 1499. D. Stroud *Capability Brown* 1975, 161,227. L. Fleming *and* A. Gore *English garden* 1979, 81 (Paston Manor?) D. Watkin *English vision* 1982, 9. D. Jacques *Georgian gardens* 1983, 19.

Grimston Park, Grimston, N. Yorks
Cottage Gdnr v. 21, 1851, 7–8. G.C. ii 1880, 300–02, 305; ii 1881, 468,469,656,657; ii 1908, 66–67. *J. Hort. Cottage Gdnr* N.S., v. 27, 1893, 56–58; N.S., v. 37, 1898, 128–30. C.L. v. 10 1901, 464–70; v. 87, 1940, 252–56, 276–80. C. Holme *Gardens of England in Northern counties* 1911, pls. 49–51. G. Jekyll *Garden ornament* 1918, 106. Lady Rockley *Historic gardens of England* 1938, 202–03. L. Fleming *and* A. Gore *English garden* 1979, 187,191.

Grocers' Company *see* London

Groombridge Place, Groombridge, Kent
C.L. v. 2, 1897, 350–52; v. 12, 1902, 624–31,657–62; v. 118, 1955, 1376–79; v. 119, 1956, 986–89. H.I. Triggs *Formal gardens in England and Scotland* 1902, 32–33. C. Holme *Gardens of England in Southern & Western counties* 1907, pls. 62–64. T. Wright *Gardens of Britain* v. 4, 1978, 55–56.

Grotto House, Basildon, Berks
W.B. Cooke *and* S. Owen *The Thames* v. 1, 1811, 41.

Grove near Newbury, Berks
Gentleman's Mag. 1772, 561.

Grove, Rickmansworth, Herts
D.C. Webb *Observations and remarks* 1812, 162–65.

Grove, Stanmore, Harrow, London
J.C. Loudon *Encyclopardia of Gdning* 1822, 1226. G.C. ii 1889, 526–27; ii 1900, 335–36.

Grove, Highgate, London
W. Keane *Beauties of Middlesex* 1850, 239–41. J. MacGregor *Gardens of celebrities . . . in and around London* 1918, 237–54. J. Harris *Artist and the country house* 1979, 73.

Grove, Streatham, Lambeth, London
Gdning World v. 12, 1895, 221.

Grove, Teddington, Twickenham, London
Gdning World v. 4, 1888, 742–43.

Grove, Epsom, Surrey
E.W. Brayley *and* J. Britton *Topographical history of Surrey* v. 4, 369.

Grove, Dumfries, Dumfries and Galloway
Scottish Gdnr and Northern Forester v. 8, 1913, 577–78.

Grove End Road (Sir Lawrence Alma-Tadema), St John's Wood, London
C.L. v. 32, 1912, 716–18.

Grove Hall, Grove, Notts
Garden v. 68, 1905, 56–57. D. Stroud *Humphry Repton* 1962, 63. J. Harris *Catalogue of British drawings . . . in American collections* 1971, 129. G. Carter *et al. Humphry Repton* 1982, 160.

Grove Hill, Camberwell, Southwark, London
[J.C. Lettsom] *Grove-hill: an horticultural sketch* 1794; 1804. O. Manning *and* W. Bray *History . . . of Surrey* v. 3, 1814, 398. E.W. Brayley *and* J. Britton *Topographical history of Surrey* v. 3, 274. V.C.H. *Surrey* v. 4, 1912, 26.

Grove House, Old Windsor, Berks
C.L. v. 165, 1979, 1838,1840.

Grove House, St John, Margate, Kent
C. Greenwood *Epitome of county history . . . v. 1: Kent* 1838, 330.

Grove House, Isleworth, Hounslow, London
W. Angus *Seats* 1787, pl. 32. W. Keane *Beauties of Middlesex* 1850, 243–45.

Grove Lodge, Fulham, Hammersmith, London
C.J. Fèret *Fulham old and new* v. 3, 1900, 48,49.

Grove Place near Romsey, Hants
C.L. v. 16, 1904, 774–81.

Grovelands, Southgate, Enfield, London
W. Keane *Beauties of Middlesex* 1850, 120–22.
G. Carter *et al. Humphry Repton* 1982, 158.

Gubbins *see* Gobions

Gudgeon, Thomas *see* Stoke Newington

Guildford Castle, Guildford, Surrey
G.M. v. 5, 1829, 573–74. *C.L.* v. 157, 1975, 1056.

Guilsborough Grange, Guilsborough, Northants
J. Anthony *Gardens of Britain* v. 6, 1979, 80–81.

Guincho, Helen's Bay, Co. Down, Ulster
J. Royal Hort. Soc. 1964, 318–23. *G.C.* v. 161 no. 24, 1967, 16–17. *International Dendrology Society Year Book* 1974, 32–33. Ulster Architectural Heritage Society *Northern gardens* 1982, 19.

Guisborough Hall, Guisborough, Cleveland
J. Beeverell *Les delices de la Grande Bretagne* v. 5, 1707, 872. J. Kip *Nouveau theatre de la Grande Bretagne* v. 1, 1724. *Gdning World* v. 18, 1901, 141.

Gumley Hall, Gumley, Leics
J. Throsby *Select views in Leicestershire* v. 1, 1790, 286. J. Nichols *History . . . of county of Leicester* v. 2, 1798, 589; v. 3, 1804, 1125. V.C.H. *Leicester* v. 5, 1964, 117.

Gunby Hall, Gunby, Lincs
Official guide. *C.L.* v. 94, 1943, 816–19. *G.C.* ii 1963, 21. M. Allan *Fisons guide* 1970, 193–94. *J. Royal Hort. Soc.* 1971, 216–17. J. Anthony *Gardens of Britain* v. 6, 1979, 81–83. G.S. Thomas *Gardens of National Trust* 1979, 139–40.

Gunnersbury Park, Hounslow, London
D. Defoe *Tour* v. 3, 1742, 290–91. R. *and* J. Dodsley *London and its environs described* v. 3, 1761, 111. W. Angus *Seats* 1787, pl. 47. *G.M.* v. 9, 1833, 518–20. W. Keane *Beauties of Middlesex* 1850, 88–91. *G.C.* i 1880, 145,147; ii 1881, 72–73; i 1891, 591; ii 1893, 426–27,467–68; i 1898, 314; i 1899, 333; i 1902, 228,309; ii 1902, 20; ii 1906, 101–03,121–22,123; ii 1910, 276–77,278,283. *Garden* v. 19, 1881, 227–30; v. 24, 1883, 384,385; v: 61, 1902, 140–41. *J. Hort. Cottage Gdnr* N.S., v. 11, 1885, 18–19; N.S. v. 39, 1899, 80–82; N.S. v. 43, 1901, 132–33; N.S., v. 52, 1906, 412–13, 475. *Gdning World* v. 7, 1891, 666. *Gdnrs Mag.* 1902, 160–61; 1906, 496–98. *C.L.* v. 8, 1900, 656–65; v. 57, 1925, 562–63; v. 172, 1982, 1480–82. B. Jones *Follies & grottoes* 1974, 329.

Gunthorpe Hall, Gunthorpe, Norfolk
G.M. v. 17, 1841, 272. J. Grigor *Eastern arboretum* 1841, 233.

Gunton, Norfolk
J.P. Neale *Views* v. 3, 1820. *G.M.* v. 17, 1841, 31.
J. Grigor *Eastern arboretum* 1841, 132–34. F.O. Morris *Series of picturesque views* v. 4, 59. *Gdning World* v. 2, 1885, 25–26. *G.C.* ii 1894, 369–70; ii 1913, 291–92.
B. Jones *Follies & grottoes* 1974, 360. P. Willis *Charles Bridgeman* 1977, 179. G. Carter *et al. Humphry Repton* 1982, 158–59.

Guthrie Castle near Forfar, Tayside
M. Allan *Fisons guide* 1970, 340.

Guy's Cliff near Warwick, Warwickshire
J.P. Neale *Views* v. 4, 1821. R. Ackermann *Repository* v. 7, 1826, pl. 1. W.W.J. Gendall *Views* v. 1, 1830, 71. F.O. Morris *Series of picturesque views* v. 1, 53. *C.L.* v. 1, 1897, 154–56; v. 7, 1900, 176–82. C. Holme *Gardens of England in Midland & Eastern counties* 1908, pl. 66.

Gwersyllt House, Gwersyllt, Clwyd
J. Harris *Artist and the country house* 1979, 245.

Gwydir Castle, Llanrwst, Gwynedd
C.L. v. 9, 1901, 772–79.

Gwynns, Woodford, Redbridge, London
F.G. Emmison *Catalogue of maps in Essex Record Office* 3rd Supplt, 1968, 15.

Gwysaney Hall near Mold, Clwyd
C.L. v. 174, 1983, 900–01.

Gyrn near Mostyn, Clwyd
J.P. Neale *Views* 2nd Series, v. 1, 1824.

Habberley Hall near Shrewsbury, Shropshire
V.C.H. *Shropshire* v. 8, 1968, 240.

Hackbridge near Sutton, London
Architectural Review v. 67, 1930, 69–71.

Hackfall near Ripon, N. Yorks
Society of Gentlemen *England displayed* v. 2, 1769, 128–29. A. Young *Six months tour through North of England* v. 2, 1771, 306–12. R.J. Sulivan *Tour* v. 2, 1785, 135–36. D. Defoe *Tour* v. 3, 1778, 145–46. W. Bray *Sketch of tour into Derbyshire and Yorkshire* 1783, 80–83. *New display of the beauties of England* v. 2, 1787, 435–39. R. Warner *Tour through Northern*

counties of England v. 1, 1802, 273–80. T. Pennant *Tour from Alston-Moore to Harrowgate* 1804, 54–56. *History of Ripon* 1806, 231–38. H. Skrine *Three successive tours* 1813, xv–xvi. W. Gilpin *Observations on several parts of England* v. 2, 1808, 187–94. Duke of Rutland *Journal of a tour to the northern parts of Great Britain* 1813, 129–32. N. Whittock *and* H. Gastineau *Picturesque beauties of England and Wales* 1830, 4. T. Allen *New . . . history of county of York* 1831, 413–14. Viscount Torrington *Diaries* v. 3, 1936, 51–52. *C.L.* v. 156, 1974, 1450. B. Jones *Follies & grottoes* 1974, 60–63. *Mr. Aislabies' gardens: three North Yorkshire gardens* 1981.

Hackness Hall, Hackness, N. Yorks
J. Hort. Cottage Gdnr v. 54, 1875, 116–18. *C.L.* v. 49, 1921, 338–44.

Hackney (Sir Thomas Cooke), London
Archaeologia v. 12, 1796, 186.

Hackney Commons *see* London

Hackney Theological Seminary, London
Historical MSS Commission *Architectural history* v. 1, 1969, item 635.

Hackwood near Basingstoke, Hants
P. Sandby *Collection of one hundred and fifty select views* v. 1, 1781, pl. 19. J. Britton *and* E.W. Brayley *Beauties of England and Wales* v. 6, 1805, 272–74. J.P. Neale *Views* v. 2, 1819. R. Ackermann *Repository* v. 6, 1825, pl. 13. W.W.J. Gendall *Views* v. 2, 1830, 17. J. Hewetson *Architectural and picturesque views of . . . Hampshire* 1830. E.F. Prosser *Select illustrations of Hampshire* 1833. *Journey-book of England: Hampshire* 1841, 63–64. *Gdning World* v. 3, 1886, 89–90. *C.L.* v. 13, 1903, 48–54; v. 33, 1913, 706–14,742–50. G. Jekyll *Garden ornament* 1918, 156. V.C.H. *Hampshire* v. 4, 1911, 115,119. N. Pevsner *and* D. Lloyd *Hampshire and the Isle of Wight* 1967, 262.

Haddo House near Ellon, Grampian
F.O. Morris *Series of picturesque views* v. 4, 49. *G.C.* i 1879, 299–300,305. *C.L.* v. 140, 1960, 378–81.

Haddon Hall near Bakewell, Derbyshire
Official guide. C. Burlington *Modern universal British traveller* 1779, 107. S. Rayner *History and antiquities of Haddon Hall* 1836, 39–40,49. D. Morison *Views of Haddon Hall* 1842. *C.L.* v. 9, 1901, 693–703; v. 106, 1949, 1651–56,1884–88; v. 131, 1962, 1498–1500. H.I. Triggs *Formal gardens in England and Scotland* 1902, 34–35. G. Jekyll *Garden ornament* 1918, 79,163. P. Coats *Great gardens of Britain* 1967, 106–11. M. Allan *Fisons guide* 1970, 222–23. H. Evans *Beautiful gardens of Britain* 1974, 99–100. J. Anthony *Gardens of Britain* v. 6, 1979, 83–86.

Hadham Hall, Little Hadham, Herts
J.E. Cussans *History of Hertfordshire* v. 1, 1870, 192.
J. Harris *Artist and the country house* 1979, 22.
R. Strong *Renaissance garden in England* 1979, 181–82.

Hadlow Castle, Hadlow, Kent
C. Greenwood *Epitome of county history . . . v. 1: Kent* 1838, 129.

Hadzor near Droitwich, Hereford and Worcester
J. Hort. Cottage Gdnr v. 33, 1865, 231. *C.L.* v. 10, 1901, 208–13.

Hadspen House near Castle Cary, Somerset
Garden 1979, 5–10. A. Lees–Milne *and* R. Verey *Englishwoman's garden* 1980, 63–66. J. Sales *West Country gardens* 1980, 153–56.

Haffield near Ledbury, Hereford and Worcester
G.M. v. 12, 1836, 114–16. R. Sidwell *West Midland gardens* 1981, 55–57.

Hafod, Dyfed
G. Cumberland *An attempt to describe Hafod* 1796.
G. Lipscomb *Journey into South Wales* 1799, 127–36.
R. Warner *Second walk through Wales* 1799, 149–54.
W. Gilpin *Observations on River Wye* 1800, 80–82. Mr. Malkin [*A new tour in Wales*] In J. Pinkerton v. 2, 1808, 648–53,659. J.E. Smith *Tour to Hafod* 1810. H. Skrine *Two successive tours throughout . . . Wales* 1812, 122–24. E. Inglis-Jones *Peacocks in Paradise* 1950.

Hafodunos near Llanrwst, Gwynedd
J. Hort. Cottage Gdnr N.S., v. 38, 1899, 45–46.

Hagley, Hereford and Worcester
Official guide. W. Toldervy *England and Wales described in a series of letters* 1762, 281. Society of Gentlemen *England displayed* v. 2, 1769, 15,16–17. T. Whately *Observations on modern gardening* 1771, 194–206; 1801, pl. 6. A. Young *Six months tour through North of England* v. 3, 1771, 286–96. J. Heeley *Description of Hagley Park* 1777. J. Heeley *Letters on the beauties of Hagley, Envil and The Leasowes* v. 1, 1777, 97–231. D. Defoe *Tour* v. 2, 1778, 274–79. R.J. Sulivan *Tour* v. 2, 1785, 20–25. *New display of the beauties of England* v. 2, 1787, 377–79. *Companion to The Leasowes, Hagley and Enville* 1789, 43–87. W. Pitt *General view of agriculture of . . . Stafford* 1796, 95. *Gentleman's Mag.* v. 71 pt 2, 1801, 593. R. Warner *Tour through Northern counties of England* v. 1, 1802, 69–70. W. Marshall *On planting and rural ornament* v. 1, 1803, 321–27. W. Gilpin *Observations on several parts of England* v. 1, 1808, 64–68. L. Simond *Journal* v. 2, 1815, 98–99. J.C. Loudon *Encyclopaedia of gardening* 1822, 1237–38. J.P. Neale *Views* v. 5, 1822. British Museum *Catalogue of maps, prints* 1829, 139. *J. Hort.*

Hagley (*Cont.*)

Cottage Gdnr v. 32, 1864, 509–10. *G.C.* ii 1881, 588; i 1887, 731–32. R. Pococke *Travels through England* v. 1, 1888, 223–30; v. 2, 1889, 233–35. *C.L.* v. 38, 1915, 520–28; v. 122, 1957, 546–49. Viscount Torrington *Diaries* v. 1, 1934, 46–47. M. Williams *Letters of William Shenstone* 1939, passim. O. Siren *China and gardens of Europe of 18th century* 1950, 41. *Connoisseur Year Book* 1954, 11–17. E. Malins *English landscaping and literature* 1966, 56–65. N. Pevsner *Worcestershire* 1968, 178. Dumbarton Oaks *Picturesque garden and its influence outside the British Isles* 1974, 49–55. B. Jones *Follies & grottoes* 1974, 55–56. *Landscape Design* no. 111, 1975, 10–12. *Burlington Mag.* v. 118, 1976, 214–25. M.R. Brownell *Alexander Pope & the arts of Georgian England* 1978, 219–23. R. Sidwell *West Midland gardens* 1981, 57–58. *Landscape Research* v. 7 no. 1, 1982, 20. K. Rorschach *Early Georgian landscape garden* 1983, 38–40, 42–43.

Haigh Hall, Haigh, Greater Manchester
J. Beeverell *Les delices de la Grande Bretagne* v. 5, 1707, 872. L. Knyff *and* J. Kip *Britannia illustrata* v. 1, 1714. E. Baines *History . . . of Lancaster* v. 3, 1836, 553. *G.C.* ii 1878, 235–36; ii 1890, 351–52. J. Harris *Artist and the country house* 1979, 219.

Hailes Abbey near Winchcombe, Glos
R. Atkyns *Ancient and present state of Glostershire* 1712, 470. L. Knyff *and* J. Kip *Britannia illustrata* v. 2, 1715.

Haileybury near Hertford, Herts
Gdn History v. 6 no. 2, 1978, 16–19. G. Carter *et al. Humphry Repton* 1982, 154.

Haimes Place near Cheltenham, Glos
J. Harris *Gardens of delight* 1978, 48.

Haines Hill, Cornwall
D. Stroud *Humphry Repton* 1962, 148.

Haining near Selkirk, Borders
J.P. Neale *Views* v. 6, 1823.

Hainton Hall, Hainton, Lincs
D. Stroud *Capability Brown* 1975, 227.

Haldon House near Exeter, Devon
R. Polwhele *History of Devonshire* v. 2, 1793, 182. *G.C.* ii 1882, 53–54. J. Harris *Artist and the country house* 1979, 290.

Hale Hall near Speke, Merseyside
J.P. Neale *Views* 2nd Series, v. 1, 1824. E. Baines *History . . . of Lancaster* v. 3, 1836, 747. D. Jacques *Georgian gardens* 1983, pl. 4.

Hales Place near Canterbury, Kent
G. Virtue *Picturesque beauties of Great Britain: Kent* 1829, 116.

Hales Place, Tenterden, Kent
Architectural Review v. 43, 1918, 43–47.

Haling House, Croydon, London
D. Stroud *Humphry Repton* 1962, 49. G. Carter *et al. Humphry Repton* 1982, 162.

Hall, Tendring, Essex
Gdn Design 1932, 43–47.

Hall, Bradford-on-Avon, Wilts
C. Holme *Gardens of England in Southern & Western counties* 1907, pls. 23–24. *C.L.* v. 5, 1899, 304–08; v. 132, 1962, 840–44, 900, 1020.

Hall, Leighton, Powys
C.L. v. 12, 1902, 528–35. R. Haslam *Powys* 1979, 118–19.

Hall Barn, Beaconsfield, Bucks
Society of Gentlemen *England displayed* v. 1, 1769, 282. T. Whately *Observations on modern gardening* 1801, pl. 1. J.C. Loudon *Encyclopaedia of gardening* 1822, 1233. British Museum *Catalogue of maps, prints* 1829, 141. *G.M.* v. 9, 1833, 647. *C.L.* v. 4, 1898, 432–35; v. 26, 1909, 260–66; v. 37, 1915, 118; v. 91, 1942, 564–67, 612–16, 662. *Gdnrs Mag.* 1907, 897–900. E. Cecil *History of gardening in England* 1910, 224–25. G. Jekyll *Garden ornament* 1918, 205, 286. N. Pevsner *Buckinghamshire* 1960, 151–52. L. Fleming *and* A. Gore *English garden* 1979, 54–58.

Hall Garth, Goodmanham, Humberside
C.L. v. 129, 1961, 392–95.

Hall-i'-th'-Wood, Bolton, Greater Manchester
C.L. v. 21, 1907, 774–83. G. Jekyll *Garden ornament* 1918, 153. G. Beard *Thomas H. Mawson* 1976, 53.

Hall Leys Pleasure Gardens, Matlock, Derbyshire
Historical MSS Commission *Architectural history* v. 4, 1972, item 4360.

Hall Place, Maidenhead, Berks
C.L. v. 83, 1938, 246–51, 272.

Hall Place, West Meon, Hants
C.L. v. 95, 1944, 860–63, 904; v. 156, 1974, 602–04.

Hall Place, Leigh, Kent
Garden v. 11, 1877, 468–70. *J. Hort. Cottage Gdnr* v. 58, 1877, 74–75. *C.L.* v. 8, 1900, 776–81; v. 51, 1922,

Hall Place (*Cont.*)

80–87. M. Allan *Fisons guide* 1970, 46–47. T. Wright *Gardens of Britain* v. 4, 1978, 56–58.

Hallingbury Place, Hallingbury, Essex
J.P. Neale *Views* v. 1, 1818. T. Wright *History . . . of Essex* v. 2, 1836, 322. *J. Hort. Cottage Gdnr* N.S., v. 44, 1902, 430,432. *Garden* 1913, 598–600; 1920, 54–55. *C.L.* v. 36, 1914, 390–96; v. 46, 1919, 440–41. F.G. Emmison *Catalogue of maps in Essex Record Office* 2nd Supplt, 1964, 35. D. Stroud *Capability Brown* 1975, 227.

Halnaby Hall near Darlington, N. Yorks
C.L. v. 73, 1933, 334–38.

Halnaker Park, Chichester, W. Sussex
J. Brown *Gardens of a golden afternoon* 1982, 176.

Halse near Brackley, Northants
Northamptonshire Past and Present v. 5 no. 3, 1975, 225.

Halston near Oswestry, Shropshire
T. Pennant *Tour in Wales* v. 1, 1778, 234–35, pl. 20. *Picturesque views of the principal seats* 1788.

Halswell House near Goathurst, Somerset
A. Young *Farmer's tour through East of England* v. 4, 1771, 14–21. W. Watts *Seats* 1779, pl. 15. J. Collinson *History . . . of Somersetshire* v. 1, 1791, 81. J.B. Burke *Visitation* 2nd Series, v. 1, 1855, 110–11. *C.L.* v. 24, 1908, 702–10. N. Pevsner *South and West Somerset* 1958, 189. B. Jones *Follies & grottoes* 1974, 384–85. *Gdn History* v. 5 no. 3, 1977, 27–32. J. Harris *Artist and the country house* 1979, 282.

Halton Hall, Halton, Lancs
E. Baines *History . . . of Lancaster* v. 4, 1836, 587.

Halton House, Halton, Bucks
G.C. ii 1889, 379–80,383,436–37. *J. Hort. Cottage Gdnr* N.S., v. 27, 1893, 199–201; N.S., v. 35, 1897, 315–17. *C.L.* v. 1, 1897, 664–66; v. 154, 1973, 1062–64. *Gdnrs Mag.* 1900, 449–55.

Halton Place, N. Yorks
T.D. Whitaker *History and antiquities of the Deanery of Craven* 1878, 157.

Ham, Wantage, Oxfordshire
R. Bisgrove *Gardens of Britain* v. 3, 1978, 87.

Ham Frith Farm, Newham, London
F.G. Emmison *Catalogue of maps in Essex Record Office* 1st Supplt, 1952, 21.

Ham House (Farm), Weybridge, Surrey
Short account of the principal seats and gardens in and about Richmond and Kew [1760s?] 16–17. R. and J. Dodsley *London and its environs described* v. 3, 1761, 132.

Ham House, Richmond, London
Official guide. T. Badeslade and J. Rocque *Vitruvius Brittanicus* 1739, pls. 65–66. J.P. Neale *Views* v. 4, 1821. R. Ackermann *Repository* v. 9, 1827, pl. 13. W.W.J. Gendall *Views* v. 2, 1830, 113. N. Whittock and H. Gastineau *Picturesque beauties of England and Wales* 1830, 37. *G.M.* v. 11, 1835, 684. *G.C.* ii 1884, 69–70. *J. Hort. Cottage Gdnr* N.S., v. 22, 1891, 11–12. *Gdning World* v. 7, 1891, 671. *C.L.* v. 6, 1899, 144–50; v. 47, 1920, 372–78,404,444–47; v. 58, 1925, 998–1001; v. 158, 1975, 902–03. M.R. Gloag *Book of English gardens* 1906, 177–94. C. Holme *Gardens of England in Southern & Western counties* 1907, pls. 65–66. V.C.H. *Surrey* v. 3, 1911, 529. *Gdnrs Mag.* 1915, 406–07. J. Evelyn *Diary* v. 4, 1955, 143–44. *Gdn History* v. 3 no. 4, 1975, 58. *Landscape Design* no. 113, 1976, 26–28. R.I.B.A. *Catalogue* v. S, 1976, 95. M. Binney and A. Hills *Elysian gardens* 1979, 54–55. J. Harris *Artist and the country house* 1979, 56,109. G.S. Thomas *Gardens of National Trust* 1979, 149–50. M. Hadfield et al. *British gardeners* 1980, 110.

Hambleden Manor House, Hambleden, Bucks
R. Bisgrove *Gardens of Britain* v. 3, 1978, 88.

Hamels near Ware, Herts
H. Chauncy *Historical antiquities of Hertfordshire* 1700, 227. J. Kip *Nouveau theatre de la Grande Bretagne* v. 4, 1729. M. Macartney *English houses & gardens* 1908, pl. 13.

Hamels, Boars Hill, Oxford
G.C. ii 1935, 37.

Hamilton Palace, Hamilton, Strathclyde
G.M. v. 18, 1842, 338–41. J.C. Loudon *Arboretum et fruticetum Britannicum* v. 1, 1844, 92–93. *Scottish Gdnr* v. 11, 1862, 170–73. F.O. Morris *Series of picturesque views* v. 6, 9. *J. Hort. Cottage Gdnr* v. 34, 1865, 273–74,294–95,315. A.A. Tait *Landscape garden in Scotland* 1980, passim.

Hammerfield near Tonbridge, Kent
C.L. v. 9, 1901, 208–12.

Hampden House, Hampden, Bucks
C.L. v. 7, 1900, 304–08.

Hampstead Heath *see* London

Hampstead Marshall near Newbury, Berks
J. Beeverell *Les delices de la Grande Bretagne* v. 5, 1707, 872. L. Knyff and J. Kip *Britannia illustrata* v. 1, 1714. H. Overton *Britannia illustrata* c.1724, pl. 11. *G.M.*

Hampstead Marshall (*Cont.*)

v. 10, 1834, 115–17. *Architectural Review* v. 19, 1906, 155–63. M. Macartney *English houses & gardens* 1908, pl. 27. *C.L.* v. 33, 1913, 454–58. G. Jekyll *Garden ornament* 1918, 8–10.

Hampstead Wells, Hampstead, Camden, London
W. Wroth *London pleasure gardens of the eighteenth century* 1896, 177–83.

Hampton, Balbriggan, Co. Dublin, Eire
G.M. v. 2, 1827, 146–47.

Hampton. Bushey Park, London
S. Switzer *Hydrostaticks and hydraulicks* v. 2, 1729, 403, pl. 34. J.P. Neale *Views* v. 2, 1819. W. Keane *Beauties of Middlesex* 1850, 105–08. E. Law *Chestnut Avenue, Bushey Park* 1919. *G.C.* ii 1963, 136–37. C.M. Anstead and G.D. Heath *Bushey Park* 1965. *C.L.* v. 145, 1969, 1090–91. G. Williams *Royal Parks of London* 1978, 173–97. A. Hellyer *Gardens of genius* 1980, 78–81. D.o.E. *and* Directorate of Ancient Monuments and Historic Buildings *Hampton Court and Bushy Park* 1983. *See also* Hampton Court Palace

Hampton Court near Leominster, Hereford and Worcester
J. Beeverell *Les delices de la Grande Bretagne* v. 5, 1707, 872. R. Atkyns *Ancient and present state of Glostershire* 1712, 452. L. Knyff *and* J. Kip *Britannia illustrata* v. 1, 1714. C. Campbell *Vitruvius Britannicus* v. 3, 1725, pl. 75. Society of Gentlemen *England displayed* v. 2, 1769, 41. *Copper Plate Mag.* v. 3, pl. 135. J.P. Neale *Views* 2nd Series, v. 3, 1826. *Jones's views* 1829. *G.M.* v. 17, 1841, 415–16. F.O. Morris *Series of picturesque views* v. 2, 9. *G.C.* ii 1891, 757–58. *C.L.* v. 9, 1901, 836–42; v. 153, 1973, 450–53,518–21. H.I. Triggs *Formal gardens in England and Scotland* 1902, 37–38. Lady Rockley *Historic gardens of England* 1938, 214–15. L. Fleming *and* A. Gore *English garden* 1979, pls. 27–28. J. Harris *Artist and the country house* 1979, 118–19, 122, pls. 15–16. G. Carter *et al. Humphry Repton* 1982, 153.

Hampton Court House, Hampton, London
C.L. v. 172, 1982, 392–94.

Hampton Court Palace, Hampton, London
Official guide. J. Beeverell *Les delices de la Grande Bretagne* v. 4, 1707, 871. L. Knyff *and* J. Kip *Britannia illustrata* v. 1, 1714. H. Overton *Britannia illustrata* c.1724, pl. 2. T. Badeslade *and* J. Rocque *Vitruvius Brittanicus* 1739, pls. 4–5. S. Switzer *Ichnographia rustica* v. 1, 1742, 76,83. N. Spencer *Complete English traveller* 1771, 317. D. Defoe *Tour* v. 1, 1778, 233–34. *Archaeologia* v. 7, 1785, 124–26. D. Lysons *Historical account of those parishes in . . . Middlesex . . . not described in the Environs* 1800, 71–73. F.I. Mannskirsch *Coloured views of parks and gardens* 1813, pls. 5–6. British Museum *Catalogue of maps, prints* 1829, 142–43. *G.M.* v. 9, 1833, 478; 13, 1837, 8–9. D. Cox *Six views of Hampton Court* c.1840. J. Grundy *Stranger's guide to Hampton Court Palace and Gardens* 1849. W. Keane *Beauties of Middlesex* 1850, 158–60. *Cottage Gdnr* v. 15, 1855, 83–84,104–05. *Country Gentleman's Companion* 6 November 1855, 83–84; 13 November 1855, 104–05. N. Cole *Royal parks and gardens of London* 1877, 39–46. *J. Hort. Cottage Gdnr* v. 57, 1877, 214–15; N.S., v. 11, 1885, 160–62; N.S., v. 27, 1893, 147; v. 53, 1906, 289–90. *Garden* v. 6, 1874, 76–77; v. 20, 1881, 105–06; 1919, 431. *G.C.* ii 1888, 691–92, 737–38; i 1889, 73–74,104–05,169; ii 1893, 205–06; ii 1895, 155; ii 1907, 177–78; i 1919, 99,100; i 1961, 432–33. E. Law *History of Hampton Court Palace* 1885–91, 3 vols. *C.L.* v. 3, 1898, 499–500; v. 7, 1900, 709–12,761–63,824–27; v. 8, 1900, 815–18; v. 13, 1903, 400–09; v. 28, 1910, 349–51; v. 45, 1919, 207–08; v. 45, 1919, 711–13; v. 119, 1956, 372–73. *Gdnrs Mag.* 1902, 809–13. H.I. Triggs *Formal gardens in England and Scotland* 1902, 21–23. V.C.H. *Middlesex* v. 2, 1911, 380–86. C. Ward *Royal gardens* 1912, 50–60. G. Jekyll *Garden ornament* 1918, 16–17, 181. E. Law *Flower-lover's guide to gardens of Hampton Court Palace* 1923. E. Law *Hampton Court gardens old and new* 1926. *Hampton Court Palace 1689–1702; original Wren drawings from the Sir John Soanes' Museum and All Souls collections. Wren Society* v. 4, 1927, passim. C. Williams *Thomas Platter's travels in England 1599* 1932, 199,200–01. E. Yates *Hampton Court* 1935. T. Jefferson *Garden book 1766–1824* 1944, 111. P. Lindsay *Hampton Court* 1948. C. Fiennes *Journeys* 1949, 356–57. M. Sands *Gardens of Hampton Court* 1950. N. Pevsner *Middlesex* 1951, 82–84. *J.R.I.B.A.* v. 58, 1951, 112–13. G.H. Chettle *Hampton Court Palace* 1955. J. Evelyn *Diary* v. 3, 1955, 324–25; v. 4, 645. D. Green *Gardener to Queen Anne* 1956, passim. R. Church *Royal Parks of London* 1965, 53–60. P. Coats *Great gardens of Britain* 1967, 212–21. Historical MSS Commission *Architectural history* v. 2, 1970, item 1513; v. 3, 1971, item 2870; v. 4, 1972, item 4111. *J. Royal Hort. Soc.* 1970, 127–28,321–22; 1971, 371–72. D. Green *Gardens and parks at Hampton Court and Bushy* 1974. H. Thurston *Royal parks for the people* 1974, 70–75. D. Stroud *Capability Brown* 1975, 122–23. H.M. Colvin *History of the King's works* v. 4, 1982, 26,132,138–39,142,143–44,146; v. 5, 1976, 170–74. P. Willis *Charles Bridgeman* 1977, 179–80. G. Williams *Royal parks of London* 1978, 173–97. T. Wright *Gardens of Britain* v. 4, 1978, 217–18. L. Fleming *and* A. Gore *English garden* 1979, 49. J. Harris *Artist and the country house* 1979, 106,120,129. R. Strong *Renaissance garden in England* 1979, 25–34. M. Hadfield *et al. British gardeners* 1980, 189. G. Plumptre *Royal gardens* 1981, 126–57. D.o.E. *and* Directorate of Ancient Monuments and Historic Buildings *Hampton Court and*

Hampton Court Palace (*Cont.*)
Bushy Park 1983. B. Cherry *and* N. Pevsner *London 2: South* 1983, 497–500.

Hampton House *see* Garrick's Villa

Hampton Lodge, Seale, Surrey
G. Carter *et al. Humphry Repton* 1982, 162.

Hamptons, West Peckham, Kent
C. Greenwood *Epitome of county history . . . v. 1: Kent* 1838, 140.

Hampworth Lodge near Salisbury, Wilts
G. Beard *Thomas H. Mawson* 1976, 53.

Hams Hall near Coleshill, Warwickshire
J.P. Neale *Views* v. 4, 1821.

Hamstead, Handsworth, Birmingham, W. Midlands
S. Shaw *History . . . of Staffordshire* v. 2, 1801, 112.
J. Nightingale *Topographical . . . description of Staffordshire* 1810, 838.

Hamstead Mount, Staffs
C.L. v. 141, 1967, 782–83.

Hamsterley Hall, Hamsterley, Co. Durham
C.L. v. 86, 1939, 418–22.

Hamwood, Dunboyne, Co. Meath, Eire
Cottage Gdnr v. 28, 1862, 251–54, 274–75. *J. Hort. Cottage Gdnr* v. 47, 1872, 295–96; N.S., v. 41, 1900, 468–69. *Irish Gdning* v. 8, 1913, 87–88. E. Malins *and* P. Bowe *Irish gardens and demesnes* 1980, 76.

Hanbury Hall near Droitwich, Hereford and Worcester
Official guide. F.O. Morris *Series of picturesque views* v. 5, 65. *C.L.* v. 10, 1901, 368–74; v. 39, 1916, 502–08; v. 143, 1968, 18–22. N. Pevsner *Worcestershire* 1968, 186. G.S. Thomas *Gardens of National Trust* 1979, 150.

Hanch Hall, Lichfield, Staffs
R. Sidwell *West Midland gardens* 1981, 166–67.

Handcross Park near Cuckfield, W. Sussex
G.C. ii 1883, 653.

Handley near Towcester, Northants
Northamptonshire Past and Present v. 5 no. 3, 1975, 225–26.

Handstyle House, Liverpool, Merseyside
Cottage Gdnr v. 15, 1855, 38–42.

Hanford House near Blandford, Dorset
J. Hutchins *History . . . of Dorset* v. 4, 1870, 62. *C.L.*
v. 17, 1905, 558–64. J. Harris *Gardens of delight* 1978, 50.

Hanley near Edinburgh, Lothian
Gdning World v. 5, 1888, 231.

Hanmer, Sir Thomas *see* Bettisfield

Hannaford, Ashburton, Devon
G. Beard *Thomas H. Mawson* 1976, 54.

Hannayfield, Dumfriess and Galloway
G.M. v. 9, 1833, 12.

Hanover Lodge, Regent's Park, London
J. Elmes *Metropolitan improvements* 1828.

Hanover Square *see* Westminster

Hanslope Park near Stony Stratford, Bucks
H. Repton *Sketches* 1794, 24. D. Stroud *Humphry Repton* 1962, 170. M. Hadfield *et al. British gardeners* 1980, 238. G. Carter *et al. Humphry Repton* 1982, 148.

Hanwell, Oxfordshire
R. Plot *Natural history of Oxfordshire* 1705, 240. V.C.H. *Oxford* v. 9, 1969, 114.

Hanwell Park, Ealing, London
J.B. Burke *Visitation* 2nd Series, v. 1, 1855, 86.
D. Stroud *Capability Brown* 1975, 227.

Hanworth Hall, Hanworth, Norfolk
D. Stroud *Humphry Repton* 1962, 170. G. Carter *et al. Humphry Repton* 1982, 159.

Hanworth Park, Hounslow, London
W. Keane *Beauties of Middlesex* 1850, 41–45.
H.M. Colvin *History of the King's works* v. 4, 1982, 148.

Happy Valley, Bigswell, Orkney
Scots Mag. N.S., v. 111 no. 4, 1979, 357–61.

Harcombe House near Alresford, Hants
A. Paterson *Gardens of Britain* v. 2, 1978, 91–92.

Hardington near Frome, Somerset
Proc. Somerset Archaeological and Natural History Soc. v. 122, 1977/78, 11–28. *Trans. Ancient Monuments Soc.* v. 24, 1980, 143–52.

Hardwick, Northants
Royal Commission on Historical Monuments *Inventory of historical monuments in . . . Northampton* v. 2, 1979, 72–73. C. Taylor *Archaeology of gardens* 1983, 55.

Hardwick Hall near Chesterfield, Derbyshire
Official guide. *Topographer* v. 3, 1791, 323. W. Adam *Gem of the Peak* 1851, 190–97. L. Jewitt *and* S.C. Hall *Stately homes of England* 1874, 116–52. *J. Hort. Cottage Gdnr* v. 54, 1875, 582–84. *Garden* v. 18, 1880, 572–73. *C.L.* v. 2, 1897, 434–36, 464–66; v. 8, 1900, 464–70; v. 64, 1928, 806–14. G. Jekyll *and* G.S. Elgood *Some English gardens* 1905, 52–54. G. Jekyll *Garden ornament* 1918, 411. Lady Rockley *Historic gardens of England* 1938, 118–19. *G.C.* ii 1964, 476–77. J. Anthony *Gardens of Britain* v. 6, 1979, 87–91. G.S. Thomas *Gardens of National Trust* 1979, 151–52.

Hardwick Hall, Sedgefield, Co. Durham
J. Britton *and* E.W. Brayley *Beauties of England and Wales* v. 5, 1803, 98–99. W. Elstob(?) *Walk through Hardwick Gardens* 1820. V.C.H. *County Durham* v. 3, 1928, 322. B. Jones *Follies & grottoes* 1974, 297.

Hardwick Hall near Shrewsbury, Shropshire
C.L. v. 43, 1918, 550–55.

Hardwick House, Whitchurch, Oxfordshire
C.L. v. 20, 1906, 90–97.

Hardwick House near Bury St Edmunds, Suffolk
J. Gage *History . . . of Suffolk: Thingoe Hundred* 1838, 484. *J. Hort. Cottage Gdnr* v. 40, 1868, 77; v. 53, 1875, 54–57, 74–76. *G.C.* ii 1879, 140–42, 145; ii 1889, 239–40.

Hardwicke Court near Gloucester, Glos
R. Atkyns *Ancient and present state of Glostershire* 1712, 456. L. Knyff *and* J. Kip *Britannia illustrata* v. 2, 1715. *C.L.* v. 154, 1973, 18–19. Historical MSS Commission *Architectural history* v. 2, 1970, item 1526.

Hardwicke Grange near Shrewsbury, Shropshire
J.P. Neale *Views* 2nd Series, v. 3, 1826. *Garden* v. 48, 1895, 375. B. Jones *Follies & grottoes* 1974, 580.

Hare Hall near Romford, Havering, London
G.A. Walpoole *New British traveller* 1784, 69. W. Angus *Seats* 1787, pl. 28. J.P. Neale *Views* v. 1, 1818. T. Wright *History . . . of Essex* v. 2, 1836, 446.

Harefield near Exmouth, Devon
R. Ackermann *Repository* v. 12, 1828, pl. 7. W.W.J. Gendall *Views* v. 1, 1830, 95.

Harefield Grove, Hillingdon, London
Garden v. 25, 1884, 395–96. *G.C.* i 1884, 175–76. *Gdning World* v. 2, 1886, 584–86.

Harefield Park, Hillingdon, London
W. Keane *Beauties of Middlesex* 1850, 186–87.

Harewood House, Harewood, W. Yorks
W. Watts *Seats* 1779, pl. 7. S. Shaw *Tour in 1787* 1788, 251. J.C. Loudon *Treatise on forming, improving and managing county residences* v. 2, 1806, pl. 16. J. Jewell *Tourist's companion on history and antiquities of Harewood* 1819. J.P. Neale *Views* v. 5, 1822. *Jones's views* 1829, 8–9. *G.M.* v. 6, 1830, 649–53. T. Allen *New . . . history of . . . York* v. 3, 1831, 388. E.A. Brooke *Gardens of England* 1857, pl. 40. *Florist* 1857, 42–45. F.O. Morris *Series of picturesque views* v. 1, 7. *Gdnrs Mag.* 1896, 271–78. *C.L.* v. 10, 1901, 432–40; v. 51, 1922, 243–48. C. Holme *Gardens of England in Northern counties* 1911, pls. 52–53. G. Jekyll *Garden ornament* 1918, 56, 68. *Garden* 1922, 88–89. Lady Rockley *Historic gardens of England* 1938, 196–97. D. Stroud *Humphry Repton* 1962, 110–11. M. Allan *Fisons guide* 1970, 246–47. R.I.B.A. *Catalogue* v. B, 1972, 23. *Gdn History* v. 1 no. 3, 1973, 14. D. Stroud *Capability Brown* 1975, 105–06, 228. K. Lemmon *Gardens of Britain* v. 5, 1978, 165–68. *Landscape Planning* v. 7, 1980, 121–49. G. Carter *et al. Humphry Repton* 1982, 164.

Harford Hall, Norfolk
J.P. Neale *Views* v. 3, 1820.

Haringey House, Hornsey, Haringey, London
G.M. v. 16, 1840, 584. W. Keane *Beauties of Middlesex* 1850, 48–52.

Harkstead near Ipswich, Suffolk
J. Hort. Cottage Gdnr N.S., v. 25, 1892, 555–56.

Harlaxton Manor, Harlaxton, Lincs
Copper Plate Mag. v. 5, 1802, pl. 138. *G.M.* v. 16, 1840, 329–37. F.O. Morris *Series of picturesque views* v. 2, 17. *C.L.* v. 20, 1906, 522–32; v. 82, 1937, 379–79; v. 121, 1957, 704–07. G. Jekyll *Garden ornament* 1918, 94.

Harlestone Park, Harlestone, Northants
H. Repton *Fragments* 1816, 22. J.P. Neale *Views* v. 3, 1820. D. Stroud *Humphry Repton* 1962, 147. G. Carter *et al. Humphry Repton* 1982, 160.

Harleyford near Great Marlow, Bucks
W.B. Cooke *and* S. Owen *The Thames* v. 1, 1811, 33. *Gdnrs Mag.* 1904, 87–90. *C.L.* v. 27, 1910. 810–19. D. Stroud *Capability Brown* 1975, 228. J. Harris *Artist and the country house* 1979, 281.

Harlow Car Gardens, Harrogate, N. Yorks
Official guide. *J. Royal Hort. Soc.* 1952, 314–20; 1960, 469–76; 1964, 415–23. *G.C.* v. 160 no. 18, 1966, 15–15; v. 189 no. 1, 1981, 27–29. M. Allan *Fisons guide* 1970, 247–49. H. Evans *Beautiful gardens of Britain* 1974, 109–10. K. Lemmon *Gardens of Britain* v. 5, 1978, 74–80. *C.L.* v. 168, 1980, 834–36. *Garden* 1983, 85–90.

Harsley Hall near Northallerton, N. Yorks
K. Lemmon *Gardens of Britain* v. 5, 1978, 80. I. Hall *Samuel Buck's Yorkshire sketchbook* 1979, 325.

Harlsey Manor near Northallerton, N. Yorks
K. Lemmon *Gardens of Britain* v. 5, 1978, 81–82.

Harraton Hall, Harraton, Co. Durham
J. Harris *Artist and the country house* 1979, 78.

Harrington Hall, Harrington, Northants
Northamptonshire Past and Present v. 5 no. 5, 1977, 394,395–97. *C.L.* v. 156, 1974, 18–21; v. 166, 1979, 2142–44. *Gdn History* v. 5 no. 3, 1977, 11. M. Binney and A. Mills *Elysian gardens* 1979, 12. Royal Commission on Historical Monuments *Inventory of historical monuments in . . . Northampton* v. 2, 1979, 75–77, pl. 26. C. Taylor *Archaeology of gardens* 1983, 22,23–24.

Harringworth, Northants
Northamptonshire Past and Present v. 5 no. 3, 1975, 226. Royal Commission on Historical Monuments *Inventory of the historical monuments in . . . Northampton* v. 4, 1982, 189.

Harristown near Naas, Co. Kildare, Eire
J.B. Burke *Visitation* 2nd Series, v. 1, 1855, 131–32. B. Jones *Follies & grottoes* 1974, 116. Knight of Glin and P. Bowe *Gardens of outstanding historic interest in . . . Ireland* 1980.

Harrock Hall near Parbold, Lancs
Scottish Gdnr v. 15, 1866, 343–44.

Harrow Manor House, Harrow on the Hill, London
J. Harris *Artist and the country house* 1979, 344–45.

Harrowden Hall, Great Harrowden, Northants
C.L. v. 24, 1908, 910–19; v. 156, 1974, 1086–89. G. Jekyll *Garden ornament* 1918, 35,39,126.

Hartbury House, Hartbury, Glos
Gdnrs Mag. 1913, 117–19,120. *G.C.* ii 1938, 135. G. Beard *Thomas H. Mawson* 1976, 54.

Hartham Park near Chippenham, Wilts
A. Robertson *Topographical survey of the Great Road* part 2 1792, 68–69. *J. Hort. Cottage Gdnr* v. 54, 1875, 423–26; N.S. v. 52, 1906, 76–77. C. Holme *Gardens of England in Southern & Western counties* 1907, pls. 67–68. *C.L.* v. 26, 1909, 196–204. G. Jekyll *Garden ornament* 1918, 214,258,336,338.

Hartland Abbey, Hartland, Devon
R. Polwhele *History of Devonshire* v. 2, 1793. *C.L.* v. 174, 1983, 602–05.

Hartlebury Castle, Hartlebury, Hereford and Worcester
S. and N. Buck *Buck's antiquities* v. 2, 1774, pl. 318. E.H. Pearce *Hartlebury Castle* 1926. *C.L.* v. 150, 1971, 672–75.

Hartsfield near Betchworth, Surrey
Garden v. 2, 1872, 84–85.

Hartsholme Hall near Lincoln, Lincs
J. Hort. Cottage Gdnr v. 55, 1876, 192–94.

Hartwell, Northants
Northamptonshire Past and Present v. 5 no. 3, 1975, 226.

Hartwell House near Aylesbury, Bucks
Copper Plate Mag. v. 1, 1792, pl. 42. *Picturesque views of the principal seats* 1788. G. Lipscomb *History . . . of Buckingham* v. 2, 1847, 313. J.B. Burke *Visitation* v. 1, 1852, 12. *G.C.* ii 1885, 133–34; ii 1905, 233–34. *C.L.* v. 9, 1901, 740–47; v. 35, 1914, 378–84,418–21; v. 165, 1979, 707–09. R. Pococke *Travels through England* v. 1, 1888, 161. D. Stroud *Capability Brown* 1975, 228. R. Bisgrove *Gardens of Britain* v. 3, 1978, 89. J. Harris *Artist and the country house* 1979, 188–89, pl. 20. L. Fleming and A. Gore *English garden* 1979, pls. 40–44. *Royal Soc. of Arts J.* v. 128, 1980, 284–94.

Harviestoun Castle near Dollar, Central
Scottish Gdnr and Northern Forester v. 7, 1912, 429–30.

Hascombe Court, Hascombe, Surrey
Gdn Design no. 3, 1930, 103–13. *C.L.* v. 92, 1942, 554–57. P. Coats *Great gardens of Britain* 1967, 246–51. R. Webber *Percy Cane* 1975, 72–75, 184. T. Wright *Gardens of Britain* v. 4, 1978, 218–20.

Haselbech Hall, Haselbech, Northants
G.C. ii 1899, 449.

Haseley Court, Little Haseley, Oxfordshire
C.L. v. 127, 1960, 268–71,329; v. 133, 1963, 1230–32. *G.C.* ii 1961, 156–57. P. Coats *Great gardens of Britain* 1967, 272–81. R. Bisgrove *Gardens of Britain* v. 3, 1978, 90–91.

Haseley Manor, Haseley, Warwickshire
J. Hort. Cottage Gdnr N.S., v. 25, 1892, 173–74.

Hasells near Sandy, Beds
H. Repton *Sketches* 1794, 6–7. D. Stroud *Humphry Repton* 1962, 53. Historical MSS Commission *Architectural history* v. 3, 1971, item 3387. G. Carter et al. *Humphry Repton* 1982, 147.

Haslingfield Hall, Haslingfield, Cambs
Royal Commission on Historical Monuments

Haslingfield Hall (*Cont.*)

Inventory of historical monuments in . . . Cambridge v. 1, 1968, pl. 28.

Hassobury near Bishop's Stortford, Essex
Historical MSS Commission *Architectural history* v. 1, 1969, item 445.

Hatch, Churt, Surrey
C.L. v. 158, 1975, 554–55.

Hatch Court, Hatch Beauchamp, Somerset
J. Collinson *History . . . of Somersetshire* v. 1, 1791, 44. C.L. v. 136, 1964, 1034–37,1140.

Hatch House near Hindon, Wilts
C.L. v. 45, 1919, 526–27.

Hatchford Park near Cobham, Surrey
W. Keane *Beauties of Surrey* 1849, 40–42. *Surrey Archaeological Collections* v. 61, 1964, 81.

Hatchlands, East Clandon, Surrey
C.L. v. 39, 1916, 176–84; v. 114, 1953, 870–73. D. Stroud *Humphry Repton* 1962, 170. J. Harris *Catalogue of British drawings . . . in American collections* 1971, 176,177. G.S. Thomas *Gardens of National Trust* 1979, 152–53. J. Brown *Miss Gertrude Jekyll* 1981, 16–17. G. Carter et al. *Humphry Repton* 1982, 162.

Hatfield near Ledbury, Hereford and Worcester
Garden v. 1, 1872, 266–68.

Hatfield Forest Lake near Hatfield Broad Oak, Essex
C.L. v. 142, 1967, 986–89.

Hatfield Hall, Hatfield, Yorks
W. Watts *Seats* 1779, pl. 20.

Hatfield House, Hatfield, Herts
Official guide. W. Watts *Seats* 1779, pl. 53. R. Clutterbuck *History . . . of the county of Hertford* v. 2, 1821, 342. G.M. v. 5, 1829, 672; v. 12, 1836, 294. L. Jewitt and S.C. Hall *Stately homes of England* 1874, 294–307. F.O. Morris *Series of picturesque views* v. 2, 7. *J. Hort. Cottage Gdnr* v. 46, 1871, 299–303; N.S., v. 19, 1889, 136–37; N.S., v. 36, 1898, 209–13,216–17. G.C. 9 May 1874, 8 p.; ii 1887, 72,75,77,79,85; ii 1898, 100–01; ii 1901, 435; ii 1914, 78; ii 1915, 257–58,259,260. *Garden* v. 19, 1881, 647–51; v. 59, 1901, 211. *Gdnrs Mag.* 1906, 21–25. C.L. v. 1, 1897, 491–93,519–22; v. 8, 1900, 176–83; v. 22, 1907, 872–83,907; v. 61, 1927, 390–97, 426–34; v. 175, 1984, 662–64, 770–72. H.I. Triggs *Formal garden in England and Scotland* 1902, 18–19. M.R. Gloag *Book of English gardens* 1906, 197–218. C. Holme *Gardens of England in Southern & Western counties* 1907, pls. 70–73. V.C.H. *Hertford* v. 3, 1912, 100. G. Jekyll *Garden ornament* 1918, 246,265. *Gdning Illustrated* 1927, 288–89. Lady Rockley *Historic gardens of England* 1938, 114–15. J. Evelyn *Diary* v. 2, 1955, 80. N.T. Newton *Design on the land* 1971, 195. N. Pevsner *Hertfordshire* 1977, 170. R. Bisgrove *Gardens of Britain* v. 3, 1978, 91–94. R. Strong *Renaissance garden in England* 1979, 103–10.

Hatherop, Glos
R. Atkyns *Ancient and present state of Glostershire* 1712, 464. L. Knyff and J. Kip *Britannia illustrata* v. 2, 1715. V.C.H. *Gloucester* v. 7, 1981, 91.

Hatherton Lodge near Nantwich, Cheshire
J.B. Burke *Visitation* v. 1, 1852, 229.

Hatley St George near Royston, Cambs
J. Beeverell *Les delices de la Grande Bretagne* v. 5, 1707, 872. L. Knyff and J. Kip *Britannia illustrata* v. 1, 1714. M. Macartney *English houses & gardens* 1908, pl. 32.

Hatton Grange near Shifnal, Shropshire
C.L. v. 143, 1968, 466–70. R. Sidwell *West Midland gardens* 1981, 119.

Hatton House, Hatton, Warwickshire
G. Beard *Thomas H. Mawson* 1976, 54.

Hatton House near Ratho, Lothian
C.L. v. 30, 1911, 408–15.

Haughley (Hawleigh) **Park**, Haughley, Suffolk
H. Davy *Views* 1827.

Haughton near Nantwich, Cheshire
G.C. i 1904, 250–51.

Haughton near Tuxford, Notts
J. Beeverell *Les delices de la Grande Bretagne* v. 5, 1707, 872. L. Knyff and J. Kip *Britannia illustrata* v. 1, 1714.

Havelet, Guernsey, Channel Islands
W. Berry *History of the Island of Guernsey* 1815, 162.

Haverholme Priory near Sleaford, Lincs
C.L. v. 13, 1903, 112–17.

Havering Park, Romford, Havering, London
G.C. ii 1893, 436–37; i 1909, 407,408,409. F.G. Emmison *Catalogue of maps in Essex Record Office* 1st Supplt, 1952, 25,32.

Haverland Park near Norwich, Norfolk
G.M. v. 17, 1841, 32. J. Grigor *Eastern arboretum* 1841, 151–52.

Hawarden Castle, Hawarden, Clwyd
F.O. Morris *Series of picturesque views* v. 6, 65. *J. Hort.*

Hawarden Castle (*Cont.*)
Cottage Gdnr N.S., v. 3, 1881, 449–50. *G.C.* ii 1882, 433,436; ii 1896, 167. *C.L.* v. 141, 1967, 1516–19, 1676–80. R.I.B.A. *Catalogue* v. G-K, 1973, 58. Historical MSS Commission *Architectural history* v. 5, 1974, item 5165.

Hawkesyard Park near Armitage, Staffs
J. Hort. Cottage Gdnr v. 47, 1872, 347–49. *G.C.* ii 1890, 40–41.

Hawkstone Park near Wem, Shropshire
Description of Hawkstone 1766. T. Rodenhurst *Description of Hawkstone* 1783 and subsequent editions to 1811. J. Boswell *Life of Samuel Johnson* 1791 (entry for 25 July 1774). *Copper Plate Mag.* v. 4, pl. 191. R. Warner *Tour through Northern counties* v. 2, 1802, 173–82. E. Butcher *Excursion from Sidmouth to Chester* 1805, 173–79. H. Skrine *Two successive tours throughout . . . Wales* 1812, 175–80. J. Nightingale *Beauties of England and Wales* v. 13 pt 1, 1813, 285–93. J.P. Neale *Views* 2nd Series, v. 3, 1826. C. Hulbert *Stranger's friend* 1830, 8–13. Prince Pückler-Muskau *Tour* 1833, 82–83. F.O. Morris *Series of picturesque views* v. 6, 61. *G.C.* ii 1875, 495–96,519; ii 1893, 469. *C.L.* v. 123, 1958, 640–43; v. 124, 1958, 18–21,72–75,368–71. N. Pevsner *Shropshire* 1958, 145–46. *Publications of Bedfordshire Historical Record Soc.* v. 47, 1968, 136–37. P. Hunt *Garden lover's companion* 1974, 107–08. B. Jones *Follies & grottoes* 1974, 78–84. L. Fleming *and* A. Gore *English garden* 1979, 165–66. *Landscape Research* v. 7 no. 1, 1982, 22.

Hawksworth near Otley, W. Yorks
I. Hall *Samuel Buck's Yorkshire sketchbook* 1979, 204.

Hawleigh *see* Haughley

Hawley Hall, Hawley, Hants
R. Ackermann *Repository* v. 11, 1828, pl. 20. W.W.J. Gendall *Views* v. 2, 1830, 109.

Hawley House, Sutton at Hone, Kent
C. Greenwood *Epitome of county history . . . v. 1: Kent* 1838, 71.

Hawstead near Bury St Edmunds, Suffolk
Bibliotheca topographica Britannica v. 5 no. 23, 1790, 92–94,160–61.

Hawthornden Castle, Lasswade, Lothian
Scottish Gdnr v. 3, 1854, 41–43. G.A. Little *Scotland's gardens* 1981, 87.

Hay Castle, Hay-on-Wye, Powys
S. *and* N. Buck *Buck's antiquities* v. 2, 1774, pl. 355.

Hayes Place, Hayes, Bromley, London
G.C. ii 1881, 74.

Hayle Place, Loose, Kent
C. Greenwood *Epitome of county history . . . v. 1: Kent* 1838, 179.

Haystoun near Peebles, Borders
G.A. Little *Scotland's gardens* 1981, 87–88.

Hazelbury Manor, Box, Wilts
C.L. v. 59, 1926, 274–81.

Hazelhatch, Burrows Cross, Shere, Surrey
J. Brown *Gardens of a golden afternoon* 1982, 162.

Hazelwood, King's Langley, Herts
G.C. ii 1891, 766–67.

Hazelwood, Silverdale, Lancs
G. Beard *Thomas H. Mawson* 1976, 54.

Hazelwood near Sligo, Co. Sligo, Eire
E. Malins *and* Knight of Glin *Lost demesnes* 1976, 83.

Hazelwood Castle, Stutton, N. Yorks
C.L. v. 122, 1957, 1380–83. B. Jones *Follies & grottoes* 1974, 367.

Headbourne Worthy near Winchester, Hants
Gdn Design 1932, 26–27. M. Allan *Fisons guide* 1970, 113.

Headfort House near Kells, Co. Meath, Eire
Irish Gdning v. 8, 1913, 87–88; v. 12, 1917, 136–37. R.H.S. *Conifers in cultivation* 1932, 216–18,220. *New Flora and Silva* v. 1, 1929, 121–22. *C.L.* v. 79, 1936, 300–05,326,352–58. *G.C.* ii 1944, 120,121. *J. Royal Hort. Soc.* 1959, 358–66. E. Malins *and* Knight of Glin *Lost demesnes* 1976, 91–92. Knight of Glin *and* P. Bowe *Gardens of outstanding historic interest in . . . Ireland* 1980. E. Malins *and* P. Bowe *Irish gardens and demesnes* 1980, 73–76.

Headington Hill Hall, Headington, Oxfordshire
Cottage Gdnr v. 21, 1858, 100–01. *J. Hort. Cottage Gdnr* v. 60, 1878, 450–51. *G.C.* ii 1901, 111.

Headley Court, Epsom, Surrey
C.L. v. 32, 1912, 18–25.

Headon Hall, Headon, Notts
N. Pevsner *Nottinghamshire* 1979, 142.

Heale House, Woodford, Wilts
C.L. v. 37, 1915, 272–77. G. Jekyll *Garden ornament* 1918, 141. J. Sales *West Country gardens* 1980, 210–13.

Heanton Satchville near Hatherleigh, Devon
T. Badeslade *and* J. Rocque *Vitruvius Brittanicus* 1739, pls. 73–74. British Museum *Catalogue of maps, prints* 1829, 147. *G.M.* v. 19, 1843, 242–43. *Architectural History* v. 7, 1964, 28–29,70.

Heaselands near Haywards Heath, W. Sussex
Sussex Life v. 1 no. 3, 1965, 26–28. *C.L.* v. 140, 1966, 536–38. M. Allan *Fisons guide* 1970. 48. T. Wright *Gardens of Britain* v. 4, 1978, 151–52.

Heath Bank House near Cheadle, Greater Manchester
Cottage Gdnr v. 23, 1859, 93–94.

Heath Hall, Wakefield, W. Yorks
C.L. v. 144, 1968, 692–95,756–59,816–19. I. Hall *Samuel Buck's Yorkshire sketchbook* 1979, 142.

Heath House, Hampstead, London
J. Harris *Artist and the country house* 1979, 213.

Heath House, Tean, Staffs
C.L. v. 133, 1963, 18–21,62–65,383.

Heath House, Headley near Epsom, Surrey
J. Brown *Gardens of a golden afternoon* 1982, 173.

Heathcote, Ilkley, W. Yorks
C.L. v. 28, 1910, 54–65. L. Weaver *Houses and gardens by E.L. Lutyens* 1913, 183–96. A.S. Butler *et al. Architecture of Sir Edwin Lutyens* v. 2, 1950, 11. J. Brown *Gardens of a golden afternoon* 1982, 109,169. M. *and* R. Tooley *Gardens of Gertrude Jekyll in Northern England* 1982, 54.

Heathcote, Sir Thomas *see* Thames Ditton

Heatherbank, Weybridge, Surrey
G.C. i 1884, 110–11. *C.L.* v. 8, 1900, 304–10.

Heathfield Park, Heathfield, E. Sussex
H. Repton *Observations* 1803, 72–75. T.W. Horsfield *History . . . of Sussex* v. 1, 1835, 574. D. Stroud *Humphry Repton* 1962, 170. B. Jones *Follies & grottoes* 1974, 320–21. G. Carter *et al. Humphry Repton* 1982, 163.

Heathwaite, Windermere, Cumbria
G. Beard *Thomas H. Mawson* 1976, 54.

Heaton Mount, Heaton, W. Yorks
Bradford Illustrated Weekly Telegraph *Series of picturesque views* 1885.

Heaton Park near Manchester, Greater Manchester
J. Aikin *Description of the country . . . round Manchester* 1795, 236. J.P. Neale *Views* 2nd Series, v. 1, 1824. E. Baines *History . . . of Lancaster* v. 2, 1836, 563. F.O. Morris *Series of picturesque views* v. 4, 21. *C.L.* v. 36, 1914, 710–17; v. 58, 1925, 322–28. N. Pevsner *Lancaster: 1* 1969, 329–30. B. Jones *Follies & grottoes* 1974, 334.

Heckfield Place, Heckfield, Hants
E.F. Prosser *Select illustrations of Hampshire* 1833. *G.C.* 1872, 1457–60,1524–25; i 1878, 140–42,145; i 1881, 12–13,16–17; ii 1881, 433,821; ii 1882, 743–44; i 1884, 371–72,378; i 1889, 528; ii 1889, 210–11. *Garden* v. 7, 1875, 446–47. *J. Hort. Cottage Gdnr* v. 5, 1882, 430–32,433; N.S., v. 18, 1889, 5–6. *Gdning World* v. 1, 1884, 183. *C.L.* v. 4, 1898, 688–92.

Hedenham Hall, Hedenham, Norfolk
J. Harris *Artist and the country house* 1979, 318.

Hedingham Castle, Hedingham, Essex
P. Muilman *History of Essex* v. 2, 1769, 101.

Hedsor near Great Marlow, Bucks
A. Robertson *Topographical survey of the Great Road* pt 1, 1792, 87–88. J. *and* J. Boydell *History of the River Thames* v. 1, 1794, 274. J.C. Loudon *Encyclopaedia of gardening* 1822, 1233. *G.M.* v. 9, 1833, 646. *G.C.* i 1900, 153,154–55; i 1909, 42–43. *Gdnrs Mag.* 1907, 249–52.

Heffleton near Wareham, Dorset
J. Hutchins *History . . . of Dorset* v. 1, 1861, 417.

Heights, Witley, Surrey
G.C. i 1907, 197–98.

Heights of Abraham, Matlock Bath, Derbyshire
J. Anthony *Gardens of Britain* v. 6, 1979, 93–96.

Heligan near St Austell, Cornwall
G.C. ii 1896, 747–48. *Cornish Gdn* no. 26, 1983, 41–49.

Helmdon, Northants
Royal Commission on Historical Monuments *Inventory of the historical monuments in . . . Northampton* v. 4, 1982, 85–86.

Helmingham Hall, Helmingham, Suffolk
F.O. Morris *Series of picturesque views* v. 3, 21. *C.L.* v. 4, 1898, 720–24; v. 120, 1956,378–81. C. Holme *Gardens of England in Midland & Eastern counties* 1908, pls. 47–48. Architectural MSS Commission *Architectural history* v. 3, 1971, item 2687. M. Binney *and* A. Hills *Elysian gardens* 1979, 23.

Hemingford Grey near St Ives, Cambs
C. Holme *Gardens of England in Midland & Eastern counties* 1908, pls. 70–71.

Hemington, Northants
Royal Commission on Historical Monuments *Inventory of historical monuments in . . . Northampton* 1975, 52–54.

Hempstead, Gloucester, Glos
J.N. Brewer *Delineations of Gloucestershire* 1825, 154. J. Harris *Artist and the country house* 1979, 116.

Hemsted Park near Cranbrook, Kent
Cottage Gdnr v. 28, 1862, 626–27. F.O. Morris *Series of picturesque views* v. 6, 57.

Henbury near Bristol, Avon
R. Atkyns *Ancient and present state of Glostershire* 1712, 473. L. Knyff and J. Kip *Britannia illustrata* v. 2, 1715. *C.L.* v. 6, 1899, 776–81. J. Harris *Gardens of delight* 1978, 39.

Hendon Hall, Barnet, London
W. Keane *Beauties of Middlesex* 1850, 237–38. V.C.H. *Middlesex* v. 5, 1976, 9.

Hendon House, Barnet, London
W. Keane *Beauties of Middlesex* 1850, 8–9.

Hendon Place, Barnet, London
W. Keane *Beauties of Middlesex* 1850, 124–25.

Hendon Rectory, Barnet, London
G.M. v. 14, 1838, 220–34. J.C. Loudon *Villa gardener* 1850, 327–38.

Hendre, Monmouth, Gwent
G.C. ii 1900, 261–62,276. *Gdnrs Mag.* 1903, 643–46.

Hendregadredd near Tremadoc, Gwynedd
J.B. Burke *Visitation* v. 2, 1853, 52.

Henfield (William Borrer), W. Sussex
G.M. v. 14, 1838, 501–03.

Hengistbury Head near Bournemouth, Hants
G. Beard *Thomas H. Mawson* 1976, 38,55.

Hengrave Hall, Hengrave, Suffolk
J.B. Burke *Viositation* v. 1, 1852, 73. F.O. Morris *Series of picturesque views* v. 3, 71. *G.C.* i 1881, 723–25,729; i 1912, 5. *C.L.* v. 2, 1897, 624–26; v. 27, 1910, 558–68. Historical MSS Commission *Architectural history* v. 3, 1971, item 2901. M. Binney and A. Hills *Elysian gardens* 1979, 21.

Henham Hall, Henham, Suffolk
J.P. Neale *Views* v. 4, 1821. H. Davy *Views* 1827. A. Suckling *History . . . of Suffolk* v. 2, 1848, 368. D. Stroud *Humphry Repton* 1962, 63,170. Historical MSS Commission *Architectual history* v. 1, 1969, items 212,461. G. Carter et al. *Humphry Repton* 1982, 162.

Henham Old Hall, Henham, Suffolk
A. Suckling *History . . . of Suffolk* v. 2, 1848, 354.

Henley Hall, Tasley, Shropshire
C.L. v. 100, 1946, 302–05,348–49. R. Sidwell *West Midland gardens* 1981, 120–21.

Henllys, Llanfaes, Gwynedd
J.B. Burke *Visitation* v. 1, 1852, 157.

Hensol, Mossdale, Dumfries and Galloway
G.A. Little *Scotland's gardens* 1981, 260–61.

Henstead near Beccles, Suffolk
H. Davy *Views* 1827.

Hergest Croft, Kington, Hereford and Worcester
M. Allan *Fisons guide* 1970, 275–76. *International Dendrology Soc. Year Book* 1973, 19–22. *C.L.* v. 157, 1975, 494–96. *G.C.* v. 186 no. 8, 1979, 21–22. *Garden* 1980, 133–39,196–201. A. Lees-Milne and R. Verey *Englishman's garden* 1982, 28–31.

Hermes House, Islington, London
J. Harris *Artist and the country house* 1979, 207.

Hermitage, North End, Fulham, London
J. Harris *Artist and the country house* 1979, 324–25, pl. 26.

Hermitage, Priors Marston, Warwickshire
R. Sidwell *West Midland gardens* 1981, 212–14.

Hermitage, Dunkeld, Tayside
Connoisseur v. 187, 1974, 196–201.

Heron Court near Christchurch, Hants
E.F. Prosser *Select illustrations of Hampshire* 1833.

Heronden near Sandwich, Kent
C.L. v. 128, 1960, 284–87,333.

Heron's Ghyll near Uckfield, E. Sussex
C.L. v. 13, 1903, 638–42.

Heronsgate, Rickmansworth, Herts
R. Bisgrove *Gardens of Britain* v. 3, 1978, 94–95.

Herriard's House, Herriard, Hants
E.F. Prosser *Select illustrations of Hampshire* 1833. D. Stroud *Humphry Repton* 1962, 170. G. Carter et al. *Humphry Repton* 1982, 153.

Herringston near Dorchester, Dorset
C.L. v. 34, 1913, 674–78.

Herstmonceux Castle, Herstmonceux, E. Sussex
C.L. v. 43, 1918, 242–48,270–76; v. 78, 1935, 566–72,606–12.

Herterton House, Cambo, Northumberland
A. Lees-Milne *and* R. Verey *Englishman's garden* 1982, 88–91.

Hesketh Park *see* Merseyside

Hesleyside near Bellingham, Northumberland
J.P. Neale *Views* 2nd Series, v. 2, 1825. D. Stroud *Capability Brown* 1975, 228–29.

Heslington Hall, York, N. Yorks
J.P. Neale *Views* v. 5, 1822. *Jones's views* 1829, 46. C.L. v. 8, 1900, 624–30; v. 15, 1904, 700–01; v. 34, 1913, 90–97; v. 150, 1971, 532–34. H.I. Triggs *Formal gardens in England and Scotland* 1902, 28. C. Holme *Gardens of England in Northern counties* 1911, pls. 54–57.

Hestercombe near Taunton, Somerset
A. Young *Farmer's tour through the East of England* v. 4, 1771, 2–9. J. Collinson *History . . . of Somersetshire* v. 3, 1791, 258. C.L. v. 24, 1908, 486–94,522–32; v. 61, 1927, 598–605,638–45; v. 160, 1976, 822–26. L. Weaver *Houses and gardens by E.L. Lutyens* 1913, 140–57. G. Jekyll *Garden ornament* 1918, 71,189,307,339,348,391,433. Lady Rockley *Historic gardens of England* 1938, 252–53. A.S. Butler *et al. Architecture of Sir Edwin Lutyens* v. 2, 1950, 12. *J. Institute of Landscape Architects* no. 61, 1963, 8–11. R.I.B.A. *Catalogue: Lutyens* 1973, 23. G.C. v. 180 no. 23, 1976, 29–31. A. Hellyer *Gardens of genius* 1980, 132–37. J. Sales *West Country gardens* 1980, 156–59. *Landscape Design* no. 133, 1981, 26–27. J. Brown *Gardens of a golden afternoon* 1982, 82–85,168.

Hethersett, Seale, Surrey
C.L. v. 159, 1976, 1582–83.

Heveningham Hall, Heveningham, Suffolk
W. Watts *Seats* 1779, pl. 43. J.P. Neale *Views* v. 4, 1821. J.C. Loudon *Encyclopaedia of gardening* 1822, 1235. H. Davy *Views* 1827. C.L. v. 23, 1908, 594–603; v. 58, 1925, 432–40; v. 77, 1935, 50. G. Jekyll *Garden ornament* 1918, 120,193,435. M. Allan *Fisons guide* 1970, 194–95. N. Pevsner *Suffolk* 1974, 271. D. Stroud *Capability Brown* 1975, 198,229. D. Jarrett *English landscape* 1978, 123–27. L. Fleming *and* A. Gore *English garden* 1979, 122.

Hever Castle, Edenbridge, Kent
C.L. v. 2, 1897, 266–68; v. 22, 1907, 522–35,558–67; v. 169, 1981, 66–69; v. 174, 1983, 25. G.C. ii 1961, 194–96. *Connoisseur* v. 158, 1965, 215–25. P. Coats *Great gardens of Britain* 1967, 112–17. *Park Administration* February 1967, 44–45. M. Allan *Fisons guide* 1970, 49–50. R.I.B.A. *Catalogue* v. O-R, 1976, 35. J. Newman *West Kent and the Weald* 1976, 325. T. Wright *Gardens of Britain* v. 4, 1978, 60–65. A. Hellyer *Gardens of genius* 1980, 120–23. *Garden Design* no. 1, 1982, 33. *Landscape Architecture* v. 72, 1982, 26–33.

Hewell Grange near Bromsgrove, Hereford and Worcester
J.P. Neale *Views* v. 5, 1822. C. Holme *Gardens of England in Midland & Eastern counties* 1908 pl. 74. *Garden* v. 59, 1901, 412–13. C.L. v. 12, 1902, 732–41; v. 33, 1913, 669. G.C. i 1904, 209–10; ii 1913, 138; v. 187 no. 17, 1980, 31–33. *J. Hort. Cottage Gdnr* N.S., v. 48, 1904, 160–61. G. Jekyll *Garden ornament* 1918, 73,242. D. Stroud *Humphry Repton* 1962, 170. M. Binney *and* A. Hills *Elysian gardens* 1979, 6,28. L. Fleming *and* A. Gore *English garden* 1979, 203. G. Carter *et al. Humphry Repton* 1982, 163.

Hexton Manor, Hexton, Herts
Cottage Gdnr v. 19, 1857, 276–77,293–94. R. Bisgrove *Gardens of Britain* v. 3, 1978, 95–96.

Hexworthy, Lawhitton, Cornwall
Architectural History v. 7, 1964, 29,71.

Heydon near Aylsham, Norfolk
G.M. v. 17, 1841, 33. J. Grigor *Eastern arboretum* 1841, 160–61. J.B. Burke *Visitation* v. 1, 1852, 70. C.L. v. 172, 1982, 318–21.

Heyns Green, Layer Marney, Essex
F.G. Emmison *Catalogue of maps in Essex Record Office* 1st Supplt, 1952, 26.

Heythrop near Chipping Norton, Oxfordshire
J.P. Neale *Views* v. 3, 1820. F.O. Morris *Series of picturesque views* v. 6, 77. *Garden* v. 19, 1881, 301–03. C.L. v. 18, 1905, 270–77. V.C.H. *Oxford* v. 11, 1983, 49,129,135.

Heywood near Westbury, Wilts
G.C. i 1897, 46–48.

Heywood, Ballinakill, Co. Laois, Eire
G. Jekyll *Garden ornament* 1918, 383,436–37,440,443. C.L. v. 45, 1919, 16–22,42–47. A.S. Butler *et al. Architecture of Sir Edwin Lutyens* v. 2, 1950, 14. R.I.B.A. *Catalogue: Lutyens* 1973, 23. E. Malins *and* Knight of Glin *Lost demesnes* 1976, 94–96. E. Malins *and* P. Bowe

Irish gardens and demesnes 1980, 158–59. J. Brown *Gardens of a golden afternoon* 1982, 86–89,169.

Hickleton, S. Yorks
G.C. i 1904, 104. Historical MSS Commission *Architectural history* v. 2, 1970, item 1565.

Hickstead Place, Twineham, W. Sussex
B. Jones *Follies & grottoes* 1974, 402.

Hidcote Manor near Chipping Campden, Glos
Official guide. *C.L.* v. 67, 1930, 286–94; v. 68, 1930, 231–33. *Listener* 22 August 1934, 321–23. Lady Rockley *Historic gardens of England* 1938, 240–41. *J. Royal Hort. Soc.* 1949, 476–81; 1960, 346–47. *Garden* 1978, 423–28. G.C. i 1960, 318–20; ii 1964, 238; ii 1965, 34–35. P. Coats *Great gardens* 1963, 232–39. E. Hyams *English garden* 1964, 151–55. H. Evans *Beautiful gardens of Britain* 1974, 37–38. *National Trust Year Book* 1977–78, 18–29. L. Fleming *and* A. Gore *English garden* 1979, 210, pl. 132. G.S. Thomas *Gardens of National Trust* 1979, 153–56. A. Hellyer *Gardens of genius* 1980, 137–41. J. Sales *West Country gardens* 1980, 67–71. T. Hinde *Stately gardens of Britain* 1983, 118–25.

Hidcote Vale, Chipping Campden, Glos
J. Sales *West Country gardens* 1980, 71–72.

High Ashurst near Mickleham, Surrey
E.W. Brayley *and* J. Britton *Topographical history of Surrey* v. 4, 457,458.

High Beeches near Crawley, W. Sussex
Gdn History v. 7 no. 1, 1979, 4–7. *C.L.* v. 175, 1984, 810–12.

High Coxlease, Lyndhurst, Hants
G. Jekyll *and* L. Weaver *Gardens for small country houses* 1913, 13–16.

High Ercall, Shropshire
C.L. v. 47, 1920, 234–36.

High Fearnley near Bradford, W. Yorks
I. Hall *Samuel Buck's Yorkshire sketchbook* 1979, 157.

High Glanau near Trellech, Gwent
C.L. v. 65, 1929, 251,822–29,854–60; v. 166, 1979, 2270–73. Lady Rockley *Historic gardens of England* 1938, 248–49.

High Grove, Reading, Berks
Florist 1856, 248–49.

High Legh Hall near Knutsford, Cheshire
W. Watts *Seats* 1779, pl. 64. *Landscape & Garden* v. 4 no. 3, 1937, 145–49. D. Stroud *Humphry Repton* 1962, 78. G. Carter *et al. Humphry Repton* 1982, 150.

High Leigh, Hoddesdon, Herts
J. Hort. Cottage Gdnr v. 34, 1865, 292–93.

High Street House, Chiddingstone, Kent
J. Harris *History of Kent* 1719, 75.

High Trees, Redhill, Surrey
G.C. ii 1904, 86–87.

Higham Ferrers, Northants
Northamptonshire Past and Present v. 5 no. 3, 1975, 226–27.

Higham House, Walthamstow, Waltham Forest, London
F.G. Emmison *Catalogue of maps in Essex Record Office* 2nd Supplt, 1964, 29.

Highams, Woodford Green, Redbridge, London
D. Stroud *Humphry Repton* 1962, 170. G. Carter *et al. Humphry Repton* 1982, 151.

Highbury, Birmingham, W. Midlands
G.C. ii 1884, 519–20; ii 1894, 699–700; ii 1900, 193–94,208; ii 1904, 361–62,363,391–92; i 1905, 24. *J. Hort. Cottage Gdnr* N.S., v. 32, 1896, 227–33,234,235. *Garden* v. 60, 1901, 298–99. *Gdnrs Mag.* 1903, 255–56.

Highbury Barn, Islington, London
W. Wroth *London pleasure gardens of the eighteenth century* 1896, 161–66.

Highbury Fields *see* London

Highclere Castle, Highclere, Hants
A. Robertson *Topographical survey of the Great Road* pt. 1, 1792, 145–46. *G.M.* v. 7, 1831, 135; v. 10, 1834, 245–59. E.F. Prosser *Select illustrations of Hampshire* 1833. J.B. Burke *Visitation* v. 1, 1852, 1–2. *Florist* 1856, 276–77. *Garden* v. 1, 1872, 613–14. W. Robinson *English flower garden* 1883, xi–xii. G.C. ii 1894, 211–12. *J. Hort. Cottage Gdnr* N.S., v. 58, 1909, 298–99,305. *C.L.* v. 125, 1959, 1378–81; v. 126, 1959, 18–21; v. 168, 1980, 1471. N. Pevsner *and* D. Lloyd *Hampshire and the Isle of Wight* 1967, 290–91. R.I.B.A. *Catalogue* v. B. 1972, 23. D. Stroud *Capability Brown* 1975, 160. A. Paterson *Gardens of Britain* v. 2, 1978, 93–95.

Highcliffe Castle near Christchurch, Hants
W. Watts *Seats* 1779, pl. 55. F.O. Morris *Series of picturesque views* v. 5, 75. *C.L.* v. 91, 1942, 806–09.

Highcroft, Burley, Hants
A. Paterson *Gardens of Britain* v. 2, 1978, 95.

Highdown near Goring, W. Sussex
C.L. v. 58, 1925, 316–17; v. 81, 1937, 198–203. *Kew Bulletin* 1925, 1–6. F. Stern *A chalk garden* 1960. E. Hyams *English garden* 1964, 166–70. *J. Royal Hort. Soc.* 1967, 104–08. M. Allan *Fisons guide* 1970, 50–51. *Sussex Life* v. 6 no. 3, 1970, 62–63.

Higher Leigh Manor, Combe Martin, Devon
Garden 1982, 322–23.

Higher Trap, Padiham, Lancs
G. Beard *Thomas H. Mawson* 1976, 55.

Highfield, Gloucester, Glos
J.N. Brewer *Elineations of Gloucestershire* 1825, 195.

Highgate Cemetery, Haringey, London
R.I.B.A. J. April 1968, 179–83. C.L. v. 159, 1976, 848–50. Friends of Highgate Cemetery *Highgate Cemetery* 1978. J.S. Curl *Celebration of death* 1980, 224–27.

Highgrove near Tetbury, Glos
J.N. Brewer *Delineations of Gloucestershire* 1825, 193.

Highhead Castle, Ivegill, Cumbria
C.L. v. 50, 1921, 480–87.

Highlands, Ticehurst, E. Sussex
T.W. Horsfield *History . . . of Sussex* v. 1, 1835, 590.

Highlands *see* Hylands

Highmount, Guildford, Surrey
G. Jekyll *and* L. Weaver *Gardens for small country houses* 1913, 46–54.

Highnam Court, Highnam, Glos
S. Rudder *New history of Gloucestershire* 1779, 342. J.N. Brewer *Delineations of Gloucestershire* 1825, 143. *Florist* 1855, 136–39. G.C. ii 1892, 177–78. C.L. v. 5, 1899, 400–04; v. 14, 1903, 644–46; v. 107, 1950, 1376–80. *Garden* v. 65, 1904, 424,425. D. Verey *Gloucestershire* v. 2, 1970, 271. V.C.H. *Gloucester* v. 10, 1972, 20.

Hildersham Hall, Hildersham, Cambs
V.C.H. *Cambridge* v. 6, 1978, 63.

Hill (Hull) near Berkeley, Glos
R. Atkyns *Ancient and present state of Glostershire* 1712, 479.

Hill, Hampstead, Camden, London
T.H. Mawson *Art & craft of garden making* 1907, 65,79,113,216,236,271,272–77. G.C. ii 1912, 482–83. *Architectural Review* v. 34, 1913, pls. 12–13. C.L. v. 43, 1918, 186–93. G. Beard *Thomas H. Mawson* 1976, 20–21,55.

Hill Court near Ross, Hereford and Worcester
C.L. v. 139, 1966, 286–89.

Hill End, Hitchin, Herts
J. Brown *Gardens of a golden afternoon* 1982, 171.

Hill Hall, Theydon Mount, Essex
P. Muilman *History of Essex* v. 3, 1770, 391. W. Watts *Seats* 1779, pl. 18. P. Morant *History . . . of Essex* v. 1, 1816, 157. J.P. Neale *Views* 2nd Series, v. 1, 1824. G. Virtue *Picturesque beauties of Great Britain: Essex* 1831, 35. T. Wright *History . . . of Essex* v. 2, 1836, 370. C.L. v. 20, 1906, 18–27; v. 41, 1917, 448–54,472–77, 496. G. Jekyll *Garden ornament* 1918, 117. V.C.H. *Essex* v. 4, 1956, 281. G. Carter *et al. Humphry Repton* 1982, 15.

Hill House, Braintree, Essex
F.G. Emmison *Catalogue of maps in Essex Record Office* 2nd Supplt, 1964, 32.

Hill House, Wickwar, Glos
C.L. v. 161, 1977, 1798–99. A. Lees-Milne *and* R. Verey *Englishman's garden* 1980, 146–48. J. Sales *West Country gardens* 1980, 72–74.

Hill House, Stanstead Abbots, Herts
R. Bisgrove *Gardens of Britain* v. 3, 1978, 96–97.

Hill House, Bromley, London
J. Hassell *Seats near London* 1804–05.

Hill House, Streatham, Lambeth, London
W. Keane *Beauties of Surrey* 1849, 80–81.

Hill House, Langport, Somerset
J. Hort. Cottage Gdnr N.S., v. 15, 1887, 278–79.

Hill of Tarvit, Cupar, Fife
C.L. v. 32, 1912, 926–31; v. 172, 1982, 442–45. G.A. Little *Scotland's gardens* 1981, 152–53.

Hill Park *see* Valence

Hill Pasture near Broxted, Essex
C.L. v. 129, 1961, 1202–04. M. Allan *Fisons guide* 1970, 207.

Hill Top, Oxenholme, Cumbria
G. Beard *Thomas H. Mawson* 1976, 55.

Hillbarn House, Great Bedwyn, Wilts
C.L. v. 163, 1978, 966–68. J. Sales *West Country gardens* 1980, 213–14.

Hillfield Gardens near Reigate, Surrey
G.C. 1872, 1557–59, 1621–22.

Hillier Arboretum, Romsey, Hants
M. Allan *Fisons guide* 1970, 98. C.L. v. 164, 1978, 610–12. *International Dendrology Society Year Book* 1978, 7–16.

Hillingdon Court, Uxbridge, Hillingdon, London
Florist 1856, 243–44. G.C. i 1907, 319–20. *J. Hort. Home Farmer* N.S., v. 66, 1913, 564–65.

Hillingdon House, Uxbridge, Hillingdon, London
Copper Plate Mag. v. 1, 1792, pl. 46. W. Keane *Beauties of Middlesex* 1850, 150–51, 191–93. *Cottage Gdnr* v. 14, 1855, 310–12.

Hillingdon Place, Uxbridge, Hillingdon, London
Gdning World v. 1, 1884, 199.

Hillington Hall, Hillington, Norfolk
J. Grigor *Eastern arboretum* 1841, 178–83. G.C. ii 1893, 771–72.

Hills, W. Sussex
D. Stroud *Capability Brown* 1975, 118, 229.

Hillsborough, Co. Down, Ulster
Ulster Architectural Heritage Society *Northern gardens* 1982, 20.

Hillside, Sevenoaks, Kent
G.C. ii 1947, 22.

Hillside, Four Oaks, W. Midlands
G.C. v. 161 no. 22, 1967, 20–21. R. Webber *Percy Cane* 1975, 144, 152.

Hillside House, Ceres, Fife
G.A. Little *Scotland's gardens* 1981, 153.

Hilly Fields *see* London

Hilton, Cambs
D. Stroud *Capability Brown* 1975, 229.

Hilton Castle *see* Hylton

Hilton House, Cupar, Fife
G.A. Little *Scotland's gardens* 1981, 153–54.

Hilton Park, Essington, Staffs
W. Pitt *General view of agriculture of . . . Stafford* 1796, 96. G. Carter *et al. Humphry Repton* 1982, 161.

Himley Hall, Himley, Staffs
W. Pitt *General view of agriculture of . . . Stafford* 1796, 94. S. Shaw *History . . . of Staffordshire* v. 2, 1801, 224. D. Stroud *Capability Brown* 1975, 154.

Hinchingbrooke near Huntingdon, Cambs
S. *and* N. Buck *Buck's antiquities* v. 1, 1774, pl. 119. J.P. Neale *Views* v. 2, 1819. G.C. ii 1881, 751–52, 756, 757. *Gdnrs Mag.* 1905, 21–25. C.L. v. 22, 1907, 630–36; v. 65, 1929, 482–88. V.C.H. *Huntingdon* v. 2, 1932, 136. C. Fiennes *Journeys* 1949, 67. P.G.M. Dickinson *Maps in the County Record Office, Huntingdon* 1968, 20.

Hindhead Court near Haslemere, Surrey
M. Parsons *English house grounds* 1924, 55–59.

Hindlip Hall, Hindlip, Hereford and Worcester
J. Hort. Cottage Gdnr v. 48, 1872, 447–50. G.C. i 1887, 475–76.

Hintlesham Hall, Hintlesham, Suffolk
H. Davy *Views* 1827. C.L. v. 64, 1928, 232–38.

Hinton Admiral near Christchurch, Hants
C. Holme *Gardens of England in Southern & Western counties* 1907, pls. 74–76. C.L. v. 28, 1910, 494–98. G. Jekyll *Garden ornament* 1918, 157.

Hinton Ampner House, Hinton Ampner, Hants
C.L. v. 101, 1947, 326–29; v. 122, 1957, 536–38. P. Coats *Great gardens of Britain* 1967, 166–73. A. Paterson *Gardens of Britain* v. 2, 1978, 98–100. A. Lees-Milne *and* R. Verey *Englishman's garden* 1982, 52–55.

Hinton Hall, Haddenham, Cambs
Proc. Cambridgeshire Antiquarian Soc. v. 67, 1977, 85–102.

Hinton House, Hinton Charterhouse, Avon
Historical MSS Commission *Architectural history* v. 3, 1971, item 2920.

Hinton House, Hinton St George, Somerset
J. Collinson *History . . . of Somersetshire* v. 2, 1791, 165. J.P. Neale *Views* 2nd Series, v. 4, 1828. V.C.H. *Somerset* v. 4, 1978, 42.

Hinton St Mary Manor, Dorset
A. Paterson *Gardens of Britain* v. 2, 1978, 32.

Hinton Waldrist, Oxfordshire
C.L. v. 92, 1942, 1130–33.

Hinwick Hall, Hinwick, Beds
C.L. v. 30, 1911, 628–34.

Hinwick House, Hinwick, Beds
C.L. v. 128, 1960, 618–21,676,733. J. Harris *Artist and the country house* 1979, 151.

Hirsel near Coldstream, Borders
H. Maxwell *Scottish gardens* 1911, 73–76. *C.L.* v. 76, 1934, 698–700. G.A. Little *Scotland's gardens* 1981, 88–89.

Hitcham Grange near Maidenhead, Bucks
J. Hort. Cottage Gdnr N.S., v. 42, 1901, 478,479.

Hitchin Priory, Hitchin, Herts
C.L. v. 58, 1925, 592–98.

Hitherbury, Guildford, Surrey
C.L. v. 10, 1901, 297–300.

Hoar Cross Hall, Burton upon Trent, Staffs
C.L. v. 11, 1902, 592–600. C. Holme *Gardens of England in Midland & Eastern counties* 1908, pls. 75–76. M. Binney *and* A. Hills *Elysian gardens* 1979, 2. R. Sidwell *West Midland gardens* 1981, 167–68.

Hockley House, Bramdean, Hants
A. Paterson *Gardens of Britain* v. 2, 1978, 101.

Hoddington House near Basingstoke, Hants
E.F. Prosser *Select illustrations of Hants* 1833.

Hodges, Shipton Moyne, Glos
C.L. v. 141, 1967, 502–04. *J. Royal Hort. Soc.* 1967, 382–88. J. Sales *West Country gardens* 1980, 74–77.

Hodnet Hall, Hodnet, Shropshire
Official guide. *C.L.* v. 123, 1958, 1416–17. *J. Royal Hort. Soc.* 1958, 498–503. M. Allan *Fisons guide* 1970, 277–78. B. Jones *Follies & grottoes* 1974, 277–78. *G.C.* v. 186 no. 12, 1979, 35–37. R. Sidwell *West Midland gardens* 1981, 121–25.

Hodsock Priory near Blyth, Notts
J. Anthony *Gardens of Britain* v. 6, 1979, 96–97.

Hogarth House, Chiswick, Hounslow, London
J. MacGregor *Gardens of celebrities . . . in and around London* 1918, 227–36.

Hoghton Tower, Hoghton, Lancs
C.L. v. 17, 1905, 198–206. V.C.H. *Lancaster* v. 6, 1911, 46. J. Harris *Artist and the country house* 1979, 266. *Connoisseur* v. 207, 1981, 255–59.

Holbecks, Hadleigh, Suffolk
G. Carter *et al. Humphry Repton* 1982, 162.

Holcombe House, near Stroud, Glos
C.L. v. 88, 1940, 542–46.

Holcombe House, Hendon, Barnet, London
V.C.H. *Middlesex* v. 5, 1976, 7.

Holcot Manor, Holcot, Beds
V.C.H. *Bedford* v. 3, 1912, 386.

Holdenby House, Holdenby, Northants
C.L. v. 32, 1912, 528–38; v. 166, 1979, 1286–89,1398–1401,2144. *Architectural Review* v. 33, 1933, pl. 15. *Northamptonshire Past and Present* v. 5 no. 5, 1977, 389,390,392–95. M. Binney *and* A. Hills *Elysian gardens* 1979, 14. Royal Commission on Historical Monuments *Inventory of the historical monuments in . . . Northampton* v. 3, 1981, 106–09. C. Taylor *Archaeology of gardens* 1983, 43–46.

Holderness House, Humberside
G. Poulson *History . . . of Seigniory of Holderness* v. 2, 1841, 322,341.

Hole Park, Rolvenden, Kent
C. Greenwood *Epitome of county history . . . v. 1: Kent* 1838, 240. M. Allan *Fisons guide* 1970, 52–53. T. Wright *Gardens of Britain* v. 4, 1978, 65–66.

Holehird, Windermere, Cumbria
Official guide. G. Beard *Thomas H. Mawson* 1976, 55.

Holeyn Hall near Wylam, Northumberland
J. Hort. Cottage Gdnr v. 60, 1878, 390–91; N.S., v. 15, 1887, 340,341.

Holker Hall, Holker, Cumbria
E. Baines *History . . . of Lancaster* v. 4, 1836, 733. F.O. Morris *Series of picturesque views* v. 6, 41. M. Allan *Fisons guide* 1970, 249. Historical MSS Commission *Architectural history* v. 4, 1972, item 4144. G. Beard *Thomas H. Mawson* 1976, 26,55. *C.L.* v. 167, 1980, 1470–73.

Holkham Hall, Holkham, Norfolk
A. Young *Six weeks tour through Southern counties of England and Wales* 1768, 20–21. *Description of Holkham House* 1775. D. Defoe *Tour* v. 1, 1778, 63. W. Watts *Seats* 1779, pl. 39. Duke of Rutland *Journal of a tour to the northern parts of Great Britain* 1813, 27–29. J. Blome *New description of Holkham* 1816. J. Dawson *Stranger's guide to Holkham* 1817. R. Havell *Series of picturesque views* 1818, pl. 16. J.C. Loudon *Encyclopaedia of gardening* 1822, 1235. *General history of County of Norfolk* v. 2, 1829, 591–92. *G.M.* v. 16, 1840, 666–67. J. Grigor *Eastern arboretum* 1841, 69–76. J.B. Burke *Visitation* 2nd Series, v. 1, 1855, 72–73. E.A. Brooke *Gardens of England* 1857, pls. 29–30. *C.L.* v. 2, 1897,

Holkham Hall (*Cont.*)

752–54; v. 23, 1908, 822–34; v. 130, 1961, 1143; v. 143, 1968, 1310–14; v. 156, 1974, 1554–57,1642–45; v. 167, 1980, 298–301. G.C. i 1898, 86–87. G. Jekyll *Garden ornament* 1918, 162. J. Lees-Milne *Earls of creation* 1962, 244–47. N. Pevsner *North-West and South Norfolk* 1962, 203–04. D. Stroud *Humphry Repton* 1962, 36–38. *Publications of Bedfordshire Historical Record Soc.* v. 47, 1968, 143–44. M. Allan *Fisons guide* 1970, 196–97. J. Harris *Catalogue of British drawings . . . in American collections* 1971, 176. *Apollo* v. 100, 1974, 136. B. Jones *Follies & grottoes* 1974, 361. D. Stroud *Capability Brown* 1975, 229. R.I.B.A. *Catalogue* v. S, 1976, 20. *Gdn History* v. 6 no. 2, 1978, 22–25. M. Binney *and* A. Hills *Elysian gardens* 1979, 16. L. Fleming *and* A. Gore *English garden* 1979, 128–29, pl. 108. *Landscape Design* no. 129, 1980, 26–29. G. Carter *et al. Humphry Repton* 1982, 159.

Holland House, Kensington, London
R. Havell *Series of picturesque views* 1817, pl. 12. W. Keane *Beauties of Middlesex* 1850, 131–35. C. McIntosh *Book of the garden* 1853–55, pl. 24. *J. Hort. Cottage Gdnr* v. 34, 1865, 256–57; v. 48, 1872, 150–52; v. 51, 1874, 35–37; N.S., v. 42, 1901, 213–17. *Garden* v. 4, 1873, 483–84; v. 53, 1898, 335–36,339; v. 61, 1902, 423–25. G.C. ii 1884, 5–6,17; i 1899, 225,227,229,267–68,269; i 1902, 425–28,429,431,436, 437; ii 1910, 233; ii 1921, 23. *Gdning World* v. 7, 1891, 745; v. 18, 1902, 685. C.L. v. 1, 1897, 632–34; v. 13, 1903, 272–80. C. Dixon *Catalogue of plants* 1901. *Gdnrs Mag.* 1902, 401–06; 1916, 116–17. H.I. Triggs *Formal gardens in England and Scotland* 1902, 33–34. M.R. Gloag *Book of English gardens* 1906, 221–40. C. Holme *Gardens of England in Southern & Western counties* 1907, pls. 77–81. G. Jekyll *Garden ornament* 1918, 174. J. MacGregor *Gardens of celebrities . . . in and around London* 1918, 198–226. J. Harris *Catalogue of British drawings . . . in American collections* 1971, 21. *J. Gdn History* v. 3 no. 2, 1983, 130–33.

Holland Park *see* London

Hollies near Leeds, W. Yorks
K. Lemmon *Gardens of Britain* v. 5, 1978, 169–71.

Hollingbury Park *see* Brighton

Holly Grove House, Windsor, Berks
R. Ackermann *Repository* v. 2, 1823, pl. 8. W.W.J. Gendall *Views* v. 2, 1830, 61–62.

Holly Hill near Stoke Poges, Bucks
G.C. i 1914, 334.

Holly Hill near Forest Row, E. Sussex
J. Hort. Home Farmer N.S., v. 67, 1913, 371–72,373.

Hollybrook House, Skibbereens, Co. Cork, Eire
E. Malins *and* P. Bowe *Irish gardens and demesnes* 1980, 152–53.

Hollywell Lodge, Co. Cavan, Eire
J.P. Neale *Views* v. 6, 1823.

Holmbush, Beeding, W. Sussex
T.W. Horsfield *History . . . of Sussex* v. 2, 1835, 222. J.B. Burke *Visitation* v. 1, 1852, 24.

Holme, Cliviger, Lancs
T.D. Whitaker *History of the original parish of Whalley and Honor of Clitheroe* 1818, 353.

Holme, Regent's Park, London
R. Ackermann *Repository* v. 12, 1828, pl. 19. J. Elmes *Metropolitan improvements* 1828. W.W.J. Gendall *Views* v. 1, 1830, 70. W. Keane *Beauties of Middlesex* 1850, 30–33. C.L. v. 86, 1939, 444–48.

Holme Lacy, Hereford and Worcester
S. Shaw *Tour to West of England in 1788* In J. Pinkerton, v. 2, 1808, 217. F.O. Morris *Series of picturesque views* v. 1, 27. *J. Hort. Cottage Gdnr* v. 58, 1877, 493–95; v. 59, 1878, 10–13,50–52; N.S., v. 67, 1913, 353–55. G.C. i 1897, 79–80. C.L. v. 2, 1899, 80–85; v. 25, 1909, 870–78. G. Jekyll *Garden ornament* 1918, 131, 270–71,328,415.

Holme Park, Sonning, Berks
H. Repton *Sketches* 1794, 85–86. J.P. Neale *Views* 2nd Series, v. 4, 1828. *Jones's views* 1829. *Gdning World* v. 11, 1894, 168. D. Stroud *Humphry Repton* 1962, 80. G. Carter *et al. Humphry Repton* 1982, 148.

Holme Pierrepont Hall near Nottingham, Notts
J.P. Neale *Views* v. 3, 1820. *Jones's views* 1829. C.L. v. 166, 1979, 842–45. J. Anthony *Gardens of Britain* v. 6, 1979, 97–98. M. Binney *and* A. Hills *Elysian gardens* 1979, 53. N. Pevsner *Nottinghamshire* 1979, 148.

Holmefield, Aigburth, Merseyside
L. Fleming *and* A. Gore *English garden* 1979, 199.

Holmes, St Boswells, Borders
G.A. Little *Scotland's gardens* 1981, 89–91.

Holmesdale House near Reigate, Surrey
W. Keane *Beauties of Surrey* 1849, 68–69.

Holmewood, Cheshunt, Herts
G.C. ii 1897, 338–39; i 1901, 280–82.

Holt, Upham, Hants
C.L. v. 135, 1964, 1396–99,1472.

Holt, Harrow Weald, Harrow, London
G.C. ii 1908, 276–77.

Holt Castle, Holt, Hereford and Worcester
C.L. v. 88, 1940, 54–57.

Holwood, Keston, Bromley, London
H. Repton *Sketches* 1794, 57–58. *Copper Plate Mag.* v. 2, pl. 72. R. Ackermann *Repository* v. 12, 1828, pl. 32. J.P. Neale *Views* 2nd Series, v. 4, 1828. W.W.J. Gendall *Views* v. 1, 1830, 108. *Gdning World* v. 5, 1888, 134. G.C. ii 1890, 745–46. D. Stroud *Humphry Repton* 1962, 69. G. Carter *et al. Humphry Repton* 1982, 155.

Holyrood Palace, Edinburgh, Lothian
J.C. Loudon *Arboretum et fruticetum Britannicum* v. 1, 1844, 94–95. C. Ward *Royal gardens* 1912, 91–104. *Scottish Gdnr and Northern Forester* v. 8, 1913, 417–19. E.S. Rohde *Story of the garden* 1932, 125. L. Roper *Royal gardens* 1953, 94–96. C.L. v. 161, 1977, 1386.

Holywell House near St Albans, Herts
Historical MSS Commission *Architectural history* v. 2, 1970, item 2045.

Home Close, Sibford, Oxfordshire
Architectural Review v. 51, 1922, 178–79.

Home House, Worthing, W. Sussex
G.C. ii 1894, 345. *Worthing Gazette* 15 March 1950.

Home Place, Holt, Norfolk
C.L. v. 26, 1909, 634–42. *Garden* 1920, 587.

Home Place, Limpsfield, Surrey
G.C. ii 1903, 206.

Homestall, East Grinstead, W. Sussex
C.L. v. 73, 1933, 99.

Homewood, Knebworth, Herts
L. Weaver *Houses and gardens by E.L. Lutyens* 1913, 63–67. J. Brown *Gardens of a golden afternoon* 1982, 165.

Honiley near Warwick, Warwickshire
W. Dugdale *Antiquities of Warwickshire* v. 2, 1730, 644.

Honing Hall, Honing, Norfolk
G.M. v. 17, 1841, 272. J. Grigor *Eastern arboretum* 1841, 229–30. D. Stroud *Humphry Repton* 1962, 66. G. Carter *et al. Humphry Repton* 1982, 159.

Honingham Hall, Honingham, Norfolk
J. Grigor *Eastern arboretum* 1841, 288–92.

Honington Hall, Honington, Warwickshire
J.P. Neale *Views* 2nd Series, v. 1, 1824. C.L. v. 15, 1904, 942–52; v. 48, 1920, 630–36; v. 164, 1978, 1082–85. G. Jekyll *Garden ornament* 1918, 287. J. Harris *Gardens of delight* 1978, 42–44. M. Hadfield *et al. British gardeners* 1980, 206.

Honsdon House *see* Hunsdon House

Hoo, St Paul's Walden, Herts
H. Chauncy *Historical antiquities of Hertfordshire* 1700, 510. R.I.B.A. *Catalogue* v. B, 1972, 113. D. Stroud *Capability Brown* 1975, 229–30. N. Pevsner *Hertfordshire* 1977, 331.

Hoo, Willingdon, E. Sussex
L. Weaver *Houses and gardens by E.L. Lutyens* 1913, 118–20. A.S. Butler *Architecture of Sir Edwin Lutyens* v. 2, 1950, 14. J. Brown *Gardens of a golden afternoon* 1982, 166.

Hook near Titchfield, Hants
E.F. Prosser *Select illustrations of Hampshire* 1833.

Hook End Farm, Checkendon, Oxfordshire
Gdn Design 1933, 9–13.

Hook Norton Manor, Hook Norton, Oxfordshire
R. Bisgrove *Gardens of Britain* v. 3, 1978, 98.

Hoole House, Chester, Cheshire
G.M. v. 14, 1838, 353–63. J.C. Loudon *Villa gardener* 1850, 315–27. G.C. ii 1882, 747, 753.

Hooton near Birkenhead, Cheshire
W. Watts *Seats* 1779, pl. 23. D. Stroud *Humphry Repton* 1962, 78. R.I.B.A. *Catalogue* v. B, 1972, 115. G. Carter *et al. Humphry Repton* 1982, 150.

Hooton Roberts near Rotherham, S. Yorks
J. Kip *Nouveau theatre de la Grande Bretagne* v. 4, 1729. J. Harris *Artist and the country house* 1979, 149.

Hop Castle, Chieveley, Berks
B. Jones *Follies & grottoes* 1974, 288.

Hope End, Ledbury, Hereford and Worcester
Gdn History v. 8 no. 1, 1980, 64–65.

Hopetoun House near South Queensferry, Lothian
Official guide. W. Gilpin *Observations relative chiefly to picturesque beauty* v. 1, 1792, 68–70. J.C. Loudon *Arboretum et fruticetum Britannicum* v. 1, 1844, 102. R. Pococke *Tours in Scotland* 1887, 298. G.C. i 1896, 453–54; ii 1905, 196–97. *Gdnrs Mag.* 1906, 675–81; 1911, 431–33. *J. Hort. Cottage Gdnr* N.S., v. 46, 1903, 223–27. C.L. v. 119, 1956, 16–19. *Park Administration*

Hopetoun House (*Cont.*)
no. 10, 1966, 52–53. M. Allan *Fisons guide* 1970, 325. C. McWilliam *Lothian* 1978, 258. A.A. Tait *Landscape garden in Scotland* 1980, passim. G.A. Little *Scotland's gardens* 1981, 91–92.

Hopton Court near Worcester, Hereford and Worcester
J. Loudon *Treatise on forming, improving and managing country residences* v. 2, 1806, pls. 29–30.

Hopton Hall near Wirksworth, Derbyshire
B. Jones *Follies & grottoes* 1974, 308.

Hopton House, Hambledon, Hants
B. Jones *Follies & grottoes* 1974, 336.

Horham Hall near Thaxted, Essex
G. Virtue *Picturesque beauties of Great Britain: Essex* 1831, 30. T. Wright *History . . . of Essex* v. 2, 1836, 236. *C.L.* v. 18, 1905, 18–25.

Hornby Castle, Hornby, N. Yorks
F.O. Morris *Series of picturesque views* v. 5, 1.

Horseheath Hall, Horseheath, Cambs
V.C.H. *Cambridge* v. 6, 1978, 72.

Horsford Hall, Horsford, Norfolk
J. Grigor *Eastern arboretum* 1841, 135–36.

Horsted Place, Little Horsted, E. Sussex
C.L. v. 124, 1958, 276–79; v. 154, 1973, 6–8. T. Wright *Gardens of Britain* v. 4, 1978, 152–53.

Horton Court near Chipping Sodbury, Avon
C.L. v. 71, 1932, 122–27.

Horton House, Horton, Northants
J.P. Neale *Views* v. 3, 1820. R.I.B.A. *Catalogue* v. G-K, 1973, 13. B. Jones *Follies & grottoes* 1974, 139–40. T. Wright *Arbours & grottoes* 1979. Royal Commission on Historical Monuments *Inventory of historical monuments in . . . Northampton* v. 2, 1979, 66–69, pl. 21. C. Taylor *Archaeology of gardens* 1983, 61.

Horwood House, Little Horwood, Bucks
C.L. v. 54, 1923, 644–51.

Hotham Hall, Hotham, Humberside
K. Lemmon *Gardens of Britain* v. 5, 1978, 40.

Hotham House, Hotham, Humberside
K. Lemmon *Gardens of Britain* v. 5, 1978, 40–41.

Hothfield Place, Hothfield, Kent
J. Hort. Cottage Gdnr v. 48, 1872, 467–68.

Houghton Hall, Sancton, Humberside
C.L. v. 138, 1965, 1734–37, 1782. R.I.B.A. *Catalogue: Lutyens* 1973, 24. K. Lemmon *Gardens of Britain* v. 5, 1978, 42.

Houghton Hall, Houghton, Norfolk
C. Campbell *Vitruvius Britannicus* v. 3, 1725, 27–28. I. Ware *Plans, elevations and sections . . . of Houghton in Norfolk* 1735. W. Watts *Seats* 1779, pl. 46. H. Walpole *Essay on modern gardening* 1785, 53,55. J.P. Neale *Views* v. 3, 1820. J. Grigor *Eastern arboretum* 1841, 192–97. *C.L.* v. 49, 1921, 14–22; v. 131, 1962, 526. P. Willis *Charles Bridgeman* 1977, 180. *Architectural History* v. 7, 1964, 29–30,72.

Houghton Lodge near Stockbridge, Hants
C.L. v. 109, 1951, 1190–93.

Houghton Park House, Beds
T. Fisher *Collections . . . for Bedfordshire* 1812–36.

Houndsell Place near Wadhurst, E. Sussex
C.L. v. 124, 1958, 126–29.

Houndstall House, Mark Cross, E. Sussex
C.L. v. 43, 1918, 108–14.

Houndwood House, Reston, Borders
G.A. Little *Scotland's gardens* 1981, 92.

House (Sir Frederick Gibberd), Harlow, Essex
G.C. v. 161 no. 12, 1967, 16–18. *C.L.* v. 168, 1980, 2340–42.

House-in-the-Wood, Bartley, Hants
M. Allan *Fisons guide* 1970, 95.

House of Pitmuies, Friockheim, Tayside
G.A. Little *Scotland's gardens* 1981, 193–96.

House of Urrard, Killiecrankie, Tayside
G.A. Little *Scotland's gardens* 1981, 154.

Hove. Athaeum, E. Sussex
A. Dale *Fashionable Brighton 1820–1860* 1947, 153–55, pls. 33, 74. J. and J. Ford *Images of Brighton* 1981, 119–20.

Hove. Brunswick Square, E. Sussex
A. Dale *Fashionable Brighton 1820–1860* 1947, 118,132, pls. 58,60.

Hove. Chalybeate Spring, E. Sussex
J. and J. Ford *Images of Brighton* 1981, 76–77.

Hoveton Hall, Hoveton St Peter, Norfolk
J. Grigor *Eastern arboretum* 1841, 162–63. G. Carter *et al. Humphry Repton* 1982, 159. *Garden* 1983, 365.

Hoveton House, Hoveton St John, Norfolk
G.M. v. 17, 1841, 271. J. Grigor *Eastern arboretum* 1841, 214. D. Stroud *Humphry Repton* 1962, 146–47,170. G. Carter *et al. Humphry Repton* 1982, 159.

Hovingham Hall, Hovingham, N. Yorks
Copper Plate Mag. v. 4, pl. 194. *C.L.* v. 17, 1905, 162–67; v. 62, 1927, 884–92. C. Holme *Gardens of England in Northern counties* 1911, pl. 58. Historical MSS Commission *Architectural history* v. 4, 1972, item 4156.

Howard's House, Cardington, Beds
R. Bisgrove *Gardens of Britain* v. 3, 1978, 98–99.

Howick House near Preston, Lancs
J. Hort. Cottage Gdnr v. 58, 1877, 110–111; N.S., v. 13, 1886, 542–44.

Howick Hall, Howick, Northumberland
F.O. Morris *Series of picturesque views* v. 6, 63. *G.C.* i 1884, 112. *J. Royal Hort. Soc.* 1974, 263–71. A. Lees-Milne *and* R. Verey *Englishwoman's garden* 1980, 72–77. *C.L.* v. 171, 1982, 952–54. T. Hinde *Stately gardens of Britain* 1983, 146–51.

Howsham Hall, Howsham, N. Yorks
J.P. Neale *Views* v. 5, 1822. *Jones's views* 1829, 20. F.O. Morris *Series of picturesque views* v. 1, 13. *C.L.* v. 17, 1905, 450–53; v. 78, 1935, 194–99,220.

Howth Castle near Dublin, Co. Dublin, Eire
T. Milton *Seats . . . in Ireland* 1783–93, 27. *Delineator* 1831, 53. *C.L.* v. 40, 1916, 14–21; v. 67, 1930, 743–46; v. 68, 1930, 286–92. *J. Royal Hort. Soc.* 1950, 316–17. M. Allan *Fisons guide* 1970, 358–59. E. Malins *and* Knight of Glin *Lost demesnes* 1976, 25,26. J. Harris *Artist and the country house* 1979, 178. Knight of Glin *and* P. Bowe *Gardens of outstanding historic interest in . . . Ireland* 1980. E. Malins *and* P. Bowe *Irish gardens and demesnes* 1980, 157–58. J. Brown *Gardens of a golden afternoon* 1982, 171.

Huddington Court, Huddington, Hereford and Worcester
C.L. v. 80, 1936, 116–22. Lady Rockley *Historic gardens of England* 1938, 94–95.

Hudson, Thomas *see* Twickenham

Hughenden Manor, High Wycombe, Bucks
F.O. Morris *Series of picturesque views* v. 5, 27. *G.C.* ii 1882, 425–26,432. *C.L.* v. 1, 1897, 463–65; v. 113, 1953, 1604–07; v. 171, 1982, 216–17. R. Bisgrove *Gardens of Britain* v. 3, 1978, 99–100. G.S. Thomas *Gardens of National Trust* 1979, 156–57.

Huish near Torrington, Devon
R. Ackermann *Repository* v. 11, 1828, pl. 26.
W.W.J. Gendall *Views* v. 2, 1830, 89.

Hull *see* Hill

Hull. Botanic Garden, Humberside
P.W. Watson *Dendrologia Britannica* v. 1, 1823, xii–xvi. T. Allen *New . . . history of . . . York* v. 2, 1831, 97. *J. Hort. Cottage Gdnr* v. 39, 1868, 424. *G.C.* i 1877, 599. *Garden* v. 23, 1883, 295–96.

Hulton Hall, Lancs
E. Baines *History . . . of Lancaster* v. 3, 1836, 40.

Hume Towers, Bournemouth, Dorset
G.C. i 1884, 733–34.

Humewood near Baltinglass, Co. Wicklow, Eire
Knight of Glin *and* P. Bowe *Gardens of outstanding historic interest in . . . Ireland* 1980.

Hungerdown House, Seagry, Wilts
M. Allan *Fisons guide* 1970, 96. *J. Royal Hort. Soc.* 1975, 12–20. R. Webber *Percy Cane* 1975, 83–87,186. J. Sales *West Country gardens* 1980, 215–18. A. Lees-Milne *and* R. Verey *Englishman's garden* 1982, 32–35. *C.L.* v. 173, 1983, 514–16.

Hungerton Hall, Hungerton, Lincs
Copper Plate Mag. v. 5, 1802, pl. 258. *G.M.* v. 16, 1840, 569–72.

Hunsdon House, Hunsdon, Herts
H. Chauncy *Historical antiquities of Hertfordshire* 1700, 195. J.P. Neale *Views* v. 2, 1819. J.E. Cussans *History of Hertfordshire* v. 1, 1870, 46.

Hunstanton Hall, Hunstanton, Norfolk
G.M. v. 17, 1841, 271. J. Grigor *Eastern arboretum* 1841, 198–99. *J. Hort. Cottage Gdnr* v. 52, 1874, 57–58. *C.L.* v. 8, 1900, 208–14; v. 59, 1926, 552–59. Lady Rockley *Historic gardens of England* 1938, 124–25.

Huntercombe Manor near Taplow, Bucks
Official guide. *C.L.* v. 5, 1899, 560–65; v. 105, 1949, 1374–77,1438–41. *G.C.* ii 1913, 353–54,402. J. Evelyn *Diary* v. 4, 1955, 177.

Huntfield, Biggar, Strathclyde
S.M. McCosh *Between two gardens: the diary of two Border gardens* 1982.

Hunting Lodge near Odiham, Hants
C.L. v. 173, 1983, 1093.

Huntington, Ascot Heath, Berks
C.L. v. 48, 1920, 287–88.

Hunton Court Lodge, Hunton, Kent
C. Greenwood *Epitome of county history . . . v. 1: Kent* 1838, 144.

Huntroyde Hall near Burnley, Lancs
J. Hort. Cottage Gdnr v. 34, 1865, 477–78; v. 35, 1866, 196–97.

Hurlingham House, Fulham, London
W. Keane *Beauties of Middlesex* 1850, 166–68. D. Stroud *Humphry Repton* 1962, 170. *G.C.* v. 192 no. 2, 1982, 28–29. G. Carter *et al. Humphry Repton* 1982, 157.

Hursley Park, Hursley, Hants
J.P. Neale *Views* v. 2, 1819. E.F. Prosser *Select illustrations of Hampshire* 1833. *C.L.* v. 12, 1902, 776–81; v. 26, 1909, 562–69. *G.C.* i 1904, 201–02.

Hurst Lodge, Hurst, Berks
R. Bisgrove *Gardens of Britain* v. 3, 1978, 100.

Hurst Mill, Petersfield, Hants
A. Paterson *Gardens of Britain* v. 2, 1978, 103–05.

Hurstbourne Priors near Andover, Hants
B. Jones *Follies & grottoes* 1974, 336. J. Harris *Artist and the country house* 1979, 197. L. Fleming and A. Gore *English garden* 1979, 86.

Hurstbourne Tarrant near Andover, Hants
W. Cobbett *Rural rides* v. 1, 1912, 7.

Hurstside, Molesey, Surrey
G.C. ii 1882, 491.

Hurts Hall near Saxmundham, Suffolk
H. Davy *Views* 1827.

Hurtwood, Holmbury St Mary, Surrey
C.L. v. 30, 1911, 742–79. G. Jekyll and L. Weaver *Gardens for small country houses* 1913, 75–76.

Husheath Manor near Goudhurst, Kent
C.L. v. 136, 1964, 154–56. P. Coats *Great gardens of Britain* 1967, 180–85. T. Wright *Gardens of Britain* v. 4, 1978, 66–68.

Hut, Munstead, Godalming, Surrey
J. Brown *Gardens of a golden afternoon* 1982, 161.

Hutton Bonville Hall, Hutton Bonville, N. Yorks
I. Hall *Samuel Buck's Yorkshire sketchbook* 1979, 391.

Hutton Hall, Hutton Lowcross, Cleveland
F.O. Morris *Series of picturesque views* v. 3, 15. *J. Hort. Cottage Gdnr* v. 63, 1880, 261–62. *Gdning World* v. 18, 1902, 285–86.

Hutton Hall, Hutton, Essex
P. Muilman *History of Essex* v. 5, 1772, 28. P. Morant *History . . . of Essex* v. 1, 1816, 195.

Hutton Hall, Hutton Wandesley (?), N. Yorks
I. Hall *Samuel Buck's Yorkshire sketchbook* 1979, 238.

Hutton-in-the-Forest, Cumbria
J. Beeverell *Les delices de la Grande Bretagne* v. 5, 1707, 872. L. Knyff and J. Kip *Britannia illustrata* v. 1, 1714. F.O. Morris *Series of picturesque views* v. 6, 11. *C.L.* v. 21, 1907, 18–29; v. 137, 1965, 232–35, 286–89, 352–56. G. Jekyll *Garden ornament* 1918, 59.

Hutton John near Dacre, Cumbria
M.R. Gloag *Book of English gardens* 1906, 243–56. C. Holme *Gardens of England in Northern counties* 1911, pls. 59–60. *C.L.* v. 65, 1929, 116–23. *G.C.* ii 1930, 41. Lady Rockley *Historic gardens of England* 1938, 100–101.

Hyde, East Hyde, Beds
C.G. v. 22, 1859, 386–88.

Hyde, Bridport, Dorset
J. Hutchins *History . . . of Dorset* v. 2, 1863, 12.

Hyde, Ingatestone, Essex
F.G. Emmison *Catalogue of maps in Essex Record Office* 2nd Supplt, 1964, 23.

Hyde near Handcross, W. Sussex
T. Wright *Gardens of Britain* v. 4, 1978, 154–55.

Hyde Crook, Frampton, Dorset
M. Allan *Fisons guide* 1970, 97. A. Paterson *Gardens of Britain* v. 2, 1978, 32–33.

Hyde Hall, Rettenden, Essex
C.L. v. 155, 1974, 1178–80.

Hyde Hall near Sawbridgeworth, Herts
H. Chauncy *Historical antiquities of Hertfordshire* 1700, 182. J.P. Neale *Views* v. 2, 1819.

Hyde Hall near Denton, Greater Manchester
J. Aikin *Description of the country . . . round Manchester* 1795, 451.

Hyde Park *see* London

Hylands (Highlands), Widford, Essex
J.P. Neale *Views* v. 1, 1818. G. Virtue *Picturesque beauties of Great Britain: Essex* 1831, 28. T. Wright *History . . . of Essex* v. 1, 1836, 164. G.C. i 1881, 763. D. Stroud *Humphry Repton* 1962, 170. F.G. Emmison *Catalogue of maps in Essex Record Office* 1st Supplt, 1952, 31; 2nd Supplt, 1964, 27. G. Carter *et al. Humphry Repton* 1982, 151.

Hylton Castle, Hylton, Tyne and Wear
J.P. Neale *Views* v. 1, 1818.

Ibstone House, Ibstone, Bucks
R. Bisgrove *Gardens of Britain* v. 3, 1978, 101.

Ickwell Bury, Ickwell, Beds
C.L. v. 117, 1955, 1174–77, 1234–37.

Ickworth near Bury St Edmunds, Suffolk
Official guide. *G.C.* ii 1881, 74–75, 104–05; ii 1911, 418. *C.L.* v. 18, 1905, 870–77; v. 58, 1925, 668–75; v. 117, 1955, 678–81. M. Allan *Fisons guide* 1970, 198–99. D. Stroud *Capability Brown* 1925, 230. G.S. Thomas *Gardens of National Trust* 1979, 157–58. J.L. Phibbs *Ickworth* National Trust, 1980.

Iford Manor, Iford, Wilts
C.L. v. 22, 1907, 450–61; v. 34, 1913, 484–85; v. 52, 1922, 242–48, 272–77; v. 133, 1963, 726; v. 151, 1972, 1214–16. *Architectural Review* v. 33, 1913, 11–14, 28–30, pls. 5–6, 10–11. G. Jekyll *Garden ornament* 1918, 144, 175. L. Fleming *and* A. Gore *English garden* 1979, 212–13. J. Sales *West Country gardens* 1980, 218–21.

Ightham Court, Ightham, Kent
J. Harris *History of Kent* 1719, 162. J. Kip *Supplement du Nouveau theatre de la Grande Bretagne* 1728, pl. 16. T. Badeslade *Thirty six different views . . . in Kent* 1750s, pl. 15. *C.L.* v. 123, 1958, 1424–27.

Ightham Mote, Ightham, Kent
Garden v. 27, 1885, 19, 30, 31, 34. *G.C.* i 1889, 135–36. *C.L.* v. 1, 1897, 406–09; v. 7, 1900, 336–41; v. 21, 1907, 414–25. Lady Rockley *Historic gardens of England* 1938, 84–85.

Ilam Hall, Ilam, Staffs
A. Young *Farmer's tour through East of England* v. 1, 1771, 190–91. J. Boswell *Life of Samuel Johnson* 1791 (entry at beginning of 1777). W. Pitt *General view of agriculture of . . . Stafford* 1796, 195–96. J. Nightingale *Topographical . . . description of Staffordshire* 1810, 976–80. W. Adam *Gem of the Peak* 1851, 217–20. F.O. Morris *Series of picturesque views* v. 1, 41.

Ilmington Manor, Ilmington, Warwickshire
C.L. v. 67, 1930, 399–400; v. 173, 1983, 1296–98. R. Sidwell *West Midland gardens* 1981, 214–15.

Ilnacullin *see* Garinish, Co. Cork

Ilsington House near Dorchester, Dorset
G.C. ii 1882, 265–66; i 1894, 350.

Ilsom near Tetbury, Glos
J. Sales *West Country gardens* 1980, 77–78.

Imber Court, Thames Ditton, Surrey
G.C. ii 1899, 305.

Imberhorne Park near East Grinstead, W. Sussex
Historical MSS Commission *Architectural history* v. 2, 1970, item 1610.

Impney Hall near Droitwich, Hereford and Worcester
G.C. ii 1881, 427; i 1890, 790; i 1904, 113–14. *J. Hort. Cottage Gdnr* N.S., v. 8, 1884, 266–67; N.S., v. 47, 1903, 288–89. *Garden* v. 64, 1903, 200, 201. *C.L.* v. 9, 1901, 592–98.

Ince Blundell Hall, Ince Blundell, Merseyside
J.P. Neale *Views* v. 2, 1819. *C.L.* v. 123, 1958, 816–19. N. Pevsner *Lancashire: 1* 1969, 129.

Ince Castle, Saltash, Cornwall
C.L. v. 141, 1967, 592–95, 648–51. P.M. Synge *Gardens of Britain* v. 1, 1977, 102–04. A. Lees-Milne *and* R. Verey *Englishwoman's garden* 1980, 41–44.

Inchmarlo, Banchory, Grampian
C.L. v. 162, 1977, 346–47. G.A. Little *Scotland's gardens* 1981, 196.

Inchyra House, Glencarse, Tayside
G.A. Little *Scotland's gardens* 1981, 154.

Inchrye near Newburgh, Fife
J.P. Neale *Views* v. 6, 1823.

Ingatestone Hall, Ingatestone, Essex
C.L. v. 83, 1937, 64–69. F.G. Emmison *Catalogue of maps in Essex Record Office* 1947, 1, 139.

Ingestre Hall, Ingestre, Staffs
Official guide. R. Plot *Natural history of Staffordshire* 1685, 225. J. Nightingale *Topographical . . . description of Staffordshire* 1810, 910. J.P. Neale *Views* v. 4, 1821. *J. Hort. Cottage Gdnr* v. 47, 1872, 215–18; N.S., v. 5, 1882, 366, 367–68. *G.C.* ii 1882, 140–42; ii 1891, 516–17; ii 1892, 581–82. *C.L.* v. 3, 1898, 720–23; v. 122, 1957, 772–75, 874–77, 924. C. Holme *Gardens of*

Ingestre Hall (*Cont.*)

England in Midland & Eastern counties 1908, pls. 77–78. M. Macartney *English houses & gardens* 1908, pl. 16. C. Fiennes *Journeys* 1949, 174. *Archaeological Journal* v. 120, 1963, 264. J. Harris *Catalogue of British drawings . . . in American collections* 1971, 65–66. D. Stroud *Capability Brown* 1975, 146–47,230.

Ingestre Rectory, Ingestre, Staffs
Historical MSS Commission *Architectural history* v. 4, 1972, item 4171.

Ingleborough (Reginald Farrer), N. Yorks
C.L. v. 62, 1927, 243–44.

Ingleby Manor, Ingleby Greenhow, N. Yorks
J. Beeverell *Les delices de la Grande Bretagne* v. 5, 1707, 872. L. Knyff *and* J. Kip *Britannia illustrata* v. 1, 1714. *G.C.* ii 1893, 233–34. M. Macartney *English houses & gardens* 1908, pl. 11. I. Hall *Samuel Buck's Yorkshire sketchbook* 1979, 312.

Ingress Abbey, Greenhithe, Kent
J. Harris *History of Kent* 1719, 309. J. Kip *Supplement du Nouveau theatre de la Grande Bretagne* 1728, pl. 18. T. Badeslade *Thirty six different views . . . in Kent* 1750s, pl. 16. W.B. Cooke *and* S. Owen *The Thames* v. 2, 1811. C. Greenwood *Epitome of county history . . . v. 1: Kent* 1838, 76. M. Macartney *English houses & gardens* 1908, pl. 53.

Inkpen Old Rectory, Inkpen, Berks
C.L. v. 93, 1943, 308–11,355. L. Fleming *and* A. Gore *English garden* 1979, 77.

Innes House near Elgin, Grampian
G.A. Little *Scotland's gardens* 1981, 196–98.

Intwood Hall, Intwood, Norfolk
J. Harris *Artist and the country house* 1979, 138.

Inveralmond House, Cramond, Lothian
Scottish Gdnr and Northern Forester v. 7, 1912, 255–56.

Inveraray Castle, Inveraray, Strathclyde
J.P. Neale *Views* v. 6, 1823. J.C. Loudon *Arboretum et fruticetum Britannicum* v. 1, 1844, 91–92. F.O. Morris *Series of picturesque views* v. 1, 75. *G.C.* ii 1876, 742, 777–78,836–38. *C.L.* v. 6, 1899, 304–08; v. 113, 1953, 2060–63. B. Faujas de Saint Fond *Journey* v. 1, 1907, 246. Historical MSS Commission *Architectural history* v. 1, 1969, items 139,494,682. A.A. Tait *Landscape garden in Scotland* 1980, passim.

Inveresk Lodge, Musselburgh, Lothian
G.C. i 1964, 427–28. M. Allan *Fisons guide* 1970, 326–27. J. *Royal Hort.Soc.* 1974, 202–05. G.A. Little *Scotland's gardens* 1981, 92–93.

Inverewe, Poolewe, Highland
Official guide. *C.L.* v. 106, 1949, 172–75. J.M. Cowan *Report on Inverewe Gardens* 1949. J. *Royal Hort. Soc.* 1950, 436–44; 1953, 243–45. J.M. Cowan *Inverewe* 1964. *G.C.* v. 160 no. 4, 1966, 10–11. M. Allan *Fisons guide* 1970, 341–42. P. Verey *Gardens of Scotland* 1976, 63–74. A. Hellyer *Gardens of genius* 1980, 50–53. D. Macleod *Oasis of the North: a Highland garden* ed. 3, 1980. G.A. Little *Scotland's gardens* 1981, 232–33.

Inverleith, Edinburgh, Lothian
C.L. v. 157, 1975, 332–33.

Invermay near Forteviot, Tayside
A.A. Tait *Landscape garden in Scotland* 1980, passim.

Inwood House near Stalbridge, Somerset
J. *Hort. Cottage Gdnr* N.S., v. 27, 1893, 311. *C.L.* v. 10, 1901, 112–19. *Garden* 1904, 184–85. C. Holme *Gardens of England in Southern & Western counties* 1907, pl. 82. G. Jekyll *Garden ornament* 1918, 35,123.

Ipswich (William Beeston Coyte), Suffolk
W.B. Coyte *Hortus botanicus Gippovicensis* 1796.

Ireland's Royal Brighton Gardens *see* Brighton

Iridge Place near Etchingham, E. Sussex
J.B. Burke *Visitation* v. 1, 1852, 172.

Irlam Hall, Irlam, Greater Manchester
E. Baines *History . . . of Lancaster* v. 3, 1836, 129.

Irnham Hall, Irnham, Lincs
J.P. Neale *Views* v. 2, 1819.

Isabella Plantation *see* Richmond Park

Island Gardens *see* London

Isle Hampstead *see* Latimers

Isleworth, Hordean, Hants
G. Beard *Thomas H. Mawson* 1976, 56.

Iselworth House, Hounslow, London
G.M. v. 13, 1837, 109–11. W. Keane *Beauties of Middlesex* 1850, 66–67.

Islington. Albert Park, London
G. Chadwick *Park and the town* 1966, 119–20,132–35, 221.

Islington Spa (New Tunbridge Wells), Clerkenwell, Islington, London
W. Wroth *London pleasure gardens of the eighteenth*

Islington Spa *(Cont.)*

century 1896, 15–24. E.B. Chancellor *Pleasure haunts of London* 1925, 385–87.

Islip Rectory, Islip, Oxfordshire
W. Kennett *Parochial antiquities . . . in . . . Ambrosden and Burcester* 1695, pl. 2.

Iver Grove, Iver, Bucks
R. Ackermann *Repository* v. 3, 1824, pl. 14.
W.W.J. Gendall *Views* v. 2, 1830, 11.

Ivies, Winchmore Hill, Enfield, London
G.C. i 1889, 779,781.

Ivy House, North End, Hampstead, London
R. Webber *Percy Cane* 1975, 70–71.

Iwerne Minster House, Iwerne Minster, Dorset
G.C. ii 1881, 471; ii 1898, 317–18. *Gdning World* v. 1, 1884, 215.

Jardine Hall near Lockerbie, Dumfries and Galloway
G.M. v. 9, 1833, 4–5.

Jarn Mound Gardens, Boars Hill, Oxford
M. Batey *Oxford gardens* 1982, 201–09.

Jasmine House, Hatch Bridge, Berks
R. Bisgrove *Gardens of Britain* v. 3, 1978, 102. *Garden* 1979, 97–100.

Jenkyn Place, Bentley, Hants
M. Parsons *English house grounds* 1924, 67–73. G.C. ii 1964, 172–73,177. C.L. v. 137, 1965, 1334–36.
A. Paterson *Gardens of Britain* v. 2, 1978, 105–09.

Jennings near Maidstone, Kent
P. Sandby *Collection of one hundred and fifty select views* v. 1, 1781, pl. 28.

Jenny's Whim, Pimlico, Westminster, London
W. Wroth *London pleasure gardens of the eighteenth century* 1896, 222–24.

Jermyns House *see* Hillier Arboretum

Jesmond Cemetery *see* Newcastle upon Tyne

Jesmond Dene, Jesmond, Tyne and Wear
C. Holme *Gardens of England in Northern counties* 1911, pls. 61–62.

Jodrell Hall near Middlewich, Cheshire
J. Hort. Cottage Gdnr N.S., v. 13, 1886, 537–38.

Johnstown Castle near Wexford, Co. Wexford, Eire
J. Harris *Artist and the country house* 1979, 359.

E. Malins *and* P. Bowe *Irish gardens and demesnes* 1980, 25–26. M.H. le Clerc *Trees and shrubs of the amenity lands of Johnstown Castle* 1980. Knight of Glin *and* P. Bowe *Gardens of outstanding historic interest in . . . Ireland* 1980.

Joldwynds near Gomshall, Surrey
G.C. ii 1881, 206. *Landscape and Gdn* v. 5, 1938, 221–23.

Jordanhill House, Glasgow, Strathclyde
A.A. Tait *Landscape garden in Scotland* 1980, passim.

Joymount, Carrickfergus, Co. Antrim, Ulster
Ulster J. of Archaeology v. 7, 1902, 96–97. C.L. Falkiner *Illustrations of Irish history and topography* 1904, 368–69.

Jubilee Gardens *see* Lambeth

Julians near Buntingford, Herts
C.L. v. 101, 1947, 1160–63; v. 102, 1947, 28–31.
P. Coats *Great gardens of Britain* 1967, 234–39.

Juniper Hill, Penn, Bucks
R. Bisgrove *Gardens of Britain* v. 3, 1978, 103.

Kailzie near Peebles, Borders
G.A. Little *Scotland's gardens* 1981, 93.

Kearnsey Court near Dover, Kent
T.H. Mawson *Art & craft of garden making* 1907, 94. *Architectural Review* v. 28, 1910, 71–72. G.C. i 1913, 438. G. Beard *Thomas H. Mawson* 1976, 56.

Keats House, Hampstead, London
Gdn History v. 3 no. 4, 1975, 35–39.

Kedleston Hall, Kedleston, Derbyshire
Official guide. A. Young *Farmer's tour through East of England* v. 1, 1771, 202–04. W. Watts *Seats* 1779, pl. 22. W. Bray *Sketch of a tour into Derbyshire* 1783, 116. J.P. Neale *Views* v. 1, 1818. W. Adam *Gem of the Peak* 1851, 203–05. G.M. v. 15, 1839, 450. L. Jewitt *and* S.C. Hall *Stately homes of England* 1877, 93–111. C.L. v. 10, 1901, 240–45; v. 34, 1913, 892–99; v. 163, 1978, 194–97. G. Jekyll *Garden ornament* 1918, 363. M. Allan *Fisons guide* 1970, 225. N. Pevsner *Derbyshire* 1978, 258. J. Anthony *Gardens of Britain* v. 6, 1979, 98–102. N. Nichols *Local maps of Derbyshire to 1770* 1980, 110. D. Watkin *English vision* 1982, 57.

Keele Hall, Keele, Staffs
F.O. Morris *Series of picturesque views* v. 3, 9. *Cottage Gdnr* v. 17, 1856, 106–08. *J. Hort. Cottage Gdnr* v. 30, 1863, 234–37,274–76. G.C. 1871, 1452–53; 1872, 109–12; ii 1883, 720–22; i 1893, 9,10–11,17,19; i 1916, 330–31. C.L. v. 23, 1908, 306–11.

Keevil Manor, Keevil, Wilts
G.C. i 1902, 141. C.L. v. 15, 1904, 702–08.

Keffolds, Haslemere, Surrey
G. Beard *Thomas H. Mawson* 1976, 56.

Keillour Castle near Methven, Tayside
C.L. v. 140, 1966, 372–74. G.A. Little *Scotland's gardens* 1981, 154–55.

Keir near Edinburgh, Lothian
Gdnrs Mag. 1900, 672–74.

Keir House near Dunblane, Central
Scottish Gdnr v. 4, 1855, 11–13. *J. Hort. Cottage Gdnr* N.S., v. 5, 1882, 550–52. G.C. i 1893, 537–38,545. *Garden* v. 60, 1901, 550–52. M. Allan *Fisons guide* 1970, 327–28. C.L. v. 158, 1975, 326–29,506–10. *Garden* 1980, 7–15. G.A. Little *Scotland's gardens* 1981, 155.

Keith Hall near Inverurie, Grampian
G.C. i 1878, 591–92,593,597.

Keithock, Brechin, Tayside
G.A. Little *Scotland's gardens* 1981, 198–99.

Kelburne Castle near Largs, Strathclyde
H. Maxwell *Scottish gardens* 1911, 144–48.

Keldgate Manor, Beverley, Humberside
K. Lemmon *Gardens of Britain* v. 5, 1978, 42–43.

Kelham Hall, Kelham, Notts
J.P. Neale *Views* v. 3, 1820. *Jones's views* 1829. F.O. Morris *Series of picturesque views* v. 4, 43. *Gdning World* v. 6, 1890, 756–57. J. Anthony *Gardens of Britain* v. 6, 1979, 102–03.

Kellaways near Chippenham, Wilts
J. Sales *West Country gardens* 1980, 221–23.

Kellie Castle near Pittenweem, Fife
G. Jekyll and G.S. Elgood *Some English gardens* 1905, 47–51. C.L. v. 20, 1906, 126–31; v. 168, 1980, 486–92. H. Maxwell *Scottish gardens* 1911, 91–95. P. Verney *Gardens of Scotland* 1976, 75–83. G.A. Little *Scotland's gardens* 1981, 155–56.

Kelling Place, Holt, Norfolk
Architectural Review v. 19, 1906, 70–75.

Kelly House, Tavistock, Devon
C.L. v. 6, 1899, 16–20.

Kelmarsh Hall, Kelmarsh, Northants
J.P. Neale *Views* v. 3, 1820. C.L. v. 73, 1933, 198–203.

Kelmscott House, Hammersmith, London
J. MacGregor *Gardens of celebrities . . . in and around London* 1918, 271–96.

Kelmscott Manor, Kelmscott, Oxfordshire
C.L. v. 50, 1921, 224–29,256–62.

Kelsey Manor, Beckenham, Bromley, London
Gdning World v. 4, 1887, 53–54.

Kelsterton, Clwyd
Garden v. 39, 1891, 209.

Kelston (Kelweston), near Bath, Avon
J. Collinson *History . . . of Somersetshire* v. 1, 1791, 128. D. Stroud *Capability Brown* 1975, 230.

Kelvedon Hall, Kelvedon Hatch, Essex
C.L. v. 89, 1941, 386–89; v. 131, 1962, 506–08. P. Coats *Great gardens of Britain* 1967, 174–79.

Kelweston *see* Kelston

Kemp Town Gardens *see* Brighton

Kempsford near Fairford, Glos
R. Atkyns *Ancient and present state of Glostershire* 1712, 490. L. Knyff and J. Kip *Britannia illustrata* v. 2, 1715. V.C.H. *Gloucester* v. 7, 1981, 99,101.

Kempshott Park near Basingstoke, Hants
E.F. Prosser *Select illustrations of Hampshire* 1833.

Kempton Park near Kingston upon Thames, Surrey
J.C. Loudon *Encyclopaedia of gardening* 1822, 1226.

Ken Hill near Snettisham, Norfolk
C.L. v. 142, 1967, 1654,1656.

Kenegie near Gulval, Cornwall
W. Borlase *Natural history of Cornwall* 1758, pl. 5.

Kenfield Hall near Petham, Kent
C. Greenwood *Epitome of county history . . . v. 1: Kent* 1838, 394. *J. Hort. Cottage Gdnr* v. 44, 1870, 145–47. G.C. ii 1884, 711–12. R.I.B.A. *Catalogue* v. G-K, 1973, 113.

Kenilworth Castle, Kenilworth, Warwickshire
W. Gilpin *Observations on several parts of England* v. 1, 1808, 48–49. E. Burritt *Walks in the Black Country and its green borderland* 1868, 406–12. A.F. Sieveking *Praise of gardens* 1899, 82–83. E.S. Rohde *Story of the garden* 1932, 82. *Medieval Archaeology* v. 8, 1964, 222–23; v. 9, 1965, 156–61. R. Strong *Renaissance garden in England* 1979, 50–51.

Kenmare House, Kenmare, Co. Kerry, Eire
G.C. ii 1887, 97–98.

Kenmure Castle near New Galloway, Dumfries and Galloway
Scottish Gdnr and Northern Forester v. 8, 1913, 167–68.

Kennington, Lambeth, London
H.M. Colvin History of the King's Works v. 2, 1963, 968.

Kennington Park see London

Kensal Green Cemetery, Brent, London
J.S. Curl Celebration of death 1980, 214–23.

Kensington Palace and Gardens see London

Kentchurch Court, Kentchurch, Hereford and Worcester
J.P. Neale Views 2nd Series, v. 4, 1828. Garden v. 13, 1878, 73. C.L. v. 140, 1966, 1632–35.

Kentish Town (William Stukeley), Camden, London
C.L. v. 174, 1983, 1248–50.

Kentwell Hall near Sudbury, Suffolk
C.L. v. 12, 1902, 464–71. M. Binney and A. Hills Elysian gardens 1979, 23.

Kenwood, Hampstead, Camden, London
Picturesque views of the principal seats 1788. Copper Plate Mag. v. 1, 1792, pl. 32. D. Lysons Environs of London v. 3, 1795, 349–50. H. Boswell Historical descriptions of new and picturesque views 1800. R. Ackermann Repository v. 5, 1825, pl. 30. W.W.J. Gendall Views v. 2, 1830, 76. W. Keane Beauties of Middlesex 1850, 60–65. J.C. Loudon Villa gardener 1850, 452–64. F.O. Morris Series of picturesque views v. 3, 37. G.C. ii 1921, 19,46. Architectural Review v. 58, 1925, 162–63. B. Jones Follies & grottoes 1974, 330. G. Carter et al. Humphry Repton 1982, 157.

Kepwick Hall near Thirsk, N. Yorks
K. Lemmon Gardens of Britain v. 5, 1978, 83–84.

Keswick Hall, Keswick, Norfolk
J. Grigor Eastern arboretum 1841, 271.

Ketteringham Park, Ketteringham, Norfolk
J. Grigor Eastern arboretum 1841, 278–80.

Kettlethorpe Hall near Wakefield, W. Yorks
B. Jones Follies & grottoes 1974, 251–52.

Ketton Cottage, Ketton, Leics
Garden v. 45, 1894, 41–42.

Kew (Sir Henry Capel), Richmond, London
Archaeologia v. 12, 1796, 185. J. Evelyn Diary v. 4, 144,347,576. See also Kew. Royal Botanic Gardens

Kew. Royal Botanic Gardens, Richmond, London
There are too many references to Kew Gardens in G.C. and J. Hort. Cottage Gdnr, etc. to list here. The Kewensia Collection at Kew should also be consulted for further references.
Official guide. T. Badeslade and J. Rocque Vitruvius Brittanicus 1739, pls. 9–10. Description of the royal gardens at Richmond in Surry c.1740s. W. Chambers Plans, elevations, sections, and perspective views of the gardens and buildings at Kew in Surry 1763. J. Hill Hortus Kewensis 1768. G. Bickham and P. Norbury Description of the Gardens and buildings at Kew c.1771. G.L. le Rouge Jardins Anglo-Chinois a la mode 2^e cahier, 1776, pls. 7,13,15; 4^e cahier, 1776, pls. 22–26; 6^e cahier, 1777, pls. 4–5,30; 7^e cahier, 1779, pl. 28. D. Defoe Tour v. 1, 1778, 227. New display of the beauties of England v. 2, 1787, 278–83. W. Aiton Hortus Kewensis 1789. W.T. Aiton Hortus Kewensis ed. 2, 1810–13. J. and J. Boydell History of the River Thames v. 2, 1796, 40–49. F.I. Mannskirsch Views of parks and gardens 1813, pls. 7–8. G.E. Papendick Kew Gardens c.1820. British Museum Catalogue of maps, prints 1829, 172. C.F. Partington National history and views of London v. 1, 1834, 53–55. E.W. Brayley and J. Britton Topographical history of Surrey v. 3, 144–51,171–72. P.H. Gosse Wanderings through the conservatories at Kew 1856. N. Cole Royal parks and gardens of London 1877, 47–52. J. Smith Records of Royal Botanic Gardens, Kew 1880. Bulletin of Miscellaneous Information, Kew [Kew Bulletin] no. 60, 1891, 279–327. F. Kielmansegge Diary 1902, 77–78. B. Faujas de Saint Fond Journey through England and Scotland v. 1, 1907, 77–85. Home Counties Mag. v. 7, 1907, 1–12,85–98,157–70,229–42. W.J. Bean Royal Botanic Gardens, Kew 1908. T.M. Martin Kew Gardens 1908. Art J. 1909, 201–06. V.C.H. Surrey v. 3, 1911, 485. H. Walpole Visits to country seats. Walpole Society v. 7, 1927/28, 23–24,38. Landscape and Garden v. 5 Spring 1936, 16–22. T. Jefferson Garden book 1766–1824 1944, 114. O. Siren China and gardens of Europe of 18th century 1950, 70–76. C.L. v. 67, 1930, 792–94; v. 125, 1959, 1260–62; v. 170, 1981, 401–05; v. 173, 1983, 1342–44. J. Royal Hort. Soc. 1959, 256–64; 1970, 335–48. W.B. Turrill Royal Botanic Gardens, Kew 1959. W.B. Turrill Joseph Dalton Hooker 1963. J. Kew Guild 1965, 576–87. M. Allan Hookers of Kew 1785–1911 1967. E. Hyams Great botanical gardens of the world 1969, 104–21. Historical MSS Commission Architectural history v. 2, 1970, item 1393; v. 5, 1974, items 5128,5229. J. Harris Catalogue of British drawings . . . in American collections 1971, 54–57. I. Nairn and B. Cherry Surrey 1971, 323–30. Kew Bulletin 1972, 295–303. R.I.B.A. Catalogue v. C-F, 1972, 17; v. L-N, 1973, 98; Wyatt family, 1974. H.M. Colvin History of

Kew. Royal Botanic Gardens (*Cont.*)

the King's Works v. 6, 1973, passim. M. Bingham *Making of Kew* 1975. R.W. King *World of Kew* 1976. L.M. Brockway *Science and colonial expansion* 1979. L. Fleming *and* A. Gore *English garden* 1979, 133–35. J. Harris *Artist and the country house* 1979, 277. M. Hadfield *et al. British gardeners* 1980, 62–65,66. *Arboricultural J.* v. 5, 1981, 173–88. *Gdn History* v. 9 no. 1, 1981, 50–55. *Garden* 1982, 173–80. *J. Gdn History* v. 2 no. 1, 1982, 44–45; no. 3, 1982, 233–72. N. Hepper *Royal Botanic Gardens, Kew* 1982. K. Rorschach *Early Georgian landscape garden* 1983, 64–73. B. Cherry *and* N. Pevsner *London 2: South* 1983, 506–12.
see also Richmond Gardens

Kexby, N. Yorks
I. Hall *Samuel Buck's Yorkshire sketchbook* 1979, 47.

Kidbrooke Park near East Grinstead, W. Sussex
J.P. Neale *Views* v. 4, 1821. *C.L.* v. 79, 1936, 404–09. D. Stroud *Humphry Repton* 1962, 147. J. Harris *Artist and the country house* 1979, 263. G. Carter *et al. Humphry Repton* 1982, 163.

Kiddington, Oxfordshire
D. Stroud *Capability Brown* 1975, 47,230.

Kidlington, Oxfordshire
G. Beard *Thomas H. Mawson* 1976, 56.

Kiftsgate Court near Chipping Campden, Glos
Official guide. *J. Royal Hort. Soc.* 1951, 159–65. A. Lees-Milne *and* R. Verey *Englishwoman's garden* 1980, 35–40. J. Sales *West Country gardens* 1980, 79–81. T. Hinde *Stately gardens of Britain* 1983, 140–45.

Kilarden, Rosneath, Strathclyde
G.A. Little *Scotland's gardens* 1981, 233–34.

Kilbogget, Killiney, Co. Dublin, Eire
C.L. v. 169, 1981, 1236–38.

Kilbryde, Corbridge, Northumberland
J. Royal Hort. Soc. 1967, 84–88, 284–87.

Kilburn Wells, Hampstead, Camden, London
W. Wroth *London pleasure gardens of the eighteenth century* 1896, 194–96.

Kilconquhar House, Kilconquhar, Fife
M. Binney *and* A. Hills *Elysian gardens* 1979, 26.

Kilcoy Castle, Muir of Ord, Highland
G.A. Little *Scotland's gardens* 1981, 234.

Kildale Hall, Kildale, N. Yorks
J.W. Ord *History . . . of Cleveland* 1846, 425.

Kildangan, Co. Kildare, Eire
E. Malins *and* P. Bowe *Irish gardens and demesnes* 1980, 79–80. Knight of Glin *and* P. Bowe *Gardens of outstanding historic interest in . . . Ireland* 1980.

Kildonan, Helmsdale, Highland
G.A. Little *Scotland's gardens* 1981, 234–35.

Kildrum, Co. Donegal, Eire
G.C. v. 161 no. 316, 1967, 20–21.

Kildrummy Castle, Kildrummy, Grampian
G.A. Little *Scotland's gardens* 1981, 199–200.

Kildwick Hall, Kildwick, N. Yorks
C.L. v. 29, 1911, 126–33. G. Jekyll *Garden ornament* 1918, 142.

Kilgraston near Bridge of Earn, Tayside
J.P. Neale *Views* 2nd series, v. 4, 1828.

Kilkenny Castle, Co. Kilkenny, Eire
J. Hort. Cottage Gdnr N.S., v. 59, 1909, 538–39. E. Malins *and* Knight of Glin *Lost demesnes* 1976, 7. J. Harris *Artist and the country house* 1979, 107.

Kilkerran near Maybole, Strathclyde
G.M. v. 9, 1833, 9. *C.L.* v. 157, 1975, 1114–17,1178–81. A.A. Tait *Landscape garden in Scotland* 1980, passim.

Killakee near Dublin, Co. Dublin, Eire
C. McIntosh *Book of the garden* 1853–55, pl. 20. E. Malins *and* P. Bowe *Irish gardens and demesnes* 1980, 39.

Killarney House, Killarney, Co. Kerry, Eire
G.C. i 1909, 180–81,187,189; ii 1913, 173. E. Malins *and* E. Bowe *Irish gardens and demesnes* 1980, 154–55.

Killerton near Exeter, Devon
Official guide. R. Ackermann *Repository* v. 11, 1828, pl. 25. W.W.J. Gendall *Views* 1830, 95. J. Britton *and* E.W. Brayley *Devonshire & Cornwall* 1832, 34. *G.M.* v. 19, 1843, 240–42. *Garden* v. 23, 1883, 35–36. *G.C.* ii 1903, 365,386; i 1964, 140–41; v. 187 no. 18, 1980, 6–8. C. Holme *Gardens of England in Southern & Western counties* 1907, pls. 83–85. *C.L.* v. 120, 1956, 339; v. 123, 1958, 1132–33. *J. Royal Hort. Soc.* 1960, 348; 1971, 219; 1972, 17–21. M. Allan *Fisons guide* 1970, 127–28. H. Evans *Beautiful gardens of Britain* 1974, 15–16. P.M. Synge *Gardens of Britain* v. 1, 1977, 53–58. G.S. Thomas *Gardens of National Trust* 1979, 158–60.

A. Hellyer *Gardens of genius* 1980, 82–85. Manpower Services commission *Killerton* 1980.

Killua Castle, Killua, Co. Westmeath, Eire
E. Malins *and* Knight of Glin *Lost demesnes* 1976, 185,186.

Killymoon Castle, Co. Tyrone, Ulster
A. Rowan *North West Ulster* 1979, 334.

Kilmacurragh near Rathdrum, Co. Wicklow, Eire
Irish Gdning v. 9, 1914, 99–101. *New Flora and Silva* v. 1, 1928, 120. R.H.S. *Conifers in cultivation* 1932, 214–15. *J. Royal Hort. Soc.* 1958, 456–58. E. Malins *and* P. Bowe *Irish gardens and demesnes* 1980, 127–29.

Kilmahew Castle near Cardross, Strathclyde
G.C. ii 1938, 354–55.

Kilmory Castle, Lochgilphead, Strathclyde
Scottish Gdnr v. 4, 1855, 14–15.

Kilnside, Paisley, Strathclyde
G.C. ii 1887, 653–54.

Kilnwick Hall, Kilnwick, Humberside
Historical MSS Commission *Architectural history* v. 3, 1971, items 3001, 3280.

Kilravock Castle near Nairn, Highland
G.M. v. 15, 1839, 628.

Kilruddery near Bray, Co. Wicklow, Eire
J.P. Neale *Views* v. 6, 1823. E. Malins *and* Knight of Glin *Lost demesnes* 1976, 10–12. *C.L.* v. 162, 1977, 78–81,146–49. J. Harris *Artist and the country house* 1979, 365. Knight of Glin *and* P. Bowe *Gardens of outstanding historic interest in . . . Ireland* 1980.

Kilwarlin, Co. Down, Ulster
Gdn History v. 11 no. 1, 1983, 65–69.

Kimberley Hall, Kimberley, Norfolk
J.P. Neale *Views* v. 3, 1820. J. Grigor *Eastern arboretum* 1841, 274–77. F.O. Morris *Series of picturesque views* v. 5, 13. D. Stroud *Capability Brown* 1975, 112,230.

Kimbolton Castle, Kimbolton, Cambs
F.O. Morris *Series of picturesque views* v. 3, 51. V.C.H. Huntingdon v. 3, 1936, 78–79. L. Whistler *Imagination of Vanbrugh and his fellow artists* 1954, 140–42. *C.L.* v. 144, 1968, 1696–99. P.G.M. Dickinson *Maps in the County Record Office Huntingdon* 1968, 22–23. *Gdn History* v. 8 no. 2, 1980, 59,61,63.

Kimpton Hoo, Kimpton, Herts
Cottage Gdnr v. 20, 1858, 2–4, 54–55.

Kincardine Castle near Fettercairn, Grampian
J.P. Neale *Views* v. 6, 1823.

Kincardine O'Neil, Grampian
G. Beard *Thomas H. Mawson* 1976, 56.

Kincorth House near Forres, Grampian
G.A. Little *Scotland's gardens* 1981, 200.

Kinfauns Castle near Perth, Tayside
G.M. v. 13, 1837, 60–61. *Scottish Gdnr* v. 3, 1854, 102–04; v. 10, 1861, 400–01.

Kingcombe, Chipping Campden, Glos
Concrete Quarterly no. 98, 1973, 33–35.

King's Bromley near Lichfield, Staffs
J.P. Neale *Views* 2nd Series, v. 4, 1828.

Kings Chantry, Binsted, Hants
A. Paterson *Gardens of Britain* v. 2, 1978, 111–13.

King's Cliffe, Northants
Northamptonshire Past and Present v. 5 no. 3, 1975, 227.

Kings Copse House, Southend, Reading, Berks
R. Bisgrove *Gardens of Britain* v. 3, 1978, 104.

King's House Garden, Burhill, Surrey
R. Webber *Percy Cane* 1975, 71–72,184.

Kings Inch, Paisley, Strathclyde
A.A. Tait *Landscape garden in Scotland* 1980, passim.

Kings Langley, Herts
H.M. Colvin *History of the King's Works* v. 2, 1963, 971,975,976.

King's Manor, York, N. Yorks
C.L. v. 50, 1921, 544–50.

Kings Square *see* London

King's Walden Bury, King's Walden, Herts
G.C. ii 1904, 27; i 1905, 43–44; i 1925, 261. *J. Hort. Cottage Gdnr* v. 49, 1904, 121–24. *C.L.* v. 154, 1973, 858–61.

Kings Weston near Bristol, Avon
R. Atkyns *Ancient and present state of Glostershire* 1712, 476. L. Knyff *and* J. Kip *Britannia illustrata* v. 2, 1715. *Copper Plate Mag.* v. 4, pl. 176. R. Havell *Series of picturesque views* 1816, pl. 8. J.P. Neale *Views* v. 2, 1819. J.N. Brewer *Delineations of Gloucestershire* 1825, 79. *Jones's views* 1829. *C.L.* v. 6, 1899, 592–97; v. 61, 1927, 680–87; v. 113, 1953, 212–15. M. Macartney *English houses & gardens* 1908, pl. 6. H.I. Triggs *Formal*

Kings Weston (*Cont.*)
gardens in England and Scotland 1902, 38–39. G. Jekyll *Garden ornament* 1918, 219, 327, 351. *Architectural History* v. 10, 1967, 9–32. D. Stroud *Capability Brown* 1975, 230. *J. Gdn History* v. 2 no. 1, 1982, 51–52.

Kingsbury, Brent, London
G.M. v. 16, 1840, 233–41.

Kingsgate, North Foreland, Kent
B. Jones *Follies & grottoes* 1974, 351–52.

Kingsmoor, Sunningdale, Berks
R. Bisgrove *Gardens of Britain* v. 3, 1978, 104–05.

Kingston House, Stinsford, Dorset
J. Hutchins *History . . . of Dorset* v. 2, 1863, 561.

Kingston House, Kingston Bagpuize, Oxfordshire
C.L. v. 92, 1942, 890–93. *G.C.* ii 1960, 38–39. R. Bisgrove *Gardens of Britain* v. 3, 1978, 106–07.

Kingston House, Bradford-on-Avon, Wilts
Garden v. 46, 1894, 517–18.

Kingston Lacy near Wimborne, Dorset
J.P. Neale *Views* v. 1, 1818. J. Hutchins *History . . . of Dorset* v. 3, 1868, 236. *C.L.* v. 7, 1900, 496–501. C. Holme *Gardens of England in Southern & Western counties* 1907, pl. 87. G. Jekyll *Garden ornament* 1918, 118, 260.

Kingston Lisle Park, Wantage, Oxfordshire
R. Bisgrove *Gardens of Britain* v. 3, 1978, 105–06.

Kingston Maurwood, Dorset
J. Hutchins *History . . . of Dorset* v. 2, 1863, 561.
A. Paterson *Gardens of Britain* v. 2, 1978, 34–35.

Kingston Russell House near Dorchester, Dorset
C.L. v. 110, 1951, 1628–31.

Kingswood, Sydenham, Lewisham, London
G.C. i 1905, 283.

Kingswood House, Sunningdale, Berks
Gdn Design 1931, 100–09.

Kingswood Lodge, Egham, Surrey
J. Hassell *Seats near London* 1804–05. J.C. Loudon *Treatise on forming, improving and managing country residences* v. 2, 1806, pls. 24–25. W. Keane *Beauties of Surrey* 1849, 48–51.

Kingswood Warren, Kingswood, Surrey
Gdning World v. 3, 1886, 25–26.

Kingweston, Somerset
J.P. Neale *Views* 2nd Series, v. 4, 1828.

Kinloch Hourn, Highland
Trees and shrubs planted out at Kinloch Hourn, West coast of Inverness-shire 1906.

Kinlochruel near Colintraive, Strathclyde
G.C. v. 160 no. 7, 1966, 14–15.

Kinmel, Clwyd
Cottage Gdnr v. 12, 1854, 359–60. *C.L.* v. 146, 1969, 542–45.

Kinnaird Castle near Brechin, Tayside
Scottish Gdnr v. 3, 1854, 134–38. G.A. Little *Scotland's gardens* 1981, 200.

Kinnaird House, Larbert, Central
Historical MSS Commission *Architectural history* v. 4, 1972, item 4237.

Kinrara, Grampian
A.A. Tait *Landscape garden in Scotland* 1980, passim.

Kinross House, Kinross, Tayside
G.M. v. 18, 1842, 587–88. H.I. Triggs *Formal gardens in England and Scotland* 1902, 47. *C.L.* v. 32, 1912, 54–62, 90–95; v. 109, 1951, 472–75; v. 137, 1965, 666–70, 726. P. Coats *Great gardens of Britain* 1967, 78–87. H. Colvin and J. Harris *Country seat* 1970, 66. G.A. Little *Scotland's gardens* 1981, 156–58.

Kiplin Hall, Scorton, N. Yorks
C.L. v. 70, 1931, 228–32. K. Lemmon *Gardens of Britain* v. 5, 1978, 85.

Kippax Park, Kippax, W. Yorks
Historical MSS Commission *Architectural history* v. 3, 1971, item 3007.

Kippendavie near Dunblane, Central
A.A. Tait *Landscape garden in Scotland* 1980, 35–36.

Kippington near Sevenoaks, Kent
J. Harris *History of Kent* 1719, 278. J. Kip *Supplement du Nouveau theatre de la Grande Bretagne* 1728, pl. 13. T. Badeslade *Thirty six different views . . . in Kent* 1750s, pl. 17. J.P. Neale *Views* v. 2, 1819. G. Carter et al. *Humphry Repton* 1982, 155.

Kirby Cane Hall, Kirby Cane, Norfolk
G.M. v. 17, 1841, 273. J. Grigor *Eastern arboretum* 1841, 251–52.

Kirby Hall, Kirby Bedon, Norfolk
J. Grigor *Eastern arboretum* 1841, 293–94.

Kirby Hall near Gretton, Northants
Official guide. J. Morton *Natural history of Northamptonshire* 1712, 493. C.L. v. 20, 1906, 558–65; v. 122, 1957, 444,488–91. G. Jekyll *Garden ornament* 1918, 20. J. Evelyn *Diary* v. 3, 1955, 134. *House & Garden* March 1975, 134–35. *Northamptonshire Past and Present* v. 5 no. 5, 1977, 400–01. J. Anthony *Gardens of Britain* v. 6, 1979, 103–06. Royal Commission on Historical Monuments *Inventory of historical monuments in . . . Northampton* v. 2, 1979, 59–61. M. Hadfield *et al. British gardeners* 1980, 146. C. Taylor *Archaeology of gardens* 1983, 47,48. *J. Gdn History* v. 4 no. 2, 1984, 139–56.

Kirkbride near Crosshill, Strathclyde
Scottish Gdnr and Northern Forester v. 6, 1911, 673–74.

Kirkby Fleetham, N. Yorks
J. Harris *Artist and the country house* 1979, 196. *Mr Aislabie's gardens* 1981.

Kirkby Mallory Hall near Bosworth, Leics
J. Throsby *Select views in Leicestershire* v. 1, 1790, 157. J. Nichols *History . . . of county of Leicester* v. 4, 1811, 771.

Kirkconnell near Dumfries, Dumfries and Galloway
G.C. ii 1900, 141.

Kirkdale House near Creetown, Dumfries and Galloway
G.A. Little *Scotland's gardens* 1981, 261.

Kirkharle, Northumberland
D. Stroud *Capability Brown* 1975, 41–41,230. *Gdn History* v. 9 no. 2, 1981, 159–66. Tyne and Wear County Council Museums *Capability Brown and the northern landscape* 1983, 11,13,41.

Kirklands, Ancrum, Borders
G.A. Little *Scotland's gardens* 1981, 95.

Kirkleatham, Redcar, Cleveland
J. Beeverell *Les delices de la Grande Bretagne* v. 5, 1707, 872. L. Knyff *and* J. Kip *Britannia illustrata* v. 1, 1714. J.W. Ord *History . . . of Cleveland* 1846, 363. Historical MSS Commission *Architectural history* v. 1, 1969, item 108. C.L. v. 161, 1977, 18–21. T. Wright *Arbours & grottoes* 1979.

Kirklees Hall near Huddersfield, W. Yorks
J.P. Neale *Views* v. 5, 1822. *Jones's views* 1829, 19. Bradford Illustrated Weekly Telegraph *Series of picturesque views* 1885. C. Holme *Gardens of England in Northern counties* 1911, pls. 63–64. C.L. v. 24, 1908, 256–66.

Kirtling Tower, Kirtling, Cambs
F.O. Morris *Series of picturesque views* v. 4, 47. C.L. v. 69, 1931, 102–08.

Kirtlington Park, Kirtlington, Oxfordshire
D. Stroud *Capability Brown* 1975, 69,230.

Kissing Tree House, Alveston, Warwickshire
R. Sidwell *West Midland gardens* 1981, 216.

Kitley near Yealmpton, Devon
R. Ackermann *Repository* v. 11, 1828, pl. 7. W.W.J. Gendall *Views* v. 2, 1830, 47. J. Britton *and* E.W. Brayley *Devonshire & Cornwall* 1832, 42. G.M. v. 18, 1842, 542–43. *Garden* v. 44, 1893, 455. C.L. v. 86, 1939, 362–67.

Kiveton, S. Yorks
T. Badeslade *and* J. Rocque *Vitruvius Brittanicus* 1739, pls. 13–18. Historical MSS Commission *Architectural history* v. 2, 1970, item 1657.

Knapton, N. Yorks
I. Hall *Samuel Buck's Yorkshire sketchbook* 1979, 36.

Knapton near Abbeyleix, Co. Laois, Eire
Irish Gdning v. 10, 1915, 12. M. Hornibrook *Dwarf and slow-growing conifers* 1923.

Knebworth House near Stevenage, Herts
H. Chauncy *Historical antiquities of Hertfordshire* 1700, 353. J.P. Neale *Views* 2nd Series, v. 1, 1824. S.C. Hall *Baronial halls and picturesque edifices of England* 1848. *J. Hort. Cottage Gdnr* v. 52, 1874, 451–52,453; N.S., v. 19, 1889, 137–38. G.C. i 1886, 615–17; ii 1891, 7–8. C.L. v. 1, 1897, 694–96; v. 19, 1906, 486–93. B. Jones *Follies & grottoes* 1974, 344. R. Bisgrove *Gardens of Britain* v. 3, 1978, 107–08. J. Brown *Miss Gertrude Jekyll* 1981, 22. J. Brown *Gardens of a golden afternoon* 1982, 65,168.

Kneller Hall, Whitton, Twickenham, London
J. Harris *Artist and the country house* 1979, 112.

Knepp Castle near Horsham, W. Sussex
J. Dallaway *History of Western Division of . . . Sussex* v. 2 pt 32, 1830, 298. T.W. Horsfield *History . . . of Sussex* v. 2, 1835, 247.

Knights Hill near Dulwich, London
Copper Plate Mag. v. 2, pl. 84.

Knightshayes Court, Tiverton, Devon
Official guide. G.C. ii 1882, 116–17; ii 1888, 723–24; v. 160 no. 5, 1966, 10–11; v. 190 no. 19, 1981, 24–26. *J. Hort. Cottage Gdnr* N.S., v. 18, 1889, 174–76. C.L. v. 128, 1960, 664–66. *J. Royal Hort. Soc.* 1960, 431–39. M. Allan *Fisons guide* 1970, 129–30. H. Evans

Knightshayes Court (*Cont.*)
Beautiful gardens of Britain 1973, 19–20. P.M. Synge *Gardens of Britain* v. 1, 1977, 58–65. G.S. Thomas *Gardens of National Trust* 1979, 160–62. A. Lees-Milne and R. Verey *Englishwoman's garden* 1980, 20–25. Manpower Services Commission *Knightshayes* 1980. T. Hinde *Stately gardens of Britain* 1983, 168–75.

Knightstone near Crediton, Devon
C.L. v. 108, 1950, 754–58.

Knockmaroon Lodge, Dublin, Eire
Cottage Gdnr v. 27, 1862, 337–39.

Knole, Almondsbury, Avon
R. Atkyns *Ancient and present state of Glostershire* 1712, 212. L. Knyff and J. Kip *Britannia illustrata* v. 2, 1715.

Knole near Sevenoaks, Kent
Official guide. J. Beeverell *Les delices de la Grande Bretagne* v. 5, 1707, 872. L. Knyff and J. Kip *Britannia illustrata* v. 1, 1714. J. Harris *History of Kent* 1719, 278. J. Kip *Supplement du Nouveau theatre de la Grande Bretagne* 1728, pls. 3–4. T. Badeslade *Thirty six different views . . . in Kent* 1750s, pls. 18–19. P. Sandby *Collection of one hundred and fifty select views* v. 1, 1781, pl. 23. W.W.J. Gendall *Views* v. 2, 1830, 12,15–16. J.H. Brady *Visitor's guide to Knole* 1839. F.O. Morris *Series of picturesque views* v. 6, 69. L. Jewitt and S.C. Hall *Stately homes of England* 1877, 56–73. *G.C.* ii 1890, 683–84. M.R. Gloag *Book of English gardens* 1906, 259–84. M. Macartney *English houses & gardens* 1908, pl. 2. *C.L.* v. 31, 1912, 772–87,826–39. Historical MSS Commission *Architectural history* v. 2, 1970, items 1033,1646,2086. T. Wright *Gardens of Britain* v. 4, 1978, 68–69. G.S. Thomas *Gardens of National Trust* 1979, 162.

Knottfield House near Calverley, W. Yorks
Bradford Illustrated Weekly Telegraph *Series of picturesque views* 1885.

Knott's Green, Leyton, Waltham Forest, London
J. Hort. Cottage Gdnr v. 54, 1875, 50–52.

Knowle (Knoll), Cranley, Surrey
E.W. Brayley and J. Britton *Topographical history of Surrey* v. 5, 1848, 170.

Knowle Cottage, Sidmouth, Devon
C.F. Williams *Guide to illustrations and views of Knowle Cottage, Sidmouth; the elegant marine villa ornée of Thos L. Fish* 1834.

Knowlton Court near Sandwich, Kent
J. Harris *History of Kent* 1719, 171. J. Kip *Supplement du Nouveau theatre de la Grande Bretagne* 1728, pl. 9. T. Badeslade *Thirty six different views . . . in Kent* 1750s, pl. 21. J.P. Neale *Views* 2nd Series, v. 2, 1825. *C.L.* v. 39, 1916, 534–40.

Knowsley Hall, Knowsley, Merseyside
H. Skrine *Three successive tours in the north of England* 1813, 4. J.P. Neale *Views* 2nd Series, v. 1, 1824. *Jones's views* 1829. E. Baines *History . . . of Lancaster* v. 4, 1836, 11. *Cottage Gdnr* v. 14, 1855, 72–73. *J. Hort. Cottage Gdnr* v. 51, 1874, 490–92; N.S., v. 60, 1910, 187–91. *G.C.* ii 1882, 682–83; i 1886, 716; ii 1890, 463–64. F.O. Morris *Series of picturesque views* v. 1, 55. C. Holme *Gardens of England in the Northern counties* 1911, pls. 65–68. *C.L.* v. 34, 1913, 54. N. Pevsner *Lancashire: 1* 1969, 134. D. Stroud *Capability Brown* 1975, 231. J. Harris *Artist and the country house* 1979, 236.

Knypersley Hall, Knypersley, Staffs
Cottage Gdnr v. 14, 1855, 461–62.

Kyle House, Kyleakin, Isle of Skye, Highland
G.A. Little *Scotland's gardens* 1981, 235.

Kylemore Castle, Kylemore, Co. Galway, Eire
E. Malins and P. Bowe *Irish gardens and demesnes* 1980, 51.

Kymnel Manor near Chislehurst, Bromley, London
Florist 1853, 204–07.

Kyre Park, Kyre Wyard, Hereford and Worcester
C.L. v. 41, 1917, 252–58,276–83. G. Jekyll *Garden ornament* 1918, 233. V.C.H. *Worcester* v. 4, 1924, 279.

La Colline, Jersey, Channel Islands
C.L. v. 149, 1971, 820–22.

La Moye Manor, Jersey, Channel Islands
C.L. v. 149, 1971, 820–22.

Lacock Abbey, Lacock, Wilts
J.P. Neale *Views* 2nd Series, v. 3, 1826. *C.L.* v. 13, 1903, 176–81. G.S. Thomas *Gardens of National Trust* 1979, 163. J. Sales *West Country gardens* 1980, 224–25.

Lacy House, Isleworth, Hounslow, London
W. Angus *Seats of the nobility* 1787, pl. 36. W.B. Cooke and S. Owen *The Thames* v. 2, 1811. J. Harris *Artist and the country house* 1979, 331.

Ladham House, Goudhurst, Kent
C.L. v. 121, 1957, 476–78. T. Wright *Gardens of Britain* v. 4, 1978, 69–72.

Ladiston (Ledestown), Mullingar, Co. Westmeath, Eire
Remarks on the management of orchidaceous plants with a

Ladiston *(Cont.)*

catalogue of those in the collection of J.C. Lyons 1843. E.C. Nelson *John Lyons and his orchid manual* 1983. *Orchid Review* v. 91, 1983, 74–77.

Lady St Mary, Wareham, Dorset
C.L. v. 159, 1976, 532–34.

Laines, Plumpton, E. Sussex
C.L. v. 172, 1982, 909–12.

Lainston House near Winchester, Hants
C.L. v. 45, 1919, 252–59.

Lake House, Wanstead, Redbridge, London
F.G. Emmison *Catalogue of maps in Essex Record Office* 3nd Supplt, 1968, 9.

Lake House, Wilsford, Wilts
C.L. v. 23, 1908, 198–203; v. 81, 1937, 326–31.

Laleham, Surrey
D. Stroud *Capability Brown* 1975, 231.

Lamanch, Newlands, Borders
I.H. Adams *Descriptive list of plans* v. 1, 1966, 127.

Lamb House, Rye, E. Sussex
G.S. Thomas *Gardens of National Trust* 1979, 163.

Lambay Castle, Lambay Island, Co. Dublin, Eire
C.L. v. 66, 1929, 86–94,120. A.S. Butler *et al. Architecture of Sir Edwin Lutyens* v. 2, 1950, 11. Knight of Glin *and* P. Bowe *Gardens of outstanding historic interest in . . . Ireland* 1980. E. Malins *and* P. Bowe *Irish gardens and demesnes* 1980, 155–57. J. Brown *Gardens of a golden afternoon* 1982, 70–71,100–01,168.

Lambden near Greenlaw, Borders
G.A. Little *Scotland's gardens* 1981, 95–96.

Lambeth (Capt. Foster), London
Archaeologia v. 12, 1796, 190.

Lambeth (Tradescant), London
Philosophical Trans. Royal Hort. Soc. v. 46, 1749–50, 160–61. D. Lysons *Environs of London* v. 1, 1792, 330. M. Allan *The Tradescants* 1964, passim. *J. Gdn History* v. 2 no. 1, 1982, 1–16. P. Leith Ross *The John Tradescants* 1984.
See also St Mary's Church, Lambeth

Lambeth. Archbishop's Park, London
M.P.G. Draper *Lambeth's open spaces* 1979, 47.

Lambeth. Brockwell Park, London
M.P.G. Draper *Lambeth's open spaces* 1979, 48–49.

Lambeth. Jubilee Gardens, London
M.P.G. Draper *Lambeth's open spaces* 1979, 46.

Lambeth. Myatt's Fields, London
M.P.G. Draper *Lambeth's open spaces* 1979, 50–51.

Lambeth. Ruskin Park, London
M.P.G. Draper *Lambeth's open spaces* 1979, 51–52.

Lambeth. Streatham Memorial Garden, London
M.P.G. Draper *Lambeth's open spaces* 1979, 53.

Lambeth. Vauxhall Park, London
M.P.G. Draper *Lambeth's open spaces* 1979, 54.

Lambeth Palace, Lambeth, London
L. Knyff *and* J. Kip *Britannia illustrata* v. 1, 1714. *Bibliotheca topographica Britannica* v. 2 no. 27, 1790, 76–77. D. Lysons *Environs of London* v. 1, 1792, 268. *Archaeologia* v. 12, 1796, 187–88. V.C.H. *Surrey* v. 4, 1912, 45. J. MacGregor *Gardens of celebrities . . . in and around London* 1918, 29–61. D. Gardiner *Story of Lambeth Palace* 1930. C.L. v. 77, 1935, 574–76. G.L.C. *Survey of London* v. 23: *South Bank and Vauxhall* 1951, 102–03. G. Taylor *Old London gardens* 1953, 53–60. J. Evelyn *Diary* v. 5, 1955, 80,213.

Lambton Castle, Durham, Co. Durham
J.P. Neale *Views* v. 1, 1818. R. Surtees *History . . . of County . . . of Durham* v. 2, 1820, 170. G.M. v. 10, 1834, 121–22. E. MacKenzie *and* M. Ross *Historical . . . view of . . . Durham* v. 1, 1834, 137. *J. Hort. Cottage Gdnr* v. 50, 1873, 293–96,313–15; N.S., v. 15, 1887, 207–09. G.C. i 1877, 341,343,375–76,400–01; i 1882, 529,532, 533; i 1884, 671–72. F.O. Morris *Series of picturesque views* v. 3, 5. *Garden* v. 31, 1887, 249,253. *Gdning World* v. 14, 1897, 70. C. Holme *Gardens of England in Northern counties* 1911, pls. 69–71. C.L. v. 139, 1966, 664–67,726–29.

Lamellen near St Tudy, Cornwall
P.M. Synge *Gardens of Britain* v. 1, 1977, 105–07.

Lamer, Welwyn, Herts
D. Stroud *Humphry Repton* 1962, 54. G. Carter *et al. Humphry Repton* 1982, 81,100,154.

Lamorran near Truro, Cornwall
J. Hort. Cottage Gdnr v. 58, 1877, 177–80,217–18.

Lamport Hall, Lamport, Northants
Official guide. J.P. Neale *Views* v. 3, 1820. *Cottage Gdnr* v. 23, 1859, 84–86. *J. Hort. Cottage Gdnr* v. 47, 1872, 501–03. G.C. ii 1897, 209–10,217,219,395. C.L. v. 3, 1898, 518–20; v. 49, 1921, 672–79; v. 112, 1952, 932–35,1106–09; v. 128, 1960, 1104–07,1164–67. J. Anthony *Gardens of Britain* v. 6, 1979, 107–10. Royal

Lamport Hall (*Cont.*)

Commission on Historical Monuments *Inventory of the historical monuments in . . . Northampton* v. 3, 1981, 116–19.

Lanarth, St Keverne, Cornwall
J. Royal Hort. Soc. 1945, 63–72.

Langdale Chase, Troutbeck, Ambleside, Cumbria
G. Beard *Thomas H. Mawson* 1976, 56–57.

Langdon Court near Plymouth, Devon
J. Harris *Artist and the country house* 1979, 131.

Langford Grove Park, Langford, Essex
F.G. Emmison *Catalogue of maps in Essex Record Office* 3rd Supplt, 1968, 21.

Langham Hall, Langham, Essex
P. Muilman *History of Essex* v. 6, 1772, 242. P. Morant *History . . . of Essex* v. 2, 1816, 242. *Gdn Design* 1938, 127–29.

Langham Old Hall, Langham, Leics
R.I.B.A. *Catalogue* v. G–K, 1973, 61.

Langholm Cottage, Dumfries and Galloway
A.A. Tait *Landscape garden in Scotland* 1980, passim.

Langley Grange near Loddon, Norfolk
C.L. v. 170, 1981, 758–60.

Langley Park, Colnbrook, Bucks
A. Robertson *Topographical survey of the Great Road* pt 1, 1792, 160–61. *Copper Plate Mag.* v. 2, pl. 70. *G.M.* v. 9, 1833, 650. J.B. Burke *Visitation* v. 1, 1852, 39. *Garden* v. 66, 1904, 189–91. *G.C.* i 1915, 7–8; i 1965, 14–15.

Langley Park, Beckenham, Bromley, London
E. Hasted *History . . . of . . . Kent* v. 1, 1778, 85. H. Repton *Sketches* 1794, 22–24. D. Stroud *Humphry Repton* 1962, 49,170. R.I.B.A. *Catalogue* v. O–R, 1976, 119–20. M. Hadfield *et al. British gardeners* 1980, 238. G. Carter *et al. Humphry Repton* 1982, 50,155–56.

Langley Park, Langley, Norfolk
J.P. Neale *Views* v. 3, 1820. J. Grigor *Eastern arboretum* 1841, 266–68. *C.L.* v. 62, 1927, 16–22. D. Stroud *Capability Brown* 1975, 129,231.

Langleys, Great Waltham, Essex
P. Morant *History . . . of Essex* v. 2, 1816, 88. P. Muilman *History of Essex* v. 1, 1771, 325. *Connoisseur* v. 140, 1957, 211–17. G. Carter *et al. Humphry Repton* 1982, 151.

Langton Hall, West Langton, Leics
J.P. Neale *Views* v. 2, 1819. *Jones's views* 1829.
J. Anthony *Gardens of Britain* v. 6, 1979, 110–11.

Langton Hall, Langton, Lincs
J. Hort. Cottage Gdnr v. 52, 1874, 497–500.

Langton House, Langton Long Blandford, Dorset
G.M. v. 11, 1835, 332–33. J. Hutchins *History . . . of Dorset* v. 1, 1861, 285. *J. Hort. Cottage Gdnr* v. 35, 1866, 182–83.

Langtons, Hornchurch, Havering, London
V.C.H. *Essex* v. 7, 1978, 29.

Lanhydrock near Bodmin, Cornwall
Official guide. C.S. Gilbert *Historical survey of . . . Cornwall* v. 2, 1820, 637. R. Ackermann *Repository* v. 10, 1827, pl. 8. W.W.J. Gendall *Views* v. 1, 1830, 19. J. Britton *and* E.W. Brayley *Devonshire & Cornwall* 1832, 27. F.O. Morris *Series of picturesque views* v. 5, 39. *C.L.* v. 14, 1903, 890–96; v. 147, 1970, 542–44. Lady Rockley *Historic gardens of England* 1938, 162–63. *Architectural History* v. 7, 1964, 31,75. M. Allan *Fisons guide* 1970, 130–31. H. Evans *Beautiful gardens of Britain* 1974, 5–6. P.M. Synge *Gardens of Britain* v. 1, 1977, 107–10. G.S. Thomas *Gardens of National Trust* 1979, 164–65. A. Hellyer *Gardens of genius* 1980, 110–14. Manpower Services Commission *Lanhydrock* 1982.

Lansdown, Bath, Avon
B. Jones *Follies & grottoes* 1974, 283.

Lansdowne Park, Helensburgh, Strathclyde
Scottish Gdnr and Northern Forester v. 8, 1913, 513–15.

Larbert House, Larbert, Central
Gdning World v. 17, 1900, 267–68. *Scottish Gdnr and Northern Forester* v. 8, 1913, 381–82.

Larch Wood, Beachamwell, Norfolk
C.L. v. 171, 1982, 550–52. A. Lees-Milne *and* R. Verey *Englishman's garden* 1982, 104–07.

Larches, Alderley Edge, Cheshire
G.C. i 1896, 327–28.

Larmer Gardens, Tollard Royal, Wilts
B. Jones *Follies & grottoes* 1974, 256.

Lartington Hall, Lartington, Co. Durham
W. Angus *Seats* 1787, pl. 23. I. Hall *Samuel Buck's Yorkshire sketchbook* 1979, 368.

Lasborough House near Tetbury, Glos
T.D. Fosbrooke *Abstracts of . . . county of Gloucester* v. 1, 1807, 410.

Lascombe, Puttenham, Surrey
J. Brown *Gardens of a golden afternoon* 1982, 161.

Lathallan near Colinsburgh, Fife
G.M. v. 7, 1831, 21–22.

Lathom House, Lathom, Lancs
H. Repton *Sketches* 1794, 43–47. J.P. Neale *Views* v. 2, 1819. *Jones's views* 1829. E. Baines *History . . . of Lancaster* v. 4, 1836, 255. *Cottage Gdnr* v. 25, 1861, 289–90, 333. F.O. Morris *Series of picturesque views* v. 5, 53. *G.C.* ii 1890, 555–56. D. Stroud *Capability Brown* 1962, 170. G. Carter et al. *Humphry Repton* 1982, 156.

Latimers, Latimer, Bucks
J. Hort. Cottage Gdnr v. 32, 1864, 333–36, 347–48; v. 52, 1874, 567–68. D. Stroud *Capability Brown* 1975, 231.

Launde Abbey, Launde, Leics
G.M. v. 7, 1831, 422–23.

Lauriston Castle, Edinburgh, Lothian
Scottish Gdnr v. 1, 1852, 396–98.

Laverstoke House, Laverstoke, Hants
E.F. Prosser *Select illustrations of Hampshire* 1833.

Lavington Park, East Lavington, W. Sussex
G.C. i 1914, 410–11. *C.L.* v. 58, 1925, 130–35.

Lawers, Tayside
J.P. Neale *Views* v. 6, 1823. *C.L.* v. 58, 1925, 550–55.

Lawford Place, Lawford, Essex
F.G. Emmison *Catalogue of maps in Essex Record Office* 2nd Supplt, 1964, 20.

Lawn, Langley, Essex
F.G. Emmison *Catalogue of maps in Essex Record Office* 2nd Supplt, 1964, 17.

Laws, Kingennie, Tayside
C.L. v. 76, 1934, 244–46.

Lawton Hall near Congleton, Cheshire
F.O. Morris *Series of picturesque views* v. 3, 77.

Laxton Hall, Laxton, Northants
J.P. Neale *Views* 2nd Series, v. 1, 1824. D. Stroud *Humphry Repton* 1962, 148, 170. G. Carter et al. *Humphry Repton* 1982, 160.

Layer Marney Tower, Layer Marney, Essex
C.L. v. 35, 1914, 270–78, 306–14. G. Virtue *Picturesque beauties of Great Britain: Essex* 1831, 2.

Lazenby Hall near Northallerton, N. Yorks
I. Hall *Samuel Buck's Yorkshire sketchbook* 1979, 9.

Le Clos de Chemin, Jersey, Channel Islands
C.L. v. 149, 1971, 820–22.

Lea near Gainsborough, Lincs
F.O. Morris *Series of picturesque views* v. 1, 37.

Lea near Godalming, Surrey
G.F. Prosser *Select illustrations of . . . Surrey* 1828. B. Jones *Follies & grottoes* 1974, 199–201.

Lea Rhododendron Gardens near Matlock, Derbyshire
M. Allan *Fisons guide* 1970, 226–27. J. Anthony *Gardens of Britain* v. 6, 1979, 112.

Leaden Hall, Leavenheath, Suffolk
J. Royal Hort. Soc. 1970, 246–51.

Leadenham House, Leadenham, Lincs
C.L. v. 137, 1965, 1528–31.

Leasowes, Halesowen, W. Midlands
R. Dodsley *Description of The Leasowes* 1764. Society of Gentlemen *England displayed* v. 2, 1769, 51–55. T. Whately *Observations on modern gardening* 1771, 162–71. J. Heeley *Description of The Leasowes* 1777. J. Heeley *Letters on the beauties of Hagley, Envil and The Leasowes* v. 2, 1777, 96–239. C. Burlington *Modern universal British traveller* 1779, 131. P. Sandby *Collection of one hundred and fifty select views* v. 1, 1781, pl. 57. R.J. Sulivan *Tour . . . in 1778* v. 2, 1785, 26–32. D. Defoe *Tour* v. 2, 1778, 273–74. *New display of the beauties of England* v. 2, 1787, 204–18. S. Johnson *Works* v. 4: *Lives of the poets* 1787, 216–17. R. Graves *Recollection of some particulars in the life of the late William Shenstone, Esq.* 1788. *Companion to The Leasowes, Hagley, and Enville* 1789, 1–40. *Copper Plate Mag.* v. 1, 1792, pl. 15. G. Lipscomb *Journey into South Wales* 1799, 299–310. *Description of Hagley, Envil and The Leasowes* c.1800. W. Marshall *On planting and rural ornament* v. 1, 1803, 314–21. W. Gilpin *Observations on several parts of England* v. 1, 1808, 58–64. L. Simond *Journal* v. 2, 1815, 97–98. F. Calvert *Picturesque views . . . in Shropshire* 1831, 119–20. E. Burritt *Walks in the Black Country and its green borderland* 1868, 236–37. J. Wesley *Journal* v. 4, 1903, 221. *Papers of Manchester Literary Club* v. 37, 1911, 99–119. *C.L.* v. 66, 1929, 861–62; v. 108, 1950, 1490–91; v. 133, 1963, 250–51. Viscount Torrington *Diaries* v. 1, 1934, 47–48. A.R. Humphreys *William Shenstone* 1937.

Leasowes (Cont.)

M. Williams *Letters of William Shenstone* 1939, passim.
T. Jefferson *Garden book 1766–1824* 1944, 113.
H.F. Clark *English landscape garden* 1948, 45–53.
O. Siren *China and the gardens of Europe of the eighteenth century* 1950, 36–40. E. Malins *English landscaping and literature* 1966, 65–79. *Landscape Design* no. 99, 1972, 11–13. A. Parreaux *and* M. Plaissant *Jardins et paysages: le style Anglais* 1977, 139–52. M.R. Brownell *Alexander Pope & the arts of Georgian England* 1978, 235–41. *Apollo* v. 110, 1979, 202–09. L. Fleming *and* A. Gore *English garden* 1979, 107–09. C. Thacker *History of gardens* 1979, 198–203. *Gdn History* v. 8 no. 2, 1980, 64–65; v. 9 no. 1, 1981, 69. M. Hadfield *et al. British gardeners* 1980, 260. K. Rorschach *Early Georgian landscape garden* 1983, 40–42, 44–45. D. Jacques *Georgian gardens* 1983, 53.

Leckhampton near Cheltenham, Glos
R. Atkyns *Ancient and present state of Glostershire* 1712, 530. L. Knyff *and* J. Kip *Britannia illustrata* v. 2, 1715.

Leckie near Gargunnock, Central
H. Maxwell *Scottish gardens* 1911, 158–60.

Ledestown *see* Ladiston

Ledston Hall, Ledston, W. Yorks
J.P. Neale *Views* v. 5, 1822. *C.L.* v. 21, 1907, 942–50; v. 84, 1938, 556–61, 584; v. 106, 1949, 607. P. Willis *Charles Bridgeman* 1977, 180. J. Harris *Artist and the country house* 1979, 192–93.

Lee Ford, Budleigh Salterton, Devon
M. Allan *Fisons guide* 1970, 131–32.

Lee Grove, Lewisham, London
C. Greenwood *Epitome of county history . . . v. 1: Kent* 1838, 22.

Lee Hall, Gateacre, Liverpool, Merseyside
J. Hort. Cottage Gdnr N.S., v. 1, 1880, 192–93.

Lee Place (C. Boone), Kent
J. Evelyn *Diary* v. 4, 1955, 288, 337.

Lee Place near Lanark, Strathclyde
J.P. Neale *Views* 2nd Series, v. 4, 1828. *G.M.* v. 18, 1842, 389–90.

Lee Priory, Ickham, Kent
E. Hasted *History . . . of Kent* v. 3, 1790, 664.
J.P. Neale *Views* 2nd Series, v. 2, 1825. C. Greenwood *Epitome of county history . . . v. 1: Kent* 1838, 354.
J. Harris *Artist and the country house* 1979, 338.

Leeds. Botanical Gardens, W. Yorks
G.M. v. 15, 1839, 305–16. G. Chadwick *Park and the town* 1966, 85.

Leeds Abbey (Priory), Leeds, Kent
J. Harris *History of Kent* 1719, 176. J. Kip *Supplement du Nouveau theatre de la Grande Bretagne* 1728, pl. 22.
T. Badeslade *Thirty six different views . . . in Kent* 1750s, pl. 22.

Leeds Castle, Leeds, Kent
W.W.J. Gendall *Views* v. 1, 1830, 100. F.O. Morris *Series of picturesque views* v. 2, 45. *C.L.* v. 1, 1897, 435–37; v. 34, 1913, 806–14, 856–63; v. 80, 1936, 568–74. Lady Rockley *Historic gardens of England* 1938, 82–83. T. Wright *Gardens of Britain* v. 4, 1978, 72–73.

Lees Court near Faversham, Kent
J. Harris *History of Kent* 1719, 280. T. Badeslade *Thirty six different views . . . in Kent* 1750s, pl. 23. J.P. Neale *Views* 2nd Series, v. 4, 1828. *C.L.* v. 52, 1922, 178–83.
G. Beard *Thomas H. Mawson* 1976, 57.

Leesthorpe Hall near Melton Mowbray, Leics
J. Throsby *Select views in Leicestershire* v. 1, 1790, 291.
J. Nichols *History . . . of county of Leicester* v. 3, 1804, 1126.

Leeswood near Mold, Clwyd
C.L. v. 94, 1943, 200–03, 244–47.

Leez Priory, Little Leighs, Essex
C.L. v. 35, 1914, 486–93.

Leggatts Park, Potters Bar, Herts
R. Bisgrove *Gardens of Britain* v. 3, 1978, 108–09.

Leicester. Abbey Park, Leics
J. Hort. Cottage Gdnr N.S., v. 21, 1890, 94–97. *Gdning World* v. 2, 1885, 24; v. 8, 1891, 118–19.

Leicester. Arboretum near Evington, Leics
Arboricultural Assoc. J. v. 2 no. 4, 1973, 110–13.

Leicester. University Botanic Garden, Leics
M. Allan *Fisons guide* 1970, 216. J. Anthony *Gardens of Britain* v. 6, 1979, 113–17. *Garden* 1979, 209–13.

Leicester Grange near Nuneaton, Warwickshire
Bibliotheca topographica Britannica v. 7 no. 7, 1790, 347–49.

Leicester Square *see* London

Leigh Park, Leigh, Essex
F.G. Emmison *catalogue of maps in Essex Record Office* 2nd Supplt, 1964, 15.

Leigh Park near Havant, Hants
E.F. Prosser *Select illustrations of Hampshire* 1833. *Notices of the Leigh Park Estate* 1836. *J. Hort. Cottage Gdnr* v. 37, 1867, 404–05. *Garden* v. 34, 1888, 385–86.

Leigh Place near Godstone, Surrey
C.L. v. 15, 1904, 342–47.

Leigham Court, Streatham, Lambeth, London
Garden v. 28, 1885, 563–64,565.

Leighton Hall near Carnforth, Lancs
C.L. v. 109, 1951, 1452–55.

Leighton House, Kensington, London
J. MacGregor *Gardens of celebrities . . . in and around London* 1918, 297–320.

Leith Hall, Huntley, Grampian
C.L. v. 83, 1938, 280–82. *J. Royal Hort. Soc.* 1961, 453. G.A. Little *Scotland's gardens* 1981, 203.

Leith Hill Place, Dorking, Surrey
O. Manning *and* W. Bray *History . . . of Surrey* v. 2, 1809, 161. G.S. Thomas *Gardens of National Trust* 1979, 165.

Lennoxlove near Haddington, Lothian
C.L. v. 35, 1914, 522–29.

Lennoxwood, Windlesham, Surrey
G. Jekyll *Garden ornament* 1918, 151.

Leonardslee near Horsham, W. Sussex
Official guide. *C.L.* v. 2, 1897, 343–45; v. 8, 1900, 282–85; v. 26, 1909, 48–50; v. 56, 1924, 98–99; v. 125, 1959, 876–78; v. 161, 1977, 630–32. *G.C.* ii 1906, 253–54,272–73; i 1907, 300; ii 1911, 275,357; i 1914, 111. *Gdnrs Mag.* 1908, 106–08. E.G. Loder *List of trees and shrubs* 1913. A.E. Pease *Edmund Loder* 1923, passim. M. Allan *Fisons guide* 1970, 53–54. T. Wright *Gardens of Britain* v. 4, 1978, 155–61. A. Hellyer *Gardens of genius* 1980, 73–78. T. Hinde *Stately gardens of Britain* 1983, 86–93.

Lepe House, Exbury, Hants
A. Paterson *Gardens of Britain* v. 2, 1978, 113–14.

Les Vaux, Jersey, Channel Islands
C.L. v. 149, 1971, 820–22.

Letheringsett Hall, Letheringsett, Norfolk
C.L. v. 141, 1967, 18–21.

Letton Park, Letton, Norfolk
G.M. v. 17, 1841, 272. J. Grigor *Eastern arboretum* 1841, 234.

Lettsom, John Coakley *see* Camberwell

Level, Pillowell, Glos
J. Sales *West Country gardens* 1980, 83–85.

Leven, Fife
B. Jones *Follies & grottoes* 1974, 254–55.

Leven Grove, Cleveland
J. Graves *History of Cleveland* 1808, 173–74.

Levens Hall, Levens, Cumbria
Official guide. *G.C.* ii 1874, 263–66; ii 1891, 671,674. F.O. Morris *Series of picturesque views* v. 6, 49. *Garden* v. 24, 565–66. *C.L.* v. 6, 1899, 656–61; v. 60, 1926, 538–46,610–17; v. 145, 1969, 62–63; v. 147, 1970, 782–84. H.I. Triggs *Formal gardens in England and Scotland* 1902, 27–28. G. Jekyll *and* G.S. Elgood *Some English gardens* 1905, 63–66. C. Holme *Gardens of England in Northern counties* 1911, pls. 72–80. G. Jekyll *Garden ornament* 1918, 276,287,421. Lady Rockley *Historic gardens of England* 1938, 138–39. P. Coats *Great gardens of Britain* 1963, 52–57. *Gdn History* v. 3 no. 4, 1975, 66–78.

Leverington Hall, Leverington, Cambs
C.L. v. 103, 1948, 126–28.

Lewiston Manor near Sherborne, Dorset
G. Beard *Thomas H. Mawson* 1976, 57.

Lexden Park near Colchester, Essex
F.G. Emmison *Catalogue of maps in Essex Record Office* 1947, 37; 1st Supplt, 1952, 27.

Leybourne Castle near Maidstone, Kent
J. Kip *Supplement du Nouveau theatre de la Grande Bretagne* 1728, pl. 23.

Leyswood near Crowborough, E. Sussex
G.C. ii 1887, 272–73; i 1888, 205,333. *J. Hort.* N.S., v. 68, 1914, 79–82.

Leyton Grange, Waltham Forest, London
J. Kip *Nouveau theatre de la Grande Bretagne* v. 4, 1729.

Lickleyhead Castle near Insch, Grampian
C.L. v. 82, 1937, 444–48.

Lifton House, Lifton, Devon
R. Ackermann *Repository* v. 12, 1828, pl. 8. W.W.J. Gendall *Views* v. 1, 1830, 87. J. Britton *and* E.W. Brayley *Devonshire & Cornwall* 1832, 103.

Lightwater Manor near Bagshot, Surrey
J. Royal Hort. Soc. 1961, 251–56.

Lilburn Tower, Lilburn, Northumberland
J. Hodgson *History of Northumberland* pt. 2, v. 2, 1832.
F.O. Morris *Series of picturesque views* v. 6, 19. *Garden* v. 49, 1896, 149.

Lilford Hall, Lilford, Northants
Garden v. 46, 1894, 169; v. 66, 1904, 139–40. *C.L.* v. 6, 1900, 112–17; v. 166, 1979, 2142–43. Lady Rockley *Historic gardens in England* 1938, 194–95. *Northamptonshire Past and Present* v. 5 no. 3, 1975, 227. M. Binney and A. Hills *Elysian gardens* 1979, 10. J. Harris *Artist and the country house* 1979, 265.

Lilleshall near Newport, Shropshire
C.L. v. 4, 1898, 80–83; v. 10, 1901, 584–85. G. Jekyll *Garden ornament* 1918, 315. J. Harris *Catalogue of British drawings . . . in American collections* 1971, 306,307. M. Binney and A. Hills *Elysian gardens* 1979, 37.

Lilliesden, Hawkhurst, Kent
J. Hort. Cottage Gdnr v. 38, 1867, 238–39.

Lillingstone Lovell, Bucks
R. Plot *Natural history of Oxfordshire* 1705, 175,266.

Lillington Manor, Leamington, Warwickshire
P. Willis *Charles Bridgeman* 1977, 181.

Lime Close, Drayton, Oxfordshire
R. Bisgrove *Gardens of Britain* v. 3, 1978, 110–11.

Lime Grove, Putney, Wandsworth, London
E.W. Brayley and J. Britton *Topographical history of Surrey* v. 3, 480.

Lime Kiln, Claydon, Suffolk
C.L. v. 157, 1975, 1670–72. *Garden* 1981, 283–85.

Limeburners, Ironbridge, Shropshire
R. Sidwell *West Midland gardens* 1981, 126–27.

Limes, Muswell Hill, Haringey, London
W. Keane *Beauties of Middlesex* 1850, 148–50.

Limpsfield, Surrey
Garden v. 61, 1902, 175–76.

Lincoln's Inn Fields see London

Linden Hall, Borwick, Lancs
J.B. Burke *Visitation* v. 2, 1853, 240.

Lindertis near Kirriemuir, Tayside
J.P. Neale *Views* v. 6, 1823.

Lindisfarne Castle, Holy Island, Northumberland
Gdn History v. 8 no. 3, 1980, 32–36,39. J. Brown *Gardens of a golden afternoon* 1982, 167. M. and R. Tooley *Gardens of Gertrude Jekyll in Northern England* 1982, 10–15,55.

Lindley Hall near Hinckley, Leics
J. Throsby *Select views in Leicestershire* v. 1, 1790, 292. J. Nichols *History . . . of county of Leicester* v. 4, 1811, 647.

Lindridge near Newton Abbot, Devon
R. Polwhele *History of Devonshire* v. 2, 1793, 149. *C.L.* v. 84, 1938, 356–60.

Ling Beeches, Scarcroft, W. Yorks
K. Lemmon *Gardens of Britain* v. 5, 1978, 176–78. A. Lees-Milne and R. Verey *Englishwoman's garden* 1980, 106–10.

Lingwood near Scone, Tayside
Scottish Gdnr and Northern Forester v. 7, 1912, 237–38.

Links, Hythe, Kent
R.I.B.A. *Catalogue* v. G-K, 1973, 141.

Linley Hall, Linley, Shropshire
G.C. ii 1880, 747–48. *C.L.* v. 130, 1961, 502–05,558.

Linlithgow Palace, Linlithgow, Lothian
Scottish Gdnr v. 11, 1862, 374–75.

Linton Park, Linton, Kent
Cottage Gdnr v. 23, 1859, 143–45,160–63; v. 26, 1861, 101–02; v. 27, 1861, 185–88,218–20,238–40,258. *J. Hort. Cottage Gdnr* v. 35, 1866, 189–90,208–09. *G.C.* i 1890, 639–40. *C.L.* v. 9, 1901, 364–65; v. 99, 1946, 578–81.

Lion House, Stamford Hill, Hackney, London
W. Keane *Beauties of Middlesex* 1850, 249.

Liscard Hall, Birkenhead, Merseyside
G.C. i 1886, 784–85.

Liscombe House near Leighton Buzzard, Bucks
G. Lipscombe *History . . . of Buckingham* v. 3, 1847, 467.

Lisle Combe, Isle of Wight
A. Paterson *Gardens of Britain* v. 2, 1978, 163–64.

Lismore Castle, Lismore, Co. Waterford, Eire
J. Hort. Cottage Gdnr v. 57, 1877, 273. *G.C.* ii 1901, 269. *J. Royal Hort. Soc.* 1960, 480–82. *C.L.* v. 136, 1964, 336–40. E. Malins and Knight of Glin *Lost demesnes* 1976, 179,180. Knight of Glin and P. Bowe *Gardens of outstanding historic interest in . . . Ireland* 1980.

Lisnabrucka House, Clifden, Co. Galway, Eire
Irish Gdning v. 12, 1917, 18–19.

Lissadell near Sligo, Co. Sligo, Eire
F.H. Purchas *Some interesting Irish experiments on Sir Jasslyn Gore-Booth's Lissadell estate* 1905. *Irish Gdning* v. 3, 1908, 39. E. Malins *and* P. Bowe *Irish gardens and demesnes* 1980, 138–40.

Lissanoure Castle, Lough Guile, Co. Antrim, Ulster
Ulster Architectural Heritage Society *Northern gardens* 1982, 20.

Lisselane near Clonakilty, Co. Cork, Eire
E. Malins *and* P. Bowe *Irish gardens and demesnes* 1980, 117–19.

Liston Hall, Liston, Essex
P. Muilman *History of Essex* v. 2, 1769, 152. P. Morant *History . . . of Essex* v. 2, 1816, 319.

Lisways Hall near Lichfield, Staffs
S. Shaw *History . . . of Staffordshire* v. 1, 1798, pl. 19.

Little Aston Hall near Lichfield, Staffs
S. Shaw *History . . . of Staffordshire* v. 2, 1801, 52. J. Nightingale *Topographical . . . description of Staffordshire* 1810, 823. *G.C.* i 1880, 12,17.

Little Birch Hall, Birch, Essex
P. Muilman *History of Essex* v. 6, 1772, 156. P. Morant *History . . . of Essex* v. 2, 1816, 184.

Little Blakenham, Suffolk
C.L. v. 157, 1975, 698–700.

Little Boarhunt, Liphook, Hants
G. Jekyll *and* L. Weaver *Gardens for small country houses* 1913, 55–59.

Little Bowden, Pangbourne, Berks
R. Bisgrove *Gardens of Britain* v. 3, 1978, 111–12.

Little Compton, Warwickshire
R. Atkyns *Ancient and present state of Glostershire* 1712, 366. L. Knyff *and* J. Kip *Britannia illustrata* v. 2, 1715. H.I. Triggs *Formal gardens in England and Scotland* 1902, 38. M. Macartney *English houses & gardens* 1908, pl. 21. *C.L.* v. 86, 1939, 64–68,90.

Little Court, Buntingford, Herts
H. Chauncy *Historical antiquities of Hertfordshire* 1700, 131. D. Stroud *Humphry Repton* 1962, 53. G. Carter *et al. Humphry Repton* 1982, 154.

Little Durnford near Wilton, Wilts
R. Pococke *Travels through England* v. 2, 1889, 135–36.

Little Glemham, Suffolk
Historical MSS Commission *Architectural history* v. 2, 1970, item 1719. M. Binney *and* A. Hills *Elysian gardens* 1979, 18.

Little Green, Compton, W. Sussex
D. Stroud *Humphry Repton* 1962, 68,171. Historical MSS Commission *Architectural history* v. 2, 1970, item 1277. G. Carter *et al. Humphry Repton* 1982, 163.

Little Grove, East Barnet, London
D. Stroud *Capability Brown* 1975, 216.

Little Haugh Hall, Norton, Suffolk
C.L. v. 123, 1958, 1238–41. J. Harris *Artist and the country house* 1979, 235.

Little Hay, Burley, Hants
A. Paterson *Gardens of Britain* v. 2, 1978, 115–17.

Little Holme, Guildford, Surrey
G. Jekyll *and* L. Weaver *Gardens for small country houses* 1913, 78–80.

Little Moreton Hall, Congleton, Cheshire
National Trust no. 26, 1976, 12. G.S. Thomas *Gardens of National Trust* 1979, 165–66.

Little Offley, Herts
H. Chauncy *Historical antiquities of Hertfordshire* 1700, 406.

Little Onn Hall, Church Eaton, Staffs
T.H. Mawson *Art & craft of garden making* 1907, 163,267–72. C. Holme *Gardens of England in Midland & Eastern counties* 1908, pl. 79. G. Beard *Thomas H. Mawson* 1976, 57. R. Sidwell *West Midland gardens* 1981, 170–72.

Little Paddocks, Sunninghill, Berks
C.L. v. 75, 1934, 494–95.

Little Paston, Fulmer, Bucks
R. Bisgrove *Gardens of Britain* v. 3, 1978, 113.

Little Pednor Farm, Chesham, Bucks
G. Jekyll *Garden ornament* 1918, 232.

Little Ridge near Tisbury, Wilts
C.L. v. 32, 1912, 566–74.

Little Tangley, Wonersh, Surrey
J. Brown *Gardens of a golden afternoon* 1982, 163.

Little Thakeham near Pulborough, W. Sussex
C.L. v. 26, 1909, 292–99. L. Weaver *Houses and gardens by E.L. Lutyens* 1913, 103–16. G. Jekyll *Garden*

Little Thakeham *(Cont.)*
ornament 1918, 301. J. Brown *Gardens of a golden afternoon* 1982, 166.

Little Walden Park near Saffron Walden, Essex
F.G. Emmison *Catalogue of maps in Essex Record Office* 1st Supplt, 1952, 22.

Little Wyrley Hall, Little Wyrley, Staffs
J. Harris *Artist and the country house* 1979, 365.

Littleberries, Hendon, Barnet, London
E.T. Evans *History and topography of the parish of Hendon* 1890, 253.

Littlebury near Saffron Walden, Essex
F.G. Emmison *Catalogue of maps in Essex Record Office* 1947, 44.

Littlecote Park near Hungerford, Wilts
J.P. Neale *Views* v. 5, 1822. *J. Hort. Cottage Gdnr* v. 36, 1866, 486–87. *C.L.* v. 12, 1902, 400–09; v. 62, 1927, 664–71; v. 139, 1966, 367; v. 138, 1965, 1406–09, 1678–81. J. Harris *Artist and the country house* 1979, 145. J. Sales *West Country gardens* 1980, 225–26. *V.C.H. Wiltshire* v. 12, 1983, 30,33.

Littleton near Staines, Surrey
W. Keane *Beauties of Middlesex* 1850, 178–81.

Livermere Park, Great Livermere, Suffolk
H. Repton *Sketches* 1794, 5–6. J.P. Neale *Views* v. 4, 1821. D. Stroud *Humphry Repton* 1962, 54. M. Binney and A. Hills *Elysian gardens* 1979, 39. J. Harris *Artist and the country house* 1979, 236–37. G. Carter *et al. Humphry Repton* 1982, 162.

Liverpool. Botanic Gardens, Merseyside and Cheshire
Catalogue of plants 1808. J.C. Loudon *Encyclopaedia of gardening* 1822, 1243. *G.C.* i 1886, 785–86,793,826; i 1964, 620–21; ii 1964, 10–11,396–97; i 1965, 38–39,48; v. 188 no. 7, v. 63, 1911, 601. M. Allan *Fisons guide* 1970, 227–28. *Northern Gdnr* v. 27 no. 1, 1972, 19–26. *C.L.* v. 175, 1984, 1058–60.

Liverpool. Prince's Park, Merseyside
N. Pevsner *Lancashire: 1* 1969, 233.

Liverpool. Sefton Park, Merseyside
G.C. 1872, 1004–05. *Garden* v. 2, 1872, 124–26. *Gdning World* v. 13, 1896, 25. C. Holme *Gardens of England in Northern counties* 1911, pls. 112–13. N. Pevsner *Lancashire: 1* 1969, 233–34. *Landscape Design* no. 139, 1982, 11–14.

Liverpool. Stanley Park, Merseyside
N. Pevsner *Lancashire: 1* 1969, 212.

Liverpool House, Walmer, Kent
C. Greenwood *Epitome of county history . . . v. 1: Kent* 1838, 430.

Llanarth Court, Llanarth, Gwent
D. Williams *History of Monmouthshire* 1796, pl. 21.
J.C. Loudon *Treatise on forming, improving and managing country residences* v. 2, 1806, pl. 15.
J.P. Neale *Views* v. 2, 1819.

Llanbedrog near Pwllheli, Gwynedd
J.B. Burke *Visitation* 2nd Series, v. 1, 1855, 79.

Llanblethian near Cowbridge, S. Glamorgan
Historical MSS Commission *Architectural history* v. 2, 1970, item 1723.

Llandilo, Gwent
D. Williams *History of Monmouthshire* 1796, pl. 34.

Llanerch House near Denbigh, Clwyd
R.C. Hoare *Collection of forty-eight views* 1806, pl. 14.
J.C. Loudon *Encyclopaedia of gardening* 1822, 1248. *Gdn Design* 1938, 108–15. R. Webber *Percy Cane* 1975, 62–63,187–88. L. Fleming and A. Gore *English garden* 1979, pl. 24. J. Harris *Artist and the country house* 1979, pl. 3.

Llangedwyn, Clwyd
Garden v. 28, 1885, 371,377,378. *C.L.* v. 22, 1907, 944–53.

Llangibby, Gwent
D. Williams *History of Monmouthshire* 1796, 294, pl. 26.

Llanover Court, Llanover, Gwent
G.C. i 1911, 273–74.

Llantarnam Abbey, Llantarnam, Gwent
R. Ackermann *Repository* v. 12, 1828, pl. 14.
W.W.J. Gendall *Views* v. 1, 1830, 86.

Llantrithyd Place, Llantrithyd, S. Glamorgan
Royal Commission on Ancient and Historical Monuments in Wales *Inventory of the ancient monuments in Glamorgan* v. 4, 1981, 176.

Llanvihangel Court, Llanvihangel Crucorney, Gwent
C.L. v. 39, 1916, 618–23.

Llanwern House near Newport, Gwent
D. Williams *History of Monmouthshire* 1796, pl. 30.
Scottish Gdnr and Northern Forester v. 8, 1913, 149–50.
C.L. v. 42, 1917, 580–86.

Llewenny Hall near Denbigh, Clwyd
W. Angus *Seats* 1787, pl. 15. R.C. Hoare *Collection of*

Llewenny Hall (*Cont.*)
forty-eight views 1806, pls. 7–9. D. Stroud *Capability Brown* 1975, 232.

Lochinch near Castle Kennedy, Dumfries and Galloway
C.L. v. 8, 1900, 840–45; v. 76, 1934, 300–05; v. 150, 1971, 384–86. *G.C.* i 1956, 234–35. P. Coats *Great gardens of Britain* 1967, 208–11. *Scots Mag.* v. 109 no. 2, 1978, 134–37. M. Binney *and* A. Hills *Elysian gardens* 1979, 24. A. Hellyer *Gardens of genius* 1980, 191–93.

Lochnaw Castle, Lochnaw, Dumfries and Galloway
J. Hort. Cottage Gdnr N.S., v. 21, 1890, 495–96.

Lochryan, Dumfries and Galloway
Scottish Gdnr and Northern Forester v. 7, 1912, 301–02.

Lochside near Yetholm, Borders
G.A. Little *Scotland's gardens* 1981, 96–97.

Locke Park *see* Barnsley

Lockinge, Wantage, Oxfordshire
G.C. i 1877, 76–77,81; ii 1882, 788–89; ii 1889, 405–06; i 1890, 40,41,161,163; ii 1896, 433,434–35; ii 1905, 312; i 1906, 65–68. *J. Hort. Cottage Gdnr* N.S., v. 34, 1897, 201–03,208–09; N.S., v. 42, 1901, 501. *Gdnrs Mag.* 1902, 713–17. *C.L.* v. 4, 1898, 48–51.

Lockington Hall, Lockington, Leics
J. Nichols *History . . . of county of Leicester* v. 3, 1804, 873.

Lockleys near Welwyn, Herts
C.L. v. 48, 1920, 48–55.

Locko Park near Derby, Derbyshire
F.O. Morris *Series of picturesque views* v. 4, 29. Historical MSS Commission *Architectural history* v. 3, 1971, item 3505. N. Pevsner *Derbyshire* 1978, 264. H. Nichols *Local maps of Derbyshire to 1770* 1980, 59,60.

Loddington Hall, Loddington, Leics
J. Throsby *Select views in Leicestershire* v. 1, 1790, 294. J. Nichols *History . . . of county of Leicester* v. 3, 1804, 1132.

Lodge near Ludlow, Shropshire
F. Calvert *Picturesque views . . . in Shropshire* 1831, 125.

Loen near Bewdley, Hereford and Worcester
R. Sidwell *West Midland gardens* 1981, 63–64.

Logan, Ardwell, Dumfries and Galloway
Official guide. *G.C.* ii 1901, 126. *Garden* 1924, 602–03. *C.L.* v. 116, 1954, 426–29. P. Coats *Great gardens of Britain* 1967, 258–65. M. Allan *Fisons guide* 1970, 305–06. *Amateur Gdning* v. 89 no. 4568, 1972, 26–27. G.A. Little *Scotland's gardens* 1981, 262.

Londesborough Park, Londesborough, Humberside
J. Beeverell *Les delices de la Grande Bretagne* v. 5, 1707, 872. L. Knyff *and* J. Kip *Britannia illustrata* v. 1, 1714. *J. Hort. Cottage Gdnr* N.S., v. 38, 1899, 342–43. *G.C.* ii 1905, 21–22. C. Holme *Gardens of England in Northern counties* 1911, pls. 81–86. I. Hall *Samuel Buck's Yorkshire sketch book* 1979, 24. *Gdn History* v. 8 no. 1, 1980, 69–90.

London. Alexandra Park, Wood Green, Haringey
R. Carrington *Alexandra Park and Palace* 1975.

London. Bakers' Company
J. Gdn History v. 2 no. 2, 1982, 101–02.

London. Battersea Park, Wandsworth
Garden v. 10, 1876, 470–72; v. 18, 1880, 617–19; v. 37, 1890, 431–32. *J. Hort. Cottage Gdnr* v. 32, 1864, 214–15; v. 34, 1865, 124–26; v. 40, 1868, 131–32,167,298–99; v. 56, 1876, 408–09. *G.C.* i 1887, 742; ii 1909, 420–21,437–38. N. Cole *Royal parks and gardens of London* 1877, 31–34. *Gdning World* v. 12, 1895, 60–61. L.C.C. *Guide to Battersea Park* 1904. J.J. Sexby *Municipal parks . . . of London* 1905, 1–23. W. Johnson *Battersea Park as a centre for nature study* 1910. *C.L.* v. 102, 1947, 684–85. *Architects' J.* v. 113, 1951, 420–23. L.C.C. *Battersea Park 1858–1958* 1958. G. Chadwick *Park and the town* 1960, 125–31,160–61.

London. Blackheath, Lewisham
J.J. Sexby *Municipal parks . . . of London* 1905, 24–29.

London. Bloomsbury Square, Camden
H. Overton *Britannia illustrata* c.1724, pl. 69. G. Carter *et al. Humphry Repton* 1982, 156.

London. Brockwell Park, Lambeth
J.J. Sexby *Municipal parks . . . of London* 1905, 71–79. *Lambethan* no. 12, 1963–68, 10–11.

London. Charterhouse Square, Islington
H. Overton *Britannia illustrata* c.1724, pl. 73.

London. Clapham Common, Lambeth
J.J. Sexby *Municipal parks . . . of London* 1905, 95–115.

London. Clissold Park, Hackney
J.J. Sexby *Municipal parks . . . of London* 1905, 320–33.

London. Crystal Palace, Hyde Park and Sydenham
P. Brannon *Park and the Crystal Palace* 1851. *Florist* 1853, 274–76; 1854, 153–55,179–81; 1855, 323–24; 1857, 204–06; 1860, 279–80. *Scottish Gdnr* v. 2, 1853,

378–79; v. 3, 1854, 211–13. *Cottage Gdnr* v. 12, 1854, 209–13,401–02,422–23; v. 13, 1854, 38–40,56–59; v. 15, 1855, 2–4,18–19,34–35. *J. Hort. Cottage Gdnr* v. 53, 1875, 313–16. *Garden* v. 10, 1876, 590–92. N. Cole *Royal parks and gardens of London* 1877, 53–58. *Landscape & Gdn* v. 4 no. 1, 1937, 26–27. *Architectural Review* v. 129, 1961, 122–27. G. Chadwick *Park and the town* 1966, passim. *C.L.* v. 144, 1968, 1252–53. A. Bird *Paxton's Palace* 1976.

London. Deptford Park, Lewisham
J.J. Sexby *Municipal parks . . . of London* 1905, 122–30.

London. Drapers' Company
J. Gdn History v. 2 no. 2, 1982, 87–92.

London. Dulwich Park, Southwark
G.C. ii 1891, 65–66; i 1892, 807–09. *Gdning World* v. 9, 1892, 119–20. J.J. Sexby *Municipal parks . . . of London* 1905, 80–94.

London. Festival Gardens, Southwark
C.L. v. 109, 1951, 1898,1900,1902.

London. Finsbury Park, Islington
G.C. ii 1889, 184–85. J.J. Sexby *Municipal parks . . . of London* 1905, 309–20.

London. Golden Square, Westminster
H. Overton *Britannia illustrata* c.1724, pl. 70.

London. Goldsmiths' Company
J. Gdn History v. 2 no. 2, 1982, 103–12.

London. Gray's Inn, Holborn
W.R. Douthwaite *Gray's Inn* 1886. *G.C.* ii 1950, 150. G. Taylor *Old London gardens* 1953, 36–41.

London. Green Park, Westminster
J.T. Smith *Antiquities of Westminster* 1807. R. Ackermann *Repository* v. 4, 1810, 245; v. 12, 1814, pl. 22. W.B. Cooke and S. Owen *History of London and its environs* v. 2, 1811, pl. 21. J.B. Papworth *Select views of London* 1816, pls. 8–9. *G.M.* v. 1, 1826, 282–83. T.M. Baynes *Parks of London* c.1830, pl. 4. *C.L.* v. 45, 1919, 775–76. H. Thurston *Royal parks for the people* 1974, 43–48. G. Williams *Royal parks of London* 1978, 49–63. Land Use Consultants *Green Park* 1983.

London. Greenwich Park, Greenwich
Gdning World v. 14, 1898, 601–02. A.D. Webster *Greenwich Park* 1902. *J. Hort. Cottage Gdnr* N.S., v. 54, 1907, 434–36. *G.C.* ii 1925, 32. *C.L.* v. 119, 1956, 372–73; v. 138, 1965, 864–67; v. 158, 1975, 1344–46. Ministry of Public Buildings and Works *Trees in Greenwich Park* 1964. R. Church *Royal parks of London* 1965, 37–44. H. Thurston *Royal parks for the people* 1974, 76–81. P. Willis *Charles Bridgeman* 1978, 178–79. G. Williams *Royal parks of London* 1978, 15–19,134–50.

London. Grocers' Company
J. Gdn History v. 2 no. 2, 1982, 96–101.

London. 17 Grove End Road, St Johns Wood
R.I.B.A. *Catalogue* v. A, 1968, 21.

London. Hackney Commons, Hackney
J.J. Sexby *Municipal parks . . . of London* 1905, 334–74.

London. Hampstead Heath, Hampstead
J.J. Sexby *Municipal parks . . . of London* 1905, 375–412.

London. Hanover Square, Westminster
H. Overton *Britannia illustrata* c.1724, pl. 67.

London. Highbury Fields, Islington
J.J. Sexby *Municipal parks . . . of London* 1905, 436–46.

London. Hilly Fields, Lewisham
J.J. Sexby *Municipal parks . . . of London* 1905, 116–22.

London. Holland Park, Kensington
G.C. ii 1889, 619–20; v. 179 no. 23, 1976, 20–23. *Landscape Design* no. 126, 1979, 29–32.

London. Hyde Park, Westminster
G.M. v. 1, 1826, 280–82; v. 15, 1839, 131–34. British Museum *Catalogue of maps, prints* 1829, 204. T.M. Baynes *Parks of London* c.1830, pl. 3. C.F. Partington *National history and views of London* v. 1, 1834, 27–28. P. Brannon *Hyde Park and the Crystal Palace* 1851. *J. Hort. Cottage Gdnr* v. 46, 1871, 237–39; v. 56, 1876, 448–50. N. Cole *Royal parks and gardens of London* 1877, 19–24. *G.C.* ii 1888, 12; v. 164 no. 14, 1968, 16–17. J. Ashton *Hyde Park from Domesday Book to date* 1896. A. Tweedie *Hyde Park* 1908. E. Dancy *Hyde Park* 1937. A.P. Oppé *Drawings of Paul and Thomas Sandby* 1947, 50–53. *C.L.* v. 103, 1948, 81. R. Church *Royal parks of London* 1965, 15–22. *J. Royal Hort. Soc.* 1968, 214–18. Historical MSS Commission *Architectural history* v. 2, 1970, item 1895. N. Pevsner *London* v. 1, 1973, 589–91. T. Thurston *Royal parks for the people* 1974, 15–26. P. Willis *Charles Bridgeman* 1977, 180. G. Williams *Royal parks of London* 1978, 64–77,91––133. Land Use Consultants *Hyde Park* 1983.

London. Island Gardens, Poplar, Tower Hamlets
J.J. Sexby *Municipal parks . . . of London* 1905, 447–57.

London. Kennington Park, Lambeth
J.J. Sexby *Municipal parks . . . of London* 1905, 141–57.

London. Kensington Palace and Gardens, Kensington
Official guide. T. Tickell *Kensington Gardens* 1722. H. Overton *Britannia illustrata* c.1724, pl. 3. J. Kip *Nouveau theatre de la Grande Bretagne* v. 4, 1729. T. Badeslade *and* J. Rocque *Vitruvius Brittanicus* 1739, pls. 2–3. S. Switzer *Ichnographia rustica* v. 1, 1742, 83. F.I. Mannskirsch *Views of parks and gardens* 1813, pls. 1–2. W.H. Pyne *History of the royal residences* v. 2, 1819. British Museum *Catalogue of maps, prints* 1829, 171. J. Sargeant *Views in Kensington Gardens* 1831. C.F. Partington *National history and views of London* v. 1, 1834, 60–61. *G.M.* v. 13, 1837, 145–57; v. 15, 1839, 131–34; v. 18, 1842, 382–83; v. 19, 1843, 285–92; v. 19, 1843, 650–51. *J. Hort. Cottage Gdnr* N.S., v. 56, 1876, 368–69. *G.C.* ii 1880, 208–09; i 1897, 395; ii 1909, 265. N. Cole *Royal parks and gardens of London* 1877, 7–10. *Garden* v. 13, 1878, 243–44. *Architectural Review* v. 6, 1899, 40–42; v. 32, 1912, 3–5; v. 48, 1920, pls. v–vi. *C.L.* v. 14, 1903, 825–26; v. 16, 1904, 622–24; v. 61, 1927, 168–74; v. 138, 1965, 1318–20. W.L. Rutton *Making of Kensington Gardens* 1904. *Home Counties Mag.* v. 6, 1904, 145–59. *Gdnrs Mag.* 1910, 670–71. C. Ward *Royal gardens* 1912, 82–90. *J. British Archaeological Association* v. 14, 1951, 8–10. G. Taylor *Old London gardens* 1953, 168–72. J. Evelyn *Diary* v. 5, 1955, 8,237,606. D. Green *Gardener to Queen Anne* 1956, passim. W. Gaunt *Kensington* 1958. R. Church *Royal parks of London* 1965, 23–27. *J. Royal Hort. Soc.* 1968, 214–18. D. Hudson *Kensington Palace* 1968. H. Thurston *Royal parks for the people* 1974, 27–34. H.M. Colvin *History of the King's Works* v. 5, 1976, 191–94,203–04; v. 6, 1973, 348–49. P. Willis *Charles Bridgeman* 1977, 180. G. Williams *Royal parks of London* 1978, 91–133. L. Fleming *and* A. Gore *English garden* 1979, 64. Land Use Consultants *Kensington Gardens* 1983.

London. Kings Square, Soho, Westminster
H. Overton *Britannia illustrata* c.1724, pl. 71.

London. Lambeth
M.P.G. Draper *Lambeth's open spaces* 1979.

London. Leicester Square, Westminster
H. Overton *Britannia illustrata* c.1724, pl. 72. *Garden* v. 6, 1874, 1. J.J. Sexby *Municipal parks . . . of London* 1905, 466–86. M. Hadfield *et al. British gardeners* 1980, 131.

London. Lincoln's Inn Fields, Camden
J.J. Sexby *Municipal parks . . . of London* 1905, 487–510. *G.C.* i 1895, 261–62. G. Hurst *Short history of Lincoln's Inn* 1946. G. Taylor *Old London gardens* 1953, 26–28.

London. Marylebone Park, Westminster
London and Middlesex Antiquarian Soc. v. 21, 1967, 178.

London. Maryon Park, Greenwich
J.J. Sexby *Municipal parks . . . of London* 1905, 166–71.

London. Peckham Rye Park, Southwark
J.J. Sexby *Municipal parks . . . of London* 1905, 176–89.

London. Primrose Hill, Camden
D.o.E. *and* Directorate of Ancient Monuments and Historic Buildings *Regent's Park & Primrose Hill* 1983.

London. Ravenscourt Park, Hammersmith
J. Hort. Cottage Gdnr N.S., v. 43, 1901, 242–43,247. J.J. Sexby *Municipal parks . . . of London* 1905, 518–26.

London. Red Lion Square, Camden
H. Overton *Britannia illustrata* c.1724, pl. 68. J.J. Sexby *Municipal parks . . . of London* 1905, 510–17.

London. Regent's Park, Westminster
J. White *Some account of the proposed improvements of the western part of London* 1814. J. Elmes *Metropolitan improvements* 1828. *G.M.* v. 15, 1839, 322–25; v. 16, 1840, 321–22,514–17,605–06. *Florist* 1848, 181; 1849, 197–98; 1854, 314–15. W. Keane *Beauties of Middlesex* 1850, 19–24. *G.C.* 1871, 547–48; ii 1883, 720,721; ii 1889, 184; ii 1936, 63–64; ii 1937, 55; ii 1964, 556–57,595. *Garden* v. 1, 1872, 234–36. *J. Hort. Cottage Gdnr* N.S., v. 56, 1876, 283–84; N.S., v. 57, 1877, 234–35. N. Cole *Royal parks and gardens of London* 1877, 15–18,35–38. P.E.F. Perrédès *London botanic gardens* 1906, 40–48. A.D. Webster *Regent's Park and Primrose Hill* 1911. J. Summerson *John Nash* 1949, passim. R. Church *Royal parks of London* 1965, 28–36. G. Chadwick *Park and the town* 1966, passim. A. Saunders *Regent's Park* 1969. N.T. Newton *Design on the land* 1971, 226. H. Thurston *Royal parks for the people* 1974, 49–59. *Architectural History* v. 20, 1977, 56–62. G. Williams *Royal parks of London* 1978, 198–220. *London J.* v. 6 no. 2, 1980, 135–46. D.o.E. *and* Directorate of Ancient Monuments and Historic Buildings *Regent's Park & Primrose Hill* 1983. D. Jacques *Georgian gardens* 1983, 204–05.

London. Royal Victoria Gardens, Greenwich
J.J. Sexby *Municipal parks . . . of London* 1905, 457–65.

London. St James's Park, Westminster
J. Beeverell *Les delices de la Grande Bretagne* v. 4, 1707, 837. H. Overton *Britannia illustrata* c.1724, pl. 5. J.T. Smith *Antiquities of Westminster* 1807, pls. 4, 45,90. F.I. Mannskirsch *Views of parks and gardens* 1813, pls. 3–4. R. Ackermann *Repository* v. 12, 1814, pl. 17. J.B. Papworth *Select views of London* 1816, pls. 8–9. *G.M.* v. 1, 1826, 283; v. 18, 1842, 381–82.

London. St James's Park (*Cont.*)

British Museum *Catalogue of maps, prints* 1829, 204–05. T.M. Baynes *Parks of London* c.1830, pl. 1. C.F. Partington *National history and views of London* v. 1, 1834, 99–102. J. Dennis *Landscape gardener* 1835, 41. *Garden* v. 4, 1873, 381–82. N. Cole *Royal parks and gardens of London* 1877, 25–26. *G.C.* ii 1888, 68; i 1911, 200–01. E. Cecil *History of gardening in England* 1910, 180–85. *C.L.* v. 45, 1919, 776; v. 119, 1956, 372–73; v. 150, 1971, 550. *Architectural Review* v. 110, 1951, 292–98. D. Green *Gardener to Queen Anne* 1956, passim. *London Naturalist* no. 44, 1965, 128–38. R. Church *Royal parks of London* 1965, 7–14. G. Chadwick *Parks and the town* 1966, passim. J. Harris *Catalogue of British drawings . . . in American collections* 1971, 38. H.M. Colvin *History of the King's Works* v. 6, 1973, 292. N. Pevsner *London* v. 1, 1973, 642. H. Thurston *Royal parks for the people* 1974, 43–48. D. Stroud *Capability Brown* 1975, 232. P. Willis *Charles Bridgeman* 1977, 182. *History Today* v. 28, 1978, 264–69. G. Williams *Royal parks of London* 1978, 21–48. J. Harris *Artist and the country house* 1979, 113. T. Wright *Arbours & grottos* 1979. Land Use Consultants *St James Park* 1983. D. Jacques *Georgian gardens* 1983, 82.

London. Skinners Company
J. Gdn History v. 2 no. 2, 1982, 102–03.

London. Southwark Park, Southwark
J.J. Sexby *Municipal parks . . . of London* 1905, 190–99.

London. Spa Green, Clerkenwell
J.J. Sexby *Municipal parks . . . of London* 1905, 530–42.

London. Stationers Company
J. Gdn History v. 2 no. 2, 1982, 92–96.

London. Streatham Common, Lambeth
J.J. Sexby *Municipal parks . . . of London* 1905, 224–34.

London. Sydenham Park, Lewisham
Architectural Review v. 129, 1961, 122–27.

London. Telegraph Hill, Lewisham
J.J. Sexby *Municipal parks . . . of London* 1905, 130–40.

London. Temple, Westminster
G. Taylor *Old London gardens* 1953, 28–36.

London. Thames Embankment
J. Hort. Cottage Gdnr v. 44, 1870, 393–95. *Garden* v. 1, 1871, 47–48. *Gdnrs Mag.* v. 14, 1871, 309–10,14. J.J. Sexby *Municipal parks . . . of London* 1905, 262–308.

London. Tooting Bec Common, Wandsworth
J.J. Sexby *Municipal parks . . . of London* 1905, 209–24.

London. Vauxhall Park, Lambeth
J. Hort. Cottage Gdnr N.S., v. 21, 1890, 21.

London. Victoria Park, Tower Hamlets
Commissioner of Woods and Forests *18th report 1841: Appendix.* W. Robinson *History . . . of . . . Hackney* v. 1, 1842, 202–06. *G.C.* 1871, 1548; ii 1874, 227–28, 229. *Garden* v. 1, 1872, 327–29. *J. Hort. Cottage Gdnr* v. 56, 1876, 489–90; N.S., v. 36, 1898, 155–56. N. Cole *Royal parks and gardens of London* 1877, 27–30. *Gdning World* v. 14, 1897, 74. J.J. Sexby *Municipal parks . . . of London* 1905, 553–71. N. Pevsner *London* v. 2, 1952, 173. *East London Papers* v. 5 no. 2, 1962, 73–90. G. Chadwick *Park and the town* 1966, passim. N.T. Newington *Design on the land* 1971, 228. C. Poulsen *Victoria Park* 1976.

London. Wandsworth Common, Wandsworth
J.J. Sexby *Municipal parks . . . of . . . London* 1905, 235–49.

London. Waterlow Park, Camden
J.J. Sexby *Municipal parks . . . of London* 1905, 575–98.

London. Welsh Harp, Brent
C.L. v. 138, 1965, 188,191.

London. West Ham Park, Newham
G. Pagenstecher *Story of West Ham Park* 1895.

London Botanic Garden (William Curtis), Lambeth, London
W. Curtis *Catalogue of the British, medicinal, culinary and agricultural plants cultivated in the London Botanic Garden* 1783. *Chronica Botanica* v. 9, 1945, 75, pl. 9.

London Botanic Garden (William Salisbury), Chelsea, London
Gentleman's Mag. 1810, 113–14. W. Salisbury *Botanist's companion* v. 1, 1816, frontispiece. *G.C.* i 1900, 65–66.

London Spa, Clerkenwell, Islington, London
W. Wroth *London pleasure grounds of the eighteenth century* 1896, 29–32.

Long Ashton Court, Long Ashton, Avon
J. Collinson *History . . . of Somersetshire* v. 2, 1791, 294.

Long Barn near Sevenoaks, Kent
C.L. v. 169, 1981, 924–26. J. Brown *Gardens of a golden afternoon* 1982, 175.

Long View, Reigate, Surrey
R. Webber *Percy Cane* 1975, 175,184.

Longford Castle, Odstock, Wilts
W. Angus *Seats* 1787, pl. 10. J.P. Neale *Views* 2nd Series, v. 4, 1828. *G.M.* v. 8, 1832, 548–51. *G.C.* ii 1876, 9–10; ii 1880, 588–89; i 1886, 44,45; ii 1892, 61–62; ii 1911, 283–84,302–03. *J. Hort. Cottage Gdnr* N.S., v. 7, 1883, 274–76; N.S., v. 41, 1900, 292–93. *Garden* v. 33, 1888, 453–54; v. 57, 1900, 467. *C.L.* v. 4, 1898, 176–79; v. 70, 1931, 648–55,696,724; v. 136, 1964, 608–11. H.I. Triggs *Formal gardens in England and Scotland* 1902, 13. C. Holme *Gardens of England in Southern & Western counties* 1907, pls. 88–89. G. Jekyll *Garden ornament* 1918, 108. Lady Rockley *Historic gardens of England* 1938, 204–05. C. Fiennes *Journeys* 1949, 57–58. N. Pevsner *Wiltshire* 1975, 308. D. Stroud *Capability Brown* 1975, 233. M. Binney and A. Hills *Elysian gardens* 1979, 33. L. Fleming and A. Gore *English garden* 1979, 30. J. Harris *Artist and the country house* 1979, 104.

Longford Hall, Longford, Derbyshire
C.L. v. 17, 1905, 630–36.

Longford Hall near Stretford, Greater Manchester
Cottage Gdnr v. 27, 1862, 353–54,417–18. *G.C.* ii 1875, 195–96,226–27.

Longford Hall, Longford, Shropshire
C.L. v. 132, 1962, 354–58.

Longhurst, Northumberland
J. Hodgson *History of Northumberland* pt 2, v. 2, 1832, 163.

Longleat near Warminster, Wilts
Official guide. J. Beeverall *Les delices de la Grande Bretagne* v. 5, 1707, 872. L. Knyff and J. Kip *Britannia illustrata* v. 1, 1714. H. Overton *Britannia illustrata* c.1724, pl. 10. C. Campbell *Vitruvius Britannicus* v. 3, 1725, pls. 63–64. S. Switzer *Ichnographia rustica* v. 1, 1742, 78–79. J. Britton *Beauties of Wiltshire* v. 2, 1801, 31–33. H. Repton *Fragments* 1816, 115–23. J.P. Neale *Views* v. 5, 1822. R. Havell *Series of picturesque views* 1823. *G.M.* v. 9, 1833, 425. J. Dennis *Landscape gardener* 1835, 14–15. R.R. Pocock *Views of Longleat House* c.1840. *Florist* 1856, 259–61. *J. Hort. Cottage Gdnr* v. 50, 1873, 9–11. F.O. Morris *Series of picturesque views* v. 5, 35. *Garden* v. 16, 1879, 481–85. *G.C.* ii 1885, 743–45; ii 1890, 695–96; ii 1891, 271–72. *C.L.* v. 2, 1897, 154–56; v. 12, 1902, 496–503; v. 105, 1949, 926,990–93. *Architectural Review* v. 8, 1901, 2–4. G. Jekyll *Garden ornament* 1918, 187,238. H. Walpole *Visits to country seats. Walpole Society* v. 7, 1927–28, 45. D. Green *Gardener to Queen Anne* 1956, 9–12. D. Stroud *Humphry Repton* 1962, 131–32. M. Allan *Fisons guide* 1970, 100. *Quarterly J. of Forestry* v. 66 no. 3, 1972, 258–60. N. Pevsner *Wiltshire* 1975, 313. D. Stroud *Capability Brown* 1975, 85–86,233.
D. Burnett *Longleat* 1978. L. Fleming and A. Gore *English garden* 1979, 65. J. Harris *Artist and the country house* 1979, 69. J. Sales *West Country gardens* 1980, 227–32. J. Johnson *Excellent Cassandra* 1981, 66–67. *J. Gdn History* v. 2 no. 1, 1982, 51. G. Carter *et al. Humphry Repton* 1982, 163. *Gdn History* v. 11 no. 1, 1983, 12–14,30–31.

Longnor Hall, Longnor, Shropshire
D. Stroud *Humphry Repton* 1962, 133. *C.L.* v. 135, 1964, 328–31,396. V.C.H. *Shropshire* v. 8, 1968, 110. G. Carter *et al. Humphry Repton* 1982, 161.

Longstock Park near Stockbridge, Hants
G.C. v. 180 no. 2, 1976, 22–23. M. Allan *Fisons guide* 1970, 101–02. *Garden* 1978, 189–94. A. Paterson *Gardens of Britain* v. 2, 1978, 118–19.

Longworth, Lugwardine, Hereford and Worcester
J.P. Neale *Views* 2nd Series, v. 4, 1828.

Loraine, St Ives, Cornwall
G.C. ii 1965, 540–41.

'Lord Cobham's Head', Islington, London
W. Wroth *London pleasure gardens of the eighteenth century* 1896, 68–69.

Loseley near Guildford, Surrey
O. Manning and W. Bray *History . . . of Surrey* v. 1, 1804, 98. G.F. Prosser *Select illustrations of . . . Surrey* 1828. W. Keane *Beauties of Surrey* 1849, 123–24. *Garden* v. 30, 1886, 469. *Architectural Review* v. 29, 1911, 40–43. *C.L.* v. 5, 1899, 272–74; v. 77, 1935, 544–49; v. 146, 1969, 802–05. G. Jekyll *Garden ornament* 1918, 100. Lady Rockley *Historic gardens of England* 1938, 130–31. Architectural MSS Commission *Architectural history* v. 3, 1971, item 3137.

Lotherton Hall, Aberford, W. Yorks
Gdn History v. 6 no. 2, 1978, 11–15. K. Lemmon *Gardens of Britain* v. 5, 1978, 180–83.

Loudoun Castle, Strathclyde
J.C. Loudon *Arboretum et fruticetum Britannicum* v. 1, 1844, 101.

Lough Key Forest Park, Co. Roscommon, Eire
Knight of Glin and P. Bowe *Gardens of outstanding historic interest in . . . Ireland* 1980.

Loughcrew near Oldcastle, Co. Meath, Eire
Cottage Gdnr v. 27, 1861, 298–301; v. 27, 1862, 310–12. *G.C.* ii 1884, 244–45. E. Malins and P. Bowe *Irish gardens and demesnes* 1980, 20–26.

Loughfea near Carrickmacross, Co. Monaghan, Ulster
E. Malins *and* P. Bowe *Irish gardens and demesnes* 1980, 31.

Low Ham, Somerset
Proc. Somerset Archaeological and Natural History Soc. 1977/78, 11–28.

Lower Eatington Hall near Shipston on Stour, Warwickshire
J.P. Neale *Views* v. 4, 1821.

Lower Hall, Worfield, Shropshire
C.L. v. 161, 1977, 492–94. R. Sidwell *West Midland gardens* 1981, 127–30.

Lower Sandhill, Halland, E. Sussex
R. Webber *Percy Cane* 1975, 165.

Lowesby Hall, Lowesby, Leics
G.M. v. 7, 1831, 428–29. *C.L.* v. 18, 1905, 342–48; v. 37, 1915, 626–33; v. 39, 1916, 105. Lady Rockley *Historic gardens of England* 1938, 164–65. M. Binney and A. Hills *Elysian gardens* 1979, 20.

Lowther Castle, Lowther, Cumbria
J. Beeverell *Les delices de la Grande Bretagne* v. 5, 1707, 872. L. Knyff *and* J. Kip *Britannia illustrata* v. 1, 1714. C. Campbell *Vitruvius Britannicus* v. 3, 1725, pl. 76. J.C. Loudon *Encyclopaedia of gardening* 1822, 1244. J.P. Neale *Views* v. 5, 1822. *G.M.* v. 7, 1831, 548–49. J.B. Burke *Visitation* 2nd Series, v. 1, 1855, 29. F.O. Morris *Series of picturesque views* v. 2, 65. *G.C.* i 1876, 496–98,534–36; ii 1884, 455–56; ii 1893, 334; i 1897, 307–08. L. Jewitt *and* S.C. Hall *Stately homes of England* 1877, 291–316. H.I. Triggs *Formal gardens in England and Scotland* 1902, 42. C. Holme *Gardens of England in Northern counties* 1911, pls. 87–93. *Garden* 1915, 626–28. C. Fiennes *Journeys* 1949, 199. D. Stroud *Capability Brown* 1975, 114–15,233. J. Harris *Artist and the country house* 1979, 153. Tyne and Wear County Council Museums *Capability Brown and the northern Landscape* 1983, 31,42. D. Jacques *Georgian gardens* 1983, 78,199.

Loxford Hall, Ilford, Redbridge, London
J. Hort. Cottage Gdnr v. 45, 1871, 419; v. 53, 1875, 472–75.

Loxley Hall, Loxley, Staffs
J.P. Neale *Views* v. 4, 1821. R. Sidwell *West Midland gardens* 1981, 216–18.

Lucan House, Lucan, Co. Dublin, Eire
T. Milton *Seats . . . in Ireland* 1783–93, 5.

Ludgvan near Penzance, Cornwall
G.C. ii 1962, 297. *Cornish Gdn* no. 24, 1981, 28–29. *International Dendrology Soc. Year Book* 1981, 99–100.

Ludstone Hall, Claverley, Shropshire
C.L v. 111, 1952, 92–95,222–25. R. Sidwell *West Midland gardens* 1981, 130–32.

Luffness, Aberlady, Lothian
G.A. Little *Scotland's gardens* 1981, 97.

Luggala near Roundwood, Co. Wicklow, Eire
E. Malins *and* Knight of Glin *Lost demesnes* 1976, 169–71.

Lullingstone Castle, Eynsford, Kent
C.L. v. 34, 1913, 602–08; v. 173, 1983, 1053. J. Harris *Artist and the country house* 1979, 82. S. Pittman *Lullingstone Park* 1983.

Lululaund, Bushey, Herts
G. Beard *Thomas H. Mawson* 1976, 57.

Lulworth Castle, East Lulworth, Dorset
J. Kip *Nouveau theatre de la Grande Bretagne* v. 4, 1729. W. Watts *Seats* 1779, pl. 71. *Copper Plate Mag.* v. 4, pl. 198. J.P. Neale *Views* 2nd Series, v. 4, 1828. J. Hutchins *History . . . of Dorset* v. 1, 1861, 374. *C.L.* v. 59, 1926, 52–60. Historical MSS Commission *Architectural history* v. 1, 1969, item 580. J. Harris *Artist and the country house* 1979, 131.

Lumley Castle, Chester-le-Street, Co. Durham
Society of Gentlemen *England displayed* v. 2, 1769, 166. S. *and* N. Buck *Buck's antiquities* v. 1, 1774, pl. 86. C. Burlington *Modern universal British traveller* 1779, 591. G.A. Walpoole *New British traveller* 1784, 148. W. Angus *Seats* 1787, pl. 37. J.P. Neale *Views* v. 1, 1818. F.O. Morris *Series of picturesque views* v. 4, 9. *Garden* v. 49, 1896, 303. D. Jacques *Georgian gardens* 1983, 88.

Lupset Hall near Wakefield, W. Yorks
I. Hall *Samuel Buck's Yorkshire sketchbook* 1979, 148.

Luscombe Castle near Totnes, Devon
J.P. Neale *Views* v. 1, 1818. R. Ackermann *Repository* v. 12, 1828, pl. 7. W.W.J. Gendall *Views* v. 2, 1830, 78. *G.M.* v. 8, 1832, 566–67; v. 18, 1842, 533–34. J. Britton *and* E.W. Brayley *Devonshire & Cornwall* 1832, 63. *G.C.* i 1882, 743–44,745. *C.L.* v. 119, 1956, 248–51,292. D. Stroud *Humphry Repton* 1962, 106. L. Fleming *and* A. Gore *English garden* 1979, 154–56. G. Carter *et al. Humphry Repton* 1982, 75,150–51.

Luss near Dumbarton, Strathclyde
Copper Plate Mag. v. 1, 1792, pl. 30.

Luton Hoo near Luton, Beds
Official guide. Society of Gentlemen *England displayed* v. 1, 1769, 352. D. Defoe *Tour* v. 3, 1778, 52–53. W. Watts *Seats* 1779, pl. 69. *Bibliotheca topographica Britannica* v. 4 no. 8, 1790, 65. *J. Hort. Cottage Gdnr* v. 48. 1872, 310–12; N.S., v. 38, 1899, 30–31. *Garden* v. 8, 1875, 248–49. *G.C.* i 1885, 787–88; ii 1886, 490–91; i 1889, 594–95; ii 1889, 72; i 1897, 93,95,108. P. Coats *Great gardens of Britain* 1967, 124–29. M. Allan *Fisons guide* 1970, 15–16. D. Stroud *Capability Brown* 1975, 133–34. R. Bisgrove *Gardens of Britain* v. 3, 1978, 114–15. *Bedfordshire Mag.* v. 18, 1982, 275–77.

Luttrellstown, Co. Dublin, Eire
E. Malins *and* Knight of Glin *Lost demesnes* 1976, 74–77. Knight of Glin *and* S. Bowe *Gardens of outstanding historic interest in . . . Ireland* 1980.

Luxborough near Waltham Abbey, Essex
J. Harris *Artist and the country house* 1979, 337.

Lyddington Bede House, Lyddington, Leics
C.L. v. 26, 1909, 126–34. G. Jekyll *Garden ornament* 1918, 199.

Lydiard, Lydiard Tregoze, Wilts
C.L. v. 103, 1948, 578–81. V.C.H. *Wiltshire* v. 9, 1970, 80.

Lydiate Hall, Lydiate, Lancs
Historical MSS Commission *Architectural history* v. 3, 1971, item 3146.

Lydney Park, Lydney, Glos
Official guide. S. Rudder *New history of Gloucestershire* 1779, 524. J. Sales *West Country gardens* 1980, 85–87. *C.L.* v. 169, 1981, 1585–88.

Lyegrove near Chipping Sodbury, Avon
C.L. v. 66, 1929, 864–70; v. 129, 1961, 494–96; v. 156, 1974, 316–17. P. Coats *Great gardens of Britain* 1967, 222–27. A. Lees-Milne *and* R. Verey *Englishwoman's garden* 1980, 149–52. J. Sales *West Country gardens* 1980, 87–90.

Lyme Park near Disley, Cheshire
Official guide. W. Watts *Seats* 1779, pl. 79. J.P. Neale *Views* 2nd Series, v. 1, 1824. W. Adam *Gem of the Peak* 1851, 325–28. J.B. Burke *Visitation* 2nd Series, v. 1, 1855, 34. *C.L.* v. 16, 1904, 906–15; v. 156, 1974, 1724–27,1858–61,1998. G. Jekyll *Garden ornament* 1918, 239. Lady Rockley *Historic gardens of England* 1938, 152–53. *J. Royal Hort. Soc.* 1971, 214–15. B. Jones *Follies & grottoes* 1974, 296. J. Harris *Artist and the country house* 1979, 143. G.S. Thomas *Gardens of National Trust* 1979, 166–68.

Lyme Park *see* Stockport

Lymore near Montgomery, Powys
C.L. v. 23, 1908, 342–49.

Lympne Castle, Lympne, Kent
C.L. v. 28, 1910, 682–89.

Lyne, Newdigate, Surrey
E.W. Brayley *and* J. Britton *Topographical history of Surrey* v. 4, 290.

Lyneham near Plymouth, Devon
Architectural History v. 7, 1964, 31,75.

Lynford Hall, Lynford, Norfolk
G.C. ii 1884, 359–61,365. *C.L.* v. 14, 1903, 758–65.

Lyng Rectory, Lyng, Norfolk
G. Carter *et al. Humphry Repton* 1982, 159.

Lynsted, Kent
L. Knyff *and* J. Kip *Britannia illustrata* v. 2, 1715. C. Greenwood *Epitome of county history . . . v. 1: Kent* 1838, 206. J. Harris *Artist and the country house* 1979, 112.

Lyons near Celbridge, Co. Kildare, Eire
J.P. Neale *Views* 2nd Series, v. 2, 1825. *J. Hort. Cottage Gdnr* v. 29, 1863, 261–63,277–79.

Lypiatt Park near Stroud, Glos
R. Atkyns *Ancient and present state of Glostershire* 1712, 701. L. Knyff *and* J. Kip *Britannia illustrata* v. 2, 1715. *C.L.* v. 8, 1900, 688–94. *Lily Yearbook* 1948, 1–3. V.C.H. *Gloucester* v. 11, 1976, 112,113.

Lytchett Heath, Lytchett Matravers, Dorset
J. Royal Hort. Soc. 1931, 56–60. Lady Rockley *Historic gardens of England* 1938, 246–47.

Lytes Cary near Ilchester, Somerset
C.L. v. 102, 1947, 128–31,228–31; v. 172, 1982, 634–36. *J. Royal Hort. Soc.* 1971, 221. G.S. Thomas *Gardens of National Trust* 1979, 168. J. Sales *West Country gardens* 1980, 160–62.

Lytham Hall, Lytham, Lancs
J. Hort. Cottage Gdnr v. 48, 1872, 383–85,406–07. C. Holme *Gardens of England in Northern counties* 1911, pls. 94–95. *C.L.* v. 128, 1960, 130–33.

Lythe, Ellesmere, Shropshire
R. Sidwell *West Midland gardens* 1981, 132–33.

Lythe Hill, Haslemere, Surrey
G.C. i 1883, 789–90.

Lyveden New Bield, Oundle, Northants
Northamptonshire Past and Present v. 5 no. 3, 1975, 227–28; v. 5 no. 5, 1977, 397–400. *Archaeological J.* v. 129, 1972, 154–60. *C.L.* v. 166, 1979, 2144. J. Anthony *Gardens of Britain* v. 6, 1979, 117–19. G.S. Thomas *Gardens of National Trust* 1979, 169. C. Taylor *Archaeology of gardens* 1983, 18,21,46–47.

Mabie near Dumfries, Dumfries and Galloway
Scottish Gdnr and Northern Forester v. 8, 1913, 625–26.

Mabledon Park near Tonbridge, Kent
C. Greenwood *Epitome of county history . . . v. 1: Kent* 1838, 125.

Maby Hall, Cheshire
G. Beard *Thomas H. Mawson* 1976, 58.

Mackerye End, Harpenden, Herts
C.L. v. 119, 1956, 108–11. R. Bisgrove *Gardens of Britain* v. 3, 1978, 116.

Madeley Court, Madeley, Shropshire
C.L. v. 42, 1917, 12–17; v. 131, 1962, 723.

Madeley Manor, Madeley, Staffs
R. Plot *Natural history of Staffordshire* 1685, 223.

Madingley Hall, Madingley, Cambs
J. Beeverell *Les delices de la Grande Bretagne* v. 5, 1707, 872. L. Knyff and J. Kip *Britannia illustrata* v. 1, 1714. J.P. Neale *Views* 2nd Series v. 1, 1824. *C.L.* v. 32, 1912, 454–65. D. Stroud *Capability Brown* 1975, 79–80.

Madresfield Court near Great Malvern, Hereford and Worcester
J. Hort. Cottage Gdnr v. 41, 1869, 392; N.S., v. 18, 1889, 278–80. *Garden* v. 33, 1888, 49–50. *Gdning World* v. 1, 1884, 77–78. *G.C.* i 1893, 100–01,105; i 1899, 50–51; ii 1909, 389–90,399,411–12. *J. Hort. N.S.*, v. 68, 1914, 221–26. *C.L.* v. 21, 1907, 450–60; v. 176, 1984, 6–8. G. Jekyll *Garden ornament* 1918, 109,393. V.C.H. *Worcester* v. 4, 1924, 119. G. Beard *Thomas H. Mawson* 1976, 58. M. Binney and A. Hills *Elysian gardens* 1979, 20. R. Sidwell *West Midland gardens* 1981, 64–69.

Madryn near Pwllheli, Gwynedd
J.B. Burke *Visitation* 2nd Series, v. 1, 1855, 33.

Maenan Hall near Eglwys Fach, Gwynedd
C.L. v. 129, 1961, 334–37.

Maer Hall, Shropshire
G. Beard *Thomas H. Mawson* 1976, 58.

Maesllwch Castle near Hay, Powys
G.M. v. 13, 1837, 205–06.

Maesruddud, Newport, Gwent
G. Beard *Thomas H. Mawson* 1976, 58.

Magnolia House, Yoxford, Suffolk
C.L. v. 155, 1974, 872–74. A. Lees-Milne and R. Verey *Englishman's garden* 1982, 120–23.

Magnolias, Merrington, Shropshire
R. Sidwell *West Midland gardens* 1981, 133–34.

Maiden Bradley House, Maiden Bradley, Wilts
C.L. v. 9, 1901, 464–68.

Maiden Erlegh near Reading, Berks
D. Stroud *Capability Brown* 1975, 233. G. Carter et al. *Humphry Repton* 1982, 148.

Maidstone. Cemetery, Kent
J. Hort. Cottage Gdnr v. 22, 1872, 256–58.

Maidwell Hall, Maidwell, Northants
G.C. ii 1960, 116–17,130.

Mainhouse near Kelso, Borders
G.A. Little *Scotland's gardens* 1981, 98.

Malahide Castle, Malahide, Co. Dublin, Eire
C.L. v. 101, 1947, 710–13; v. 159, 1976, 1172–73. M. Stones *Endemic flora of Tasmania* 1967–80, 6v. *University of Washington Arboretum Bulletin* 1980, 10–16. E. Malins and P. Bowe *Irish gardens and demesnes* 1980, 171–72. Knight of Glin and P. Bowe *Gardens of outstanding historic interest in . . . Ireland* 1980.

Malcolm House, Batsford, Glos
M. Allan *Fisons guide* 1970, 160.

Malleny House near Balerno, Lothian
H. Maxwell *Scottish gardens* 1911, 83–84. G.A. Little *Scotland's gardens* 1981, 98–100.

Malling Abbey, West Malling, Kent
Historical MSS Commission *Architectural history* v. 3, 1971, item 3155.

Malmesbury House, Salisbury, Wilts
C.L. v. 130, 1961, 882–85,1002.

Malone *see* Cranmore

Malshanger near Basingstoke, Hants
G.C. ii 1899, 185.

Malsis Hall near Glusburn, N. Yorks
Bradford Illustrated Weekly Telegraph *Series of picturesque views* 1885.

Malvern Hall near Solihull, W. Midlands
J. Harris *Artist and the country house* 1979, 355.

Mamhead near Exmouth, Devon
R. Polwhele *History of Devonshire* v. 2, 1793, 154. J. Britton *and* E.W. Brayley *Beauties of England and Wales* v. 4, 1803, 99. J.P. Neale *Views* v. 1, 1818. *Jones's views* 1829. J. Britton *and* E.W. Brayley *Devonshire & Cornwall* 1832, 64. G.M. v. 11, 1835, 127–32; v. 18, 1842, 491–94,531–32. *Cottage Gdnr* v. 21, 1858, 115–17. F.O. Morris *Series of picturesque views* v. 3, 7. G.C. i 1882, 796–98,805. C.L. v. 117, 1955, 1366–69,1428. B. Jones *Follies & grottoes* 1974, 313. D. Stroud *Capability Brown* 1975, 97–98. R.I.B.A. *Catalogue* v. S, 1976, 14. M. Binney *and* A. Hills *Elysian gardens* 1979, 21.

Manchester. Botanic Garden, Greater Manchester
Hort. Register v. 1, 1831, 106–09. *J. Hort. Cottage Gdnr* v. 36, 1866, 235–36; v. 46, 1871, 439–40. G.C. i 1883, 629; i 1888, 744; i 1890, 763–64; i 1897, 390–91. *Gdning World* v. 10, 1894, 807.

Manchester. Victoria Park, Greater Manchester
G. Chadwick *Park and the town* 1966, 35. Historical MSS Commission *Architectural history* v. 3, 1971, item 3402.

Manderston near Duns, Borders
C.L. v. 41, 1917, 60–65; v. 145, 1969, 1354–56; v. 165, 1979, 390–93,542–45. G.A. Little *Scotland's gardens* 1981, 100–01.

Manley Hall, Manchester, Greater Manchester
J. Hort. Cottage Gdnr v. 40, 1868, 335–38,457–58; v. 41, 1869, 6–7,80–81.

Manley Hall near Lichfield, Staffs
G.M. v. 15, 1839, 457.

Manor Close, Aspley Guise, Beds
R. Bisgrove *Gardens of Britain* v. 3, 1978, 29.

Manor House, Bledlow, Bucks
R. Bisgrove *Gardens of Britain* v. 3, 1978, 117.

Manor House, Little Marlow, Bucks
R. Bisgrove *Gardens of Britain* v. 3, 1978, 119.

Manor House, Cranborne, Dorset
A. Lees-Milne *and* R. Verey *Englishwoman's garden* 1980, 116–21.

Manor House, Sandford Orcas, Dorset
C.L. v. 139, 1966, 462–66.

Manor House, Basingstoke, Hants
G.C. i 1908, 26.

Manor House, Donington-le-Heath, Leics
J. Anthony *Gardens of Britain* v. 6, 1979, 73–74.

Manor House, Bampton, Oxfordshire
A. Lees-Milne *and* R. Verey *Englishwoman's garden* 1980, 92–96.

Manor House, Clifton Hampden, Oxfordshire
R. Bisgrove *Gardens of Britain* v. 3, 1978, 118.

Manor House, Milton, Oxfordshire
C.L. v. 104, 1948, 1274–77.

Manor House, Sutton Courtenay, Oxfordshire
C.L. v. 69, 1931, 610–16,646–52. R. Bisgrove *Gardens of Britain* v. 3, 1978, 120.

Manor House, Mells, Somerset
C.L. v. 42, 1917, 444–50; v. 93, 1943, 748–51. J. Brown *Gardens of a golden afternoon* 1982, 166.

Manor House, Stoke D'Abernon, Surrey
C.L. v. 90, 1941, 956–59,1010.

Manor House, Hove, E. Sussex
C.L. v. 48, 1920, 114–20.

Manor House, Earnley, W. Sussex
Architectural Review v. 71, 1932, 54–55.

Manor House of St Helena, Guernsey, Channel Islands
W. Berry *History of the Island of Guernsey* 1815, 144.

Manor of Dean, Tillington, W. Sussex
Sussex Life v. 4 no. 6, 1968, 28–29.

Manresa House, Roehampton, Wandsworth, London
G.C. ii 1889, 495–96.

Manse of Fyvie, Grampian
H. Maxwell *Scottish gardens* 1908, 130–38.

Mansion House, Highgate, Haringey, London
M. Macartney *English houses & gardens* 1908, pl. 42.

Manydown near Basingstoke, Hants
E.F. Prosser *Select illustrations of Hampshire* 1833.

Maple Hayes near Lichfield, Staffs
J.P. Neale *Views* 2nd Series, v. 2, 1825.

Mapledurham House, Mapledurham, Oxfordshire
C.L. v. 20, 1906, 274–76; v. 149, 1971, 1152–56,1216. *G.C.* ii 1914, 334,335. B. Jones *Follies & grottoes* 1974, 294–95.

Mapperton House near Beaminster, Dorset
C.L. v. 10, 1901, 16–20; v. 34, 1913, 490–97; v. 131, 1962, 66–69,176,80. A. Paterson *Gardens of Britain* v. 2, 1978, 35–36.

Mar Lodge near Castleton, Grampian
A.A. Tait *Landscape garden in Scotland* 1980, passim.

Marble Hall, Vauxhall, Lambeth, London
W. Wroth *London pleasure gardens of the eighteenth century* 1896, 281–82.

Marble Hill near Dunfanaghy, Co. Donegal, Eire
C.L. v. 165, 1979, 538–40.

Marble Hill House, Twickenham, Richmond, London
Official guide. *Short account of the principal seats and gardens in and around Richmond and Kew,* [1760s?] 6. W. Keane *Beauties of Middlesex* 1850, 143–44. *Architectural Review* 1901, 23–26. *C.L.* v. 7, 1900, 236–37. J. Lees-Milne *Earls of creation* 1962, 79–92. G.L.C. *Marble Hill House* 1966. M.P.G. Draper *Marble Hill House and its owners* 1970.

Marbury Hall, Marbury, Cheshire
G. Ormerod *History of the County Palatine and City of Chester* v. 1, 1882, 634.

Marches, Willowbrook, Bucks
J. Brown *Gardens of a golden afternoon* 1982, 175.

Marchmont near Duns, Borders
C.L. v. 57, 1925, 310–18,354. G.A. Little *Scotland's gardens* 1981, 101.

Marden Hill near Hertford, Herts
C.L. v. 89, 1941, 328–31.

Marden Park near Caterham, Surrey
Archaeologia v. 12, 1796, 187. W. Keane *Beauties of Surrey* 1849, 62–64. *G.C.* i 1903, 261–62,264. J. Evelyn *Diary* v. 4, 1955, 121; v. 5, 425–26. G. Beard *Thomas H. Mawson* 1976, 58. J. Greenwood *History of Woldingham and Marden Park* 1976.

Marelands, Bentley, Hants
C.L. v. 91, 1942, 948–51.

Margam Park, Port Talbot, W. Glamorgan
Official guide. E.D. Clarke *Tour through South of England* 1793, 193–94. R. Warner *Second walk through Wales* 1799, 82–86. J. Evans *Letters written during a tour through South Wales* 1804, 138–39. B.H. Malkin *Scenery, antiquities and biography of South Wales* v. 2, 1807, 516–17. D.C. Webb *Observations and remarks* 1812, 368–69. J.C. Loudon *Encyclopaedia of gardening* 1822, 1248. *J. Hort. Cottage Gdnr* v. 60, 1878, 110–12, 129–31; N.S. v. 16, 1888, 68–70. *G.C.* ii 1881, 622, 628–29,655–56; i 1894, 134–36; i 1909, 129–30. *Gdnrs Mag.* 1905, 99–101. *C.L.* v. 11, 1902, 432–41; v. 119, 1956, 256,336–39; v. 158, 1975, 696–97; v. 163, 1978, 210. G. Jekyll *Garden ornament* 1918, 92,104,218. *Post-Medieval Archaeology* v. 10, 1976, 161–75. J. Harris *Artist and the country house* 1979, 127. Royal Commission on Ancient and Historical Monuments in Wales *Inventory of the ancient monuments in Glamorgan* v. 4, 1981, 323–31, pls. 30–31,33.

Margate. Grotto, Kent
B. Jones *Follies & grottoes* 1974, 172–74.

Marholm, Northants
Northamptonshire Past and Present v. 5 no. 3, 1975, 228.

Marine Villa, West Cowes, Isle of Wight
R. Ackermann *Repository* v. 10, 1827, pl. 32. W.W.J. Gendall *Views* v. 1, 1830, 112.

Marino near Dublin, Co. Dublin, Eire
T. Milton *Seats . . . in Ireland* 1783–93, 9. *Delineator* 1831, 73. *C.L.* v. 65, 1929, 837. E. Malins *and* Knight of Glin *Lost demesnes* 1976, 138–41,143. *Moorea* v. 2, 1983, 29–38.

Mariston *see* Marystow

Mark Hall, Harlow, Essex
D. Stroud *Humphry Repton* 1962, 171. G. Carter *et al. Humphry Repton* 1982, 151.

Markeaton Hall, Markeaton, Derbyshire
J.P. Neale *Views* 2nd Series, v. 1, 1824. N. Nichols *Local maps of Derbyshire to 1770* 1980, 64.

Markree Castle near Collooney, Co. Sligo, Eire
E. Malins *and* P. Bowe *Irish gardens and demesnes* 1980, 140–41.

Marks Hall near Colchester, Essex
T. Wright *History . . . of Essex* v. 1, 1836, 371. *C.L.* v. 11, 1902, 144–48. F.G. Emmison *Catalogue of maps in Essex Record Office* 1947, 59; 3rd Supplt, 1968, 5.

Markyate Cell, Markyate, Herts
G. Jekyll *and* L. Weaver *Gardens for small country houses* 1913, xxiii–xxviii. *Garden* 1915, 568–69.

Marlands, Sampford Arundel, Somerset
G.C. i 1965, 330–31. J. Sales *West Country gardens* 1980, 163–64.

Marlborough House, Pall Mall, Westminster, London
J. Kip *Nouveau theatre de la Grande Bretagne* v. 4, 1729. *G.C.* i 1910, 308. C. Ward *Royal gardens* 1912, 73–81. J. MacGregor *Gardens of celebrities . . . in and around London* 1918, 139–53.

Marlborough House, Preshute, Wilts
W. Stukeley *Itinerarium curiosum* v. 1, 1776, pls. 3,62. H.S. Hughes *The gentle Hertford: her life and letters* 1940, passim. C. Fiennes *Journeys* 1949, 331. V.C.H. *Wiltshire* v. 12, 1983, 160,170.

Marlee House, Kinloch, Tayside
I.H. Adams *Descriptive list of plans* v. 3, 1974, 111.

Marlesford Hall, Marlesford, Suffolk
H. Davy *Views* 1827.

Marley Hall near Exmouth, Devon
Gdning World v. 11, 1894, 235. *G.C.* ii 1898, 54–55,70–71.

Marndhill, Ardington, Oxfordshire
R. Bisgrove *Gardens of Britain* v. 3, 1978, 121.

Marple Hall, Marple, Greater Manchester
C.L. v. 45, 1919, 222–27.

Marsh Baldon House, Marsh Baldon, Oxfordshire
V.C.H. *Oxford* v. 5, 1957, 32.

Marsh Court, Stockbridge, Hants
C.L. v. 33, 1913, 562–71; v. 71, 1932, 316–22,354–59. L. Weaver *Houses and gardens by E.L. Lutyens* 1913, 75–93. G. Jekyll *Garden ornament* 1918, 326. A.S. Butler *et al. Architecture of Sir Edwin Lutyens* v. 2, 1950, 11. L. Fleming *and* A. Gore *English garden* 1979, 208–09. J. Brown *Gardens of a golden afternoon* 1982, 72–78,165.

Marsh Lane, Harlow, Essex
A. Lees-Milne *and* R. Verey *Englishman's garden* 1982, 68–71.

Marshalls, Romford, Havering, London
F.G. Emmison *Catalogue of maps in Essex Record Office* 1st Supplt, 1952, 32.

Marston Hall, Marston, Lincs
N. Pevsner *and* J. Harris *Lincolnshire* 1964, 604. *C.L.* v. 138, 1965, 612–15,688–92. J. Anthony *Gardens of Britain* v. 6, 1979, 119–21.

Marston House, Marston Bigott, Somerset
T. Badeslade *and* J. Rocque *Vitruvius Brittanicus* 1739, pls. 69–70. J.P. Neale *Views* v. 3, 1820. R. Pococke *Travels* v. 2, 1889, 40. *Proc. Somerset Archaeological and Natural History Soc.* v. 118, 1974, 15–24.

Marston Park, Marston Montgomery, Derbyshire
N. Nichols *Local maps of Derbyshire to 1770* 1980, 116.

Marwood Hill near Barnstaple, Devon
P.M. Synge *Gardens of Britain* v. 1, 1977, 65–68. *C.L.* v. 169, 1981, 448–50. A. Lees-Milne *and* R. Verey *Englishman's garden* 1982, 128–31.

Marybone House (Benjamin Hyett), Gloucester, Glos
J. Harris *Gardens of delight* 1978, 14–15. *Bristol and Gloucestershire Archaeological Soc. Trans.* v. 99, 1981, 123–25.

Marylebone Gardens, Westminster, London
W. Wroth *London pleasure gardens of the eighteenth century* 1896, 93–110. E.B. Chancellor *Pleasure haunts of London* 1925, 348–57.

Marylebone Park *see* London

Maryon Park *see* London

Marystow House, Marystow, Devon
R. Ackermann *Repository* v. 8, 1826, pl. 19. W.W.J. Gendall *Views* v. 1, 1830, 80.

Massingberd, William Burrell *see* South Ormesby

Mathern Palace, Mathern, Gwent
Garden v. 57, 1900, 57,58,59,77–78. *C.L.* v. 28, 1910, 718–25; v. 166, 1979, 2154–57.

Matson House, Matson, Glos
J.N. Brewer *Delineations of Gloucestershire* 1825, 94. *C.L.* v. 108, 1950, 1990–94.

Maugersbury Manor, Maugersbury, Glos
R. Atkyns *Ancient and present state of Glostershire* 1712, 695. L. Knyff *and* J. Kip *Britannia illustrata* v. 2, 1715.

Mavisbank near Loanhead, Lothian
A.A. Tait *Landscape garden in Scotland* 1980, passim.

Mawley Hall near Cleobury Mortimer, Shropshire
R. Sidwell *West Midland gardens* 1981, 135–36.

Maxstoke Castle, Maxstoke, Warwickshire
C.L. v. 19, 1906, 54–65; v. 47, 1920, 170–78.

Maxwelton House near Moniaive, Dumfries and Galloway
G.A. Little *Scotland's gardens* 1981, 262–64.

May Place, Crayford, Bexley, London
C. Greenwood *Epitome of county history . . . v. 1: Kent* 1838, 42.

Maybo near Dumfries, Dumfries and Galloway
J. Loudon *Treatise on forming, improving and managing country residences* v. 2, 1806, 647–48, pl. 31.

Meaford Hall, Meaford, Staffs
F. Calvert *Picturesque views . . . in Staffordshire & Shropshire* 1830, 38.

Meer Hall *see* Mere Hall

Meggernie near Killin, Tayside
J.P. Neale *Views* v. 6, 1823.

Megginch Castle near Errol, Tayside
G.A. Little *Scotland's gardens* 1981, 158–60.

Melbourne Hall, Melbourne, Derbyshire
Official guide. *J. Hort. Cottage Gdnr* v. 55, 1876, 34–35. L. Jewitt *and* S.C. Hall *Stately homes of England* 1877, 186–202. C.L. v. 6, 1899, 368–73; v. 10, 616–17; v. 63, 1928, 492–99,526–33; v. 132, 1962, 716; v. 157, 1975, 228–30. H.I. Triggs *Formal gardens in England and Scotland* 1902, 30–31. G. Jekyll *and* G.S. Elgood *Some English gardens* 1904, 18–22. C. Holme *Gardens of England in Midland & Eastern counties* 1908, pls. 80–85. G. Jekyll *Garden ornament* 1918, 69,127,349. Lady Rockley *Historic gardens of England* 1938, 140–41. D. Green *Gardener to Queen Anne* 1956, 41–47. R. Lister *Great works of craftsmanship* 1967, 101–13. M. Allan *Fisons guide* 1970, 228–29. N.T. Newton *Design on the land* 1971, 198. N. Pevsner *Derbyshire* 1978, 279. D. Jarrett *English landscape garden* 1978, 22–23. J. Anthony *Gardens of Britain* v. 6, 1979, 121–26.

Melbury House, Melbury Sampford, Dorset
J.P. Neale *Views* 2nd Series, v. 4, 1828. J. Hutchins *History . . . of Dorset* v. 2, 1863, 672. F.O. Morris *Series of picturesque views* v. 2, 29. C.L. v. 6, 1899, 208–13. H. Walpole *Visits to country seats. Walpole Society* v. 7, 1927–28,48.

Melchet Court near Romsey, Hants
British Museum *Catalogue of maps, prints* 1829, 223. G.C. i 1881, 137–38; ii 1928, 121,130–31. *J. Hort. Cottage Gdnr* N.S., v. 52, 1906, 32–33. V.C.H. *Hampshire* v. 4, 1911, 542. *Architectural Review* v. 60, 1926, 59–65. C.L. v. 68, 1930, 176–83,271.

Melcombe Bingham, Dorset
C.L. v. 7, 1900, 768–74.

Meldon Hall, Meldon, Northumberland
C.L. v. 139, 1966, 406–09.

Melford Hall, Long Melford, Suffolk
Official guide. J.P. Neale *Views* 2nd Series, v. 2, 1825. C.L. v. 10, 1901, 496–503; v. 82, 1937, 116–21,142; v. 133, 1963, 919. G. Jekyll *Garden ornament* 1918, 224. G.S. Thomas *Gardens of National Trust* 1979, 169–70.

Mellerstain, Gordon, Borders
Official guide. C.L. v. 38, 1915, 648–56; v. 124, 1958, 416–19,476. *Park Administration* no. 7, 1968, 32–33. G.A. Little *Scotland's gardens* 1981, 101–03.

Mells Park, Mells, Somerset
J. Brown *Gardens of a golden afternoon* 1982, 174.

Melplash Court, Melplash, Dorset
A. Paterson *Gardens of Britain* v. 2, 1978, 36–37.

Melton Constable, Norfolk
J. Beeverell *Les delices de la Grande Bretagne* v. 5, 1707, 872. L. Knyff *and* J. Kip *Britannia illustrata* v. 1, 1714. S. *and* N. Buck *Buck's antiquities* v. 1, 1774, pl. 201. W. Watts *Seats* 1779, pl. 38. J.P. Neale *Views* v. 3, 1820. J. Grigor *Eastern arboretum* 1841, 303. F.O. Morris *Series of picturesque views* v. 6, 73. C.L. v. 18, 1905, 378–84; v. 64, 1928, 364–70,402. M. Macartney *English houses & gardens* 1908, pl. 39. G. Jekyll *Garden ornament* 1918, 116. N. Pevsner *North-East Norfolk and Norwich* 1962, 197. *Architectural History* v. 7, 1964, 31,76. B. Jones *Follies & grottoes* 1974, 362. D. Stroud *Capability Brown* 1975, 112.

Melton Park, Melton, Norfolk
J. Grigor *Eastern arboretum* 1841, 190–91.

Melville Castle near Lasswade, Lothian
W. Angus *Seats* 1787, pl. 29. G.C. ii 1884, 298–99; ii 1895, 543–44.

Melville House near Ladybank, Fife
G. Jekyll *Garden ornament* 1918, 255. C.L. v. 30, 1911, 1006–12.

Membland near Modbury, Devon
G.C. i 1885, 205–06,213,238–39,245.

Menabilly near Fowey, Cornwall
C.S. Gilbert *Historical survey of . . . Cornwall* v. 2,

Menabilly (*Cont.*)
1820, 875–76. *G.C.* i 1886, 817,818,821; i 1903, 234–36. B. Jones *Follies & grottoes* 1974, 298–99.

Menacuddle near St Austell, Cornwall
C.S. Gilbert *Historical survey of . . . Cornwall* v. 2, 1820, 866–67.

Mentmore Towers, Mentmore, Bucks
G.C. i 1879, 747–48,779–80; i 1890, 488,489; i 1899, 389. *J. Hort. Cottage Gdnr* N.S., v. 5, 1882, 478–80,481; N.S., v. 40, 1900, 219–24,225. *Garden* v. 62, 1902, 305–06. *J. Hort. Home Farmer* N.S., v. 65, 1912, 55.

Meols Hall, Meols, Merseyside
N. Pevsner *Lancashire: 2* 1969, 100. *C.L.* v. 153, 1973, 274–77.

Merdon Manor, Hursley, Hants
A. Paterson *Gardens of Britain* v. 2, 1978, 120–21.

Mere Hall near Droitwich, Hereford and Worcester
F.O. Morris *Series of picturesque views* v. 6, 15. *C.L.* v. 8, 1900, 808–14.

Merevale Hall, Merevale, Warwickshire
F.O. Morris *Series of picturesque views* v. 3, 59. *C.L.* v. 145, 1969, 598–601.

Mereworth Castle, Mereworth, Kent
N. Spencer *Complete English traveller* 1771, 56. E. Hasted *History . . . of Kent* v. 2, 1782, 268. J.P. Neale *Views* 2nd Series, v. 2, 1825. *J. Hort. Cottage Gdnr* N.S., v. 16, 1888, 531–32. *G.C.* i 1890, 761–62. *C.L.* v. 47, 1920, 808–16,912–19. P. Coats *Great gardens of Britain* 1967, 282–87. B. Jones *Follies & grottoes* 1974, 156–57. P. Willis *Charles Bridgeman* 1977, 181.

Merlin's Cave, Clerkenwell, Islington, London
W. Wroth *London pleasure gardens of the eighteenth century* 1896, 54–55.

Merly, Canford Magna, Dorset
J. Hutchins *History . . . of Dorset* v. 3, 1868, 304. G. Carter *et al. Humphry Repton* 1982, 151.

Merrow Grange, Merrow, Surrey
M. Binney *and* A. Hills *Elysian gardens* 1979, 43. *Gdn History* v. 11 no. 2, 1983, 157–66.

Mersham Hatch, Mersham, Kent
E. Hasted *History . . . of Kent* v. 3, 1790, 286. J.P. Neale *Views* 2nd Series, v. 3, 1826. F.O. Morris *Series of picturesque views* v. 5, 45. *C.L.* v. 49, 1921, 368–75; v. 58, 1925, 218–26.

Merton Place, Merton, London
W. Angus *Seats* 1787, pl. 55.

Mertoun, St Boswells, Borders
C.L. v. 139, 1966, 1392–95. G.A. Little *Scotland's gardens* 1981, 103.

Metcombe Brake, Devon
P.M. Synge *Gardens of Britain* v. 1, 1977, 68–69.

Methley Hall, Methley, W. Yorks
J.P. Neale *Views* v. 5, 1822. *C.L.* v. 21, 1907, 702–09.

Methven Castle, Methven, Tayside
G.M. v. 13, 1837, 124. *G.C.* ii 1883, 811–12.

Michaelstowe Hall near Harwich, Essex
G.C. ii 1926, 230,231,232.

Michel Grove, Arundel, W. Sussex
H. Repton *Observations* 1803, 175–76,179–82. R. Ackermann *Repository* v. 10, 1827, pl. 1. *G.M.* v. 5, 1829, 588–89. W.W.J. Gendall *Views* v. 2, 1830, 79. D. Stroud *Humphry Repton* 1962, 171. G. Carter *et al. Humphry Repton* 1982, 163.

Michelham Priory near Hailsham, E. Sussex
Landscape Design no. 137, 1982, 31–32.

Michelmersh Court, Michelmersh, Hants
A. Paterson *Gardens of Britain* v. 2, 1978, 123.

Mickleham Hall, Mickleham, Surrey
G. Carter *et al. Humphry Repton* 1982, 162.

Middle Hill, Broadway, Hereford and Worcester
J.P. Neale *Views* 2nd Series, v. 3, 1826. J. Harris *Artist and the country house* 1979, 345.

Middlefield, Great Shelford, Cambs
J. Brown *Gardens of a golden afternoon* 1982, 170.

Middlethorpe Hall near York, N. Yorks
Royal Commission on Historical Monuments *Inventory of the historical monuments in the City of York* v. 3, 1972, 121, pl. 198. I. Hall *Samuel Buck's Yorkshire sketchbook* 1979, 43.

Middleton near Castleton, Co. Westmeath, Eire
J.B. Burke *Visitation* 2nd Series, v. 1, 1855, 152.

Middleton Hall near Llanarthney, Dyfed
J.P. Neale *Views* v. 5, 1822. J.B. Burke *Visitation* 2nd Series, v. 1, 1855, 179.

Middleton House near Edinburgh, Lothian
Copper Plate Mag. v. 2, pl. 59.

Middleton Lodge, Middleton Tyas, N. Yorks
K. Lemmon *Gardens of Britain* v. 5, 1978, 85–87.

Middleton Park, Middleton Stoney, Oxfordshire
Gdn History v. 4 no. 1, 1976, 54–56. J. Brown *Gardens of a golden afternoon* 1982, 176.

Midelney Manor near Langport, Somerset
C.L. v. 76, 1934, 548–53.

Midford Castle near Bath, Avon
C.L. v. 95, 1944, 376–79. B. Jones *Follies & grottoes* 1974, 285.

Midgham House, Midgham, Berks
R. Ackermann *Repository* v. 8, 1826, pl. 32. W.W.J. Gendall *Views* v. 1, 1830, 52.

Midhurst. King Edward VII Sanitorium, W. Sussex
J. Brown *Miss Gertrude Jekyll* 1981, 23–25.

Milborne St Andrew, Dorset
J. Hutchins *History . . . of Dorset* v. 2, 1863, 598. J. Harris *Artist and the country house* 1979, 294.

Milbourne Hall, Milbourne, Northumberland
J. Hodgson *History of Northumberland* pt 2 v. 3, 1840.

Milford Hall, Baswich, Staffs
V.C.H. *Stafford* v. 5, 1959, 4.

Mill Garden, Warwick, Warwickshire
R. Sidwell *West Midland gardens* 1981, 219–20.

Mill Hill, Brandsby, N. Yorks
C.L. v. 37 Supplt to 22 May 1915, 2–6.

Mill House, Corpusty, Norfolk
A. Lees-Milne *and* R. Verey *Englishman's garden* 1982, 84–87.

Mill House, Sutton Courtenay, Oxfordshire
R. Bisgrove *Gardens of Britain* v. 3, 1978, 123–24.

Mill House, Fittleworth, W. Sussex
R. Webber *Percy Cane* 1975, 155,185. T. Wright *Gardens of Britain* v. 4, 1978, 161–62.

Millburn Tower near Edinburgh, Lothian
A.A. Tait *Landscape garden in Scotland* 1980, passim.

Millearne near Auchterarder, Tayside
C.L. v. 151, 1972, 452–56.

Millichope Park, Munslow, Shropshire
C.L. v. 161, 1977, 310–13,370. R. Sidwell *West Midland gardens* 1981, 137–38.

Millmead, Bramley, Surrey
G. Jekyll *and* L. Weaver *Gardens for small country houses* 1913, 1–9. L. Weaver *Houses and gardens by E.L. Lutyens* 1913, 164–66. *Garden* 1919, 130–31. J. Brown *Gardens of a golden afternoon* 1982, 111–20,167.

Millwater near Ripley, Surrey
G.C. ii 1926, 48,49,50,51.

Milnerfield, Bingley, W. Yorks
Bradford Illustrated Weekly Telegraph *Series of picturesque views* 1885.

Milnes Bridge House near Huddersfield, W. Yorks
J.P. Neale *Views* v. 5, 1822.

Milton, Cambs
D. Stroud *Humphry Repton* 1962, 41. G. Carter *et al. Humphry Repton* 1982, 149.

Milton, Dorset
D. Stroud *Capability Brown* 1975, 118–20.

Milton near Peterborough, Northants
W. Angus *Seats* 1787, pl. 13. *C.L.* v. 32, 1912, 638–48; v. 129, 1961, 1148–51,1273–74. D. Stroud *Humphry Repton* 1962, 63–64. R. Webber *Percy Cane* 1975, 152–53,179. G. Carter *et al. Humphry Repton* 1982, 160.

Milton Abbey, Milton Abbas, Dorset
W. Watts *Seats* 1779, pl. 33. F.O. Morris *Series of picturesque views* v. 2, 23. *G.C.* ii 1882, 267–68,273. *J. Hort. Cottage Gdnr* N.S., v. 5, 1882, 87–88. *C.L.* v. 11, 1902, 208–13; v. 37, 1915, 734–41,770–76; v. 139, 1960, 1586–89. R.I.B.A. *Catalogue* v. B, 1972, 113. B. Jones *Follies & grottoes* 1974, 71. D. Stroud *Capability Brown* 1975, 118–20.

Milton Brodie near Forres, Grampian
G.C. ii 1958, 19.

Milton Court, Dorking, Surrey
C.L. v. 10, 1901, 528–35. *G.C.* i 1903, 389–90.

Milton Lockhart near Carluke, Strathclyde
G.M. v. 18, 1842, 388–89.

Milton Lodge near Wells, Somerset
C.L. v. 59, 1926, 478–85; v. 161, 1977, 1214–16. J. Sales *West Country gardens* 1980, 164–66.

Milton Manor, Milton, Oxfordshire
R. Bisgrove *Gardens of Britain* v. 3, 1978, 124.

Milton Park, Castor, Cambs
H. Repton *Sketches* 1794, 6. *G.C.* i 1882, 267. *Garden* v. 40, 1891, 391–92. V.C.H. *Northampton* v. 2, 1906, 476–77,478. B. Jones *Follies & grottoes* 1974, 369. G. Carter *et al. Humphry Repton* 1982, 160.

Miltown House, Castlemaine, Co. Kerry, Eire
J.P. Neale *Views* v. 6, 1823.

Minchenden House, Southgate, Enfield, London
G.M. v. 15, 1839, 511–12. W. Keane *Beauties of Middlesex* 1850, 95–97.

Minley Manor, Minley, Hants
J. Hort. Cottage Gdnr v. 32, 1864, 433–34; N.S., v. 35, 1897, 124–25. *G.C.* ii 1891, 695–96,707; ii 1904, 9. *C.L.* v. 6, 1899, 808–13. *Gdnrs Mag.* 1905, 531–34. G. Jekyll *Garden ornament* 1918, 260.

Minstead Manor House, Minstead, Hants
E.F. Prosser *Select illustrations of Hampshire* 1833.

Minterne House, Minterne Magna, Dorset
C.L. v. 11, 1902, 528–33. M. Allan *Fisons guide* 1970, 102. A. Paterson *Gardens of Britain* v. 2, 1978, 37–38. *C.L.* v. 167, 1980, 498–501,574–77.

Miserden Park, Miserden, Glos
R. Atkyns *Ancient and present state of Glostershire* 1712, 560. L. Knyff *and* J. Kip *Britannia illustrata* v. 2, 1915. J. Sales *West Country gardens* 1980, 90–92.

Misterton Hall, Misterton, Leics
J. Throsby *Select views in Leicestershire* v. 1, 1790, 296.

Mistley Hall, Mistley, Essex
P. Muilman *History of Essex* v. 6, 1772, 31. P. Morant *History . . . of Essex* v. 1, 1816, 460. T. Wright *History . . . of Essex* v. 2, 1836, 780. F.G. Emmison *Catalogue of maps in Essex Record Office* 1947, 23–24. J. Harris *Artist and the country house* 1979, 293.

Mitcham Grove, Mitcham, Merton, London
R. Ackermann *Repository* v. 8, 1826, pl. 14. W.W.J. Gendall *Views* v. 1, 1830, 79.

Moat Bank near Lichfield, Staffs
J. Hort. Cottage Gdnr v. 55, 1876, 116–17.

Moccas Court, Moccas, Hereford and Worcester
W. Angus *Seats* 1787, pl. 19. D. Stroud *Humphry Repton* 1962, 171. D. Stroud *Capability Brown* 1975, 233–34. *C.L.* v. 160, 1976, 1474–77,1554–57. R. Sidwell *West Midland gardens* 1981, 69–70. G. Carter *et al. Humphry Repton* 1982, 153.

Mochrum Park, Penninghame, Dumfries and Galloway
Scottish Gdnr and Northern Forester v. 8, 1913, 273–74.

Moditonham House, Botus, Cornwall
J.P. Neale *Views* v. 1, 1818. C.S. Gilbert *Historical survey of . . . Cornwall* v. 2, 1820, 438–39. *Jones's views* 1829.

Moggerhanger Park near Sandy, Beds
G. Carter *et al. Humphry Repton* 1982, 147.

Moidrum Castle *see* Moydrum Castle

Moigne Combe near Owermoigne, Dorset
A. Paterson *Gardens of Britain* v. 2, 1978, 38–39.

Moira, Co. Down, Ulster
C. Smith *and* W. Harris *Antient and present state of the County of Down* 1744, 103–04. J.C. Loudon *Arboretum et fruticetum Britannicum* v. 1, 1844, 111. *C.L.* v. 172, 1982, 1406–07. *Belfast Natural History and Philosophical Soc. Proceedings and Reports* v. 10, 1977/82, 47–48.

Monchelsea Place *see* Boughton

Moncrieffe House near Perth, Tayside
G.M. v. 13, 1837, 122–23. *G.C.* ii 1876, 552,553,557.

Mongewell near Wallingford, Oxfordshire
G.M. v. 10, 1834, 4–5.

Monkton House, Singleton, W. Sussex
L. Weaver *Houses and gardens by E.L. Lutyens* 1913, 123–26. J. Brown *Gardens of a golden afternoon* 1982, 166.

Monreith near Whithorn, Dumfries and Galloway
H. Maxwell *Scottish gardens* 1911, 35–39. Historical MSS Commission *Architectural history* v. 5, 1974, item 5360.

Montacute House, Montacute, Somerset
Official guide. L. Knyff *and* J. Kip *Britannia illustrata* v. 2, 1715. J. Collinson *History . . . of Somersetshire* v. 3, 1791, 314. J.P. Neale *Views* 2nd Series, v. 4, 1828. *C.L.* v. 3, 1898, 464–66,496–98; v. 15, 1904, 810–21; v. 37, 1915, 820–27,870–75; v. 118, 1955, 850–53,960, 1020. H.I. Triggs *Formal gardens in England and Scotland* 1902, 11–12. G. Jekyll *and* G.S. Elgood *Some English gardens* 1905, 55–57. C. Holme *Gardens of England in Southern & Western counties* 1907, pl. 91. *Architectural Review* v. 35, 1914, 139–42, pls. 3–7. G. Jekyll *Garden ornament* 1918, 82–83,100,203,215. Lady Rockley *Historic gardens of England* 1938, 116–17. *J. Royal Hort. Soc.* 1960, 348–49. *G.C.* ii 1965, 134–35; v. 160 no. 12, 1966, 14–15. N.T. Newton *Design on the land* 1971,

Montacute House (*Cont.*)
191. R.I.B.A. *Catalogue* v. B, 1972, 15. H. Evans *Beautiful gardens of Britain* 1974, 21–22. G.S. Thomas *Gardens of National Trust* 1979, 170–72. J. Sales *West Country gardens* 1980, 166–70.

Montagu House, Great Russell Street, Camden, London
L. Knyff *and* J. Kip *Britannia illustrata* v. 2, 1715. H. Overton *Britannia illustrata* c.1724, pl. 15.

Montague Cottage, Blairlogie, Central
Scottish Gdnr and Northern Forester v. 7, 1912, 596–98.

Monteviot near Jedburgh, Borders
C.L. v. 143, 1968, 1414–16. R. Webber *Percy Cane* 1975, 89–91.

Montreal, Sevenoaks, Kent
E. Hasted *History . . . of Kent* v. 1, 1778, 354. P. Sandby *Collection of one hundred and fifty select views* v. 1, 1781, pl. 27. J.P. Neale *Views* v. 2, 1819. F. Hull *Catalogue of estate maps 1590 to 1840 in the Kent County Archive Office* 1973, 235. G. Carter *et al. Humphry Repton* 1982, 156.

Montrose near Dublin, Co. Dublin, Eire
Cottage Gdnr v. 28, 1862, 133–34.

Montville, Guernsey, Channel Islands
W. Berry *History of Island of Guernsey* 1815, 160.

Monymusk House, Monymusk, Grampian
R. Pococke *Tours in Scotland* 1887, 200. C.L. v. 152, 1972, 1046–50. A.A. Tait *Landscape garden in Scotland* 1980, passim.

Monzie Castle, Monzie, Tayside
J.C. Nattes *Scotia depicta* 1804, pl. 15. J.P. Neale *Views* v. 6, 1823.

Moonhill, Cuckfield, W. Sussex
T.H. Mawson *Art & craft of garden making* 1907, 150. G. Beard *Thomas H. Mawson* 1976, 59.

Moor Close, Binfield, Berks
C.L. v. 54, 1924, 875–76. *Studio* v. 87, 1924, 28–31. *Architectural Review* v. 57, 1925, 22–25,156,157,158. R.I.B.A. *Catalogue* v. G-K, 1973, 108.

Moor Court near Kington, Hereford and Worcester
G.C. i 1875, 172–73,177.

Moor Crab, Windermere, Cumbria
G. Beard *Thomas H. Mawson* 1976, 59.

Moor End Farm, Broxted, Essex
F.G. Emmison *Catalogue of maps at Essex Record Office* 2nd Supplt, 1964, 16.

Moor-End, Northants
Northamptonshire Past and Present v. 5 no. 3, 1975, 228.

Moor Hall, Cookham, Berks
J. Hort. Cottage Gdnr N.S., v. 42, 1901, 96–97.

Moor Hall, Harlow, Essex
T. Wright *History . . . of Essex* v. 2, 1836, 289. F.G. Emmison *Catalogue of maps in Essex Record Office* 1947, 23; 1st Supplt, 1952, 26,31. Historical MSS Commission *Architectural history* v. 5, 1974, item 5156. G. Carter *et al. Humphry Repton* 1982, 151.

Moor Park near Rickmansworth, Herts
T. Whately *Observations on modern gardening* 1771, 4–6. W. Marshall *Planting and ornamental gardening* 1785, 569–90. H. Walpole *Essay on modern gardening* 1785, 37–43. W. Temple *Works* v. 3, 1814: *Of gardening* 235–37. R. Clutterbuck *History . . . of county of Hertford* v. 1, 1815, 194. J.P. Neale *Views* v. 2, 1819. J.C. Loudon *Encyclopaedia of gardening* 1822, 1233. R. Ackermann *Repository* v. 5, 1825, pl. 13. W.W.J. Gendall *Views* v. 2, 1830, 124. *Cottage Gdnr* v. 14, 1855, 185–86. *J. Hort. Cottage Gdnr* v. 46, 1871, 339–42; v. 52, 1874, 356–57. *Garden* v. 11, 1877, 541. G.C. ii 1886, 293–94, 297. C. Holme *Gardens of England in Southern & Western counties* 1907, pls. 92–93. V.C.H. *Hertford* v. 2, 1908, 378. C.L. v. 31, 1912, 18–26. H. Walpole *Visits to country seats. Walpole Society* v. 7, 1927–28,24. E.S. Rohde *Story of the garden* 1932, 143–44. T. Jefferson *Garden book 1766–1824* 1944, 114. D. Stroud *Capability Brown* 1975, 69–70,234. G. Beard *Thomas H. Mawson* 1976, 59. N. Pevsner *Hertfordshire* 1977, 252–53. P. Willis *Charles Bridgeman* 1977, 181. J. Harris *Artist and the country house* 1979, 273. H.M. Colvin *History of the King's Works* v. 4, 1982, 167,168.

Moor Park near Farnham, Surrey
Society of Gentlemen *England displayed* v. 1, 1769, 226. D. Defoe *Tour* v. 1, 1778, 197–98. S. Shaw *Tour to West of England in 1788* In J. Pinkerton, v. 2, 1808, 314. C.L. v. 11, 1902, 832–34; v. 106, 1949, 1578–81; v. 118, 1955, 598; v. 155, 1974, 76–77. W. Cobbett *Rural rides* v. 1, 1912, 28. I. Nairn *and* B. Cherry *Surrey* 1971, 373. *Gdn History* v. 2 no. 1, 1973, 70. J. Harris *Artist and the country house* 1979, 116. M. Hadfield *et al. British gardeners* 1980, 278.

Moor Place near Much Hadham, Herts
H. Chauncy *Historical antiquities of Hertfordshire* 1700, 160. C.L. v. 119, 1956, 156–59. R. Bisgrove *Gardens of Britain* v. 3, 1978, 125.

Moorend near Berkeley, Glos
G.M. v. 19, 1843, 705–07.

Moorland Garden, Rivington, Lancs
N. Pevsner *Lancashire: 2* 1969, 210.

Moot, Downton, Wilts
C.L. v. 25, 1909, 54–62. G. Jekyll *Garden ornament* 1918, 198. M. Binney *and* A. Hills *Elysian gardens* 1979, 44. V.C.H. *Wiltshire* v. 11, 1980, 30.

Moraston near Ross, Hereford and Worcester
C.L. v. 141, 1967, 782–83.

More, Sir Thomas *see* Beaufort House, Chelsea

Moreby Hall, Stillingfleet, N. Yorks
C.L. v. 21, 1907, 234–44. C. Holme *Gardens of England in Northern counties* 1911, pls. 96–97. I. Hall *Samuel Buck's Yorkshire sketchbook* 1979, 46.

Moreton Hall near Congleton, Cheshire
J. Hort. Cottage Gdnr v. 33, 1865, 90–91. F.O. Morris *Series of picturesque views* v. 3, 69.

Moreton Hall near Whalley, Lancs
E. Baines *History . . . of Lancaster* v. 3, 1836, 192.

Moreton House, Moreton, Dorset
J. Hutchins *History . . . of Dorset* v. 1, 1774, 148.

Moreton Paddox, Moreton Morrell, Warwickshire
G.C. i 1915, 323; ii 1916, 132,133,137. M. Binney *and* A. Hills *Elysian gardens* 1979, 16.

Morleys, Wallsbank, Shropshire
R. Sidwell *West Midland gardens* 1981, 138–39.

Morrab Gardens, Penzance, Cornwall
G.C. ii 1962, 282–84. *Cornish Gdn* no. 25, 1982, 28–35.

Morton Hall, Morton, Norfolk
J. Grigor *Eastern arboretum* 1841, 58–60.

Morton Hall near Edinburgh, Lothian
Gdning World v. 3, 1886, 280; v. 15, 1899, 601–02,620. *Scottish Gdnr and Northern Forester* v. 6, 1911, 645–46.

Morval near East Looe, Cornwall
J. Britton *and* E.W. Brayley *Devonshire & Cornwall* 1832, 47. C.L. v. 15, 1904, 90–94.

Morville Hall, Morville, Shropshire
F. Calvert *Picturesque views . . . in Shropshire* 1831, 133. C.L. v. 112, 1952, 464–67,532–35. J. Harris *Artist and the country house* 1979, 204. G.S. Thomas *Gardens of National Trust* 1979, 172–73. R. Sidwell *West Midland gardens* 1981, 139–41.

Moseley Hall, Birmingham, W. Midlands
J.P. Neale *Views* v. 5, 1822. D. Stroud *Humphry Repton* 1962, 171. J. Harris *Catalogue of British drawings . . . in American collections* 1971, 176. G. Carter *et al. Humphry Repton* 1982, 164.

Moseley Old Hall near Wolverhampton, West Midlands
Official guide. C.L. v. 137, 1965, 959. G.S. Thomas *Gardens of National Trust* 1979, 173–74. R. Sidwell *West Midland gardens* 1981, 173.

Moselle Villa, Totteham, Haringey, London
W. Keane *Beauties of Middlesex* 1850, 199–200.

Mosley Hill, Aigburth, Merseyside
Scottish Gdnr v. 7, 1858, 359–61.

Moss House, Shenstone, Staffs
S. Shaw *History . . . of Staffordshire* v. 2, 1801, 47.

Mostyn Hall, Mostyn, Clwyd
C.L. v. 59, 1926, 200–07.

Mote near Maidstone, Kent
J. Harris *History of Kent* 1719, 192. J. Kip *Supplement du Nouveau theatre de la Grande Bretagne* 1728, pl. 8. T. Badeslade *Thirty six different views . . . in Kent* 1750s, pl. 24. W. Watts *Seats* 1779, pl. 55. J.P. Neale *Views* 2nd Series, v. 2, 1825. W.H. Ireland *History . . . of Kent* v. 3, 1829, 637. *J. Hort. Cottage Gdnr* v. 40, 1868, 319–21. G.C. ii 1885, 458; ii 1888, 349–51.

Mote Mount, Mill Hill, Barnet, London
G.C. i 1959, 222.

Mothecombe House, Mothecombe, Devon
C.L. v. 120, 1956, 190–93. *Architectural History* v. 7, 1964, 31–32,76.

Mottisfont Abbey, Mottisfont, Hants
Official guide. E.F. Prosser *Select illustrations of Hampshire* 1833. C.L. v. 50, 1921, 652–59; v. 115, 1954, 1310–13,1398–1401; v. 167, 1980, 822–24. *J. Royal Hort. Soc.* 1960, 349. G.C. ii 1963, 82–83. A. Paterson *Gardens of Britain* v. 2, 1978, 124–26. G.S. Thomas *Gardens of National Trust* 1979, 174–76. *Garden* 1982, 303–07.

Mottistone Manor, Mottistone, Isle of Wight
C.L. v. 65, 1929, 362–68. A. Paterson *Gardens of Britain* v. 2, 1978, 165–66.

Moulsham Hall, Chelmsford, Essex
P. Muilman *History of Essex* v. 1, 1771, 84. P. Morant *History . . . of Essex* v. 2, 1816, 3. F.G. Emmison *Catalogue of maps in Essex Record Office* 1947, 1.

Moulton, Northants
Northamptonshire Past and Present v. 5 no. 3, 1975, 228–29.

Moulton Hall, Middleton Tyas, N. Yorks
C.L. v. 79, 1936, 253–55.

Moulton Manor, Middleton Tyas, N. Yorks
C.L. v. 79, 1936, 250–52.

Moulton Paddocks, Moulton, Suffolk
J. Hort. Home Farmer N.S., v. 64, 1912, 205–10.

Moundsmere Manor, Preston Candover, Hants
C.L. v. 27, 1910, 378–85. A. Paterson *Gardens of Britain* v. 2, 1978, 126–28.

Mount, Ifield, W. Sussex
J. Hort. Cottage Gdnr N.S., v. 58, 1909, 32–33.

Mount Bellew near Ballinasloe, Co. Galway, Eire
J.P. Neale *Views* v. 6, 1823. E. Malins *and* Knight of Glin *Lost demesnes* 1976, 67.

Mount Clare, Roehampton, Wandsworth, London
W. Watts *Seats* 1779, pl. 62. E.W. Brayley *and* J. Britton *Topographical history of Surrey* v. 3, 482. C.L. v. 77, 1935, 90–94,118. Lady Rockley *Historic gardens of England* 1938, 186–87. D. Stroud *Capability Brown* 1975, 169.

Mount Congreve near Waterford, Co. Waterford, Eire
E. Hyams *Irish gardens* 1967, 86–90. E. Malins *and* P. Bowe *Irish gardens and demesnes* 1980, 166–68. Knight of Glin *and* P. Bowe *Gardens of outstanding historic interest in . . . Ireland* 1980.

Mount Edgcumbe, Cremyll, Cornwall
T. Badeslade *and* J. Rocque *Vitruvius Brittanicus* 1739, pls. 94–95. *The World* 25 August 1789. G. Lipscomb *Journey into Cornwall* 1799, 219–23. J. Britton *and* E.W. Brayley *Beauties of England and Wales* v. 4, 1803, 189–90. Duke of Rutland *Journal of a tour round the southern coasts of England* 1805, 132–34,202–03. *A walk round Mount Edgcumbe* 1808 and subsequent editions to 1841. W. Gilpin *Observations on the Western parts of England* 1808, 215–19. S. Shaw *Tour to West of England in 1788*. In J. Pinkerton, v. 2, 1808, 268,269–70. R. Warner *Tour through Cornwall* 1809, 73–80. L. Simond *Journal* v. 1, 1815, 7–9. W. Clarke *Eight views of Mount Edgcumbe* 1820. C.S. Gilbert *Historical survey of . . . Cornwall* v. 2, 1820, 374–80. R. Ackermann *Repository* v. 7, 1826, pl. 19. W. Payne *Picturesque views in Devonshire, Cornwall, etc.* 1826, pls. 10, 12. R. Havell *The tour, or select views on the southern coast* 1827, pl. 18. W.W.J. Gendall *Views* v. 1, 1830, 81–86. J. Britton *and* E.W. Brayley *Devonshire & Cornwall* 1832, 37–41. G.M. v. 18, 1842, 547–48. J.B. Burke *Visitation* v. 2, 1853, 29–31. *Cottage Gdnr* v. 21, 1858, 147–49. *Garden* v. 1, 1872, 552–53,554. *J. Hort. Cottage Gdnr* v. 58, 1877, 402–04,419–21. G.C. ii 1882, 7,17,39; v. 178 no. 8, 1975, 22–25. L. Jewitt *and* S.C. Hall *Stately homes of England* 1874, 54–72. F.O. Morris *Series of picturesque views* v. 2, 57. R. Pococke *Travels through England* v. 1, 1888, 107–08. *Illustrated London News* v. 105, 1894, 110–14. *Pall Mall Gazette* May 1897, 4–6. C.L. v. 11, 1902, 317–19; v. 119, 1956, 746; v. 128, 1960, 1550–53,1598–1601; v. 129, 1961, 188. L. Melville *Life and letters of William Beckford* 1910, 123. C. Fiennes *Journeys* 1949, 254. *Architectural History* v. 7, 1964, 32,77–78. B. Jones *Follies & grottoes* 1974, 300. L. Fleming *and* A. Gore *English garden* 1979, 142–43,145,162–64.

Mount Felix near Walton-on-Thames, Surrey
W. Keane *Beauties of Surrey* 1849, 13–15.

Mount Gardens *see* Flora Tea Gardens

Mount Grove, Hampstead, Camden, London
G.M. v. 15, 1839, 1–9. W. Keane *Beauties of Middlesex* 1850, 252–54.

Mount Henry, Dalkey, Co. Dublin, Eire
Irish Gdning v. 9, 1913, 74–75,81–82.

Mount Ievers near Six-Mile-Bridge, Co. Clare, Eire
C.L. v. 132, 1962, 1152–55. E. Malins *and* Knight of Glin *Lost demesnes* 1976, 24,25.

Mount Juliet near Thomastown, Co. Kilkenny, Eire
Knight of Glin *and* P. Bowe *Gardens of outstanding historic interest in . . . Ireland* 1980.

Mount Kennedy near Newtown Mount Kennedy, Co. Wicklow, Eire
Delineator 1831, 47. C.L. v. 138, 1965, 1128–31,1256. E. Malins *and* Knight of Glin *Lost demesnes* 1976, 171. J. Harris *Artist and the country house* 1979, 302.

Mount Melville near St Andrews, Fife
J.P. Neale *Views* 2nd Series, v. 2, 1825. G.M. v. 7, 1831, 681. A.A. Tait *Landscape garden in Scotland* 1980, passim.

Mount Merrion, Co. Dublin, Eire
G.C. i 1895, 301,303–04. *J. Hort. Cottage Gdnr* N.S., v. 30, 1895, 338–40. E. Malins *and* Knight of Glin *Lost demesnes* 1976, 104–06. *Moorea* v. 3, 1984, 22.

Mount Morris, Westenhanger, Kent
J. Harris *History of Kent* 1719, 156. J. Kip *Supplement du Nouveau theatre de la Grande Bretagne* 1728, pl. 21.

Mount Morris (*Cont.*)

T. Badeslade *Thirty six different views . . . in Kent* 1750s, pl. 25. H.I. Triggs *Formal gardens in England and Scotland* 1902, 39–40. M. Macartney *English houses & gardens* 1908, pl. 47.

Mount Shannon near Limerick, Co. Limerick, Eire
E. Malins *and* Knight of Glin *Lost demesnes* 1976, 73–74.

Mount Stewart near Newtownards, Co. Down, Ulster
Official guide. *J. Royal Hort. Soc.* 1935, 521–31; 1950, 241–43. *C.L.* v. 78, 1935, 356–62,380–86; v. 145, 1969, 1261–64,1302–06; v. 167, 1980, 646–49,754–58,1406. *Gdn Design* no. 33, 1938, 8–13. *G.C.* ii 1960, 240–41, 245; ii 1962, 80–81. P. Coats *Great gardens of Britain* 1967, 200–07. E. Hyams *Irish gardens* 1967, 124–34. M. Allan *Fisons guide* 1970, 364–65. H. Evans *Beautiful gardens of Britain* 1974, 127–28. E. Malins *and* Knight of Glin *Lost demesnes* 1976, 110–11. G.S. Thomas *Gardens of National Trust* 1979, 176–79. A. Hellyer *Gardens of genius* 1980, 124–28. E. Malins *and* P. Bowe *Irish gardens and demesnes* 1980, 100–05. Ulster Architectural Heritage Society *Northern gardens* 1982, 20.

Mount Stuart, Isle of Bute, Strathclyde
W. Watts *Seats* 1779, pl. 73. G. Beard *Thomas H. Mawson* 1976, 59.

Mount Usher, Ashford, Co. Wicklow, Eire
Official guide. *Garden* v. 32, 1887, 121; v. 60, 1901, 92–93. *G.C.* ii 1903, 81–82,186–87,192; v. 190 no. 6, 1981, 26–27. *Irish Gdning* v. 8, 1913, 135–36; v. 10, 1915, 108; v. 14, 1919, 145–46; v. 16, 1921, 73–74. *New Flora & Silva* v. 1, 1928, 119–20. *C.L.* v. 80, 1936, 12–18; v. 155, 1974, 1282–85. *J. Royal Hort. Soc.* 1947, 237–40; 1950, 245–47; 1966, 111–13. E.H. Walpole *Mount Usher, 1868–1952* 1952. E. Hyams *Irish gardens* 1967, 25–41. M. Allan *Fisons guide* 1970, 266–67. E. Malins *and* P. Bowe *Irish gardens and demesnes* 1980, 123–27. Knight of Glin *and* P. Bowe *Gardens of outstanding historic interest in . . . Ireland* 1980.

Mountains near Witham, Essex
C.L. v. 57, 1925, 388–95.

Mountgerald, Kiltearn, Highland
I.H. Adams *Descriptive list of plans* v. 3, 1974, 117.

Mounton House near Chepstow, Gwent
C.L. v. 37, 1915, 208–17,233–34; v. 42, 1917, 84–91; v. 166, 1979, 2270–73. G. Jekyll *Garden ornament* 1918, 149,302–04,369.

Mountwilson House near Edenderry, Co. Offaly, Eire
Irish Gdning v. 17, 1922, 57.

Moxhull Hall near Coleshill, Warwickshire
J.P. Neale *Views* v. 4, 1821.

Moyclare, Liskeard, Cornwall
M. Allan *Fisons guide* 1970, 132–33. A. Lees-Milne *and* R. Verey *Englishwoman's garden* 1980, 111–12.

Moydrum Castle near Athlone, Co. Westmeath, Eire
J.P. Neale *Views* v. 6, 1823.

Moyer House, Leyton, Waltham Forest, London
F.G. Emmison *Catalogue of maps in Essex Record Office* 3rd Supplt, 1968, 3.

Moyles Court near Ringwood, Hants
C.L. v. 26, 1909, 876–81.

Moyns Park near Haverhill, Essex
P. Muilman *History of Essex* v. 2, 1769, 241. T. Wright *History . . . of Essex* v. 1, 1836, 332. *C.L.* v. 12, 1902, 560–67; v. 70, 1931, 592–97. C. Holme *Gardens of England in Midland & Eastern counties* 1908, pl. 86.

Mucklagh near Aughrim, Co. Wicklow, Eire
Irish Gdning v. 9, 1913, 60–61; v. 10, 1915, 93.

Muckross Abbey, Muckross, Co. Kerry, Eire
G.C. i 1887, 763–64; ii 1918, 185–86. M. Allan *Fisons guide* 1970, 368–69. E. Malins *and* Knight of Glin *Lost demesnes* 1976, 156–67.

Muirhouse, Davidson's Mains, Edinburgh, Lothian
Scottish Gdnr and Northern Forester v. 7, 1912, 693–94.

Mulberry Garden, Clerkenwell, Islington, London
W. Wroth *London pleasure gardens of the eighteenth century* 1896, 40–42.

Mulgrave Castle near Whitby, N. Yorks
J.P. Neale *Views* 2nd Series, v. 2, 1825. *Jones's views* 1829, 25. F.O. Morris *Series of picturesque views* v. 2, 11. D. Stroud *Humphry Repton* 1962, 80. G. Carter *et al. Humphry Repton* 1982, 164.

Mullaboden near Naas, Co. Kildare, Eire
Irish Gdning v. 2, 1907, 63,81; v. 7, 1912, 26–27.

Mulroy House near Milford, Co. Donegal, Eire
E. Malins *and* P. Bowe *Irish gardens and demesnes* 1980, 133–34.

Muncaster Castle, Muncaster, Cumbria
F.O. Morris *Series of picturesque views* v. 3, 17. *G.C.* ii 1893, 502–03. *J. Hort. Cottage Gdnr* v. 51, 1905, 84. *C.L.* v. 87, 1940, 570–74,592,612–16. *Gdning Illustrated* v. 71, 1954, 115–17. M. Allan *Fisons guide* 1970, 252–53. B. Jones *Follies & grottoes* 1974, 305.

Munches near Dalbeattie, Dumfries and Galloway
G.M. v. 9, 1833, 6–7.

Munstead Oaks near Godalming, Surrey
J. Brown *Miss Gertrude Jekyll* 1981, 30–31.

Munstead Orchard near Godalming, Surry
J. Brown *Gardens of a golden afternoon* 1982, 162.

Munstead Place near Godalming, Surrey
J. Brown *Gardens of a golden afternoon* 1982, 161.

Munstead Wood near Godalming, Surrey
Garden v. 23, 1883, 298,299. *G.C.* i 1890, 133–34; i 1914, 101–02. G. Jekyll *Wood and garden* 1899. G. Jekyll *Home and garden* 1900. *C.L.* v. 8, 1900, 730–39; v. 40, 1916, 161; v. 170, 1981, 1971. L. Weaver *Houses and gardens by E.L. Lutyens* 1913, 12–19. L. Fleming and A. Gore *English garden* 1979, pl. 130. J. Brown *Gardens of a golden afternnon* 1982, 35–53,61.

Muntham Court, Findon, W. Sussex
T.W. Horsfield *History . . . of Sussex* v. 2, 1835, 203. *G.C.* ii 1884, 615–16,625. *Gardens* v. 35, 1889, 139. *C.L.* v. 21, 1907, 162–72.

Murieston House, Mid Calder, Lothian
Scottish Gdnr and Northern Forester v. 6, 1911, 717–18.

Murthly Castle, Murthly, Tayside
G.C. i 1901, 262,265. *C.L.* v. 38, 1915, 456–63. G. Jekyll *Garden ornament* 1918, 202.

Myatt's Fields *see* Lambeth

Myddelton House, Enfield, London
W. Keane *Beauties of Middlesex* 1850, 72–73. *Garden* 1909, 315. *Gdnrs Mag.* 1910, 26–27. *G.C.* i 1914, 17–18; ii 1960, 446–47. E.A. Bowles: *My garden in Spring* 1914; *My garden in Summer* 1914; *My garden in Autumn and Winter* 1915. *J. Royal Hort. Soc.* 1941, 225–29; 1954, 512–19. M. Allan *E.A. Bowles and his garden at Myddelton House* 1973.

Myddelton Lodge near Ilkley, W. Yorks
Bradford Illustrated Weekly Telegraph Series of picturesque views 1885.

Myles's, Kelvedon Hatch, Essex
V.C.H. Essex v. 4, 1956, 68.

Mynthurst near Reigate, Surrey
G. Jekyll and G.S. Elgood *Some English gardens* 1904, 115–17.

Myres Castle near Auchtermuchty, Fife
G.A. Little *Scotland's gardens* 1981, 161.

Naburn Hall, Naburn, N. Yorks
I. Hall *Samuel Buck's Yorkshire sketchbook* 1979, 44.

Nacton, Suffolk
D. Stroud *Humphry Repton* 1962, 171. G. Carter *et al.* *Humphry Repton* 1982, 47,48,162.

Nailsea Court, Nailsea, Avon
C.L. v. 32, 1912, 890–98. *Architectural Review* v. 33, 1913, 99. G. Jekyll *Garden ornament* 1918, 208.

Nanswhydyn near St Columb Major, Cornwall
W. Borlase *Natural history of Cornwall* 1758, pl. 8. *C.L.* v. 132, 1962, 775.

Nant-Eos near Aberystwyth, Dyfed
J.B. Burke *Visitation* v. 1, 1852, 244.

Nant-y-Glyn, Colwyn Bay, Clwyd
G.C. ii 1882, 295–96.

Narford Hall, Narford, Norfolk
C. Campbell *Vitruvius Britannicus* v. 3, 1725, pl. 95. *Architectural History* v. 7, 1964, 32,79–80.

Naseby Woolleys, Northants
C.L. v. 174, 1983, 216.

Nash Court near Faversham, Kent
J. Hort. Cottage Gdnr v. 50, 1873, 273–76. *Gdning World* v. 3, 1887, 458. *G.C.* i 1888, 39–40.

Nashdom, Taplow, Bucks
C.L. v. 32, 1912, 292–98. L. Weaver *Houses and gardens by E.L. Lutyens* 1913, 238–46. G. Jekyll *Garden ornament* 1918, 66. J. Brown *Gardens of a golden afternoon* 1982, 168.

Naughton House near Balmerino, Fife
G.A. Little *Scotland's gardens* 1981, 161–62.

Navestock, Essex
P. Muilman *History of Essex* v. 4, 1770, 48. P. Morant *History . . . of Essex* v. 1, 1816, 183. F.G. Emmison *Catalogue of maps in Essex Record Office* 1947, 12,36. *V.C.H. Essex* v. 4, 1956, 144. D. Stroud *Capability Brown* 1975, 234.

Naworth Castle, Naworth, Cumbria
G.C. ii 1890, 153–54. *C.L.* v. 29, 1911, 414–22. C. Holme *Gardens of England in Northern counties* 1911, pl. 98.

Nawton Tower, Nawton, N. Yorks
C.L. v. 132, 1962, 188–90. R. Webber *Percy Cane* 1975, 80,176. K. Lemmon *Gardens of Britain* v. 5, 1978, 87–90.

Nead-an-Eoin, Plockton, Highland
G.A. Little *Scotland's gardens* 1981, 235–36.

Neale near Cong, Co. Mayo, Eire
E. Malins *and* Knight of Glin *Lost demesnes* 1976, 141,142.

Neidpath Castle, near Peebles, Borders
Royal Commission on Ancient and Historical Monuments of Scotland *Peebleshire: an inventory of the ancient monuments* v. 2, 1967, 257,259.

Ness Gardens *see* Liverpool. Botanic Gardens

Nether Hall near Bury St Edmunds, Suffolk
F.O. Morris *Series of picturesque views* v. 4, 57.

Nether Lypiatt near Stroud, Glos
C.L. v. 75, 1934, 512–17.

Nether Swell Manor, Stow-on-the-Wold, Glos
C.L. v. 28, 1910, 754–60. G. Jekyll *Garden ornament* 1918, 128.

Nether Winchendon House, Aylesbury, Bucks
C.L. v. 127, 1960, 924–27. R. Bisgrove *Gardens of Britain* v. 3, 1978, 126. M. Binney *and* A. Hills *Elysian gardens* 1979, 22.

Netheravon near Amesbury, Wilts
T. Wright *Arbours & grottos* 1979.

Netherby Hall near Longtown, Cumbria
W. Hutchinson *History of county of Cumberland* v. 2, 1794, 533–34. *J. Hort. Cottage Gdnr* v. 57, 1877, 100–03. *G.C.* ii 1890, 65–66. C.L. v. 105, 1949, 142–45,198.

Netherbyres, Eyemouth, Borders
G.A. Little *Scotland's gardens* 1981, 103–04.

Netherhall near Maryport, Cumbria
F.O. Morris *Series of picturesque views* v. 6, 23. *J. Hort. Cottage Gdnr* N.S., v. 43, 1901, 58,59.

Netherplace near Mauchline, Strathclyde
Scottish Gdnr and Northern Forester v. 8, 1913, 497–98.

Netherton Hall near Newton Abbot, Devon
Architectural History v. 7, 1964, 32–33,81.

Nettlecombe Court, Nettlecombe, Somerset
W. Angus *Seats* 1787, pl. 3, 1791, 540. *G.M.* v. 18, 1842, 482–88.

Nettleham Hall, Nettleham, Lincs
C. Taylor *Archaeology of gardens* 1983, 37–38.

Nettlestead Place, Nettlestead, Kent
C.L. v. 124, 1958, 832–35,886–89.

Nevill Holt, Leics
C.L. v. 25, 1909, 270–80.

New Chapel House, Lingfield, Surrey
C.L. v. 60, 1926, 631–33.

New Georgia, Hampstead, Camden, London
W. Wroth *London pleasure gardens of the eighteenth century* 1896, 187–88.

New Globe Gardens, Mile End Road, London
E.B. Chancellor *Pleasure haunts of London* 1925, 411–12. C.L. v. 131, 1962, 727,916.

New Hailes near Edinburgh, Lothian
C.L. v. 42, 1917, 228–32.

New Hall, Boreham, Essex
P. Morant *History . . . of Essex* v. 2, 1768, 14. P. Muilman *History of Essex* v. 1, 1771, 127. W. Watts *Seats* 1779, pl. 4. G. Virtue *Picturesque beauties of Great Britain: Essex* 1831, 13. T. Wright *History . . . of Essex* v. 1, 1836, 102. C.L. v. 36, 1914, 550–54. F.G. Emmison *Catalogue of maps in Essex Record Office* 1947, 54; 3rd Supplt, 1968, 8. J. Evelyn *Diary* v. 3, 1955, 180.

New Hall near Sutton Coldfield, W. Midlands
C. Holme *Gardens of England in Midland & Eastern counties* 1908, pl. 87.

New High Riley, Accrington, Lancs
B. Jones *Follies & grottoes* 1974, 353.

New Lodge *see* White Lodge

New Mills, Glos
S. Rudder *New history of Gloucestershire* 1779, 714.

New Park, Petersham, Richmond, London
J. Beeverell *Les delices de la Grande Bretagne* v. 5, 1707, 872. L. Knyff *and* J. Kip *Britannia illustrata* v. 1, 1714. D. Defoe *Tour* v. 1, 1778, 226–27. British Museum *Catalogue of maps, prints* 1829, 266. R. Pococke *Travels through England* v. 2, 1889, 261. J. Harris *Artist and the country house* 1979, 144, pl. 11. C.L. v. 172, 1982, 984–86.

New Park near Devizes, Wilts
J. Britton *Beauties of Wiltshire* v. 2, 1801, 198–99. J.P. Neale *Views* v. 5, 1822. D. Stroud *Humphry Repton* 1962, 171. G. Carter *et al*. *Humphry Repton* 1982, 163.

New Place, Shedfield, Hants
G. Beard *Thomas H. Mawson* 1976, 59. J. Brown *Gardens of a golden afternoon* 1982, 104–05,169.

New Place, Gilston, Herts
H. Chauncy *Historical antiquities of Hertfordshire* 1700, 190. M. Macartney *English houses & gardens* 1908, pl. 7.

New Place, Haslemere, Surrey
Garden 1921, 388–89. M. Parsons *English house grounds* 1924, 49–53.

New Place, Stratford-on-Avon, Warwickshire
M. Allan *Fisons guide* 1970, 166–67. R. Sidwell *West Midland gardens* 1981, 227–29.

New Posso, Borders
G.M. v. 18, 1842, 438–39. J.C. Loudon *Arboretum et fruticetum Britannicum* v. 1, 1844, 93–94.

New Tunbridge Wells *see* Islington Spa

New Wells, Clerkenwell, Islington, London
W. Wroth *London pleasure gardens of the eighteenth century* 1896, 33–36.

Newark Park, Ozleworth, Glos
J.N. Brewer *Delineations of Gloucestershire* 1825, 194. *C.L.* v. 154, 1973, 795.

Newbattle Abbey, Newbattle, Lothian
Copper Plate Mag. v. 3, pl. 118. *G.C.* ii 1891, 278,283. *C.L.* v. 12, 1902, 336–43. H.I. Triggs *Formal gardens in England and Scotland* 1902, 46–47. *House and Gdn* v. 4, 1903, 143–47. G. Jekyll *Garden ornament* 1918, 252. C. McWilliam *Lothian* 1978, 349–50.

Newbold Revel near Coventry, W. Midlands
C.L. v. 13, 1903, 304–11. G. Jekyll *Garden ornament* 1918, 97.

Newburgh Priory, Coxwold, N. Yorks
Official guide. A. Young *Six months tour through North of England* v. 2, 1771, 458–59. *C.L.* v. 18, 1905, 666–76; v. 155, 1974, 426–29,482–85. K. Lemmon *Gardens of Britain* v. 5, 1978, 90–92. J. Harris *Artist and the country house* 1979, 133.

Newby Hall, Newby, N. Yorks
Official guide. J. Beeverell *Les delices de la Grande Bretagne* v. 5, 1707, 872. L. Knyff *and* J. Kip *Britannia illustrata* v. 1, 1714. J.P. Neale *Views* v. 5, 1822. *G.M.* v. 13, 1837, 201–03. *G.C.* ii 1901, 257–58; i 1957, 628–29. *C.L.* v. 19, 1906, 90–99; v. 35, 1914, 878–85; v. 81, 1937, 658–64,688,714; v. 125, 1959, 510–12; v. 156, 1974, 1006; v. 165, 1979, 1802. C. Fiennes *Journeys* 1949, 84. P. Coats *Great gardens of Britain* 1967, 88–93. N. Pevsner *Yorkshire: West Riding* 1967, 376. M. Allan *Fisons guide* 1970, 253–54. K. Lemmon *Gardens of Britain* v. 5, 1978, 93–97.

Newcastle upon Tyne (Sir William Blackett), Tyne and Wear
J. Beeverell *Les delices de la Grande Bretagne* v. 5, 1707, 872.

Newcastle upon Tyne. Jesmond Cemetery, Tyne and Wear
C.L. v. 170, 1981, 68–69.

Newcombe House, Crediton, Devon
J. Hort. Cottage Gdnr N.S., v. 14, 1887, 30–32.

Newdigate House, Nottingham, Notts
M. Macartney *English houses & gardens* 1908, pl. 52.

Newhall near Penicuit, Lothian
C. McWilliam *Lothian* 1978, 355.

Newhouse, Downton, Wilts
V.C.H. *Wiltshire* v. 11, 1980, 31.

Newhouse Park, Dawlish, Devon
C.L. v. 131, 1962, 1111.

Newlands, Harrow on the Hill, London
G.C. i 1902, 28–29; ii 1912, 149.

Newliston near Kirkliston, Lothian
J.C. Loudon *Encyclopaedia of gardening* 1822, 1255. *C.L.* v. 39, 1916, 270–77. Historical MSS Commission *Architectural history* v. 2, 1970, item 1904. C. McWilliam *Lothian* 1978, 355–56. A.A. Tait *Landscape garden in Scotland* 1980, passim.

Newnham Hall, Newnham, Northants
B. Jones *Follies & grottoes* 1974, 369.

Newnham Paddox near Rugby, Warwickshire
J. Beeverell *Les delices de la Grande Bretagne* v. 5, 1707, 872. L. Knyff *and* J. Kip *Britannia illustrata* v. 1, 1714. *G.C.* ii 1884, 491. *J. Hort. Cottage Gdnr* N.S., v. 27, 1893, 268; N.S., v. 43, 1901, 154–55. H. Walpole *Visits to country seats. Walpole Society* v. 7, 1927–28, 63. *Warwickshire History* v. 1, 1969, 3–17. D. Stroud *Capability Brown* 1975, 54,71,234.

Newsells Bury, Barkway, Herts
H. Chauncy *Historical antiquities of Hertfordshire* 1700, 100.

Newstead, Wimbledon, Merton, London
Garden v. 2, 1872, 486–87.

Newstead Abbey, Newstead, Notts
Official guide. N. Spencer *Complete English traveller* 1771, 492. C. Burlington *Modern universal British traveller* 1779, 542. P. Sandby *Collection of one hundred and fifty select views* v. 1, 1781, pls. 43–44. R. Ackermann *Repository* v. 4, 1824, pl. 25. W.W.J. Gendall *Views* v. 2, 1830, 73. W. Adam *Gem of the Peak* 1851, 197–202. F.O. Morris *Series of picturesque views* v. 1, 77. *J. Hort. Cottage Gdnr* v. 57, 1877, 9–12; N.S., v. 9, 1884, 101–02. *C.L.* v. 3, 1898, 208–10,240–43; v. 9, 1901, 798–99; v. 42, 1917, 468–74,492–97; v. 155, 1974, 1122–25,1190–93,1560. C. Holme *Gardens of England in Midland & Eastern counties* 1908, pls. 88–89. G. Jekyll *Garden ornament* 1918, 345,380. M. Allan *Fisons guide* 1970, 230–31. J. Harris *Catalogue of British drawings . . . in American collections* 1971, 129. B. Jones *Follies & grottoes* 1974, 375–76. J. Anthony *Gardens of Britain* v. 6, 1979, 126–35. J. Harris *Artist and the country house* 1979, 234.

Newtimber Place, Newtimber, W. Sussex
C.L. v. 40, 1916, 780–85.

Newton, Little Newton, Northants
Northamptonshire Past and Present v. 5 no. 5, 1977, 396,397. Royal Commission on Historical Monuments *Inventory of historical monuments in . . . Northampton* v. 2, 1979, 113–15.

Newton Ferrars near Callington, Cornwall
C.L. v. 15, 1904, 54–63; v. 84, 1938, 604–08. G. Jekyll *Garden ornament* 1918, 26,61,64,84. *Architectural History* v. 7, 1964, 33,69.

Newton Green Hall, Leeds, W. Yorks
C. Holme *Gardens of England in Northern counties* 1911, pls. 99–100. G. Beard *Thomas H. Mawson* 1976, 60.

Newton Hall near Stocksfield, Northumberland
J. Hort. Cottage Gdnr v. 58, 1877, 455–58.

Newton Hall near Newcastle upon Tyne, Tyne and Wear
J. Hort. Cottage Gdnr N.S., v. 15, 1887, 340–41,344.

Newton House, Alves, Grampian
J.B. Burke *Visitation* 2nd Series, v. 1, 1855, 155.

Newton House near Insch, Grampian
G.A. Little *Scotland's gardens* 1981, 204.

Newton House *see* Dynevor Castle

Newton Park, Newton St Loe, Avon
J. Collinson *History . . . of Somersetshire* v. 3, 1791, 343. D. Stroud *Humphry Repton* 1962, 171. D. Stroud *Capability Brown* 1975, 234. G. Carter *et al. Humphry Repton* 1982, 161.

Newton Surmaville near Yeovil, Somerset
C.L. v. 112, 1952, 676–79.

Newton Valence Manor House, Newton Valence, Hants
E.F. Prosser *Select illustrations of Hampshire* 1833.

Newtonairds near Dumfries, Dumfries and Galloway
Scottish Gdnr and Northern Forester v. 7, 1912, 357–58.

Nibley near Dursley, Glos
R. Atkyns *Ancient and present state of Glostershire* 1712, 579. L. Knyff *and* J. Kip *Britannia illustrata* v. 2, 1715. S. Rudder *New history of Gloucestershire* 1779, 574.

Niddrie Marischal, Edinburgh, Lothian
Scottish Gdnr and Northern Forester v. 6, 1911, 741–42.

Ninewells, Great Shelford, Cambs
G.C. ii 1889, 5–6.

Nocton Hall, Nocton, Lincs
C.L. v. 10, 1901, 402–06.

Node, Welwyn, Herts
Cottage Gdnr v. 19, 1857, 194–96. *J. Hort.* N.S., v. 68, 1914, 149–51. *G.C.* ii 1921, 312–13.

Nonsuch, Cheam, Sutton, London
Archaeologia v. 7, 1785, 119–20. D. Lysons *Environs of London* v. 1, 1792, 152,154. P. Hentzner *Travels in England* 1797, 58–59. W. Gilpin *Observations on the Western parts of England* 1808, 3. *G.M.* v. 7, 1831, 430–32. *Gentleman's Mag.* 1837, 135–44. E.W. Brayley *and* J. Britton *Topographical history of Surrey* v. 4, 410,411. W. Keane *Beauties of Surrey* 1849, 95–99. J.B. Burke *Visitation* v. 1, 1852, 214–16. *Surrey Archaeological Collections* v. 5, 1871, 145–46. *Gdning World* v. 2, 1886, 794. *V.C.H. Surrey* v. 3, 1911, 270. C. Williams *Thomas Platter's travels in England 1599* 1932, 191,195–97. J. Evelyn *Diary* v. 3, 1955, 427–28. *C.L.* v. 130, 1961, 1008–10. J. Dent *Quest for Nonsuch* 1962. R. Strong *Renaissance garden in England* 1979, 38–43,63–69. H.M. Colvin *History of the King's Works* v. 4, 1982, 190,202.

Norbiton Place, Kingston, London
T.K. Cromwell *Excursions . . . through Surrey* 1821, 51–53. G.F. Prosser *Select illustrations of . . . Surrey* 1828. N. Whittock *and* H. Gastineau *Picturesque beauties of England and Wales* 1830, 60. *G.M.* v. 15, 1839, 426–29. *J. Hort. Cottage Gdnr* v. 55, 1876, 392–93.

Norbury Park near Dorking, Surrey
J.P. Neale *Views* 2nd Series, v. 4, 1828. G.F. Prosser *Select illustrations of . . . Surrey* 1828. E.W. Brayley and J. Britton *Topographical history of Surrey* v. 4, 448, 452–54. W. Keane *Beauties of Surrey* 1849, 107–09. J.B. Burke *Visitation* v. 2, 1853, 221; 2nd Series, v. 1, 1855, 246–47. *G.C.* i 1882, 667–68.

Nork, Banstead, Surrey
G.F. Prosser *Select illustrations of . . . Surrey* 1828.

Norman Court near Stockbridge, Hants
G.M. v. 9, 1833, 16. E.F. Prosser *Select illustrations of Hampshire* 1833. *G.C.* ii 1882, 42. *Gdning World* v. 1, 1884, 263. G. Carter *et al. Humphry Repton* 1982, 153.

Normanby Park, Normanby, Lincs
C.L. v. 30, 1911, 170–76; v. 130, 1961, 346–49.

Normanhurst near Battle, E. Sussex
F.O. Morris *Series of picturesque views* v. 6, 51. *G.C.* ii 1881, 399–400; ii 1885, 197–98; ii 1892, 427–28; ii 1912, 279–80. G. Beard *Thomas H. Mawson* 1976, 60.

Normanton Hall, Normanton, Lincs
Historical MSS commission *Architectural history* v. 2, 1970, item 1916.

Normanton Park, Normanton, Leics
J.P. Neale *Views* v. 3, 1820. *J. Hort. Cottage Gdnr* v. 51, 1874, 511–13. *G.C.* i 1882, 219. *C.L.* v. 33, 1913, 198–206. G. Jekyll *Garden ornament* 1918, 254. G. Carter *et al. Humphry Repton* 1982, 160.

Normanton Turville Hall, Normanton Turville, Leics
J. Throsby *Select views in Leicestershire* v. 1, 1790, 297.

Norris Castle near East Cowes, Isle of Wight
R. Ackermann *Repository* v. 8, 1826, pl. 1. W.W.J. Gendall *Views* v. 1, 1830, 97. J.B. Burke *Visitation* v. 2, 1853, 89. *C.L.* v. 4, 1898, 28–29. G. Carter *et al. Humphry Repton* 1982, 155.

Norris Green, Merseyside
J. Hort. Cottage Gdnr v. 54, 1875, 511–13; N.S., v. 12, 1886, 510. *G.C.* i 1879, 718–19, 725.

North Bierley Hall, North Bierley, W. Yorks
Gdn History v. 1 no. 3, 1973, 47–50. I. Hall *Samuel Buck's Yorkshire sketchbook* 1979, 155.

North Cheam Park, Sutton, London
W. Keane *Beauties of Surrey* 1849, 93–95.

North Cray Place, North Cray, Bexley, London
E. Hasted *History . . . of . . . Kent* v. 1, 1778, 154. D. Stroud *Capability Brown* 1975, 235.

North Grimston, Grimston, N. Yorks
I. Hall *Samuel Buck's Yorkshire sketchbook* 1979, 34.

North Luffenham Hall, North Luffenham, Leics
C.L. v. 45, 1919, 400–06.

North Merchiston, Edinburgh, Lothian
A.A. Tait *Landscape garden in Scotland* 1980, passim.

North Mymms Park, North Mymms, Herts
G.C. ii 1900, 254–55. *C.L.* v. 75, 1934, 38–44, 66, 90–95; v. 157, 1975, 560–62. Lady Rockley *Historic gardens of England* 1938, 242–43. N. Pevsner *Hertfordshire* 1977, 263. R. Bisgrove *Gardens of Britain* v. 3, 1978, 128–29.

North Ockendon Hall, North Ockendon, Essex
F.G. Emmison *Catalogue of maps in Essex Record Office* 2nd Supplt, 1964, 15.

North Rode Hall near Congleton, Cheshire
Cottage Gdnr v. 20, 1858, 195–96. *J. Hort. Cottage Gdnr* v. 30, 1863, 270–71.

North Stoneham Park, North Stoneham, Hants
E.F. Prosser *Select illustrations of Hampshire* 1833. *G.M.* v. 11, 1835, 162. D. Stroud *Capability Brown* 1975, 241.

North Stoneham Parsonage, North Stoneham, Hants
G.M. v. 11, 1835, 59.

Northaw House, Potters Bar, Herts
G.C. ii 1901, 93.

Northbourne Court, Northbourne, Kent
C.L. v. 57, 1925, 954–61; v. 128, 1960, 278–79. T. Wright *Gardens of Britain* v. 4, 1978, 73–76.

Northcourt near Brighstone, Isle of Wight
J.P. Neale *Views* v. 2, 1819. R. Ackermann *Repository* v. 7, 1826, pl. 31. W.W.J. Gendall *Views* v. 1, 1830, 127–28.

Northerwood near Emery Down, Hants
E.F. Prosser *Select illustrations of Hampshire* 1833.

Northrepps, Norfolk
D. Stroud *Humphry Repton* 1962, 66. G. Carter *et al. Humphry Repton* 1982, 159.

Northwick Park, Northwick, Hereford and Worcester
A. Rushout *Picturesque scenery in Northwick Park, Worcestershire* 1815.

Norton Conyers near Ripon, N. Yorks
C.L. v. 7, 1900, 624–29. G. Jekyll *Garden ornament*

Norton Conyers (*Cont.*)
1918, 42. K. Lemmon *Gardens of Britain* v. 5, 1978, 97–98. J. Harris *Artist and the country house* 1979, 291.

Norton Hall, Norton, Derbyshire
N. Nicholls *Local maps of Derbyshire to 1770* 1980, 129–30.

Norton Hall near Daventry, Northants
J.P. Neale *Views* 2nd Series, v. 2, 1825. Royal Commission on Historical Monuments *Inventory of the historical monuments in . . . Northampton* v. 3, 1981, 157. G. Carter *et al. Humphry Repton* 1982, 160.

Norton Manor, Sutton Scotney, Hants
A. Paterson *Gardens of Britain* v. 2, 1978, 128.

Norton Park near Evesham, Hereford and Worcester
C.L. v. 11, 1902, 776–83.

Norton Place near Market Rasen, Lincs
B. Howlett *Selection of views in county of Lincoln* 1805.

Norwood Cemetery, West Norwood, Lambeth, London
J.S. Curl *Celebration of death* 1980, 257–58.

Norwood Hall, Sheffield, S. Yorks
J. Harris *Artist and the country house* 1979, 203.

Noseley Hall, Noseley, Leics
J. Throsby *Select views in Leicestershire* v. 1, 1790, 299.

Nostell Priory near Wakefield, W. Yorks
Official guide. J.P. Neale *Views* v. 5, 1822. *Jones's views* 1829, 23–24. F.O. Morris *Series of picturesque views* v. 5, 63. Bradford Illustrated Weekly Telegraph *Series of picturesque views* 1885. *J. Hort. Cottage Gdnr* N.S., v. 11, 1885, 340–41; N.S., v. 31, 1895, 554–55. *Gdning World* v. 15, 1899, 537–39. *C.L.* v. 36, 1914, 582–89; v. 111, 1952, 1492–95. *Park Administration* July 1964, 42–44. N. Pevsner *Yorkshire: West Riding* 1967, 382. Historical MSS Commission *Architectural history* v. 1, 1969, item 709. K. Lemmon *Gardens of Britain* v. 5, 1978, 183–86. G.S. Thomas *Gardens of National Trust* 1979, 179. D. Jacques *Georgian gardens* 1983, 41.

Notgrove Manor, Notgrove, Glos
C.L. v. 36, 1914, 678–83. G. Jekyll *Garden ornament* 1918, 37,308.

Nottingham (Marshal Tallard), Notts
J. Beeverell *Les delices de la Grande Bretagne* v. 5, 1707, 872. M. Hadfield *et al. British gardeners* 1980, 188.

Nottingham. Colwick Park, Notts
E.S.P. Evans *Colwick Park* 1967.

Nottingham. University, Notts
Architect and Building News 5 May 1955, 531–33.

Notton Lodge near Lacock, Wilts
J. Sales *West Country gardens* 1980, 235.

Nowton Court, Nowton, Suffolk
G.C. ii 1883, 557–58.

Nun Monkton Priory, Nun Monkton, N. Yorks
J. Harris *Artist and the country house* 1979, 241. *C.L.* v. 168, 1980, 1650–53.

Nuneham Park, Nuneham Courtenay, Oxfordshire
Official guide. P. Sandby *Virtuosi's museum* 1778, pl. 76. P. Sandby *Collection of one hundred and fifty select views* v. 1, 1781, pls. 45–48. W. Angus *Seats* 1787, pl. 38. J. and J. Boydell *History of the River Thames* v. 1, 1794, 180–200. H. Meister *Letters* 1799, 273. S. Shaw *Tour to West of England in 1788* In J. Pinkerton, v. 2, 1808, 197–98. W.B. Cooke *and* S. Owen *The Thames* v. 1, 1811, 39–40. J. Hodgson *and* F.C. Laird *Beauties of England and Wales* v. 12, pt 2, 1813, 279–85. J.P. Neale *Views* v. 3, 1820. British Museum *Catalogue of maps, prints* 1829, 242. *G.M.* v. 10, 1834, 97–98. *Tombleson's Thames* 1834. *Florist* 1855, 301–05. E.A. Brooke *Gardens of England* 1857, pl. 41. *Cottage Gdnr* v. 12, 1854, 156–59. *J. Hort. Cottage Gdnr* v. 36, 1866, 255–56; v. 38, 1867, 294–95, 313–15, 351–52, 404–05. F.O. Morris *Series of picturesque views* v. 6, 31. *G.C.* ii 1882, 165–66; i 1908, 9, 10–11, 21; ii 1912, 26–27, 32. *Gdning World* v. 6, 1890, 665. *Gdnrs Mag.* 1913, 7–10, 11. *C.L.* v. 34, 1913, 746–55; v. 90, 1941, 866–70, 910–13; v. 144, 1968, 541–42, 640–42; v. 156, 1974, 1024–28. H. Walpole *Correspondence*; edited by W.S. Lewis, v. 28, 1955, 105. V.C.H. *Oxford* v. 5, 1957, 238–39. *Gdn History* v. 1 no. 2, 1973, 13–20; v. 3 no. 4, 1975, 19. J. Sherwood *and* N. Pevsner *Oxfordshire* 1974, 728–30. P. Willis *Furor hortensis* 1974, 57–71. D. Stroud *Capability Brown* 1975, 189–93, 235. A. Parreaux *and* M. Plaissant *Jardins et paysages: le style Anglais* 1977, 247–55. R. Bisgrove *Gardens of Britain* v. 3, 1978, 129–30. D. Jarrett *English landscape garden* 1978, 130–33. M. Binney and A. Hills *Elysian gardens* 1979, 18. J. Harris *Artist and the country house* 1979, 278. M. Batey *Oxford gardens* 1982, 115, 118–22, 136. *J. Gdn History* v. 2 no. 1, 1982, 55–56.

Nunhead Cemetery, Southwark, London
C.L. v. 158, 1975, 146–48. Ancient Monuments Society *Nunhead Cemetery, London,* 1977. J.S. Curl *Celebration of death* 1980, 229–34.

Nunnery of St Bridget near Douglas, Isle of Man
Proc. Isle of Man Natural History and Antiquarian Soc. v. 8 no. 3, 1976/78, 247–48, 265–66.

Nunnington Hall, Nunnington, N. Yorks
C.L. v. 63, 1928, 148–55.

Nunnykirk near Morpeth, Northumberland
J. Hodgson *History of Northumberland* pt 2 v. 2, 1832.

Nunton House, Nunton, Wilts
J. Sales *West Country gardens* 1980, 236–37.

Nunwell near Brading, Isle of Wight
R. Worsley *History of the Isle of Wight* 1781. *C.L.* v. 159, 1976, 402–05, 470–73.

Nurstead Court, Nurstead, Kent
C. Greenwood *Epitome of county history . . . v. 1: Kent* 1838, 225.

Nuthall Temple, Nottingham, Notts
C.L. v. 53, 1923, 570–76; v. 150, 1971, 548–50.
T. Wright *Arbours & grottos* 1979.

Nutley near Booterstown, Co. Dublin, Eire
Flora and Sylva v. 1, 1903, 164–65.

Nutwell Court near Topsham, Devon
G. Tod *Plans, elevations and sections of hot-houses* 1807, 16, 19, pls. 14, 20. R. Ackermann *Repository* v. 4, 1824, pls. 30–31. W.W.J. Gendall *Views* v. 2, 1830, 115, 117–18. *G.M.* v. 19, 1843, 239–40.

Nymans, Handcross, W. Sussex
Official guide. L. Messel *Garden flora: trees and shrubs grown in the gardens at Nymans, 1890–1915* 1918. *C.L.* v. 72, 1932, 292–97, 320–25, 346–52; v. 175, 1984, 1362–65. *J. Royal Hort. Soc.* 1940, 203–10; 1954, 174–79; 1960, 349–50; 1971, 482–91. *G.C.* ii 1963, 154–55. E. Hyams *English garden* 1964, 156–59. *Sussex Life* v. 1 no. 1, 1965, 24–25. P. Coats *Great gardens of Britain* 1967, 118–23. M. Allan *Fisons guide* 1970, 55–56. H. Evans *Beautiful gardens of Britain* 1974, 67–68. T. Wright *Gardens of Britain* v. 4, 1978, 163–70. L. Fleming *and* A. Gore *English garden* 1979, pl. 133. G.S. Thomas *Gardens of National Trust* 1979, 179–90. A. Hellyer *Gardens of genius* 1980, 145–50. *Connoisseur* v. 207, 1981, 100–03.

Nynehead Court, Nynehead, Somerset
M. Binney *and* A. Hills *Elysian gardens* 1979, 22.

Oak Lodge, Kensington, London
J. Hort. Cottage Gdnr v. 42, 1869, 281–82. *Garden* v. 3, 1873, 50–51.

Oakbank, Kippen, Central
Scottish Gdnr and Northern Forester v. 6, 1911, 659–60.

Oakery, Beckenham, Bromley, London
C. Greenwood *Epitome of county history . . . v. 1: Kent* 1838, 31.

Oakes Park, Norton, S. Yorks
Historical MSS Commission *Architectural history* v. 5, 1974, items 5329, 5387. K. Lemmon *Gardens of Britain* v. 5, 1978, 137–38.

Oakfield, Mortimer, Berks
R. Bisgrove *Gardens of Britain* v. 3, 1978, 130–31.

Oakfield, Penshurst, Kent
C.L. v. 48, 1920, 413–15.

Oakhill near Cheshunt, Herts
G.M. v. 15, 1839, 515–16.

Oakholme, Sheffield, S. Yorks
Gdning World v. 3, 1886, 153.

Oakingham *see* Wokingham

Oaklands, Bristol, Avon
G.C. ii 1909, 325–26.

Oaklands near Okehampton, Devon
R. Ackermann *Repository* v. 8, 1826, pl. 25. W.W.J. Gendall *Views* v. 1, 1830, 67. J. Britton *and* E.W. Brayley *Devonshire & Cornwall* 1832, 73.

Oaklands House, Manchester, Greater Manchester
Cottage Gdnr v. 22, 1859, 164–65.

Oakleigh near Burnley, Lancs
Gdning World v. 3, 1886, 246–47.

Oakley Court near Windsor, Berks
G.C. i 1906, 382–83.

Oakley Great Park *see* Cirencester House

Oakley Hall near Basingstoke, Hants
J. Hort. Cottage Gdnr N.S., v. 25, 1892, 190–91.

Oakley Park near Eye, Suffolk
C.L. v. 23, 1908, 18–26.

Oakly Park near Ludlow, Shropshire
J.P. Neale *Views* 2nd Series, v. 3, 1826. *G.M.* v. 14, 1838, 212–13. *C.L.* v. 119, 1956, 380–81. D. Stroud *Capability Brown* 1975, 172–73, 235.

Oaks, Woodmansterne, Surrey
J.P. Neale *Views* v. 4, 1821. G.F. Prosser *Select illustrations of . . . Surrey* 1828.

Oakville, Clonmel, Co. Cork, Eire
Garden v. 46, 1894, 193.

Oakwood near Maidstone, Kent
J. Hort. Cottage Gdnr v. 45, 1871, 334–35.

Oakwood near Wylam, Northumberland
G.C. ii 1898, 65.

Oakwood, Funtington, W. Sussex
J. Dallaway *History of Western Division of . . . Sussex* v. 1, 1815, 107.

Oakwood near Newcastle upon Tyne, Tyne and Wear
Gdnrs Mag. 1904, 341–43, 345.

Oakwood *see* Royal Horticultural Society Gardens

Oakworth House near Keighley, W. Yorks
J. Hort. Cottage Gdnr N.S., v. 1, 1880, 241, 259–60, 326. Bradford Illustrated Weekly Telegraph *Series of picturesque views* 1885.

Oare House, Oare, Wilts
C.L. v. 63, 1928, 334–41. *House & Gdn* November 1974, 142–43. J. Sales *West Country gardens* 1980, 238–39.

Oatlands near Weybridge, Surrey
T. Badeslade *and* J. Rocque *Vitruvius Brittanicus* 1739, pls. 67–68. R. *and* J. Dodsley *London and its environs described* v. 4, 1761, 60. *Short account of the principal seats and gardens in and about Richmond and Kew*, [1760s?], 18. *Copper Plate Mag.* v. 2, pls. 74, 86. W.B. Cooke *and* S. Owen *The Thames* v. 1, 1811, 35. G.F. Prosser *Select illustrations of . . . Surrey* 1828. British Museum *Catalogue of maps, prints* 1829, 247. *G.M.* v. 13, 1837, 112. E.W. Brayley *and* J. Britton *Topographical history of Surrey* v. 2, 1841, 388–89. W. Keane *Beauties of Surrey* 1849, 18–20. F. Kielmansegge *Diary* 1902, 79–80. *Architectural Review* v. 103, 1948, 216–17. *C.L.* v. 103, 1948, 924–25. J. Evelyn *Diary* v. 4, 1955, 566. B. Jones *Follies & grottoes* 1974, 158–60. *History Today* v. 25, 1975, 204–07. J. Harris *Artist and the country house* 1979, 268. T. Wright *Arbours & grottos* 1979. *Gdn History* v. 8 no. 3, 1980, 77–81, 106; v. 9 no. 2, 1981 136–56. H.M. Colvin *History of the King's Works* v. 4, 1982, 214, 215–16.

Observatory, Campden Hill, London
W. Keane *Beauties of Middlesex* 1850, 231–32.

Ochtertyre near Crieff, Tayside
J.P. Neale *Views* 2nd Series, v. 4, 1828. *G.C.* ii 1876, 809–10, 813.

Ockenden near Cuckfield, W. Sussex
G.C. ii 1881, 301–02.

Ockham Mill, Ripley, Surrey
C.L. v. 91, 1942, 1230–33.

Ockham Park near Ripley, Surrey
J.P. Neale *Views* 2nd Series, v. 3, 1826. G.F. Prosser *Select illustrations of . . . Surrey* 1828. E.W. Brayley *and* J. Britton *Topographical history of Surrey* v. 2, 1841, 116, 118. W. Keane *Beauties of Surrey* 1849, 117–18.

Ockwells Manor near Bray, Berks
C.L. v. 54, 1924, 52–60.

Oddington near Stow-on-the-Wold, Glos
J.P. Neale *Views* 2nd Series, v. 1, 1824. J. Harris *Catalogue of British drawings . . . in American collections* 1971, 127.

Odell Castle, Odell, Beds
R. Bisgrove *Gardens of Britain* v. 3, 1978, 131. *Bedfordshire Mag.* v. 18, 1982, 223–27.

Odiham, Hants
H.M. Colvin *History of the King's Works* v. 2, 1963, 767–68.

Offchurch Bury, Offchurch, Warwickshire
J.P. Neale *Views* v. 4, 1821.

Offington Park, Worthing, W. Sussex
G.C. ii 1894, 278–80.

Offley Place, Offley, Herts
H. Chauncy *Historical antiquities of Hertfordshire* 1700, 405. R. Ackermann *Repository* v. 9, 1827, pl. 20. W.W.J. Gendall *Views* v. 1, 1830, 51. G. Carter *et al. Humphry Repton* 1982, 154.

Ogston Hall near Alfreton, Derbyshire
J. Hort. Cottage Gdnr v. 51, 1874, 204–06.

Okeover Hall, Okeover, Staffs
R. Plot *Natural history of Staffordshire* 1685, 227. *C.L.* v. 11, 1902, 176–82; v. 27, 1910, 342–49; v. 135, 1964, 172–76, 568, 645–49. C. Holme *Gardens of England in Midland & Eastern counties* 1908, pls. 90–91. G. Jekyll *Garden ornament* 1918, 62. J. Harris *Artist and the country house* 1979, 217.

Olantigh near Wye, Kent
W. Watts *Seats* 1779, pl. 78. *G.C.* ii 1884, 601. *C.L.* v. 146, 1969, 222–26, 282–85, 334.

Old Ballikinrain, Balfron, Central
G.A. Little *Scotland's gardens* 1981, 162–63.

Old Bell House, Ludford, Shropshire
M. Parsons *English house grounds* 1924, 21–31.

Old Buckhurst House near East Grinstead, W. Sussex
C.L. v. 46, 1919, 488–95, 518–25.

Old Conna Hill, Bray, Co. Wicklow, Eire
Irish Gdning v. 4, 1909, 103; v. 7, 1912, 67–69; v. 13, 1918, 81–83, 85. *J. Royal Hort. Soc.* 1950, 244–45.

Old Forge, Henley-on-Thames, Oxfordshire
R. Webber *Percy Cane* 1975, 165.

Old Hall, Nether Hambleton, Leics
C.L. v. 68, 1930, 372–77.

Old Hall, East Bergholt, Suffolk
J. Harris *Artist and the country house* 1979, 354.

Old Hall, Shadingfield, Suffolk
A. Suckling *History . . . of Suffolk* v. 1, 1846, 73.

Old Hall, Heath, W. Yorks
C.L. v. 22, 1907, 90–96.

Old House, Rotherwick, Hants
A. Paterson *Gardens of Britain* v. 2, 1978, 129–31.

Old Lodge, Nutley, E. Sussex
Sussex Life v. 1 no. 4, 1965, 56–57.

Old Manor, Little Hempston, Devon
C.L. v. 74, 1933, 120–26.

Old Manse of Marnoch, Banff, Grampian
G.A. Little *Scotland's gardens* 1981, 204–06.

Old Mansion, Boldre, Hants
C.L. v. 60, 1926, 350–56.

Old Meadows, West Drayton, Hillingdon, London
Gdn Design 1930, 158–61.

Old Melrose, Melrose, Borders
I.H. Adams *Descriptive list of plans* v. 3, 1974, 126.

Old Park House, Enfield, London
V.C.H. *Middlesex* v. 5, 1976, 230.

Old Parsonage, Marlow, Bucks
R. Webber *Percy Cane* 1975, 143, 177.

Old Place, Lindfield, W. Sussex
Garden v. 35, 1889, 281; 1921, 464–66. *C.L.* v. 8, 1900, 432–40; v. 22, 1907, 414–23. C. Holme *Gardens of England in Southern & Western counties* 1907, pls. 94–97. *G.C.* i 1930, 247.

Old Place of Mochrum, Mochrum, Dumfries and Galloway
C.L. v. 32, 1912, 162–67.

Old Rectory, Burghfield, Berks
C.L. v. 163, 1978, 666–68. A. Lees-Milne *and* R. Verey *Englishwoman's garden* 1980, 88–91.

Old Rectory, Naunton, Glos
A. Lees-Milne *and* R. Verey *Englishwoman's garden* 1982, 116–19.

Old Rectory near Droitwich, Hereford and Worcester
R. Sidwell *West Midland gardens* 1981, 72–73.

Old Rectory, Orford, Suffolk
C.L. v. 161, 1977, 850–52.

Old Rectory, Oxhill, Warwickshire
R. Sidwell *West Midland gardens* 1981, 221.

Old Rectory, Whichford, Warwickshire
R. Sidwell *West Midland gardens* 1981, 222–23.

Old Rectory Cottage, Tidmarsh, Berks
A. Lees-Milne *and* R. Verey *Englishman's garden* 1982, 24–27.

Old School, Langord, Oxfordshire
A. Lees-Milne *and* R. Verey *Englishman's garden* 1982, 16–19.

Old Sneyd Park, Bristol, Avon
G.C. ii 1884, 588–89. *J. Hort. Cottage Gdnr* v. 51, 1905, 156–57.

Old Stones, Blackawton, Devon
B. Jones *Follies & grottoes* 1974, 310.

Old Surrey Hall, East Grinstead, W. Sussex
C.L. v. 66, 1929, 352–58.

Old Swinford Castle, Old Swinford, W. Midlands
Garden v. 34, 1888, 597.

Old Vicarage, Bucklebury, Berks
C.L. v. 146, 1969, 146–48. R. Bisgrove *Gardens of Britain* v. 3, 1978, 141–42.

Old Vicarage, Firle, E. Sussex
C.L. v. 158, 1975, 762–64.

Old Warden, Beds
J. Hort. Cottage Gdnr N.S., v. 1, 1880, 98–99; N.S.,

Old Warden (*Cont.*)
v. 67, 1913, 502–05. *G.C.* ii 1885, 404; v. 189 no. 24, 1981, 25–27. *Gdnrs Mag.* 1902, 547–50. *Gdn History* v. 3 no. 4, 1975, 40–43. *C.L.* v. 161, 1977, 364–66. M. Binney *and* A. Hills *Elysian gardens* 1979, 62. *Bedfordshire Mag.* v. 18, 1982, 201–05.

Old Wilsley, Cranbrook, Kent
C.L. v. 104, 1948, 26,78–81.

Oldbury Court, Oldbury-on-Severn, Glos
D. Stroud *Humphry Repton* 1962, 171. Historical MSS Commission *Architectural history* v. 3, 1971, item 3339. G. Carter *et al. Humphry Repton* 1982, 153.

Oldershaw near Lichfield, Staffs
G.M. v. 12, 1836, 310–11.

Oldfield Grange, Coggeshall, Essex
P. Muilman *History of Essex* v. 6, 1772, 116.

Oldham. Alexandra Park, Greater Manchester
G.C. ii 1925, 321–22; i 1930, 399; ii 1938, 207.

Oldlands Hall near Uckfield, E. Sussex
J. Hort. Cottage Gdnr v. 54, 1875, 246–47.

Oldtown near Naas, Co. Kildare, Eire
E. Malins *and* Knight of Glin *Lost demesnes* 1976, 28.

Olney (William Cowper), Bucks
C.L. v. 138, 1965, 1032–33.

Ombersley Court, Ombersley, Hereford and Worcester
Historical MSS Commission *Architectural history* v. 2, 1970, item 1933.

Ongar Park, Essex
F.G. Emmison *Catalogue of maps in Essex Record Office* 1st Supplt, 1952, 28; 2nd Supplt, 1964, 22.

Orchard Cottage, Gretton, Glos
A. Lees-Milne *and* R. Verey *Englishwoman's garden* 1980, 122–24.

Orchard Cottage near Undercliffe, Isle of Wight
R. Ackermann *Repository* v. 7, 1826, pl. 20. W.W.J. Gendall *Views* v. 1, 1830, 89.

Orchard Farm near Broadway, Hereford and Worcester
R. Sidwell *West Midland gardens* 1981, 73–75.

Orchard Portman, Somerset
J. Beeverell *Les delices de la Grande Bretagne* v. 5, 1707, 872. L. Knyff *and* J. Kip *Britannia illustrata* v. 1, 1714.

Orchardleigh Park near Frome, Somerset
C.L. v. 10, 1901, 808–15. C. Holme *Gardens of England in Southern & Western counties* 1907, pls. 98–101. J. Sales *West Country gardens* 1980, 173–74. *Trans. Ancient Monuments Soc.* v. 27, 1983, 119–45.

Orchards, Munstead, Godalming, Surrey
C.L. v. 10, 1901, 272–79; v. 23, 1908, 522–31. L. Weaver *Houses and gardens by E.L. Lutyens* 1913, 23–35. G. Jekyll *Garden ornament* 1918, 146,396,397, 424. R.I.B.A. *Catalogue: Lutyens* 1973, 40. J. Brown *Gardens of a golden afternoon* 1982, 55–60,163.

Orchill House, Ardoch, Tayside
I.H. Adams *Descriptive list of plans* v. 3, 1974, 97.

Ord, John *see* Walham Green

Ordsall Hall, Manchester
V.C.H. Lancaster v. 4, 1911, 214.

Orford Hall, Orford, Cheshire
Gdn History v. 9 no. 1, 1981, 71–72.

Organ Hall, Aldenham, Herts
D. Stroud *Humphry Repton* 1962, 171. G. Carter *et al. Humphry Repton* 1982, 154.

Oriel Temple near Collon, Co. Louth, Eire
E. Malins *and* Knight of Glin *Lost demesnes* 1976, 107–09.

Orielton near Pembroke, Dyfed
J.P. Neale *Views* v. 5, 1822.

Orleans House, Twickenham, London
J. Macky *Journey through England* v. 1, 1722, 63,64. D. Lysons *Supplement to . . . Environs of London* 1811, 312–13. W. Keane *Beauties of Middlesex* 1850, 212–15.

Ormesby House, Ormesby, Norfolk
J.P. Neale *Views* v. 3, 1820.

Ormidale near Tighnabruaich, Strathclyde
G. Beard *Thomas H. Mawson* 1976, 60.

Ormonde Lodge *see* Richmond Gardens

Orsett Hall, Orsett, Essex
G.C. i 1908, 129–30.

Orton Hall, Orton, Cambs
J. Hort. Cottage Gdnr N.S., v. 17, 1888, 3–4. *G.C.* i 1930, 128–29.

Orwell Park, Orwell, Suffolk.
J.P. Neale *Views* v. 4, 1821. *G.C.* ii 1876, 198–99,205, 229–30.

Osbaston Hall, Osbaston, Leics
J. Throsby *Select views in Leicestershire* v. 1, 1790, 304.

Osberton near Worksop, Notts
J. Hort. Cottage Gdnr N.S., v. 33, 1896, 204–06.

Osborne (R.P. Blachford), Isle of Wight
R. Worsley *History of Isle of Wight* 1781.

Osborne, East Cowes, Isle of Wight
Official guide. *G.C.* i 1897, 396–99; i 1901, 55,57. *J. Hort. Cottage Gdnr* N.S., v. 34, 1897, 563–65. C. Ward *Royal gardens* 1912, 61–72. N. Pevsner *and* D. Lloyd *Hampshire and the Isle of Wight* 1967, 758–59. *C.L.* v. 171, 1982, 426.

Osmaston Manor, Osmaston, Derbyshire
J. Britton *and* E.W. Brayley *Beauties of England and Wales* v. 3, 1802, 395. *G.M.* v. 15, 1839, 450. *J. Hort. Cottage Gdnr* v. 54, 1875, 402–05,428–30. *G.C.* ii 1901, 46. *C.L.* v. 12, 1902, 48–55. C. Holme *Gardens of England in Midland & Eastern counties* 1908, pls. 92–95.

Osterley Park, Osterley, Hounslow, London
Official guide. W. Watts *Seats* 1779, pl. 70. S. Shaw *Tour to West of England in 1788* In J. Pinkerton, v. 2, 1808, 182. W. Keane *Beauties of Middlesex* 1850, 227–31. *G.C.* ii 1885, 261–62,267–68,272; ii 1933, 229. *C.L.* v. 60, 1926, 782–91,818–26; v. 143, 1968, 141. *V.C.H. Middlesex* v. 3, 1962, 102. G.S. Thomas *Gardens of National Trust* 1979, 190–91. Manpower Services Commission *Osterley Park* 1980.

Ote Hall, Wivelsfield, E. Sussex
G.C. ii 1905, 249–50.

Oteley Park near Ellesmere, Shropshire
G.C. ii 1883, 216–17.

Otley Hall, Otley, Suffolk
C.L. v. 65, 1929, 152–56.

Otterington Hall, Otterington, N. Yorks
K. Lemmon *Gardens of Britain* v. 5, 1978, 99–100. *C.L.* v. 173, 1983, 228–30.

Ottershaw Park, Ottershaw, Surrey
G.F. Prosser *Select illustrations of . . . Surrey* 1828. E.W. Brayley *and* J. Britton *Topographical history of Surrey* v. 2, 1841, 225–26. W. Keane *Beauties of Surrey* 1849, 38–40.

Otton Hall, Tadcaster, N. Yorks
Garden v. 61, 1902, 88.

Ouborough, Godstone, Surrey
C.L. v. 92, 1942, 362–65.

Oulton Hall, Oulton, W. Yorks
D. Stroud *Humphry Repton* 1962, 148–49,171. G. Carter *et al. Humphry Repton* 1982, 164.

Oulton Park near Tarporley, Cheshire
C.L. v. 23, 1908, 774–80. G. Jekyll *Garden ornament* 1918, 264.

Ouston *see* Owston

Ovenden near Sevenoaks, Kent
C.L. v. 47, 1920, 620–27.

Over Court, Over, Avon
R. Atkyns *Ancient and present state of Glostershire* 1712, 214. L. Knyff *and* J. Kip *Britannia illustrata* v. 2, 1715.

Over Hall, Gestingthorpe, Essex
P. Muilman *History of Essex* v. 2, 1769, 174. P. Morant *History . . . of Essex* v. 2, 1816, 305.

Overbecks, Salcombe, Devon
G.C. ii 1961, 380–81.

Overbury Court, Overbury, Hereford and Worcester
R. Sidwell *West Midland gardens* 1981, 76–78.

Overstone Hall, Overstone, Northants
Northamptonshire Past and Present v. 5 no. 3, 1975, 229. Royal Commission on Historical Monuments *Inventory of historical monuments in . . . Northampton* v. 2, 1979, 122.

Overstrand Hall, Overstrand, Norfolk
J. Brown *Gardens of a golden afternoon* 1982, 163.

Oving House, Oving, Bucks
C.L. v. 124, 1958, 1172–75,1232.

Owermoigne Moor, Owermoigne, Dorset
A. Paterson *Gardens of Britain* v. 2, 1978, 40–41.

Owl House, Lamberhurst, Kent
M. Allan *Fisons guide* 1970, 56–57. T. Wright *Gardens of Britain* v. 4, 1978, 77–78.

Owlpen Manor, Owlpen, Glos
C.L. v. 20, 1906, 486–92; v. 110, 1951, 1460–63. G. Jekyll *and* L. Weaver *Gardens for small country houses* 1913, xix–xxii. G. Jekyll *Garden ornament* 1918,

54,281. Lady Rockley *Historic gardens of England* 1938, 98–99.

Owston (Ouston) **Park**, Owston, S. Yorks
D. Stroud *Humphry Repton* 1962, 171. Historical MSS Commission *Architectural history* v. 3, 1971, item 3255. *Garden* 1983, 366.

Owthorpe, Notts
L. Hutchinson *Memoirs of life of Colonel Hutchinson* 1905, 365–66.

Oxburgh Hall, Oxborough, Norfolk
Official guide. C.L. v. 1, 1897, 548–50; v. 13, 1903, 470–77; v. 167, 1980, 1480–82. *J. Royal Hort. Soc.* 1960, 350. G.C. ii 1963, 3. M. Allan *Fisons guide* 1970, 199–200. G.S. Thomas *Gardens of National Trust* 1979, 191–92.

Oxenfoord Castle near Dalkeith, Lothian
W. Angus *Seats* 1787, pl. 14. *Gdning World* v. 5, 1889, 774. G.C. ii 1905, 195. A.A. Tait *Landscape garden in Scotland* 1980, passim.

Oxenford Grange, Peper Harow, Surrey
B. Jones *Follies & grottoes* 1974, 396.

Oxenhoath near Tonbridge, Kent
J. Harris *History of Kent* 1719, 236. J. Kip *Nouveau theatre de la Grande Bretagne* v. 4, 1729, pl. 36. T. Badeslade *Thirty six different views . . . in Kent* 1750s, pl. 26.

Oxford. Botanic Garden, Oxfordshire
Official guide. J. Bobart *Catalogus plantarum horti medici Oxoniensis* 1648. D. Logan *Oxonia illustrata* 1675, pl. 12. R. Plot *Natural history of Oxfordshire* 1705, 174,265–66,274. J. Beeverell *Les delices de la Grande Bretagne* v. 3, 1707, 534. A. Evans *Vertumnus. An epistle to Mr Jacob Bobart* 1713. R. Ackermann *History of University of Oxford* v. 2, 1814, 241. J. Skelton *Oxonia antiqua restaurata* v. 1, 1823. W. Williams *Oxonia depicta* 1732–33, pl. 8. *G.M.* v. 10, 1834, 110–14. C. Daubeny *Oxford Botanic Garden* 1850. *Cottage Gdnr* v. 9, 1853, 180–81. G.C. i 1885, 540,541,724,732–33; ii 1887, 153–54; i 1889, 769–70; ii 1907, 357–58; ii 1923, 22–23; i 1928, 330. R.T. Günther *Oxford gardens* 1912, 1–196. C.L. v. 53, 1923, 917–19; v. 150, 1971, 142–45. *Report of Botanical Exchange Club* 1923, 335–67. E.S. Rohde *Oxford's college gardens* 1932, 142–63. V.C.H. *Oxford* v. 3, 1954, 49–50. J. Evelyn *Diary* v. 3, 1955, 109–10,386. E. Hyams *Great botanical gardens of the world* 1969, 102–03. Historical MSS Commission *Architectural history* v. 2, 1970, item 1939. *Nature* v. 233, 1971, 455–56. *Amateur Gdning* v. 90 no. 4642, 1973, 18–19. J. Sherwood *and* N. Pevsner *Oxfordshire* 1974, 267–68. R. Bisgrove *Gardens of Britain* v. 3, 1978, 142–44. L. Fleming *and* A. Gore *English garden* 1979,

41. *Gdn History* v. 9 no. 1, 1981, 68–69. M. Batey *Oxford gardens* 1982, passim. S. Raphael *et al. Of Oxfordshire gardens* 1982, 3–23. D. Sturdy *Twelve Oxford gardens* 1982.

Oxford. All Souls College, Oxfordshire
E.S. Rohde *Oxford's college gardens* 1932, 59–67. V.C.H. *Oxford* v. 3, 1954, 173. M. Batey *Oxford gardens* 1982, 21–27.

Oxford. Balliol College, Oxfordshire
D. Logan *Oxonia illustrata* 1675, pl. 14. R. Plot *Natural history of Oxfordshire* 1705, 149. J. Beeverell *Les delices de la Grande Bretagne* v. 3, 1707, 559. W.A. Delamotte *Original views of Oxford* 1843. C. Rundt *Views of the colleges of Oxford* c.1845. M. Macartney *English houses & gardens* 1908, pl. 56. R.T. Günther *Oxford gardens* 1912, 229–30. E.S. Rohde *Oxford's college gardens* 1932, 26–32. V.C.H. *Oxford* v. 3, 1954, 94. M. Batey *Oxford gardens* 1982, 150–51.

Oxford. Brasenose College, Oxfordshire
D. Logan *Oxonia illustrata* 1675, pl. 25. R. Plot *Natural history of Oxfordshire* 1705, 266.

Oxford. Christ Church College, Oxfordshire
D. Logan *Oxonia illustrata* 1675, pl. 27. J. Skelton *Oxonia antiqua restaurata* v. 1, 1823. *G.M.* v. 10, 1834, 105–07. M. Macartney *English houses & gardens* 1908, pl. 57. E.S. Rohde *Oxford's college gardens* 1932, 93–98. M. Batey *Oxford gardens* 1982, 18,65–66,72–74,116, 210. D. Sturdy *Twelve Oxford gardens* 1982.

Oxford. Corpus Christi College, Oxfordshire
D. Logan *Oxonia illustrata* 1675, pl. 26. R. Plot *Natural history of Oxfordshire* 1705, 176. W. Williams *Oxonia depicta* 1732–33, pl. 40. J. Skelton *Oxonia antiqua restaurata* v. 1, 1823. E.S. Rohde *Oxford's college gardens* 1932, 82–90. D. Sturdy *Twelve Oxford gardens* 1982.

Oxford. Exeter College, Oxfordshire
R. Plot *Natural history of Oxfordshire* 1705, 266. J. Skelton *Oxonia antiqua restaurata* v. 2, 1823. W.A. Delamotte *Original views of Oxford* 1843. C. Rundt *Views of the colleges of Oxford* c.1845. R.T. Günther *Oxford gardens* 1912, 225–27. E.S. Rohde *Oxford's college gardens* 1932, 50–53.

Oxford. Gloucester Hall, Oxfordshire
D. Logan *Oxonia illustrata* 1675, pl. 40.

Oxford. Jesus College, Oxfordshire
D. Logan *Oxonia illustrata* 1675, pl. 31. J. Beeverell *Les delices de la Grande Bretagne* v. 3, 1707, 554. J. Skelton *Oxonia antiqua restaurata* v. 1, 1823. F. Crisp *Mediaeval gardens* v. 2, 1924, fig. 240.

Oxford. Keble College, Oxfordshire
J. Royal Hort. Soc. 1971, 18-23.

Oxford. Lady Margaret Hall, Oxfordshire
E.S. Rohde *Oxford's college gardens* 1932, 164-67.
M. Batey *Oxford gardens* 1982, 175.

Oxford. Lincoln College, Oxfordshire
R.T. Günther *Oxford gardens* 1912, 227-28.

Oxford. Magdalen College, Oxfordshire
D. Logan *Oxonia illustrata* 1675, pl. 24. R. Plot *Natural history of Oxfordshire* 1705, 161,174. *G.M.* v. 10, 1834, 105. *C.L.* v. 20, 1906, 621-28. C. Holme *Gardens of England in Southern & Western counties* 1907, pl. 90. R.T. Günther *Oxford gardens* 1912, 209-22. E.S. Rohde *Oxford's college gardens* 1932, 68-81. M. Batey *Oxford gardens* 1982, 91-103,129-32. G. Carter et al. *Humphry Repton* 1982, 160. D. Sturdy *Twelve Oxford gardens* 1982.

Oxford. Merton College, Oxfordshire
D. Logan *Oxonia illustrata* 1675, pl. 15. R.T. Günther *Oxford gardens* 1912, 207-09. E.S. Rohde *Oxford's college gardens* 1932, 19-26.

Oxford. New College, Oxfordshire
D. Logan *Oxonia illustrata* 1675, pl. 19. R. Plot *Natural history of Oxfordshire* 1705, 172,266. W. Williams *Oxonia depicta* 1732-33, pl. 14. R. Southey *Letters of Espriella* v. 2, 1807, 69. M. Macartney *English houses & gardens* 1908, pl. 58. R.T. Günther *Oxford gardens* 1912, 222-25. F. Crisp *Mediaeval gardens* v. 2, 1924, fig. 110. E.S. Rohde *Oxford's college gardens* 1932, 35-49. V.C.H. *Oxford* v. 3, 1954, 154. *G.C.* ii 1962, 406-07. J. Buxton *New College Oxford: a note on the garden* 1976. *C.L.* v. 165, 1979, 1186-89. L. Fleming and A. Gore *English garden* 1979, 23. M. Batey *Oxford gardens* 1982, 9-10,42-43,75-76,81-83. D. Sturdy *Twelve Oxford gardens* 1982.

Oxford. Oriel College, Oxfordshire
D. Logan *Oxonia illustrata* 1675, pl. 17. V.C.H. *Oxford* v. 3, 1954, 127.

Oxford. Pembroke College, Oxfordshire
D. Logan *Oxonia illustrata* 1675, pl. 33. J. Beeverell *Les delices de la Grande Bretagne* v. 3, 1707, 569. W. Williams *Oxonia depicta* 1732-33, pl. 56. J. Skelton *Oxonia antiqua restaurata* v. 1, 1823. R.T. Günther *Oxford gardens* 1912, 207. E.S. Rohde *Oxford's college gardens* 1932, 133-35.

Oxford. Queen's College, Oxfordshire
D. Logan *Oxonia illustrata* 1675, pl. 18. J. Skelton *Oxonia antiqua restaurata* v. 1, 1823. J.R. Magrath *Queen's College* v. 2, 1921, 85. E.S. Rohde *Oxford's college gardens* 1932, 53-58. M. Batey *Oxford gardens* 1982, 7-8.

Oxford. St Catherine's College, Oxfordshire
M. Batey *Oxford gardens* 1982, 229-32.

Oxford. St Hilda's College, Oxfordshire
E.S. Rohde *Oxford's college gardens* 1932, 179-86.

Oxford. St Hugh's College, Oxfordshire
E.S. Rohde *Oxford's college gardens* 1932, 173-79. *St Hugh's Chronicle* no. 25, 1952. M. Batey *Oxford gardens* 1982, 181-87.

Oxford. St John's College, Oxfordshire
D. Logan *Oxonia illustrata* 1675, pl. 29. R. Plot *Natural history of Oxfordshire* 1705, 172. J. Beeverell *Les delices de la Grande Bretagne* v. 3, 1707, 562. W. Williams *Oxonia depicta* 1732-33, pl. 48. J. Skelton *Oxonia antiqua restaurata* v. 2, 1823. *G.M.* v. 10, 1834, 104-05. W.A. Delamotte *Original views of Oxford* 1843. *C.L.* v. 17, 1905, 705-09. R.T. Günther *Oxford gardens* 1912, 230-31. E.S. Rohde *Oxford's college gardens* 1932, 113-23. *J. Royal Hort. Soc.* 1941, 237-41. V.C.H. *Oxford* v. 3, 1954, 253,257. M. Batey *Oxford gardens* 1982, 18,85,116-17,160-61.

Oxford. Somerville College, Oxfordshire
E.S. Rohde *Oxford's college gardens* 1932, 167-73.

Oxford. Trinity College, Oxfordshire
D. Logan *Oxonia illustrata* 1675, pl. 28. J. Beeverell *Les delices de la Grande Bretagne* v. 3, 1707, 560. W. Williams *Oxonia depicta* 1732-33, pl. 45. R. Southey *Letters of Espriella* v. 2, 1807, 69. J. Skelton *Oxonia antiqua restaurata* v. 2, 1823. British Museum *Catalogue of maps, prints* 1829, 254. *G.M.* v. 10, 1834, 104. R.T. Günther *Oxford gardens* 1912, 228-29. *C.L.* v. 67, 1930, 352-59. E.S. Rohde *Oxford's college gardens* 1932, 99-112. M. Batey *Oxford gardens* 1982, 88-89.

Oxford. University College, Oxfordshire
D. Logan *Oxonia illustrata* 1675, pl. 13. J. Skelton *Oxonia antiqua restaurata* v. 1, 1823. R.T. Günther *Oxford gardens* 1912, 209. E.S. Rohde *Oxford's college gardens* 1932, 32-34. V.C.H. *Oxford* v. 3, 1954, 81. D. Sturdy *Twelve Oxford gardens* 1982.

Oxford. Wadham College, Oxfordshire
D. Logan *Oxonia illustrata* 1675, pl. 32. R. Plot *Natural history of Oxfordshire* 1705, 240,268. J. Beeverell *Les delices de la Grande Bretagne* v. 3, 1707, 565. W. Williams *Oxonia depicta* 1732-33, pl. 55. J. Skelton *Oxonia antiqua restaurata* v. 1, 1823. T.G. Jackson *Wadham College* 1893. *C.L.* v. 17, 1905, 513-19. C. Holme *Gardens of England in Southern & Western counties* 1907, pl. 131. M. Macartney *English houses & gardens* 1908,

Oxford. Wadham College *(Cont.)*

pl. 59. R.T. Günther *Oxford gardens* 1912, 233–36.
F. Crisp *Mediaeval gardens* v. 2, 1924, fig. 109.
E.S. Rohde *Oxford's college gardens* 1932, 124–33.
V.C.H. *Oxford* v. 3, 1954, 287. M. Batey *Oxford gardens* 1982, 43–46. D. Sturdy *Twelve Oxford gardens* 1982.

Oxford. Worcester College, Oxfordshire
J. Skelton *Oxonia antiqua restaurata* v. 2, 1823.
R.T. Günther *Oxford gardens* 1912, 232–33.
E.S. Rohde *Oxford's college gardens* 1932, 135–41. *C.L.* v. 104, 1948, 938–41. V.C.H. *Oxford* v. 3, 1954, 309.
M. Batey *Oxford gardens* 1982, 126–27,190. D. Sturdy *Twelve Oxford gardens* 1982.

Oxley Manor near Wolverhampton, W. Midlands
F.O. Morris *Series of picturesque views* v. 4, 55.

Oxnead Hall, Oxnead, Norfolk
J. Britton *Architectural antiquities of Great Britain* v. 2, 1809, 98.

Oxney Court near Dover, Kent
C. Greenwood *Epitome of county history . . . v. 1: Kent* 1838, 434.

Oxney Park, Ringwould, Kent
J.P. Neale *Views* 2nd Series, v. 2, 1825.

Oxton near Exeter, Devon
R. Ackermann *Repository* v. 10, 1827, pl. 20.
W.W.J. Gendall *Views* v. 1, 1830, 116–20. *G.C.* i 1882, 632–33.

Packington Hall near Lichfield, Staffs
G.M. v. 12, 1836, 563.

Packington Hall, Great Packington, Warwickshire
J.P. Neale *Views* v. 4, 1821. *Garden* v. 1, 1872, 647–48.
C.L. v. 2, 1897, 98–100; v. 148, 1970, 102–06.
D. Stroud *Capability Brown* 1975, 56,235.

Packwood House, Hockley Heath, W. Midlands
Official guide. *C.L.* v. 11, 1902, 16–24; v. 56, 1924, 218–24,250–57. C. Holme *Gardens of England in Midland & Eastern counties* 1908, pl. 96. G. Jekyll *Garden ornament* 1918, 71. *Landscape and Gdn* v. 2 no. 2, 1935, 61–64. Lady Rockley *Historic gardens of England* 1938, 128–29. *G.C.* ii 1963, 366–67. M. Allan *Fisons guide* 1970, 163–64. *J. Royal Hort. Soc.* 1971, 211–12.
H. Evans *Beautiful gardens of Britain* 1974, 89–90.
R. Strong *Renaissance garden in England* 1979, 211–14.
G.S. Thomas *Gardens of National Trust* 1979, 192–93.
R. Sidwell *West Midland gardens* 1981, 223–24.
T. Hinde *Stately gardens of Britain* 1983, 20–25.

Paddington House (John Symmons), London
W. Salisbury *Hortus Paddingtonensis* 1797.

Paddockhurst near Worth, W. Sussex
G.C. i 1897, 247; ii 1900, 401.

Painshill near Cobham, Surrey
D. Defoe *Tour* v. 3, 1742, 395–97. R. and J. Dodsley *London and its environs described* v. 5, 1761, 101.
A. Young *Six weeks tour through southern counties of England and Wales* 1768, 187–92. Society of Gentlemen *England displayed* v. 1, 1769, 224. T. Whately *Observations on modern gardening* 1771, 184–92; 1801, pl. 5.
G.L. le Rouge *Jardins Anglo-Chinois a la mode* 6^e cahier, 1777, pl. 3. H. Walpole *Essay on modern gardening* 1785, 75,77. *New display of the beauties of England* v. 2, 1787, 295–99. *Picturesque views of the principal seats* 1788. J.C. Loudon *Encyclopaedia of gardening* 1822, 1228. J.P. Neale *Views* 2nd Series, v. 1, 1824.
G.F. Prosser *Select illustrations of . . . Surrey* 1828.
British Museum *Catalogue of maps, prints* 1829, 257.
G.M. v. 9, 1833, 479. E.W. Brayley and J. Britton *Topographical history of Surrey* v. 2, 1841, 371–78.
W. Keane *Beauties of Surrey* 1849, 33–37. J.B. Burke *Visitation* v. 1, 1852, 217–19. R. Pococke *Travels through England* v. 2, 1889, 166. *C.L.* v. 1, 1897, 239–41,268–70; v. 15, 1904, 414–21; v. 107, 1950, 1471; v. 123, 1958, 18–21,62–65; v. 166, 1979, 2332–35; v. 170, 1981, 638–40. F. Kielmansegge *Diary* 1902, 55–57. E. Cecil *History of gardening in England* 1910, 249–50. G. Jekyll *Garden ornament* 1918, 125.
H. Walpole *Visits to country seats. Walpole Society* v. 7, 1927/28, 36–37. *Architectural Review* v. 82, 1937, 147–50. Lady Rockley *Historic gardens of England* 1938, 176–77. T. Jefferson *Garden book 1766–1824* 1944, 112.
H.F. Clark *English landscape garden* 1948, 43–45.
O. Siren *China and gardens of Europe of 18th century* 1950, 42–46. I. Nairn and B. Cherry *Surrey* 1971, 404.
Gdn History v. 2 no. 1, 1973, 39–68; v. 3 no. 1, 1974, 77–82; v. 3 no. 2, 1975, 23–28; v. 8 no. 1, 1980, 91–106; v. 8 no. 2, 1980, 21; v. 9 no. 1, 1981, 62–67; v. 11 no. 2, 1983, 112–24,173–74. B. Jones *Follies & grottoes* 1974, 39–44. *Landscape Design* no. 109, 1975, 17–19.
L. Fleming and A. Gore *English garden* 1979, 105.
J. Harris *Artist and the country house* 1979, 286.
M. Hadfield et al. *British gardeners* 1980, 141–42. *J. Gdn History* v. 2 no. 1, 1982, 46. D. Taylor *Book of Cobham* 1982. *Painshill Park Trust Newsletter* 1983 to date. D. Jacques *Georgian gardens* 1983, 91. Land Use Consultants *Painshill* 1984.

Painshill Cottage, Cobham, Surrey
Surrey Archaeological Collections v. 67, 1970, 98–99.

Painswick House, Painswick, Glos
D. Verey *Gloucestershire* v. 1, 1970, 364. J. Harris *Gardens of delight* 1978, 16–17. J. Harris *Artist and the country house* 1979, 208, pl. 22. *J. Garden History* v. 4 no. 2, 1984, 163–78.

Pakenham Hall near Castlepollard, Co. Westmeath, Eire
G.M. v. 11, 1835, 682–83. F. Malins *and* Knight of Glin *Lost demesnes* 1976, 19,20.

Palace House, Beaulieu, Hants
C.L. v. 20, 1906, 702–09. G. Jekyll *Garden ornament* 1918, 350.

Palmer's Farm near Tunbridge Wells, Kent
C.L. v. 172, 1982, 2068–69.

Palmerstown House near Naas, Co. Kildare, Eire
G. Jekyll *and* G.S. Elgood *Some English gardens* 1904, 99–100.

Pampisford Hall, Pampisford, Cambs
G.C. i 1884, 575–76. V.C.H. *Cambridge* v. 6, 1978, 107.

Pancras Wells, Camden, London
W. Wroth *London pleasure gardens of the eighteenth century* 1896, 123–26.

Panmure House near Carnoustie, Tayside
Scottish Gdnr and Northern Forester v. 8, 1913, 525–26.

Pan's Lodge, Painswick, Glos
J. Harris *Gardens of delight* 1978, 18–19. *Gloucester and Avon Life* October, 1982.

Panshanger, Hertingfordbury, Herts
J.P. Neale *Views* v. 2, 1819. E.A. Brooke *Gardens of England* 1857, pl. 43. J.E. Cussans *History of Hertfordshire* v. 2, 1874, 70. F.O. Morris *Series of picturesque views* v. 2, 53. C.L. v. 6, 1899, 176–81; v. 79, 1936, 38–44; v. 165, 1979, 1179. G.C. ii 1908, 325–26. G. Jekyll *Garden ornament* 1918, 121. Lady Rockley *Historic gardens of England* 1938, 188–89. *East Herts Archaeological Soc. Trans.* v. 14 no. 1, 1959, 42–58. D. Stroud *Humphry Repton* 1962, 108,172. G. Carter *et al. Humphry Repton* 1982, 154.

Pantglas near Llandeilo, Dyfed
J.B. Burke *Visitation* v. 1, 1852, 203.

Pantygoitre near Usk, Gwent
D. Williams *History of Monmouthshire* 1796, pl. 35.

Papillon Hall, Lubenham, Leics
C.L. v. 31, Supplt 4 May 1912, xiv–xviii. L. Weaver *Houses and gardens by E.L. Lutyens* 1913, 112–18. A.S. Butler *et al. Architecture of Sir Edwin Lutyens* v. 2, 1950, 11. J. Brown *Gardens of a golden afternoon* 1982, 166–67.

Papplewick Hall, Papplewick, Notts
C.L. v. 134, 1963, 600–03.

Paradise, Oxford, Oxfordshire
D. Sturdy *Twelve Oxford gardens* 1982.

Parcevall Hall, Appletreewick, N. Yorks
M. Allan *Fisons guide* 1970, 255–56. K. Lemmon *Gardens of Britain* v. 5, 1978, 101–04.

Parham Old Hall, Parham, Suffolk
C.L. v. 25, 1909, 702–07.

Parham Park, Parham, W. Sussex
Official guide. J.P. Neale *Views* 2nd series, v. 4, 1828. *Garden* v. 35, 1889, 477. C.L. v. 11, 1902, 496–504; v. 109, 1951, 1716–19. M. Allan *Fisons guide* 1970, 57–58.

Park Hill, Streatham, Lambeth, London
W. Keane *Beauties of Surrey* 1849, 76–77. *Garden* v. 29, 1886, 568,569. G.C. ii 1894, 400–01.

Park House, Parson's Green, Hammersmith, London
W. Keane *Beauties of Middlesex* 1850, 242–43.

Park Place near Henley-on-Thames, Oxfordshire
A. Robertson *Topographical survey of the Great Road* pt 1, 1792, 101–10. J. *and* J. Boydell *History of the River Thames* v. 1, 1794, 250–55. J. Britton *and* E.W. Brayley *Beauties of England and Wales* v. 1, 1801, 183,187–90. W.B. Cooke *and* S. Owen *The Thames* v. 1, 1811, 43. L. Simond *Journal of a tour . . . in . . . 1810 and 1811* v. 2, 1815, 114. R. Havell *Series of picturesque views* 1823, pl. 1. J.C. Loudon *Encyclopaedia of gardening* 1822, 1236. G.M. v. 9, 1833, 660–62. *Tombleson's Thames* 1834. *Cottage Gdnr* v. 18, 1857, 211–12. *Garden* v. 16, 1879, 572–75. *Gdning World* v. 9, 1893, 817–18. G.C. i 1894, 728–29. *J. Hort. Cottage Gdnr* N.S., v. 31, 1895, 330–32. C.L. v. 127, 1960, 640–42. N. Pevsner *Berkshire* 1966, 193. B. Jones *Follies & grottoes* 1974, 289. J. Harris *Artist and the country house* 1979, 229. *J. Gdn History* v. 2 no. 1, 1982, 56–57.

Parkstead House, Roehampton, Wandsworth, London
Surrey Archaeological Collections 1980, 197–221.

Parnham House near Beaminster, Dorset
C.L. v. 24, 1908, 288–97.

Passenham Manor, Stony Stratford, Bucks
J. Brown *Gardens of a golden afternoon* 1982, 176.

Pasturewood House, Holmbury St Mary, Surrey
J. Brown *Gardens of a golden afternoon* 1982, 164.

Patshull near Wolverhampton, Staffs
W. Pitt *General view of agriculture of . . . Stafford* 1796, 96. J. Nightingale *Topographical . . . description of*

Patshull (*Cont.*)
Staffordshire 1810, 856. *Gdning World* v. 7, 1890, 42. G.C. i 1891, 701–02; i 1895, 273. C. Fiennes *Journeys* 1949, 229–30. D. Stroud *Capability Brown* 1975, 235–36.

Paulerspury, Northants
Northamptonshire Past and Present v. 5 no. 3, 1975, 229–30.

Paultons near Romsey, Hants
W. Gilpin *Remarks on forest scenery* v. 2, 1794, 228–30. E.F. Prosser *Select illustrations of Hampshire* 1833. *G.M.* v. 11, 1835, 163. C. Holme *Gardens of England in Southern & Western counties* 1907, pls. 102–03. C.L. v. 84, 1938, 276–81. D. Stroud *Capability Brown* 1975, 236.

Pavilion, Isleworth, Hounslow, London
C.L. v. 152, 1972, 1272–74.

Pax Hill, Lindfield, W. Sussex
Garden v. 35, 1889, 549–50.

Paxton House, Paxton, Borders
C.L. v. 142, 1967, 364–65,422–23,470–71. A.A. Tait *Landscape garden in Scotland* 1980, passim.

Peacock Place, Basildon, Berks
B. Jones *Follies & grottoes* 1974, 276.

Peake House, Sidmouth, Devon
G.M. v. 19, 1843, 238–39.

Pearce Memorial Garden *see* Thame

Peasholm Glen, Scarborough, N. Yorks
G.C. v. 162 no. 11, 1967, 16–17.

Peckforton Castle near Tarporley, Cheshire
F.O. Morris *Series of picturesque views* v. 4, 65.

Peckham (Lord Trevor), London
D. Defoe *Tour* v. 3, 1742, 292–93.

Peckham (Peter Collinson), Southwark, London
P. Kalm *Account of his visit to England* 1892, 66–68,87. N.G. Brett-James *Life of Peter Collinson* 1926, passim.

Peckham (Mr Thomas), Southwark, London
G.M. v. 14, 1838, 463–64.

Peckham Rye Park *see* London

Peckover House, Wisbech, Cambs
Official guide. *J. Royal Hort. Soc.* 1960, 350. M. Allan *Fisons guide* 1970, 200–01. *Garden* 1975, 596–99.

G.S. Thomas *Gardens of National Trust* 1979, 193–94. C.L. v. 167, 1980, 248–50. G.C. v. 194 no. 12, 1983, 31–33.

Pelling Place, Windsor, Berks
W. Angus *Seats* 1787, pl. 51. R. Ackermann *Repository* v. 3, 1824, pls. 7–8. W.W.J. Gendall *Views* v. 1, 1830, 53–55.

Pencarrow near Bodmin, Cornwall
R. Ackermann *Repository* v. 7, 1826, pl. 14. W.W.J. Gendall *Views* v. 1, 1830, 105. J.B. Burke *Visitation* v. 2, 1853, 59. *J. Hort. Cottage Gdnr* v. 59, 1878, 69–71. G.C. i 1900, 234. *J. Royal Hort. Soc.* 1946, 364–69. C.L. v. 116, 1954, 200. P.M. Synge *Gardens of Britain* v. 1, 1977, 110–13.

Pendarves near Camborne, Cornwall
W. Borlase *Natural history of Cornwall* 1758, pl. 14. C.S. Gilbert *Historical survey of . . . Cornwall* v. 2, 1820, 694–95. G.M. v. 13, 1837, 122; v. 14, 1838, 418–21.

Pendell Court near Redhill, Surrey
P. Sandby *Collection of one hundred and fifty select views* v. 1, 1781, pl. 62. G.C. ii 1878, 310–11; i 1886, 598–99. *Garden* v. 19, 1881, 147–50; v. 21, 1882, 325–26. W. Robinson *English flower garden* 1883, xv–xviii.

Pengwern Place near St Asaph, Clwyd
J.P. Neale *Views* v. 5, 1822.

Penheale Manor, Egloskerry, Cornwall
C.L. v. 57, 1925, 484–91,524. J. Brown *Gardens of a golden afternoon* 1982, 173.

Penicuik House, Penicuik, Lothian
J.P. Neale *Views* 2nd Series, v. 2, 1825. G.C. ii 1901, 70–71. C.L. v. 144, 1968, 383–87,448–51. P. Willis *Furor hortensis* 1974, 31–40. C. McWilliam *Lothian* 1978, 387–88.

Penjerrick near Falmouth, Cornwall
G.C. ii 1889, 749; i 1901, 309,310. *Garden* v. 55, 1899, 31. M. Allan *Fisons guide* 1970, 133–34. P.M. Synge *Gardens of Britain* v. 1, 1977, 113–15. *Cornish Gdn* no. 23, 1980, 17–20; no. 25, 47–50.

Penllergaer, W. Glamorgan
J. Hort. Cottage Gdnr N.S., v. 13, 1886, 75–76. *Gdnrs Mag.* 1895, 594–96.

Penn Hall near Wolverhampton, W. Midlands
S. Shaw *History . . . of Staffordshire* v. 2, 1801, 218.

Penninghame House, Penninghame, Dumfries and Galloway
J. Hort. Cottage Gdnr v. 58, 1877, 325–27. *Scottish Gdnr and Northern Forester* v. 8, 1913, 117–18.

Pennoyre near Brecon, Powys
J.B. Burke *Visitation* v. 2, 1853, 175.

Penns in the Rocks near Groombridge, E. Sussex
C.L. v. 129, 1961, 644–47,704; v. 155, 1974,1624–26. T. Wright *Gardens of Britain* v. 4, 1978, 171–72. *Garden* 1981, 134–41.

Penpont near Brecon, Powys
H. Skrine *Two successive tours throughout . . . Wales* 1812, 43–46. J.P. Neale *Views* v. 5, 1822.

Penrhyn Castle, Bangor, Gwynedd
F.O. Morris *Series of picturesque views* v. 2, 59. *G.C.* ii 1878, 591–92,597; ii 1887, 43; ii 1891, 453–54; ii 1892, 695–96; i 1914, 37–38,41,42,51–52,125; i 1963, 242–43. *J. Hort. Cottage Gdnr* N.S., v. 31, 1895, 131. *C.L.* v. 13, 1903, 674–79. *J. Royal Hort. Soc.* 1960, 350–51; 1971, 214. M. Allan *Fisons guide* 1970, 279. G.S. Thomas *Gardens of National Trust* 1979, 194–96. Manpower Services Commission *Penrhyn Castle* (map only), 1981.

Penrice Castle, Penrice, W. Glamorgan
C.L. v. 158, 1975, 694–97. Royal Commission on Ancient and Historical Monuments in Wales *Inventory of the ancient monuments in Glamorgan* v. 4, 1981, 303.

Penshurst Place, Penshurst, Kent
Official guide. J. Harris *History of Kent* 1719, 236. J. Kip *Supplement du Nouveau theatre de la Grande Bretagne* 1728, pl. 2. T. Badeslade *Thirty six different views . . . in Kent* 1750s, pl. 27. E. Hasted *History . . . of Kent* v. 1, 1778, 415. J.P. Neale *Views* 2nd Series, v. 4, 1828. F.O. Morris *Series of picturesque views* v. 4, 69. L. Jewitt *and* S.C. Hall *Stately homes of England* 1874, 172–91. *Garden* v. 19, 1881, 393–95; v. 46, 1894, 25–26. *C.L.* v. 1, 1897, 576–78; v. 5, 1899, 336–39; v. 9, 1901, 172–73; v. 30, 1911, 844–54,894,902; v. 94, 1943, 1040–41; v. 109, 1951, 860–64; v. 151, 1972, 554–58,618–21. H.I. Triggs *Formal gardens in England and Scotland* 1902, 14–15. G. Jekyll *and* G.S. Elgood *Some English gardens* 1904, 82–86. C. Holme *Gardens of England in Southern and Western counties* 1907, pls. 104–09. M. Macartney *English houses & gardens* 1908, pl. 1. G. Jekyll *Garden ornament* 1918, 21. J. Evelyn *Diary* v. 3, 1955, 72. *Park Administration* February 1966, 44–45,47. *G.C.* v. 165 no. 16, 1969, 35. M. Allan *Fisons guide* 1970, 58–59. F. Hull *Catalogue of estate maps 1590 to 1840 in the Kent County Archive Office* 1973, 76. H. Evans *Beautiful gardens of Britain* 1974, 69–70. T. Wright *Gardens of Britain* v. 4, 1978, 78–84.

Pentillie Castle near Saltash, Cornwall
C.S. Gilbert *Historical survey of . . . Cornwall* v. 2, 1820, 440–41. W.W.J. Gendall *Views* v. 1, 1830, 73. J. Britton *and* E.W. Brayley *Devonshire & Cornwall* 1832, 16. *G.M.* v. 18, 1842, 548–49. *J. Hort. Cottage Gdnr* v. 58, 1877, 346–48. *G.C.* i 1896, 23–24; i 1901, 329–30. *Gdning World* v. 13, 1896, 231. C. Holme *Gardens of England in Southern & Western counties* 1907, pls. 110–11. D. Stroud *Humphry Repton* 1962, 77. G. Carter *et al. Humphry Repton* 1982, 150.

Peper Harow near Godalming, Surrey
G.F. Prosser *Select illustrations of . . . Surrey* 1828. N. Whittock *and* H. Gastineau *Picturesque beauties of England and Wales* 1830, 61. *G.M.* v. 11, 1835, 506–08. E.W. Brayley *and* J. Britton *Topographical history of Surrey* v. 5, 1848, 232–33. W. Keane *Beauties of Surrey* 1849, 125–30. F.O. Morris *Series of picturesque views* v. 4, 13. *C.L.* v. 58, 1925, 1002–09. D. Stroud *Capability Brown* 1975, 236.

Peplow Hall, Hodnet, Shropshire
R. Sidwell *West Midland gardens* 1981, 44.

Percy Lodge, Winchmore Hill, Enfield, London
G.C. ii 1896, 269–70.

Perridge House near Ide, Devon
R. Ackermann *Repository* v. 10, 1827, pl. 31. W.W.J. Gendall *Views* v. 1, 1830, 21.

Perry Hall, Sutton Coldfield, W. Midlands
F. Calvert *Picturesque views . . . in Staffordshire & Shropshire* 1830, 73. C. Radclyffe *Views of Perry Barr Hall* 1838. J. Harris *Artist and the country house* 1979, 322.

Perry Hill House, Lewisham, London
C. Greenwood *Epitome of county history . . . v. 1: Kent* 1838, 24.

Peterborough Abbey, Cambs
J. Harvey *Mediaeval gardens* 1981, 85.

Peterborough House, Fulham, Hammersmith, London
D. Lysons *Environs of London* v. 2, 1795, 363; *Supplement* 1811, 433. C.J. Fèret *Fulham old and new* v. 2, 1900, 150,153,154,155,156.

Peterborough House, Chelsea, London
Z.C. von Uffenbach *London in 1710* 1934, 139–41.

Petersham Lodge, Richmond, London
J. of Warburg and Courtauld Institutes v. 30, 1967, 444–46. J.D. Hunt *and* P. Willis *The genius of the place* 1975, 148–50.

Petham, Kent
C. Greenwood *Epitome of county history . . . v. 1: Kent* 1838, 396.

Petwood, Woodhall Spa, Lincs
C.L. v. 38, 1915, 198–204. G. Jekyll *Garden ornament* 1918, 207.

Petworth House, Petworth, W. Sussex
Official guide. L. Simond *Journal of a tour . . . in . . . 1810 and 1811* v. 2, 1815, 249–51. T.W. Horsfield *History . . . of Sussex* v. 2, 1835, 178. *J. Hort. Cottage Gdnr* v. 30, 1863, 186–87. *G.C.* ii 1878, 491–92,523–24. *C.L.* v. 58, 1925, 818–26,862; v. 153, 1973, 1870; v. 154, 1973, 620–21; v. 157, 1975, 1686–87. I. Nairn *and* N. Pevsner *Sussex* 1965, 307. F.W. Steer *et al. Petworth House archives: a catalogue* West Sussex Record Office, 1968–79. 2 vols, passim. Historical MSS Commission *Architectural history* v. 4, 1972, items 3725,4480,4482. D. Stroud *Capability Brown* 1975, 68–69,236. *Apollo* v. 105, 1977, 334–39,380–81. T. Wright *Gardens of Britain* v. 4, 1978, 172–77. L. Fleming *and* A. Gore *English garden* 1979, 123. J. Harris *Artist and the country house* 1979, 84–85,339. G.S. Thomas *Gardens of National Trust* 1979, 196–97. *Sussex Archaeological Collections* v. 118, 1980, 373–77.

Philiberds *see* Cresswells Manor House

Philiphaugh near Selkirk, Borders
F.O. Morris *Series of picturesque views* v. 3, 65. *Scottish Gdnr and Northern Forester* v. 7, 1912, 621–22.

Philorth House, Philorth, Grampian
J. Harris *Artist and the country house* 1979, 169.

Phoenix Park *see* Dublin

Phoenix Park Lodge, Dublin, Co. Dublin, Eire
J. Hort. Cottage Gdnr v. 44, 1870, 473–76.

Picton Castle near Haverfordwest, Dyfed
W. Watts *Seats* 1779, pl. 2. F.O. Morris *Series of picturesque views* v. 1, 21. *C.L.* v. 127, 1960, 18–21, 170–73.

Piercefield near Chepstow, Gwent
A. Young *Six weeks tour through southern counties of England and Wales* 1768, 135–44. Society of Gentlemen *England displayed* v. 2, 1769, 33–35. T. Whately *Observations on modern gardening* 1771, 236–42. W. Marshall *Planting and ornamental gardening* 1785, 616–26. J. Heath *Descriptive account of Persfield and Chepstow* 1795. Duke of Rutland *Journal of a tour through North and South Wales* 1805, 44–47. S. Shaw *Tour to West of England in 1788* In J. Pinkerton, v. 2, 1808, 229. R.J. Sulivan *Tour . . . in 1778* v. 1, 1785, 226–30. J.C. Ibbetson *et al. Picturesque guide to Bath* 1793, 257–60. D. Williams *History of Monmouthshire* 1796, 338–41, pl. 36. W. Gilpin *Observations on the River Wye* 1800, 57–61. J.T. Barber *Tour throughout South Wales and Monmouthshire* 1803, 255–62. W. Marshall *On planting and rural ornament* v. 1, 1803, 286–98. C. Heath *Historical and descriptive accounts of . . . Chepstow including . . . Piercefield* 1805. H. Skrine *Two successive tours throughout . . . Wales* 1812, 18–20. C. *and* T.H. Fielding *Picturesque illustrations of the River Wye* 1821, pl. 26. R. Ackermann *Repository* v. 5, 1825, pl. 31. T.D. Fosbroke *Wye tour* 1826, 90–106. British Museum *Catalogue of maps, prints* 1829, 268. W.W.J. Gendall *Views* v. 2, 1830, 134. T.H. Fielding *Picturesque description of the River Wye* 1841, pl. 10. R. Pococke *Travels through England* 1889, 215. W. Coxe *Historical tour through Monmouthshire* 1904, 312–20. Viscount Torrington *Diaries* v. 1, 1934, 28–30. *Gdn History* v. 8 no. 3, 1980, 107,109,111. D. Jacques *Georgian gardens* 1983, 62.

Pierremont, Bradford, W. Yorks
Bradford Illustrated Weekly Telegraph *Series of picturesque views* 1885.

Pierrepont near Farnham, Surrey
Garden v. 29, 1886, 228,229. *C.L.* v. 14, 1903, 506–11.

Pierrepont House, Nottingham, Notts
L. Fleming *and* A. Gore *English garden* 1979, pl. 25. J. Harris *Artist and the country house* 1979, 114–15,130, pl. 10.

Pilewell *see* Pylewell

Pilton Manor, Pilton, Somerset
J. Sales *West Country gardens* 1980, 175.

Pinbury, Duntisbourne Rouse, Glos
C.L. v. 27, 1910, 630–36.

Pinehanger near Farnham, Surrey
T. Wright *Gardens of Britain* v. 4, 1978, 222–23.

Pinewood House near Woking, Surrey
T. Wright *Gardens of Britain* v. 4, 1978, 223–24.

Pinkie House, Musselburgh, Lothian
C.L. v. 30, 1911, 240–47. C. McWilliam *Lothian* 1978, 338.

Pinmore near Girvan, Strathclyde
Scottish Gdnr and Northern Forester v. 7, 1912, 113–14.

Pinner Hill House near Harrow, London
J.B. Burke *Visitation* 2nd Series, v. 1, 1855, 64.

Pirton Hall, Pirton, Herts
Historical MSS Commission *Architectural history* v. 3, 1971, item 3291.

Pishiobury near Bishop's Stortford, Herts
H. Chauncy *Historical antiquities of Hertfordshire* 1700, 179. J.P. Neale *Views* v. 2, 1819. D. Stroud *Capability Brown* 1975, 236. J. Harris *Artist and the country house* 1979, 110.

Pitchford Hall, Pitchford, Shropshire
J.P. Neale *Views* 2nd Series, v. 2, 1825. *C.L.* v. 9, 1901, 144–51; v. 41, 1917, 352–58, 376–81. Lady Rockley *Historic gardens of England* 1938, 90–91. V.C.H. *Shropshire* v. 8, 1968, 119. Historical MSS Commission *Architectural history* v. 3, 1971, item 3292. R. Sidwell *West Midland gardens* 1981, 145. L. Fleming *and* A. Gore *English garden* 1979, 138–39.

Pitfour House near Mintlaw, Grampian
J. Hort. Cottage Gdnr v. 48, 1872, 115–16, 132–34. *J. Gdn History* v. 3 no. 4, 1983, 322–31.

Pitmedden House, Pitmedden, Grampian
Official guide *J. Royal Hort. Soc.* 1953, 242–43; 1961, 452–53. *G.C.* v. 160 no. 17, 1966, 10–11. R.J. Prentice *Pitmedden and its great garden* 1966. *C.L.* v. 150, 1971, 402–04; v. 157, 1975, 1187. M. Allan *Fisons guide* 1970, 343–44. *Gdn History* v. 3 no. 4, 1975, 28, 29, 31. P. Verney *Gardens of Scotland* 1976, 28–33. M. Binney and A. Hills *Elysian gardens* 1979, 56–57. A. Hellyer *Gardens of genius* 1980, 13–14. G.A. Little *Scotland's gardens* 1981, 206–08.

Pitsea Hall, Pitsea, Essex
F.G. Emmison *Catalogue of maps in Essex Record Office* 3rd Supplt, 1968, 12.

Pittencrieff Park and Glen *see* Dunfermline

Pixholme Court, Dorking, Surrey
Gdn Design 1931, 152–61. *C.L.* v. 81, 1937, 230–32.

Place House, Horton, Bucks
Gentleman's Mag. v. 61, 1791, pt 2, 715.

Place House, Fowey, Cornwall
G. Beard *Thomas H. Mawson* 1976, 60.

Place House, Padstow, Cornwall
W. Borlase *Natural history of Cornwall* 1758, pl. 4.

C.S. Gilbert *Historical survey of . . . Cornwall* v. 2, 1820, 650–51. J. Britton *and* E.W. Brayley *Devonshire & Cornwall* 1832, 31.

Plaish Hall, Plaish, Shropshire
C.L. v. 41, 1917, 520–26. G. Jekyll *Garden ornament* 1918, 118.

Plaistow House, Bromley, London
J. Hassell *Seats near London* 1804–05.

Plas, Tan-y-Bwlch, Gwynedd
J. Hort. Cottage Gdnr N.S., v. 16, 1888, 218–20.

Plas Brondanw near Tremadoc, Gwynedd
C.L. v. 69, 1931, 130–36; v. 122, 1957, 434–37.

Plas Coch near Llanfair, Anglesey, Gwynedd
J.B. Burke *Visitation* 2nd Series, v. 1, 1855, 103.

Plas Newydd, Llanfairpwll, Anglesey, Gwynedd
Official guide. H. Repton *Observations* 1803, 105–06. J.P. Neale *Views* v. 5, 1822. *J. Hort. Cottage Gdnr* v. 50, 1873, 219, 236–37. *C.L.* v. 118, 1955, 1198–1201; v. 135, 1964, 1588–89; v. 160, 1976, 722–24. D. Stroud *Humphry Repton* 1962, 172. G.S. Thomas *Gardens of National Trust* 1979, 198–99. G. Carter *et al. Humphry Repton* 1982, 164.

Plas Penglais, Aberystwyth, Dyfed
A. Hellyer *Gardens of genius* 1980, 63–66.

Plas-yn-Rhin, Pwllheli, Gwynedd
G.S. Thomas *Gardens of National Trust* 1979, 199.

Plashwood near Stowmarket, Suffolk
H. Davy *Views* 1827.

Pleasaunce, Overstrand, Norfolk
J. Hort. Cottage Gdnr N.S., v. 59, 1909, 490–91. *G.C.* ii 1911, 260–61. J. Brown *Gardens of a golden afternoon* 1982, 164.

Pleasley Vale, Pleasley, Derbyshire
J. Hort. Cottage Gdnr v. 52, 1874, 144–46.

Plowden Hall, Plowden, Shropshire
C.L. v. 157, 1975, 318.

Plumber, Lydlinch, Dorset
J. Hutchins *History . . . of Dorset* v. 4, 1870, 189.

Plumpton House, Whepstead, Suffolk
J. Gage *History . . . of Suffolk: Thingoe Hundred* 1838, 395.

Plumpton Park, Plumpton, Northants
Northamptonshire Past and Present v. 5 no. 3, 1975, 230.

Plumpton Place, Plumpton, E. Sussex
C.L. v. 73, 1933, 522–28. J. Brown *Gardens of a golden afternoon* 1982, 148–50,175.

Plumstead Hall, Plumstead, Norfolk
G.M. v. 17, 1841, 272–73. J. Grigor *Eastern arboretum* 1841, 235–36.

Pluscarden Abbey near Elgin, Grampian
G.A. Little *Scotland's gardens* 1981, 208–09.

Plympton House, Plympton, Devon
C.L. v. 74, 1933, 146–51.

Podenhale, Wentworth, Surrey
Gdn Design 1938, 48–52.

Point Pleasant (Bank Farm) near Richmond, London
D. Stroud *Humphry Repton* 1962, 166. G. Carter *et al. Humphry Repton* 1982, 74,162.

Polam Hill, Darlington, Co. Durham
G.M. v. 13, 1837, 441.

Poles near Hertford, Herts
Cottage Gdnr v. 19, 1857, 128–30,143–44. *J. Hort. Cottage Gdnr* v. 47, 1872, 527; v. 48, 1872, 14–16.

Polesden Lacey near Great Bookham, Surrey
Official guide. J.P. Neale *Views* 2nd Series, v. 1, 1824. G.F. Prosser *Select illustrations of . . . Surrey* 1828. E.W. Brayley *and* J. Britton *Topographical history of Surrey* v. 4, 471. W. Keane *Beauties of Surrey* 1849, 114–15. C.L. v. 103, 1948, 478–81,526; v. 169, 1981, 445. *J. Royal Hort. Soc.* 1960, 351–52. G.C. ii 1965, 373–74,380. M. Allan *Fisons guide* 1970, 60. H. Evans *Beautiful gardens of Britain* 1974, 55–56. T. Wright *Gardens of Britain* v. 4, 1978, 224–29. G.S. Thomas *Gardens of National Trust* 1979, 199–200.

Pollards, Chalfont St Giles, Bucks
J. Brown *Gardens of a golden afternoon* 1982, 167.

Pollok near Barrhead, Strathclyde
G.M. v. 13, 1837, 167–71. H. Maxwell *Scottish gardens* 1911, 54–60. C.L. v. 33, 1913, 126–33; v. 76, 1934, 388–93. G. Jekyll *Garden ornament* 1918, 206. M. Allan *Fisons guide* 1970, 307.

Poltalloch near Lochgilphead, Strathclyde
C. McIntosh *Book of the garden* 1853–55, pl. 6. *Gdning World* v. 7, 1890, 5,21–22; v. 10, 1893, 148.

Poltimore House, Poltimore, Devon
R. Ackermann *Repository* v. 10, 1827, pl. 2. W.W.J. Gendall *Views* v. 2, 1830, 67. *Architectural History* v. 7, 1964, 35,91–92.

Pontrilas Court, Pontrilas, Hereford and Worcester
R. Sidwell *West Midland gardens* 1981, 80.

Pontypool Park, Pontypool, Gwent
D. Williams *History of Monmouthshire* 1796, 326–27, pl. 28. J.B. Burke *Visitation* v. 2, 1853, 7. B. Jones *Follies & grottoes* 1974, 184–86.

Pope's Villa, Twickenham, London
J. Serle *Plan of Mr Pope's garden and grotto, etc.* 1745. W. Watts *Seats* 1779, pl. 48. H. Walpole *Essay on modern gardening* 1785, 63. *Topographer* v. 1, 1789, 471–74. J. *and* J. Boydell *History of the River Thames* v. 2, 1796, 3–6. W.B. Cooke *and* S. Owen *The Thames* v. 1, 1811. W. Keane *Beauties of Middlesex* 1850, 10–15. *J. Hort. Cottage Gdnr* N.S., v. 15, 1887, 118–19. S. Felton *Gleanings on gardens* 1897, 96–101. *South Atlantic Quarterly* v. 42, 1943, 289–95. T. Jefferson *Garden book 1766–1824* 1944, 111. *Huntingdon Library Quarterly* v. 12, 1948–49,141–62. O. Siren *China and gardens of Europe of 18th century* 1950, 20–24. A. Pope *Correspondence* 1956 5 vols, passim. V.C.H. *Middlesex* v. 3, 1962, 143. C. Camden *Restoration and 18th century literature* 1963, 69–83,143–53. F.W. Hilles *and* H. Bloom *From sensibility to romanticism* 1965, 3–29. C. Hussey *English gardens and landscapes, 1700–1750* 1967, 41–44. C.L. v. 143, 1968, 512–14,812. P. Quennell *Alexander Pope, the education of genius, 1688–1728* 1968. M. Mack *Essential articles for study of Alexander Pope* 1968, 97–121. M. Mack *Garden and the city* 1969, 237–43. *Eighteenth-century studies* v. 5, 1972, 450–55. *Times Literary Supplement* 22 June 1973, 715–16. *Durham University J.* v. 65 no. 3, 1973, 248–59. J.D. Hunt *and* P. Willis *Genius of the place* 1975, 247–53. *Gdn History* v. 4 no. 1, 1976, 30–53,57–87; v. 5 no. 2, 1977, 9–23. *Notes & Queries* v. 24, 1977, 243–45. M.R. Brownell *Alexander Pope & the arts of Georgian England* 1978, passim. J. Harris *Artist and the country house* 1979, 184,322. M. Hadfield *et al. British gardeners* 1980, 228–29. Marble Hill House *Alexander Pope's villa . . . catalogue of exhibition* 1980. *J. Gdn History* v. 1 no. 1, 1981, 35–36. D. Watkin *English vision* 1982, 4–5. K. Rorschach *Early Georgian landscape garden* 1983, 11–15.

Porkington near Oswestry, Shropshire
J.P. Neale *Views* v. 3, 1820. F. Calvert *Picturesque views . . . in Shropshire* 1831, 123.

Port Eliot near St Germans, Cornwall
H. Repton *Observations* 1803, 192–94. C.S. Gilbert *Historical survey of . . . Cornwall* v. 2, 1820, 409.

Port Eliot (*Cont.*)

R. Ackermann *Repository* v. 7, 1826, pl. 32.
W.W.J. Gendall *Views* v. 1, 1830, 110. J. Britton *and*
E.W. Brayley *Devonshire & Cornwall* 1832, 22. *Cottage Gdnr* v. 23, 1860, 208–10. *C.L.* v. 104, 1948, 778,828–31,882. D. Stroud *Humphry Repton* 1962, 69. G. Carter *et al. Humphry Repton* 1982, 150.

Port Lympne near Hythe, Kent
C.L. v. 53, 1923, 678–84; v. 66, 1929, 513–17; v. 72, 1932, 285–87; v. 79, 1936, 276–82. Lady Rockley *Historic gardens of England* 1938, 258–59. *G.C.* i 1939, 241. L. Fleming *and* A. Gore *English garden* 1979, 218–19, pls. 134–35. *Landscpe Design* no. 143, 1983, 31–33.

Portaferry House, Portaferry, Co. Down, Ulster
J. Stevenson *Two centuries of life in Down* 1920, 446.

Porters Park near Shenley, Herts
J. Hort. Cottage Gdnr N.S., v. 58, 1909, 400–01.

Portledge House near Bideford, Devon
Architectural History v. 7, 1964, 35,93.

Portmeirion, Penrhyndeudraeth, Gwynedd
G.C. ii 1962, 170–71. *C.L.* v. 160, 1976, 726–29,798–801. A. Hellyer *Gardens of genius* 1980, 36–38.

Portnall Park near Sunningdale, Berks
G.F. Prosser *Select illustrations of . . . Surrey* 1828.

Possingworth near Waldron, E. Sussex
J. Hort. Cottage Gdnr v. 46, 1871, 318. *Garden* v. 1, 1872, 592,593.

Postern, Tonbridge, Kent
C.L. v. 169, 1981, 1306–08.

Potholm near Eskdale, N. Yorks
J. Hort. Cottage Gdnr v. 54, 1875, 360–61.

Potterspury, Northants
Northamptonshire Past and Present v. 5 no. 3, 1975, 230. Royal Commission on Historical Monuments *Inventory of the historical monuments in . . . Northampton* v. 4, 1982, 119.

Poulett Lodge, Twickenham, London
Gdning World v. 5, 1889, 408; v. 6, 1890, 596.

Poundisford Lodge near Taunton, Somerset
C.L. v. 39, 1916, 786–91.

Poundisford Park near Taunton, Somerset
C.L. v. 39, 1916, 758–63.

Poundon, Bucks
G. Beard *Thomas H. Mawson* 1976, 60.

Powderham Castle, Powderham, Devon
Society of Gentlemen *England displayed* v. 1, 1769, 30. S. *and* N. Buck *Buck's antiquities* v. 1, 1774, pls. 67–68. R. Polwhele *History of Devonshire* v. 2, 1793, 171. G. Tod *Plans, elevations and sections of hot-houses* 1807, 14, pl. 10. J.P. Neale *Views* v. 1, 1818. R. Ackermann *Repository* v. 5, 1825, pl. 20. *Jones's views* 1829. W.W.J. Gendall *Views* v. 2, 1830, 10. J. Britton *and* E.W. Brayley *Devonshire & Cornwall* 1832, 32. *G.M.* v. 18, 1842, 532. *G.C.* i 1882, 589–90; ii 1903, 291. *J. Hort. Cottage Gdnr* N.S., v. 10, 1885, 236–37. *C.L.* v. 23, 1908, 486–92; v. 134, 1963, 18–21. Historical MSS Commission *Architectural history* v. 3, 1971, item 3307.

Powerscourt, Co. Wicklow, Eire
P. Luckombe *Tour through Ireland* 1783, 27. British Museum *Catalogue of maps, prints* 1829, 276. F.O. Morris *Series of picturesque views* v. 3, 31. *J. Hort. Cottage Gdnr* v. 45, 1871, 236–38,321–23. *G.C.* i 1895, 556; i 1911, 218–19. *Gdnrs Mag.* 1909, 473–74. R.H.S. *Conifers in cultivation* 1932, 213–14,220. *C.L.* v. 100, 1946, 1062–67,1158–61,1206–09. *J. Royal Hort. Soc.* 1950, 243–45; 1958, 458–59; 1966, 88–90. P. Coats *Great gardens of Britain* 1967, 202–09. E. Hyams *Irish gardens* 1967, 91–97. M. Allan *Fisons guide* 1970, 370–71. B. Jones *Follies & grottoes* 1974, 440. E. Malins *and* Knight of Glin *Lost demesnes* 1976, 24,26–27. J. Harris *Artist and the country house* 1979, 283, pl. 25. E. Malins *and* P. Bowe *Irish gardens and demesnes* 1980, 82–94. Knight of Glin *and* P. Bowe *Gardens of outstanding historic interest in . . . Ireland* 1980.

Powfoulis, Airth, Central
I.H. Adams *Descriptive list of plans* v. 2, 1970, 129.

Powis Castle, Welshpool, Powys
Official guide. Society of Gentlemen *England displayed* v. 2, 1769, 271. S. *and* N. Buck *Buck's antiquities* v. 2, 1774, pl. 414. *Topographer* v. 4, 1791, 17. J.C. Loudon *Encyclopaedia of gardening* 1822, 1249. F.O. Morris *Series of picturesque views* v. 6, 59. *G.C.* ii 1879, 787–88,793; ii 1894, 310–12; i 1964, 505–06; i 1966, 401–02. *Garden* v. 44, 1893, 321–22. *C.L.* v. 9, 1901, 16–24; v. 41, 1917, 108–15,132–39; v. 79, 1936, 564–72,598–604; v. 168, 1980, 935–38. J. Loveday *Diary* 1890, 16. *Architectural Review* v. 34, 1913, pl. 10. G. Jekyll *Garden ornament* 1918, 46, 130,133. Lady Rockley *Historic gardens of England* 1938, 136–37. *Connoisseur Year Book* 1954, 26–33. *J. Royal Hort. Soc.* 1960, 352; 1962, 438–46; 1971, 213–14. *J. Institute of Landscape Architects* no. 76, 1966, 2–4. P. Coats *Great gardens of Britain* 1967, 136–45. C. Hussey *English gardens and landscapes 1700–1750* 1967, 53–56.

Powis Castle (*Cont.*)

M. Allan *Fisons guide* 1970, 281–82. H. Evans *Beautiful gardens of Britain* 1974, 115–16. *Gdn History* v. 3 no. 4, 1975, 51,52. D. Jarrett *English landscape garden* 1978, 24–27. L. Fleming *and* A. Gore *English garden* 1979, 67. R. Haslam *Powys* 1979, 195–96. G.S. Thomas *Gardens of National Trust* 1979, 201–03. A. Hellyer *Gardens of genius* 1980, 17–20. Manpower Services Commission *Powis Castle* 1981. T. Hinde *Stately gardens of Britain* 1983, 26–31.

Powys, Sidmouth, Devon
P.M. Synge *Gardens of Britain* v. 1, 1977, 69–70.

Poynton Lodge, Poynton, Cheshire
J. Harris *Artist and the country house* 1979, 300.

Poynton Towers, Poynton, Cheshire
J. Harris *Artist and the country house* 1979, 206.

Poxwell Manor, Poxwell, Dorset
G. Jekyll *Garden ornament* 1918, 32. *C.L.* v. 35, 1914, 558–62.

Poyle Park near Farnham, Surrey
G.C. ii 1880, 814,815,817.

Presdales near Ware, Herts
G.C. ii 1902, 229.

Preshaw House, Corhampton, Hants
E.F. Prosser *Select illustrations of Hampshire* 1833.

Preston Deanery, Northants
Northamptonshire Past and Present v. 5 no. 3, 1975, 230.

Preston Hall near Maidstone, Kent
J. Harris *History of Kent* 1719, 32. J. Kip *Supplement du Nouveau theatre de la Grande Bretagne* 1728, pl. 12. T. Badeslade *Thirty six different views . . . in Kent* 1750s, pl. 28. E. Hasted *History . . . of Kent* v. 2, 1782, 174. F.O. Morris *Series of picturesque views* v. 3, 75. *Cottage Gdnr* v. 21, 1859, 381–82. *J. Hort. Cottage Gdnr* v. 35, 1866, 286–87; v. 46, 1871, 260–63. *G.C.* ii 1884, 461–62; ii 1893, 236–38.

Preston Hall, Dalkeith, Lothian
Scottish Gdnr v. 3, 1854, 294–97. *C.L.* v. 130, 1961, 394–97,455. C. McWilliam *Lothian* 1978, 397.

Preston House, Cirencester, Glos
G.C. i 1879, 811–12.

Preston Park *see* Brighton

Prestonfield, Edinburgh, Lothian
J.C. Loudon *Arboretum et fruticetum Britannicum* v. 1, 1844, 92. A.A. Tait *Landscape garden in Scotland* 1980, passim. *Gdn History* v. 8 no. 3, 1980, 93,97,98.

Prestwold Hall, Prestwold, Leics
J. Throsby *Select views in Leicestershire* v. 1, 1790, 305. J. Nichols *History . . . of county of Leicester* v. 3, 1804, 1133. J.P. Neale *Views* v. 2, 1819. *Jones's views* 1829. *G.M.* v. 7, 1831, 426–27. J.B. Burke *Visitation* v. 1, 1852, 23. *C.L.* v. 125, 1959, 828–31,948–51.

Prestwood, Staffs
S. Shaw *History . . . of Staffordshire* v. 2, 1801, 234. D. Stroud *Humphry Repton* 1962, 51. G. Carter *et al. Humphry Repton* 1982, 161.

Prideaux Place, Padstow, Cornwall
J. Hort. Cottage Gdnr N.S., v. 40, 1900, 289–90. *G.C.* ii 1911, 219–20. *Architectural History* v. 7, 1964, 33–34, 84–86.

Primrose Hill *see* London

Prince's Park *see* Liverpool

Prinknash Park near Gloucester, Glos
J.N. Brewer *Delineations of Gloucestershire* 1825, 149. *Trans. Bristol and Gloucestershire Archaeological Soc.* v. 7, 1882/83, 267–306. *C.L.* v. 20, 1906, 414–18.

Prior Park, Bath, Avon
D. Defoe *Tour* v. 2, 1778, 230–31. W. Watts *Seats* 1779, pl. 75. *C.L.* v. 7, 1900, 48–53; v. 52, 1922, 545; v. 165, 1979, 873–76. *G.C.* i 1902, 130. *Apollo* v. 98, 1973, 366–74. D. Stroud *Capability Brown* 1975, 236. J. Harris *Gardens of delight* 1978, 61–62. J. Sales *West Country gardens* 1980, 175–76.

Priorwood, Melrose, Borders
Scottish Field v. 124 no. 918, 1978, 73.

Priory, Beech Hill, Berks
R. Bisgrove *Gardens of Britain* v. 3, 1978, 145–46.

Priory, Hatfield Peverel, Essex
P. Muilman *History of Essex* v. 4, 1770, 119. *G.C.* i 1899, 312–14. F.G. Emmison *Catalogue of maps in Essex Record Office* 1947, 19.

Priory, Kemerton, Hereford and Worcester
R. Sidwell *West Midland gardens* 1981, 81–84. A. Lees-Milne *and* R. Verey *Englishman's garden* 1982, 72–75.

Priory, St Helens, Isle of Wight
R. Worsley *History of Isle of Wight* 1781.

Priory, Sea View, Isle of Wight
J. Brown *Gardens of a golden afternoon* 1982, 175.

Priory, Bidston, Merseyside
C. Holme *Gardens of England in Northern counties* 1911, pls. 101–03.

Priory, Reigate, Surrey
G.F. Prosser *Select illustrations of . . . Surrey* 1828. W. Keane *Beauties of Surrey* 1849, 69–70. *C.L.* v. 43, 1918, 340–44.

Priory, Leamington, Warwickshire
G.M. v. 16, 1840, 585–86.

Priory, Warwick, Warwickshire
C.L. v. 103, 1948, 78–79, 335–36.

Priory of Lady St Mary, Wareham, Dorset
M. Allan *Fisons guide* 1970, 104. *C.L.* v. 159, 1976, 532–34.

Promenade Grove *see* Brighton

Prospect House, Woodford, Redbridge, London
P. Muilman *History of Essex* v. 4, 1770, 204. P. Morant *History . . . of Essex* v. 1, 1816, 39.

Pudleston Court, Pudleston, Hereford and Worcester
J.B. Burke *Visitation* v. 1, 1852, 144.

Pull Court, Bushley, Hereford and Worcester
N. Pevsner *Worcestershire* 1968, 114.

Purley Hall, Purley, Berks
C.L. v. 147, 1970, 310–13. D. Stroud *Humphry Repton* 1962, 80. B. Jones *Follies & grottoes* 1974, 288–89. P. Willis *Charles Bridgeman* 1977, 181. R. Bisgrove *Gardens of Britain* v. 3, 1978, 146–47. J. Harris *Artist and the country house* 1979, 330, 363. G. Carter *et al. Humphry Repton* 1982, 148.

Purser's Cross, Fulham, Hammersmith, London
J.C. Loudon *Arboretum et fruticetum Britannicum* v. 1, 1844, 72–73. W. Keane *Beauties of Middlesex* 1850, 37–41.

Pusey House, Faringdon, Oxfordshire
Official guide. *C.L.* v. 128, 1960, 553–55; v. 160, 1976, 1958–61. P. Coats *Great gardens of Britain* 1967, 66–71. R. Bisgrove *Gardens of Britain* v. 3, 1978, 147–48. *Garden* 1980, 103–07. A. Lees-Milne *and* R. Verey *Englishwoman's garden* 1980, 67–71. *Architectural Digest* v. 38, 1981, 100–05. T. Hinde *Stately gardens of Britain* 1983, 160–67.

Puslinch near Plympton, Devon
C.L. v. 74, 1933, 524–29.

Putteridge Park, Luton, Beds
J. Brown *Miss Gertrude Jekyll* 1981, 28–29. J. Brown *Gardens of a golden afternoon* 1982, 172.

Putteridgebury near Luton, Beds
Scottish Gdnr v. 11, 1862, 339–46. *Cottage Gdnr* v. 28, 1862, 491–92, 512–13. *J. Hort. Cottage Gdnr* v. 31, 1864, 113–15, 176–77, 250–51; v. 47, 1872, 443–45.

Pye Nest near Halifax, W. Yorks
J.B. Burke *Visitation* v. 1, 1855, 210. Bradford Illustrated Weekly Telegraph *Series of picturesque views* 1885.

Pylewell Park near Lymington, Hants
T. Badeslade *and* J. Rocque *Vitruvius Brittanicus* 1739, pls. 102–03. P. Coats *Great gardens of Britain* 1967, 228–33. M. Allan *Fisons guide* 1970, 105. A. Paterson *Gardens of Britain* v. 2, 1978, 135–36.

Pynes near Exeter, Devon
R. Ackermann *Repository* v. 5, 1825, pl. 8. W.W.J. Gendall *Views* v. 1, 1830, 45–47. F.O. Morris *Series of picturesque views* v. 6, 27.

Pyrford Court, Pyrford, Surrey
E.W. Brayley *and* J. Britton *Topographical history of Surrey* v. 2, 1841, 147–48. *G.C.* ii 1924, 45–46, 347; ii 1957, 150–51. *C.L.* v. 135, 1964, 1118–19. P. Coats *Great gardens of Britain* 1967, 252–57. M. Allan *Fisons guide* 1970, 17–18.

Pyrgo Park, Havering, London
F.G. Emmison *Catalogue of maps in Essex Record Office* 1st Supplt, 1952, 2.

Quadrangle, Munstead, Surrey
J. Brown *Gardens of a golden afternoon* 1982, 162.

Quarry Gardens, Bellie, Grampian
I.H. Adams *Descriptive list of plans* v. 2, 1970, 107.

Quarry Park *see* Shrewsbury

Quarry Wood, Burghclere, Hants
M. Allan *Fisons guide* 1970, 18–19.

Quarters, Alresford, Essex
C.L. v. 124, 1958, 1040–41.

Quebec House, Westerham, Kent
C.L. v. 421, 1917, 252–59.

Queen Hoo Hall near Tewin, Herts
C.L. v. 131, 1962, 594–98.

Queen's Park see Brighton

Queensbery House near Drumlanrig, Dumfries and Galloway
W. Gilpin *Observations, relative chiefly to picturesque beauty* v. 2, 1792, 83–85.

Quenby Hall near Hungarton, Leics
A. Young *Farmer's tour through East of England* v. 1, 1771, 80–81. J. Throsby *Select views in Leicestershire* v. 1, 1790, 307. J. Nichols *History . . . of county of Leicester* v. 3, 1800, 296; v. 3, 1804, 1128. G.M. v. 7, 1831, 423. C.L. v. 16, 1904, 342–49; v. 30, 1911, 550–57,590–97. *Architectural Review* v. 29, 1911, 96–97. J. Anthony *Gardens of Britain* v. 6, 1979, 135–37. J. Harris *Artist and the country house* 1979, 239.

Quendon Hall, Quendon, Essex
P. Muilman *History of Essex* v. 3, 1770, 34. P. Morant *History . . . of Essex* v. 2, 1816, 581. F.G. Emmison *Catalogue of maps in Essex Record Office* 1st Supplt, 1952, 7.

Quernmore Park, Quernmore, Lancs
E. Baines *History . . . of Lancaster* v. 4, 1836, 547. Historical MSS Commission *Architectural history* v. 5, 1974, item 5448.

Quex Park, Birchington, Kent
C. Greenwood *Epitome of county history . . . v. 1: Kent* 1838, 327. G.C. ii 1902, 424. B. Jones *Follies & grottoes* 1974, 207–08.

Quidenham Park, Quidenham, Norfolk
J.P. Neale *Views* 2nd Series, v. 1, 1824.

Quinta, Swettenham, Cheshire
A. Lees-Milne *and* R. Verey *Englishman's garden* 1982, 96–99.

Quinton Castle, Quinton, Co. Down, Ulster
B. Jones *Follies & grottoes* 1974, 429.

Quorndon Hall, Quorndon, Leics
J. Throsby *Select views in Leicestershire* v. 1, 1790, 309. J. Nichols *History . . . of county of Leicester* v. 3, 1800, 101; v. 3, 1804, 1128. *Gdning World* v. 4, 1888, 773–74. G.C. ii 1892, 121–22.

Raby Castle near Staindrop, Co. Durham
Official guide. Society of Gentlemen *England displayed* v. 2, 1769, 168. A. Young *Six months tour through North of England* v. 2, 1771, 430–35. J.P. Neale *Views* v. 1, 1818. *Jones's views* 1829. *Florist* 1859, 107–10.

F.O. Morris *Series of picturesque views* v. 2, 15. L. Jewitt *and* S.C. Hall *Stately homes of England* 1877, 242–45. J. *Hort. Cottage Gdnr* v. 60, 1878, 278–79,296–98; N.S., v. 15, 1887, 156–57. G.C. i 1882, 640,680,702–03; ii 1896, 520–22. C.L. v. 2, 1897, 321–24; v. 38, 1915, 760–68,804–10. Lady Rockley *Historic gardens of England* 1938, 78–79. B. Jones *Follies & grottoes* 1974, 319. T. Wright *Arbours & grottos* 1979. *Gdn History* v. 8 no. 2, 1980, 51,53–54.

Rackheath Park, Rackheath, Norfolk
G.M. v. 17, 1841, 271. J. Grigor *Eastern arboretum* 1841, 202.

Racton Tower near Chichester, W. Sussex
M. Binney *and* A. Hills *Elysium gardens* 1978, 51.

Radier Manor, Jersey, Channel Islands
C.L. v. 149, 1971, 820–22.

Radley, Oxfordshire
D. Stroud *Capability Brown* 1975, 237.

Radnor House, Twickenham, London
J.H. Pye *Peep into the principal seats and gardens in and about Twickenham* 1775, 9–10. J. Boydell *Collection of views in England and Wales* 1790, pl. 30.

Radway Grange, Radway, Warwickshire
C.L. v. 100, 1946, 440–43,486–89.

Raeden House, Grampian
H. Maxwell *Scottish gardens* 1911, 184–86.

Reagill near Shap, Cumbria
B. Jones *Follies & grottoes* 1974, 250.

Raehills near Lockerbie, Dumfries and Galloway
G.M. v. 9, 1833, 5.

Ragdale Old Hall, Ragdale, Leics
C.L. v. 19, 1906, 126–31.

Ragley Hall near Alcester, Warwickshire
J. Beeverell *Lew delices de la Grande Bretagne* v. 5, 1707, 872. L. Knyff *and* J. Kip *Britannia illustrata* v. 1, 1714. J.P. Neale *Views* v. 4, 1821. C.L. v. 6, 1899, 430–31; v. 13, 1903, 571; v. 54, 1924, 438–45; v. 123, 1958, 938–41. M. Macartney *English houses & gardens* 1908, pl. 46. D. Stroud *Capability Brown* 1975, 237.

Ragman's Castle, Twickenham, London
Short account of the principal seats and gardens in and about Richmond and Kew [1760s?], 7.

Railshead see Gordon House

Rainham Hall, Rainham, Havering, London
C.L. v. 47, 1920, 760–68.

Raith House near Kirkaldy, Fife
Cottage Gdnr v. 16, 1856, 308–10.

Ramsbury Manor, Ramsbury, Wilts
J.P. Neale *Views* v. 5, 1822. *C.L.* v. 22, 1907, 198–205; v. 48, 1920, 432–39; v. 130, 1961, 1376–80,1526, 1580–83; v. 157, 1975, 194–95. V.C.H. *Wiltshire* v. 12, 1983, 21–22.

Ramsford near Gorey, Co. Wexford, Eire
Irish Naturalists J. v. 19, 1978, 274–75. E. Malins *and* P. Bowe *Irish gardens and demesnes* 1980, 47.

Ramster near Chiddingfold, Surrey
T. Wright *Gardens of Britain* v. 4, 1978, 229–30.

Randalls Park near Leatherhead, Surrey
E.W. Brayley *and* J. Britton *Topographical history of Surrey* v. 4, 433.

Ranelagh Gardens, Chelsea, London
W. Wroth *London pleasure gardens of the eighteenth century* 1896, 199–218. E.B. Chancellor *Pleasure haunts of London* 1925, 228–47. E. von Erdberg *Chinese influence on European garden structures* 1936, 177. M. Sands *Invitation to Ranelagh 1742–1803* 1946.

Ranelagh House, Chelsea, London
C.L. v. 125, 1959, 368–69. D. Stroud *Capability Brown* 1975, 226.

Rangemore Hall, Rangemore, Staffs
J. Hort. Cottage Gdnr v. 55, 1876, 53–55,74–75. *G.C.* ii 1890, 377–78. *Gdnrs Mag.* 1901, 403–07. C. Holme *Gardens of England in Midland & Eastern counties* 1908, pls. 97–98.

Rankeilour near Cupar, Fife
G. Jekyll *Garden ornament* 1918, 317.

Ranston House near Blandford, Dorset
W. Watts *Seats* 1779, pl. 8. J. Hutchins *History . . . of Dorset* v. 4, 1870, 93.

Rathcline near Lanesborough, Co. Longford, Eire
E. Malins *and* Knight of Glin *Lost demesnes* 1976, 7.

Rathgar, Dublin, Eire
Irish Gdning v. 1, 1906, 175–76; v. 4, 1909, 129–31; v. 7, 1912, 163–64.

Ravelston, Edinburgh, Lothian
Scottish Gdnr and Northern Forester v. 7, 1912, 513–14. *G.C.* ii 1890, 270–71.

Ravenfield near Rotherham, S. Yorks
T. Badeslade *and* J. Rocque *Victruvius Brittanicus* 1739, pls. 108–09. I. Hall *Samuel Buck's Yorkshire sketchbook* 1979, 258.

Ravenhurst, Bolton, Greater Manchester
G. Beard *Thomas H. Mawson* 1976, 61.

Raveningham Hall, Raveningham, Norfolk
G.M. v. 17, 1841, 274. J. Grigor *Eastern arboretum* 1841, 262–63.

Ravenscourt Park *see* London

Ravensworth Castle near Gateshead, Tyne and Wear
G.M. v. 10, 1834, 363–64. F.O. Morris *Series of picturesque views* v. 5, 17. *J. Hort. Cottage Gdnr* v. 58, 1877, 382–84.

Ravensworth House, Walham Green, Hammersmith, London
Gdn History v. 9 no. 1, 1981, 67.

Rawflat, Ancrum, Borders
I.H. Adams *Descriptive list of plans* v. 3, 1974, 124.

Rawleigh House, Barnstaple, Devon
G.C. ii 1882, 135.

Raynham Hall near Fakenham, Norfolk
W. Watts *Seats* 1779, pl. 52. J.P. Neale *Views* v. 3, 1820. J. Grigor *Eastern arboretum* 1841, 175–77. *C.L.* v. 58, 1925, 742–50; v. 131, 1962, 527. *Architectural History* v. 7, 1964, 36,95–97.

Red House, Effingham, Surrey
J. Brown *Gardens of a golden afternoon* 1982, 160.

Red House, Charterhouse, Godalming, Surrey
J. Brown *Gardens of a golden afternoon* 1982, 163.

Red Lion Square *see* London

Reddish House, Broad Chalke, Wilts
C.L. v. 121, 1957, 540–43,599.

Redford near Ockley, Surrey
G.C. ii 1932, 175,176–77.

Redgrave Hall, Redgrave, Suffolk
J.P. Neale *Views* v. 4, 1821. D. Stroud *Capability Brown* 1975, 112–13,237.

Redhouse (Sir Henry Slingsby), Yorks
C.L. v. 106, 1949, 1889.

Redland Court near Westbury on Trym, Avon
J.N. Brewer *Delineations of Gloucestershire* 1825, 45.

Redlands near Glasgow, Strathclyde
G.C. i 1890, 46–47.

Redleaf, Penshurst, Kent
C. Greenwood *Epitome of county history . . . v. 1: Kent* 1838, 111. *G.M.* v. 15, 1839, 353–79. C.G. Carus *King of Saxony's journey through England and Scotland* 1846, 44. J.C. Loudon *Villa gardener* 1850, 299–315. *Cottage Gdnr* v. 26, 1861, 4–5,26–27,64–66. *Architectural Review* v. 82, 1937, 203–06. *C.L.* v. 160, 1976, 1923–24.

Redlees, Isleworth, Hounslow, London
J. Hort. Cottage Gdnr v. 54, 1875, 92–93.

Redlynch near Wincanton, Somerset
H. Walpole *Visits to country seats. Walpole Society* v. 7, 1927/8, 44. J. Sales *West Country gardens* 1980, 176.

Rednock near Port of Menteith, Central
A.A. Tait *Landscape garden in Scotland* 1980, passim.

Redwell, Wellingborough, Northants
J. Hort. Cottage Gdnr N.S., v. 41, 1900, 357.

Reed Hall, Colchester, Essex
J. Hort. Cottage Gdnr v. 32, 1864, 310–11.

Regal Lodge, Kentford, Suffolk
Garden 1912, 451–52.

Regent's Lodge, Regent's Park, London
C.L. v. 85, 1939, 161–64.

Regent's Park (Marquess of Hertford), London
G.M. v. 5, 1829, 464–65.

Regent's Park *see* London

Relic, Highalnd
G.M. v. 11, 1835, 555–57.

Remans (Beaumont College), Old Windsor, Berks
T. Wright *Arbors & grottos* 1979.

Rempstone Hall near Corfe Castle, Dorset
A. Paterson *Gardens of Britain* v. 2, 1978, 41–42.

Rendcomb Park, Rendcomb, Glos
R. Atkyns *Ancient and present state of Glostershire* 1712, 618. L. Knyff *and* J. Kip *Britannia illustrata* v. 2, 1715. S. Rudder *New history of Gloucestershire* 1779, 621. J.N. Brewer *Delineations of Gloucestershire* 1825, 76. M. Macartney *English houses & gardens* 1908, pl. 48.

Rendlesham Hall, Rendlesham, Suffolk
H. Davy *Views* 1827. *G.C.* ii 1881, 178–79. D. Stroud *Humphry Repton* 1962, 172. B. Jones *Follies & grottoes* 1974, 393. G. Carter *et al. Humphry Repton* 1982, 162.

Renishaw near Chesterfield, Derbyshire
Official guide. *C.L.* v. 8, 1900, 560–67; v. 83, 1938, 476–80,506; v. 162, 1977, 522–25. C. Holme *Gardens of England in Midland & Eastern counties* 1908, pl. 99. O. Sitwell *Left hand, right hand* 1945–50, 5 vols, passim. *Garden* 1978, 301–08. N. Pevsner *Derbyshire* 1978, 302–03. *Gdn History* v. 8 no. 3, 1980, 37,39,42. J. Brown *Gardens of a golden afternoon* 1982, 170. M. Hadfield *et al. British gardeners* 1980, 262. M. *and* R. Tooley *Gardens of Gertrude Jekyll in Northern England* 1982, 16–19,54.

Rest Hill Farm, Over Worton, Oxfordshire
R. Bisgrove *Gardens of Britain* v. 3, 1978, 150–51.

Restoration Spring Gardens, Southwark, London
W. Wroth *London pleasure gardens of the eighteenth century* 1896, 263–64. E.B. Chancellor *Pleasure haunts of London* 1925, 365.

Rhianfa near Beaumaris, Anglesey, Gwynedd
Garden v. 17, 1880, 364–65. W. Robinson *English flower garden* 1883, xxii–xxiv.

Rhinefield House, Brockenhurst, Hants
C.L. v. 162, 1977, 640.

Rhual near Mold, Clwyd
C.L. v. 93, 1943, 1144–47.

Rhydd Court near Upton upon Severn, Hereford and Worcester
F.O. Morris *Series of picturesque views* v. 5, 23.

Ribby Hall, Ribby, Lancs
G. Beard *Thomas H. Mawson* 1976, 61.

Ribston Hall, Ribston, N. Yorks
J. Beeverell *Les delices de la Grande Bretagne* v. 5, 1707, 872. L. Knyff *and* J. Kip *Britannia illustrata* v. 1, 1714. *Florist* 1856, 267–70. *Florist & Pomologist* 1866, 245–48. *G.C.* ii 1880, 69. *Garden* v. 60, 1901, 126–27. *C.L.* v. 19, 1906, 198–205; v. 154, 1973, 1050–53,1142–45. M. Macartney *English houses & gardens* 1908, pl. 22. C. Holme *Gardens of England in Northern counties* 1911, pls. 104–08. R. Dutton *English garden* 1937, pl. 54. J. Harris *Artist and the country house* 1979, 108.

Riby, Lincs
M. Binney *and* A. Hills *Elysian gardens* 1979, 38.

Richardson, Winterbourne Bassett, Wilts
V.C.H. *Wiltshire* v. 12, 1983, 188.

Richings near Colnbrook, Bucks
R. Ackermann *Repository* v. 4, 1824, pl. 8.
W.W.J. Gendall *Views* v. 2, 1830, 129. *Gdn History* v. 4 no. 1, 1976, 47,50.

Richmond (Sir Matthew Decker), London
Society of Gentlemen *England displayed* v. 1, 1769, 222.

Richmond (Robert Dodsley), London
Gdn History v. 8 no. 2, 1980, 45–46,48.

Richmond Gardens (Ormonde Lodge, Richmond Lodge), Richmond, London
J. Laurence *New system of agriculture* 1726, frontispiece. E. Curll *Rarities of Richmond: being exact descriptions of the Royal Hermitage and Merlin's Cave* 1736. T. Badeslade *and* J. Rocque *Vitruvius Brittanicus* 1739, pls. 6–9. A. Young *Farmer's tour through East of England* v. 2, 1771, 247–48. *New display of the beauties of England* v. 2, 1787, 284–86. A. Robertson *Topographical survey of the Great Road* v. 1, 1792, 26–29. J. *and* J. Boydell *History of the River Thames* v. 2, 1796, 30,34–37. British Museum *Catalogue of maps, prints* 1829, 285. F. Kielmansegge *Diary* 1902, 73–76. A.P. Oppé *Drawings of Paul and Thomas Sandby* 1947, 48. R.I.B.A. *Catalogue* v. A, 1968, 17. *C.L. Annual* 1970, 82–83. *Architectura* v. 4 no. 2, 1974, 181–91. D. Stroud *Capability Brown* 1975, 123–28,237. H.M. Colvin *History of the King's Works* v. 5, 1976, 221–26. *Eighteenth-century Studies* v. 10, 1976, 1–20. P. Willis *Charles Bridgeman* 1977, 181–82. L. Fleming *and* A. Gore *English garden* 1979, 112. J. Harris *Artist and the country house* 1979, 171,327. K. Rorschach *Early Georgian landscape garden* 1983, 58–63.
See also Kew Gardens

Richmond Palace, Richmond, London
Surrey Archaeological Collections v. 5, 1871, 82–85,88–90. H.M. Colvin *History of the King's Works* v. 3, 1975, 125; v. 4, 1982, 226,231. R. Strong *Renaissance garden in England* 1979, 97–103.

Richmond Park, Richmond, London
British Museum *Catalogue of maps, prints* 1829, 285. E.W. Brayley *and* J. Britton *Topographical history of Surrey* v. 3, 65. T. Nelson *Richmond Park* 1883. C. De Vere *Handbook of Richmond Park* 1909. H.R. Hall *Round the year in Richmond Park* 1923. C.L. Collenette *History of Richmond Park* 1937. Ministry of Work *Trees in Richmond Park* 1961. R. Church *Royal Parks of London* 1965, 45–52. *C.L.* v. 146, 1969, 1574–75; v. 147, 1970, 77. H. Thurston *Royal parks for the people* 1974, 60–69. G. Williams *Royal parks of London* 1978, 151–72. P.F. Jones *Richmond Park* 1983.
See also White Lodge

Richmond Park. Isabella Plantation, Richmond London
C.L. v. 145, 1969, 1090–91. M. Allan *Fisons guide* 1970, 12–13. *Garden* 1980, 245–48. A. Hellyer *Gardens of genius* 1980, 81.

Rickmansworth Park, Rickmansworth, Herts
J. Harris *Artist and the country house* 1979, 263.

Riddings House, Riddings, Derbyshire
J. Hort. Cottage Gdnr v. 57, 1877, 424–26.

Riddlesworth Hall, Riddlesworth, Norfolk
J.P. Neale *Views* v. 3, 1820.

Ridgemead, Englefield Green, Surrey
C.L. v. 87, 1940, 144–48,172–76.

Ridgeway House, Mill Hill, Barnet, London
D. Lysons *Environs of London* v. 3, 1795, 8; *Supplement* 1811, 195–96. L.W. Dillwyn *Hortus Collinsonianus* 1843. J.C. Loudon *Arboretum et fruticetum Britannicum* v. 1, 1844, 56–57. N.G. Brett-James *Life of Peter Collinson* 1926, passim. N.G. Brett-James *Story of Manor and Park of Hendon* 1932, 81–85. N.G. Brett-James *Story of Mill Hill Village* 1938, 43–46. V.C.H. *Middlesex* v. 5, 1976, 8. *Gdn History* v. 9 no. 1, 1981, 59–60.

Ridglands, Wimbledon, Merton, London
G.C. i 1901, 398.

Rievaulx Terrace near Hemsley, N. Yorks
Apollo v. 95, 1972, 418. K. Lemmon *Gardens of Britain* v. 5, 1978, 70–71. L. Fleming *and* A. Gore *English garden* 1979, 125–26.
See also Duncombe Park

Riffhams near Chelmsford, Essex
T. Wright *History . . . of Essex* v. 1, 1836, 121. *Garden* 1983, 366.

Rimpton near Yeovil, Somerset
Proc. Somerset Archaeological and Natural History Soc. v. 104, 1960, 91–95.

Ringwood Hall near Chesterfield, Derbyshire
Cottage Gdnr v. 18, 1857, 358–60. *J. Hort. Cottage Gdnr* v. 55, 1876, 214–16.

Ringwould House, Ringwould, Kent
C. Greenwood *Epitome of county history . . . v. 1: Kent* 1838, 433.

Ripley Castle, Ripley, N. Yorks
Official guide. T. Allen *New . . . history of . . . York* v. 3, 1831, 422. F.O. Morris *Series of picturesque views* v. 1, 63. *J. Hort. Cottage Gdnr* N.S., v. 38, 1899, 238–39. *C.L.* v. 72, 1932, 182–88, 210–16. Historical MSS Commission *Architectural history* v. 2, 1970, item 2016. D. Stroud *Capability Brown* 1975, 238. K. Lemmon *Gardens of Britain* v. 5, 1978, 104–06.

Ripple Court, Ripple, Kent
C. Greenwood *Epitome of county history . . . v. 1: Kent* 1838, 432.

Risby Hall, Rowley, Humberside
A. Young *Six months tour through North of England* v. 1, 1771, 214–18. V.C.H. *York: East Riding* v. 4, 1979, 129.

Risden *see* Rushden Place

Rise Park, Rise, Humberside
D. Stroud *Capability Brown* 1975, 238.

Riskins, Iver, Bucks
S. Switzer *Ichnographia rustica* v. 3, 1742: Appendix, 9–10, pl. 39. M.R. Brownell *Alexander Pope & the arts of Georgian England* 1978, 229–32.

Rivenhall Place, Rivenhall, Essex
H. Repton *Sketches* 1794, 4–5. G. Virtue *Picturesque beauties of Great Britain: Essex* 1831, 30. T. Wright *History . . . of Essex* v. 1, 1836, 255. F.G. Emmison *Catalogue of maps in Essex Record Office* 1947, 10, 35, pl. 13. D. Stroud *Humphry Repton* 1962, 41. G. Carter et al. *Humphry Repton* 1982, 151.

River Hall, Sevenoaks, Kent
C. Greenwood *Epitome of county history . . . v. 1: Kent* 1838, 97.

Rivernook near Staines, Surrey
G. Beard *Thomas H. Mawson* 1976, 61.

Riversdale (Mr Drummond), Twickenham, London
Tombleson's Thames 1834.

Rivington Pike, Rivington, Lancs
G. Beard *Thomas H. Mawson* 1976, 61.

Robert Louis Stevenson Memorial Garden, Bournemouth, Dorset
Dorset Year Book 1977, 133–36.

Roby Hall, Roby, Merseyside
E. Baines *History . . . of Lancaster* v. 4, 1836, 10.

Rochdale. Falinge Park, Greater Manchester
G.C. ii 1925, 281.

Roche Abbey near Rotherham, S. Yorks
W. Gilpin *Observations, relative chiefly to picturesque beauty* v. 1, 1792, 21–24.

Rochester. Deanery, Kent
G. Jekyll and G.S. Elgood *Some English gardens* 1904, 93–95.

Rochester Castle, Rochester, Kent
Garden v. 1, 1872, 140–43.

Rochford House, Rochford, Hereford and Worcester
J. Hort. Cottage Gdnr N.S., v. 34, 1897, 15–16.

Rockbeare House, Rockbeare, Devon
R. Ackermann *Repository* v. 11, 1828, pl. 2. W.W.J. Gendall *Views* v. 2, 1830, 126. *C.L.* v. 67, 1930, 570–76. Lady Rockley *Historic gardens of England* 1938, 184–85.

Rockingham near Boyle, Co. Roscommon, Eire
B. Jones *Follies & grottoes* 1974, 72–74. E. Malins and Knight of Glin *Lost demesnes* 1976, 183–84.

Rockingham Castle, Rockingham, Northants
Official guide. *C.L.* v. 8, 1900, 80–83, 112–14; v. 50, 1921, 44–51, 76–82. G. Jekyll and G.S. Elgood *Some English gardens* 1904, 33–35. G. Jekyll *Garden ornament* 1918, 278. Lady Rockley *Historic gardens of England* 1938, 70–71. M. Allan *Fisons guide* 1970, 231–32. *Northamptonshire Past and Present* v. 5 no. 3, 1975, 230–31. J. Anthony *Gardens of Britain* v. 6, 1979, 137–39. T. Hinde *Stately gardens of Britain* 1983, 94–101.

Rockville, Black Rock, Dublin, Eire
Cottage Gdnr v. 27, 1862, 499–502, 517–19. E. Malins and P. Bowe *Irish gardens and demesnes* 1980, 59.

Rodborough Court, Stroud, Glos
G. Beard *Thomas H. Mawson* 1976, 61.

Rode Hall, Rode Heath, Cheshire
J.P. Neale *Views* 2nd Series, v. 1, 1824. *Jones's views* 1829. D. Stroud *Humphry Repton* 1962. G. Carter et al. *Humphry Repton* 1982, 150.

Rodmarton Manor, Rodmarton, Glos
C.L. v. 69, 1931, 422–27; v. 160, 1976, 1844–46; v. 164, 1978, 1178–81. A. Lees-Milne and R. Verey *Englishwoman's garden* 1980, 31–34. J. Sales *West Country gardens* 1980, 95–98. *Garden* 1982, 263–68. T. Hinde *Stately gardens of Britain* 1983, 52–59.

Roehampton Grove, Roehampton, Wandsworth, London
J. Hassell *Seats near London* 1804–05.

Roehampton House, Roehampton, Wandsworth, London
J.P. Neale *Views* 2nd Series, v. 3, 1826. *C.L.* v. 38, 1915, 232–39.

Roehampton Park, Roehampton, Wandsworth, London
J. Evelyn *Diary* v. 4, 1955, 105.

Roehampton Priory, Roehampton, Wandsworth, London
R. Ackermann *Repository* v. 9, 1827, pl. 7.
W.W.J. Gendall *Views* v. 1, 1830, 57–58.

Rokeby Hall near Barnard Castle, Co. Durham
D. Defoe *Tour* v. 3, 1778, 171–72. *C.L.* v. 2, 1897, 405–07; v. 42, 1917, 276–82, 300–05.

Rolleston Hall, Rolleston, Leics
J. Nichols *History . . . of county of Leicester* v. 2, 1798, 443.

Rolleston Hall, Rolleston, Staffs
Cottage Gdnr v. 13, 1855, 280–81. F.O. Morris *Series of picturesque views* v. 4, 7. *J. Hort. Cottage Gdnr* v. 54, 1875, 533–35; v. 55, 1876, 27–29. *G.C.* i 1896, 419–20, 421.

Rolls Park near Chigwell, Essex
J.P. Neale *Views* 2nd Series, v. 3, 1826.

Rood Ashton near Trowbridge, Wilts
Scottish Gdnr v. 14, 1865, 357–59, 375–77; v. 15, 1866, 32–34. *J. Hort. Cottage Gdnr* v. 49, 1873, 513–15; N.S., v. 11, 1885, 518–19; N.S., v. 46, 1903, 141–45. *V.C.H. Wiltshire* v. 8, 1965, 204.

Rookery near Dorking, Surrey
J.P. Neale *Views* v. 4, 1821. W.W.J. Gendall *Views* v. 2, 1830, 38–40. E.W. Brayley *and* J. Britton *Topographical history of Surrey* v. 5, 1848, 109–10. W. Keane *Beauties of Surrey* 1849, 146–48.

Rook's Nest, Lambourn, Berks
R. Bisgrove *Gardens of Britain* v. 3, 1978, 151–52.

Rook's Nest near Godstone, Surrey
W. Keane *Beauties of Surrey* 1849, 64–66. *Gdning World* v. 5, 1889, 626–27. *J. Hort. Cottage Gdnr* N.S., v. 40, 1900, 418–20.

Rooksbury near Wickham, Hants
J. Hewetson *Architectural and picturesque views of noble mansions in Hampshire* 1830. E.F. Prosser *Select illustrations of Hampshire* 1833. *J. Hort. Cottage Gdnr* N.S., v. 22, 1891, 342–43. B. Jones *Follies & grottoes* 1974, 339.

Ropes near Haslemere, Surrey
G.C. ii 1937, 297.

Rose Castle near Carlisle, Cumbria
W. Hutchinson *History of county of Cumberland* v. 2, 1794, 433, 438.

Rosebank Gardens, Malvern, Hereford and Worcester
G.C. ii 1892, 675, 677; i 1892, 497.

Rosedale House, Richmond, London
E.W. Brayley *and* J. Britton *Topographical history of Surrey* v. 3, 107.

Rosehill, Falmouth, Cornwall
G.C. ii 1905, 103–04.

Rosemoor near Torrington, Devon
Garden 1977, 210–15. P.M. Synge *Gardens of Britain* v. 1, 1977, 71–74. A. Lees-Milne *and* R. Verey *Englishwoman's garden* 1980, 97–100. *G.C.* v. 191 no. 24, 1982, 32–33.

Rosemundy House, St Agnes, Cornwall
J. Hort. Cottage Gdnr v. 58, 1877, 476–77.

Roseneath near Helensburgh, Strathclyde
J.P. Neale *Views* v. 6, 1823. *Scottish Gdnr and Northern Forester* v. 8, 1913, 261–63.

Rosherville Gardens, Gravesend, Kent
C.L. v. 131, 1962, 224–25.

Ross Priory near Balloch, Strathclyde
J.P. Neale *Views* v. 6, 1823. A.A. Tait *Landscape garden in Scotland* 1980, passim. G.A. Little *Scotland's gardens* 1981, 236.

Rossdhu near Luss, Strathclyde
Scottish Gdnr and Northern Forester v. 8, 1913, 321–23. A.A. Tait *Landscape garden in Scotland* 1980, passim.

Rossdohan Island, Co. Kerry, Eire
J. Royal Hort. Soc. 1966, 9–12. E. Hyams *Irish gardens* 1967, 67–75. *C.L.* v. 162, 1977, 84–85. A. Hellyer *Gardens of genius* 1980, 53–55. E. Malins *and* P. Bowe *Irish gardens and demesnes* 1980, 110–15. Knight of Glin *and* P. Bowe *Gardens of outstanding historic interest in . . . Ireland* 1980. *Moorea* v. 2, 1983, 39–42.

Rossie Castle near Montrose, Tayside
F.O. Morris *Series of picturesque views* v. 5, 73.

Rossie Priory near Inchture, Tayside
Scottish Gdnr v. 4, 1855, 392–94. *Scottish Gdnr and Northern Forester* v. 7, 1912, 286–88. *G.C.* ii 1876,

Rossie Priory (*Cont.*)
653,655–56; i 1877, 464–65. G.A. Little *Scotland's gardens* 1981, 163–64.

Rosslyn House, Hampstead, London
W. Keane *Beauties of Middlesex* 1850, 139–40.

Rossmore Park near Monaghan, Co. Monaghan, Ulster
F.O. Morris *Series of picturesque views* v. 3, 63.

Rostrevor, Rostrevor, Co. Down, Ulster
J. Ross-of-Bladensburg *List of trees and shrubs grown in the grounds of Rostrevor House, Co. Down* 1911. *Irish Gdning* v. 10, 1915, 115–16; v. 11, 1916, 129–31; v. 12, 1917, 137–38; v. 13, 1918, 129–32; v. 14, 1919, 114–16, 151; v. 15, 1920, 81–83; v. 16, 1921, 76,88–89,97–100, 134; v. 17, 1922, 17–18,25–26. *New Flora and Silva* v. 1, 1929, 122–23. R.H.S. *Conifers in cultivation* 1932, 215.

Rothamsted near Harpenden, Herts
G.C. i 1875, 720–21,725. N. Pevsner *Hertfordshire* 1953, 195.

Rotherfield Hall, Rotherfield, E. Sussex
C.L. v. 26, 1909, 228–36. *Architectural Review* v. 34, 1913, 19–20, pls. 12–14. G. Jekyll *Garden ornament* 1918, 177.

Rotherfield Park near Alton, Hants
E.F. Prosser *Select illustrations of Hampshire* 1833. *C.L.* v. 103, 1948, 826–29,878–81. A. Paterson *Gardens of Britain* v. 2, 1978, 137–38.

Rotherhithe, Southwark, London
H.M. Colvin *History of the King's Works* v. 2, 1963, 992.

Rotherwas near Hereford, Hereford and Worcester
J.P. Neale *Views* 2nd Series, v. 2, 1825.

Rothley, Northumberland
D. Stroud *Capability Brown* 1975, 137,238.

Rougham Hall, Rougham, Suffolk
G.C. ii 1896, 491–92.

Roughhills, Colvend near Dalbeattie, Dumfries and Galloway
G.A. Little *Scotland's gardens* 1981, 264.

Round Green House, Darfield, S. Yorks
Historical MSS Commission *Architectural history* v. 2, 1970, item 1324.

Roundhay Park, Leeds, W. Yorks
C. Goodall *Illustrated royal handbook to Roundhay Park* 1872. *Thoresby Society Miscellanea* v. 2, 1889, 215–49.

B. Jones *Follies & grottoes* 1974, 404. K. Lemmon *Gardens of Britain* v. 5, 1978, 159–60.

Roundlewood, Crieff, Tayside
Scottish Gdnr and Northern Forester v. 7, 1912, 681–82.

Rounton Grange, East Rounton, N. Yorks
C.L. v. 37, 1915, 906–12.

Rous Lench Court, Rous Lench, Hereford and Worcester
C.L. v. 6, 1899, 336–42. V.C.H. *Worcester* v. 3, 1913, 498. G. Jekyll *Garden ornament* 1918, 154. N. Pevsner *Worcestershire* 1968, 256. M. Binney *and* A. Hills *Elysian gardens* 1979, 5.

Rousdon House, Rousdon, Devon
G.C. i 1903, 17–18.

Rousham House, Rousham, Oxfordshire
R. Plot *Natural history of Oxfordshire* 1705, 266. *C.L.* v. 27, 1910, 306–15; v. 99, 1946, 1084–87,1130–33. *Art J.* 1912, 33–41. G. Jekyll *Garden ornament* 1918, 125, 129,228,247. H. Walpole *Visits to country seats. Walpole Society* v. 7, 1927/28, 25–26. Lady Rockley *Historic gardens of England* 1938, 158–59. M. Jourdain *Work of William Kent* 1948, 80–81. O. Siren *China and gardens of Europe of 18th century* 1950, 32–34. *Connoisseur* v. 153, 1963, 158–65. *G.C.* i 1964, 272. C. Hussey *English gardens and landscapes 1700–1750* 1967, 147–53. P. Coats *Great gardens of Britain* 1967, 186–93. *Studio International* v. 186, 1973, 121–25. *Apollo* v. 100, 1974, 282–91. B. Jones *Follies & grottoes* 1974, 378.
J. Sherwood *and* N. Pevsner *Oxfordshire* 1974, 743–46. J. St Bodfan Gruffyd *Protecting historic landscapes* 1977, 37–44. P. Willis *Charles Bridgeman* 1977, 182.
R. Bisgrove *Gardens of Britain* v. 3, 1978, 153–54. D. Jarrett *English landscape garden* 1978, 30–41.
L. Fleming *and* A. Gore *English garden* 1979, 101–04. J. Harris *Artist and the country house* 1979, 282.
M. Hadfield *et al. British gardeners* 1980, 44,188.
M. Batey *Oxford gardens* 1982, 104–05. D. Watkin *English vision* 1982, 24–27. T. Hinde *Stately gardens of Britain* 1983, 32–39. K. Rorschach *Early Georgian landscape garden* 1983, 19–20,25. Victoria and Albert Museum *The common chronicle* 1983, 29. V.C.H. *Oxford* v. 11, 1983, 161,193. *Gdn History* v. 11 no. 2, 1983, 125–32. D. Jacques *Georgian gardens* 1983, 38.

Rowallane, Saintfield, Co. Down, Ulster
Official guide. *Irish Gdning* v. 7, 1912, 161–63; v. 14, 1919, 81–82,97–99,150–51. *G.C.* ii 1928, 210–11; i 1929, 355; ii 1960, 240–41,245; ii 1962, 130–31. *New Flora and Silva* v. 2, 1930, 171–79,230–38. *C.L.* v. 79, 1936, 220–26. *J. Royal Hort. Soc.* 1956, 473–80; 1964, 365–72. P. Coats *Great gardens of Britain* 1967, 72–77. E. Hyams *Irish gardens* 1967, 115–23. M. Allan *Fisons*

Rowallane (*Cont.*)
guide 1970, 372–73. G.S. Thomas *Gardens of National Trust* 1979, 203–05. E. Malins *and* P. Bowe *Irish gardens and demesnes* 1980, 130–32.

Rowfant near East Grinstead, W. Sussex
C.L. v. 50, 1921, 686–92.

Royal Botanic Society *see* London. Regent's Park

Royal Fort (The Fort), Bristol, Avon
H. Repton *Observations* 1803, 7–9. *C.L.* v. 39, 1916, 646–52. J. Harris *Catalogue of British drawings . . . in American collections* 1971, 176,177. G. Carter *et al. Humphry Repton* 1982, 161.

Royal Horticultural Society, Chiswick, Hounslow, London
Catalogue of fruits cultivated in the garden of Horticultural Society of London at Chiswick 1826; ed. 3, 1842. W. Keane *Beauties of Middlesex* 1850, 170–73. *Scottish Gdnr* v. 1, 1852, 219–21; v. 7, 1858, 356–58,450–52, 513–17. *J. Hort. Cottage Gdnr* v. 46, 1871, 359–61; N.S., v. 7, 1883, 338–39. *Gdning World* v. 5, 1889, 308. *G.C.* ii 1895, 233–34. *C.L.* v. 3, 1898, 616–17. *J. Royal Hort. Soc.* 1940, 391–98. H.R. Fletcher *Story of the Royal Horticultural Society 1804–1968* 1969, passim.

Royal Horticultural Society, South Kensington, London
A. Murray *Book of the Royal Horticultural Society 1862–1863* 1863. N. Cole *Royal parks and gardens of London* 1877, 11–14. H.R. Fletcher *Story of the Royal Horticultural Society 1804–1968* 1969, passim. G.L.C. *Survey of London v. 38: Museums area of South Kensington and Westminster* 1975, 124–32.

Royal Horticultural Society Gardens (includes Oakwood), Wisley, Surrey
Official guide. *G.C.* i 1883, 178,183; ii 1887, 225–26, 365–66; i 1889, 522–23; ii 1893, 497,499 (Oakwood); i 1914, 229,230,231. *Gdning World* v. 2, 1886, 806–07 (Oakwood). *C.L.* v. 2, 1897, 319–21,371–72; v. 6, 1899, 230–34; v. 6, 1899, 230–34; v. 8, 1900, 304–10; v. 10, 1901, 101–04 (Oakwood); v. 73, 1933, 170–75; v. 153, 1973, 743–46; v. 166, 1979, 646–48. *Gdnrs Mag.* 1903, 826–28. *J. Hort. Cottage Gdnr* N.S., v. 48, 1904, 29–30. *J. Royal Hort. Soc.* 1946, 215–24; 1949, 133–44; 1964, 363–64; 1970, 104–07. *Architect and Building News* v. 226, 1964, 667–70. H. Evans *Beautiful gardens of Britain* 1974, 59–60. T. Wright *Gardens of Britain* v. 4, 1978, 236–43.

Royal Victoria Park *see* Bath

Roydon Hall near Yalding, Kent
C.L. v. 87, 1940, 198–202.

Royds Hall near Bradford, W. Yorks
Garden v. 45, 1894, 83.

Roynton Cottage, Rivington Pike, Lancs
G. Beard *Thomas H. Mawson* 1976, 62.

Royton Hall, Greater Manchester
J. Aikin *Description of the country . . . round Manchester* 1795, 239.

Rozel Manor, Jersey, Channel Islands
C.L. v. 149, 1971, 732–34.

Ruckmans, Oakwood Hill, Surrey
L. Weaver *Houses and gardens by E.L. Lutyens* 1913, 5–6. J. Brown *Gardens of a golden afternoon* 1982, 161.

Rudding Park near Harrogate, N. Yorks
Official guide. H. Repton *Sketches* 1794, 58–59. *C.L.* v. 105, 1949, 254–57,310; v. 149, 1971, 1592–94. D. Stroud *Humphry Repton* 1962, 53. H. Evans *Beautiful gardens of Britain* 1974, 107–08. K. Lemmon *Gardens of Britain* v. 5, 1978, 106–10. G. Carter *et al. Humphry Repton* 1982, 164.

Rufford Abbey near Ollerton, Notts
T. Quincy *Short tour in the Midland counties* 1775, 87–88. *J. Hort. Cottage Gdnr* v. 58, 1877, 233–36. *G.C.* i 1908, 249,250. *Gdnrs Mag.* 1910, 471–73. J. Anthony *Gardens of Britain* v. 6, 1979, 140–44. N. Pevsner *Nottinghamshire* 1979, 302–03.

Rufford Hall, Rufford, Lancs
J.P. Neale *Views* v. 2, 1819. E. Baines *History . . . of Lancaster* v. 3, 1836, 432.

Rufford Old Hall, Rufford, Lancs
E. Baines *History . . . of Lancaster* v. 3, 1836, 431. *C.L.* v. 66, 1929, 528–35.

Rug near Corwen, Clwyd
H. Repton *Observations* 1803, 138–40. *J. Hort. Cottage Gdnr* N.S., v. 20, 1890, 68–70. D. Stroud *Humphry Repton* 1962, 79–80. G. Carter *et al. Humphry Repton* 1982, 165. *Garden* 1983, 366. *C.L.* v. 174, 1983, 906–09,986–89.

Ruperra near Caerphilly, Mid Glamorgan
J.P. Neale *Views* v. 5, 1822.

Rushbrooke Hall, Rushbrooke, Suffolk
C.L. v. 14, 1903, 542–51. T. Wright *Arbors & grottos* 1979.

Rushden Place, Rushden, Herts
H. Chauncy *Historical antiquities of Hertfordshire* 1700, 78.

Rushen Abbey, Isle of Man
Proc. Isle of Man Natural History and Antiquarian Soc. v. 8 no. 3, 1976/78, 246–47.

Rushton Hall, Rushton, Northants
J. Morton *Natural history of Northamptonshire* 1712, 493. J.P. Neale *Views* 2nd Series, v. 3, 1826. F.O. Morris *Series of picturesque views* v. 4, 11. *C.L.* v. 26, 1909, 454–61. *Garden* v. 47, 1895, 267. G. Beard *Thomas H. Mawson* 1976, 62.

Ruskin Park *see* Lambeth

Russborough near Blessington, Co. Wicklow, Eire
C.L. v. 81, 1937, 94–99; v. 134, 1963, 1464–67, 1623, 1686–87.

Russell House, Broadway, Hereford and Worcester
C.L. v. 29, 1911, 57–61.

Russell Park near Watford, Herts
G. Beard *Thomas H. Mawson* 1976, 62.

Russell Square, Bloomsbury, Camden, London
G. Carter *et al. Humphry Repton* 1982, 157.

Ruthin Castle, Ruthin, Clwyd
J. Hort. Cottage Gdnr N.S., v. 22, 1891, 306–07.

Ruxley Lodge near Esher, Surrey
J. Hort. Cottage Gdnr N.S., v. 15, 1887, 143–44. *G.C.* ii 1892, 492; i 1899, 294–95.

Rycote near Thame, Oxford
R. Plot *Natural history of Oxfordshire* 1705, 161. J. Beeverell *Les delices de la Grande Bretagne* v. 5, 1707, 872. L. Knyff *and* J. Kip *Britannia illustrata* v. 1, 1714. M. Macartney *English houses & gardens* 1908, pl. 9. R. Dutton *English garden* 1937, pl. 49. D. Stroud *Capability Brown* 1975, 159–60. J. Harris *Artist and the country house* 1979, 103.

Rydal Hall, Rydal, Cumbria
C. Holme *Gardens of England in Northern counties* 1911, pls. 109–10. G. Beard *Thomas H. Mawson* 1976, 62.

Ryelands near Lancaster, Lancs
Gdning World v. 3, 1886, 213–14.

Rymans near Chichester, W. Sussex
T. Wright *Gardens of Britain* v. 4, 1978, 177–79.

Ryshworth Hall, Bingley, W. Yorks
Bradford Illustrated Weekly Telegraph *Series of picturesque views* 1885. I. Hall *Samuel Buck's Yorkshire sketchbook* 1979, 158.

Sacombe Park, Sacombe, Herts
P. Willis *Charles Bridgeman* 1977, 182.

Sadler's Wells, Clerkenwell, Islington
W. Wroth *London pleasure gardens of the eighteenth century* 1896, 43–53.

Saighton Grange, Saighton, Cheshire
H.I. Triggs *Formal gardens in England and Scotland* 1902, 35. C. Holme *Gardens of England in Midland & Eastern counties* 1908, pls. 100–02. *C.L.* v. 23, 1908, 738–48.

St Adrians, Crail, Fife
G.A. Little *Scotland's gardens* 1981, 164–65.

St Alban's Court, Nonington, Kent
C. Greenwood *Epitome of county history . . . v. 1: Kent* 1838, 349. *Architectural Review* v. 21, 1967, 298–301.

St Albans House, Windsor, Berks
J. Beeverell *Les delices de la Grande Bretagne* v. 5, 1707, 872. L. Knyff *and* J. Kip *Britannia illustrata* v. 1, 1714. M. Macartney *English houses & gardens* 1908, pl. 25.

St Andrews Priory, St Andrews, Fife
G.M. v. 7, 1831, 679–80.

St Andrews University. Botanic Garden, St Andrews, Fife
Scottish Field v. 122 no. 870, 1975, 64.

St Anne's, Clontarf, Co. Dublin, Eire
Garden v. 26, 1884, 512–15, 517. *G.C.* i 1898, 202. G. Jekyll *and* G.S. Elgood *Some English gardens* 1904, 101–03. *Irish Gdning* v. 3, 1908, 155; v. 13, 1917, 50. *Irish Landscape J.* v. 1, 1971, 23–25. E. Malins *and* P. Bowe *Irish gardens and demesnes* 1980, 47–50.

St Ann's Hill, Chertsey, Surrey
G.M. v. 13, 1837, 113–14. E.W. Brayley *and* J. Britton *Topographical history of Surrey* v. 2, 1841, 236–38. W. Keane *Beauties of Surrey* 1849, 45–48. R. Webber *Percy Cane* 1975, 100–01, 184. B. Jones *Follies & grottoes* 1974, 395.

St Audries near Watchet, Somerset
J. Collinson *History . . . of Somersetshire* v. 3, 1791, 497. *G.C.* ii 1884, 555–56; ii 1888, 627–28.

St Catherine's Court near Bath, Avon
C.L. v. 4, 1898, 792–96; v. 13, 1903, 494–96; v. 20, 1906, 738–47, 774–79. R. Blomfield *Formal garden in England* 1901, 115. *G.C.* i 1902, 343; ii 1909, 361. H.I. Triggs *Formal gardens in England and Scotland* 1902, 13–14. R.S. Nichols *English pleasure gardens* 1903, 139. G. Jekyll *Garden ornament* 1918, 52, 55, 72, 75,

St Catherine's Court *(Cont.)*

282. Lady Rockley *Historic gardens of England* 1938, 112–13. N.T. Newton *Design on the land* 1971, 188.

St Catherine's Farm near Bredon's Norton, Hereford and Worcester
R. Sidwell *West Midland gardens* 1981, 84–85.

St Catherine's Lodge, Regent's Park, Westminster, London
R.I.B.A. *Catalogue* v. G–K, 1973, 119.

St Chad's Well, Camden, London
W. Wroth *London pleasure gardens of the eighteenth century* 1896, 72–74.

St Clairtown near Kirkaldy, Fife
G.M. v. 15, 1839, 50–57.

St Cleran's near Loughrea, Co. Galway, Eire
J.P. Neale *Views* v. 6, 1823.

St Clere, Kemsing, Kent
C.L. v. 131, 1962, 450–53, 518–21; v. 143, 1968, 973. Historical MSS Commission *Architectural history* v. 3, 1971, item 2989.

St Columb's near Church Hill, Co. Donegal, Eire
C.L. v. 157, 1975, 1326–30. E. Malins *and* P. Bowe *Irish gardens and demesnes* 1980, 134–35.

St Donat's Castle, St Donat's, S. Glamorgan
C.L. v. 22, 1907, 270–79, 315.

St Enda, Fathfarnham, Co. Dublin, Eire
Irish Gdning v. 6, 1911, 26–28.

St Fagan's Castle, St Fagan's, S. Glamorgan
J. Hort. Cottage Gdnr N.S., v. 1, 1880, 264–65; N.S., v. 40, 1900, 484–86. *Gdnrs. Mag.* 1898, 622–23. *C.L.* v. 12, 1902, 366–77. *G.C.* i 1912, 179–81, 182. G. Jekyll *Garden ornament* 1918, 124. *Amgueddfa* no. 24, 1976, 30–37. M. Binney *and* A. Hills *Elysian gardens* 1979, 18. Royal Commission on Ancient and Historical Monuments in Wales *Inventory of the ancient monuments in Glamorgan* v. 4, 1981, 252.

St Fort near Leuchars, Fife
Scottish Gdnr and Northern Forester v. 9, 1914, 109–10.

St George's Hill, Weybridge, Surrey
J. Royal Hort. Soc. 1956, 84–93.

St Giles's House, Wimborne St Giles, Dorset
G.C. i 1881, 561–62; ii 1909, 213–14. R. Pococke *Travels through England* v. 2, 1889, 137–38. *C.L.* v. 16, 1904, 270–72; v. 37, 1915, 336–42; v. 94, 1943, 552; v. 125, 1959, 1252. J. Newman *and* N. Pevsner *Dorset* 1972, 472–73.

St Helena Gardens, Rotherhithe, Southwark, London
W. Wroth *London pleasure gardens of the eighteenth century* 1896, 238–40.

St Ives, Bingley, W. Yorks
Bradford Illustrated Weekly Telegraph *Series of picturesque views* 1885.

St James's Palace, Westminster, London
L. Knyff *and* J. Kip *Britannia illustrata* v. 1, 1714. H. Overton *Britannia illustrata* c.1724, pl. 4. R. Strong *Renaissance garden in England* 1979, 19, 161, 188–89. H.M. Colvin *History of the King's Works* v. 4, 1982, 245.

St James's Park *see* London

St John's, Ryde, Isle of Wight
R. Worsley *History of the Isle of Wight* 1781. D. Stroud *Humphry Repton* 1962, 106. G. Carter *et al. Humphry Repton* 1982, 155.

St John's, Sutton at Hone, Kent
C. Greenwood *Epitome of county history . . . v. 1: Kent* 1838, 72.

St John's Jerusalem near Dartford, Kent
T. Wright *Gardens of Britain* v. 4, 1978, 84–85. G.S. Thomas *Gardens of National Trust* 1979, 205–06.

St Julians, Sevenoaks, Kent
C. Greenwood *Epitome of county history . . . v. 1: Kent* 1838, 97. D. Jacques *Georgian gardens* 1983, 188.

St Leonard's Hill near Windsor, Berks
R. Ackermann *Repository* v. 3, 1824, pl. 13. W.W.J. Gendall *Views* v. 2, 1830, 8–9. *G.M.* v. 9, 1833, 652. *C.L.* v. 9, 1901, 368–72. G. Carter *et al. Humphry Repton* 1982, 148.

St Loe's, Henley-in-Arden, Warwickshire
C.L. v. 54, 1923, 473–74.

St Margaret's, Twickenham, London
R. Ackermann *Repository* v. 3, 1824, pls. 19–20. W.W.J. Gendall *Views* v. 2, 1830, 68, 71. *G.M.* v. 13, 1837, 111–12. W. Keane *Beauties of Middlesex* 1850, 98–101. A.C.B. Urwin *Railshead* 1974, 14–15.

St Mary's Church (Tradescant Trust Museum), Lambeth, London
Official guide. M.P.G. Draper *Lambeth's open spaces* 1979, 52. *G.C.* v. 189 no. 3, 1981, 24–25.

St Mary's Isle, Kirkcudbright, Dumfries and Galloway
G.M. v. 9, 1833, 7. *Garden* v. 68, 1905, 191–92.

Saint Mary's Pleasance, Haddington, Lothian
G.A. Little *Scotland's gardens* 1981, 105–08.

St Michael's Mount near Penzance, Cornwall
P.M. Synge *Gardens of Britain* v. 1, 1977, 115–17.
G.S. Thomas *Gardens of National Trust* 1979, 206.

St Nicholas, Wallingford, Oxfordshire
R. Bisgrove *Gardens of Britain* v. 3, 1978, 156.

St Nicholas near Richmond, N. Yorks
J. Royal Hort. Soc. 1931, 155–64. *C.L.* v. 80, 1936, 626–32. M. Allan *Fisons guide* 1970, 258–59. K. Lemmon *Gardens of Britain* v. 5, 1978, 110–12. A. Lees-Milne *and* R. Verey *Englishwoman's garden* 1980, 78–79.

St Osyth's Priory, St Osyth, Essex
G.C. i 1895, 37–39. *C.L.* v. 14, 1903, 304–09; v. 44, 1918, 550–56,576; v. 124, 1958, 360–61. F.G. Emmison *Catalogue of maps in Essex Record Office* 1947, 60; 2nd Supplt, 1964, 12,26.

St Paul's Walden Bury, St Paul's Walden, Herts
C.L. v. 119, 1956, 472–75,532–35. P. Coats *Great gardens of Britain* 1967, 56–65. C. Hussey *English gardens and landscapes 1700–1750* 1967, 84–88. M. Allan *Fisons guide* 1970, 19–20. *Studio International* v. 193, 1977, 90–94. R. Bisgrove *Gardens of Britain* v. 3, 1978, 156–57.

St Peter's, Dalbeattie, Dumfries and Galloway
G.M. v. 9, 1833, 12–13.

St Peter's Home, Woolverstone, Suffolk
J. Brown *Gardens of a golden afternoon* 1982, 165.

St Pierre near Chepstow, Gwent
R. Ackermann *Repository* v. 6, 1825, pl. 2.
W.W.J. Gendall *Views* v. 2, 1830, 43.

St Roche's Arboretum, West Dean, W. Sussex
T. Wright *Gardens of Britain* v. 4, 1978, 179–80.

St Serf's House, Roehampton, Wandsworth, London
C.L. v. 48, 1920, 566–73.

St Valery near Bray, Co. Wicklow, Eire
E. Malins *and* Knight of Glin *Lost demesnes* 1976, 177.

St Vincent near Wrotham, Kent
J. Harris *Artist and the country house* 1979, 281.

St Vincent's, Grantham, Lincs
J. Hort. Cottage Gdnr N.S., v. 5, 1882, 157–58.

St Wolstans near Celbridge, Co. Kildare, Eire
Copper Plate Mag. v. 1, 1792, pl. 6.

Salford Hall near Salford Priors, Warwickshire
C.L. v. 30, 1911, 932–38.

Salhouse Hall, Salhouse, Norfolk
J. Grigor *Eastern arboretum* 1841, 305–07.

Saling Grove, Great Saling, Essex
D. Stroud *Humphry Repton* 1962, 54. G. Carter *et al. Humphry Repton* 1982, 151.

Saling Hall, Great Saling, Essex
A. Lees-Milne *and* R. Verey *Englishman's garden* 1982, 76–79.

Salisbury, Richard Anthony *see* Chapel Allerton

Salisbury, William *see* London Botanic Garden

Salisbury Green, Edinburgh, Lothian
Gdning World v. 1, 1885, 745–46; v. 4, 1887, 277–78.

Salisbury Hall, London Colney, Herts
C.L. v. 126, 1959, 596–99. R. Bisgrove *Gardens of Britain* v. 3, 1978, 158.

Salle Park, Sall, Norfolk
J. Grigor *Eastern arboretum* 1841, 159.

Saltram, Plympton, Devon
Official guide. W. Angus *Seats* 1787, pl. 21.
G. Lipscomb *Journey into Cornwall* 1799, 320–22.
D.C. Webb *Observations and remarks* 1812, 75.
R. Ackermann *Repository* v. 6, 1825, pl. 1.
W.W.J. Gendall *Views* v. 2, 1830, 41. J. Britton *and* E.W. Brayley *Devonshire & Cornwall* 1832, 52. *G.C.* ii 1903, 413–14. Lady Rockley *Historic gardens of England* 1938, 166–67. *C.L.* v. 142, 1967, 594–97. M. Allan *Fisons guide* 1970, 134–35. *J. Royal Hort. Soc.* 1971, 219. P.M. Synge *Gardens of Britain* v. 1, 1977, 75–77. G.S. Thomas *Gardens of National Trust* 1979, 206–08.

Saltwood Castle, Saltwood, Kent
T. Wright *Gardens of Britain* v. 4, 1978, 86–87.

Saltwood Vicarage, Saltwood, Kent
J. Hort. Cottage Gdnr N.S., v. 2, 1881, 50–51. *G.C.* ii 1902, 257.

Salutation, Sandwich, Kent
L. Weaver *Houses and gardens by E.L. Lutyens* 1913, 256–60. *C.L.* v. 132, 1962, 564–67,650–54; v. 170,

Salutation (*Cont.*)
1981, 849; v. 174, 1983, 506–08,616. *Architects J.* v. 174, 1981, 426–27. J. Brown *Gardens of a golden afternoon* 1982, 171.

Samares Manor, Jersey, Channel Islands
C.L. v. 139, 1971, 732–34.

Samlesbury Hall, Samlesbury, Lancs
C.L. v. 17, 1905, 452–56.

Sanctuary of the Hermit Finch, Burley on the Hill, Leics
B. Jones *Follies & grottoes* 1974, 182–84.

Sand Hutton Hall, Sand Hutton, N. Yorks
C. Holme *Gardens of England in Northern counties* 1911, pl. 111.

Sandbeck Park near Tickhill, S. Yorks
A. Young *Farmer's tour through East of England* v. 1, 1771, 299–303. D. Defoe *Tour* v. 3, 1778, 108–09. W. Watts *Seats* 1779, pl. 10. T. Allen *New . . . history of . . . York* v. 3, 1831, 126. F.O. Morris *Series of picturesque views* v. 5, 15. E. Cecil *History of gardening in England* 1910, 254–56. *C.L.* v. 138, 1965, 880–83, 966,1024–27. Historical MSS Commission *Architectural history* v. 2, 1970, item 2052. D. Stroud *Capability Brown* 1975, 138–40,238. K. Lemmon *Gardens of Britain* v. 5, 1978, 138. L. Fleming *and* A. Gore *English garden* 1979, 132–33. Tyne and Wear County Council Museums *Capability Brown and the northern landscape* 1983, 33,34,43.

Sanderstead Court, Croydon, London
J.P. Neale *Views* v. 4, 1821.

Sandford Orcas near Sherborne, Dorset
C.L. v. 21, 1907, 341–45.

Sandford Park, Sandford-on-Thames, Oxfordshire
C.L. v. 87, 1940, 480–84. J. Sherwood *and* N. Pevsner *Oxfordshire* 1974, 751.

Sandgate Lodge, Sullington, W. Sussex
J. Dallaway *History of Western Division of . . . Sussex* v. 2 no. 2, 1830, 123.

Sandhill Park near Bishop's Lydeard, Somerset
J. Collinson *History . . . of Somersetshire* v. 2, 1791, 494. J.P. Neale *Views* 2nd Series, v. 4, 1828. *Jones's views* 1829.

Sandhills, Bletchingley, Surrey
G.C. v. 160 no. 3, 1966, 18–19.

Sandhoe near Hexham, Northumberland
J. Hort. Cottage Gdnr v. 44, 1870, 177–78.

Sandhouse, Witley, Surrey
C.L. v. 28, 1910, 296–302.

Sandhurst Lodge, Sandhurst, Berks
Garden v. 62, 1902, 164–65. *C.L.* v. 16, 1904, 308–11.

Sandlands near Hythe, Kent
G. Virtue *Picturesque beauties of Great Britain: Kent* 1829, 58.

Sandleford Priory, Berks
D. Stroud *Capability Brown* 1975, 195–97. J. Harris *Artist and the country house* 1979, 267.

Sandling Park near Hythe, Kent
T. Wright *Gardens of Britain* v. 4, 1978, 88–91.

Sandon Hall, Sandon, Staffs
J.P. Neale *Views* v. 4, 1821. *J. Hort.* N.S., v. 69, 1914, 84–86. M. Allan *Fisons guide* 1970, 283–84. B. Jones *Follies & grottoes* 1974, 390.

Sandringham, Norfolk
F.O. Morris *Series of picturesque views* v. 3, 1. *J. Hort. Cottage Gdnr* v. 47, 1872, 59–62,103–06; v. 52, 1874, 100; N.S., v. 26, 1893, 178–80,204–05; N.S., v. 59, 1909, 442–43. *G.C.* i 1891, 759–60; ii 1892, 267–68; i 1902, 402–11; ii 1902, 113,115,118,355,358; ii 1905, 440; i 1906, 104,184; i 1910, 319,321; i 1937, 311. *Gdnrs Mag.* 1897, 414–16,417. *C.L.* v. 11, 1902, 806–18; v. 12, 1902, 104–06; v. 73, 1933, 582–86; v. 75, 1934, 116–24,439; v. 77, 1935, 452–54; v. 167, 1980, 1382–84; v. 168, 1980, 396. C. Ward *Royal gardens* 1912, 121–46. *J. Royal Hort. Soc.* 1932, 165–74. Lady Rockley *Historic gardens of England* 1938, 208–09. L. Roper *Royal gardens* 1953, 64–85. M. Allan *Fisons guide* 1970, 203–04. G. Plumptre *Royal gardens* 1981, 10–33.

Sandwell Park, West Bromwich, W. Midlands
W. Pitt *General view of agriculture of . . . Stafford* 1796, 96. S. Shaw *History . . . of Staffordshire* v. 2, 1801, 128. J. Nightingale *Topographical . . . description of Staffordshire* 1810, 840,1201. F. Calvert *Picturesque views . . . in Staffordshire & Shropshire* 1830, 65.

Sandy Lodge, Sandy, Beds
M. Allan *Fisons guide* 1970, 159. Historical MSS Commission *Architectural history* v. 4, 1972, item 4562.

Sandymount Castle, Dublin, Eire
E. Malins *and* P. Bowe *Irish gardens and demesnes* 1980, 137.

Sandywell Park near Cheltenham, Glos
R. Atkyns *Ancient and present state of Glostershire* 1712, 400. L. Knyff *and* J. Kip *Britannia illustrata* v. 2, 1715. S. Rudder *New history of Gloucestershire* 1779, 415.

Sandywell Park (*Cont.*)
H.I. Triggs *Formal garden in England and Scotland* 1902, 39. M. Macartney *English houses & gardens* 1908, pl. 29.

Sansaw Hall, Clive, Shropshire
Gdnrs Mag. 1913, 413–14,415. R. Sidwell *West Midland gardens* 1981, 146–47.

Santry Court, Santry, Co. Dublin, Eire
Lady Domvile *Santry House* c.1840. E. Malins *and* Knight of Glin *Lost demesnes* 1976, 14. E. Malins *and* P. Bowe *Irish gardens and demesnes* 1980, 42.

Sapperton near Cirencester, Glos
R. Atkyns *Ancient and present state of Glostershire* 1712, 636. L. Knyff *and* J. Kip *Britannia illustrata* v. 2, 1715. V.C.H. *Gloucester* v. 11, 1976, 91.

Sarsden near Chipping Norton, Oxfordshire
W. Kennett *Parochial antiquities . . . in the counties of Oxford and Bucks* 1695, 683, pls. 8–9. M. Macartney *English houses & gardens* 1908, pl. 20. D. Stroud *Humphry Repton* 1962, 172. G. Carter *et al. Humphry Repton* 1982, 160.

Sarsden Glebe, Churchill, Oxfordshire
R. Bisgrove *Gardens of Britain* v. 3, 1978, 160–61.

Sauchieburn House near Stirling, Central
Scottish Gdnr and Northern Forester v. 8, 1913, 661–62.

Saughton House, Edinburgh, Lothian
Scottish Gdnr and Northern Forester v. 9, 1914, 345–46.

Saunders Grove near Baltinglass, Co. Wicklow, Eire
E. Malins *and* Knight of Glin *Lost demesnes* 1976, 15.

Saunders Hill, Padstow, Cornwall
C.S. Gilbert *Historical survey of . . . Cornwall* v. 2, 1820, 652. J.P. Neale *Views* 2nd Series, v. 2, 1825. *Jones's views* 1829.

Sausmarez Manor, Guernsey, Channel Islands
W. Berry *History of Island of Guernsey* 1815, 137,140.

Savage's House, Bishops Tachbrook, Warwickshire
R. Sidwell *West Midland gardens* 1981, 226–27.

Savill Gardens *see* Windsor Great Park

Sawston Hall, Sawston, Cambs
Official guide. *C.L.* v. 115, 1954, 1902–05, 1998,2092. V.C.H. *Cambridge* v. 6, 1978, 251.

Saxham Hall, Great Saxham, Suffolk
J. Gage *History . . . of Suffolk* 1838, 109.

Saxonbury Lodge near Tunbridge Wells, E. Sussex
T.W. Horsfield *History . . . of Sussex* v. 1, 1835, 407.

Sayes Court, Deptford, Lewisham, London
Archaeologia v. 12, 1796, 188. D. Lysons *Environs of London* v. 4, 1798, 363–64. T. Pennant *Journey from London to Isle of Wight* v. 1, 1801, 9–10. J. Britton *and* E.W. Brayley *Beauties of England and Wales* v. 7, 1808, 458. *Cottage Gdnr* v. 16, 1856, 134–35. J. Evelyn *Directions for the gardiner at Says-Court* (ed. by G. Keynes) 1932. *Illustrated London News* v. 221, 1952, 348–49. G. Taylor *Old London gardens* 1953, 112–21. J. Evelyn *Diary* v. 3, 1955, 80–81,370; v. 5, 552. *C.L.* v. 134, 1963, 1263. J.D. Hunt *and* P. Willis *Genius of the place* 1975, 63. R. Strong *Renaissance garden in England* 1979, 222.

Scampston Hall, Scampston, N. Yorks
C.L. v. 115, 1954, 946–49,1035. D. Stroud *Capability Brown* 1975, 173–75,238. P. Willis *Charles Bridgeman* 1977, 182. J. Harris *Artist and the country house* 1979, 287.

Scarisbrick near Southport, Lancs
D. Stroud *Humphry Repton* 1962, 125. G. Carter *et al. Humphry Repton* 1982, 156.

Scawby Hall, Scawby, Humberside
J. Hort. Cottage Gdnr v. 52, 1874, 93–94.

Schaw Park near Alloa, Central
Scottish Gdnr and Northern Forester v. 8, 1913, 101–02.

Scone Palace, Scone, Tayside
J.P. Neale *Views* v. 6, 1823. *G.M.* v. 13, 1837, 123–24. F.O. Morris *Series of picturesque views* v. 1, 83. *G.C.* i 1877, 496–97. *J. Hort. Cottage Gdnr* N.S., v. 10, 1885, 90–91,132. A.A. Tait *Landscape garden in Scotland* 1980, passim. G.A. Little *Scotland's gardens* 1981, 165–67.

Scone Pinetum, Scone, Tayside
C.L. v. 156, 1974, 1854–55.

Scorrier near Redruth, Cornwall
Historical MSS Commission *Architectural history* v. 2, 1970, item 1606.

Scotney Castle near Lamberhurst, Kent
Official guide. *C.L.* v. 11, 1902, 688–93; v. 48, 1920, 12–19; v. 120, 1956, 470–73,526; v. 146, 1969, 958–63; v. 165, 1979, 1522–25. *G.C.* i 1961, 530–32. Lady Rockley *Historic gardens of England* 1938, 80–81. M. Allan *Fisons guide* 1970, 61–62. H. Evans *Beautiful gardens of Britain* 1974, 71–72. T. Wright *Gardens of Britain* v. 4, 1978, 91–95. G.S. Thomas *Gardens of*

Scotney Castle (*Cont.*)
National Trust 1979, 209. A. Hellyer *Gardens of genius* 1980, 32–35.

Scottow Park, Scottow, Norfolk
G.M. v. 17, 1841, 33. J. Grigor *Eastern arboretum* 1841, 164.

Scott's Grotto, Ware, Herts
B. Jones *Follies & grottoes* 1974, 169–71.

Scraptoft Hall, Scraptoft, Leics
J. Throsby *Select views in Leicestershire* v. 1, 1790, 312. J. Nichols *History . . . of county of Leicester* v. 3, 1804, 1126. C. Holme *Gardens of England in Midland & Eastern counties* 1908, pl. 104. B. Jones *Follies & grottoes* 1974, 356.

Scrivelsby Court, Scrivelsby, Lincs
D. Stroud *Humphry Repton* 1962, 172. G. Carter *et al. Humphry Repton* 1982, 156.

Seacox Heath near Hawkhurst, Kent
J. Hort. Cottage Gdnr v. 52, 1874, 299–301.

Seacroft Hall, Leeds, W. Yorks
Historical MSS Commission *Architectural history* v. 5, 1974, items 5432, 5504.

Seaforde near Clough, Co. Down, Ulster
Ulster Architectural Heritage Society *Northern gardens* 1982, 21.

Seaforth House, Seaforth, Merseyside
J.P. Neale *Views* v. 2, 1819.

Seaham Hall, Seaham, Co. Durham
Historical MSS Commission *Architectural history* v. 2, 1970, item 2076.

Seaton Delaval near Blyth, Northumberland
W. Hutchinson *View of Northumberland* v. 2, 1778, 329, 331, 333. *C.L.* v. 54, 1923, 860–68. J. Harris *Gardens of delight* 1978, 37.

Seaton House *see* Gordon House

Seavenhampton *see* Sevenhampton

Seckford Hall near Woodbridge, Suffolk
C.L. v. 27, 1910, 90–95.

Sedbury Hall, Gilling West, N. Yorks
B. Jones *Follies & grottoes* 1974, 364.

Sedgebrook Manor, Sedgebrook, Lincs
C.L. v. 115, 1954, 152–55.

Sedgefield (Dr Kearsley), Sedgefield, Co. Durham
Historical MSS Commission *Architectural history* v. 3, 1971, item 3398.

Sedgwick near Kendal, Cumbria
G.C. 1874, 484–86.

Sedgwick Park, Horsham, W. Sussex
C.L. v. 9, 1901, 560–67; v. 62, 1927, 459–62; v. 91, 1942, 1086–89, 1134–37. C. Holme *Gardens of England in Southern & Western counties* 1907, pls. 114–15. G. Jekyll *Garden ornament* 1918, 160. *G.C.* ii 1924, 422–23; i 1925, 329; i 1956, 524–25.

Seething Hall, Seething, Norfolk
J. Grigor *Eastern arboretum* 1841, 246.

Sefton Park near Slough, Bucks
D. Stroud *Humphry Repton* 1962, 173. G. Carter *et al. Humphry Repton* 1982, 148.

Sefton Park *see* Liverpool

Selsdon, Croydon, London
J.P. Neale *Views* v. 4, 1821. R. Ackermann *Repository* v. 11, 1828, pl. 8. W.W.J. Gendall *Views* v. 2, 1830, 57. E.W. Brayley *and* J. Britton *Topographical history of Surrey* v. 4, 105. W. Keane *Beauties of Surrey* 1849, 60–61. *G.C.* i 1902, 211–12.

Selsley near Woodchester, Glos
T. Wright *Arbors & grottos* 1979.

Selwood Cottage, Frome, Somerset
W. Robinson *English flower garden* 1883, xxvii.

Sennicots, Funtington, W. Sussex
T.W. Horsfield *History . . . of Sussex* v. 2, 1835, 74.

Sennowe Park near Fakenham, Norfolk
C.L. v. 170, 1981, 2298–2301.

Senwick House, Borgue, Dumfries and Galloway
G.A. Little *Scotland's gardens* 1981, 264–65.

Serlby Hall near Blyth, Notts
Official guide. J.P. Neale *Views* v. 3, 1820. *Jones's views* 1829. *G.C.* i 1914, 161–62, 163. *C.L.* v. 125, 1959, 654–57, 708, 766. Historical MSS Commission *Architectural history* v. 3, 1971, item 3639. J. Harris *Artist and the country house* 1979, 213. N. Pevsner *Nottinghamshire* 1979, 308.

Sevenhampton near Cheltenham, Glos
L. Knyff *and* J. Kip *Britannia illustrata* v. 2, 1715.

Sevenhampton Place, Sevenhampton, Wilts
J. Sales *West Country gardens* 1980, 240–41.

Sevenoaks (Thomas Fuller), Kent
J. Kip *Supplement du Nouveau theatre de la Grande Bretagne* 1728, pl. 28.

Severn End, Hanley Castle, Hereford and Worcester
Garden v. 46, 1894, 389. *C.L.* v. 6, 1899, 464–67; v. 158, 1975, 194–97,266–69.

Sewerby Hall near Bridlington, Humberside
K. Lemmon *Gardens of Britain* v. 5, 1978, 44–48.

Sezincote near Moreton-in-Marsh, Glos
Official guide. J. Martin *Views of Sezincote House* c.1818. J.P. Neale *Views* v. 2, 1819. F.O. Morris *Series of picturesque views* v. 3, 49. *J. Hort. Cottage Gdnr* N.S., v. 53, 1906, 552–53. *G.C.* ii 1912, 170,171,172,173. *Architectural Review* v. 69, May 1931, 161–66, pls. 3–5. *C.L.* v. 85, 1939, 502–06,528–32; v. 160, 1976, 600–02. D. Stroud *Humphry Repton* 1962, 172. P. Coats *Great gardens of Britain* 1967, 130–35. D. Verey *Gloucestershire* v. 1, 1970, 393–94. R.I.B.A. *Catalogue* v. C–F, 1972, 38,64–65; v. O–R, 1976, 120. L. Fleming *and* A. Gore *English garden* 1979, pls. 97–98. P. Conner *Oriental architecture in the west* 1979, 121–24. M. Shellim *Oil paintings of India and the East by Thomas Daniell and William Daniell* 1979, 86–90. *Gdn History* v. 8 no. 1, 1980, 46–66; v. 8 no. 3, 1980, 14. M. Archer *Early views of India* 1980, 230–31. J. Sales *West Country gardens* 1980, 99–102. G. Carter *et al. Humphry Repton* 1982, 153. T. Hinde *Stately gardens of Britain* 1983, 54–61.

Shabden Park near Redhill, Surrey
G.F. Prosser *Select illustrations of . . . Surrey* 1828.

Shadwell Park, Rushford, Norfolk
C.L. v. 136, 1964, 18–21; v. 164, 1978, 1974–75. *J. Royal Soc. of Arts* v. 129, 1981, 678–81.

Shalford House, Guildford, Surrey
J.P. Neale *Views* 2nd Series, v. 3, 1826.

Shambellie near Dumfries, Dumfries and Galloway
Scottish Gdnr and Northern Forester v. 8, 1913, 370.

Shane's Castle near Antrim, Co. Antrim, Ulster
J. Hort. Cottage Gdnr N.S., v. 22, 1891, 228–30. *G.C.* ii 1962, 298–99. E. Malins *and* Knight of Glin *Lost demesnes* 1976, 80–83. Ulster Architectural Heritage Society *Northern gardens* 1982, 21.

Shapwick, Somerset
J. Collinson *History . . . of Somersetshire* v. 3, 1791, 427.

Shardeloes near Amersham, Bucks
T. Badeslade *and* J. Rocque *Vitruvius Brittanicus* 1739, pls. 100–01. H. Repton *Observations* 1803, 64,65. S. Shaw *Tour to West of England in 1788* In J. Pinkerton, v. 2, 1808, 185. *Connoisseur* v. 148, 1961, 268–75. D. Stroud *Humphry Repton* 1962, 172. Historical MSS Commission *Architectural history* v. 3, 1971, item 3401. G. Carter *et al. Humphry Repton* 1982, 148.

Sharnden near Mayfield, E. Sussex
Studio v. 87, 1924, 193–97. R. Webber *Percy Cane* 1975, 61–62,185.

Sharow Hall, Sharow, N. Yorks
K. Lemmon *Gardens of Britain* v. 5, 1978, 113.

Sharpham House near Totnes, Devon
C.L. v. 145, 1969, 952–55,1014. D. Stroud *Capability Brown* 1975, 238.

Sharpitor near Salcombe, Devon
M. Allan *Fisons guide* 1970, 136. P.M. Synge *Gardens of Britain* v. 1, 1977, 78–81. G.S. Thomas *Gardens of National Trust* 1979, 209–10.

Sharps Place, Kent
J. Kip *Nouveau theatre de la Grande Bretagne* v. 2, 1724. T. Badeslade *Thirty six different views of . . . Kent* 1750s.

Sharsted Court near Sittingbourne, Kent
C.L. v. 107, 1950, 586,658–62.

Shavington (Shenton) **Hall** near Market Drayton, Shropshire
R. Ackermann *Repository* v. 10, 1827, pl. 13. W.W.J. Gendall *Views* v. 2, 1830, 75. G. Carter *et al. Humphry Repton* 1982, 161.

Shaw Hall near Eccles, Greater Manchester
E. Baines *History . . . of Lancaster* v. 3, 1836, 451.

Shaw House, Newbury, Berks
C.L. v. 28, 1910, 328–38. *Gdn History* v. 5 no. 3, 1977, 35–39.

Shawford House near Winchester, Hants
C.L. v. 48, 1920, 172–79.

Shawms, Stafford, Staffs
G. Beard *Thomas H. Mawson* 1976, 63.

Sheen (Sir William Temple), Richmond, London
Archaeologia v. 12, 1796, 184–85. J. Evelyn *Diary* v. 4, 1955, 143. *C.L.* v. 155, 1974, 76–77.

Sheen Lodge, Richmond, London
W. Robinson *English flower garden* 1883, xxx–xxxii.

Sheen Palace, Richmond, London
H.M. Colvin *History of the King's Works* v. 2, 1963, 995,996,1001.

Sheffield. Botanical Gardens, S. Yorks
G.M. v. 15, 1839, 453–55. J. Law *Catalogue . . . of the rare and interesting plants now in . . . Sheffield Botanical Gardens* 1849. *Scottish Gdnr* v. 1, 1852, 378–80. *United Gdnrs' & Land Stewards' J.* 1845, 681–82. *Cottage Gdnr* v. 16, 1856, 6–8. B. Hobson *What to observe in the conservatories . . .* 1880. *G.C.* ii 1897, 144,146.
A.L. Winning *Sheffield Botanical Gardens* 1970.
K. Lemmon *Gardens of Britain* v. 5, 1978, 139–45. *C.L.* v. 138, 1965, 1633; v. 173, 1983, 920–22.

Sheffield House, Kensington, London
Gdn History v. 11 no. 1, 1983, 18,26.

Sheffield Park near Uckfield, E. Sussex
Official guide. A. Young *Farmer's tour through East of England* v. 3, 1771, 145–46. W. Watts *Seats* 1779, pl. 3. H. Repton *Observations* 1803, 82–83. J.P. Neale *Views* v. 4, 1821. T.W. Horsfield *History . . . of Sussex* v. 1, 1835, 378. *G.C.* i 1937, 339; ii 1937, 207; ii 1964, 199–200. *C.L.* v. 109, 1951, 1552–57; v. 126, 1959, 286–88. *J. Royal Hort. Soc.* 1960, 352–53. D. Stroud *Humphry Repton* 1962, 39. M. Allan *Fisons guide* 1970, 62–63. H. Evans *Beautiful gardens of Britain* 1974, 61–62. D. Stroud *Capability Brown* 1975, 238–39. T. Wright *Gardens of Britain* v. 4, 1978, 180–85. G.S. Thomas *Gardens of National Trust* 1979, 210–12. A. Hellyer *Gardens of genius* 1980, 196–200. G. Carter et al. *Humphry Repton* 1982, 163. T. Hinde *Stately gardens of Britain* 1983, 47–53.

Sheldon Manor near Chippenham, Wilts
C.L. v. 34, 1913, 638–45. J. Sales *West Country gardens* 1980, 241–42.

Shelleys near Twyford, Berks
J. Royal Hort. Soc. 1974, 350–58.

Shelton Abbey near Arklow, Co. Wicklow, Eire
F.O. Morris *Series of picturesque views* v. 4, 61.

Shendish near Kings Langley, Herts
Garden 1914, 402–03.

Shennanton Hall, Kirkcowan, Dumfries and Galloway
Scottish Gdnr and Northern Forester v. 7, 1912, 61–62.

Shenstone, Staffs
S. Shaw *History . . . of Staffordshire* v. 2, 1801, 46.

Shenstone Court, Shenstone, Staffs
G. Beard *Thomas H. Mawson* 1976, 63.

Shenton *see* Shavington

Shenton Hall, Shenton, Leics
J. Nichols *History . . . of county of Leicester* v. 4, 1811, 528.

Shenvilles, Margaretting, Essex
F.G. Emmison *Catalogue of maps in Essex Record Office* 1947, 1.

Shephalbury, Shephall, Herts
J.E. Cussans *History of Hertfordshire* v. 2, 1874, 102.

Shepherd's Hill near Uckfield, E. Sussex
C.L. v. 158, 1975, 906–09.

Shepperton, Surrey
W. Keane *Beauties of Middlesex* 1850, 225–26.

Sherard, James *see* Eltham

Sherborne, Glos
R. Atkyns *Ancient and present state of Glostershire* 1712, 645. L. Knyff and J. Kip *Britannia illustrata* v. 2, 1715.

Sherborne Castle, Sherborne, Dorset
J. Hutchins *History . . . of Dorset* v. 4, 1870, 265.
J.P. Neale *Views* 2nd Series, v. 4, 1828. *Jones's views* 1829. S. Felton *Gleanings on gardens* 1897, 88–95. *C.L.* v. 28, 1910, 424–32. *Notes and Queries* v. 22, 1975, 490–91. D. Stroud *Capability Brown* 1975, 239. *Gdn History* v. 4 no. 1, 1976, 57–87; v. 4 no. 3, 1976, 5–8.

Sherbourne Park, Sherbourne, Warwickshire
R. Sidwell *West Midland gardens* 1981, 229–30. *C.L.* v. 174, 1983, 1660,1662–63.

Sherfield Court, Sherfield-upon-Loddon, Hants
G.C. ii 1904, 235–37. A. Paterson *Gardens of Britain* v. 2, 1978, 139–41.

Sheriff Hutton, N. Yorks
Official guide. *C.L.* v. 140, 1966, 548–51,628–31. Historical MSS Commission *Architectural history* v. 3, 1971, item 2545.

Sheriffmuir near Dunblane, Central
G.C. i 1885, 337–38.

Sheringham Hall, Upper Sheringham, Norfolk
H. Repton *Fragments* 1816, 195–212. *C.L.* v. 121, 1957, 192–95. D. Stroud *Humphry Repton* 1962, 152.
E. Malins *Red books of Humphry Repton* 1976, 27–30.
M. Hadfield *et al. British gardeners* 1980, 239. *Landscape*

Sheringham Hall (*Cont.*)

Design no. 135, 1981, 26-28. G. Carter *et al. Humphry Repton* 1982, 55,159. D. Watkin *English vision* 1982, 82-83.

Shermanbury Park, Shermanbury, W. Sussex
T.W. Horsfield *History . . . of Sussex* v. 2, 1835, 259.

Shernfold Park near Frant, E. Sussex
T.W. Horsfield *History . . . of Sussex* v. 1, 1835, 406.

Sherwood Park, Tunbridge Wells, Kent
G.C. ii 1881, 590-92.

Shibden Hall near Halifax, W. Yorks
Bradford Illustrated Weekly Telegraph *Series of picturesque views* 1885.

Shillinglee Park, Fisherstreet, W. Sussex
C.L. v. 80, 1936, 142-47. B. Jones *Follies & grottoes* 1974, 400-01.

Shinfield Grange, Shinfield, Berks
J. Royal Hort. Soc. 1971, 84-92. R. Bisgrove *Gardens of Britain* v. 3, 1978, 161-63.

Shiplake Court, Shiplake, Oxfordshire
C.L. v. 4, 1898, 16-19; v. 20, 1906, 594-602. *Garden* v. 58, 1900, 29-30. G.C. ii 1903, 274,286.

Shipley, Northants
Northamptonshire Past and Present v. 5 no. 3, 1975, 231.

Shipley Hall near Ilkeston, Derbyshire
G.C. ii 1883, 211-12; i 1903, 44. *Gdning World* v. 1, 1885, 760-62. *Garden* v. 58, 1900, 433-34. *Gdnrs Mag.* 1902, 287-91. N. Nichols *Local maps of Derbyshire to 1770* 1980, 146.

Shipton Court, Shipton-under-Wychwood, Oxfordshire
J. Skelton *Engraved illustrations of principal antiquities of Oxfordshire* 1823. J.P. Neale *Views* 2nd Series, v. 1, 1824. C.L. v. 7, 1900, 144-50.

Shipton Hall, Shipton, Glos
C.L. v. 27, 1910, 414-22.

Shipton Moyne, Glos
R. Atkyns *Ancient and present state of Glostershire* 1712, 646. L. Knyff *and* J. Kip *Britannia illustrata* v. 2, 1715.

Shirburn Castle, Shirburn, Oxfordshire
Copper Plate Mag. v. 1, 1792, pl. 21. J.P. Neale *Views* v. 3, 1820. J.C. Loudon *Encyclopaedia of gardening* 1822, 1236. C.L. v. 7, 1900, 80-84. V.C.H. *Oxford* v. 8, 1964, 181. J. Sherwood *and* N. Pevsner *Oxfordshire* 1974, 762-63.

Shirecliffe Hall, Sheffield, S. Yorks
G.C. ii 1885, 472.

Shirenewton Hall near Chepstow, Gwent
G.C. i 1896, 728.

Shireoaks Hall, Shireoaks, Notts
Gdn History v. 3 no. 4, 1975, 32. M. Binney *and* A. Hills *Elysian gardens* 1979, 60. N. Pevsner *Nottinghamshire* 1979, 312-13.

Shirley House, Shirley, Croydon, London
J.P. Neale *Views* v. 4, 1821. N. Whittock *and* H. Gastineau *Picturesque beauties of England and Wales* 1830, 63. W. Keane *Beauties of Surrey* 1849, 57-58. G.C. ii 1904, 330-31.

Shirley Vicarage, Shirley, Croydon, London
G.C. ii 1890, 239-40. C.L. v. 3, 1898, 624-26. *J. Hort. Cottage Gdnr* N.S., v. 38, 1899, 408-09.

Shobdon Court, Shobdon, Hereford and Worcester
L. Knyff *and* J. Kip *Britannia illustrata* v. 2, 1715. *G.M.* v. 14, 1838, 213-15. G.C. i 1877, 469,471-72; i 1892, 425-26. *J. Hort. Cottage Gdnr* v. 57, 1877, 484-86. R. Pococke *Travels through England* v. 2, 1889, 219-20. C.L. v. 20, 1906, 666-74; v. 115, 1954, 101; v. 139, 1966, 533,1031. M. Macartney *English houses & gardens* 1908, pl. 51. G. Jekyll *Garden ornament* 1918, 28. B. Jones *Follies & grottoes* 1974, 53-54.

Shortacres, Crailing, Borders
I.H. Adams *Descriptive list of plans* v. 3, 1974, 124.

Shortgrove near Saffron Walden, Essex
F.G. Emmison *Catalogue of maps in Essex Record Office* 2nd Supplt, 1964, 18. Historical MSS Commission *Architectural history* v. 4, 1972, item 4597. D. Stroud *Capability Brown* 1975, 239-40.

Shotesham Park, Shotesham, Norfolk
J. Grigor *Eastern arboretum* 1841, 237-38. C.L. v. 142, 1967, 312-13.

Shotover House near Oxford, Oxfordshire
F. Kielmansegge *Diary* 1902, 114-15. C.L. v. 59, 1926, 240-46; v. 162, 1977, 1912-14,1978-79. Lady Rockley *Historic gardens of England* 1938, 160-61. V.C.H. *Oxford* v. 5, 1957, 276. B. Jones *Follies & grottoes* 1974, 51-52. J. Sherwood *and* N. Pevsner *Oxfordshire* 1974, 765. M. Batey *Oxford gardens* 1982, 106-08.

Shottesbrooke, Berks
J.P. Neale *Views* 2nd Series, v. 4, 1828. *Jones's views* 1829. C.L. v. 33, 1913, 162-68.

Shrewsbury. Quarry Park, Shropshire
Gdning World v. 3, 1886, 8–9. *G.C.* ii 1895, 337–38. B. Jones *Follies & grottoes* 1974, 381.

Shrewsbury House, Plumstead, Greenwich, London
C. Greenwood *Epitome of county history . . . v. 1: Kent* 1838, 44.

Shrubland Park near Coddenham, Suffolk
Cottage Gdnr v. 10, 1853, 495–97; v. 11, 1854, 5–7; v. 16, 1856, 452–54,469–71; v. 17, 1856, 39–41; v. 19, 1857, 17–20,32–35,80–82,97–99. *Florist* 1856, 151–55. E.A. Brooke *Gardens of England* 1857, pls. 18–21. *G.C.* 1867, 1099–1100,1123,1170–72; 1868, 9–10,31,55; ii 1888, 328–29; ii 1890, 278,279. *Garden* v. 1, 1872, 350–51. *C.L.* v. 10, 1901, 560–67; v. 114, 1953, 948–51,1654–57,1734–38. C. Holme *Gardens of England in Midland & Eastern counties* 1908, pls. 105–06. Lady Rockley *Historic gardens of England* 1938, 200–01. Historical MSS Commission *Architectural history* v. 2, 1970, item 2324. B. Jones *Follies & grottoes* 1974, 393. N. Pevsner *Suffolk* 1974, 418. L. Fleming *and* A. Gore *English garden* 1979, 188.

Shrublands, Windermere, Cumbria
C. Holme *Gardens of England in Northern counties* 1911, pls. 115–16. G. Beard *Thomas H. Mawson* 1976, 63.

Shuckburgh Hall near Daventry, Warwickshire
R. Sidwell *West Midland gardens* 1981, 230–31.

Shugborough near Stafford, Staffs
Official guide. T. Pennant *Journey from Chester to London* 1782, 68–69, pls. 4–5. G.A. Walpoole *New British traveller* 1784, 101. W. Pitt *General view of agriculture of . . . Stafford* 1796, 97. W. Gilpin *Observations on several parts of England* v. 1, 1808, 71–75. J. Nightingale *Topographical . . . description of Staffordshire* 1810, 1084–88. J.P. Neale *Views* v. 4, 1821. *G.M.* v. 1, 1826, 407–09. F. Calvert *Picturesque views . . . in Staffordshire & Shropshire* 1830, 12. *J. Hort. Cottage Gdnr* v. 48, 1872, 172–74. *C.L.* v. 115, 1954, 510–13,677, 1126–29,1220–23; v. 150, 1971, 546–48; v. 161, 1977, 578–81; v. 175, 1984, 831. *Archaeological J.* v. 120, 1963, 264. *Connoisseur* v. 164, 1967, 211–15. *Publications of Bedfordshire Historical Record Soc.* v. 47, 1968, 137,161. *Collections for a History of Staffordshire* 4th Series, v. 6, 1970, 86–110. *J. Royal Hort. Soc.* 1971, 213. Historical MSS Commission *Architectural history* v. 5, 1974, item 5376. B. Jones *Follies & grottoes* 1974, 389–90. N. Pevsner *Staffordshire* 1974, 236,238. P. Conner *Oriental architecture in the West* 1979, 51–52. L. Fleming *and* A. Gore *English garden* 1979, 137,138. J. Harris *Artist and the country house* 1979, 290–91. G.S. Thomas *Gardens of National Trust* 1979, 212–14. T. Wright *Arbors & grottos* 1979. R. Sidwell *West Midland gardens* 1981, 175–76. D. Watkin *English vision* 1982, 30.

Shurdington, Glos
R. Atkyns *Ancient and present state of Glostershire* 1712, 240. L. Knyff *and* J. Kip *Britannia illustrata* v. 2, 1715. *C.L.* v. 176, 1984, 194–95.

Shute House, Shute, Devon
R. Polwhele *History of Devonshire* v. 2, 1793, 315. Historical MSS Commission *Architectural history* v. 2, 1970, item 2108.

Shute House, Donhead St Mary, Wilts
A. Lees-Milne *and* R. Verey *Englishwoman's garden* 1980, 134–38.

Shutlanger, Northants
Royal Commission on Historical Monuments *Inventory of the historical monuments in . . . Northampton* v. 4, 1982, 131–32.

Sibdon Castle, Sibdon Carwood, Shropshire
C.L. v. 141, 1967, 1372–76.

Sidbury Manor near Sidmouth, Devon
Gdning World v. 13, 1897, 377–78.

Sidegarth, Staveley, Cumbria
G. Beard *Thomas H. Mawson* 1976, 63.

Sigglesthorpe Hall near Hornsea, Humberside
K. Lemmon *Gardens of Britain* v. 5, 1978, 43–44.

Silverstone, Northants
Northamptonshire Past and Present v. 5 no. 3, 1975, 231.

Silwood Park near Ascot, Berks
J.P. Neale *Views* v. 1, 1818.

Singleton Abbey, Swansea, W. Glamorgan
J. Hort. Cottage Gdnr N.S., v. 11, 1885, 200–02; N.S., v. 60, 1878, 50–51.

Sir John Oldcastle Tavern, Camden, London
W. Wroth *London pleasure gardens of the eighteenth century* 1896, 70–71.

Sissinghurst Castle, Sissinghurst, Kent
Official guide. *C.L.* v. 92, 1942, 410–13,458–61, 506–09. *J. Royal Hort. Soc.* 1953, 400–08; 1966, 370–75; 1971, 217–18. E. Hyams *English garden* 1964, 163–66. *G.C.* 1967 v. 161 no. 19, 4–5. P. Coats *Great gardens of Britain* 1967, 254–63. P. Nicholson *V. Sackville-West's garden book* 1968. M. Allan *Fisons guide* 1970, 64–65. H. Evans *Beautiful gardens of Britain* 1974, 77–78. A. Scott-James *Sissinghurst: the making of*

Sissinghurst Castle (*Cont.*)
a garden 1975. *Garden* 1978, 385–89. T. Wright *Gardens of Britain* v. 4, 1978, 95–104. G.S. Thomas *Gardens of National Trust* 1979, 214–16. A. Hellyer *Gardens of genius* 1980, 141–45. *Connoisseur* v. 207, 1981, 260–62. *Garden Design* v. 1 no. 1, 1982, 26–31; v. 1 no. 2, 1982, 60–63.

Sissinghurst Place, Sissinghurst, Kent
M. Allan *Fisons guide* 1970, 65–66.

Siston Court, Siston, Avon
R. Atkyns *Ancient and present state of Glostershire* 1712, 654. L. Knyff *and* J. Kip *Britannia illustrata* v. 2, 1715. T.D. Fosbrooke *Abstracts of . . . county of Gloucester* v. 2, 1807, 56. *C.L.* v. 18, 1905, 486–91.

Sizergh Castle near Kendal, Cumbria
Official guide. J.P. Neale *Views* 2nd Series, v. 1, 1824. *G.C.* i 1964, 537–38. G.S. Thomas *Gardens of National Trust* 1979, 216–17. *C.L.* v. 173, 1983, 768–70.

Skeffington Hall, Skeffington, Leics
J. Throsby *Select views in Leicestershire* v. 1, 1790, 207. J. Nichols *History . . . of county of Leicester* v. 3, 1800, 440; 1804, 1133.

Skeldon House near Dalrymple, Strathclyde
G.A. Little *Scotland's gardens* 1981, 265.

Skells, Redditch, Hereford and Worcester
G. Beard *Thomas H. Mawson* 1976, 63.

Skelton Castle, Skelton, Cleveland
J. Graves *History of Cleveland* 1803, 364. J.W. Ord *History . . . of Cleveland* 1846, 245. I. Hall *Samuel Buck's Yorkshire sketchbook* 1979, 338.

Skene House, Skene, Grampian
I.H. Adams *Descriptive list of plans* v. 1, 1966, 8.

Skibo Castle near Dornoch, Highland
G. Beard *Thomas H. Mawson* 1976, 63.

Skinners Company *see* London

Skipton Castle, Skipton, N. Yorks
B. Jones *Follies & grottoes* 1974, 145.

Skirsgill House near Penrith, Cumbria
J.P. Neale *Views* 2nd Series, v. 3, 1826. *Jones's views* 1829.

Skisdon Lodge, St Kew, Cornwall
C.S. Gilbert *Historical survey of . . . Cornwall* v. 2, 1820, 610.

Skreens near Chelmsford, Essex
P. Muilman *History of Essex* v. 1, 1771, 297. F.G. Emmison *Catalogue of maps in Essex Record Office* 1949, 5.

Slade, Cornwood, Devon
P.M. Synge *Gardens of Britain* v. 1, 1977, 81–82.

Slains Castle, Slains, Grampian
G. Beard *Thomas H. Mawson* 1976, 63–64.

Slane Castle, Slane, Co. Meath, Eire
J.N. Brewer *Beauties of Ireland* v. 2, 1826, 203. *G.M.* v. 2, 1827, 149. D. Stroud *Capability Brown* 1975, 246. E. Malins *and* Knight of Glin *Lost demesnes* 1976, 89–90. *C.L.* v. 168, 1980, 382–85. Knight of Glin *and* P. Bowe *Gardens of outstanding historic interest in . . . Ireland* 1980.

Slape Manor, Netherbury, Dorset
A. Paterson *Gardens of Britain* v. 2, 1978, 42–43.

Slaugham Place, Slaugham, W. Sussex
C.L. v. 87, 1940, 269–71.

Slebech Park, Slebech, Dyfed
G.C. ii 1882, 621–22,625.

Sledmere House, Sledmere, Humberside
Official guide. *C.L.* v. 106, 1949, 972–76,1064,1140. N. Pevsner *Yorkshire: York and the East Riding* 1972, 346. D. Stroud *Capability Brown* 1975, 240. K. Lemmon *Gardens of Britain* v. 5, 1978, 48–49.

Sleightholmedale Lodge near Fadmoor, N. Yorks
K. Lemmon *Gardens of Britain* v. 5, 1978, 114–16.

Slindon House, Slindon, W. Sussex
J.P. Neale *Views* v. 4, 1821. *Garden* v. 34, 1888, 505–06.

Slyfield Manor near Leatherhead, Surrey
C.L. v. 83, 1938, 400–05,424.

Smallhythe Place, Tenterden, Kent
G.S. Thomas *Gardens of National Trust* 1979, 217–18.

Smeaton Manor near Northallerton, N. Yorks
K. Lemmon *Gardens of Britain* v. 5, 1978, 116–17.

Smeaton-Hepburn, Lothian
H. Maxwell *Scottish gardens* 1908, 212–16.

Smedmore near Corfe Castle, Dorset
J. Hutchins *History . . . of Dorset* v. 1, 1861, 568. *C.L.* v. 77, 1935, 62–67. A. Paterson *Gardens of Britain* v. 2, 1978, 43–44.

Smethwick Grove, Staffs
F. Calvert *Picturesque views . . . in Staffordshire & Shropshire* 1830, 128.

Smithills Hall, Bolton, Greater Manchester
E. Baines *History . . . of Lancaster* v. 3, 1836, 45. *C.L.* v. 12, 1902, 592–99; v. 66, 1929, 488–96. C. Holme *Gardens of England in Northern counties* 1911, pls. 118–20. V.C.H. *Lancaster* v. 5, 1911, 19.

Smith's Hall, East Farleigh, Kent
J. Harris *History of Kent* 1719, 120. J. Kip *Supplement du Nouveau theatre de la Grande Bretagne* 1728, pl. 19. T. Badeslade *Thirty six different views . . . in Kent* 1750s, pl. 29.

Snelston Hall, Snelston, Derbyshire
J.B. Burke *Visitation* 2nd Series, v. 1, 1855, 228.

Sneyd Park, Westbury on Trym, Avon
R. Atkyns *Ancient and present state of Glostershire* 1712, 804. L. Knyff *and* J. Kip *Britannia illustrata* v. 2, 1715.

Snitterfield House, Snitterfield, Warwickshire
J. Harris *Artist and the country house* 1979, 227.

Snitterton Hall near Matlock, Derbyshire
C.L. v. 129, 1961, 178–81,228.

Snowshill Manor near Broadway, Glos
C.L. v. 62, 1927, 470–77; v. 163, 1978, 1358–60; v. 167, 1980, 1178–80. G.S. Thomas *Gardens of National Trust* 1979, 218–19. J. Sales *West Country gardens* 1980, 102–06.

Soho Manufactuary, Handsworth, Birmingham, W. Midlands
S. Shaw *History . . . of Staffordshire* v. 2, 1801, 121. J. Nightingale *Topographical . . . description of Staffordshire* 1810, 840.

Soldon, Holsworthy, Devon
Architectural History v. 7, 1964, 37,100.

Somerford Park near Congleton, Cheshire
J. Hort. Cottage Gdnr v. 32, 1864, 453–54.

Somerhill near Tonbridge, Kent
E. Hasted *History . . . of Kent* v. 2, 1782, 341.
J.P. Neale *Views* 2nd Series, v. 3, 1826.
C. Greenwood *Epitome of county history . . . v. 1: Kent* 1838, 126. *Garden* v. 27, 1885, 59–60. *Gdnrs Mag.* 1899, 360–63. *C.L.* v. 52, 1922, 310–17. C. Fiennes *Journeys* 1949, 137. J. Harris *Artist and the country house* 1979, 352.

Somerley Park near Ringwood, Hants
G.M. v. 11, 1835, 331. *G.C.* ii 1885, 441–42. *C.L.* v. 123, 1958, 108–11,156. R.I.B.A. *Catalogue* v. A, 1968, 29.

Somerleyton Hall, Somerleyton, Suffolk
J.P. Neale *Views* v. 4, 1821. H. Davy *Views* 1827. A. Suckling *History . . . of Suffolk* v. 2, 1848, 47. *Florist* 1857, 327–29,368–70; 1858, 29. *Garden* v. 1, 1872, 489–90,510–11. F.O. Morris *Series of picturesque views* v. 4, 71. L. Jewitt *and* S.C. Hall *Stately homes of England* 1877, 212–17. *Gdnrs Mag.* 1912, 7–10,30. M. Allan *Fisons guide* 1970, 204–05. *C.L.* v. 171, 1982, 1668–72.

Somerset House, Strand, Westminster, London
J. Beeverell *Les delices de la Grande Bretagne* v. 4, 1707, 835. L. Knyff *and* J. Kip *Britannia illustrata* v. 1, 1714. H. Overton *Britannia illustrata* c.1724, pl. 54. J.T. Smith *Antiquities of Westminster* 1807, pl. 81. H.M. Colvin *History of the King's Works* v. 4, 1982, 255,257.

Somerton Hall, West Somerton, Norfolk
J.P. Neale *Views* 2nd Series, v. 1, 1824.

Sophia Lodge, Clewer, Berks
R. Ackermann *Repository* v. 2, 1823, pls. 25–26. W.W.J. Gendall *Views* v. 2, 1830, 131–33.

Sorrel Sykes Farm, Aysgarth, N. Yorks
B. Jones *Follies & grottoes* 1974, 233.

Sotterley Hall, Sotterley, Suffolk
H. Davy *Views* 1827.

South Bank, Ipswich, Suffolk
G.C. ii 1882, 339–40.

South Bantaskine near Falkirk, Central
Scottish Gdnr and Northern Forester v. 7, 1912, 465–66. H. Maxwell *Scottish gardens* 1911, 77–79.

South Dalton House, South Dalton, Humberside
T. Badeslade *and* J. Rocque *Vitruvius Brittanicus* 1739, pls. 90–91. V.C.H. *York: East Riding* v. 4, 1979, 88. H. Colvin *and* J. Harris *Country seat* 1970, 117.

South Hill House, Mendip Hills, Somerset
R. Ackermann *Repository* v. 10, 1827, pl. 19.

South Lodge, Southgate, Enfield, London
J.C. Loudon *Encyclopaedia of gardening* 1822, 1226. *G.M.* v. 15, 1839, 513–14. V.C.H. *Middlesex* v. 5, 1976, 231.

South Lodge near Horsham, W. Sussex
G.C. i 1895, 485–86; i 1906, 98,99. T. Wright *Gardens of Britain* v. 4, 1978, 186–89.

South Ormsby, Lincs
L. Fleming *and* A. Gore *English garden* 1979, pl. 85. *Gdn History* v. 8 no. 2, 1980, 52,54–55.

South Shields. Harton Cemetery, Tyne and Wear
J. Hort. Cottage Gdnr N.S., v. 37, 1898, 63–65; N.S., v. 46, 1903, 316–17. *Gdnrs Mag.* v. 45, 1902, 858.

South Stoneham House near Southampton, Hants
J. Hort. Cottage Gdnr N.S., v. 49, 1904, 438–39.
J. Harris *Artist and the country house* 1979, 211.

South Weald Manor near Brentwood, Essex
F.G. Emmison *Catalogue of maps in Essex Record Office* 1947, 25.

South Wingfield Manor, South Wingfield, Derbyshire
J. Harris *Artist and the country house* 1979, 126.

South Wraxall Manor, South Wraxall, Wilts
C.L. v. 17, 1905, 54–64; v. 73, 1933, 720.

Southam de la Bere, Southam, Glos
R. Atkyns *Ancient and present state of Glostershire* 1712, 356. L. Knyff *and* J. Kip *Britannia illustrata* v. 2, 1715. C.L. v. 22, 1907, 594–601. Lady Rockley *Historic gardens of England* 1938, 126–27.

Southampton. Botanic Gardens, Hants
W.B. Page *Page's prodromus . . . plants . . . cultivated in the Southampton Botanic Gardens* 1818.

Southbourne, Dorset
B. Jones *Follies & grottoes* 1974, 255–56.

Southgate Grove, Southgate, Enfield, London
J.C. Loudon *Encyclopaedia of gardening* 1822, 1226.

Southgate House, Southgate, Enfield, London
G.C. ii 1899, 354–56.

Southgate Lodge, Enfield, London
G.M. v. 15, 1839, 512–13. W. Keane *Beauties of Middlesex* 1850, 182–84.

Southill near Wanstrow, Somerset
J. Collinson *History . . . of Somersetshire* v. 2, 1791, 210.

Southill Park, Biggleswade, Beds
T. Badeslade *and* J. Rocque *Vitruvius Brittanicus* 1739, pls. 84–85. W. Watt *Seats* 1779, pl. 37. R. Ackermann *Repository* v. 6, 1825, pl. 7. W.W.J. Gendall *Views* v. 1, 1830, 33. C.L. v. 68, 1930, 42–48. Lady Rockley *Historic gardens of England* 1938, 182–83. N. Pevsner *Bedfordshire and county of Huntingdon* 1968, 147. Historical MSS Commission *Architectural history* v. 3, 1971, item 3446. D. Stroud *Capability Brown* 1975, 240. R. Bisgrove *Gardens of Britain* v. 3, 1978, 164. D. Jacques *Georgian gardens* 1983, 142.

Southport. Hesketh Park, Merseyside
Gdn History Soc. Newsletter no. 16, 1972, 7–9.

Southwark Park *see* London

Southwick Hall, Southwick, Northants
C.L. v. 131, 1962, 1298–1301,1364.

Southwick House, Caulkerbush, Dumfries and Galloway
G.A. Little *Scotland's gardens* 1981, 267.

Southwick Park, Southwick, Hants
J. Beeverell *Les delices de la Grande Bretagne* v. 5, 1707, 872. L. Knyff *and* J. Kip *Britannia illustrata* v. 1, 1714. J.P. Neale *Views* v. 2, 1819. E.F. Prosser *Select illustrations of Hampshire* 1833. J. Harris *Artist and the country house* 1979, 330.

Southwood, Bickley, Bromley, London
G.C. ii 1905, 107–08.

Southwood Hall, Highgate, Haringey, London
W. Keane *Beauties of Middlesex* 1850, 86–87.

Spa Fields Pantheon, Clerkenwell, London
W. Wroth *London pleasure gardens of eighteenth century* 1896, 25–28.

Spa Green *see* London

Spa House, Cheltenham, Glos
J. Harris *Gardens of delight* 1978, 22–23.

Spains Hall, Finchingfield, Essex
T. Wright *History . . . of Essex* v. 1, 1836, 650. C.L. v. 11, 1902, 48–53; v. 172, 1982, 2076–79; v. 173, 1983, 18–21. F.G. Emmison *Catalogue of maps in Essex Record Office* 1st Supplt, 1952, 3. N. Pevsner *Essex* 1954, 331. G. Carter *et al. Humphry Repton* 1982, 151.

Spaniards Inn, Hampstead, Camden, London
W. Wroth *London pleasure gardens of eighteenth century* 1896, 184–86.

Spedan Tower, Hampstead, London
Gdn Design 1936, 105–11.

Speke Hall, Speke, Merseyside
C.L. v. 13, 1903, 336–42; v. 51, 1922, 16–22. G. Jekyll and G.S. Elgood *Some English gardens* 1904, 76–78. C. Holmes *Gardens of England in Northern counties* 1911, pls. 121–23. G.S. Thomas *Gardens of National Trust* 1979, 219.

Spence, Joseph *see* Byfleet

Spetchley Park, Spetchley, Hereford and Worcester
J.P. Neale *Views* v. 5, 1822. C.L. v. 40, 1916, 42–48, 70–75. M. Allan *Fisons guide* 1970, 169–70. B. Jones *Follies & grottoes* 1974, 342. T. Wright *Arbours & grottos* 1979. R. Sidwell *West Midland gardens* 1981, 85–87.

Spinners, Boldre, Hants
A. Paterson *Gardens of Britain* v. 2, 1978, 144–45.

Spixworth Park, Spixworth, Norfolk
G.M. v. 17, 1841, 271. J. Grigor *Eastern arboretum* 1841, 215–16.

Spofforth near Wetherby, W. Yorks
G.M. v. 6, 1830, 531–33.

Spring Garden, Stepney, Tower Hamlets, London
W. Wroth *London pleasure gardens of eighteenth century* 1896, 88–89.

Spring Gardens, Vauxhall, Lambeth, London
W. Wroth *London pleasure gardens of eighteenth century* 1896, 286–89. E.B. Chancellor *Pleasure haunts of London* 1925, 197–202.

Spring Gardens, Charing Cross, Westminster, London
E.B. Chancellor *Pleasure haunts of London* 1925, 194–97.

Spring Grove, Hounslow, London
G. Tod *Plans, elevations and sections of hot-houses* 1807, 15, pl. 11. G.M. v. 9, 1833, 649. W. Keane *Beauties of Middlesex* 1850, 67–71. J. Hort. Cottage Gdnr N.S., v. 32, 1896, 425–26.

Spring Park, Woodchester, Glos
J.N. Brewer *Delineations of Gloucestershire* 1825, 38.

Spring Vale near Stone, Staffs
F. Calvert *Picturesque views . . . in Staffordshire & Shropshire* 1830, 44.

Springfield, Poole, Dorset
J. Hutchins *History . . . of Dorset* v. 1, 1861, 44.

Springfield, Lisburn, Co. Antrim, Ulster
Scottish Gdnr and Northern Forester v. 7, 1912, 549–50. *Irish Gdning* v. 10, 1915, 114.

Springfields near Spalding, Lincs
J. Royal Hort. Soc. 1971, 177–80. J. Anthony *Gardens of Britain* v. 6, 1979, 144–48.

Springhill, Moneymore, Co. Londonderry, Ulster
G.S. Thomas *Gardens of National Trust* 1979, 219–20.

Springwood, Dartford, Kent
G.C. ii 1888, 634.

Sprotborough Hall, Sprotbrough, S. Yorks
J. Beeverell *Les delices de la Grande Bretagne* v. 5, 1707, 872. L. Knyff and J. Kip *Britannia illustrata* v. 1, 1714. J.P. Neale *Views* v. 5, 1822. *Jones's views* 1829, 36. C.L. v. 51, 1922, 174–80. I. Hall *Samuel Buck's Yorkshire sketchbook* 1979, 69.

Sproughton Chantry near Ipswich, Suffolk
J.P. Neale *Views* v. 4, 1821.

Sprowston Park, Sprowston, Norfolk
G.M. v. 17, 1841, 271. J. Grigor *Eastern arboretum* 1841, 200–01.

Spye Park near Calne, Wilts
A. Robertson *Topographical survey of the Great Road* pt. 2, 1792, 55–57. R. Warner *Excursions from Bath* 1801, 209. G.C. ii 1891, 667–68.

Squerryes Court, Westerham, Kent
J. Harris *History of Kent* 1719, 329. J. Kip *Supplement du Nouveau theatre de la Grande Bretagne* 1728, pl. 25. T. Badeslade *Thirty six different views . . . in Kent* 1750s, pl. 30. R. Pococke *Travels through England* v. 2, 1889, 74. M. Macartney *English houses & gardens* 1908, pl. 38. C.L. v. 143, 1968, 1580–83,1752; v. 153, 1973, 386.

Stackpole Court, Stackpole Elidor, Dyfed
J.P. Neale *Views* v. 5, 1822. G.C. i 1909, 218.

Stafford House (Frome Billet), West Stafford, Dorset
H. Repton *Fragments* 1816, 101–05. J. Hutchins *History . . . of Dorset* v. 2, 1863, 512. C.L. v. 131, 1962, 654–57,712–15. D. Stroud *Humphry Repton* 1962, 169. G. Carter et al. *Humphry Repton* 1982, 151.

Stafford House, Westminster, London
Historical MSS Commission *Architectural history* v. 3, 1971, item 2840.

Stagenhoe Park near Stevenage, Herts
H. Chauncy *Historical antiquities of Hertfordshire* 1700, 414. *Gdnrs Mag.* 1910, 338–40.

Staghurst, Berkhamsted, Herts
Garden 1917, 212–13.

Stainborough Castle *see* Wentworth Castle

Stainsby, Yorks
I. Hall *Samuel Buck's Yorkshire sketchbook* 1979, 332.

Stakehill House, Castleton, Greater Manchester
G.C. ii 1884, 246. *Gdning World* v. 6, 1890, 632–33.

Stalbridge House, Stalbridge, Dorset
J. Hutchins *History . . . of Dorset* v. 3, 1868, 671.

Stanage Park near Knighton, Powys
H. Repton *Fragments* 1816, 33–39. *C.L.* v. 8, 1900, 368–73. *G.C.* i 1927, 164,353. D. Stroud *Humphry Repton* 1962, 132. R. Haslam *Powys* 1979, 276. G. Carter *et al. Humphry Repton* 1982, 76,165.

Stancliffe near Bakewell, Derbyshire
G.C. ii 1884, 807–08; ii 1886, 210–11.

Stancombe Park near Dursley, Glos
B. Jones *Follies & grottoes* 1974, 247–50. *C.L.* v. 169, 1981, 26–28. J. Sales *West Country gardens* 1980, 107–08.

Standen near East Grinstead, W. Sussex
Official guide. *C.L.* v. 27, 1910, 666–72; v. 147, 1970, 494–97; v. 173, 1983, 1100–02. G.S. Thomas *Gardens of National Trust* 1979, 220–21.

Standish Hall near Wigan, Greater Manchester
J.P. Neale *Views* 2nd Series, v. 4, 1828.

Standlynch Manor, Standlynch, Wilts
V.C.H. *Wiltshire* v. 11, 1980, 70.

Standon Lordship near Hertford, Herts
H. Chauncy *Historical antiquities of Hertfordshire* 1700, 220.

Stanfield Hall near Wymondham, Norfolk
J.P. Neale *Views* v. 3, 1820.

Stanford Hall near Lutterworth, Leics
J. Throsby *Select views in Leicestershire* v. 1, 1790, 179. *C.L.* v. 124, 1958, 1284–87,1472–75.

Stanford Hall, Stanford on Soar, Notts
T. Badeslade *and* J. Rocque *Vitruvius Brittanicus* 1739, pls. 106–07. R. Thornton *Thornton's history* v. 1, 1797, 9–10. J.P. Neale *Views* v. 3, 1820.

Stanford Park near Worcester, Hereford and Worcester
W. Cobbett *rural rides* v. 2, 1912, 118.

Stanley Hall near Bridgnorth, Shropshire
J.P. Neale *Views* v. 3, 1820. F. Calvert *Picturesque views . . . in Shropshire* 1831, 122.

Stanley Park *see* Liverpool

Stanmer Park near Brighton, E. Sussex
J.P. Neale *Views* v. 4, 1821. *Garden* v. 35, 1889, 595. *Sussex Archaeological Collections* v. 117, 1979, 195–99.

Stanmore House, Stanmore, Harrow, London
W. Keane *Beauties of Middlesex* 1850, 138–39. *G.C.* ii 1913, 277–78. D. Stroud *Humphry Repton* 1962, 172. G. Carter *et al. Humphry Repton* 1982, 158.

Stanstead Bury, Stanstead Abbots, Herts
H. Chauncy *Historical antiquities of Hertfordshire* 1700, 195.

Stanstead Lodge, Stanstead Abbots, Herts
R. Bisgrove *Gardens of Britain* v. 3, 1978, 165.

Stansted Hall, Stansted Mountfitchet, Essex
F.G. Emmison *Catalogue of maps in Essex Record Office* 2nd Supplt, 1964, 19. D. Stroud *Humphry Repton* 1962, 54–55. G. Carter *et al. Humphry Repton* 1982, 152.

Stansted Park near Chichester, W. Sussex
J. Beeverell *Les delices de la Grande Bretagne* v. 5, 1707, 872. L. Knyff *and* J. Kip *Britannia illustrata* v. 1, 1714. H. Overton *Britannia illustrata* c. 1724, pl. 14. M. Macartney *English houses & gardens* 1908, pl. 40. I. Nairn *and* N. Pevsner *Sussex* 1965, 336–37. D. Stroud *Capability Brown* 1975, 240–41. *C.L.* v. 171, 1982, 346–49,478.

Stanton Court near Evesham, Glos
C.L. v. 30, 1911, 780–85.

Stanton Fitzwarren near Swindon, Wilts
C.L. v. 92, 1942, 314–17.

Stanton Harcourt near Witney, Oxfordshire
Garden v. 48, 1895, 137. *G.C.* ii 1956, 462–63. *C.L.* v. 131, 1962, 1018–20.

Stanway House, Stanway, Glos
R. Atkyns *Ancient and present state of Glostershire* 1712, 685. L. Knyff *and* J. Kip *Britannia illustrata* v. 2, 1715. *C.L.* v. 5, 1899, 816–20; v. 40, 1916, 630–37; v. 136, 1964, 1647,1708–11. J. Harris *Artist and the country house* 1979, 210.

Stanwick Park, Richmond, N. Yorks
C.L. v. 7, 1900, 208–12.

Stapleford Park, Stapleford, Leics
Official guide. J. Throsby *Select views in Leicestershire* v. 1, 1790, 147. J. Nichols *History . . . of county of Leicester* v. 3, 1804, Appendix, 69. J. Anthony *Gardens of Britain* v. 6, 1979, 148–50.

Stapleton, Bristol, Avon
D. Stroud *Humphry Repton* 1962, 172. G. Carter *et al. Humphry Repton* 1982, 153.

Stapleton Park near Pontefract, W. Yorks
J.P. Neale *Views* v. 5, 1822. *Jones's views* 1829, 29. I. Hall *Samuel Buck's Yorkshire sketchbook* 1979, 62.

Star and Garter Tavern and Gardens, Westminster, London
W. Wroth *London pleasure gardens of eighteenth century* 1896, 220–21.

Stationers Company *see* London

Staunton Harold near Ashby-de-la-Zouch, Leics
J. Beeverell *Les delices de la Grande Bretagne* v. 5, 1707, 872. L. Knyff *and* J. Kip *Britannia illustrata* v. 1, 1714. J. Throsby *Select views in Leicestershire* v. 1, 1790, 126. J. Nichols *History . . . of county of Leicester* v. 3, 1804, 717. M. Macartney *English houses & gardens* 1908, pl. 54. *C.L.* v. 33, 1913, 490–96, 526–33. G. Jekyll *Garden ornament* 1918, 11. J. Harris *Artist and the country house* 1979, 121, 269.

Steadstone, Dumfries and Galloway
C.L. v. 170, 1981, 576–78.

Steane Park, Steane, Northants
C.L. v. 84, 1938, 12–17. *Northamptonshire Past and Present* v. 5 no. 4, 1976, 314–18. Royal Commission on Historical Monuments *Inventory of the historical monuments in . . . Northampton* v. 4, 1982, 56, 58.

Steart Hill House, Little Horwood, Bucks
R. Bisgrove *Gardens of Britain* v. 3, 1978, 166–67. *Garden* 1979, 231–36.

Stede Hill, Harrietsham, Kent
C. Greenwood *Epitome of county history . . . v. 1: Kent* 1838, 160.

Steephill Botanic Garden, Ventnor, Isle of Wight
A. Paterson *Gardens of Britain* v. 2, 1978, 168–70.

Steine *see* Brighton

Stepleton House, Stepleton Iwerne, Dorset
C.L. v. 71, 1932, 42–48.

Sternfield House, Saxmundham, Suffolk
J. Royal Hort. Soc. 1962, 181–86.

Stevenson House near Haddington, Lothian
G.A. Little *Scotland's gardens* 1981, 108–09.

Stevenstone near Torrington, Devon
G.M. v. 19, 1843, 243–44. F.O. Morris *Series of picturesque views* v. 6, 21. R.I.B.A. *Catalogue* v. B, 1972, 56.

Stewards Park, Romford, Havering, London
F.G. Emmison *Catalogue of maps in Essex Record Office* 1st Supplt, 1952, 2.

Stewartry, Threave, Dumfries and Galloway
Scottish Field v. 123 no. 901, 1977, 22–23.

Stibbington Hall, Stibbington, Cambs
C.L. v. 16, 1904, 304–07.

Stilemans, Godalming, Surrey
C.L. v. 81, 1937, 63–65.

Stillorgan near Dublin, Eire
B. Jones *Follies & grottoes* 1974, 122–23. E. Malins *and* Knight of Glin *Lost demesnes* 1976, 8–9. J. Harris *Artist and the country house* 1979, 298–99.

Stinsford House near Dorchester, Dorset
G.C. i 1899, 83–84.

Stirling Castle, Stirling, Central
D. Defoe *Tour* v. 2, 1778, 753–54. *G.M.* v. 18, 1842, 603–04. *C.L.* v. 161, 1977, 1386. C. Taylor *Archaeology of gardens* 1983, 58.

Stirling. University *see* Airthrey Castle

Stisted Hall, Stisted, Essex
G. Virtue *Picturesque beauties of Great Britain: Essex* 1831, 52. T. Wright *History . . . of Essex* v. 2, 1836, 12.

Stobhall near Perth, Tayside
H.I. Triggs *Formal gardens in England and Scotland* 1902, 43–44. H. Maxwell *Scottish gardens* 1911, 181–83. *C.L.* v. 35, 1914, 738–44; v. 132, 1962, 468–71. G.A. Little *Scotland's gardens* 1981, 167.

Stock House, Stock Gaylard, Dorset
J. Hutchins *History . . . of Dorset* v. 3, 1868, 686.

Stockgrove Park near Leighton Buzzard, Beds
C.L. v. 86, 1939, 334–38.

Stockport. Lyme Park, Greater Manchester
Parks and Recreation v. 41 no. 6, 1971, 44–49.

Stocks near Tring, Herts
G. Beard *Thomas H. Mawson* 1976, 64.

Stockton House, Stockton, Wilts
G.C. i 1895, 230. C.L. v. 18, 1905, 558–68; v. 175, 1984, 336–37.

Stockwood Park near Luton, Beds
Cottage Gdnr v. 23, 1859, 21–24.

Stoke Albany, Northants
Northamptonshire Past and Present v. 5 no. 3, 1975, 231.

Stoke Bishop, Bristol, Avon
R. Atkyns *Ancient and present state of Glostershire* 1712, 804. L. Knyff *and* J. Kip *Britannia illustrata* v. 2, 1715. J.N. Brewer *Delineations of Gloucestershire* 1825, 190.

Stoke College, Stoke by Clare, Suffolk
J. Brown *Gardens of a golden afternoon* 1982, 164.

Stoke Court, Stoke Poges, Bucks
R. Bisgrove *Gardens of Britain* v. 3, 1978, 167–68.

Stoke Edith Park (Stoke Park), Stoke Edith, Hereford and Worcester
H. Repton *Observations* 1803, 137–38,149. J.P. Neale *Views* v. 2, 1819. British Museum *Catalogue of maps, prints* 1829, 320. C.L. v. 13, 1903, 744–48; v. 26, 1909, 420–29. *C.L. Annual* 1951, 81–88. G. Jekyll *Garden ornament* 1918, 248. C. Fiennes *Journeys* 1949, 45,233. D. Stroud *Humphry Repton* 1962, 51. *Connoisseur* v. 200, 1979, 86–91. G. Carter *et al. Humphry Repton* 1982, 153.

Stoke Farm, Bucks
W.W.J. Gendall *Views* v. 2, 1830, 114.

Stoke Newington (Thomas Gudgeon), Hackney, London
J. Hassell *Seats near London* 1804–05.

Stoke Park *see* Stoke Edith Park

Stoke Park, Stoke Gifford, Avon
R. Atkyns *Ancient and present state of Glostershire* 1712, 690. L. Knyff *and* J. Kip *Britannia illustrata* v. 2, 1715. *Copper Plate Mag.* v. 4, pl. 154. D. Verey *Gloucestershire* v. 2, 1970, 350. J. Harris *Artist and the country house* 1979, 231. T. Wright *Arbours & grottos* 1979.

Stoke Park, Stoke Poges, Bucks
H. Repton *Sketches* 1794, 56–57. J. Penn *Historical . . . account of Stoke Park* 1813. J.P. Neale *Views* v. 1, 1818. R. Ackermann *Repository* v. 3, 1824, pl. 31. W.W.J. Gendall *Views* v. 1, 1830, 129. *G.M.* v. 9, 1833, 528–29,641–43; v. 19, 1843, 586–89. *Florist* 1853, 285–88. *Gdning World* v. 8, 1892, 468–69. G.C. ii 1893, 653–54. C.L. v. 1, 1897, 724–26; v. 14, 1903, 168–74. *Garden* v. 60, 1901, 70. G. Jekyll *Garden ornament* 1918, 359. N. Pevsner *Buckinghamshire* 1960, 247. D. Stroud *Humphry Repton* 1962, 173. D. Stroud *Capability Brown* 1975, 49. J. Harris *Artist and the country house* 1979, 295. G. Carter *et al. Humphry Repton* 1982, 148. *Garden* 1983, 366. D. Jacques *Georgian gardens* 1983, pl. 8.

Stoke Park, Stoke Bruerne, Northants
C.L. v. 114, 1953, 280–83. *Northamptonshire Past and Present* v. 5 no. 3, 1975, 231.

Stoke Park near Guildford, Surrey
W. Keane *Beauties of Surrey* 1849, 121–22.

Stoke Park, Seend, Wilts
A. Robertson *Topographical survey of the Great Road* pt. 2, 1792, 90–92. J. Britton *Beauties of Wiltshire* v. 2, 1801, 202–03. R.I.B.A. *Catalogue* v. C–F, 1972, 112.

Stoke Place, Stoke Poges, Bucks
R. Ackermann *Repository* v. 4, 1824, pl. 12. W.W.J. Gendall *Views* v. 2, 1830, 35–36. *G.M.* v. 9, 1833, 525–28.

Stoke Poges Memorial Garden, Stoke Poges, Bucks
Official guide. *Landscape & Gdn* v. 1 no. 2, 1934, 17. C.L. v. 80, 1936, 124–25.

Stoke Rochford House, Stoke Rochford, Lincs
Copper Plate Mag. v. 5, 1802, pl. 111. *J. Hort. Cottage Gdnr* v. 51, 1874, 406–08. G.C. i 1879, 44–45; ii 1880, 495,499. C.L. v. 10, 1901, 592–97. G. Jekyll *Garden ornament* 1918, 248.

Stokesay Castle, Stokesay, Shropshire
C.L. v. 8, 1900, 714–18; v. 15, 1904, 270–72; v. 157, 1975, 713.

Stokesay Court, Stokesay, Shropshire
C.L. v. 9, 1901, 272–77.

Ston Easton Park, Ston Easton, Somerset
J. Collinson *History . . . of Somersetshire* v. 2, 1791, 155. C.L. v. 97, 1945, 508–11. D. Stroud *Humphry Repton* 1962, 68. G. Carter *et al. Humphry Repton* 1982, 161.

Stonard House, Stamford Hill, Hackney, London
W. Keane *Beauties of Middlesex* 1850, 71–72.

Stone Cottage, Hambleton, Leics
C.L. v. 162, 1977, 738–39. A. Lees-Milne *and* R. Verey *Englishman's garden* 1982, 44–47.

Stone Hall, Easton, Suffolk
G. Jekyll *and* G.S. Elgood *Some English gardens* 1904, 90–92.

Stone House Cottage near Kidderminster, Hereford and Worcester
R. Sidwell *West Midland Gardens* 1981, 87–88.

Stone Lodge *see* White Lodge

Stoneacre, Otham, Kent
C.L. v. 67, 1930, 420–26, 468.

Stonefield near Tarbet, Highland
H. Maxwell *Scottish gardens* 1911, 61–64.

Stoneham Park, Stoneham, Hants
R. Ackermann *Repository* v. 6, 1825, pl. 25. W.W.J. Gendall *views* v. 2, 1830, 29. J. Hewetson *Architectural and picturesque views of . . . Hampshire* 1830. D. Stroud *Capability Brown* 1975, 241.

Stonehouse, Whitchurch, Bucks
R. Bisgrove *Gardens of Britain* v. 3, 1978, 168–69.

Stonehouse Court, Stonehouse, Glos
T.D. Fosbrooke *Abstracts of . . . county of Gloucester* v. 1, 1807, 344.

Stonelands, Dawlish, Devon
C.L. v. 133, 1963, 702–04.

Stonelands near East Grinstead, W. Sussex
Garden v. 48, 1895, 57. J. Harris *Catalogue of British drawings . . . in American collections* 1971, 178, 179. G. Carter *et al. Humphry Repton* 1982, 163.

Stoneleigh Abbey, Stoneleigh, Warwickshire
J. Hort. Cottage Gdnr v. 48, 1872, 347–48, 365–66; N.S., v. 37, 1898, 228–30. *G.C.* ii 1890, 328; ii 1898, 320–21, 323. *C.L.* v. 1, 1897, 186–88; v. 6, 1899, 528–33; v. 10, 1901, 104–05; v. 19, 1906, 630–37; v. 160, 1976, 1974–75. *C.L. Annual* 1950, 46–47. *Gdnrs Mag.* 1901, 111–12. *Garden* v. 60, 1901, 205–07. G. Jekyll *Garden ornament* 1918, 70, 245, 342. *Gdn Design* 1935, 73–78. R. Webber *Percy Cane* 1975, 186. *Gdn History* v. 5 no. 1, 1977, 21–29. G. Carter *et al. Humphry Repton* 1982, 163.

Stonely Woods, Fadmoor, N. Yorks
R. Webber *Percy Cane* 1975, 78–80, 186–87.

Stonor Park, Stonor, Oxfordshire
J.P. Neale *Views* v. 3, 1820. *C.L.* v. 103, 1948, 976; v. 108, 1950, 1094–99; v. 158, 1975, 1794–97. V.C.H. *Oxford* v. 8, 1964, 142. J. Harris *Artist and the country house* 1979, 134.

Stonyhurst College near Clitheroe, Lancs
C.L. v. 28, 1910, 534–42, 574–83; v. 84, 1938, 60–65, 84, 87. V.C.H. *Lancaster* v. 7, 1912, 9–10. G. Jekyll *Garden ornament* 1918, 200–01. N. Pevsner *Lancashire* v. 2, 1969, 242.

Stonypath, Dunsyre, Strathclyde
C.L. v. 162, 1977, 928–30; v. 168, 1980, 1662. *J. Gdn History* v. 1 no. 2, 1981, 113–44. G.A. Little *Scotland's gardens* 1981, 267–68.

Stoodleigh Court, Stoodleigh, Devon
G.C. ii 1882, 103.

Stormont, Lord *see* Wandsworth

Stormont Castle, Belfast, Co. Down, Ulster
Scottish Gdnr and Northern Forester v. 8, 1913, 429–31. Ulster Architectural Heritage Society *Northern gardens* 1982, 21.

Stoughton Hall, Stoughton, Leics
J. Throsby *Select views in Leicestershire* v. 1, 1790, 319. J. Nichols *History . . . of county of Leicester* v. 3, 1804, 1127. *G.M.* v. 7, 1831, 425.

Stourhead, Stourton, Wilts
Official guide. J. Hannay *Journal of eight days journey* v. 1, 1757, 137–42. D. Defoe *Tour* v. 1, 1778, 317–21. R.J. Sulivan *Tour . . . in 1778* v. 1, 1785, 131–37, 143–46. *Description of house and gardens at Stourhead* 1800; 1818. J. Britton *Beauties of Wiltshire* v. 2, 1801, 13–20. R. Warner *Excursions from Bath* 1801, 104–15. W. Gilpin *Observations on the Western parts of England* 1808, 120–23. L. Simond *Journal of a tour . . . in . . . 1810 and 1811* v. 1, 1815, 200–01. R.C. Hoare *Modern history of South Wiltshire* v. 1, 1822, 63. R. Havell *Series of picturesque views* 1823, pl. 13. *G.M.* v. 9, 1833, 426; v. 11, 1835, 335–38. J.P. Neale *Views* v. 5, 1822. J.B. Burke *Visitation* v. 1, 1852, 90–92. R. Pococke *Travels through England* v. 2, 1889, 43. *C.L.* v. 9, 1901, 432–39; v. 57, 1925, 592–43. *C.L.* v. 9, 1901, 432–39; v. 57, 1925, 592–94; v. 83, 1938, 608–14. J. Wesley *Journal* v. 4, 1903, 161. H. Walpole *Visits to country seats.* Walpole Society v. 7, 1927/28, 43. Lady Rockley *Historic gardens of England* 1938, 174–75. O. Siren *China and gardens of Europe of eighteenth century* 1950, 47–51. *J. Royal Hort. Soc.* 1960, 353. P. Coats *Great gardens of Britain* 1963, 136–43. *Art Bulletin* v. 47, 1965, 83–116; v. 61, 1979, 68–77. *G.C.* i 1965, 480–81. E. Malins *English landscaping and literature* 1966, 49–56. C. Hussey *Great gardens and landscapes, 1700–1750* 1967, 158–64. *Apollo* v. 88, 1968, 210–14. K. Woodbridge *Landscape and antiquity: aspects of English culture at Stourhead, 1718–1838* 1970. K. Woodbridge *Stourhead landscape* 1971. Historical MSS Commission *Architectural history* v. 3, 1971, item

Stourhead *(Cont.)*

3482. *Burlington Mag.* v. 114, 1972, 636. H. Evans *Beautiful gardens of Britain* 1974, 31–32. B. Jones *Follies & grottoes* 1974, 44–48. N. Pevsner *Wiltshire* 1975, 497–500. *Gdn History* v. 4 no. 1, 1976, 88–109; v. 7 no.2, 1979, 102–04; v. 8 no. 3, 1980, 96,98,101. D. Jarrett *English landscape garden* 1978, 56–65. M.R. Brownell *Alexander Pope & the arts of Georgian England* 1978, 241–46. National Trust *Conservation of the garden at Stourhead: report and recommendations* 1978. L. Fleming *and* A. Gore *English garden* 1979, pls. 67–74,76. G.S. Thomas *Gardens of National Trust* 1979, 221–24. M. Hadfield *et al. British gardeners* 1980, 151–53. A. Hellyer *Gardens of genius* 1980, 27–30. J. Sales *West Country gardens* 1980, 243–49. *J. Gdn History* v. 2 no. 1, 1982, 49–50,59–70. Manpower Services Commission *Stourhead* 1982. T. Hinde *Stately gardens of Britain* 1983, 40–45. K. Rorschach *Early Georgian landscape garden* 1983, 74–79.

Stourton near Knaresborough, N. Yorks
F.O. Morris *Series of picturesque views* v. 2, 27.
D. Stroud *Capability Brown* 1975, 198–99.

Stover Lodge near Newton Abbot, Devon
R. Polwhele *History of Devonshire* v. 2, 1793.

Stow near Kilkhampton, Cornwall
C.S. Gilbert *Historical survey of . . . Cornwall* v. 2, 1820, 552–55. *C.L.* v. 131, 1962, 528. *Architectural History* v. 7, 1964, 37,104.

Stowe near Buckingham, Bucks
Official guide. G. West *Stowe: the garden* 1732; 1753. S. Bridgeman *General plan of the woods, park and gardens of Stowe* 1739; 1746. D. Defoe *Tour* v. 3, 1742, 271–87; v. 2, 1778, 176–80. B. Seeley (and after 1797) J. Seeley *Description of the house and gardens . . . at Stow* (periodically revised and reissued from 1744 to 1838—see J. Harris *Country house index* 1971, 41–42). W. Gilpin *Dialogue upon the gardens of Lord Viscount Cobham at Stowe* 1748; 1749; 1751. G. Bickham *Beauties of Stow* 1750; 1753; 1756. J.-B. Châtelain *Sixteen views of Stowe in 1752* 1753. T. Whately *Observations on modern gardening* 1771, 213–27, 243–44. A. Young *Farmer's tour through East of England* v. 1, 1771, 32–42. G.L. le Rouge *Jardins Anglo-Chinois a la mode* 2^e cahier, 1776 pls. 1–5; 4^e cahier, 1776, pls. 1, 18–21. W. Bray *Sketch of tour into Derbyshire and Yorkshire* 1783, 21–27. *New display of the beauties of England* v. 1, 1787, 47–55. H. Meister *Letters* 1799, 268–70. J. Britton *and* E.W. Brayley *Beauties of England and Wales* v. 1, 1801, 286–300. W. Marshall *On planting and rural ornament* v. 1, 1803, 298–304. S. Shaw *Tour to West of England in 1788* In J. Pinkerton v. 2, 1808, 189–90. J.P. Neale *Views* v. 1, 1818. *G.M.* v. 7, 1831, 389–90. Prince Pückler-Muskau *Tour in England, Ireland and France* 1833, 93. F.O. Morris *Series of picturesque views* v. 2, 41. *G.C.* ii 1878, 427–28. J. Wesley *Journal* v. 4, 1903, 160–61. E. Cecil *History of gardening in England* 1910, 231–32. A. Dobson *At Prior Park and other papers* 1912, 180–209. *C.L.* v. 35, 1914, 18–26,90–99; v. 102, 1947, 526–29,578–81,626–29; v. 108, 1950, 1002–06; v. 109, 1951, 119; v. 122, 1957, 68–71,390–93; v. 124, 1958, 464–66; v. 128, 1960, 1586–88; v. 130, 1961, 464; v. 140, 1966, 260–63; v. 145, 1969, 6–9,78–80; v. 151, 1972, 1254–56,1416–17; v. 155, 1974, 852–53; v. 173, 1983, 1166–67. *Bucks Architectural and Archaeological Soc. Records* v. 10, 1916, 51–59. G. Jekyll *Garden ornament* 1918, 180,194,216,362. *Architects J.* v. 57, 1923, 566–76. *Architect and Building News* v. 141, 1935, 70–71. R. Dutton *English garden* 1937, pls. 78,84. T. Jefferson *Garden book 1766–1824* 1944, 112. M. Jourdain *Work of William Kent* 1948, 78–79. O. Siren *China and gardens of Europe of eighteenth century* 1950, 26–32. A. MacDonald *Stowe House and School* 1951. R.P. Croom-Johnson *Origin of Stowe School* 1953. L. Whistler *Imagination of Vanburgh and his fellow artists* 1954, 178–88,190–93. Bucks Record Office *Hand-list of the Stowe collection in the Huntington Library, California* 1956. N. Pevsner *Buckinghamshire* 1960, 253,256–62. *Connoisseur* v. 155, 1964, 173–76. E. Malins *English landscaping and literature* 1966, 912–16. *Stoic* v. 22, 1967, 210–16,261–65, 268–69; v. 23, 1967, 5–11,65–80,116–20,158–64; v. 24, 1970, 57–64,171–82,209–15; v. 25, 1972/3, 62–68,109–15, 164–69,201–05. P. Coats *Great gardens of Britain* 1967, 42–49. C. Hussey *English gardens and landscapes, 1700–1750* 1967, 89–113. A. Lefèvre *Les parcs et les jardins* 1971, 212–18. J. Harris *Catalogue of British drawings . . . in American collections* 1971, 182–83. *Connaissance des Arts* no. 241, 1972, 66–75. *Eighteenth-century Studies* v. 6, 1972, 85–98. *Studies on Voltaire and the eighteenth century* no. 90, 1972, 1791–98. *Apollo* v. 97, 1973, 542–71. *Burlington Mag.* v. 115, 1973, 150–57. *Victorian Studies* v. 17, 1973, 508. H. Evans *Beautiful gardens of Britain* 1974, 47–48. G.B. Tobey *History of landscape architecture* 1973, 132–36. Dumbarton Oaks *Picturesque garden and its influence outside the British Isles* 1974, 34–49. B. Jones *Follies & grottoes* 1974, 135–38. P. Willis *Furor hortensis* 1974, 49–56. D. Stroud *Capability Brown* 1975, 47–53,241. A. Parreaux *and* M. Plaissant *Jardins et paysages: le style Anglais* 1977, 99–106. P. Willis *Charles Bridgeman* 1977, 106–27. *Architectural History* v. 20, 1977, 31–44; v. 21, 1978, 93. R. Bisgrove *Gardens of Britain* v. 3, 1978, 169–72. M.R. Brownell *Alexander Pope & the arts of Georgian England* 1978, 195–207. D. Jarrett *English landscape garden* 1978, 18,42–52. P. Connor *Oriental architecture in the West* 1979, 45–47. L. Fleming *and* A. Gore *English garden* 1979, 98–99, pls. 60–66. C. Thacker *History of gardens* 1979, 189. M. Hadfield *et al. British gardeners* 1980, 46,47,51,167,168. *J. Gdn History* v. 2 no. 1, 1982, 53–55. D. Watkin *English*

Stowe (*Cont.*)

vision 1982, 14–23. *Architectural Review* v. 173 no. 1033, 1983, 53–57. K. Rorschach *Early Georgian landscape garden* 1983, 26–33. C.N. Gowing *and* G.B. Clarke *Views of Stowe: drawings . . . by John Claude Nattes in the Buckinghamshire County Museum* 1983.

Stowe Nine Churches, Northants
Northamptonshire Past and Present v. 5 no. 3, 1975, 231.

Stowell Hill, Templecombe, Somerset
J. Sales *West Country gardens* 1980, 178–79.

Stowlangtoft Hall, Stowlangtoft, Suffolk
F.O. Morris *Series of picturesque views* v. 3, 27.

Stracathro House near Brechin, Tayside
J.B. Burke *Visitation* v. 1, 1852, 45.

Stradbally, Co. Laois, Eire
E. Malins *and* Knight of Glin *Lost demesnes* 1976, 23–24. J. Harris *Artist and the country house* 1979, 177.

Straffan House, Straffan, Co. Kildare, Eire
J. Hort. Cottage Gdnr v. 29, 1863, 167–69,183–86. *G.C.* i 1896, 680–81,789; i 1901, 134–36. *Garden* v. 59, 1901, 203–04. *Irish Gdning* v. 5, 1911, 117; v. 9, 1913, 59,147–49.

Stratfield Saye House near Reading, Hants
Official guide. *G.M.* v. 9, 1833, 673–77. E.F. Prosser *Select illustrations of Hampshire* 1833. *J. Hort. Cottage Gdnr* v. 49, 1873, 225–27,244–45. *G.C.* i 1896, 7–8, 44–45; v. 183 no. 20, 1978, 12–14. *Gdnrs Mag.* 1896, 711–13. *Garden* v. 54, 1898, 405. *C.L.* v. 104, 1948, 1050–53,1106–09. *Landscape Design* no. 124, 1978, 33–35.

Strathallan Castle near Crieff, Tayside
Gdning World v. 9, 1892, 212.

Strathtyrum near St Andrews, Fife
G.M. v. 7, 1831, 681–82; v. 10, 1834, 531–32.

Stratton Park, East Stratton, Hants
J.P. Neale *Views* v. 2, 1819. R. Ackermann *Repository* v. 6, 1825, pl. 19. *Jones's views* 1829. W.W.J. Gendall *Views* v. 2, 1830, 53. J. Hewetson *Architectural and picturesque views . . . in Hampshire* 1830. E.F. Prosser *Select illustrations of Hampshire* 1833. *G.C.* ii 1878, 337–38; ii 1883, 197–98. C. Holme *Gardens of England in Northern counties* 1907, 116–18. D. Stroud *Humphry Repton* 1962, 173. G. Carter *et al. Humphry Repton* 1982, 153.

Stratton Park, Stratton, Norfolk
G.M. v. 16, 1840, 667–68. J. Grigor *Eastern arboretum* 1841, 83–89.

Stratton Strawless near Norwich, Norfolk
Gdning World v. 1, 1885, 471.

Strawberry Hill, Twickenham, London
P. Sandby *Collection of one hundred and fifty select views* v. 1, 1781, pls. 33–34. *Picturesque views of the principal seats* 1788. W. Gilpin *Observations relative chiefly to picturesque beauty* v. 2, 1792, 194–95. J. *and* J. Boydell *History of River Thames* v. 2, 1796, 2. E.W.V. Chase *Horace Walpole, gardenist* 1943. J. Doyle *Strawberry Hill* 1972. B. Jones *Follies & grottoes* 1974, 333.

Streatham, Lambeth, London
Copper Plate Mag. v. 1, 1792, pl. 26. D. Stroud *Humphry Repton* 1962, 173. G. Carter *et al. Humphry Repton* 1982, 162.

Streatham (Lord William Russell), Lambeth, London
J. Hassell *Seats near London* 1804–05.

Streatham Common *see* London

Streatham Hall near Exeter, Devon
G.C. ii 1882, 300–02,305. *C.L.* v. 5, 1899, 496–500.

Streatham Memorial Garden *see* Lambeth

Streatlam Castle, Streatlam, Co. Durham
R. Surtees *History . . . of county . . . of Durham* v. 4, 1840. *C.L.* v. 38, 1915, 836–43.

Stretton Hall, Stretton, Staffs
R. Sidwell *West Midland gardens* 1981, 176.

Strixton, Northants
C.L. v. 166, 1979, 2143–44. Royal Commission on Historical Monuments *Inventory of historical monuments in . . . Northampton* v. 2, 1979, 140–42.

Strombolo House, Chelsea, London
W. Wroth *London pleasure gardens of eighteenth century* 1896, 219.

Strone House near Cairndow, Strathclyde
M. Allan *Fisons guide* 1970, 308. *C.L.* v. 163, 1978, 1673–74. G.A. Little *Scotland's gardens* 1981, 236–37.

Stroud House near Haslemere, Surrey
G.M. v. 5, 1829, 574–76.

Stubbers, North Ockendon, Havering, London
Trans. Essex Archaeological Soc. N.S., v. 21, 1937, 54. D. Stroud *Humphry Repton* 1962, 173. *V.C.H. Essex*

v. 7, 1978, 113. G. Carter *et al. Humphry Repton* 1982, 152.

Studley Castle, Studley, Warwickshire
F.O. Morris *Series of picturesque views* v. 3, 33.

Studley Priory, Studley, Oxfordshire
C.L. v. 24, 1908, 54–62.

Studley Royal near Ripon, N. Yorks
Society of Gentlemen *England displayed* v. 2, 1769, 127–28. A. Young *Six months tour through North of England* v. 2, 1771, 300–06. D. Defoe *Tour* v. 3, 1778, 142–44. R.J. Sulivan *Tour . . . in 1778* v. 2, 1785, 123. *New display of the beauties of England* v. 2, 1787, 432–35. R. Warner *Tour through northern counties of England* v. 1, 1802, 263–72. T. Pennant *Tour from Alston-Moor to Harrowgate and Brimham Crags* 1804, 74–75. *History of Ripon* 1806, 207–21. W. Gilpin *Observations on several parts of England* v. 2, 1808, 175–85. H. Skrine *Three successive tours in North of England* 1813, xii–xv. British Museum *Catalogue of maps, prints* 1829, 321. G.M. v. 12, 1836, 557–62. W. Westall [*Views of Fountains Abbey and Studley Park*] 1846. *J. Hort. Cottage Gdnr* v. 30, 1863, 28–29, 45–47; v. 55, 1876, 464–65, 493–94. G.C. ii 1880, 101–02; ii 1965, 158–59. F.O. Morris *Series of picturesque views* v. 5, 41. C.L. v. 8, 1900, 696–704; v. 70, 1931, 94–99, 128, 154–59, 180–86; v. 130, 1961, 284–87; v. 153, 1973, 335; v. 173, 1983, 912–14. C. Holme *Gardens of England in Northern counties* 1911, pl. 125. C. Hussey *Great gardens and landscapes 1700–1750* 1967, 132–39. N. Pevsner *Yorkshire: West Riding* 1967, 502–04. *Publications of Bedfordshire Historical Record Soc.* v. 47, 1968, 132, 149–50. *Quarterly Newsletter. Garden History Soc.* no. 8, 1968, 15–18. Historical MSS Commission *Architectural history* v. 2, 1970, item 2171; v. 3, 1971, items 3219, 3493. *Gdn History* v. 1 no. 1, 1972, 22–23. *York Georgian Soc. Annual Report* 1974, 17–24. H. Evans *Beautiful gardens of Britain* 1974, 113–14. B. Jones *Follies & grottoes* 1974, 28, 30. *Landscape Design* no. 115, 1976, 8–11. K. Lemmon *Gardens of Britain* v. 5, 1978, 118–20. L. Fleming *and* A. Gore *English garden* 1979, 82–83. J. Harris *Artist and the country house* 1979, 194–95. A. Hellyer *Gardens of genius* 1980, 24–26. *Mr Aislabie's gardens: three North Yorkshire gardens landscaped during 18th century by John Aislabie . . . and his son William* New Arcadians, 1981. *Garden* 1983, 301–05.

Stukeley, William *see* Grantham; Kentish Town

Sturry Court, Sturry, Kent
C.L. v. 51, 1922, 668–76. *Architectural Review* v. 62, 1927, 129–33.

Sudbourne Hall, Sudbourne, Suffolk
C.L. v. 9, 1901, 240–45.

Sudbrooke Cottage, Ham, Richmond, London
A. Lees-Milne *and* R. Verey *Englishman's garden* 1982, 108–11.

Sudbrooke Holme, Sudbrooke, Lincs
Cottage Gdnr v. 21, 1859, 228–29. C. Holme *Gardens of England in Midland & Eastern counties* 1908, pls. 108–13.

Sudbury Court, Whittlesey, Cambs
Landscape Design May 1980, 22–23.

Sudbury Hall, Sudbury, Derbyshire
Official guide. C.L. v. 77, 1935, 622–27. B. Jones *Follies & grottoes* 1974, 217. N. Pevsner *Derbyshire* 1978, 334. J. Anthony *Gardens of Britain* v. 6, 1979, 152–54. J. Harris *Artist and the country house* 1979, 130. G.S. Thomas *Gardens of National Trust* 1979, 224. N. Nichols *Local maps of Derbyshire to 1770* 1980, 153.

Sudeley Castle, Sudeley, Glos
J.B. Burke *Visitation* v. 1, 1852, 25. F.O. Morris *Series of picturesque views* v. 1, 15. C. Holme *Gardens of England in Midland & Eastern counties* 1908, pls. 114–16. C.L. v. 25, 1909, 486–95; v. 130, 1961, 744–45; v. 88, 1940, 454–58, 478–83. G. Jekyll *Garden ornament* 1918, 272–73. Lady Rockley *Historic gardens in England* 1938, 192–93. J. Sales *West Country gardens* 1980, 109–10.

Sufton Court, Sufton, Hereford and Worcester
H. Repton *Observations* 1803, 110–12. D. Stroud *Humphry Repton* 1962, 92. G. Carter *et al. Humphry Repton* 1982, 153–54.

Sugnall near Eccleshall, Staffs
Gdn History v. 9 no. 1, 1981, 26–39.

Sulby near Market Harborough, Northants
J.P. Neale *Views* v. 3, 1820.

Sulgrave Manor, Sulgrave, Northants
C.L. v. 71, 1932, 722–28. J. Anthony *Gardens of Britain* v. 6, 1979, 154–57.

Sullingstead, Hascombe, Surrey
C.L. v. 31, Supplt 4 May 1912, xxvii–viii. L. Weaver *Houses and gardens by E.L. Lutyens* 1913, 11–12. J. Brown *Gardens of a golden afternoon* 1982, 162.

Summer Castle, Fillingham, Lincs
B. Howlett *Selection of views in county of Lincoln* 1805.

Summerfield, Bowdon, Greater Manchester
Cottage Gdnr v. 21, 1859, 363–64.

Sunbury House, Sunbury, Surrey
C.L. v. 118, 1955, 801.

Sunbury Place, Sunbury, Surrey
J. Harris *Artist and the country house* 1979, 300.

Sunbury Villa, Sunbury, Surrey
W. Keane *Beauties of Middlesex* 1850, 46–48.

Sunderland Hall near Selkirk, Borders
H. Maxwell *Scottish gardens* 1911, 124–30.

Sundorne Castle near Shrewsbury, Shropshire
J.P. Neale *Views* 2nd Series, v. 3, 1826. F. Calvert *Picturesque views . . . in Shropshire* 1831, 133. F.O. Morris *Series of picturesque views* v. 6, 39.

Sundridge Park, Bromley, London
W. Angus *Seats* 1787, pl. 56. D. Stroud *Humphry Repton* 1962, 98. G. Carter *et al. Humphry Repton* 1982, 156. *Garden* 1983, 366.

Sundridge Place near Tonbridge, Kent
J. Harris *History of Kent* 1719, 305. J. Kip *Nouveau theatre de la Grande Bretagne* v. 2, 1724. T. Badeslade *Thirty six different views . . . in Kent* 1750s, pl. 31. M. Macartney *English houses & gardens* 1908, pl. 5.

Sunning Hill near Reading, Berks
J.P. Neale *Views* v. 1, 1818. D. Stroud *Humphry Repton* 1962, 50. G. Carter *et al. Humphry Repton* 1982, 148. *Garden* 1983, 366.

Sunningdale Park, Sunningdale, Berks
G.C. ii 1885, 647–49. *J. Hort. Cottage Gdnr* N.S., v. 39, 1899, 9–11.

Sunny Hill, Llandudno, Gwynedd
G.C. ii 1903, 114–15.

Sunte House near Haywards Heath, W. Sussex
J. Royal Hort. Soc. 1968, 422–30. *International Dendrology Soc. Year Book* 1978, 55–57. T. Wright *Gardens of Britain* v. 4, 1978, 189–92.

Surbiton Place, Surbiton, Kingston, London
G.F. Prosser *Select illustrations of . . . Surrey* 1828.

Surrenden Dering near Ashford, Kent
J.P. Neale *Views* 2nd Series v. 3, 1826. *J. Hort. Cottage Gdnr* v. 43, 1870, 84–85, 108.

Surrey Zoological Gardens, Southwark, London
G.M. v. 7, 1831, 692–94. C.F. Partington *National history and views of London* v. 2, 1834, 213.

Sustead Old Hall, Sustead, Norfolk
G. Carter *et al. Humphry Repton* 1982, 159. *Gdn History* v. 11 no. 1, 1983, 57–64.

Sutton Court, Stowey, Avon
J. Collinson *History . . . of . . . Somersetshire* v. 2, 1791, 96. C.L. v. 27, 1910, 126–31.

Sutton Courtenay Manor near Abingdon, Berks
C.L. v. 15, 1904, 198–204. Lady Rockley *Historic gardens of England* 1938, 234–35. *J. Institute of Landscape Architects* no. 28, 1953, 5–8.

Sutton End near Petworth, W. Sussex
M. Allan *Fisons guide* 1970, 66–67.

Sutton Hall, Sutton, Derbyshire
R. Ackermann *Repository* v. 9, 1827, pl. 1. W.W.J. Gendall *Views* v. 2, 1830, 31. C.L. v. 45, 1919, 166–73.

Sutton House, Howth, Co. Dublin, Eire
C.L. v. 80, 1936, 354–55.

Sutton Park, Sutton-on-the-Forest, N. Yorks
C.L. v. 125, 1959, 204–07; v. 158, 1975, 1068–70. K. Lemmon *Gardens of Britain* v. 5, 1978, 120–22. A. Hellyer *Gardens of genius* 1980, 101–04.

Sutton Place, Sutton-at-Hone, Kent
C. Greenwood *Epitome of county history . . . v. 1: Kent* 1838, 72.

Sutton Place near Guildford, Surrey
Official guide. G.M. v. 7, 1831, 365. W. Keane *Beauties of Surrey* 1849, 120–21. C.L. v. 4, 1898, 824–27; v. 35, 1914, 198–206, 234–42; v. 71, 1932, 202–07. *Architectural Review* v. 34, 1913, 25–28, 49–53. M.R. Gloag *Book of English gardens* 1906, 297–318. G.C. i 1911, 386–87; i 1928, 37. *Gdnrs Mag.* 1911, 8–10. *J. Hort.* N.S., v. 68, 1914, 11–14. Lady Rockley *Historic gardens of England* 1938, 108–09. *Architects J.* v. 176, 28 July 1982, 16–18. *Landscape Design* no. 145, 1983, 8–14. Sutton Place Heritage Trust *Renaissance at Sutton Place* 1983, 44–51.

Suttons, Epping, Essex
G. Carter *et al. Humphry Repton* 1982, 152.

Swadelands, Lenham, Kent
C. Greenwood *Epitome of county history . . . v. 1: Kent* 1838, 157.

Swainson, Isaac *see* Twickenham

Swainston near Newport, Isle of Wight
R. Worsley *History of Isle of Wight* 1781.

Swainston (*Cont.*)

R. Ackermann *Repository* v. 5, 1825, pl. 26.
W.W.J. Gendall *Views* v. 2, 1830, 82.

Swakeleys near Uxbridge, Hillingdon, London
J.P. Neale *Views* v. 2, 1819. W. Keane *Beauties of Middlesex* 1850, 140–42. G.C. ii 1889, 408–09,415. C.L. v. 26, 1909, 526–32.

Swallow Hayes near Wolverhampton, W. Midlands
R. Sidwell *West Midland gardens* 1981, 148–52.

Swallowfield Park, Swallowfield, Berks
G.M. v. 9, 1833, 677–78. J.B. Burke *Visitation* v. 1, 1852, 219–20,223. C.L. v. 13, 1903, 548. G.C. i 1903, 97–98,101. V.C.H. *Berkshire* v. 3, 1923, 268. J. Evelyn *Diary* v. 4, 1955, 481–82.

Swanborough Manor near Lewes, E. Sussex
C.L. v. 76, 1934, 472–77.

Swangrove, Badminton, Avon
C.L. v. 86, 1939, 626–29.

Swanmore Park, Swanmore, Hants
G.C. ii 1884, 246–47. *J. Hort. Cottage Gdnr* N.S., v. 9, 1884, 439–40; v. 17, 1888, 92–93; v. 32, 1896, 38–39; v. 49, 1904, 528–29. *Gdning World* v. 4, 1887, 40–41. C.L. v. 5, 1899, 208–12. *Garden* v. 68, 1905, 24.

Swarcliffe Hall near Ripley, N. Yorks
Historical MSS Commission *Architectural history* v. 5, 1974, items 5432,5565.

Sway, Hants
B. Jones *Follies & grottoes* 1974, 264–65.

Swaylands near Penshurst, Kent
C. Holme *Gardens of England in Southern & Western counties* 1907, pl. 119. C.L. v. 19, 1906, 870–75.

Sweeney Hall near Oswestry, Shropshire
F. Calvert *Picturesque views . . . in Shropshire* 1831, 123.

Swell near Stow-on-the-Wold, Glos
R. Atkyns *Ancient and present state of Glostershire* 1712, 705. L. Knyff *and* J. Kip *Britannia illustrata* v. 2, 1715.

Swerford. Old Rectory, Oxfordshire
C.L. v. 168, 1980, 1071–74.

Swillington Hall near Leeds, W. Yorks
J. Beeverell *Les delices de la Grande Bretagne* v. 5, 1707, 872. L. Knyff *and* J. Kip *Britannia illustrata* v. 1, 1714. J.P. Neale *Views* 2nd Series, v. 1, 1824.

Swinbrook House, Swinbrook, Oxfordshire
R. Bisgrove *Gardens of Britain* v. 3, 1978, 172.

Swinfen near Lichfield, Staffs
S. Shaw *History . . . of Staffordshire* v. 2, 1801, 30.

Swinford Old Manor near Ashford, Kent
C.L. v. 1, 1897, 350–53.

Swinnerton *see* Swynnerton

Swinton Park, Masham, N. Yorks
Society of Gentlemen *England displayed* v. 2, 1769, 152. J.P. Neale *Views* 2nd Series, v. 4, 1828. *Jones's views* 1829, 54–56. Bradford Illustrated Weekly Telegraph *Series of picturesque views* 1885. G.C. i 1896, 131–32. C.L. v. 139, 1966, 788–92,944–48. K. Lemmon *Gardens of Britain* v. 5, 1978, 123.

Swiss Gardens, New Shoreham, W. Sussex
F. Coghlan *Brighton and its environs* 1838, 74–76. W.H. *Mason's fashionable hand-book for visitors to Brighton* [1841], 34–35. R.S. Lundie *Railway excursionist's hand-book to Brighton* 1851, 42–43. F. Coghlan *Beauties of Brighton and its environs* 1862, 67–72. *Amateur Historian* v. 3 no. 8, 1958, 319–24.

Swithland Hall, Swithland, Leics
F.O. Morris *Series of picturesque views* v. 2, 37.

Swynnerton Park, Swynnerton, Staffs
J.P. Neale *Views* v. 4, 1821. *J. Hort. Cottage Gdnr* v. 36, 1866, 446–47. D. Stroud *Capability Brown* 1975, 147, 241.

Sydenham House, Marystow, Devon
Garden v. 44, 1893, 157–58. G. Jekyll *Garden ornament* 1918, 23. C.L. v. 5, 1899, 528–32; v. 37, 1915, 176–82; v. 119, 1956, 1420–23; v. 120, 1956, 16.

Sydenham Park *see* London

Sydling Court, Sydling St Nicholas, Dorset
Picturesque views of the principal seats 1788. J. Hutchins *History . . . of Dorset* v. 4, 1870, 500.

Sydnope Hall near Matlock, Derbyshire
J. Hort. Cottage Gdnr v. 51, 1874, 222–24,239.

Syndale near Faversham, Kent
C. Greenwood *Epitome of county history . . . v. 1: Kent* 1838, 253. *J. Hort. Cottage Gdnr* v. 42, 1869, 319–21.

Syon Hill, Brentford, Hounslow, London
D. Stroud *Capability Brown* 1975, 241–42.

Syon House, Hounslow, London
Official guide. R. and J. Dodsley *London and its environs described* v. 6, 1761, 7,14. Society of Gentlemen *England displayed* v. 1, 1769, 209–10. S. and N. Buck *Buck's antiquities* v. 1, 1774, pl. 181. W. Watts *Seats* 1779, pl. 49. *New display of the beauties of England* v. 2, 1787, 64–66. H. Boswell *Historical descriptions of new and picturesque views* 1800. W.B. Cooke and S. Owen *The Thames* v. 2, 1811. R. Havell *Series of picturesque views* 1815, pl. 3. R. Ackermann *Repository* v. 1, 1823, pls. 26–27. *G.M.* v. 2, 1827, 107–08; v. 5, 1829, 502–15; v. 14, 1838, 443. W.W.J. Gendall *Views* v. 2, 1830, frontispiece, 7–8. Prince Pückler-Muskau *Tour in England, Ireland and France* 1833, 61. J.W. Thompson *Practical treatise on construction of stoves* 1838, 13–15. G.J. Aungier *History and antiquities of Syon Monastery* 1840, 120–24. W. Keane *Beauties of Middlesex* 1850, 195–98. C. McIntosh *Book of the garden* 1853–55, pl. 16. *Cottage Gdnr* v. 13, 1855, 260–62. *Garden* v. 4, 1873, 14–17. *G.C.* ii 1882, 359–61,369; ii 1884, 197–98; i 1892, 628–29; v. 163 no. 17, 1936, 17–21; v. 185 no. 3, 1979, 38–41; v. 185 no. 4, 1979, 37–41; v. 185 no. 5, 1979, 30–32. *J. Hort. Cottage Gdnr* N.S., v. 16, 1888, 152–55; v. 32, 1896, 540–42. *Gdning World* v. 12, 1896, 739–40. *Gdnrs Mag.* 1898, 328–29. *C.L.* v. 5, 1899, 112–16; v. 46, 1919, 874–81. A. Bruce Jackson *Catalogue of hardy trees and shrubs in the grounds of Syon House* 1910. *Southern Eastern Naturalist* 1917, 62–64. J. MacGregor *Gardens of celebrities . . . in and around London* 1918, 94–113. E.S. Rohde *Story of the garden* 1932, 76–78. J. Evelyn *Diary* v. 3, 1955, 415. G. Taylor *Old London gardens* 1953, 47–52. *Park Administration* Nov. 1962, 24–26. *V.C.H. Middlesex* v. 3, 1962, 100. M. Allan *Fisons guide* 1970, 23–25. Historical MSS Commission *Architectural history* v. 4, 1972, items 4180,4183. D. Stroud *Capability Brown* 1975, 103,242. J. Harris *Artist and the country house* 1979, 129,272,313. Tyne and Wear County Council Museums *Capability Brown and the northern landscape* 1983, 19.

Syston *see* Siston

Tabley House near Knutsford, Cheshire
R. Ackermann *Repository* v. 2, 1823, pl. 1.
W.W.J. Gendall *Views* v. 2, 1830, 120,122. *C.L.* v. 54, 1923, 50–58,84. J. Harris *Artist and the country house* 1979, 274.

Tabramhill Gardens near Nottingham, Notts
J. Anthony *Gardens of Britain* v. 6, 1979, 157–58.

Taddyforde near Exeter, Devon
Garden v. 27, 1885, 335–36,347.

Talbot Manor, Fincham, Norfolk
C.L. v. 128, 1960, 1486–87; v. 171, 1982, 550–52.
M. Allan *Fisons guide* 1970, 207–08.

Tandridge Court near Godstone, Surrey
W. Keane *Beauties of Surrey* 1849, 66–67.

Tangley Manor near Guildford, Surrey
G.C. i 1893, 473–74.

Tankersley Park near Barnsley, S. Yorks
J. Kip *Nouveau theatre de la Grande Bretagne* v. 4, 1729.
Yorkshire Archaeological J. v. 47, 1975, 110–14,116.
J. Harris *Artist and the country house* 1979, 149.

Tapeley Park, Westleigh, Devon
Architectural Review v. 61, 1927, 210–13. B. Jones *Follies & grottoes* 1974, 315.

Taplow, Bucks
D. Stroud *Capability Brown* 1975, 182. G. Carter *et al. Humphry Repton* 1982, 148.

Taplow Court, Taplow, Bucks
G.M. v. 9, 1833, 657–58. *G.C.* ii 1886, 229–30; i 1908, 372–73. *Garden* 1913, 325–27. C. Holme *Gardens of England in Southern & Western counties* 1907, pls. 121–22.

Taplow House, Taplow, Bucks
J. and J. Boydell *History of the River Thames* v. 1, 1794, 278–79. *G.M.* v. 9, 1833, 658–60; v. 13, 1837, 6–7.

Taplow Lodge, Taplow, Bucks
G.M. v. 9, 1833, 656–57.

Tarrant Gunville, Dorset
Royal Commission on Historical Monuments *Inventory of historical monuments in . . . Dorset* v. 4, 1972, 92–93, pl. 72.

Tarrant Rushton House near Blandford, Dorset
J. Hort. Cottage Gdnr v. 34, 1865, 143–45,170–71.
A. Paterson *Gardens of Britain* v. 2, 1978, 44–45.

Tattershall Castle, Tattershall, Lincs
C.L. v. 38, 1915, 18–26,55.

Tatton Park near Knutsford, Cheshire
Official guide. H. Repton *Sketches* 1794, 8–9,30–35, 50–53. J. Aikin *Description of the country . . . round Manchester* 1795, 423. J.P. Neale *Views* v. 1, 1818.
R. Ackermann *Repository* v. 2, 1823, pl. 13.
W.W.J. Gendall *Views* v. 1, 1830, 43. *G.M.* v. 7, 1831, 549–50. *J. Hort. Cottage Gdnr* N.S., v. 41, 1900, 59–60.
C.L. v. 19, 1906, 414–21; v. 136, 1964, 162–65,292–96; v. 159, 1976, 884–86. C. Holme *Gardens of England in*

Tatton Park (*Cont.*)
Midland & Eastern counties 1908, pls. 117–18. *G.C.* ii 1961, 188–89; ii 1965, 182–83; i 1966, 187; ii 1966, 12. D. Stroud *Humphry Repton* 1962, 78–79. J. Pratt *Tatton Park: a family portrait* 1969. M. Allan *Fisons guide* 1970, 233–34. N. Pevsner and E. Hubbard *Cheshire* 1971, 356. G.S. Thomas *Gardens of National Trust* 1979, 224–26. G. Carter et al. *Humphry Repton* 1982, 150.

Taverham Hall, Taverham, Norfolk
J. Grigor *Eastern arboretum* 1841, 57–58.

Tavistock. Abbey and Hostel, Devon
G. Carter et al. *Humphry Repton* 1982, 151.

Tawstock House, Tawstock, Devon
R. Polwhele *History of Devonshire* v. 2, 1793, 409.

Tayfield, Newport-on-Tay, Fife
G.A. Little *Scotland's gardens* 1981, 167–69.

Taymouth Castle near Aberfeldy, Tayside
T. Pennant *Tour in Scotland* 1772, 80–81. W. Gilpin *Observations, relative chiefly to picturesque beauty* v. 1, 1792, 157–59. J.P. Neale *Views* v. 6, 1823. H. Skrine *Three successive tours in North of England* 1813, 53–54. F.O. Morris *Series of picturesque views* v. 2, 31. R. Pococke *Tours in Scotland* 1887, 235–36. *Gdning World* v. 17, 1900, 104–05. *Scottish Gdnr and Northern Forester* v. 6, 1911, 705–06; v. 7, 1912, 633–34. *C.L.* v. 136, 1964, 912–13, 978–79. I.H. Adams *Descriptive list of plans* v. 1, 1966, 134. *Publications of Bedfordshire Historical Record Soc.* v. 47, 1968, 154–55. B. Jones *Follies & grottoes* 1974, 188–91. J. Harris *Artist and the country house* 1979, 198–99. A.A. Tait *Landscape garden in Scotland* 1980, passim.

Tealing, Tayside
I.H. Adams *Descriptive list of plans* v. 3, 1974, 12.

Teddesley near Penkridge, Staffs
W. Pitt *General view of agriculture of . . . Stafford* 1796, 94. E.A. Brooke *Gardens of England* 1857, pls. 31–32. Historical MSS Commission *Architectural history* v. 2, 1970, item 2189.

Teddington Grove, Twickenham, London
G.M. v. 13, 1837, 10–12; v. 15, 1839, 424–26.

Tedsmore Hall near Oswestry, Shropshire
G.C. ii 1884, 74–75.

Tehidy House near Redruth, Cornwall
W. Borlase *Natural history of Cornwall* 1758, pl. 10. W. Watts *Seats* 1779 pl. 34. C.S. Gilbert *Historical survey of . . . Cornwall* v. 2, 1820, 690–91. J. Britton and E.W. Brayley *Devonshire & Cornwall* 1832, 43. *J. Hort. Cottage Gdnr* v. 59, 1878, 109–11.

Telegraph Cottage, Kingston Hill, London
C.L. v. 160, 1976, 1383–84.

Telegraph Hill *see* London

Telegraph House near Compton, W. Sussex
T. Wright *Gardens of Britain* v. 4, 1978, 192–94.

Temple, Sir William *see* Sheen

Temple Cottage, Newington, Kent
B. Jones *Follies & grottoes* 1974, 350.

Temple Dinsley near Hitchin, Herts
H. Chauncy *Historical antiquities of Hertfordshire* 1700, 396. *C.L.* v. 29, 1911, 562–72. L. Weaver *Houses and gardens by E.L. Lutyens* 1913, 221–31. G. Jekyll *Garden ornament* 1918, 38, 215. J. Brown *Gardens of a golden afternoon* 1982, 170.

Temple Hill, Blackrock, Co. Dublin, Eire
Cottage Gdnr v. 28, 1862, 30–31, 46–47.

Temple House, Great Marlow, Bucks
G.C. ii 1898, 191–92.

Temple Newsam near Leeds, W. Yorks
J. Beeverell *Les delices de la Grande Bretagne* v. 5, 1707, 872. L. Knyff and J. Kip *Britannia illustrata* v. 1, 1714. *Jones's views* 1829, 27. J.B. Burke *Visitation* v. 1, 1852, 92. F.O. Morris *Series of picturesque views* v. 1, 71. *Garden* v. 60, 1901, 80–81. *G.C.* ii 1908, 5. *Leeds Art Calendar* no. 53, 1964, 4–9. N. Pevsner *Yorkshire West Riding* 1967, 350. D. Stroud *Capability Brown* 1975, 115–18, 242. K. Lemmon *Gardens of Britain* v. 5, 1978, 187–89. J. Harris *Artist and the country house* 1979, 316–17. Tyne and Wear County Council Museums *Capability Brown and the northern landscape* 1983, 31–32, 42.

Temple of Flora, Lambeth, London
W. Wroth *London pleasure gardens of eighteenth century* 1896, 266–67.

Templeogue near Dublin, Co. Dublin, Eire
E. Malins and Knight of Glin *Lost demesnes* 1976, 18.

Tempo Manor, Tempo, Co. Fermanagh, Ulster
A. Rowan *North West Ulster* 1979, 500. E. Malins and P. Bowe *Irish gardens and demesnes* 1980, 132–33. Ulster Architectural Heritage Society *Northern gardens* 1982, 21–22.

Tendring Hall, Stoke-by-Nayland, Suffolk
G.C. ii 1879, 363–64. D. Stroud *Humphry Repton* 1962, 54. G. Carter et al. *Humphry Repton* 1982, 162.

Terling Place, Terling, Essex
T. Wright *History . . . of Essex* v. 1, 1836, 239.
F.G. Emmison *Catalogue of maps in Essex Record Office* 1st Supplt, 1952, 1,17.

Terregles near Dumfries, Dumfries and Galloway
G.M. v. 9, 1833, 4. *Scottish Gdnr and Northern Forester* v. 8, 1913, 369. *G.C.* ii 1899, 290.

Teston, Kent
E. Hasted *History . . . of Kent* v. 2, 1782, 292.

Testwood near Southampton, Hants
D. Stroud *Capability Brown* 1975, 242.

Tew *see* Great Tew

Tewin House, Tewin, Herts
J. Harris *Artist and the country house* 1979, 216–17.

Tewin Water, Tewin, Herts
J.P. Neale *Views* v. 2, 1819. *G.C.* ii 1898, 214. *Gdning World* v. 15, 1899, 755–56. D. Stroud *Humphry Repton* 1962, 173. G. Carter *et al. Humphry Repton* 1982, 154.

Tewkesbury Lodge, Forest Hill, Lewisham, London
J. Hort. Home Farmer N.S., v. 66, 1913, 11–13.

Thame. Pearce Memorial Garden, Oxfordshire
Architectural Review v. 59, 1926, 234–36.

Thame Park, Thame, Oxfordshire
C.L. v. 26, 1909, 90–97; v. 122, 1957, 1092–95, 1148–51.

Thames Ditton (Sir Thomas Heathcote), Surrey
P. Sandby *Collection of one hundred and fifty select views* v. 1, 1781, pl. 64.

Thames Embankment *see* London

Thanckes near Devonport, Cornwall
C.S. Gilbert *Historical survey of . . . Cornwall* v. 2, 1820, 394–95.

Thatched Rest, Welwyn, Herts
G. Beard *Thomas H. Mawson* 1976, 64.

Theobalds near Cheshunt, Herts
Archaeologia v. 7, 1785, 121. D. Lysons *Environs of London* v. 4, 1796, 34,37. P. Hentzner *Travels in England* 1797, 38. J. Britton and E.W. Bayley *Beauties of England and Wales* v. 7, 1808, 242. J.C. Loudon *Encyclopaedia of gardening* 1822, 1233. *G.M.* v. 15, 1839, 514–15; v. 16, 1840, 587–88; v. 17, 1841, 92–93. A.F. Sieveking *Praise of gardens* 1899, 126. E. Cecil *History of gardening in England* 1910, 328–31. V.C.H.
Hertford v. 3, 1912, 448. *C.L.* v. 57, 1925, 781. E.S. Rohde *Story of the garden* 1932, 80–81. J. Evelyn *Diary* v. 2, 1955, 81. R. Strong *Renaissance garden in England* 1979, 51–56. H.M. Colvin *History of the King's Works* v. 4, 1982, 277.

Thicket Priory near York, N. Yorks
F.O. Morris *Series of picturesque views* v. 6, 37.

Thickthorn Hall near Hethersett, Norfolk
J. Grigor *Eastern arboretum* 1841, 272–73.

Thimbleby Hall, Thimbleby, N. Yorks
K. Lemmon *Gardens of Britain* v. 5, 1978, 124–25.

Thirkleby near Thirsk, N. Yorks
J.P. Neale *Views* v. 5, 1822. *Jones's views* 1829, 26.

Thirlestane Castle near Selkirk, Borders
G.M. v. 18, 1842, 578–81. J. Harris *Artist and the country house* 1979, 109.

Thomastown, Co. Tipperary, Eire
J.P. Neale *Views* v. 6, 1823. E. Malins *and* Knight of Glin *Lost demesnes* 1976, 5–6.

Thoor Ballylee, Co. Galway, Eire
E. Malins *and* P. Bowe *Irish gardens and demesnes* 1980, 145–47.

Thoresby Park near Ollerton, Notts
Official guide. C. Campbell *Vitruvius Britannicus* v. 3, 1725, 81–82. H. Repton *Observations* 1803, 37–40. J.P. Neale *Views* v. 3, 1820. *J. Hort. Cottage Gdnr* v. 55, 1876, 449–52. *Garden* v. 8, 1880, 425–29. *G.C.* ii 1889, 182. W. Robinson *English flower garden* 1883, x. C. Holme *Gardens of England in Midland & Eastern counties* 1908, pl. 119. *Gdnrs Mag.* 1910, 473–74. H. Walpole *Visits to country seats. Walpole Society* v. 7, 1927/8, 74. D. Stroud *Humphry Repton* 1962, 56. M. Allan *Fisons guide* 1970, 235. Historical MSS Commission *Architectural history* v. 3, 1971, items 3423,3604. D. Stroud *Capability Brown* 1975, 242–43. *C.L.* v. 165, 1979, 2082–85; v. 166, 1979, 18–21. J. Anthony *Gardens of Britain* v. 6, 1979, 158–60. J. Harris *Artist and the country house* 1979, 121. N. Pevsner *Nottinghamshire* 1979, 350. G. Carter *et al. Humphry Repton* 1982, 160.

Thornbridge Hall near Bakewell, Derbyshire
G.C. ii 1898, 221,222,223.

Thornbury, Sheffield, S. Yorks
Gdning World v. 1, 1885, 647.

Thornbury Castle, Thornbury, Avon
C.L. v. 22, 1907, 702–12; v. 118, 1955, 598. Lady Rockley *Historic gardens of England* 1938, 76–77.

Thornbury Park, Thornbury, Avon
J.B. Burke *Visitation* v. 1, 1852, 84; 2nd Series v. 1, 1855, 215.

Thorncroft, Leatherhead, Surrey
E.W. Brayley *and* J. Britton *Topographical history of Surrey* v. 4, 428.

Thorndon Hall near Brentwood, Essex
Official guide. W. Watts *Seats* 1779, pl. 17. G.A. Walpoole *New British traveller* 1784, 69. H. Boswell *Historical descriptions of new and picturesque views* 1800. T. Wright *History . . . of Essex* v. 2, 1836, 553. J.C. Loudon *Arboretum et fruticetum Britannicum* v. 1, 1844, 58. F.G. Emmison *Catalogue of maps in Essex Record Office* 1947, 13,23,30,31, pls. 18–20. Garden History Society *Occasional Paper* no. 2, 1970, 27–40. D. Stroud *Capability Brown* 1975, 243. G. Carter et al. *Humphry Repton* 1982, 152.

Thorney Abbey House near Peterborough, Cambs
C.L. v. 46, 1919, 392–400.

Thorngrove near Worcester, Hereford and Worcester
J. Hort. Cottage Gdnr v. 49, 1873, 79–81.

Thornhaugh, Northants
Northamptonshire Past and Present v. 5 no. 3, 1975, 231.

Thornton Castle near Laurencekirk, Grampian
Scottish Gdnr and Northern Forester v. 7, 1912, 271–72.

Thornton Hall, Ulceby, Lincs
G. Beard *Thomas H. Mawson* 1976, 64.

Thornton Manor, Thornton Hough, Merseyside
C. Holme *Gardens of England in Northern counties* 1911, pls. 126–28. N. Pevsner *and* E. Hubbard *Cheshire* 1971, 360. G. Beard *Thomas H. Mawson* 1976, 64.

Thornton Watlass near Bedale, N. Yorks
I. Hall *Samuel Buck's Yorkshire sketchbook* 1979, 395.

Thornwood Lodge, Camden, London
W. Keane *Beauties of Middlesex* 1850, 145–46.

Thorp Perrow, Firby, N. Yorks
G.M. v. 15, 1839, 211–12. *G.C.* ii 1878, 11–13,208–09, 405; i 1889, 204,205. K. Lemmon *Gardens of Britain* v. 5, 1978, 125–30. *C.L.* v. 169, 1981, 566–68.

Thorpe Hall, Thorpe-le-Soken, Essex
C.L. v. 48, 1920, 833–34. *G.C.* i 1939, 379.

Thorpe Hall, Louth, Lincs
M. *and* R. Tooley *Gardens of Gertrude Jekyll in Northern England* 1982, 54.

Thorpe Hall near Peterborough, Northants
C.L. v. 16, 1904, 234–43; v. 46, 1919, 300–09; v. 48, 1920, 833–34. G. Jekyll *Garden ornament* 1918, 246.

Thorpe Mandeville Manor, Thorpe Mandeville, Northants
C.L. v. 84, 1938, 180–84. Royal Commission on Historical Monuments *Inventory of the historical monuments in . . . Northampton* v. 4, 1982, 146,148.

Thrale Place, Streatham, Lambeth, London
Picturesque views of the principal seats 1788. *Copper Plate Mag.* v. 1, 1792, pl. 14.

Threave Gardens, Threave, Dumfries and Galloway
Official guide. *C.L.* v. 156, 1974, 382–84. *Northern Gardener* v. 29 no. 2, 1975, 42–45. P. Verney *Gardens of Scotland* 1976, 140–51.

Three Ash Farm (Althorne Lodge), Althorne, Essex
F.G. Emmison *Catalogue of maps in Essex Record Office* 3rd Supplt, 1968, 16.

Throcking House, Throcking, Herts
H. Chauncy *Historical antiquities of Hertfordshire* 1700, 118.

Thrumpton Hall, Thrumpton, Notts
R. Thoroton *Thoroton's history* v. 1, 1797, 36. *Garden* v. 37, 1890, 267–68. *C.L.* v. 125, 1959, 1138–41,1194, 1254–57.

Thrybergh Park near Rotherham, S. Yorks
F.O. Morris *Series of picturesque views* v. 1, 33.

Thuborough, Sutcombe, Devon
Architectural History v. 7, 1964, 38,106.

Thundercliffe Grange, Rotherham, S. Yorks
I. Hall *Samuel Buck's Yorkshire sketchbook* 1979, 96.

Thurcroft, Rotherham, S. Yorks
I. Hall *Samuel Buck's Yorkshire sketchbook* 1979, 79.

Thurnham Hall, Thurnham, Lancs
J.P. Neale *Views* 2nd Series, v. 2, 1825. *Jones's views* 1829.

Thursford Hall, Thursford, Norfolk
J.P. Neale *Views* v. 3, 1820.

Tichborne House near Alresford, Hants
E.F. Prosser *Select illustrations of Hampshire* 1833.

Tidworth House, South Tidworth, Hants
G.M. v. 10, 1834, 470–73; v. 19, 1843, 582–84. *Cottage Gdnr* v. 16, 1856, 276–77. *Florist* 1856, 170–73,194–97. G.C. ii 1891, 451–52. E.F. Prosser *Select illustrations of Hampshire* 1833.

Tigbourne Court, Witley, Surrey
International Studio v. 17, 1902, 21–24. C.L. v. 18, 1905, 414–22. L. Weaver *Houses and gardens by E.L. Lutyens* 1913, 41–47. J. Brown *Gardens of a golden afternoon* 1982, 164.

Tilgate House near Crawley, W. Sussex
J. Hort. Cottage Gdnr N.S., v. 45, 1902, 222,224.

Tillingbourne near Dorking, Surrey
W. Keane *Beauties of Surrey* 1849, 145–46.

Tillypronie near Aboyne, Grampian
G.A. Little *Scotland's gardens* 1981, 209–10.

Tilstone Lodge, Tilstone Fearnall, Cheshire
J. Royal Hort. Soc. 1975, 80–83.

Tintinhull House near Yeovil, Somerset
Official guide. *J. Royal Hort. Soc.* 1955, 24–32. C.L. v. 119, 1956, 736–39,798–801. G.C. i 1962, 118–19, 125; ii 1965, 134–35. M. Allan *Fisons guide* 1970, 107–08. H. Evans *Beautiful gardens of Britain* 1974, 23–24. G.S. Thomas *Gardens of National Trust* 1979, 226–27. J. Sales *West Country gardens* 1980, 180–83.

Tirley Garth, Tarporley, Cheshire
G. Beard *Thomas H. Mawson* 1976, 64–65. C.L. v. 171, 1982, 702–05.

Tissington Hall, Tissington, Derbyshire
J.P. Neale *Views* 2nd Series, v. 1, 1824. C.L. v. 5, 1899, 144–48; v. 160, 1976, 214–17,286–89. C. Holme *Gardens of England in Midland & Eastern counties* 1908, pls. 121–22. G. Jekyll *Garden ornament* 1918, 67.

Titsey Place, Titsey, Surrey
J.P. Neale *Views* v. 4, 1821. E.W. Brayley *and* J. Britton *Topographical history of Surrey* v. 4, 204.

Tittenhurst, Sunninghill, Berks
G.C. ii 1904, 283–84,285; v. 154, 316–17. *Gdnrs Mag.* 1906, 253–57. C.L. v. 75, 1934, 265–67; v. 77, 1935, 268–73.

Tivoli, Co. Cork, Eire
E. Malins *and* Knight of Glin *Lost demesnes* 1976, 113–14.

Tixall, Staffs
J.P. Neale *views* v. 4, 1821. F. Calvert *Picturesque views . . . in Staffordshire & Shropshire* 1830, 34. *Archaeological J.* v. 120, 1963, 264. D. Stroud *Capability Brown* 1975, 153–54.

Tocknells Court, Painswick, Glos
C.L. v. 37, 1915, 518–23. G. Jekyll *Garden ornament* 1918, 76.

Toddington, Beds
J. Britton *Historical . . . sketch of Toddington* 1840.

Toddington Manor, Toddington, Glos
R. Atkyns *Ancient and present state of Glostershire* 1712, 781. L. Knyff *and* J. Kip *Britannia illustrata* v. 2, 1715. G.M. v. 17, 1841, 418–20. F.O. Morris *Series of picturesque views* v. 5, 69. C.L. v. 15, 1904, 630–35. *Gdnrs Mag.* 1915, 8–10. M. Binney *and* A. Hills *Elysian gardens* 1979, 36.

Tofts Hall, West Tofts, Norfolk
G. Carter *et al. Humphry Repton* 1982, 159.

Tollymore Park near Newcastle, Co. Down, Ulster
Delineator 1831, 55. J.C. Loudon *Arboretum et fruticetum Britannicum* v. 1, 1844, 110. G.C. ii 1957, 169; i 1962, 248–49. B. Jones *Follies & grottoes* 1974, 91–93. E. Malins *and* Knight of Glin *Lost demesnes* 1976, 118–22. T. Wright *Arbors & grottos* 1979, Ulster Architectural Heritage Society *Northern gardens* 1982, 22.

Tonacombe near Moorwinstow, Cornwall
C.L. v. 74, 1933, 500–06. Lady Rockley *Historic gardens of England* 1938, 92–93.

Tong Castle, Tong, Shropshire
W. Angus *Seats* 1787, pl. 20. J.P. Neale *Views* 2nd Series, v. 2, 1825. F. Calvert *Picturesque views . . . in Shropshire* 1831, 118. C.L. v. 100, 1946, 578–81. B. Jones *Follies & grottoes* 1974, 125–28. D. Stroud *Capability Brown* 1975, 148. L. Fleming *and* A. Gore *English garden* 1979, 121. *Landscape Research* v. 7 no. 1, 1982, 20.

Tong Hall, Bradford, W. Yorks
J.P. Neale *Views* v. 5, 1822. *Jones's views* 1829, 45.

Tongswood near Hawkhurst, Kent
G.C. ii 1925, 151–52,153. *Architectural Review* v. 63, 1928, 44–47.

Tooting Bec Common *see* London

Torre Abbey, Torquay, Devon
R. Ackermann *Repository* v. 11, 1828, pl. 31. W.W.J. Gendall *Views* v. 1, 1830, 134.

Torosay Castle, Mull, Strathclyde
G.A. Little *Scotland's gardens* 1981, 237–38.

Torpel, Northants
Northamptonshire Past and Present v. 5 no. 3, 1975, 231–32.

Torry Hill near Lenham, Kent
Cottage Gdnr v. 26, 1861, 178–79. *J. Hort. Cottage Gdnr* v. 30, 1863, 308–09.

Tortworth Court, Tortworth, Avon
R. Atkyns *Ancient and present state of Glostershire* 1712, 784. L. Knyff *and* J. Kip *Britannia illustrata* v. 2, 1715. T.D. Fosbrooke *Abstracts of . . . county of Gloucester* v. 2, 1807, 40. *J. Hort. Cottage Gdnr* v. 50, 1873, 155–58; N.S., v. 59, 1909, 586–87; v. 68, 1914, 272–73. *G.C.* ii 1880, 433, 435–36, 465, 466–67; v. 188 no. 8, 1980, 11–13. *C.L.* v. 5, 1899, 592–97; v. 81, 1937, 5–7.

Totesham *see* Tutsham

Totley Hall, Totley, S. Yorks
Garden v. 49, 1896, 461–62.

Tottenham Park near Marlborough, Wilts
A. Robertson *Topographical survey of the Great Road* pt. 2, 1792, 20–23. J.P. Neale *Views* v. 5, 1822. *G.M.* v. 7, 1831, 136–39; v. 10, 1834, 413–19. *Florist* 1854, 273–75. *Scottish Gdnr* v. 3, 1854, 311–13. N. Pevsner *Wiltshire* 1975, 529. D. Stroud *Capability Brown* 1975, 92–95.

Totteridge Park, Barnet, London
T. Badeslade *and* J. Rocque *Vitruvius Brittanicus* 1739, pls. 77–78. Historical MSS Commission *Architectural history* v. 2, 1970, item 2221; v. 3, 1971, item 3532.

Touch, Cambusbarron, Central
C.L. v. 138, 1965, 440–43. I.H. Adams *Descriptive list of plans* v. 3, 1974, 129. G.A. Little *Scotland's gardens* 1981, 169.

Tournaig, near Poolewe, Highland
G.A. Little *Scotland's gardens* 1981, 238.

Tower Court, Ascot, Berks
G.C. i 1930, 268.

Tower of Lethendy, Meikleour, Tayside
G.A. Little *Scotland's gardens* 1981, 169–70.

Tower of London, Tower Hamlets, London
H.M. Colvin *History of the King's Works* v. 2, 1963, 717, 723.

Towers, Didsbury, Greater Manchester
G.C. i 1878, 464–65.

Towerville, Helensburgh, Strathclyde
J. Hort. Cottage Gdnr v. 37, 1867, 25–26.

Towie Barclay near Turiff, Grampian
Leopard no. 25, 1976/77, 12.

Towneley Hall near Burnley, Lancs
Official guide. E. Baines *History . . . of Lancaster* v. 3, 1836, 253. *C.L.* v. 34, 1913, 228–33.

Townhill Park near Southampton, Hants
C.L. v. 53, 1923, 536–41; v. 74, 1933, 394–96. Lady Rockley *Historic gardens of England* 1938, 256–57.

Townley Hall near Drogheda, Co. Louth, Eire
G.M. v. 2, 1827, 148–49. *C.L.* v. 104, 1948, 178, 181, 231. E. Malins *and* Knight of Glin *Lost demesnes* 1976, 90–91.

Tradescant Trust Museum *see* St Mary's Church

Tradescants *see* Lambeth

Trafalgar House near Salisbury, Wilts
G.M. v. 9, 1833, 15–16. F.O. Morris *Series of picturesque views* v. 3, 23. *C.L.* v. 98, 1945, 68–71. P. Willis *Charles Bridgeman* 1977, 183.

Trafford Park, Greater Manchester
Gdning World v. 2, 1885, 184–86.

Tranby Croft, Hessle, Humberside
J. Hort. Cottage Gdnr N.S., v. 38, 1899, 256–57.

Traquair House, Traquair, Borders
G.M. v. 18, 1842, 440. *C.L.* v. 20, 1906, 198–205; v. 106, 1949, 610–13. Royal Commission on the Ancient and Historical Monuments of Scotland *Peebleshire: an inventory of the ancient monuments* v. 2, 1967, 325, pls. 94, 117, 118.

Trawscoed near Aberystwyth, Dyfed
J. Hort. Cottage Gdnr N.S., v. 22, 1891, 209–10.

Trebartha Hall near Launceston, Cornwall
C.S. Gilbert *Historical survey of . . . Cornwall* v. 2, 1820, 485.

Treberfydd near Brecon, Powys
C.L. v. 140, 1966, 276–79, 322.

Tredegar House, Newport, Gwent
Official guide. J.P. Neale *Views* 2nd Series, v. 4, 1828. *J. Hort. Cottage Gdnr* N.S., v. 20, 261–63. *C.L.* v. 24,

Tredegar House *(Cont.)*

1908, 792–801; v. 164, 1978, 994–97. D. Jacques *Georgian gardens* 1983, 117.

Tredrea near St Ives, Cornwall
J. Hort. Cottage Gdnr v. 52, 1874, 361–62.

Treemans, Horsted Keynes, W. Sussex
C.L. v. 139, 1966, 506–08,518.

Tregothnan near Truro, Cornwall
J.P. Neale *Views* v. 1, 1818. C.S. Gilbert *Historical survey of . . . Cornwall* v. 2, 1820, 834–35. J. Britton and E.W. Brayley *Devonshire & Cornwall* 1832, 24. *G.M.* v. 13, 1837, 121. F.O. Morris *Series of picturesque views* v. 5, 29. *J. Hort. Cottage Gdnr* v. 58, 1877, 269–71,288–90. *G.C.* i 1909, 289–90. *Garden* 1913, 397–99. C. Fiennes *Journeys* 1949, 259. *C.L.* v. 119, 1956, 1051–54,1112–15. D. Stroud *Humphry Repton* 1962, 77. G. Carter *et al. Humphry Repton* 1982, 150.

Tregrehan near St Austell, Cornwall
G.C. ii 1939, 120. *Rhododendrons* 1983/4, 25–28.

Trelaske House near Launceston, Cornwall
C.S. Gilbert *Historical survey of . . . Cornwall* v. 2, 1820, 488.

Trelawny House, Pelynt, Cornwall
C.S. Gilbert *Historical survey of . . . Cornwall* v. 2, 1820, 916.

Trelissick near Truro, Cornwall
Official guide. C.S. Gilbert *Historical survey of . . . Cornwall* v. 2, 1820, 807–08. R. Ackermann *Repository* v. 9, 1827, pl. 8. W.W.J. Gendall *Views* v. 1, 1830, 35. J. Britton and E.W. Brayley *Devonshire & Cornwall* 1832, 42. *G.C.* ii 1894, 500; i 1895, 70,77; i 1896, 485; i 1901, 342–43; ii 1964, 96–98. *J. Royal Hort. Soc.* 1960, 353–54. *C.L.* v. 131, 1962, 54–55. P.M. Synge *Gardens of Britain* v. 1, 1977, 118–19. G.S. Thomas *Gardens of National Trust* 1979, 227–29. Manpower Services Commission *Trelissick* 1982.

Trelowarren near Helston, Cornwall
W. Borlase *Natural history of Cornwall* 1758, pl. 6. J. Britton and E.W. Brayley *Devonshire & Cornwall* 1832, 41. *G.M.* v. 13, 1837, 121. *C.L.* v. 39, 1916, 450–55.

Treloyhan near St Ives, Cornwall
G.C. i 1905, 84–85.

Tremeer near Bodmin, Cornwall
C.L. v. 128, 1960, 1018–20; v. 168, 1980, 1548–50. *G.C.* i 1965, 504–05. P.M. Synge *Gardens of Britain* v. 1, 1977, 120–23.

Tremough near Penryn, Cornwall
G.C. ii 1900, 440–41.

Trengwainton near Penzance, Cornwall
G.C. ii 1962, 26–27,31. M. Allan *Fisons guide* 1970, 138–39. *J. Royal Hort. Soc.* 1971, 220. P.M. Synge *Gardens of Britain* v. 1, 1977, 123–24. G.S. Thomas *Gardens of National Trust* 1979, 229–31. Manpower Service Commission *Trengwainton* (map only) 1982.

Trent Park, Barnet, London
W. Keane *Beauties of Middlesex* 1850, 154–56. *G.C.* i 1892, 55; ii 1896, 333; ii 1905, 132–33; ii 1932, 295; i 1934, 255. *C.L.* v. 66, 1929, 78–80; v. 69, 1931, 40–47, 237–39; v. 72, 1932, 65. J. Harris *Catalogue of British drawings . . . in American collections* 1971, 127–29.

Trentham Park, Trentham, Staffs
W. Watts *Seats* 1779 pl. 31. W. Gilpin *Observations, relative chiefly to picturesque beauty* v. 2, 1792, 183–84. W. Pitt *General view of agriculture of . . . Stafford* 1796, 204. J. Nightingale *Topographical . . . description of Staffordshire* 1810, 731,936. J.P. Neale *Views* v. 4, 1821. R. Ackermann *Repository* v. 4, 1824, pls. 1–2. F. Calvert *Picturesque views . . . in Staffordshire & Shropshire* 1830, 5. W.W.J. Gendall *Views* v. 2, 1830, 32–34. *G.M.* v. 16, 1840, 580–81. *Florist* 1854, 99–102. *Trentham and its gardens* 1857. E.A. Brooke *Gardens of England* 1857, pls. 1–5. *Scottish Gdnr* v. 7, 1858, 164–66; v. 8, 1859, 80–85. *Cottage Gdnr* v. 14, 1855, 405–06. *J. Hort. Cottage Gdnr* v. 30, 1863, 327–28, 354–56,374–76,392–95,413–15,434–37; N.S., v. 19, 1889, 532–35. *Garden* v. 1, 1872, 681–82; v. 20, 1881, 265–67,269. *G.C.* 1872, 505–08,539–40,701,832; i 1893, 623–24; ii 1905, 421,425. F.O. Morris *Series of picturesque views* v. 1, 59. L. Jewitt and S.C. Hall *Stately homes of England* 1877, 32–55. *C.L.* v. 3, 1898, 272–75, 304–07; v. 13, 1903, 240–46; v. 18, 1905, 880–82; v. 143, 1968, 176–80,228–31,240,282–85,354. H.I. Triggs *Formal gardens in England and Scotland* 1902, 26–27. *Archaeological J.* v. 120, 1963, 284. Historical MSS Commission *Architectural history* v. 1, 1969, item 683. R.I.B.A. *Catalogue* v. B, 1972, 46. *Gdn History* v. 1 no. 3, 1973, 15. D. Stroud *Capability Brown* 1975, 149–51,243. M. Binney and A. Hills *Elysian gardens* 1979, 30. J. Harris *Artist and the country house* 1979, 174,354–55. M. Hadfield *et al. British gardeners* 1980, 27. R. Sidwell *West Midland gardens* 1981, 177–79.

Trerice, St Newlyn East, Cornwall
Official guide. *J. Royal Hort. Soc.* 1971, 220. G.S. Thomas *Gardens of National Trust* 1979, 231.

Tresco Abbey, Isles of Scilly
Official guide. S. Tower *Sketches in the Isles of Scilly* v. 1848, pl. 3. I.W. North *A week in the Isles of Scilly*

Tresco Abbey (Cont.)
1850, pl. 2. *G.C.* ii 1879, 659–60,680–81; ii 1886, 558,561; ii 1935, 102–03; i 1947, 189–90; ii 1960, 494–95,504; ii 1961, 274–75,299; i 1963, 224–25,228, 241; v. 189 no. 21, 1981, 14–16. *Gdnrs Mag.* 1902, 246–47; 1908, 7–10,11. *J. Royal Hort. Soc.* 1947, 177–91,221–37; 1968, 319–26. P. Coats *Great gardens of Britain* 1963, 194–201. E. Hyams *English garden* 1964, 218–23. M. Allan *Fisons guide* 1970, 139–41. B. Jones *Follies & grottoes* 1974, 444. P.M. Synge *Gardens of Britain* v. 1, 1977, 134–41. *Architectural Digest* v. 37, 1980, 92–97. *C.L.* v. 167, 1980, 1094–97, 1190–93; v. 173, 1983, 612–14. A. Hellyer *Gardens of genius* 1980, 47–49. *Garden* 1982, 87–91.

Trevalyn Hall near Wrexham, Clwyd
J.P. Neale *Views* v. 5, 1822. *C.L.* v. 132, 1962, 78–81.

Trevereux near Limpfield, Surrey
E.W. Brayley *and* J. Britton *Topographical history of Surrey* v. 4, 153.

Trevor Hall near Llangollen, Clwyd
Copper Plate Mag. v. 2, pl. 78.

Trewan House near St Columnb Major, Cornwall
C.S. Gilbert *Historical survey of Cornwall* v. 2, 1820, 663.

Trewarthenick near Tregony, Cornwall
J. Britton *and* E.W. Brayley *Devonshire & Cornwall* 1832, 44. D. Stroud *Humphry Repton* 1962, 77–78. *Architectural History* v. 7, 1964, 38,106. G. Carter *et al. Humphry Repton* 1982, 150.

Trewithen near Probus, Cornwall
W. Borlase *Natural history of Cornwall* 1758, pl. 23. *J. Royal Hort. Soc.* 1937, 93–99. *C.L.* v. 113, 1953, 1512–15. M. Allan *Fisons guide* 1970, 141–42. *International Dendrology Soc. Year Book* 1973, 6–10. P.M. Synge *Gardens of Britain* v. 1, 1977, 142–45. *Connoisseur* v. 208, 1981, 183–85.

Treworgey near Liskeard, Cornwall
C.S. Gilbert Historical survey of . . . Cornwall v. 2, 1820, 948. *C.L.* v. 15, 1904, 378–85. G. Jekyll *Garden ornament* 1918, 113.

Tring Park, Tring, Herts
T. Badeslade *and* J. Rocque *Vitruvius Brittanicus* 1739, pls. 104–05. *G.C.* ii 1885, 37–38; ii 1893, 131,151. *C.L.* v. 1, 1897, 604–06; v. 14, 1903, 724–26. C. Holme *Gardens of England in Southern & Western counties* 1907, pls. 123–26. N. Pevsner *Hertfordshire* 1977, 370. P. Willis *Charles Bridgeman* 1977, 183–84.

Trinity Grove, Edinburgh, Lothian
Gdning World v. 6, 1890, 741–42. *G.C.* ii 1893, 455–56.

Trinity Manor, Jersey, Channel Islands
C.L. v. 149, 1971, 732–34.

Troy, Ewelme, Oxfordshire
R. Bisgrove *Gardens of Britain* v. 3, 1978, 173–74.

Troy Farm, Somerton, Oxfordshire
C.L. v. 66, 1929, 823.

Troy House near Monmouth, Gwent
J.C. Loudon *Encyclopaedia of gardening* 1822, 1238.
J. Harris *Artist and the country house* 1979, 123.

Trumpington Manor, Trumpington, Cambs
V.C.H. Cambridge v. 8, 1982, 254.

Try Hill (Col. Onslow) near Chertsey, Surrey
P. Sandby *Collection of one hundred and fifty select views* v. 1, 1781, pl. 65.

Tudor Barn, Windsor, Berks
R. Bisgrove *Gardens of Britain* v. 3, 1978, 174–75.

Tudor House, Southampton, Hants
Official guide. Garden History Society *Newsletter* no. 6, 1982, 10–11.

Tudor House, Broadway, Hereford and Worcester
C.L. v. 28, 1910, 360–64.

Tulliallan, Fife
G.M. v. 18, 1842, 589. M. Binney *and* A. Hills *Elysian gardens* 1979, 25.

Tully near Kildare, Co. Kildare, Eire
Official guide. *Irish Gdning* v. 5, 1910, 100–02; v. 6, 1911, 129–32. M. Allan *Fisons guide* 1970, 261–62. *Gdn History* v. 5 no. 1, 1977, 30–41. *C.L.* v. 164, 1978, 86–87. A. Hellyer *Gardens of genius* 1980, 39–41. Knight of Glin *and* P. Bowe *Gardens of outstanding historic interest in . . . Ireland* 1980. E. Malins *and* P. Bowe *Irish gardens and demesnes* 1980, 150–52. J. Colleram *Japanese gardens* 1981.

Tullymore Park *see* Tollymore Park

Tullynally Castle, Tullynally, Co. Meath, Eire
B. Jones *Follies & grottoes* 1974, 439–40. Knight of Glin *and* P. Bowe *Gardens of outstanding historic interest in . . . Ireland* 1980.

Tunstead Old House, Tunstead, Norfolk
G.C. ii 1965, 602–03; i 1966, 10–11.

Turkey Court, Maidstone, Kent
J. Hort. Cottage Gdnr v. 60, 1878, 334–35. *C.L.* v. 130, 1961, 1628–31.

Turnworth House, Turnworth, Dorset
J. Hutchins *History . . . of Dorset* v. 3, 1868, 469.

Turvey near Bedford, Beds
G.C. ii 1895, 515–16.

Turville Court, Turville Heath, Bucks
R. Bisgrove *Gardens of Britain* v. 3, 1978, 175–76.

Tusmore House, Tusmore, Oxfordshire
R. Plot *Natural history of Oxfordshire* 1705, 266–67. *C.L.* v. 84, 1938, 108–13. *V.C.H. Oxford* v. 6, 1959, 334.

Tutbury Castle, Tutbury, Staffs
B. Jones *Follies & grottoes* 1974, 391.

Tutsham (Totesham) **Hall**, West Farley, Kent
J. Harris *History of Kent* 1719, 121. J. Kip *Nouveau theatre de la Grande Bretagne* v. 4, 1729. T. Badeslade *Thirty six different views . . . in Kent* 1750s, pl. 34.

Twickenham (Thomas Hudson), London
Short account of the principal seats and gardens in and about Richmond and Kew [1760s?], 11–12. J. Harris *Artist and the country house* 1979, 328.

Twickenham (Isaac Swainson), London
G.M. v. 9, 1833, 521–23.

Twickenham Meadows, Twickenham, London
Copper Plate Mag. v. 1, 1792, pl. 50.

Twickenham Park, Twickenham, London
W. Angus *Seats* 1787, pl. 40. D. Lysons *Supplement to . . . Environs of London* 1811, 442–43. J.C. Loudon *Encyclopaedia of gardening* 1822, 1226. *Tombleson's Thames* 1834. A.C.B. Urwin *Twicknam Parke* 1965, 69,81. R.I.B.A. *Catalogue of Drawings Collection* v. S, 1976, 95. R. Strong *Renaissance garden in England* 1979, 120–22.

Twitts Ghyll near Mayfield, E. Sussex
C.L. v. 63, 1928, 598–605.

Twyford Abbey, Ealing, London
W. Keane *Beauties of Middlesex* 1850, 54–58.

Tylney Hall near Basingstoke, Hants
Architectural Review v. 16, 1904, 81–85. *G.C.* i 1905, 257–58,259. J. Brown *Miss Gertrude Jekyll* 1981, 20–21.

Tynan Abbey, Tynan, Co. Armagh, Ulster
J.B. Burke *Visitation* 2nd Series v. 1, 1855, 19.

Tyneham House, Tyneham, Dorset
J. Hutchins *History . . . of Dorset* v. 1, 1861, 618. *C.L.* v. 77, 1935, 348–53.

Tyninghame near Linton, Lothian
J.C. Loudon *Arboretum et fruticetum Britannicum* v. 1, 1844, 102–03. *Gdning World* v. 2, 1885, 120–21, 136–38. *J. Hort. Cottage Gdnr* N.S., v. 44, 1902, 227–33. *G.C.* ii 1905, 211–12. *C.L.* v. 12, 1902, 208–14; v. 158, 1975, 336–38,390–93. G. Jekyll *Garden ornament* 1918, 123. P. Coats *Great gardens of Britain* 1963, 100–05. *J. Royal Hort. Soc.* 1971, 338–44. P. Verney *Gardens of Scotland* 1976, 116–28. C. McWilliam *Lothian* 1978, 459. A. Hellyer *Gardens of genius* 1980, 175–78. A. Lees-Milne and R. Verey *Englishwoman's garden* 1980, 56–60. G.A. Little *Scotland's gardens* 1981, 109–11. T. Hinde *Stately gardens of Britain* 1983, 102–09.

Tyntesfield, Flax Bourton, Avon
C.L. v. 11, 1902, 624–30. *Gdnrs Mag.* 1908, 929–32.

Tyringham near Newport Pagnell, Bucks
Architectural Review v. 65, 1929, 56–64,142. *C.L.* v. 65, 1929, 740–46,780–86. Lady Rockley *Historic gardens of England* 1938, 250–51. A.S. Butler *et al. Architecture of Sir Edwin Lutyens* v. 2, 1950, 15–17. N. Pevsner *Buckinghamshire* 1960, 272. D. Stroud *Humphry Repton* 1962, 81. J. Brown *Gardens of a golden afternoon* 1982, 140–41,174–75. G. Carter *et al. Humphry Repton* 1982, 149.

Tysoe Manor, Tysoe, Warwickshire
R. Sidwell *West Midland gardens* 1981, 232–33.

Tythegston Court, Tythegston, Mid-Glamorgan
C.L. v. 162, 1977, 1006–09.

Tythrop House near Thame, Oxfordshire
J. Kip *Supplement du Nouveau theatre de la Grande Bretagne* 1728, pl. 32. J. Harris *Artist and the country house* 1979, 103.

Tyttenhanger Park near St Albans, Herts
J.P. Neale *Views* v. 2, 1819. F.O. Morris *Series of picturesque views* v. 4, 67. *C.L.* v. 18, 1905, 594–601; v. 46, 1919, 424–32.

Uckfield House, Uckfield, E. Sussex
C.L. v. 140, 1966, 80–83.

Uddens House near Wimborne Minster, Dorset
J. Hutchins *History . . . of Dorset* v. 3, 1868, 115.

Uffington House, Uffington, Lincs
G. Jekyll *Garden ornament* 1918, 87.

Ugbrooke near Chudleigh, Devon
J. Britton *and* E.W. Brayley *Devonshire & Cornwall* 1832, 102. *G.M.* v. 18, 1842, 551–52. F.O. Morris *Series of picturesque views* v. 2, 67. *C.L.* v. 142, 1967, 138–41, 203–07,266,790–93. D. Stroud *Capability Brown* 1975, 96–97,100,243.

Umberslade Hall near Henley-in-Arden, Warwickshire
G.C. ii 1889, 323–24. *J. Hort. Cottage Gdnr* N.S., v. 28, 1894, 501–02.

Underley Hall near Kirkby Lonsdale, Cumbria
F.O. Morris *Series of picturesque views* v. 4, 73. *G.C.* i 1875, 466–67,469. C. Holme *Gardens of England in Northern counties* 1911, pls. 129–31.

Underway, Porlock, Somerset
J. Royal Hort. Soc. 1952, 37–42; 1961, 347–54.

Upcerne House, Up Cerne, Dorset
J. Hutchins *History . . . of Dorset* v. 4, 1870, 156.

Updown House near Sandwich, Kent
T. Wright *Gardens of Britain* v. 4, 1978, 104–07.

Uplands, Stoke Poges, Bucks
G. Beard *Thomas H. Mawson* 1976, 65.

Uplands near Birmingham, W. Midlands
J. Hort. Cottage Gdnr N.S., v. 39, 1899, 56,57.

Uplands, Ben Rhydding, W. Yorks
G. Beard *Thomas H. Mawson* 1976, 65.

Upleatham Hall, Upleatham, Cleveland
G.C. ii 1880, 371,394.

Uppark, South Harting, W. Sussex
Official guide. J. Beeverell *Les delices de la Grande Bretagne* v. 5, 1707, 872. L. Knyff *and* J. Kip *Britannia illustrata* v. 1, 1714. H. Repton *Fragments* 1816, 91–93. J.P. Neale *Views* v. 4, 1821. M. Macartney *English homes & gardens* 1908, pl. 35. *C.L.* v. 27, 1910, 702–10; v. 89, 1941, 520–24; v. 173, 1983, 1648. D. Stroud *Humphry Repton* 1962, 134–35. M. Meade-Fetherstonhaugh *and* O. Warner *Uppark and its people* 1964. Historical MSS Commission *Architectural history* v. 3, 1971, item 3549. B. Jones *Follies & grottoes* 1974, 402. T. Wright *Gardens of Britain* v. 4, 1978, 194–95. G.S. Thomas *Gardens of National Trust* 1979, 231–32. G. Carter *et al. Humphry Repton* 1982, 163. *Sussex Archaeological Collections* v. 121, 1983, 215–19.

Upper Bilesley, Stratford-on-Avon, Warwickshire
R. Sidwell *West Midland gardens* 1981, 234–36.

Upper Dowdeswell near Cheltenham, Glos
R. Atkyns *Ancient and present state of Glostershire* 1712, 400. L. Knyff *and* J. Kip *Britannia illustrata* v. 2, 1715.

Upper Gatton Park, Gatton, Surrey
D. Stroud *Capability Brown* 1975, 226.

Upper House, Little Parndon, Essex
P. Muilman *History of Essex* v. 4, 1770, 97.

Upper Shelderton House, Clungunford, Shropshire
R. Sidwell *West Midland gardens* 1981, 152–53.

Upper Slaughter Manor, Upper Slaughter, Glos
C.L. v. 34, 1913, 454–59.

Upper Spurlands, Holmer Green, Bucks
R. Webber *Percy Cane* 1975, 126–30.

Upper Upham House, Upper Upham, Wilts
C.L. v. 51, 1922, 888–95.

Upsall Castle, Upsall, N. Yorks
K. Lemmon *Gardens of Britain* v. 5, 1978, 131.

Upton Court, Upton, Berks
C.L. v. 21, 1907, 906–10.

Upton Grey Place, Upton Grey, Hants
A. Paterson *Gardens of Britain* v. 2, 1978, 147–48.

Upton House, Stratford, Newham, London
P. Muilman *History of Essex* v. 4, 1770, 254. G. Thompson *Memoirs of . . . John Fothergill* 1782, 37–39. J.C. Lettsom *Hortus Uptonensis; or a catalogue of stove and greenhouse plants in Dr Fothergill's garden at Upton* 1783. J.C. Loudon *Arboretum et fruticetum Britannicum* v. 1, 1844, 71–72. R.H. Fox *Dr John Fothergill and his friends* 1919, 182–207.

Upton House, Edge Hill, Warwickshire
Official guide *C.L.* v. 16, 1904, 378–84; v. 80, 1936, 248–53,274–79. *Architectural Review* v. 69, 1931, 125–28, pls. 2–5. *G.C.* ii 1963, 190–91,194. M. Allan *Fisons guide* 1970, 174–75. J. Harris *Artist and the country house* 1979, 244. G.S. Thomas *Gardens of National Trust* 1979, 232–34. R. Sidwell *West Midland gardens* 1981, 236–38.

Upton Manor, Castor, Cambs
V.C.H. Northampton v. 2, 1906, 484.

Urchfont Manor, Urchfont, Wilts
V.C.H. Wiltshire v. 10, 1975, frontispiece, 178.

Vale Mascal, Bexley, London
Archaeologia Cantiana v. 82, 1967, 227–34.

Vale Royal near Northwich, Cheshire
J. Hort. Cottage Gdnr v. 47, 1872, 1512–52; N.S., v. 13, 1886, 320–21. G. Ormerod *History of the County Palatine and city of Chester* v. 2, 1882, 154.

Valence (Hill Park), Westerham, Kent
J.P. Neale *Views* v. 2, 1819. R. Pococke *Travels through England* v. 2, 1889, 73. D. Stroud *Capability Brown* 1975, 229.

Valentines, Ilford, Redbridge, London
P. Muilman *History of Essex* v. 4, 1770, 276. D. Lysons *Environs of London* v. 4, 1796, 87. *G.C.* ii 1878, 272–73, 277. V.C.H. *Essex* v. 5, 1966, 212.

Valewood, Haslemere, Surrey
G.C. i 1883, 753–54; ii 1930, 234.

Valewood Farm, Lurgashall, W. Sussex
C.L. v. 78, 1935, 298–303.

Valley Gardens, Harrogate, N. Yorks
K. Lemmon *Gardens of Britain* v. 5, 1978, 131–32.

Valleyfield near Culross, Fife
H. Repton *Observations* 1803, 100–02. D. Stroud *Humphry Repton* 1962, 120. A.A. Tait *Landscape garden in Scotland* 1980, passim. G. Carter *et al. Humphry Repton* 1982, 55, 164.

Vann, Hambledon, Surrey
C.L. v. 159, 1976, 1394–95. T. Wright *Gardens of Britain* v. 4, 1978, 230–32.

Vauxbelets, Guernsey, Channel Islands
B. Jones *Follies & grottoes* 1974, 443.

Vauxhall Gardens, Lambeth, London
R. *and* J. Dodsley *London and its environs described* v. 6, 1761, 216. British Museum *Catalogue of maps, prints* 1829, 342. W. Wroth *London pleasure gardens of eighteenth century* 1896, 286–326. E.B. Chancellor *Pleasure haunts of London* 1925, 205–27. J.G. Southworth *Vauxhall Gardens* 1941. *C.L.* v. 98, 1945, 638–39. G.L.C. *Survey of London* v. 23: *South Bank and Vauxhall* 1951, 146. A. Parreaux *and* M. Plaissant *Jardins et paysages: le style Anglais* 1977, 217–23.

Vauxhall Park *see* Lambeth

Ven House near Milborne Port, Somerset
W. Phelps *History . . . of Somersetshire* v. 1, 1836, 297. *C.L.* v. 4, 1898, 528–32; v. 29, 1911, 924–33. C. Holme *Gardens of England in Southern & Western counties* 1907, pls. 128–30. G. Jekyll *Garden ornament* 1918, 55.

Ventnor Botanic Garden, Ventnor, Isle of Wight
International Dendrology Soc. Year Book 1979, 20–33.

Vern, Marden, Hereford and Worcester
R. Webber *Percy Cane* 1975, 153–54, 182.

Vernon Mount, Co. Cork, Eire
E. Malins *and* Knight of Glin *Lost demesnes* 1976, 115.

Victoria Gardens *see* Brighton

Victoria Park *see* London; Manchester

Village Place, Beckenham, Bromley, London
C. Greenwood *Epitome of county history . . . v. 1: Kent* 1838, 31.

Vine House, Henbury, Avon
J. Royal Hort. Soc. 1968, 464–70. M. Allan *Fisons guide* 1970, 108. J. Sales *West Country gardens* 1980, 112–14.

Vine House, Haslingden, Lancs
G.C. i 1896, 758–59.

Vinery House, Allerton, Merseyside
J. Hort. Cottage Gdnr v. 42, 1869, 361–62, 380–81.

Vinters near Maidstone, Kent
Gdning World v. 1, 1885, 392–93. G. Carter *et al. Humphry Repton* 1982, 156.

Virginia Water *see* Windsor Great Park

Vyne near Basingstoke, Hants
R. Ackermann *Repository* v. 6, 1825, pl. 20. W.W.J. Gendall *Views* v. 2, 1830, 10. J. Hewetson *Architectural and picturesque views of noble mansions in Hampshire* 1830. E.F. Prosser *Select illustrations of Hampshire* 1833. *C.L.* v. 13, 1903, 838–47; v. 49, 1921, 582–89, 612–19; v. 121, 1957, 16–19. *Architectural Review* v. 30, 1911, 169–74. G. Jekyll *Garden ornament* 1918, 223, 254. N. Pevsner *and* D. Lloyd *Hampshire and the Isle of Wight* 1967, 638. A. Paterson *Gardens of Britain* v. 2, 1978, 149–50. J. Harris *Artist and the country house* 1979, 292. G.S. Thomas *Gardens of National Trust* 1979, 234.

Waddesden Manor, Waddesden, Bucks
Official guide. *G.C.* i 1885, 820–22; i 1886, 800–01; ii 1889, 39. *C.L.* v. 4, 1898, 208–11. *J. Royal Hort. Soc.* 1971, 211. *Apollo* v. 104, 111–12; v. 105, 1977, 415. R. Bisgrove *Gardens of Britain* v. 3, 1978, 176–77. *National Trust Studies* 1979, 77–89. G.S. Thomas *Gardens of National Trust* 1979, 235–36. *Connoisseur* v. 208, 1981, 260–62.

Waddon House, Croydon, London
Gdning World v. 2, 1886, 742. *G.C.* ii 1891, 67.

Waddon Manor near Dorchester, Dorset
C.L. v. 70, 1931, 536–42.

Wadworth Hall, Wadworth, S. Yorks
C.L. v. 140, 1966, 494–98.

Wakefield Lodge near Potterspury, Northants
P. Sandby *Collection of one hundred and fifty select views* v. 1, 1781, pls. 38–39. J.P. Neale *Views* v. 3, 1820. Historical MSS Commission *Architectural history* v. 3, 1971, item 3559. *C.L.* v. 154, 1973, 298–301. D. Stroud *Capability Brown* 1975, 54–55.

Wakehurst Place near Ardingly, W. Sussex
Official guide. *Garden* v. 35, 1889, 233–34. *G.C.* i 1960, 374–75. P. Coats *Great gardens of Britain* 1967, 50–55. *Sussex Life* v. 4 no. 8, 1968, 38–39; v. 7 no. 10, 1971, 26–28. M. Allan *Fisons guide* 1970, 67–68. *C.L.* v. 151, 1972, 906–08. *Garden* 1975, 284–91; 1973, 328–32. *International Dendrology Soc. Year Book* 1978, 53–55. T. Wright *Gardens of Britain* v. 4, 1978, 196–201. G.S. Thomas *Gardens of National Trust* 1979, 245–49.

Wakerley near Luffenham, Northants
Northamptonshire Past and Present v. 5 no. 3, 1975, 232; v. 5 no. 5, 1977, 401–02. Royal Commission on Historical Monuments *Inventory of historical monuments in . . . Northampton* v. 1, 1975, 105, pl. 20. *C.L.* v. 166, 1979, 2143. M. Binney *and* A. Hills *Elysian gardens* 1979, 12. C. Taylor *Archaeology of gardens* 1983, 16–18.

Wakes, Selborne, Hants
Garden v. 16, 1879, 29–30. *G.C.* ii 1903, 433,440,441. *C.L.* v. 148, 1970, 247–51. G. White *Garden-kalendar, 1751–1771* 1976.

Wakes Colne Rectory, Wakes Colne, Essex
G.C. ii 1894, 591–92.

Walcot Hall, Walcot, Shropshire
C.L. v. 86, 1939, 388–92.

Walcot House near Stamford, Northants
J. Morton *Natural history of Northamptonshire* 1712, 494.

Waldershare Park, Waldershare, Kent
J. Harris *History of Kent* 1719, 325. T. Badeslade *Thirty six different views . . . in Kent* 1750s, pl. 35. E. Hasted *History . . . of Kent* v. 4, 1799, 190. C. Greenwood *Epitome of county history . . . v. 1: Kent* 1838, 422. Historical MSS Commission *Architectural history* v. 2, 1970, item 2247. J. Newman *North East and East Kent* 1976, 483.

Walgrave, Northants
Royal Commission on Historical Monuments *Inventory of historical monuments in . . . Northampton* v. 2, 1979, 148–49.

Walham Green (John Ord), Fulham, Hammersmith, London
D. Lysons *Environs of London* v. 2, 1795, 352.

Walhampton near Lymington, Hants
C. Holme *Gardens of England in Southern & Western counties* 1907, pl. 132. *G.C.* i 1924, 379–80,397. B. Jones *Follies & grottoes* 1974, 337. G. Beard *Thomas H. Mawson* 1976, 65.

Wall Hall, Aldenham, Herts
D. Stroud *Humphry Repton* 1962, 66. G. Carter *et al. Humphry Repton* 1982, 154.

Wallingford, Oxfordshire
G.M. v. 10, 1834, 5–6.

Wallington Hall near Cambo, Northumberland
Official guide. J. Hodgson *History of Northumberland* pt. 2 v. 2, 1832. *C.L.* v. 43, 1918, 572–78,592–97; v. 147, 1970, 854–58; v. 149, 1971, 1204–07; v. 164, 1978, 1977. *G.C.* i 1962, 173. *J. Royal Hort. Soc.* 1971, 215–16; 1975, 167–72. D. Stroud *Capability Brown* 1975, 43. B. Jones *Follies & grottoes* 1974, 372–74. G.S. Thomas *Gardens of National Trust* 1979, 249–50. T. Wright *Arbours and grottos* 1979. A. Hellyer *Gardens of genius* 1980, 186–91. *Gdn History* v. 9 no. 2, 1981, 166–74.

Wallingwells near Worksop, Notts
N. Pevsner *Nottinghamshire* 1979, 363.

Wallsworth Hall near Gloucester, Glos
S. Rudder *New history of Gloucestershire* 1779, 638.

Wallwood House, Leytonstone, Waltham Forest, London
H. Repton *Fragments* 1816, 106–11. F.G. Emmison *Catalogue of maps in Essex Record Office* 1st Supplt, 1952, 17. D. Stroud *Humphry Repton* 1962, 173. G. Carter *et al. Humphry Repton* 1982, 152.

Walmer Castle, Walmer, Kent
G.C. i 1898, 121; ii 1962, 318–19. *C.L.* v. 46, 1919, 552–57.

Walmer Lodge (Place ?), Walmer, Kent
T.H. Mawson *Art & craft of garden making* 1907, 209,235. G. Beard *Thomas H. Mawson* 1976, 65.

Walmsgate Hall near Louth, Lincs
G.C. i 1910, 260,261–62.

Walpole House, Chiswick Mall, Hounslow, London
J. MacGregor *Gardens of celebrities . . . in and around London* 1918, 188–97. C.L. v. 168, 1980, 1795–98. A. Lees-Milne *and* R. Verey *Englishman's garden* 1982, 36–39.

Walsingham Abbey, Walsingham, Norfolk
J. Grigor *Eastern arboretum* 1841, 300–01.

Waltham Abbey, Waltham Holy Cross, Essex
J. Harris *and* A.A. Tait *Catalogue of the drawings by Inigo Jones, John Webb and Isaac de Caus at Worcester College, Oxford* 1979, 47.

Waltham House, Waltham Cross, Herts
C.L. v. 9, 1901, 136–38.

Walthamstow House (R. Wigram), Waltham Forest, London
J. Hassell *Seats near London* 1804–05.

Walton Hall near Brampton, Cumbria
W. Hutchinson *History of county of Cumberland* v. 1, 1794, 119.

Walton Hall, Walton-le-Dale, Lancs
E. Baines *History . . . of Lancaster* v. 3, 1836, 349.

Walton Hall near Stratford-on-Avon, Warwickshire
F.O. Morris *Series of picturesque views* v. 4, 53.

Walton Hall near Wakefield, W. Yorks
Bradford Illustrated Weekly Telegraph *Series of picturesque views* 1885.

Walton House (Mount Felix), Walton-on-Thames, Surrey
G.M. v. 5, 1829, 381–82; v. 10, 1834, 335–37; v. 13, 1837, 112–13. E.W. Brayley *and* J. Britton *Topographical history of Surrey* v. 2, 1841, 349–50.

Walton Lea near Warrington, Cheshire
J. Hort. Cottage Gdnr N.S., v. 4, 1882, 328–29. G.C. i 1897, 39,43.

Walton Old Hall, Walton Superior, Lancs
G. Beard *Thomas H. Mawson* 1976, 65.

Walton Park, Castle Douglas, Dumfries and Galloway
G.A. Little *Scotland's gardens* 1981, 271.

Waltons near Saffron Walden, Essex
J. Harris *Artist and the country house* 1979, 218.

Wandsworth (Lord Stormont), Wandsworth, London
W. Thornton *New, complete and universal history* 1786, 480.

Wandsworth Common *see* London

Wanlip Hall, Wanlip, Leics
J. Throsby *Select views in Leicestershire* v. 1, 1790, 322. J. Nichols *History . . . of county of Leicester* v. 3, 1804, 1096.

Wansley Park near Brinsley, Notts
D. Stroud *Humphry Repton* 1962, 173. G. Carter *et al. Humphry Repton* 1982, 160.

Wanstead Grove, Wanstead, Redbridge, London
J.P. Neale *Views* 2nd Series, v. 3, 1826.

Wanstead House, Wanstead, Redbridge, London
Official guide. J. Macky *Journey through England* v. 1, 1722, 20,23–24. J. Kip *Supplement du Nouveau theatre de la Grande Bretagne* 1728, pls. 5–7. Society of Gentlemen *England displayed* v. 1, 1769, 296. P. Muilman *History of Essex* v. 4, 1770, 228. N. Spencer *Complete English traveller* 1771, 189. G.L. le Rouge *Jardins Anglo-Chinois a la mode* 3^e cahier. 1776, pls. 24–28. W. Watts *Seats* 1779, pls. 56. W. Angus *Seats* 1787, pl. 53. S. Shaw *Tour to West of England in 1788* In J. Pinkerton v. 2, 1808, 179–80. *Archaeologia* v. 12, 1796, 186–87. P. Morant *History . . . of Essex* v. 1, 1816, 31. J.C. Loudon *Encyclopaedia of gardening* 1822, 1232. R. Havell *Series of picturesque views* 1823. R. Ackermann *Repository* v. 3, 1824, pl. 25. British Museum *Catalogue of maps, prints* 1829, 349. W.W.J. Gendall *Views* v. 2, 1830, 107. P. Kalm *Account of his visit to England* 1892, 87,175–76. F.G. Emmison *Catalogue of maps in Essex Record Office* 1947, 12,32,33, pl. 22; 1st Supplt, 1952, 18,29; 3rd Supplt, 1968, 10,11,12,18,20. C.L. v. 108, 1950, 294–98,684. D. Stroud *Humphry Repton* 1962, 173. V.C.H. *Essex* v. 6, 1973, 325,326. B. Jones *Follies & grottoes* 1974, 333–34. J. Harris *Artist and the country house* 1979, 323. G. Carter *et al. Humphry Repton* 1982, 152.

Warbrook House near Wokingham, Hants
C.L. v. 85, 1939, 250–54. L. Fleming *and* A. Gore *English garden* 1979, 73.

Warders, Tonbridge, Kent
C.L. v. 164, 1978, 896–98. T. Wright *Gardens of Britain* v. 4, 1978, 107–09.

Wardes, Otham, Kent
C.L. v. 46, 1919, 270–79.

Wardie Lodge near Edinburgh, Lothian
J. Hort. Cottage Gdnr v. 33, 1865, 156–57.

Wardour Castle, Wardour, Wilts
S. *and* N. Buck *Buck's antiquities* v. 2, 1774, pl. 317.
R.J. Sulivan *Tour . . . in 1778* v. 1, 1785, 125–26.
J.P. Neale *Views* v. 5, 1822. J. Rutter *Historical . . . sketch of Wardour* 1822. R.C. Hoare *Modern history of South Wiltshire* v. 4, 1829, 169. *G.M.* v. 12, 1836, 504–06. B. Jones *Follies & grottoes* 1974, 163,165.
D. Stroud *Capability Brown* 1975, 98–99,243. *J. Gdn History* v. 2 no. 1, 1982, 49.

Ware Park, Ware, Herts
J.B. Burke *Visitation* 2nd Series, v. 1, 1855, 205. *C.L.* v. 143, 1968, 973.

Waresley Park, Waresley, Cambs
J. Royal Hort. Soc. 1968, 210–14. G. Carter *et al. Humphry Repton* 1982, 155.

Warfield, Berks
British Museum *Catalogue of maps, prints* 1829, 350.
J. Harris *Artists and the country house* 1979, 171.

Warleigh House near Bath, Avon
J.P. Neale *Views* 2nd Series, v. 1, 1824. *Jones's views* 1829.

Warley near Birmingham, W. Midlands
D. Stroud *Humphry Repton* 1962, 174. G. Carter *et al. Humphry Repton* 1982, 164.

Warley Lodge, Little Warley, Essex
D. Stroud *Humphry Repton* 1962, 174. G. Carter *et al. Humphry Repton* 1982, 152.

Warley Place, Great Warley, Essex
Garden v. 51, 1897, 167,405; v. 57, 1900, 39–40; v. 68, 1905, 76–77,92,105–06,120–21. E. Willmott *Warley garden in Spring and Summer* 1909; ed 2, 1924. *Essex Naturalist* v. 17, 1912, 40–60; v. 31, 1966, 370–75. *C.L.* v. 37, 1915, 613–17; v. 76, 1934, 358–59. R.I.B.A. *Catalogue of the drawings collection: Lutyens* 1973, 23.
V.C.H. *Essex* v. 7, 1978, 167–68. *Garden* 1979, 241–46.
A. Le Lievre *Miss Willmott of Warley Place* 1980.

Warling Dean, Esher, Surrey
C.L. v. 74, 1933, 319–21.

Warmsworth Hall, Warmsworth, S. Yorks
I. Hall *Samuel Buck's Yorkshire sketchbook* 1979, 68.

Warmwell House, Warmwell, Dorset
A. Paterson *Gardens of Britain* v. 2, 1978, 45–46.

Warnford Park (Belmont), Warnford, Hants
E.F. Prosser *Select illustrations of Hampshire* 1833.
D. Stroud *Capability Brown* 1975, 217.

Warnham Court, Warnham, W. Sussex
L. Jewitt *and* S.C. Hall *Stately homes of England* 1877, 282–87. *Gdning World* v. 2, 1886, 373–74. *G.C.* i 1892, 757,760; ii 1895, 364; i 1896, 559–60. *Gdnrs Mag.* 1897, 517–20; 1908, 123–24,125.

Warren, Loughton, Essex
G. Carter *et al. Humphry Repton* 1982, 152.

Warren House, Hayes, Bromley, London
G. Beard *Thomas H. Mawson* 1976, 65.

Warren House, Kingston upon Thames, London
G.C. ii 1924, 121,127,129,131,133,417.

Warren House, Stanmore, Harrow, London
G.C. i 1909, 323,326; ii 1910, 19,21,22. *Gdnrs Mag.* 1910, 1015–17.

Warren Lodge, Thursley, Surrey
C.L. v. 164, 1978, 638. J. Brown *Gardens of a golden afternoon* 1982, 166.

Warren Towers near Newmarket, Suffolk
G. Jekyll *Garden ornament* 1918, 313.

Warter Priory, Warter, Humberside
F.O. Morris *Series of picturesque views* v. 6, 67. *J. Hort. Cottage Gdnr* N.S., v. 37, 1898, 48–49. Historical MSS Commission *Architectural history* v. 3, 1971, item 3567.

Warthill, Rayne, Grampian
J.B. Burke *Visitation* 2nd Series, v. 1, 1855, 122.

Warwick Castle, Warwick, Warwickshire
S. Ireland *Picturesque views in the Upper or Warwickshire Avon* 1795, 146–49. R. Warner *Tour through Northern counties of England* v. 2, 1802, 254–59. *Cottage Gdnr* v. 17, 1856, 222–24. F.O. Morris *Series of picturesque views* v. 1, 43. *Garden* v. 1, 1872, 705–06,707; v. 20, 1881, 345–46; 347,349; v. 38, 1890, 526–27. *J. Hort. Cottage Gdnr* N.S., v. 14, 1887, 174–75. *G.C.* i 1892, 71–73. L. Jewitt *and* S.C. Hall *Stately homes of England* 1874, 192–220. *C.L.* v. 1, 1897, 126–27; v. 35, 1914, 792–800,842–51; v. 133, 1963, 1050; v. 165, 1979, 474–76; v. 175, 1984, 421. C. Holme *Gardens of England in Midland & Eastern counties* 1908, pl. 123.
J. Evelyn *Diary* v. 3, 1955, 119–20. Historical MSS Commission *Architectural history* v. 2, 1970, item 1179.
D. Stroud *Capability Brown* 1975, 60–63,244. *Landscape Design* no. 121, 1978, 24–27. D. Jacques *Georgian gardens* 1983, 68.

Warwick Priory near Warwick, Warwickshire
Garden v. 26, 1884, 453. D. Green *Gardener to Queen Anne* 1956, passim. P. Willis *Charles Bridgeman* 1977, 184.

Wasing Place, Aldermaston, Berks
G.M. v. 6, 1830, 655–56. R. Bisgrove *Gardens of Britain* v. 3, 1978, 178–79.

Watcombe Park, Watcombe, Devon
G.C. ii 1882, 75–76; ii 1887, 463–64.

Water Eaton Manor, Water Eaton, Oxfordshire
C.L. v. 22, 1907, 666–74.

Waterlow Park *see* London

Watermouth Castle near Ilfracombe, Devon
R. Ackermann *Repository* v. 6, 1825, pl. 8. *Garden* v. 34, 1888, 195.

Waterstock Manor, Waterstock, Oxfordshire
V.C.H. *Oxford* v. 7, 1962, 221.

Waterston Manor near Puddletown, Dorset
C.L. v. 39, 1916, 208–14. G. Jekyll *Garden ornament* 1918, 140. J. Newman *and* N. Pevsner *Dorset* 1972, 443. A. Paterson *Gardens of Britain* v. 2, 1978, 46–47.

Watford Court, Watford, Northants
Royal Commission on Historical Monuments *Inventory of the historical monuments in . . . Northampton* v. 3, 1981, 193. C. Taylor *Archaeology of gardens* 1983, 62.

Watlington Park, Watlington, Oxfordshire
R. Plot *Natural history of Oxfordshire* 1705, 163–65. *C.L.* v. 125, 1959, 18–21,60–63.

Watton Abbey, Watton, Humberside
C.L. v. 78, 1935, 458–63.

Watton Woodhall near Watton-at-Stone, Herts
J.C. Loudon *Encyclopaedia of gardening* 1822, 1233.

Waverley Abbey near Farnham, Surrey
G.F. Prosser *Select illustrations of . . . Surrey* 1828. E.W. Brayley *and* J. Britton *Topographical history of Surrey* v. 5, 1848, 278. W. Keane *Beauties of Surrey* 1849, 132–33.

Wavertree Hall, Liverpool, Merseyside
S. Austin *et al. Lancashire illustrated* 1831, 44–45. E. Baines *History . . . of Lancaster* v. 3, 1836, 759.

Wayford Manor, Wayford, Somerset
C.L. v. 76, 1934, 336–41. Lady Rockley *Historic gardens of England* 1938, 120–21. *J. Royal Hort. Soc.* 1956, 528–34. J. Sales *West Country gardens* 1980, 184–86.

Weald Hall, South Weald, Essex
T. Wright *History . . . of Essex* v. 2, 1836, 534. *C.L.* v. 2, 1897, 560–62; v. 18, 1905, 522–27; v. 36, 1914, 454–61. F.G. Emmison *Catalogue of maps in Essex Record Office* 1947, 15,16. J. Harris *Artist and the country house* 1979, 150.

Weald Manor, Bampton, Oxfordshire
C.L. v. 100, 1946, 256–59.

Weir, Swainshill, Hereford and Worcester
G.S. Thomas *Gardens of National Trust* 1979, 250–51.

Welbeck Abbey near Worksop, Notts
H. Rooke *Description and sketches of some remarkable oaks in the park at Welbeck* 1790. *Copper Plate Mag.* v. 2, pl. 68. H. Repton *Sketches* 1794, 11–12,14–16,20–22, 25–28,30,36–37. J. Hodgson *and* F.C. Laird *Beauties of England and Wales* v. 12 pt 1, 1813, 351–53. J.P. Neale *Views* v. 3, 1820. J.B. Burke *Visitation* 2nd Series, v. 1, 1855, 203. L. Jewitt *and* S.C. Hall *Stately homes of England* 1877, 327–56. *G.C.* ii 1889, 182–83; ii 1891, 185–86,195,215–16; ii 1900, 269–70; ii 1924, 216–17,218. C. Holme *Gardens of England in Midland & Eastern counties* 1908, pls 124–25. *Gdnrs Mag.* 1910, 449–53. *C.L.* v. 37, 1915, 27–29; v. 64, 1928, 581–85; v. 74, 1933, 346–48. Lady Rockley *Historic gardens of England* 1938, 210–11. D. Stroud *Humphry Repton* 1962, 39–40. Historical MSS Commission *Architectural history* v. 2, 1970, items 2000,2276; v. 3, 1971, items 2745,2930,3338,3586. N. Simpson *Comments on the work of Humphry Repton at Welbeck* 1971. N. Pevsner *Nottinghamshire* 1979, 369,370,371. G. Carter *et al. Humphry Repton* 1982, 103,160.

Welburn Hall, Welburn, N. Yorks
Architectural Review v. 14, 1903, 158–64. I. Hall *Samuel Buck's Yorkshire sketchbook* 1979, 302.

Welcombe near Stratford-on-Avon, Warwickshire
J.P. Neale *Views* v. 4, 1821. *Jones's views* 1829.

Weldon, Northants
Northamptonshire Past and Present v. 5 no. 3, 1975, 232–33.

Well Head Gardens, Halifax, W. Yorks
J. Hort. Cottage Gdnr v. 30, 1863, 193–94,212–13, 229–30.

Well House, Westwood, Wilts
V.C.H. *Wiltshire* v. 11, 1980, 225.

Well Vale, Spilsby, Lincs
C.L. v. 152, 1972, 1650–54.

Wellfield, Preston, Lancs
G.C. ii 1903, 297.

Wellholme Lea, Scotby, Cumbria
G. Beard *Thomas H. Mawson* 1976, 66.

Wells. Bishops Palace, Somerset
S. *and* N. Buck *Buck's antiquities* v. 2, 1774, pl. 263.
G.C. ii 1893, 743–44. *Trees in the grounds of the Bishop's Palace, Wells* 1983.

Welsh Harp *see* London

Welton House, Welton, Humberside
G.C. ii 1890, 95. *J. Hort. Cottage Gdnr* N.S., v. 27, 1893, 12–13.

Welton Place, Welton, Northants
J.P. Neale *Views* 2nd Series, v. 2, 1825. *J. Hort. Cottage Gdnr* v. 30, 1863, 493–95; v. 34, 1865, 257.

Wembley, Harrow, London
H. Repton *Sketches* 1794, 9–11,16–19,38–39,40–41.
W. Keane *Beauties of Middlesex* 1850, 265–67.
D. Stroud *Humphry Repton* 1962, 68–69. P. Willis *Furor hortensis* 1974, 72–75. G. Carter *et al. Humphry Repton* 1982, 158.

Wemyss Castle, East Wemyss, Fife
Scottish Gdnr v. 11, 1862, 88–93.

Wenden Lofts Hall, Wenden Lofts, Essex
F.G. Emmison *Catalogue of maps in Essex Record Office* 2nd Supplt, 1964, 19.

Wenlock Abbey, Much Wenlock, Shropshire
C.L. v. 21, 1907, 558–64; v. 128, 1960, 1492. R. Sidwell *West Midland gardens* 1981, 153–55.

Wennington Hall, Wennington, Lancs
Gdnrs Mag. 1912, 136–38.

Wentworth Castle, Stainborough, S. Yorks
Official guide. J. Kip *Nouveau theatre de la Grande Bretagne* v. 4, 1729. T. Badeslade *and* J. Rocque *Vitruvius Brittanicus* 1739, pls. 55–58. Society of Gentlemen *England displayed* v. 2, 1769, 113–14.
A. Young *Six months tour through North of England* v. 1, 1771, 132–38. D. Defoe *Tour* v. 3, 1778, 122–24.
W. Bray *Sketch of a tour into Derbyshire and Yorkshire* 1783, 252–56. *New display of the beauties of England* v. 2, 1787, 409–11. J.P. Neale *Views* v. 5, 1822. *Jones's views* 1829, 10–11. *Cottage Gdnr* v. 19, 1857, 150,230–31. *J. Hort. Cottage Gdnr* N.S., v. 15, 1887, 164–65.

R. Pococke *Travels through England* v. 1, 1888, 64–65.
M. Macartney *English houses & gardens* 1908, pl. 55.
C.L. v. 56, 1924, 634–42. R. Dutton *English garden* 1937, pl. 55. N. Pevsner *Yorkshire: West Riding* 1967, 548. *Gdn History* v. 3 no. 3, 1975, 50–57. K. Lemmon *Gardens of Britain* v. 5, 1978, 145–46. J. Harris *Artist and the country house* 1979, 320. D. Jacques *Georgian gardens* 1983, pl. 2.

Westworth House *see* Wentworth Woodhouse

Wentworth Woodhouse, Wentworth, S. Yorks
Official guide. J. Kip *Nouveau theatre de la Grande Bretagne* v. 4, 1729. Society of Gentlemen *England displayed* v. 2, 1769, 117–18. N. Spencer *Complete English traveller* 1771, 506. A. Young *Six months tour through North of England* v. 1, 1771, 259–71. D. Defoe *Tour* v. 3, 1778, 116–19. W. Watts *Seats* 1779, pl. 5.
New display of the beauties of England v. 2, 1787, 416–20.
R. Warner *Tour through Northern counties of England* v. 1, 1802, 220–21. H. Repton *Observations* 1803, 13–15. J.P. Neale *Views* v. 5, 1822. *G.M.* v. 16, 1840, 185–86. F.O. Morris *Series of picturesque views* v. 1, 23.
R. Pococke *Travels through England* v. 1, 1888, 66–68.
C.L. v. 56, 1924, 436–44,476–83; v. 173, 1983, 624–27.
D. Stroud *Humphry Repton* 1962, 53–54. N. Pevsner *Yorkshire: West Riding* 1967, 545. Historical MSS Commission *Architectural history* v. 5, 1974, item 5627.
B. Jones *Follies & grottoes* 1974, 85–90. *Gdn History* v. 5 no. 3, 1977, 25–26. K. Lemmon *Gardens of Britain* v. 5, 1978, 147–49. *Landscape Research* v. 7 no. 1, 1982, 19.
G. Carter *et al. Humphry Repton* 1982, 164.

Wenvoe Castle, Wenvoe, S. Glamorgan
G.C. i 1921, 43–44.

Wergs Hall near Wolverhampton, W. Midlands
G.C. ii 1907, 394.

Werrington Park near Launceston, Cornwall
R. Warner *Walk through some of Western counties of England* 1800, 145–47. C.S. Gilbert *Historical survey of . . . Cornwall* v. 2, 1820, 522–23. *G.M.* v. 13, 1837, 121.
R. Pococke *Travels through England* v. 1, 1888, 133.
Architectural History v. 7, 1964, 38,108. B. Jones *Follies & grottoes* 1974, 301–02.

West Bank House, Heaton Mersey, Greater Manchester
G.C. i 1897, 222; i 1899, 187–88.

West Bitchfield, Northumberland
C.L. v. 88, 1940, 278–82.

West Burton near Arundel, W. Sussex
G. Jekyll *Garden ornament* 1918, 143.

West Coker, Yeovil, Somerset
G. Carter *et al. Humphry Repton* 1982, 161.

West Dean near Chichester, W. Sussex
J.P. Neale *Views* v. 4, 1821. *G.M.* v. 5, 1829, 581–83.
R. Ackermann *Repository* v. 9, 1827, pl. 32.
W.W.J. Gendall *Views* v. 2, 1830, 37. T.W. Horsfield
History . . . of Sussex v. 2, 1835, 82. *Garden* v. 34, 1888,
317–18. *C.L.* v. 6, 1899, 112–17; v. 170, 1981, 1378–81.
G.C. ii 1901, 1; ii 1905, 273–74; v. 186 no. 10, 1979,
16–17. T. Wright *Gardens of Britain* v. 4, 1978, 201–03.

West Drayton Manor, West Drayton, Hillingdon, London
V.C.H. Middlesex v. 3, 1962, 193.

West Farleigh Hall, West Farleigh, Kent
C.L. v. 43, 1918, 444–49; v. 142, 1967, 660–64.

West Farm, Barnett, London
R. Ackermann *Repository* v. 8, 1826, pl. 7.
W.W.J. Gendall *Views* v. 1, 1830, 120.

West Green House, Hartley Wintney, Hants
C.L. v. 80, 1936, 540–45; v. 174, 1983, 686,689,693.
A. Paterson *Gardens of Britain* v. 2, 1978, 150–54.
G.S. Thomas *Gardens of National Trust* 1979, 253–54.

West Grinstead Park, West Grinstead, W. Sussex
J. Dallaway *History of Western Division of . . . Sussex*
v. 2 no. 2, 1830, 308. T.W. Horsfield *History . . . of Sussex* v. 2, 1835, 251.

West Hall, Byfleet, Surrey
Garden 1911, 215.

West Ham Park *see* London

West Harling Hall, Harling, Norfolk
M. Binney *and* A. Hills *Elysian gardens* 1979, 41.

West Hill, Wandsworth, London
A. Angus *Seats* 1787, pl. 60. J. Hassell *Seats near London* 1804–05. G.F. Prosser *Select illustrations of . . . Surrey* 1828. D. Stroud *Humphry Repton* 1962, 174.
D. Stroud *Capability Brown* 1975, 237. G. Carter *et al. Humphry Repton* 1982, 162.

West Horndon Manor, West Horndon, Essex
F.G. Emmison *Catalogue of maps in Essex Record Office* 1947, 2.

West Horsley Place near Leatherhead, Surrey
J.P. Neale *Views* 2nd Series, v. 2, 1825. E.W. Brayley
and J. Britton *Topographical history of Surrey* v. 2, 1841,
98. W. Keane *Beauties of Surrey* 1849, 116. *C.L.* v. 85,

1939, 302–07,354–58; v. 171, 1982, 1194–96.
H.M. Colvin *History of King's Works* v. 4, 1982, 285.

West House, Congleton, Cheshire
J. Hort. Cottage Gdnr v. 34, 1865, 385–87.

West Lodge, Darlington, Co. Durham
G.M. v. 13, 1837, 440–41.

West Retford House, West Retford, Notts
Picturesque views of the principal seats 1788.

West Wood, Walberswick, Suffolk
A. Lees-Milne *and* R. Verey *Englishman's garden* 1980,
15–19.

West Woodhay House, Newbury, Berks
Gdn Design 1930, 5–10. R. Bisgrove *Gardens of Britain*
v. 3, 1978, 183–84.

West Wycombe Park, West Wycombe, Bucks
Official guide. G.L. le Rouge *Jardins Anglo-Chinois a la mode* 4^e cahier, 1776, pls. 16–17. *Copper Plate Mag.* v. 1,
1792, pl. 38. H. Repton *Observations* 1803, 32–35.
J.P. Neale *Views* v. 1, 1818. British Museum *Catalogue of maps, prints* 1829, 367. F.O. Morris *Series of picturesque views* v. 5, 43. *C.L.* v. 39, 1916, 16–24,48–55;
v. 73, 1933, 466–71,494; v. 155, 1974, 1618–21,
1682–85. N. Pevsner *Buckinghamshire* 1960, 286–87.
D. Stroud *Humphry Repton* 1962, 174. E.M. Elvey
Hand-list of Buckinghamshire estate maps 1963, 54.
B. Jones *Follies & grottoes* 1974, 100–07. R. Bisgrove
Gardens of Britain v. 3, 1978, 184–85. D. Jarrett *English landscape garden* 1978, 136–39. L. Fleming *and* A. Gore
English garden 1979, pl. 92. J. Harris *Artist and the country house* 1979, 200–01. G.S. Thomas *Gardens of National Trust* 1979, 254–55. M. Hadfield *et al. British gardeners* 1980, 94–95. Manpower Services Commission *West Wycombe* 1980. *Architectural Review* v. 171,
1982, 65. G. Carter *et al. Humphry Repton* 1982, 149.

Westacre High House near Swaffham, Norfolk
J.P. Neale *Views* v. 3, 1820.

Westbrook, Godalming, Surrey
C.L. v. 31, 1912, 92–97; v. 38, 1915, 119–21. G. Jekyll
and L. Weaver *Gardens for small country houses* 1913,
27–35.

Westbury Court, Westbury-on-Severn, Glos
Official guide. R. Atkyns *Ancient and present state of Glostershire* 1712, 799. L. Knyff *and* J. Kip *Britannia illustrata* v. 2, 1715. H.I. Triggs *Formal gardens in England and Scotland* 1902, 31–32. *C.L.* v. 14, 1903,
376–78; v. 24, 1908, 874–84; v. 135, 1964, 234; v. 136,
1964, 1280–83; v. 154, 1973, 864–66. M. Macartney
English houses & gardens 1908, pl. 10. G. Jekyll *Garden*

Westbury Court (*Cont.*)

ornament 1918, 334–35,347. Lady Rockley *Historic gardens of England* 1938, 150–51. *J. Royal Hort. Soc.* 1964, 494–97; 1971, 221–22. Garden History Society *Occasional Paper* no. 1, 1969, 15–18. D. Verey *Gloucestershire* v. 2, 1970, 400–01. V.C.H. *Gloucester* v. 10, 1972, 88. *Landscape Design* no. 104, 1973, 9–11. *Gdn History* v. 2 no. 2, 1974, 27–33; v. 3 no. 4, 1975, 53,54. L. Fleming *and* A. Gore *English garden* 1979, 68–69. G.S. Thomas *Gardens of National Trust* 1979, 251–53. J. Sales *West Country gardens* 1980, 114–16.

Westbury House, East Meon, Hants
K. Bilikowski *Hampshire countryside heritage: historic parks and gardens* 1983, 19.

Westcombe, Greenwich, London
W. Watts *Seats* 1779, pl. 1. P. Sandby *Collection of one hundred and fifty select views* v. 1, 1781, pl. 24. J. Harris *Artist and the country house* 1979, 258.

Westcotes, Leics
J. Throsby *Select views in Leicestershire* v. 1, 1790, 324. J. Nichols *History . . . of county of Leicester* v. 4, 1811, 567.

Westend House, Wickwar, Avon
J. Sales *West Country gardens* 1980, 117–18. A. Lees-Milne *and* R. Verey *Englishman's garden* 1982, 136–39.

Westerham, Kent
J. Harris *History of Kent* 1719, 330. T. Badeslade *Thirty six different views in . . . Kent* 1750s.

Westerlea, Edinburgh, Lothian
J. Hort. Cottage Gdnr N.S., v. 43, 1901, 583–84.

Westerton Tower near Bishop Auckland, Co. Durham
T. Wright *Arbours & grottos* 1979.

Westfield House near Ryde, Isle of Wight
E.A. Brooke *Gardens of England* 1857, pls. 35–36.

Westfields, Oakley, Beds
R. Webber *Percy Cane* 1975, 80–83,177. R. Bisgrove *Gardens of Britain* v. 3, 1978, 180–81. *C.L.* v. 170, 1981, 26–28.

Westminster Abbey Gardens, London
G. Taylor *Old London gardens* 1953, 16–22. *G.C.* i 1966, 347–48.

Westminster Palace, London
J.T. Smith *Antiquities of Westminster* 1807, passim.

Westminster Physic Garden, London
Proc. Linnean Soc. v. 164, 102–33. J. Evelyn *Diary* v. 3, 1955, 217. J.E. Dandy *Sloane Herbarium* 1958, 168.

Westmount, Kelvinside, Glasgow, Strathclyde
Gdning World v. 4, 1887, 184.

Weston near Kineton, Warwickshire
W. Dugdale *Antiquities of Warwickshire* v. 2, 1730, 583.

Weston Grove near Southampton, Hants
J. Hewetson *Architectural and picturesque views of noble mansions in Hampshire* 1830.

Weston Hall near Otley, W. Yorks
J.P. Neale *Views* v. 5, 1822. *Jones's views* 1829, 30. *C.L.* v. 124, 1958, 1112–16.

Weston Manor, Weston, Oxfordshire
C.L. v. 64, 1928, 268–74.

Weston Park, Weston under Lizard, Staffs
Official guide. *C.L.* v. 2, 1897, 592–94; v. 98, 1945, 818–21,910–13. V.C.H. *Stafford* v. 4, 1958, 170. *Archaeological J.* v. 120, 1963, 264. M. Allan *Fisons guide* 1970, 284–85. D. Stroud *Capability Brown* 1975, 148–49. D. Jarrett *English landscape* 1978, 111–15. R. Sidwell *West Midland gardens* 1981, 155–57.

Westonbirt House and **Arboretum** near Tetbury, Glos
Official guide. F.O. Morris *Series of picturesque views* v. 3, 53. *J. Hort. Cottage Gdnr* v. 50, 1873, 81–84; N.S., v. 35, 1897, 268–69,531; N.S., v. 48, 1904, 205–09. *G.C.* ii 1881, 43–46; i 1892, 299; i 1896, 483–84,517; ii 1902, 133–34,150–51; ii 1963, 352–53. *C.L.* v. 17, 1905, 414–23; v. 21, 1907, 911–16; v. 120, 1956, 522–23; v. 140, 1966, 620–22; v. 151, 1972, 1310–13. A. Bruce Jackson *Catalogue of the trees and shrubs* 1927. M. Woodward *Trees of Westonbirt* 1933. *J. Royal Hort. Soc.* 1964, 81–88; 1967, 430–35. H. Evans *Beautiful gardens of Britain* 1974, 35–36. P. Coats *Great gardens of Britain* 1967, 152–57. V.C.H. *Gloucester* v. 11, 1976, 283–84. A. Hellyer *Gardens of genius* 1980, 85–88. J. Sales *West Country gardens* 1980, 118–25.

Westover Lodge near Newport, Isle of Wight
R. Worsley *History of Isle of Wight* 1781.

Westport House, Westport, Co. Mayo, Eire
C.L. v. 137, 1965, 1010–13. E. Malins *and* Knight of Glin *Lost demesnes* 1976, 106–07. J. Harris *Artist and the country house* 1979, 179. Knight of Glin *and* P. Bowe *Gardens of outstanding historic interest in . . . Ireland* 1980.

Westrop House near Highworth, Wilts
G.C. ii 1891, 697.

Westwell near Tenterden, Kent
C.L. v. 134, 1963, 1180–83.

Westwell Manor, Westwell, Oxfordshire
R. Bisgrove *Gardens of Britain* v. 3, 1978, 182–83.

Westwick Cottage, Leverstock Green, Herts
C.L. v. 165, 1979, 1082–84. A. Lees-Milne *and*
R. Verey *Englishwoman's garden* 1980, 86–87.

Westwick Park near North Walsham, Norfolk
W. Watts *Seats* 1779, pl. 44. G.M. v. 17, 1841, 32.
J. Grigor *Eastern arboretum* 1841, 153–56.

Westwood House near Leek, Staffs
F. Calvert *Picturesque views . . . in Staffordshire &
Shropshire* 1830, 144.

Westwood Manor House, Westwood, Wilts
C.L. v. 60, 1926, 244–51.

Westwood Park near Droitwich, Hereford and Worcester
J. Beeverell *Les delices de la Grande Bretagne* v. 5, 1707, 872. L. Knyff *and* J. Kip *Britannia illustrata* v. 1, 1714.
H. Overton *Britannia illustrata* c.1724, pl. 20.
J.C. Loudon *Encyclopaedia of gardening* 1822, 1238.
F.O. Morris *Series of picturesque views* v. 5, 67.
L. Jewitt *and* S.C. Hall *Stately homes of England* 1877, 160–85. *Garden* v. 28, 1885, 651,658. C.L. v. 12, 1902, 688–97; v. 64, 1928, 50–57. V.C.H. *Worcester* v. 3, 1913, 234.

Westwoods, Windlesham, Surrey
Gdn Design 1933, 73–81. R. Webber *Percy Cane* 1975, 180,181,184.

Wetheral Priory, Cumbria
S. *and* N. Buck *Buck's antiquities* v. 1, 1774, pl. 51.

Wexham Park near Slough, Bucks
G.C. ii 1893, 490–92; ii 1899, 421–22. *Garden* v. 58, 1900, 316,317.

Wexham Springs, Stoke Poges, Bucks
R. Bisgrove *Gardens of Britain* v. 3, 1978, 186–87.

Weybridge Park, Alconbury, Cambs
P.G.M. Dickinson *Maps in the County Record Office, Huntingdon* 1968, 5.

Whaddon Hall, Whaddon, Bucks
E.M. Elvey *Hand-list of Buckinghamshire estate maps* 1963, 54.

Whalton Manor, Whalton, Northumberland
J. Brown *Gardens of a golden afternoon* 1982, 170.

Whatcombe House near Blandford, Dorset
J. Hutchins *History . . . of Dorset* v. 1, 1861, 198.

Whatton House near Hathern, Leics
J. Nichols *History . . . of county of Leicester* v. 3, 1804, 1104. J.P. Neale *Views* 2nd Series, v. 3, 1826. *Jones's views* 1829. G.M. v. 7, 1831, 427. J. Anthony *Gardens of Britain* v. 6, 1979, 161–63.

Wheatfield Manor, Wheatfield, Oxfordshire
V.C.H. *Oxford* v. 8, 1964, 263,264. *Gdn History* v. 8 no. 3, 1980, 96,99–100.

Wheatley, Doncaster, S. Yorks
Copper Plate Mag. v. 1, 1792, pl. 27.

Wherstead Park, Wherstead, Suffolk
D. Stroud *Humphry Repton* 1962, 174. G. Carter *et al. Humphry Repton* 1982, 162.

Whichford House near Chipping Norton, Oxfordshire
C.L. v. 141, 1967, 1382–84,1448–52.

Whiligh near Etchingham, E. Sussex
Tree lover no. 2, 1937, 159–60.

Whim near Lamancha, Borders
G.M. v. 13, 1837, 249–56.

Whitbourne Hall, Whitbourne, Hereford and Worcester
C.L. v. 157, 1975, 702–05.

Whitburgh, Crichton, Lothian
I.H. Adams *Descriptive list of plans* v. 3, 1974, 83.

Whitby. Botanic Garden, N. Yorks
Catalogue of the plants in the Botanic Garden at Whitby 1814.

Whitchester, Duns, Borders
G.A. Little *Scotland's gardens* 1981, 112.

White Barn House, Elmstead Market, Essex
A. Lees-Milne *and* R. Verey *Englishwoman's garden* 1980, 47–51. C.L. v. 169, 1981, 698–700.

White Craggs, Ambleside, Cumbria
G.C. ii 1964, 428–29. M. Allan *Fisons guide* 1970, 260.

White Conduit House, Islington, London
W. Wroth *London pleasure gardens of the eighteenth*

White Conduit House (*Cont.*)

century 1896, 131–39. E.B. Chancellor *Pleasure haunts of London* 1925, 375–78.

White Hill, Berkhamsted, Herts
G. Beard *Thomas H. Mawson* 1976, 66.

White Hill near Chester-le-Street, Co. Durham
G.M. v. 10, 1834, 194–97.

White Horse, Finchampstead, Berks
R. Bisgrove *Gardens of Britain* v. 3, 1978, 188–89.

White House, Sandwich Bay, Kent
R. Webber *Percy Cane* 1975, 167,183.

White House, Wrotham, Kent
J. Brown *Miss Gertrude Jekyll* 1981, 39.

White House, Highgate, Haringey, London
R. Webber *Percy Cane* 1975, 166,176.

White House *see* Kew. Royal Botanic Gardens

White House on the Cliff, Roedean, E. Sussex
J. Brown *Gardens of a golden afternoon* 1982, 174.

White Lodge, Richmond Park, London
W. Watts *Seats* 1779, pl. 16. H. Repton *Fragments* 1816, 83–85. R. Ackermann *Repository* v. 4, 1824, pl. 18. W.W.J. Gendall *Views* v. 2, 1830, 58. *C.L.* v. 53, 1923, 526–27. D. Stroud *Humphry Repton* 1962, 174. G. Carter *et al. Humphry Repton* 1982, 162.

White Webbs, Enfield, London
W. Keane *Beauties of Middlesex* 1850, 73–75.
J.B. Burke *Visitation* 2nd Series, v. 1, 1855, 171–72.

Whitechapel Botanical Garden (William Bennett), Tower Hamlets, London
G.C. ii 1918, 245–46.

Whitefield, Tetsworth, Oxfordshire
Copper Plate Mag. v. 2, pl. 64.

Whiteford House, Stoke, Cornwall
C.S. Gilbert *Historical survey of . . . Cornwall* v. 2, 1820, 477–78.

Whitehall, Shrewsbury, Shropshire
Garden v. 48, 1895, 177. *C.L.* v. 47, 1920, 200–06.

Whitehall Palace, Westminster, London
L.C.C. *Survey of London v. 13: Parish of St Margaret, Westminster* 1930, passim. *London Soc. J.* no. 380, 1967, 29–35. H.M. Colvin *History of the King's Works* v. 3, 1975, 164; v. 4, 1982, 26,314,316, pls. 26–27. J. Harris *Artist and the country house* 1979, 113,114. R. Strong *Renaissance garden in England* 1979, 34–38.

Whitehouse near Barnton, Lothian
H. Maxwell *Scottish gardens* 1911, 27–34.

Whitehurst near Chirk, Clwyd
Trans. Denbighshire Historical Soc. v. 22, 1973, 329–30.

Whiteknights, Reading, Berks
A. Robertson *Topographical survey of the Great Road* pt 1, 1792, 118–19. G. Tod *Plans, elevations and sections of hot-houses* 1807, 13,17, pls. 7,16. B. Hofland *Descriptive account of the mansion and gardens of White Knights* 1819. *G.M.* v. 4, 1828, 176; v. 6, 1830, 654–55; v. 9, 1833, 664–69; v. 11, 1835, 502–03. J.C. Loudon *Encyclopaedia of gardening* 1822, 1237. J.C. Loudon *Arboretum et fruticetum Britannicum* v. 1, 1844, 127–28.
J. Harris *Artist and the country house* 1979, 202.

Whiteway near Chudleigh, Devon
G.C. ii 1901, 238–39.

Whitfield, Wormbridge, Hereford and Worcester
R. Sidwell *West Midland gardens* 1981, 90–91.

Whitfield Court near Waterford, Co. Waterford, Eire
C.L. v. 142, 1967, 522–26.

Whitfield Hall, Whitfield, Northumberland
J. Hodgson *History of Northumberland* pt 2 v. 2, 1832.

Whitleigh near Plymouth, Devon
J.B. Burke *Visitation* v. 2, 1853, 176.

Whitley, Birdbrook, Essex
J. Britton *and* E.W. Brayley *Beauties of England and Wales* v. 5, 1803, 377–78.

Whitley Beaumont, Upper Whitley, W. Yorks
C.L. v. 111, 1952, 367. D. Stroud *Capability Brown* 1975, 244.

Whitley Park, Ham, Glos
T. Wright *Arbours & grottos* 1979.

Whitminster House, Whitminster, Glos
R.O. Cambridge *Works* 1803, xi.

Whitmore Hall, Whitmore, Staffs
C.L. v. 121, 1957, 1144–47.

Whitmore Lodge near Windsor, Berks
R. Ackermann *Repository* v. 10, 1827, pl. 11.
W.W.J. Gendall *Views* v. 2, 1830, 52.

Whitsbury Manor House, Whitsbury, Hants
G.C. ii 1960, 90–91.

Whittern, Lyonshall, Hereford and Worcester
G.C. i 1892, 201–02.

Whittingehame House near East Linton, Lothian
Gdning World v. 2, 1886, 473–74, 490. *J. Hort. Cottage Gdnr* N.S., v. 46, 1903, 31–32. A.A. Tait *Landscape garden in Scotland* 1980, passim.

Whittlebury, Northants
Cottage Gdnr v. 14, 1855, 144–45.

Whitton Court, Whitton, Shropshire
C.L. v. 41, 1917, 180–85; v. 143, 1968, 1426, 1510.

Whitton Place (Park), Twickenham, London
D. Crofts *A particular of the noble large house, gardens, the tower, temples, and other buildings and erections of the late Duke of Argyle situate at Whitton, near Hounslow in Middlesex* 1765. Society of Gentlemen *England displayed* v. 1, 1769, 215. *Short account of the principal seats and gardens in and about Richmond and Kew* [1760s?], 14–15. *Copper Plate Mag.* v. 1, 1792, pl. 48. *Trans. Linnean Soc.* v. 10, 1821, 275. J.C. Loudon *Encyclopaedia of gardening* 1822, 1226. British Museum *Catalogue of maps, prints* 1829, 354. *G.M.* v. 5, 1829, 94; v. 15, 1839, 424. J.C. Loudon *Arboretum et fruticetum Britannicum* v. 1, 1844, 57–58. W. Keane *Beauties of Middlesex* 1850, 78–81. J.B. Burke *Visitation* v. 1, 1852, 173–74. P. Kalm *Account of his visit to England* 1892, 58–59. *G.C.* i 1944, 70. *C.L.* v. 152, 1972, 142–45. P. Foster and D.H. Simpson *Whitton Park and Whitton Place* 1979. *Gdn History* v. 8 no. 3, 1980, 104, 107; v. 9 no. 1, 1981, 60–62. G. Carter et al. *Humphry Repton* 1982, 158. *Garden* 1983, 366.

Whixley, N. Yorks
J. Beeverell *Les delices de la Grande Bretagne* v. 5, 1707, 872. L. Knyff and J. Kip *Britannia illustrata* v. 1, 1714.

Wick House, Brislington, Avon
J.P. Neale *Views* v. 3, 1820.

Wicken Park, Wicken, Northants
J.P. Neale *Views* v. 3, 1820. *Northamptonshire Past and Present* v. 5 no. 3, 1975, 233.

Wickham, Hants
G.M. v. 10, 1834, 209–12.

Wickham Court, West Wickham, Bromley, London
J. Hort. Cottage Gdnr N.S., v. 9, 1884, 242. *C.L.* v. 11, 1902, 656–62. G. Jekyll *Garden ornament* 1918, 285.

Wickham Park near Croydon, London
W. Keane *Beauties of Surrey* 1849, 58–60.

Wickhamford Manor, Wickhamford, Hereford and Worcester
Lady Rockley *Historic gardens of England* 1938, 220–21.

Widcombe Manor near Bath, Avon
C.L. v. 82, 1937, 220–25. J. Harris *Gardens of delight* 1978, 67–68.

Widdicombe House near Kingsbridge, Devon
D. Stroud *Capability Brown* 1975, 244.

Widdington, Essex
F.G. Emmison *Catalogue of maps in Essex Record Office* 1st Supplt, 1952, 4.

Widdrington Castle, Northumberland
S. and N. Buck *Buck's antiquities* v. 1, 1774, pl. 224.

Widey near Plymouth, Devon
R. Ackermann *Repository* v. 11, 1828, pl. 19.
W.W.J. Gendall *Views* v. 2, 1830, 42.

Widford Lodge, Chelmsford, Essex
G.C. i 1896, 683–84.

Wierton near Maidstone, Kent
J. Harris *History of Kent* 1719, 49. J. Kip *Supplement du Nouveau theatre de la Grande Bretagne* 1728, pl. 11.
T. Badeslade *Thirty six different views . . . in . . . Kent* 1750s, pl. 36.

Wiggie, Redhill, Surrey
G.C. i 1928, 264–65.

Wightwick Manor near Wolverhampton, W. Midlands
Official guide. *C.L.* v. 133, 1963, 1242–45.
G.C. Thomas *Gardens of National Trust* 1979, 255.
R. Sidwell *West Midland gardens* 1981, 238–39.

Wigmore Park near Dorking, Surrey
Gdnrs Mag. 1906, 155–57.

Wigram, R. see Walthamstow House

Wilbury House near Newton Toney, Wilts
C.L. v. 71, 1932, 96–102; v. 126, 1959, 1014–18, 1148–51. B. Jones *Follies & grottoes* 1974, 408.
N. Pevsner *Wiltshire* 1975, 574.

Wilcot Manor, Wilcot, Wilts
V.C.H. *Wiltshire* v. 10, 1975, 195.

Wilcote House near Finstock, Oxfordshire
R. Bisgrove *Gardens of Britain* v. 3, 1978, 189.

Wilcote Manor near Finstock, Oxfordshire
R. Bisgrove *Gardens of Britain* v. 3, 1978, 190.

Wilderness (William Wilkes), Croydon, London
G.C. ii 1920, 143,144,145,146.

Wildernesse near Sevenoaks, Kent
J.P. Neale *Views* v. 2, 1819. G. Virtue *Picturesque beauties of Great Britain: Kent* 1829, 123. *G.C.* i 1909, 346,360,361. J.T. White *Parklands of Kent* 1975, 31. G. Carter *et al. Humphry Repton* 1982, 156.

Wilford Hall, Wilford, Notts
G.M. v. 4, 1828, 90–92.

Wilkes, William *see* Shirley Vicarage; Wilderness

Willersley Castle near Matlock, Derbyshire
J.P. Neale *Views* v. 1, 1818. W. Adam *Gem of the Peak* 1851, 21–22,43–44,67–75. *G.C.* ii 1886, 440–41. J. Harris *Artist and the country house* 1979, 297.

Willesley Hall, Willesley, Leics
F.O. Morris *Series of picturesque views* v. 6, 7.

Willey near Bridgnorth, Shropshire
J.P. Neale *Views* 2nd Series, v. 2, 1825. *C.L.* v. 49, 1921, 214–20.

Williamston House near Insh, Grampian
G.C. ii 1968, 15–16. M. Allan *Fisons guide* 1970, 345–46.

Williamstrip Park, Coln St Aldwyns, Glos
R. Atkyns *Ancient and present state of Glostershire* 1712, 364. L. Knyff and J. Kip *Britannia illustrata* v. 2, 1715. S. Rudder *New history of Gloucestershire* 1779, 384. J.N. Brewer *Delineations of Gloucestershire* 1825, 90. M. Macartney *English houses & gardens* 1908, pl. 49. Historical MSS Commission *Architectural history* v. 3, 1971, item 2630.

Willingham House, Market Rasen, Lincs
B. Howlett *Selection of views in county of Lincoln* 1805.

Willingham House, Ringmer, E. Sussex
B. Jones *Follies & grottoes* 1974, 321.

Willoughbridge, Elds Wood, Staffs
R. Sidwell *West Midland gardens* 1981, 180–81.

Willows, Ashton on Ribble, Lancs
G. Beard *Thomas H. Mawson* 1976, 66.

Wilsford Manor, Wilsford, Wilts
C.L. v. 20, 1906, 450–57.

Wilsley House, Cranbrook, London
C.L. v. 48, 1920, 240–46.

Wilson, George Fergusson *see* Royal Horticultural Society Gardens, Wisley

Wilson, Guy L. *see* Coleraine

Wilton Castle near Redcar, Cleveland
J.P. Neale *Views* 2nd Series, v. 4, 1828. *Jones's views* 1829, 1–2.

Wilton House, Wilton, Wilts
Official guide. I. de Caus *Wilton gardens* c.1645.
J. Beeverell *Les delices de la Grande Bretagne* v. 5, 1707, 872. C. Cambell *Vitruvius Britannicus* v. 3, 1725, 57–60. G.L. le Rouge *Jardins Anglo-Chinois a la mode* 2^e cahier, 1776, pl. 10. W. Stukeley *Itinerarium curiosam* v. 1, 1776, pl. 1. C. Burlington *Modern universal British traveller* 1779, 386. D. Defoe *Tour* v. 1, 1778, 283–84. W. Watts *Seats* 1779, pl. 82. J. Britton *Beauties of Wiltshire* v. 1, 1801, 143–46. L. Magalotti *Travels of Cosmo the Third, Grand Duke of Tuscany, through England . . . 1669.* 1821, 150. J.P. Neale *Views* v. 5, 1822. British Museum *Catalogue of maps, prints* 1829, 355. *G.M.* v. 12, 1836, 509–13. *Florist* 1856, 330–32. E.A. Brooke *Gardens of England* 1857, pls. 38–39. F.O. Morris *Series of picturesque views* v. 1, 9. L. Jewitt and S.C. Hall *Stately homes of England* 1877, 224–41. *J. Hort. Cottage Gdnr* N.S., v. 8, 1884, 10–11,27–29. *Garden* v. 48, 1895, 455–56; v. 53, 1898, 467.
H.I. Triggs *Formal gardens in England and Scotland* 1902, 15–16. *C.L.* v. 15, 1904, 774–87; v. 101, 1947, 1168–69; v. 133, 1963, 1044–48; v. 134, 1963, 206–09, 264–67. C. Holme *Gardens of England in Southern & Western counties* 1907, pls. 133–36. *G.C.* i 1910, 362, 382–83. G. Jekyll *Garden ornament* 1918, 67,129,176, 219,361. E.S. Rohde *Story of the garden* 1932, 123–25. C. Fiennes *Journeys* 1949, 9–10. J. Evelyn *Diary* v. 3, 1955, 114. R. Lister *Great works of craftsmanship* 1967, 114–30. R.I.B.A. *Catalogue* v. A, 1968, 17. M. Allan *Fisons guide* 1970, 109–10. B. Jones *Follies & grottoes* 1974, 409. N. Pevsner *Wiltshire* 1975, 582,585–86. D. Stroud *Capability Brown* 1975, 244. M. Binney and A. Hills *Elysian gardens* 1979, 34. J. Harris *Artist and the country house* 1979, 37,128,276. J. Harris and A.A. Tait *Catalogue of the drawings by Inigo Jones, John Webb and Isaac de Caus at Worcester College* 1979, 47–49,51. R. Strong *Renaissance garden in England* 1979, 122–23,147–61,214. M. Hadfield *et al. British gardeners* 1980, 97. J. Sales *West Country gardens* 1980, 249–51. *J. Gdn History* v. 2 no. 1, 1982, 47–48. K. Rorschach *Early Georgian landscape garden* 1983, 46–51.

Wilton Park near Beaconsfield, Bucks
D. Stroud *Humphry Repton* 1962, 174. G. Carter *et al. Humphry Repton* 1982, 149.

Wimbledon House, Merton, London
J. Kip *Supplement du Nouveau theatre de la Grande Bretagne* 1728, pls. 29–30. G.L. le Rouge *Jardins Anglo-Chinois a la mode* 2^e cahier, 1776, pl. 14.
D. Lysons *Environs of London* v. 1, 1792, 522,527–28.
J.C. Loudon *Encyclopaedia of gardening* 1822, 1229.
R. Ackermann *Repository* v. 5, 1825, pl. 7.
G.F. Prosser *Select illustrations of . . . Surrey* 1828.
W.W.J. Gendall *Views* v. 1, 1830, 64,121. *G.M.* v. 10, 1834, 337–46; v. 13, 1837, 115–17; v. 15, 1839, 429.
E.W. Brayley and J. Britton *Topographical history of Surrey* v. 3, 508–09. J.C. Loudon *Villa gardener* 1850, 420–52. *Surrey Archaeological Collections* v. 5, 1871, 112–29. *J. Hort. Cottage Gdnr* v. 56, 1876, 262–64. *G.C.* ii 1898, 224. E. Cecil *History of gardening in England* 1910, 317–38. V.C.H. *Surrey* v. 4, 1912, 123. J. Evelyn *Diary* v. 3, 1955, 315–16; v. 4, 130–31. *C.L.* v. 132, 1962, 248–50. C.S.S. Higham *Wimbledon Manor House under the Cecils* 1962. D. Stroud *Capability Brown* 1975, 244. R.I.B.A. *Catalogue* v. S, 1976, 96. P. Willis *Charles Bridgeman* 1977, 184. J. Harris *Artist and the country house* 1979, 102. R. Strong *Renaissance garden in England* 1979, 57–63,191–97. M. Hadfield *et al. British gardeners* 1980, 91.

Wimbledon Park, Merton, London
D. Stroud *Capability Brown* 1975, 134–35.

Wimborne St Giles, Dorset
J. Hutchins *History . . . of Dorset* v. 2, 1774, 217. *C.L.* v. 133, 1963, 1328. B. Jones *Follies & grottoes* 1974, 165–66.

Wimpole Hall, Arrington, Cambs
Official guide. J. Beeverell *Les delices de la Grande Bretagne* v. 5, 1707, 872. L. Knyff and J. Kip *Britannia illustrata* v. 1, 1714. J. Britton and E.W. Brayley *Beauties of England and Wales* v. 2, 1801, 125.
H. Repton *Observations* 1803, 123–25. British Museum *Catalogue of maps, prints* 1829, 355.
F.O. Morris *Series of picturesque views* v. 2, 71. *C.L.* v. 23, 1908, 234–41; v. 61, 1927, 806–13; v. 142, 1967, 1400–01,1466,1594; v. 166, 1979, 658–61,758–62.
M. Macartney *English houses & gardens* 1908, pl. 19.
D. Stroud *Humphry Repton* 1962, 174. Royal Commission on Historical Monuments *Inventory of historical monuments in . . . Cambridge* v. 1, 1968, 222–23, pls. 121,129,132,137. N. Pevsner *Cambridgeshire* 1970, 492. V.C.H. *Cambridge* v. 5, 1973, 264–65. B. Jones *Follies & grottoes* 1974, 56–58. D. Stroud *Capability Brown* 1975, 140–41,245. P. Willis *Charles Bridgeman* 1977, 184–85. M. Binney and A. Hills *Elysian gardens* 1979, 11. L. Fleming and A. Gore *English garden* 1979,
109. G.S. Thomas *Gardens of National Trust* 1979, 256.
M. Hadfield *et al. British gardeners* 1980, 207.
J.L. Phibbs *Wimpole Hall*, National Trust, 1980.
G. Carter *et al. Humphry Repton* 1982, 149. D. Watkin *English vision* 1982, 51. D. Jacques *Georgian gardens* 1983, 70,80, pl. 7.

Winchendon House, Winchendon, Bucks
J. Harris *Artist and the country house* 1979, 140–41, pls. 12–13.

Winchester Castle, Winchester, Hants
H.M. Colvin *History of King's Works* v. 2, 1963, 857, 863.

Winchester Deanery, Winchester, Hants
C.L. v. 51, 1922, 442–49.

Winchester War Memorial Cloister, Winchester, Hants
J. Brown *Miss Gertrude Jekyll* 1981, 44.

Winchfield Lodge, Winchfield, Hants
G.C. ii 1905, 25–26.

Windle Hall near St Helens, Merseyside
C.L. v. 174, 1983, 212–14.

Windlesham Moor, Windlesham, Surrey
C.L. v. 75, 1934, 566–70.

Windlesham Park, Windlesham, Surrey
Gdn Design 1931, 54–58.

Windlestone Hall, Windlestone, Co. Durham
C. Holme *Gardens of England in Northern counties* 1911, pls. 132–33.

Windmill Hill, Wartling, E. Sussex
T.W. Horsfield *History . . . of Sussex* v. 1, 1835, 546.

Winds Point near Malvern, Hereford and Worcester
R. Sidwell *West Midland gardens* 1981, 92.

Windsor Castle, Berks
L. Knyff and J. Kip *Britannia illustrata* v. 1, 1714.
H. Overton *Britannia illustrata* c.1724, pl. 1.
T. Badeslade and J. Rocque *Vitruvius Brittanicus* 1739, pls. 38–39. Society of Gentlemen *England displayed* v. 1, 1769, 232,236. G.L. le Rouge *Jardins Anglo-Chinois a la mode* 4^e cahier, 1776, pl. 17; 6^e cahier, 1777, pls. 2–3. D. Defoe *Tour* v. 1, 1778, 303–04. P. Sandby *Collection of one hundred and fifty select views* v. 1, 1781, pl. 5. W. Daniell [*Select views of Windsor Castle*] c.1827, pls. 9–10. *G.M.* v. 5, 1829, 604–07; v. 7, 1831, 144–50; v. 9, 1833, 654–55. British Museum *Catalogue of maps, prints* 1829, 356–57. S. Scarthwaite [*Six views of*

Windsor Castle (*Cont.*)

Windsor Castle] 1831, pl. 2. J.B. Pyne *Windsor with its surrounding scenery* c.1839. *Journey-book of England: Berkshire* 1840, 49,58–63. C.G. Carus *King of Saxony's journey through England and Scotland* 1846, 74–75,78. J. Nash *Views of the interior and exterior of Windsor Castle* 1848, pl. 22. *G.C.* 31 October 1874, Supplement; i 1897, 393–95; i 1902, 417; ii 1908, 147–48,149,339; i 1937, 307. *J. Hort. Cottage Gdnr* N.S., v. 14, 1887, 503,510. *Gdnrs Mag.* 1896, 375–82. *Gdning World* v. 13, 1897, 677–79. A.J. Hubbard *Norman Tower garden . . ., catalogue of the plants* 1910. *Garden* 1911, 296–300. C. Ward *Royal gardens* 1912, 1–31. *C.L.* v. 77, 1935, 450; v. 78, 1935, 324–30. *J. Royal Hort. Soc.* 1935, 189–95. A.P. Oppé *Drawings of Paul and Thomas Sandby* 1947, 19–33. C. Fiennes *Journeys* 1949, 359. L. Roper *Royal gardens* 1953, 28–63. J. Evelyn *Diary* v. 1, 1955, 72; v. 4, 317. H.M. Colvin *History of King's Works* v. 2, 1963, 867,869,881; v. 5, 1976, 332–33; v. 6, 1973, 381,387. N. Pevsner *Berkshire* 1966, 292–93. B. Jones *Follies & grottoes* 1974, 289–90. P. Willis *Charles Bridgeman* 1977, 185. J. Harris *Artist and the country house* 1979, 120. M. Hadfield et al. *British gardeners* 1980, 14. J. Harvey *Mediæval gardens* 1981, pl. 40. G. Plumptre *Royal gardens* 1981, 106–25.

Windsor Great Park, Berks
Official guide. *New display of the beauties of England* v. 1, 1787, 33–35. C. Burlington *Modern universal British traveller* 1779, 371. R. Ackermann *Repository* v. 1, 1823, pls. 1–2. W. Daniell [*Select views of Windsor Castle*] c.1827, pls. 8–10. W.W.J. Gendall *Views* v. 1, 1830, frontispiece, 3. *J. Royal Hort. Soc.* 1935, 189–95. A.P. Oppé *Drawings of Paul and Thomas Sandby* 1947, 33–44. L. Roper *Gardens in Royal Park at Windsor* 1959. N. Pevsner *Berkshire* 1966, 295–98. T.L. Barton *Windsor Great Park: a recreation study* 1967. Historical MSS Commission *Architectural history* v. 4, 1972, item 4764. H.M. Colvin *History of King's Works* v. 6, 1973, 395–401. *C.L.* v. 170, 1981, 326–31; v. 172, 1982, 1214–16.

Windsor Great Park. Savill Gardens, Berks
Official guide. *C.L.* v. 118, 1955, 604–06. *J. Royal Hort. Soc.* 1957, 502–12. *G.C.* i 1960, 206–07; i 1964, 246. P. Coats *Great gardens of Britain* 1963, 282–87. M. Allan *Fisons guide* 1970, 20–22. H. Evans *Beautiful gardens of Britain* 1974, 41–42. *Garden* 1976, 127–34; 1979, 398–401. R. Bisgrove *Gardens of Britain* v. 3, 1978, 190–93. A. Hellyer *Gardens of genius* 1980, 88–91. G. Plumptre *Royal gardens* 1981, 68–85.

Windsor Great Park. Virginia Water, Berks
W. Daniell [*Select views of Windsor Castle*] c.1827, pl. 12. *G.M.* v. 9, 1833, 652–54. J.B. Pyne *Windsor with its surrounding scenery* c.1839, pls. 10–11. E.W. Brayley *and* J. Britton *Topographical history of Surrey* v. 2, 1841, 291–94. E. von Erdberg *Chinese influence on European garden structures* 1936, 185–86. *C.L.* v. 103, 1948, 830–31; v. 126, 1959, 1270; v. 142, 1967, 130–31. J. Harris *Catalogue of British drawings . . . in American collections* 1971, 92–93,208–13. B. Jones *Follies & grottoes* 1974, 141–43. D. Watkin *English vision* 1982, 63.

Windsor. Frogmore, Berks
J. Britton *and* E.W. Brayley *Beauties of England and Wales* v. 1, 1801, 267. G. Tod *Plans, elevations and sections of hot-houses* 1807, pl. 19. W.H. Pyne *History of the royal residences* v. 1, 1819. J.C. Loudon *Encyclopaedia of gardening* 1822, 1237. R. Ackermann *Repository* v. 1, 1823, pls. 13–15. R. Havell *Series of picturesque views of noblemen's & gentlemen's seats* 1823. *G.M.* v. 4, 1828, 176–77; v. 9, 1833, 651; v. 19, 1843, 688–89. W.W.J. Gendall *Views* v. 1, 1830, 4,8,9. *Builder* 1843, v. 1, 39. *Florist* 1854, 68–71; 1856, 145–49; 1857, 138–41; 1859, 298–301. *Garden* 1876, 307–12. *J. Hort. Cottage Gdnr* N.S., v. 14, 1887, 508–10; v. 34, 1897, 550–58; v. 42, 1901, 90–92,100–01. *C.L.* v. 11, 1902, 736–45. *G.C.* ii 1908, 337–40,347,349,364–66; i 1937, 306. R. Bisgrove *Gardens of Britain* v. 3, 1978, 79. G. Plumptre *Royal gardens* 1981, 86–105.

Windsor. Royal Lodge, Berks
C.L. v. 85, 1939, 706–12. *House and Garden* January 1966, 33–47. G. Plumptre *Royal gardens* 1981, 50–67.

Windycroft, Hurtmore, Godalming, Surrey
Garden Design 1936, 39–44.

Wingerworth Hall near Chesterfield, Derbyshire
H. Repton *Fragments* 1816, 59–64. D. Stroud *Humphry Repton* 1962, 63. G. Carter et al. *Humphry Repton* 1982, 150.

Wingfield Castle, Wingfield, Suffolk
C.L. v. 33, 1913, 952–58.

Winkworth Arboretum near Godalming, Surrey
J. Royal Hort. Soc. 1954, 80–92. M. Allan *Fisons guide* 1970, 69. H. Evans *Beautiful gardens of Britain* 1974, 53–54. T. Wright *Gardens of Britain* v. 4, 1978, 233–36. G.S. Thomas *Gardens of National Trust* 1979, 257–58.

Winkworth Farm, Hascombe, Surrey
J. Brown *Gardens of a golden afternoon* 1982, 164.

Winns, Walthamstow, Waltham Forest, London
G.C. ii 1900, 61.

Winslade House near Exeter, Devon
G.M. v. 19, 1843, 242. *G.C.* ii 1882, 84,105–06.

Winslow Hall, Winslow, Bucks
C.L. v. 110, 1951, 572–76.

Winterborne Clenston Manor House, Dorset
J. Hutchins *History . . . of Dorset* v. 1, 1861, 190.

Winthorpe Hall, Winthorpe, Notts
R. Thoroton *Thoroton's history* v. 1, 1797, 366–67.

Winton House, Pencaitland, Lothian
G.A. Little *Scotland's gardens* 1981, 112–13.

Wintrey Park, Epping, Essex
F.G. Emmison *Catalogue of maps in Essex Record Office* 1st Supplt, 1952, 4.

Wiseton Hall, Wiseton, Notts
Picturesque views of the principal seats 1788. *Copper Plate Mag.* v. 1, 1792, pl. 5. *J. Hort. Home Farmer* N.S., v. 67, 1913, 233-34.

Wishaw near Motherwell, Strathclyde
J.P. Neale *Views* 2nd Series, v. 4, 1828.

Wiston Park, Wiston, W. Sussex
C.L. v. 25, 1909, 306–14.

Wistow Hall, Wistow, Leics
J. Throsby *Select views in Leicestershire* v. 1, 1790, 187. J. Nichols *History . . . of county of Leicester* v. 3, 1804, 1127. J.P. Neale *Views* v. 2, 1819. *Jones's views* 1829. *G.M.* v. 7, 1831, 424. *J. Hort. Cottage Gdnr* N.S., v. 40, 1900, 532–34.

Witanhurst, Highgate, Haringey, London
R. Webber *Percy Cane* 1975, 176–77.

Witchingham Hall near Reepham, Norfolk
F.O. Morris *Series of picturesque views* v. 4, 77.

Witcombe Park, Witcombe, Glos
R. Atkyns *Ancient and present state of Glostershire* 1712, 844. L. Knyff *and* J. Kip *Britannia illustrata* v. 2, 1715.

Witham Hall, Witham on the Hill, Lincs
C. Holme *Gardens of England in Midland & Eastern counties* 1908, pls. 126–29. G. Beard *Thomas H. Mawson* 1976, 66.

Withersdane Hall, Wye, Kent
T. Wright *Gardens of Britain* v. 4, 1978, 109–14.

Withington Hall, Old Withington, Cheshire
G. Ormerod *History of County Palatine and City of Chester* v. 3, 1882, 718.

Withnell Fold, Withnells, Lancs
G.C. ii 1904, 459–60.

Witley Court, Great Witley, Hereford and Worcester
F.O. Morris *Series of picturesque views* v. 1, 85. *G.C.* 1873, 812,845,860; ii 1881, 503–04. *J. Hort. Cottage Gdnr* v. 49, 1873, 11–14. *C.L.* v. 2, 1897, 126–28; v. 97, 1945, 992–95,1036–39; v. 143, 1968, 1435,1688. N. Pevsner *Worcestershire* 1968, 174. R.I.B.A. *Catalogue* v. L-N, 1973, 109. M. Binney *and* A. Hills *Elysian gardens* 1979, 75. G. Carter *et al. Humphry Repton* 1982, 164.

Witley Park, Witley, Surrey
I. Nairn *and* B. Cherry *Surrey* 1971, 531.

Whitley Park House near Worcester, Hereford and Worcester
R. Sidwell *West Midland gardens* 1981, 93–94.

Witnesham Hall, Witnesham, Suffolk
J.B. Burke *Visitation* v. 2, 1853, 202.

Wittersham House, Wittersham, Kent
J. Jekyll *Garden ornament* 1918, 31. J. Brown *Gardens of a golden afternoon* 1982, 169.

Wittington near Marlow, Bucks
C.L. v. 62, 1927, 90–95; v. 64, 1928, 81–85. *G.C.* ii 1930, 30–32,33.

Witton House, Blackburn, Lancs
J.B. Burke *Visitation* v. 1, 1852, 134.

Witton Park near North Walsham, Norfolk
G.M. v. 17, 1841, 272. J. Grigor *Eastern arboretum* 1841, 230. *Blackwell's centenary antiquarian catalogue* 1979, 100–101.

Wivenhoe Park near Colchester, Essex
T. Wright *History . . . of Essex* v. 1, 1836, 397. R. Feesey *History of Wivenhoe Park* 1963. F.G. Emmison *Catalogue of maps in Essex Record Office* 2nd Supplt, 1964, 12,34. *C.L.* v. 142, 1967, 1473.

Wiveton Hall, Wiveton, Norfolk
C.L. v. 38, 1915, 712–16.

Wo Yuen, Milford, Surrey
C.L. v. 89, 1941, 10–13.

Woburn Abbey, Woburn, Beds
Society of Gentlemen *England displayed* v. 1, 1769, 354–55. D. Defoe *Tour* v. 3, 1778, 49–50. *New display of the beauties of England* v. 1, 1787, 10. J. Britton *and* E.W. Brayley *Beauties of England and Wales* v. 1, 1801, 58–60. G. Tod *Plans, elevations and sections of hothouses* 1807, 17, pl. 15. H. Repton *Fragments* 1816, 148–76. G. Sinclair *Hortus gramineus Woburnensis* 1816. S. Dodd *Historical . . . account of Woburn* 1818.

Woburn Abbey (Cont.)

J.P. Neale *Views* v. 1, 1818. J.C. Loudon *Encyclopaedia of gardening* 1822, 1234. R. Ackermann *Repository* v. 4, 1824, pl. 24. G. Sinclair *Hortus ericaeus Woburnensis* 1825. J. Forbes *Salictum Woburnense* 1829. *G.M.* v. 5, 1829, 560–64; v. 12, 1836, 292–94. British Museum *Catalogue of maps, prints* 1829, 358. W.W.J. Gendall *Views* v. 2, 1830, 49. J.D. Parry *Guide to Woburn Abbey* 1831. J. Forbes *Hortus Woburnensis* 1833. Prince Pückler-Muskau *Tour in England, Ireland and France* 1833, 69–70. J.C. Bourne *Views of Woburn Abbey and in the park* 184–? E.A. Brooke *Gardens of England* 1857, pls. 22–23. F.O. Morris *Series of picturesque views* v. 2, 13. *G.C.* ii 1885, 615–16. F. Kielmansegge *Diary* 1902, 232–33. E.M. Erdberg *Chinese influence on European garden structures* 1936, 188. T. Jefferson *Garden book 1766–1824* 1944, 112. H.F. Clark *English landscape garden* 1948, 61–63. C. Fiennes *Journeys* 1949, 119–20. *C.L.* v. 117, 1955, 854–58,987; v. 118, 1955, 434–37; v. 138, 1965, 98,158–61; v. 173, 1983, 772–75,860–63. D. Stroud *Humphry Repton* 1962, 147. *Bedfordshire Mag.* v. 6, 1958, 234–38. N. Pevsner *Bedfordshire and county of Huntingdon* 1968, 170–71. B. Jones *Follies & grottoes* 1974, 145–46,286–87. R. Webber *Percy Cane* 1975, 177. R. Bisgrove *Gardens of Britain* v. 3, 1978, 193–94. L. Fleming *and* A. Gore *English garden* 1979, 140. J. Harris *Artist and the country house* 1979, 278. G. Carter *et al. Humphry Repton* 1982, pls. 5–6,60,66, 147.

Woburn Farm, Addlestone, Surrey
R. *and* J. Dodsley *London and its environs described* v. 6, 1761, 361. Society of Gentlemen *England displayed* v. 1, 1769, 225. T. Whately *Observations on modern gardening* 1771, 177–82; 1801, pl. 4. D. Defoe *Tour* v. 1, 1778, 224–25. *Short account of the principal seats and gardens in and about Richmond and Kew* [1760s?], 15–16. E.W. Brayley *and* J. Britton *Topographical history of Surrey* v. 2, 1841, 234–36. *G.M.* v. 13, 1837, 113. R. Pococke *Travels through England* v. 2, 1889, 260–61. H.F. Clark *English landscape garden* 1948, 40–43. I. Nairn *and* B. Cherry *Surrey* 1971, 90. *Gdn History* v. 2 no. 3, 1974, 27–60; v. 3 no. 2, 1975, 3–6; v. 7 no. 2, 1979, 82–101; v. 7 no. 3, 1979, 9–12. M.R. Brownell *Alexander Pope & the arts of Georgian England* 1978, 232–35. L. Fleming *and* A. Gore *English garden* 1979, 106–07. M. Hadfield *et al. British gardeners* 1980, 268.

Woburn House near Mill Isle, Co. Down, Ulster
G.C. ii 1962, 80. E. Malins *and* P. Bowe *Irish gardens and demesnes* 1980, 76.

Woburn Place, Addlestone, Surrey
G.C. ii 1910, 155–56,163.

Wokefield Park, Mortimer, Berks
Gdnrs Mag. 1904, 701,704,705.

Wokingham (Oakingham), Berks
T. Badeslade *and* J. Rocque *Vitruvius Brittanicus* 1739, pls. 92–93. J. Harris *Artist and the country house* 1979, 169.

Wolfeton House near Charminster, Dorset
J. Hutchins *History . . . of Dorset* v. 2, 1863, 545. *C.L.* v. 11, 1902, 304–09; v. 114, 1953, 414–17.

Wollaton Hall, Wollaton, Notts
Official guide. J. Beeverell *Les delices de la Grande Bretagne* v. 5, 1707, 872. L. Knyff *and* J. Kip *Britannia illustrata* v. 1, 1714. R. Thoroton *Thoroton's history* v. 2, 1797, 114. J.P. Neale *Views* v. 3, 1820. F.O. Morris *Series of picturesque views* v. 1, 73. *J. Hort. Cottage Gdnr* v. 39, 1868, 375–76; N.S., v. 56, 1876, 189–91. *Gdning World* v. 7, 1890, 23. *C.L.* v. 8, 1900, 496–502; v. 41, 1917, 568–75,592–93. J. Harris *Artist and the country house* 1979, 54,74, pl. 5. R. Strong *Renaissance garden in England* 1979, 56–57. J. Johnson *Excellent Cassandra: life and times of Duchess of Chandos* 1981, 42,45–46. G. Carter *et al. Humphry Repton* 1982, 160.

Wolseley Hall near Rugeley, Staffs
J. Nightingale *Topographical . . . description of Staffordshire* 1810, 731. J.P. Neale *Views* v. 4, 1821. *Jones's views* 1829. F. Calvert *Picturesque views . . . in Staffordshire & Shropshire* 1830, 21. F.O. Morris *Series of picturesque views* v. 3, 55. C. Fiennes *Journeys* 1949, 165.

Wolterton Park near Aylsham, Norfolk
W. Watts *Seats* 1779, pl. 59. J.P. Neale *Views* v. 3, 1820. *General history of county of Norfolk* v. 1, 1829, 218. *G.M.* v. 17, 1841, 30. J. Grigor *Eastern arboretum* 1841, 111–14. *C.L.* v. 24, 1908, 450–60; v. 122, 1957, 116–19. P. Willis *Charles Bridgeman* 1977, 185.

Wombwell Hall, Northfleet, Kent
C. Greenwood *Epitome of county history . . . v. 1: Kent* 1838, 227.

Wonersh Park near Guildford, Surrey
G.F. Prosser *Select illustrations of . . . Surrey* 1828. E.W. Brayley *and* J. Britton *Topographical history of Surrey* v. 5, 1848, 150. W. Keane *Beauties of Surrey* 1849, 137–38.

Wonham House near Godstone, Surrey
R. Ackermann *Repository* v. 10, 1827, pl. 25. W.W.J. Gendall *Views* v. 2, 1830, 48.

Wooburn *see* Woburn

Wood, South Tawton, Devon
G. Beard *Thomas H. Mawson* 1976, 66–67.

Wood Croft, Boars Hill, Oxfordshire
M. Batey *Oxford gardens* 1982, 194–201.

Wood End, Witley, Surrey
J. Brown *Gardens of a golden afternoon* 1982, 160.

Wood End near Thirsk, N. Yorks
J.P. Neale *Views* v. 5, 1822. *Jones's views* 1829, 35.

Wood Hall, Cockermouth, Cumbria
G. Beard *Thomas H. Mawson* 1976, 67.

Wood Hall, Sydenham, Lewisham, London
G.C. ii 1911, 142–43.

Wood Hall, Hilgay, Norfolk
G. Carter *et al. Humphry Repton* 1982, 159.

Wood Hill, Essendon, Herts
D. Stroud *Humphry Repton* 1962, 174. G. Carter *et al. Humphry Repton* 1982, 154.

Wood House near Epping, Essex
C.L. v. 126, 1959, 1300–03.

Wood House, Wanstead, Redbridge, London
F.G. Emmison *Catalogue of maps in Essex Record Office* 3rd Supplt, 1968, 20.

Wood Side, Westward, Cumbria
W. Hutchinson *History of county of Cumberland* v. 2, 1794, 399.

Woodbastwick Hall near Norwich, Norfolk
J. Grigor *Eastern arboretum* 1841, 308.

Woodbine Cottage, Torquay, Devon
G.M. v. 12, 1836, 26–28.

Woodchester Park near Stroud, Glos
C.L. v. 145, 1969, 284–88. D. Stroud *Capability Brown* 1975, 245. G. Carter *et al. Humphry Repton* 1983, 153.

Woodcote Park near Epsom, Surrey
G.F. Prosser *Select illustrations of . . . Surrey* 1828. J. Harris *Artist and the country house* 1979, 204.

Woodford Hall, Woodford, Redbridge, London
D. Stroud *Humphry Repton* 1962, 174. F.G. Emmison *Catalogue of maps in Essex Record Office* 2nd Supplt, 1964, 22. G. Carter *et al. Humphry Repton* 1982, 67,152.

Woodford, Northants
Royal Commission on Historical Monuments *Inventory of historical monuments in . . . Northampton* v. 1, 1975, 113, pl. 21.

Woodgate, Sutton Coldfield, W. Midlands
G. Jekyll *and* L. Weaver *Gardens for small country houses* 1913, 10–13.

Woodgreen Park near Cheshunt, Herts
J.E. Cussans *History of Hertfordshire* v. 2, 1874, 220.

Woodhall near Holytown, Strathclyde
Scottish Gdnr v. 12, 1863, 5–6.

Woodhall Park, Watton-at-Stone, Herts
Cottage Gdnr v. 26, 1861, 78–79,114–15. J.E. Cussans *History of Hertfordshire* v. 2, 1874, 168. *J. Hort. Cottage Gdnr* v. 62, 1879, 212–13. C.L. v. 57, 1925, 164–71, 198–205. R. Bisgrove *Gardens of Britain* v. 3, 1978, 194–95.

Woodhatch, Reigate, Surrey
G.C. ii 1901, 281.

Woodhouselee near Roslin, Lothian
J.C. Loudon *Encyclopaedia of gardening* 1822, 1251.

Woodlands, Hoddesdon, Herts
B. Jones *Follies & grottoes* 1974, 344.

Woodlands, Blackheath, Lewisham, London
Copper Plate Mag. v. 2, pl. 80. J. Hassell *Seats near London* 1804–05. J.C. Loudon *Encyclopaedia of gardening* 1822, 1231.

Woodlands, Streatham, Lambeth, London
Gdning World v. 2, 1886, 728–29.

Woodleigh Hall, Rawdon, W. Yorks
Bradford Illustrated Weekly Telegraph *Series of picturesque views* 1885.

Woodley Lodge, near Reading, Berks
J.C. Loudon *Encyclopaedia of gardening* 1822, 1237. G. Carter *et al. Humphry Repton* 1982, 148.

Woodperry near Oxford, Oxfordshire
C.L. v. 129, 1961, 18–21.

Woodrow Hill House, Amersham, Bucks
B. Jones *Follies & grottoes* 1974, 290.

Woodseat near Uttoxeter, Staffs
J. Hort. Cottage Gdnr v. 37, 1867, 426–29.

Woodside, Chenies, Bucks
L. Weaver *Houses and gardens by E.L. Lutyens* 1913, 7–11. C.L. v. 39, 1916, 767–68. A.S. Butler *Architecture of Sir Edwin Lutyens* v. 2, 1950, 11. J. Brown *Gardens of a golden afternoon* 1982, 54,160–61.

Woodside, Rickmansworth, Herts
C.L. v. 9, 1901, 400–05.

Woodside, Whetstone, Barnet, London
W. Keane *Beauties of Middlesex* 1850, 58–60.

Woodside, Howth, Co. Dublin, Eire
Irish Gdning v. 10, 1915, 86; v. 15, 1920, 84–85.

Woodside House, Berks
R. Ackermann *Repository* v. 2, 1823, pl. 27.
W.W.J. Gendall *Views* v. 2, 1830, 105. J. Harris *Gardens of delight* 1978, 30–33. L. Fleming *and* A. Gore *English garden* 1979, pls. 83–84. D. Jacques *Georgian gardens* 1983, pl. 3.

Woodside House, Paisley, Strathclyde
Gdning World v. 4, 1887, 214. *Scottish Gdnr and Northern Forester* v. 8, 1913, 565–66.

Woodsome Hall near Huddersfield, W. Yorks
C.L. v. 20, 1906, 906–14. Historical MSS Commission *Architectural history* v. 5, 1974, item 5650.

Woodstock near Inistioge, Co. Kilkenny, Eire
J. Hort. Cottage Gdnr v. 47, 1872, 461–63, 481–83, 504–05. E. Malins *and* P. Bowe *Irish gardens and demesnes* 1980, 51–53.

Woodstock Park, Woodstock, Oxfordshire
E.S. Rohde *Story of the garden* 1932, 39–40. *Arboricultural J.* v. 5, 1981, 201–13.

Woolbeding House, Woolbeding, W. Sussex
C.L. v. 102, 1947, 278–81, 328.

Woolcombe Hall near Cerne, Dorset
J. Hutchins *History . . . of Dorset* v. 2, 1774, 462.

Woollas Hall near Pershore, Hereford and Worcester
C.L. v. 20, 1906, 270–73.

Woolley Hall, Maidenhead, Berks
G. Beard *Thomas H. Mawson* 1976, 67.

Woolley Hall, Woolley, W. Yorks
Historical MSS Commission *Architectural history* v. 2, 1970, item 2331; v. 5, 1974, item 5623. I. Hall *Samuel Buck's Yorkshire sketchbook* 1979, 9, 134.

Woolleys, Hambleden, Bucks
R. Bisgrove *Gardens of Britain* v. 3, 1978, 195.

Woolpits near Shere, Surrey
G.C. ii 1891, 241–42, 245.

Woolton Farm, Bekesbourne, Kent
T. Wright *Gardens of Britain* v. 4, 1978, 115–16.

Woolton Hall near Liverpool, Merseyside
W. Watts *Seats* 1779, pl. 76. J.P. Neale *Views* v. 2, 1819. G.C. ii 1884, 436–37; ii 1892, 433. *J. Hort. Cottage Gdnr* N.S., v. 11, 1885, 90–92. L. Fleming *and* A. Gore *English garden* 1979, 197.

Woolverstone Park near Ipswich, Suffolk
Copper Plate Mag. v. 2, pl. 81. G.C. 1867, 156–58. *J. Hort. Cottage Gdnr* N.S., v. 50, 1905, 557–58. B. Jones *Follies & grottoes* 1974, 393.

Wootton Court, Wootton, Kent
E. Hasted *History . . . of Kent* v. 3, 1790, 763.

Wootton Court near Warwick, Warwickshire
Garden v. 61, 1902, 79–80.

Wootton Hall, Wootton, Staffs
J.P. Neale *Views* v. 4, 1821.

Wootton House, Wootton Fitzpaine, Dorset
J. Hutchins *History . . . of Dorset* v. 2, 1863, 274.

Wootton Lodge, Wootton, Lincs
G.M. v. 16, 1840, 579–80.

Wootton Lodge, Wootton, Staffs
C.L. v. 27, 1910, 946–55. C.L. v. 125, 522–25, 596–99. G. Jekyll *Garden ornament* 1918, 53, 65.

Wootton Manor near Polegate, E. Sussex
C.L. v. 117, 1955, 920–23.

Wootton Wawen Hall, Wootton Wawen, Warwickshire
C. Holme *Gardens of England in Midland & Eastern counties* 1908, pls. 130–31.

Worcester Park, Sutton, London
G.F. Prosser *Select illustrations of . . . Surrey* 1828. R.I.B.A. *Catalogue* v. S, 1976, 95.

Workington Hall, Workington, Cumbria
F.O. Morris *Series of picturesque views* v. 5, 57.

Worksop Manor, Worksop, Notts
Society of Gentlemen *England displayed* v. 1, 1769, 391. A. Young *Six months tour through North of England* v. 1, 1771, 332–34. S. *and* N. Buck *Buck's antiquities* v. 2, 1774, pls. 32–33. D. Defoe *Tour* v. 3, 1778, 70–71. J. Hodgson *and* F.C. Laird *Beauties of England and Wales* v. 12 pt 1, 1813, 347–49. J.P. Neale *Views* v. 3, 1820. G.M. v. 6, 1830, 34–35. G.C. ii 1882, 685–86. R. Pococke *Travels through England* v. 1, 1888, 71–72.

Worksop Manor (*Cont.*)
Publications of Bedfordshire Historical Record Soc. v. 47, 1968, 128. *C.L.* v. 153, 1973, 678–82. M. Binney *and* A. Hills *Elysian gardens* 1979, 13.

Worlingham Hall, Worlingham, Suffolk
H. Davy *Views* 1827. *C.L.* v. 147, 1970, 624–28.

Wormington Grange near Winchcombe, Glos
C.L. v. 88, 1940, 256–60.

Wormley Bury, Wormley, Herts
C.L. v. 37, 1915, 144–49. *J. Royal Hort. Soc.* 1941, 308–12.

Wormsley Grange, Wormsley, Hereford and Worcester
J. Hort. Cottage Gdnr v. 59, 1878, 358–60.

Worsley Hall, Worsley, Greater Manchester
A.E. Brooke *Gardens of England* 1857, pls. 24–25. F.O. Morris *Series of picturesque views* v. 2, 35. *Cottage Gdnr* v. 19, 1857, 245–47, 260–61; v. 21, 1859, 400; v. 22, 1859, 285–87. *G.C.* ii 1875, 70–71, 77; ii 1890, 619–20. *J. Hort. Cottage Gdnr* v. 56, 1876, 214–16, 237–39; N.S., v. 68, 1914, 401–04. *Gdnrs Mag.* 1895, 531–38. *C.L.* v. 10, 1901, 80–86. R.I.B.A. *Catalogue* v. B, 1972, 93.

Worstead House, Worstead, Norfolk
J.P. Neale *Views* v. 3, 1820. J. Grigor *Eastern arboretum* 1841, 228.

Worth Park, Worth, W. Sussex
J. Hort. Cottage Gdnr N.S., v. 25, 1892, 551–52. *G.C.* i 1897, 32–33. *Gdning World* v. 15, 1898, 57–58. *C.L.* v. 6, 1899, 400–04.

Worthing (James Bateman), W. Sussex
G.C. ii 1890, 242–43, 246.

Worthy Park near Winchester, Hants
W.W.J. Gendall *Views* v. 1, 1830, 99. J. Hewetson *Architectural and picturesque views of noble mansions in Hampshire* 1830. E.F. Prosser *Select illustrations of Hampshire* 1833.

Wortley Hall, Wortley, S. Yorks
G.M. v. 16, 1840, 105–08. *J. Hort. Cottage Gdnr* v. 57, 1877, 140–43. *Yorkshire Archaeological J.* v. 47, 1975, 115–19.

Wotton near Gloucester, Glos
R. Atkyns *Ancient and present state of Glostershire* 1712, 428. L. Knyff *and* J. Kip *Britannia illustrata* v. 2, 1715.

Wotton House, Wotton Underwood, Bucks
T. Whately *Observations on modern gardening* 1771, 84–88. *C.L.* v. 15, 1904, 126–35; v. 106, 1949, 38–41, 110–13. T. Jefferson *Garden book 1766–1824* 1944, 112. N. Pevsner *Buckinghamshire* 1960, 303. E.M. Elvey *Hand-list of Buckinghamshire estate maps* 1963, 57. D. Stroud *Capability Brown* 1975, 53, 245. J. Harris *Artist and the country house* 1979, 259.

Wotton House near Dorking, Surrey
O. Manning *and* W. Bray *History . . . of Surrey* v. 2, 1809, 145. E.W. Brayley *and* J. Britton *Topographical history of Surrey* v. 5, 1848, 33–36. W. Keane *Beauties of Surrey* 1849, 143–45. J.B. Burke *Visitation* 2nd Series, v. 1, 1855, 176–77. *C.L.* v. 4, 1898, 496–99; v. 10, 1901, 522–23; v. 119, 1956, 204–07. J. Evelyn *Diary* v. 1, 1955, 55; v. 2, 81; v. 3, 60–61. I. Nairn *and* B. Cherry *Surrey* 1971, 543–44. *Landscape Design* no. 124, 1978, 36–38.

Wrest Park, Silsoe, Beds
J. Beeverell *Les delices de la Grande Bretagne* v. 5, 1707, 872. L. Knyff *and* J. Kip *Britannia illustrata* v. 1, 1714. T. Badeslade *and* J. Rocque *Vitruvius Brittanicus* 1739, pls. 30–33. J. Britton *and* E.W. Brayley *Beauties of England and Wales* v. 1, 1801, 70. J.P. Neale *Views* v. 1, 1818. British Museum *Catalogue of maps, prints* 1829, 366. *Cottage Gdnr* v. 12, 1854, 320–21. *G.C.* ii 1885, 244; i 1900, 373–77; ii 1908, 157–59; i 1916, 235, 236. W. Treacher *Wrest and its surroundings* 1899. *C.L.* v. 16, 1904, 54–64, 90–98; v. 18, 1905, 772–73; v. 42, 1917, 112–14; v. 147, 1970, 1250–53; v. 148, 1970, 18–19; v. 155, 1974, 78–81. M.R. Gloag *Book of English gardens* 1906, 321–35. *Gdnrs Mag.* 1908, 833–36. C. Holme *Gardens of England in Midland & Eastern counties* 1908, pls. 132–36. M. Macartney *English houses & gardens* 1908, pl. 33. G. Jekyll *Garden ornament* 1918, passim. H. Walpole *Visits to country seats. Walpole Society* v. 7, 1927/8, 71. E. von Erdberg *Chinese influence on European garden structure* 1936, 188. R. Dutton *English garden* 1937, pl. 53. Lady Rockley *Historic gardens of England* 1938, 142–43. *Bedfordshire Mag.* v. 9, 1964, 183. N. Pevsner *Bedfordshire and county of Huntingdon* 1968, 173–75. M. Allan *Fisons guide* 1970, 177–78. Historical MSS Commission *Architectural history* v. 3, 1971, items 2458, 2472, 2848, 3170, 3417, 3629. H. Evans *Beautiful gardens of Britain* 1974, 81–82. B. Jones *Follies & grottoes* 1974, 287. D. Stroud *Capability Brown* 1975, 80–81, 145. R. Bisgrove *Gardens of Britain* v. 3, 1978, 196–97. T. Wright *Arbors & grottos* 1979. J. Johnson *Excellent Cassandra: life and times of Duchess of Chandos* 1981, 69.

Wrinstead Court near Lenham, Kent
C. Greenwood *Epitome of county history . . . v. 1: Kent* 1838, 161.

Writtle Park, Writtle, Essex
F.G. Emmison *Catalogue of maps in Essex Record Office* 2nd Supplt, 1964, 34.

Wrotham Park near South Mimms, Herts
W. Watts *Seats* 1779, pl. 28. W. Keane *Beauties of Middlesex* 1850, 33–37. *Cottage Gdnr* v. 18, 1857, 231–32. *G.C.* ii 1899, 276–77. *C.L.* v. 44, 1918, 404–09,458. D. Stroud *Capability Brown* 1975, 245. V.C.H. *Middlesex* v. 5, 1976, 289.

Wrottesley near Wolverhampton, Staffs
R. Plot *Natural history of Staffordshire* 1685, 210. W. Pitt *General view of agriculture of . . . Stafford* 1796, 95. S. Shaw *History . . . of Staffordshire* v. 2, 1801, 204.

Wroxall Abbey near Warwick, Warwickshire
R. Sidwell *West Midland gardens* 1981, 239–40.

Wroxham Hall, Wroxham, Norfolk
J. Grigor *Eastern arboretum* 1841, 223–24.

Wroxham House, Wroxham, Norfolk
G.M. v. 17, 1841, 271. J. Grigor *Eastern arboretum* 1841, 213.

Wroxton Abbey, Banbury, Oxfordshire
British Museum *Catalogue of maps, prints* 1829, 366. F.O. Morris *Series of picturesque views* v. 3, 43. *G.C.* ii 1885, 814; i 1886, 11–12. R. Pococke *Travels through England* v. 2, 1889, 240. *C.L.* v. 5, 1899, 240–43; v. 170, 1981, 854–57. *Gdnrs Mag.* 1907, 489–92. Publications of Bedfordshire Historical Record Soc. v. 47, 1968, 139. V.C.H. *Oxford* v. 9, 1969, 173. Historical MSS Commission *Architectural history* v. 5, 1974, items 4885, 5375. B. Jones *Follies & grottoes* 1974, 379. J. Sherwood and N. Pevsner *Oxfordshire* 1974, 863–64. *Gdn History* v. 4 no. 3, 1976, 3–4. R. Bisgrove *Gardens of Britain* v. 3, 1978, 197. P. Connor *Oriental architecture in the west* 1979, 52–53. *Landscape Research* v. 4 no. 3, 1979, 18–19. D. Jacques *Georgian gardens* 1983, 44. *Landscape Design* no. 146, 1983, 31–32.

Wyards Farm, Alton, Hants
A. Paterson *Gardens of Britain* v. 2, 1978, 154–55.

Wych Cross Place, Forest Row, E. Sussex
T.H. Mawson *Art & craft of garden making* 1907, passim. *J. Hort. Cottage Gdnr* N.S., v. 55, 1907, 372–75. *C.L.* v. 28, 1910, 934–40. G. Beard *Thomas H. Mawson* 1976, 67.

Wyck near Marshfield, Avon
R. Atkyns *Ancient and present state of Glostershire* 1712, 200. L. Knyff and J. Kip *Britannia illustrata* v. 2, 1715. *C.L.* v. 18, 1905, 742–43.

Wyck, Hitchin, Herts
C.L. v. 18, 1905, 630–35.

Wycliffe Hall near Richmond, N. Yorks
Picturesque views of the principal seats 1788. *Copper Plate Mag.* v. 1, 1792, pl. 36.

Wycombe Abbey, High Wycombe, Bucks
J. Britton and E.W. Brayley *Beauties of England and Wales* v. 1, 1801, 366. J.C. Loudon *Encyclopaedia of gardening* 1822, 1233. F.O. Morris *Series of picturesque views* v. 6, 5. *G.C.* i 1877, 687–88; ii 1882, 615–16. *Gdning World* v. 10, 1893, 36–38. R.I.B.A. *Catalogue* v. C-F, 1972, 56. D. Stroud *Capability Brown* 1975, 92. G. Carter et al. *Humphry Repton* 1982, 149.

Wyddiall Hall, Buntingford, Herts
H. Chauncy *Historical antiquities of Hertfordshire* 1700, 112. D. Stroud *Humphry Repton* 1962, 49–50. G. Carter et al. *Humphry Repton* 1982, 154.

Wye College, Wye, Kent
J. Royal Hort. Soc. 1953, 416–20; 1958, 250–53; 1960, 226–28; 1961, 281–84. *G.C.* ii 1962, 134–35,141.

Wyke House, Gillingham, Dorset
J. Hutchins *History . . . of Dorset* v. 3, 1868, 623.

Wykeham Abbey, Wykeham, N. Yorks
C. Holme *Gardens of England in Northern counties* 1911, pls. 134–35. G. Beard *Thomas H. Mawson* 1976, 67–68.

Wylds, Liss, Hants
A. Paterson *Gardens of Britain* v. 2, 1978, 156–57.

Wyncliffe Court near Chepstow, Gwent
C.L. v. 166, 1979, 2154–57,2272.

Wynnstay, Ruabon, Clwyd
P. Sandby *Collection of one hundred and fifty select views* v. 2, 1781, pl. 7. *Copper Plate Mag.* v. 1, 1792, pl. 4. J.C. Loudon *Encyclopaedia of gardening* 1822, 1248. F.O. Morris *Series of picturesque views* v. 3, 67. Viscount Torrington *Diaries* v. 1, 1934, 175–76. *C.L.* v. 151, 1972, 686–89,782–86,850–53. D. Stroud *Capability Brown* 1975, 182–83.

Wynyard Park near Stockton-on-Tees, Cleveland
F.O. Morris *Series of picturesque views* v. 3, 13. *J. Hort. Cottage Gdnr* N.S., v. 18, 1889, 258–60. *Gdnrs Mag.* 1907, 5–8,9,11. *G.C.* i 1908, 403. Historical MSS Commission *Architectural history* v. 2, 1970, item 2358.

Wytham Abbey, Wytham, Oxfordshire
J. Beeverell *Les delices de la Grande Bretagne* v. 5, 1707, 872. L. Knyff and J. Kip *Britannia illustrata* v. 1, 1714.

Wytham Abbey (Cont.)
F.O. Morris *Series of picturesque views* v. 2, 61. *Gdning World* v. 6, 1890, 646.

Yaffle Hill, Broadstone, Dorset
C.L. v. 128, 1960, 82–83. M. Allan *Fisons guide* 1970, 110–11.

Yanwath Hall, Yanwath, Cumbria
C.L. v. 14, 1903, 126–31.

Yardley Hastings, Northants
Northamptonshire Past and Present v. 5 no. 3, 1975, 233.

Yarlington Lodge near Wincanton, Somerset
J. Collinson *History . . . of Somersetshire* v. 1, 1791, 229.

Yarnton Manor, Yarnton, Oxfordshire
C.L. v. 110, 1951, 2096–99, 2162.

Yeldhall Manor near Henley-on-Thames, Oxfordshire
G.C. ii 1911, 388–89, 390.

Yester House, Yester, Lothian
J. Macky *Journey through Scotland* 1723, 31, 32–33. D. Defoe *Tour* v. 4, 1778, 53–55. *C.L.* v. 72, 1932, 94–100, 126; v. 154, 1973, 358–61, 430–33, 490. Historical MSS Commission *Architectural history* v. 3, 1971, item 3666. J. Harris *Artist and the country house* 1979, 86–87. A.A. Tait *Landscape garden in Scotland* 1980, passim.

Yew Tree, Lydart, Gwent
J. Royal Hort. Soc. 1971, 108–18. *C.L.* v. 167, 1980, 652–54.

Yewdon Manor near Henley-on-Thames, Oxfordshire
G.C. ii 1882, 747–46.

Yews, Storrs, Windermere, Cumbria
G. Beard *Thomas H. Mawson* 1976, 68.

York. Treasurer's House, N. Yorks
C.L. v. 52, 1922, 114–21.

York. University, N. Yorks
J. Institute Landscape Architects no. 78, 1967, 14–18. *C.L.* v. 150, 1971, 532–34. A. Hellyer *Gardens of genius* 1980, 208–11.
See also Heslington Hall

York Gate, Adel, W. Yorks
K. Lemmon *Gardens of Britain* v. 5, 1978, 189–94. A. Lees-Milne and R. Verey *Englishman's garden* 1982, 132–35.

Yotes Court near Mereworth, Kent
J.P. Neale *Views* 2nd Series, v. 4, 1828. *C.L.* v. 135, 1964, 1580–83, 1648.

Younger Botanic Garden *see* Benmore

Youngsbury, Wadesmill, Herts
D. Stroud *Capability Brown* 1975, 245–46. R. Bisgrove *Gardens of Britain* v. 3, 1978, 198.

County Index

England

AVON

Abbots Leigh, Bristol
Ammerdown Park, Radstock
Arnos Castle, Bristol
Ashton Court, Long Ashton
Ashwicke Hall, Marshfield
Badminton Cottage
Badminton House
Bailbrook House, Bath
Barrow Court, Flax Bourton
Bath. Royal Victoria Park
Bath. Sydney Gardens
Bath Botanic Garden
Batheaston Villa, Bath
Bitton Vicarage
Blaise Castle, Bristol
Blaise Hamlet, Bristol
Brentry Hill, Bristol
Bristol Zoo
Brockley Hall, Bristol
Camerton Court
Chelvey Court, Clevedon
Chew Court, Chew Magna
Claverton Manor, Bath
Cleve Hill, Bristol
Clevedon Court
Cold Ashton Manor, Bath
Cote Bank, Bristol
Crowe Hall, Bath
Dodington House
Dower House, Badminton
Dyrham Park, Chippenham
Essex House, Badminton
Farleigh House
Goldney House, Clifton
Grange, Charlcombe
Henbury, Bristol
Hinton House, Hinton Charterhouse
Horton Court, Chipping Sodbury
Kelston, Bath
Kings Weston, Bristol
Knole, Almondsbury
Lansdown, Bath
Long Ashton Court
Lyegrove, Chipping Sodbury
Midford Castle, Bath
Nailsea Court
Newton Park, Newton St Loe
Oaklands, Bristol
Old Sneyd Park, Bristol
Over Court
Prior Park, Bath
Redland Court, Westbury on Trym
Royal Fort, Bristol

St Catherine's Court, Bath
Siston Court
Sneyd Park, Westbury on Trym
Stapleton, Bristol
Stoke Bishop, Bristol
Stoke Park, Stoke Gifford
Sutton Court, Stowey
Swangrove, Badminton
Thornbury Castle
Thornbury Park
Tortworth Court
Tyntesfield, Flax Bourton
Vine House, Henbury
Warleigh House, Bath
Westend House, Wickwar
Wick House, Brislington
Widcombe Manor, Bath
Wyck, Marshfield

BEDFORDSHIRE

Ampthill Park, Bedford
Aspley Guise Gardens
Aspley Wood, Woburn Abbey
Battlesden, Woburn
Bedford Priory
Beeston Leasowes, Sandy
Bletsoe Castle
Chicksands Priory, Ampthill
Colworth House, Sharnbrook
Flitwick Manor
Hasells, Sandy
Hinwick Hall
Hinwick House
Holcot Manor, Holcot
Houghton Park House
Howard's House, Cardington
Hyde, East Hyde
Ickwell Bury, Ickwell
Luton Hoo, Luton
Manor Close, Aspley Guise
Moggerhanger Park, Sandy
Odell Castle, Odell
Old Warden
Putteridge Park, Luton
Putteridgebury, Luton
Sandy Lodge, Sandy
Southill Park, Biggleswade
Stockgrove Park, Leighton Buzzard
Stockwood Park, Luton
Toddington
Turvey, Bedford
Westfields, Oakley
Woburn Abbey
Wrest Park, Silsoe

BERKSHIRE

Aldermaston Court
Allanbay Park, Binfield
Ambarrow Farm, Sandhurst
Ascot House, Sunninghill
Bagnor Manor, Newbury
Basildon, Reading
Bateman's House, Windsor
Bear Place, Maidenhead
Bearwood, Wokingham
Beaumont Lodge
Benham, Newbury
Billingbear House, Binfield
Bisham Abbey
Bodens Ride, Ascot
Borlases, Waltham St Lawrence
Bucklebury. Old Vicarage
Bucklebury Place, Woolhampton
Bulmershe Court, Reading
Bussock Mayne, Snelsmore Common
Caversham Court, Reading
Caversham Park, Reading
Chilton Lodge
Cintra Lodge, Whitley
Coley Park, Reading
Coombe Lodge, Pangbourne
Coworth Park, Sunningdale
Cranbourne, Ascot
Creswells Manor House
Culham Court, Aston
Deanery, Sonning
Denford, Hungerford
Ditton House, Slough
Ditton Park, Slough
Donnington Castle House, Newbury
Donnington Grove, Speen
East Thorpe, Reading
Easthampstead Park, Easthampstead
Elcot Park, Newbury
Englefield House, Theale
Eton College
Farley, Wokingham
Folly Farm, Sulhamstead
Foxhill, Reading
Grange, Wraysbury
Greenham Common, Newbury
Grotto House, Basildon
Grove, Newbury
Grove House, Old Windsor
Hall Place, Maidenhead
Hampstead Marshall, Newbury
High Grove, Reading
Holly Grove House, Windsor
Holme Park, Sonning
Hop Castle, Chieveley
Huntingdon, Ascot Heath

County Index

Hurst Lodge, Hurst
Inkpen Old Rectory, Inkpen
Jasmine House, Hatch Bridge
Kings Copse House, Reading
Kingsmoor, Sunningdale
Kingswood House, Sunningdale
Little Bowden, Pangbourne
Little Paddocks, Sunninghill
Maiden Erlegh, Reading
Midgham House, Midgham
Moor Close, Binfield
Moor Hall, Cookham
Oakfield, Mortimer
Oakley Court, Windsor
Ockwells Manor, Bray
Old Rectory, Burghfield
Old Rectory Cottage, Tidmarsh
Old Vicarage, Bucklebury
Peacock Place, Basildon
Pelling Place, Windsor
Portnall Park, Sunningdale
Priory, Beech Hill
Purley Hall, Purley
Remans, Old Windsor
Rook's Nest, Lambourn
St Albans House, Windsor
St Leonard's Hill, Windsor
Sandhurst Lodge
Sandleford Priory
Shaw House, Newbury
Shelleys, Twyford
Shinfield Grange
Shottesbrooke
Silwood Park, Ascot
Sophia Lodge, Clewer
Sunning Hill, Reading
Sunningdale Park
Sutton Courtenay Manor, Abingdon
Swallowfield Park
Tittenhurst, Sunninghill
Tower Court, Ascot
Tudor Barn, Windsor
Upton Court
Warfield
Wasing Place, Aldermaston
West Woodhay House, Newbury
White Horse, Finchampstead
Whiteknights, Reading
Whitmore Lodge, Windsor
Windsor Castle
Windsor Great Park
Windsor Great Park. Savill Gardens
Windsor Great Park. Virginia Water
Windsor. Frogmore
Windsor. Royal Lodge
Wokefield Park, Mortimer
Wokingham
Woodley Lodge, Reading
Woodside House
Woolley Hall, Maidenhead

BUCKINGHAMSHIRE

Addington, Winslow
Ascott, Leighton Buzzard
Barry's Close, Long Crendon
Barton Hartshorne Manor
Bassetbury, High Wycombe
Baylis

Biddlesden Park
Bletchley Park
Boarstall Tower
Boswells, Wendover
Bradenham, High Wycombe
Bulstrode Park, Beaconsfield
Chalfont House, Chalfont St Peter
Chapel Farm, Amersham
Chequers Court, Princes Risborough
Chicheley Hall, Newport Pagnell
Chilton House, Thame
Claydon House, Winslow
Cliveden, Maidenhead
Coppins, Iver
Danesfield, Great Marlow
Daws Hill, High Wycombe
Delaford Park, Colnbrook
Denham Place, Uxbridge
Dorney Court
Dorneywood, Burnham Beeches
Dorton House
Dropmore, Beaconsfield
East Burnham Park
Eythrope, Aylesbury
Fawley Court
Gayhurst
Germains, Chesham
Gregories, Beaconsfield
Hall Barn, Beaconsfield
Halton House
Hambleden Manor
Hampden House
Hanslope Park, Stony Stratford
Harleyford, Great Marlow
Hartwell House, Aylesbury
Hedsor, Great Marlow
Hitcham Grange, Maidenhead
Holly Hill, Stoke Poges
Horwood House, Little Horwood
Hughenden Manor, High Wycombe
Huntercombe Manor, Taplow
Ibstone House
Iver Grove
Juniper Hill, Penn
Langley Park, Colnbrook
Latimers, Latimer
Lillingstone Lovell
Liscombe House, Leighton Buzzard
Little Paston, Fulmer
Little Pednor Farm, Chesham
Manor House, Bledlow
Manow House, Little Marlow
Marches, Willowbrook
Mentmore Towers
Nashdom, Taplow
Nether Winchendon House, Aylesbury
Old Parsonage, Marlow
Olney (W. Cowper)
Oving House
Passenham Manor, Stony Stratford
Place House, Horton
Pollards, Chalfont St Giles
Poundon
Richings, Colnbrook
Riskins, Iver
Sefton Park, Slough
Shardeloes, Amersham
Steart Hill House, Little Horwood
Stoke Court, Stoke Poges
Stoke Farm

Stoke Park, Stoke Poges
Stoke Place, Stoke Poges
Stoke Poges Memorial Garden
Stonehouse, Whitchurch
Stowe, Buckingham
Taplow Court
Taplow House
Taplow Lodge
Temple House, Great Marlow
Turville Court, Turville Heath
Tyringham, Newport Pagnell
Uplands, Stoke Poges
Upper Spurlands, Holme Green
Waddesden Manor
West Wycombe Park
Wexham Park, Slough
Wexham Springs, Stoke Poges
Whaddon Hall
Wilton Park, Beaconsfield
Winchendon House
Winslow Hall
Wittington, Marlow
Woodrow Hill House, Amersham
Woodside, Chenies
Woolleys, Hambleden
Wotton House, Wotton Underwood
Wycombe Abbey, High Wycombe

CAMBRIDGESHIRE

Abbots Ripton
Abington Hall, Great Abington
Anglesey Abbey, Lode
Babraham Hall, Cambridge
Bottisham Park
Bourn Hall, Caxton
Brampton Park, Huntingdon
Brington, Kimbolton
Buckden Palace
Burghley House, Stamford
Caldress Manor, Ickleton
Cambridge. Botanic Garden
Cambridge. Christ's College
Cambridge. Clare College
Cambridge. Corpus Christi College
Cambridge. Emmanuel College
Cambridge. Gonville College
Cambridge. Jesus College
Cambridge. King's College
Cambridge. Magdelene College
Cambridge. Queen's College
Cambridge. Pembroke College
Cambridge. St. Johns College
Cambridge. Sidney Sussex College
Cambridge. Trinity College
Cambridge. Trinity Hall
Cheveley Park, Newmarket
Conington Park
Croxton Park
Diddington
Dullingham
Elton Hall
Farm Hall, Godmanchester
Fen Ditton Hall
Gamlingay
Haslingfield Hall
Hatley St George, Royston
Hemingford Grey, St Ives
Hildersham Hall

County Index

Hilton
Hinchingbrooke, Huntingdon
Hinton Hall, Haddenham
Horseheath Hall
Kimbolton Castle
Kirtling Tower
Leverington Hall
Madingley Hall
Middlefield, Great Shelford
Milton
Milton Park, Castor
Ninewells, Great Shelford
Orton Hall
Pampisford Hall
Peckover House, Wisbech
Peterborough Abbey
Sawston Hall
Stibbington Hall
Sudbury Court, Whittlesey
Thorney Abbey House, Peterborough
Trumpington Manor
Upton Manor, Castor
Waresley Park
Weybridge Park, Alconbury
Wimpole Hall, Arrington

CHESHIRE

Adlington Hall, Macclesfield
Aldersey Hall, Chester
Arley Hall, Northwich
Aston Park, Nantwich
Baycliffe, Lymm
Booth's Hall, Knutsford
Brereton Hall
Burton Manor, Weston
Capesthorne, Macclesfield
Cholmondeley Castle
Combermere Abbey, Nantwich
Crewe. Queen's Park
Crewe Hall
Doddington Hall
Dorfold Hall, Nantwich
Eaton Hall
Edge Hall, Malpas
Hatherton Lodge, Nantwich
Haughton, Nantwich
High Legh Hall, Knutsford
Hoole Hall, Chester
Hooton, Birkenhead
Jodrell Hall, Middlewich
Larches, Alderley Edge
Lawton Hall, Congleton
Little Moreton Hall, Congleton
Lyme Park, Disley
Maby Hall
Marbury Hall, Marbury
Moreton Hall, Congleton
North Rode Hall, Congleton
Orford Hall
Oulton Park, Tarporley
Peckforton Castle, Tarporley
Poynton Lodge
Poynton Towers
Priory, Bidston
Quinta, Swettenham
Rode Hall, Rode Heath
Saighton Grange
Somerford Park, Congleton

Tabley House, Knutsford
Tatton Park, Knutsford
Tilstone Lodge, Tilstone Fearnall
Tirley Garth, Tarporley
Vale Royal, Northwich
Walton Lea, Warrington
West House, Congleton
Withington Hall, Old Withington

CLEVELAND

Acklam Hall, Middlesbrough
Grey Towers, Nunthorpe
Guisborough Hall
Guisborough Priory
Hutton Hall, Hutton Lowcross
Kirkleatham, Redcar
Leven Grove
Skelton Castle
Upleatham Hall
Wilton Castle, Redcar
Wynyard Park, Stockton-on-Tees

CORNWALL

Acton Castle, Penzance
Antony House, Saltash
Bake, St Germans
Boconnoc, Lostwithiel
Bosahan, Helford
Caerhays Castle, Tregony
Carclew, Penryn
Carnanton. St Colomb
Carne, Penzance
Catchfrench, Liskeard
Chyverton, Truro
Clowance, Helston
Cotehele, Callstock
Downes, Hayle
Enys, St Gluvias
Glendurgan, Falmouth
Glynn, Bodmin
Godolphin House
Haines Hill
Heligan, St Austell
Hexworthy, Lawhitton
Ince Castle, Saltash
Kenegie, Gulval
Lamellen, St Tudy
Lamorran, Truro
Lanarth, St Keverne
Lanhydrock, Bodmin
Loraine, St Ives
Ludgvan
Menabilly, Fowey
Menacuddle, St Austell
Moditonham House, Botus
Morrab Gardens, Penzance
Morval, East Looe
Mount Edgcumbe, Cremyll
Moyclare, Liskeard
Nanswhydyn, St Columb Major
Newton Ferrars, Callington
Pencarrow, Bodmin
Pendarves, Camborne
Penheale Manor, Egloskerry
Penjerrick, Falmouth
Pentillie Castle, Saltash

Place House, Fowey
Place House, Padstow
Port Eliot, St Germans
Prideaux Place, Padstow
Rosehill, Falmouth
Rosemundy House, St Agnes
St Michael's Mount, Penzance
Saunders Hill, Padstow
Scorrier, Redruth
Skisdon Lodge, St Kew
Stow, Kilkhampton
Tehidy House, Redruth
Thanckes, Devonport
Tonacombe, Morwinstow
Trebartha Hall, Launceston
Tredrea, St Ives
Tregothnan, Truro
Tregrehan, St Austell
Trelaske House, Launceston
Trelawny House, Pelynt
Trelissick, Truro
Trelowarren, Helston
Treloyham, St Ives
Tremeer, Bodmin
Tremough, Penryn
Trengwainton, Penzance
Trerice, St Newlyn East
Tresco Abbey, Isles of Scilly
Trewan House, St Columb Major
Trewarthenick, Tregony
Trewithen, Probus
Treworgey, Liskeard
Werrington Park, Launceston
Whiteford House, Stoke

CUMBRIA

Abbey House, Barrow-in-Furness
Above Beck, Grasmere
Acorn Bank, Temple Sowerby
Appleby Castle, Penrith
Arceby Hall
Bigland Hall, Cartmel
Blackwell, Windermere
Brackenbrough, Calthwaite
Brayton Hall
Briery Close, Windermere
Brockhole, Windermere
Brougham Hall, Penrith
Bryerswood, Sawrey
Burrow Hall, Kirkby Lonsdale
Carleton Hall
Cleve House, Windermere
Cockermouth Castle
Corbels, Windermere
Corby Castle, Great Corby
Cringlemere, Troutbeck
Dalemain, Penrith
Dallam Tower, Milnthorpe
Dove Cottage, Grasmere
Eden Hall, Edenhall
Graythwaite Hall, Ulverston
Greystoke Castle
Heathwaite, Windermere
Highhead Castle, Ivegill
Hill Top, Oxenholme
Holehird, Windermere
Holker Hall
Hutton-in-the-Forest

285

County Index

Hutton John, Dacre
Langdale Chase, Ambleside
Levens Hall
Lowther Castle
Moor Crab, Windermere
Muncaster Castle
Naworth Castle
Netherby Hall, Longtown
Netherhall, Maryport
Reagill, Shap
Rose Castle, Carlisle
Rydal Hall
Sedgwick, Kendal
Shrublands, Windermere
Sidegarth, Staveley
Sizergh Castle, Kendal
Skirsgill House, Penrith
Underley Hall, Kirkby Lonsdale
Walton Hall, Brampton
Wellholme Lea, Scotby
Wetheral Priory
White Craggs, Ambleside
Wood Hall, Cockermouth
Wood Side, Westward
Workington Hall
Yanwath Hall
Yews, Windermere

DERBYSHIRE

Alfreton Hall
Aston Lodge, Derby
Barlborough Hall, Chesterfield
Bladon, Newton Solney
Bolsover Castle
Breadsall Priory
Bretby, Burton-on-Trent
Bridge Hill, Belper
Buxton. Pavilion Gardens
Calke Abbey
Chatsworth, Bakewell
Cressbrook, Miller's Dale
Cromford House, Matlock
Darley Hall
Derby (Mr Chambers)
Derby Arboretum
Derncleugh
Derwent Hall
Doveridge House, Uttoxeter
Drakelow Hall, Burton-on-Trent
Ednaston Hall
Ednaston Manor
Elvaston Castle
Eyam Hall
Foremark, Derby
Green, Renishaw
Haddon Hall, Bakewell
Hall Leys Pleasure Gardens, Matlock
Hardwick Hall, Chesterfield
Heights of Abraham, Matlock Bath
Hopton Hall, Wirksworth
Kedleston Hall
Lea Rhododendron Gardens, Matlock
Locko Park, Derby
Longford Hall
Marston Park, Marston Montgomery
Markeaton Hall
Melbourne Hall
Norton Hall

Ogston Hall, Alfreton
Osmaston Manor
Pleasley Vale
Renishaw, Chesterfield
Riddings House
Ringwood Hall, Chesterfield
Shipley Hall, Ilkeston
Snelston Hall
Snitterton Hall, Matlock
South Wingfield Manor
Stancliffe, Bakewell
Sudbury Hall
Sutton Hall
Sydnope Hall, Matlock
Thornbridge Hall, Bakewell
Tissington Hall
Willersley Castle, Matlock
Wingerworth Hall, Chesterfield

DEVONSHIRE

Arlington Court
Ashcombe
Babbacombe
Belmont, Devonport
Berry Pomeroy Castle, Totnes
Bickleigh Castle, Exeter
Bicton, East Budleigh
Bishop's Court, Exeter
Bishopstowe, Torquay
Boringdon, Plymouth St Mary
Bovey House, Beer
Bowringsleigh, Kingsbridge
Bradfield, Collumpton
Bradiford House, Barnstaple
Bridwell, Tiverton
Broadgate, Barnstaple
Buckland Abbey, Tavistock
Buckland Filleigh, Hatherleigh
Buckland Monachorum, Tavistock
Bystock, Exmouth
Cann House, Plymouth
Casa di Sole, Salcombe
Castle Drogo, Drewsteignton
Castle Hill, South Molton
Chaddlewood, Plymouth
Chevithorne, Barton
Coleton Fishacre
Collacombe Barton
Collipriest House, Tiverton
Combe, Gittisham
Combe Royal, Kingsbridge
Coryton, Tavistock
Courtlands, Exmouth
Dartington Hall, Totnes
Dartmoor Prison, Princetown
Derncleugh, Dawlish
Downes, Crediton
Duncan House, Torquay
Dunsland House
Eastleigh, Teignmouth
Eggesford House
Endsleigh, Tavistock
Exeter. University
Flete, Ivybridge
Follaton House, Totnes
Fulford House, Dunsford
Garden House, Buckland Monachorum
Grange, Broadhembury

Great Fulford, Dunsford
Greenway House, Dartmouth
Haldon House, Exeter
Hannaford, Ashburton
Harefield, Exmouth
Hartland Abbey
Heanton Satchville, Hatherleigh
Higher Leigh Manor, Combe Martin
Huish, Torrington
Kelly House, Tavistock
Killerton, Exeter
Kitley, Yealmpton
Knightshayes Court, Tiverton
Knightstone, Crediton
Knowle Cottage, Sidmouth
Langdon Court, Plymouth
Lee Ford, Budleigh Salterton
Lifton House
Lindridge, Newton Abbot
Luscombe Castle, Totnes
Lyneham, Plymouth
Mamhead, Exmouth
Marley Hall, Exmouth
Marystow House
Marwood Hill, Barnstaple
Membland, Modbury
Metcombe Brake
Mothecombe House
Netherton Hall, Newton Abbot
Newcombe House, Crediton
Newhouse Park, Dawlish
Nutwell Court, Topsham
Oaklands, Okehampton
Old Manor, Little Hempston
Old Stones, Blackawton
Overbecks, Salcombe
Oxton, Exeter
Peake House, Sidmouth
Perridge House, Ide
Plympton House, Plympton
Poltimore House
Portledge House, Bideford
Powderham Castle
Powys, Sidmouth
Puslinch, Plympton
Pynes, Exeter
Rawleigh House, Barnstaple
Rockbeare House
Rosemoor, Torrington
Rousdon House
Saltram, Plympton
Sharpham House, Totnes
Sharpitor, Salcombe
Shute House
Sidbury Manor, Sidmouth
Slade, Cornwood
Soldon, Holsworthy
Stevenstone, Torrington
Stonelands, Dawlish
Stoodleigh Court
Stover Lodge, Newton Abbot
Streatham Hall, Exeter
Sydenham House, Marystow
Taddyforde, Exeter
Tapeley Park, Westleigh
Tavistock. Abbey and hostel
Tawstock House
Thuborough, Sutcombe
Torre Abbey, Torquay
Ugbrooke, Chudleigh

County Index

Watcombe Park
Watermouth Castle, Ilfracombe
Whiteway, Chudleigh
Whitleigh, Plymouth
Widdicombe House, Kingsbridge
Widey, Plymouth
Winslade House, Exeter
Wood, South Tawton
Woodbine Cottage, Torquay

DORSET

Abbotsbury
Anderson Manor
Athelhampton, Dorchester
Beaminster Manor
Bingham's Melcombe
Birchleaves, Weymouth
Boveridge Park, Cranborne
Branksome Tower, Great Canford
Bridehead House, Dorchester
Brookland, Charminster
Brownsea Castle, Brownsea Island
Bryanston House, Blandford Forum
Brympton D'Evercy
Bucknowle House, Corfe Castle
Came, Winterborne Came
Canford Manor, Canford Magna
Castle Hill, Duntish
Chantmarle, Cattistock
Charborough Park, Morden
Cheddington Court, Beaminster
Chettle House, Farnham
Compton Acres, Poole
Compton House, Over Compton
Cranborne Manor
Creech Grange, Corfe Castle
Crichel House, Wimborne Minster
Culeaze, Wareham
Down House, Blandford
Eastbury, Blandford
Edmondsham House
Encombe, Corfe Castle
Fleet House
Fontmell Parva, Child Okeford
Forde Abbey, Chard
Frampton Court
Gaunts House, Wimborne Minster
Hanford House, Blandford
Heffleton, Wareham
Herrington, Dorchester
Hinton St Mary Manor
Hume Towers, Bournemouth
Hyde, Bridport
Hyde Crook, Frampton
Ilsington House, Dorchester
Iwerne Minster House
Kingston House, Stinsford
Kingston Lacy, Wimborne
Kingston Maurwood
Kingston Russell House, Dorchester
Lady St Mary, Wareham
Langton House, Langton Long
    Blandford
Lewiston Manor, Sherborne
Lulworth Castle, East Lulworth
Lytchett Heath, Lytchett Matravers
Manor House, Cranborne
Manor House, Sandford Orcas

Mapperton House, Beaminster
Melbury House, Melbury Sampford
Melcome Bingham
Melplash Court
Merly, Canford Magna
Milborne St Andrew
Milton
Milton Abbey, Milton Abbas
Minterne House, Minterne Magna
Moigne Combe, Owermoigne
Moreton House
Owermoigne Moor
Parnham House, Beaminster
Plumber, Lydlinch
Poxwell Manor, Poxwell
Priory of Lady St Mary, Wareham
Ranston House, Blandford
Rempstone Hall, Corfe Castle
Robert Louis Stevenson Memorial
    Garden, Bournemouth
St Giles's House, Wimborne St Giles
Sandford Orcas, Sherborne
Sherborne Castle, Sherborne
Slape Manor, Netherbury
Smedmore, Corfe Castle
Southbourne
Springfield, Poole
Stafford House, W. Stafford
Stalbridge House
Stapleton House, Stapleton Iwerne
Stinsford House, Dorchester
Stock House, Stock Gaylard
Sydling Court
Tarrant Gunville
Tarrant Rushton House, Blandford
Turnworth House
Tyneham House
Uddens House, Wimborne Minster
Upcerne House, Up Cerne
Waddon Manor, Dorchester
Warmwell House
Waterston House, Puddleton
Whatcombe House, Blandford
Wimborne St Giles
Winterbourne Clenston Manor House
Wolfeton House, Charminster
Woolcombe Hall, Cerne
Wootton House, Wotton Fitzpaine
Wyke House, Gillingham
Yaffle Hill, Broadstone

COUNTY DURHAM

Auckland Castle
Biddick Hall, Chester-le-Street
Bishop Auckland
Bowes Museum, Barnard Castle
Brancepeth Castle
Byers Green Lodge, Bishop Auckland
Castle Eden
Chester-le-Street. Deanery Garden
Cocken Hall, Durham
Croxdale Hall
Durham. College Court
Hamsterley Hall
Hardwick Hall, Sedgefield
Harraton Hall
Lambton Castle, Durham
Lartington Hall

Lumley Castle, Chester-le-Street
Polam Hill, Darlington
Raby Castle, Staindrop
Rokeby Hall, Barnard Castle
Seaham Hall
Sedgefield (Dr Kearsley)
Streatlam Castle
West Lodge, Darlington
Westerton Tower, Bishop Auckland
White Hill, Chester-le-Street
Windlestone Hall

ESSEX

Abbey House, Waltham Abbey
Albyns, Stapleford Abbots
Alresford Hall, Wivenoe
Ardchoille, Frinton-on-Sea
Ardleigh, Chigwell
Ardleigh Park
Auberries, Bulmer
Audley End, Saffron Walden
Barrington Hall, Hatfield Broad Oak
Beacon Hill, Harwich
Bedfords, Havering atte Bower
Beeleigh Abbey, Maldon
Belchamp Hall
Belhus, Aveley
Berden Priory
Bilsdons Farm, Bobbingworth
Birchanger
Bocking Hall
Bocking Place
Boreham, Chelmsford
Bower Hall, Steeple Bumpstead
Brackwell Lodge, Bradwell-on-Sea
Braxted Lodge, Witham
Bridge End, Saffron Walden
Brightingsea Hall
Brizes, Kelvedon Hatch
Broomfield, Chelmsford
Champions Manor, Woodham Ferrars
Chesterford Park, Little Chesterford
Claybury, Woodford
Cliveden, Shenfield
Coopersale, Theydon Garnon
Copford Hall
Copped Hall, Epping
Crondon, Stock
Danbury, Chelmsford
Debden Hall
Dews Hall, Lambourne
Doddinghurst Place
Down Hall, Bishops Stortford
Durrington House, Sheering
Dynes Hall, Halstead
East Horndon Manor
Easton Lodge, Dunmow
Elsenham Hall
Faulkbourne Hall
Felix Hall, Coggeshall
Fishers Farm, Wakes Colne
Gosfield Hall
Great Bardfield Lodge
Great Bentley Lodge
Greensted Hall
Greenwoods, Stock
Hall, Tendring
Hallingbury Place

County Index

Hassobury, Bishop's Stortford
Hatfield Forest Lake, Hatfield Broad Oak
Hedingham Castle
Heyns Green, Layer Marney
Hill Hall, Theydon Mount
Hill House, Braintree
Hill Pasture, Broxted
Horham Hall, Thaxted
House, Harlow
Hutton Hall
Hyde, Ingatestone
Hyde Hall, Rettenden
Hylands, Widford
Ingatestone Hall
Kelvedon Hall, Kelvedon Hatch
Langford Grove Park, Langford
Langham Hall
Langsleys, Great Waltham
Lawford Place
Lawn, Langley
Layer Marney Tower
Leez Priory, Little Leighs
Leigh Park
Lexden Park, Colchester
Liston Hall
Little Birch Hall
Little Walden Park, Saffron Walden
Littlebury, Saffron Walden
Luxborough, Waltham Abbey
Mark Hall, Harlow
Marks Hall, Colchester
Marsh Lane, Harlow
Michaelstowe Hall, Harwich
Mistley Hall
Moor End Farm, Broxted
Moor Hall, Harlow
Moulsham Hall, Chelmsford
Mountains, Witham
Moyns Park, Haverhill
Myles's, Kelvedon Hatch
Navestock
New Hall, Boreham
North Ockendon Hall
Oldfield Grange, Coggeshall
Ongar Park
Orsett Hall
Over Hall, Gestingthorpe
Pitsea Hall
Priory, Hatfield Peverel
Quarters Alresford
Quendon Hall
Reed Hall, Colchester
Riffhams, Colchester
Rivenhall Place
Rolls Park, Chigwell
St Osyth's Priory
Saling Grove, Great Saling
Saling Hall, Great Saling
Shenvilles, Margaretting
Shortgrove, Saffron Walden
Skreens, Chelmsford
South Weald Manor, Brentwood
Spains Hall, Finchingfield
Stansted Hall, Stansted Mountfitchet
Stisted Hall
Suttons, Epping
Terling Place
Thorndon hall, Brentwood
Thorpe Hall, Thorpe-le-Soken
Three Ash Farm, Althorne

Upper House, Little Parndon
Wakes Colne Rectory
Waltham Abbey
Waltons, Saffron Walden
Warley Lodge, Little Warley
Warley Place, Great Warley
Warren, Loughton
Weald Hall, South Weald
Wenden Lofts Hall
West Horndon Manor
White Barn House, Elmstead Market
Whitley, Birdbrook
Widdington
Widford Lodge
Wintrey Park, Epping
Wivenhoe Park, Colchester
Wood House, Epping
Writtle Park

GLOUCESTERSHIRE

Abbey House, Cirencester
Abbotswood, Stow-on-the-Wold
Adlestrop, Stow-on-the-Wold
Alderley, Wotton-under-Edge
Alderley Grange, Alderley
Alkerton Grange, Stroud
Alscott Park
Amberley, Stroud
Amney
Arle Court, Cheltenham
Bagendon House, Cirencester
Barnsley House, Cirencester
Barnsley Park, Cirencester
Barrington, Burford
Batsford, Moreton-in-Marsh
Berkeley Castle
Beverston Castle, Tetbury
Bibury
Bleby House, Winchcomb
Blundwells, Broadwell
Bourton House, Bourton-on-the-Hill
Bowden Hall, Upton St Leonards
Boxwell Court
Bradley Court, Wotton-under-Edge
Broadwell
Brownshill, Painswick
Burnt Norton, Chipping Campden
Campden House, Chipping Campden
Cerney House, North Cerney
Charlton Park, Cheltenham
Charlton Kings, Cheltenham
Chavenage, Tetbury
Cirencester Abbey
Cirencester House
Clearwell
Coberley, Cheltenham
Colesbourne
Combend Manor, Elkstone
Cotswold House, North Cerney
Court House, Painswick
Court House, Shipton Moyne
Cowley Manor, Cheltenham
Daylesford, Stow-on-the-Wold
Didmarton, Tetbury
Dixton Manor, Winchcombe
Doughton Manor House, Tetbury
Dowdeswell Court
Dower House, Badminton

Dumbleton, Winchcombe
Duntisbourne Abbots, Cirencester
Eastington House
Elmore Court
Escourt Grange, Tetbury
Eyford, Stow-on-the-Wold
Fairford Park, Fairford
Flaxley Abbey
Frampton Court, Frampton on Severn
Frocester Court
Gatcombe Park, Tetbury
Great House, Cheltenham
Great Rissington Manor
Greville, Charles, Gloucester
Hailes Abbey, Winchcombe
Haimes Place, Cheltenham
Hardwicke Court, Gloucester
Hartbury House
Hatherop
Hempstead, Gloucester
Hidcote Manor, Chipping Campden
Hidcote Vale, Chipping Campden
Highfield, Gloucester
Highgrove, Tetbury
Highnam Court
Hill, Berkeley
Hill House, Wickwar
Hilles, Stroud
Hodges, Shipton Moyne
Holcombe House, Stroud
Ilsom, Tetbury
Kempsford, Fairford
Kiftsgate Court, Chipping Campden
Kingcombe, Chipping Campden
Lasborough House, Tetbury
Leckhampton, Cheltenham
Level, Pillowell
Lydney Park
Lyppiatt Park, Stroud
Malcolm House, Batsford
Marybone House (B. Hyett), Gloucester
Matson House
Maugersbury Manor
Miserden Park
Moorend, Berkeley
Nether Lypiatt, Stroud
Nether Swell Manor, Stow-on-the-Wold
New Mills
Newark Park, Ozleworth
Nibley, Dursley
Notgrove Manor
Oddington, Stow-on-the-Wold
Old Rectory, Naunton
Oldbury Court
Orchard Cottage, Gretton
Owlpen Manor
Painswick House
Pan's Lodge, Painswick
Pinbury, Duntisbourne Rouse
Preston House, Cirencester
Prinknash Park, Gloucester
Rendcomb Park
Rodborough Court, Stroud
Rodmarton Manor
Sandywell Park, Cheltenham
Sapperton, Cirencester
Selsley, Woodchester
Sevenhampton, Cheltenham
Sezincote, Moreton-in-Marsh
Sherborne

Shipton Hall
Shipton Moyne
Shurdington
Snowhill Manor, Broadway
Southam de la Bere, Southam
Spa House, Cheltenham
Spring Park, Woodchester
Stancombe Park, Dursley
Stanton Court, Evesham
Stanway House
Stonehouse Court
Sudeley Castle
Swell, Stow-on-the-Wold
Tocknells Court, Painswick
Toddington Manor
Upper Dowdeswell, Cheltenham
Upper Slaughter Manor
Wallsworth Hall, Gloucester
Westbury Court, Westbury-on-Severn
Westonbirt House & Arboretum, Tetbury
Whitley Park, Ham
Whitminster House
Williamstrip Park, Coln St Aldwyns
Witcombe Park
Woodchester Park, Stroud
Wormington Grange, Winchcombe
Wotton, Gloucester

HAMPSHIRE

Abbotstone, Alresford
Alresford House, Winchester
Amport House, Andover
Ashford Chase, Petersfield
Ashton Cottage, Bishops Waltham
Avington Park, Winchester
Avon Tyrell, Christchurch
Awbridge Danes Water, Romsey
Basing Park, Alton
Beaulieu Abbey
Beckford House, Southampton
Bentworth Lodge
Berrydowne Court, Ashe
Bevis Mount, Southampton
Bishopstoke Vicarage
Blackmoor House
Bourn Hill Cottage, Cadland
Bohunt Manor, Liphook
Bramdean House, Winchester
Bramshill Park, Winchfield
Breamore House, Fordingbridge
Broadhatch House, Bentley
Broadlands, Romsey
Brockenhurst, Lymington
Brookwood Park, Hinton Ampner
Burgate Court
Burley Grange
Busketts, Southampton
Cadland, Fawley
Cams Hall, Fareham
Chantry, 100 acres
Chawton House, Alton
Chewton Glen
Chilland, Winchester
Chilworth Manor
Cliddesdon Down House
Cold Hayes, Petersfield
Coles, Petersfield

Compton End, Winchester
Court Hall, East Meon
Cranbury Park, Winchester
Cuffnells, Lyndhurst
Daneshill, Basingstoke
Dangstein, Petersfield
Dogmersfield Park, Odiham
Dower House, Dogmersfield
Durmast House, Burley
Eaglehurst
Elvetham Park, Winchfield
Embley Park, Romsey
Eversley Rectory
Ewhurst
Exbury House
Fairfield House, Hambledon
Forest Lodge, Hythe
Foxlease, Lyndhurst
Freemantle, Southampton
Froyle House, Alton
Froyle Mill, Alton
Furzey, Minstead
Glen Eyre, Southampton
Grange, Hartley Wintney
Grange, Northington
Greatham Mill, Liss
Greywell Hill, Basingstoke
Grove Place, Romsey
Hackwood, Basingstoke
Hall Place, West Meon
Harcombe House, New Alresford
Hawley Hall
Headbourne Worthy, Winchester
Heckfield Place
Hengistbury Head, Bournemouth
Heron Court, Christchurch
Herriard's House
High Coxlease, Lyndhurst
Highclere Castle
Highcliffe Castle
Highcroft, Burley
Hillier Arboretum, Romsey
Hinton Admiral, Christchurch
Hinton Ampner House
Hockley House, Bramdean
Hoddington House, Basingstoke
Holt, Upham
Hook, Titchfield
Hopton House, Hambledon
Houghton, Stockbridge
House-in-the-Wood, Bartley
Hunting Lodge, Odiham
Hursley Park
Hurst Mill, Petersfield
Hurstbourne Priors, Andover
Hurstbourne Tarrant, Andover
Isleworth, Hordean
Jenkyn Place, Bentley
Kempshott Park, Basingstoke
Kings Chantry, Binsted
Lainston House, Winchester
Laverstoke House
Leigh Park, Havant
Lepe House, Exbury
Little Boarhunt, Liphook
Little Hay, Burley
Longstock Park, Stockbridge
Malshanger, Basingstoke
Manor House, Basingstoke
Manydown, Basingstoke

Marelands, Bentley
Marsh Court, Stockbridge
Melchet Court, Romsey
Merdon Manor, Hursley
Michelmersh Court
Minley Manor
Minstead Manor House
Mottisfont Abbey
Moundsmere Manor, Preston Candover
Moyles Court, Ringwood
New Place, Shedfield
Newton Valence Manor House
Norman Court, Stockbridge
North Stoneham Park
North Stoneham Parsonage
Northerwood, Emery Down
Norton Manor, Sutton Scotney
Oakley Hall, Basingstoke
Odiham
Old House, Rotherwick
Old Mansion, Boldre
Palice House, Beaulieu
Paultons, Romsey
Preshaw House, Corhampton
Pylewell Park, Lymington
Quarry Wood, Burghclere
Rhinefield House, Brockenhurst
Rooksbury, Wickham
Rotherfield Park, Alton
Shawford House, Winchester
Sherfield Court
Somerley Park, Ringwood
South Stoneham House, Southampton
Southampton. Botanic Gardens
Southwick Park
Spinners, Boldre
Stoneham Park
Stratfield Saye House, Reading
Stratton Park, East Stratton
Swanmore Park
Sway
Testwood
Tichborne House, Alresford
Tidworth House, South Tidworth
Townhill Park, Southampton
Tudor House, Southampton
Tylney Hall, Basingstoke
Upton Grey Place
Vyne, Basingstoke
Wakes, Selborne
Walhampton, Lymington
Warbrook House, Wokingham
Warnford Park
West Green House, Hartley Wintney
Westbury House, East Meon
Weston Grove, Southampton
Whitsbury Manor House
Wickham
Winchester Castle
Winchester War Memorial Deanery
Winchfield Lodge
Worthy Park, Winchester
Wyards Farm, Alton
Wylds, Liss

HEREFORD AND WORCESTER

Abberley Hall, Stourport
Abbey Dore Court

County Index

Abbey Gardens, Redditch
Avechurch. Bishop's Palace
Arley House, Kidderminster
Armston
Beaucastle, Bewdley
Beckford Hall
Bell's Castle, Kemerton
Belmont, Clehonger
Berrington Hall, Leominster
Birtsmorton Court, Tewkesbury
Brampton Bryan
Bredon Springs, Ashton under Hill
Bricklehampton Hall
Brinsop Court
Broadfield Court, Bodenham
Brook House, Colwall
Bryngwyn
Cleeve Prior, Evesham
Conderton Manor, Tewkesbury
Craycombe House, Evesham
Croft Castle, Leominster
Croome Court, Croome D'Abitot
Crown East Court, Martley
Davenham Bank, Malvern
Den, Cropthorne
Dinmore Manor, Hope under Dinmore
Downton Castle, Downton on the Rock
Duckswich House, Upton upon Severn
Dunley Hall, Stourport-on-Severn
Dunstall, Croome
Eastnor Castle, Ledbury
Eywood, Kington
Fawley Court, Ross-on-Wye
Foxley, Hereford
Garnons, Mansell Gamage
Garnstone, Weobley
Gatley Park, Leinthall Earls
Goodrich Court
Grafton Court
Grafton Manor, Bromsgrove
Hadzor, Droitwich
Haffield, Ledbury
Hagley
Hampton Court, Leominster
Hanbury Hall, Droitwich
Hartlebury Castle
Hatfield, Ledbury
Hergest Croft, Kington
Hewell Grange, Bromsgrove
Hill Court, Ross
Hindlip Hall
Holme Lacy
Holt Castle
Hope End, Ledbury
Hopton Court, Worcester
Huddington Court
Impney Hall, Droitwich
Kentchurch Court
Kyre Park
Loen, Bewdley
Longworth, Lugwardine
Madresfield Court, Great Malvern
Mere Hall, Droitwich
Middle Hill, Broadway
Moccas Court
Moor Court, Kington
Moraston, Ross
Northwick Park
Norton Park, Evesham
Old Rectory, Droitwich

Ombersley Court
Orchard Farm, Broadway
Overbury Court
Pontrilas Court
Priory, Kemerton
Pudleston Court
Pull Court, Bushley
Rhydd Court, Upton upon Severn
Rochford House
Rosebank Gardens, Malvern
Rotherwas, Hereford
Rous Lench Court
Russell House, Broadway
St Catherine's Farm, Bredon's Norton
Severn End, Hanley Castle
Shobdon Court
Skells, Redditch
Spetchley Park
Stanford Park, Worcester
Stoke Edith Park
Stone House Cottage, Kidderminster
Sufton Court
Thorngrove, Worcester
Tudor House, Broadway
Vern, Marden
Weir, Swainshill
Westwood Park, Droitwich
Whitbourne Hall
Whitfield, Wormbridge
Whittern, Lyonshall
Wickhamford Manor
Winds Point, Malvern
Witley Court, Great Witley
Witley Park House, Worcester
Woollas Hall, Pershore
Wormsley Grange

HERTFORDSHIRE

Aldenham House, Watford
Amwell House, Ware
Arkley Manor, West Barnet
Ashridge Park, Berkhampstead
Ashwell Bury House, Ashwell
Aspendon Hall, Buntingford
Aston Bury, Aston
Ball's Park, Hertford
Bayfordbury, Bayford
Bedwell Park, Essendon
Beech Hill Park, Potters Bar
Beechwood, Markyate
Benington Lordship
Bonningtons, Stanstead Abbots
Brairstrie House, Hatfield
Brent Pelham Hall, Buntingford
Brickendonbury, Hertford
Broadfield Grange
Brocket Hall, Hatfield
Brookmans, North Minns
Broxbourne
Burloes, Royston
Bury, St Paul's Walden
Bushey Hall
Bushey House
Camfield Place, Hatfield
Capel Manor, Waltham Cross
Carpenders Park, Watford
Cassiobury Park, Watford
Cheshunt Cottage

Cokenach, Barkway
Cole Green, Hertingfordbury
Colney House, Shenley
Cottered
Danesbury Park, Welwyn
Delrow, Watford
Derehams, South Mimms
Digswell, Hatfield
Easneye, Ware
Fanhams, Ware
Frythe, Welwyn
Gaddesden Place, Great Gaddesden
Garden House, Cottered
Gobions, Brookmans Park
Goldings, Hertford
Gorhambury, St Albans
Grange, Bishop's Stortford
Grove, Rickmansworth
Hadham Hall, Little Hadham
Haileybury, Hertford
Hamels, Ware
Hatfield House
Hazelwood, King's Langley
Heronsgate, Rickmansworth
Hexton Manor
High Leigh, Hoddesdon
Hill End, Hitchin
Hill House, Stanstead Abbots
Hitchin Priory
Holmewood, Cheshunt
Holywell House, St Albans
Homewood, Knebworth
Hoo, St Paul's Walden
Hunsdon House, Hunsdon
Hyde Hall, Sawbridgeworth
Julians, Buntingford
Kimpton Hoo
Kings Langley
King's Walden Bury
Knebworth House, Stevenage
Lamer, Welwyn
Leggatt's Park, Potters Bar
Little Court, Buntingford
Little Offley
Lockleys, Welwyn
Lululaund, Bushey
Makerye End, Harpenden
Marden Hill, Hertford
Markyate Cell
Moor Park, Rickmansworth
Moor Place, Much Hadham
New Place, Gilston
Newsells Bury, Barkway
Node, Welwyn, Herts
North Mymms Park
Northaw House, Potters Bar
Oakhill, Cheshunt
Offley Place
Organ Hall, Aldenham
Panshanger, Hertingfordbury
Pirton Hall
Pishiobury, Bishop's Stortford
Poles, Hertford
Porters Park, Shenley
Presdales, Ware
Queen Hoo Hall, Tewin
Rickmansworth Park
Rothamsted, Harpenden
Rushden Place
Russell Park, Watford

County Index

Sacombe Park
St Paul's Walden Bury
Salisbury Hall, London Colney
Scotts Grotto, Ware
Sheldish, Kings Langley
Shephalbury, Shephall
Stagenhoe Park, Stevenage
Staghurst, Berkhamsted
Standon Lordship, Hertford
Stanstead Bury, Stanstead Abbots
Stanstead Lodge, Stanstead Abbots
Stocks, Tring
Temple Dinsley, Hitchin
Tewin House
Tewin Water
Thatched Rest, Welwyn
Theobalds, Cheshunt
Throcking House
Tring Park
Tyttenhanger Park, St Albans
Wall Hall, Aldenham
Waltham House, Waltham Cross
Ware Park
Watton Woodhall, Watton-at-Stone
Westwick Cottage, Leverstock Green
White Hill, Berkhamsted
Wood Hill, Essendon
Woodgreen Park, Cheshunt
Woodhall Park, Watton-at-Stone
Woodlands, Hoddesdon
Woodside, Rickmansworth
Wormley Bury
Wrotham Park, South Mimms
Wyck, Hitchin
Wyddiall Hall, Buntingford
Youngsbury, Wadesmill

HUMBERSIDE

Beswick Beverley
Bishop Burton Hall
Boynton Hall, Carnaby
Bradley, Grimsby
Brantingham Thorpe, Brough
Burnby Hall, Pocklington
Burstwick
Burton Agnes Hall, Bridlington
Burton Constable, Hull
Cave
Cawkeld, Kilnwick
Chatt House, Burton Pidsea
Cottingham, Hull
Dalton Hall, Beverley
Elsham House
Everingham Park
Garrowby Hall, Pocklington
Hall Garth, Goodmanham
Holderness House
Hotham Hall
Hotham House
Houghton Hall, Sancton
Hull. Botanic Garden
Keldgate Manor, Beverley
Kilnwick Hall
Londesborough Park
Risby Hall, Rowley
Rise Park
Scawby Hall
Sewerby Hall, Bridlington

Sigglesthorne Hall
Sledmore House
South Dalton House
Tranby Croft, Hessle
Warter Priory
Watton Abbey
Welton House

ISLE OF WIGHT

Appley House, Ryde
Appley Towers, Ryde
Appuldurcombe House, Ventnor
Binstead, Ryde
Brooke House
Cedar Lodge, Puckpool
Dodpit House, Newbridge
East Cowes Castle
Fairlee, Newport
Farringford
Gatcombe House
Lisle Combe
Marina Villa, West Cowes
Mottistone Manor
Norris Castle, East Cowes
Northcourt, Brighstone
Nunwell, Brading
Orchard Cottage, Undercliffe
Osborne, East Cowes
Osborne (R.P. Blachford)
Priory, Sea View
Priory, St Helens
St John's, Ryde
Steephill Botanic Garden, Ventnor
Swainston, Newport
Ventnor Botanic Garden
Westfield House, Ryde
Westover Lodge, Newport

KENT

Acrise Place
Addington Park, Maidstone
Aldington West Court
Allington Castle, Maidstone
Ashen Wilderness, Chiddingstone
Ashurst Lodge, Ashurst
Avery Hill
Barham Court, Canterbury
Bayhall
Beachborough, Hythe
Bedgebury
Bedgebury Pinetum
Belmont Park, Throwley
Belvedere
Benendon School
Betteshanger Deal
Bifrons, Canterbury
Blackhurst, Tonbridge
Bore Place, Chiddingstone
Boughton, Maidstone
Bourne Park, Bishopsbourne
Brabourne, Ashford
Brackett Hill, Platt
Bradbourne, Sevenoaks
Bridge Place
Bromley Place, Rochester
Broome Park, Barham

Broomhill, Tunbridge Wells
Broughton Hall, Otford
Calverley Park, Tunbridge Wells
Canterbury. Christchurch
Chart Sutton, Maidstone
Chelsfield Rectory
Chestnut Wilderness, Chiddingstone
Chevening, Sevenoaks
Chilham Castle, Canterbury
Chilston Park, Boughton Malherbe
Chipstead Place, Sevenoaks
Clare House, West Malling
Cobham Hall
Combe Bank, Brasted
Court Lodge, Lamberhurst
Crete Hall, Northfleet
Crittenden House, Matfield
Dane Court, Tilmanstone
Dane Park, Margate
Deane, Barham
Deanery, Rochester
Denne Hill, Barham
Detling Hall, Maidstone
Dinorber House, Tunbridge Wells
Down House, Downe
Dunorlan, Tunbridge Wells
East Lodge, Lamberhurst
East Sutton Place
East Wickham House
Eastwell Park, Ashford
Elbridge House, Littlebourne
Elmwood, Isle of Thanet
Elsfield House, Maidstone
Emmetts, Ide Hill
Encombe, Sandgate
Eyhorne House, Hollingbourne
Fairlawn, Sevenoaks
Fatherwell House, Ryarsh
Finchcocks, Goudhurst
Folkestone. Winter Garden
Fowlers, Hawkhurst
Franks, Farningham
Fryars, Aylesford
Godden Green, Sevenoaks
Godinton. Ashford
Godmersham Park
Goodnestone Park, Faversham
Gore Court, Tunstall
Grange, Benendon
Grange, Maidstone
Great Comp, Maidstone
Great Culverden, Tunbridge Wells
Great Maytham, Rolvendon
Greatness, Sevenoaks
Groombridge Place
Grove House, Margate
Hadlow Castle
Hales Place, Canterbury
Hales Place, Tenterden
Hall Place, Leigh
Hammerfield, Tonbridge
Hamptons, West Peckham
Hawley House, Sutton at Hone
Hayle Place, Loose
Hemsted Park, Cranbrook
Heronden, Sandwich
Hever Castle, Edenbridge
High Street House, Chiddingstone
Hillside, Sevenoaks
Hole Park, Rolvenden

County Index

Hothfield Place
Hunton Court Lodge
Husheath Manor, Goudhurst
Ightham Court
Ightham Mote
Ingress Abbey, Greenhithe
Jennings, Maidstone
Kearnsey Court, Dover
Kenfield Hall, Petham
Kingsgate, North Foreland
Kippington, Sevenoaks
Knole, Sevenoaks
Knowlton Court, Sandwich
Ladham House, Goudhurst
Lee Place (C. Boone)
Lee Priory, Ickham
Lees Court, Faversham
Leybourne Castle, Maidstone
Lilliesden, Hawkhurst
Links, Hythe
Linton Park
Liverpool House, Walmer
Long Barn, Sevenoaks
Lullingstone Castle, Eynsford
Lympne Castle
Lynsted
Mabledon Park, Tonbridge
Maidstone. Cemetery
Malling Abbey, West Malling
Margate. Grotto
Mereworth Castle
Mersham Hatch
Montreal, Sevenoaks
Mote, Maidstone
Mount Morris, Westenhanger
Nash Court, Faversham
Nettlestead Place
Northbourne Court
Nurstead Court
Oakfield, Penshurst
Oakwood, Maidstone
Olantigh, Wye
Old Wilsley, Cranbrook
Ovenden, Sevenoaks
Owl House, Lamberhurst
Oxenhoath, Tonbridge
Oxney Court, Dover
Oxney Park, Ringwould
Palmer's Farm, Tunbridge Wells
Penshurst Place
Petham
Port Lympne, Hythe
Postern, Tonbridge
Preston Hall, Maidstone
Quebec House, Westerham
Quex Park, Birchington
Redleaf, Penshurst
Ringwould House
Ripple Court
River Hall, Sevenoaks
Rochester. Deanery
Rochester Castle
Rosherville Gardens, Gravesend
Roydon Hall, Yalding
St Alban's Court, Nonington
St Clere, Kemsing
St John's, Sutton at Hone
St John's Jerusalem, Dartford
St Julian's, Sevenoaks
St Vincent, Wrotham

Saltwood Castle
Saltwood Vicarage
Salutation, Sandwich
Sandlands, Hythe
Sandling Park, Hythe
Seacox Heath, Hawkhurst
Sevenoaks (T. Fuller)
Sharps Place
Sharsted Court, Sittingbourne
Sherwood Park, Tunbridge Wells
Sissinghurst Castle
Sissinghurst Place
Smallhythe Place, Tenterden
Smith's Hall, East Farleigh
Somerhill, Tonbridge
Springwood, Dartford
Squerryes Court, Westerham
Stede Hill, Harrietsham
Stoneacre, Otham
Sturry Court
Sundridge Place, Tonbridge
Surrenden Dering, Ashford
Sutton Place
Swadelands, Lenham
Swaylands, Penshurst
Swinford Old Manor, Ashford
Syndale, Faversham
Temple Cottage, Newington
Teston
Tongswood, Hawkhurst
Torry Hill, Lenham
Turkey Court, Maidstone
Tutsham Hall, West Farley
Updown House, Sandwich
Valence, Westerham
Vinters, Maidstone
Waldershare Park
Walmer Castle
Walmer Lodge
Warders, Tonbridge
Wardes, Otham
West Farleigh Hall
Westerham
Westwell, Tenterden
White House, Sandwich Bay
White House, Wrotham
Wierton, Maidstone
Wildernesse, Sevenoaks
Wilsley House, Cranbrook
Withersdane Hall, Wye
Wittersham House
Wombwell Hall, Northfleet
Woolton Farm, Bekesbourne
Wootton Court
Wrinstead Court, Lenham
Wye College
Yotes Court, Mereworth

LANCASHIRE

Arden, Accrington
Ashlands, Newchurch
Ashton Hall, Lancaster
Astley Hall, Chorley
Bailrigg House, Scotforth
Bank House, Warrington
Bold Hall
Borwick Hall, Carnforth
Broad Oak, Accrington

Broughton Tower
Capernwray Hall, Carnforth
Cranford, Aughtan
Cuerdon Hall, Chorley
Dyke Nook Lodge, Accrington
Gawthorpe Hall, Padiham
Gillibrand Hall, Chorley
Gisburn Park
Halton Hall
Harrock Hall, Parbold
Hazelwood, Silverdale
Higher Trap, Padiham
Hoghton Tower
Holme, Cliviger
Howick House, Preston
Hulton Hall
Huntroyde Hall, Burnley
Latham House
Leighton Hall, Carnforth
Linden Hall, Borwick
Lydiate Hall
Lytham Hall
Moorland Garden, Rivington
Moreton Hall, Whalley
New High Riley, Accrington
Oakleigh, Burnley
Quernmore Park
Ribby Hall
Rivington Pike
Roynton Cottage, Rivington Pike
Rufford Hall
Rufford Old Hall
Ryelands, Lancaster
Samlesbury Hall
Scarisbrick, Southport
Stoneyhurst College, Clitheroe
Thurnham Hall
Towneley Hall, Burnley
Vine House, Haslingden
Walton Hall, Walton-le-Dale
Walton Old Hall, Walton Superior
Wellfield, Preston
Wennington Hall
Willows, Ashton on Ribble
Withnell Fold
Witton House, Blackburn

LEICESTERSHIRE

Anstey Pastures
Ashby de la Zouch
Ashby St Ledgers
Baggariff Hall
Barkby Hall
Beaumanor, Loughborough
Belgrave Hall, Leicester
Belvoir Castle
Bosworth Hall
Bradgate Park, Leicester
Braunstone Hall, Leicester
Buckminster
Burbage Hinckley
Burley on the Hill
Burton, Burton on the Wolds
Carlton Curlieu
Carlton Hall
Cold Overton Hall
Coleorton Hall, Ashby-de-la-Zouch
Danett's Hall

County Index

Donington, Castle Donington
Edmondthorpe Hall
Enderby Hall
Exton Park
Garendon, Loughborough
Gopsall Hall, Market Bosworth
Gumley Hall
Ketton Cottage
Kirkby Mallory Hall, Bosworth
Langham Old Hall
Langton Hall, West Langton
Launde Abbey
Leesthorpe Hall, Melton Mowbray
Leicester. Abbey Park
Leicester. Arboretum, Evington
Leicester. University Botanic Garden
Lindley Hall, Hinckley
Lockington Hall
Loddington Hall
Lowesby Hall
Lyddington Bede House
Manor House, Donington-le-Heath
Misterton Hall
Nevill Holt
Normanton Park
Normanton Turville Hall
North Luffenham Hall
Noseley Hall
Old Hall, Nether Hambleton
Osbaston Hall
Papillon Hall, Lubenham
Prestwold Hall
Quenby Hall, Hungarton
Quorndon Hall
Ragdale Old Hall
Rolleston Hall
Sanctuary of the Hermit Finch, Burley on the Hill
Scraptoft Hall
Shenton Hall
Skeffington Hall
Stanford Hall, Lutterworth
Stapleford Park
Staunton Harold, Ashby-de-la-Zouch
Stone Cottage, Hambleton
Stoughton Hall
Swithland Hall
Wanlip Hall
Westcotes
Whatton House, Hathern
Willesley Hall
Wistow Hall

LINCOLNSHIRE

Ayscoughfee Hall
Barnhill
Bayon's Manor, Market Rasen
Belton House, Grantham
Bloxholm Hall, Kesteven
Blyborough, Lindsey
Bracebridge Court, Lincoln
Brocklesby Park
Casewick, Stamford
Coleby Hall, Scunthorpe
Cross O'Cliff, Lincoln
Culverthorpe, Sleaford
Dalby Hall, Spilsby

Denton House
Doddington Hall
Dunton Hall
Easton Hall
Fillingham Castle
Fulbeck Hall
Grantham (W. Stukeley)
Greatford Hall
Grimsthorpe Castle
Gunby Hall
Hainton Hall
Harlaxton Manor
Hartsholme Hall, Lincoln
Haverholme Priory, Sleaford
Hungerton Hall
Irnham Hall, Irnham
Langton Hall
Lea, Gainsborough
Leadenham House
Marston Hall
Nettleham Hall
Nocton Hall
Normanby Park
Normanton Hall
Norton Place, Market Rasen
Petwood, Woodhall Spa
Riby
St Vincent's, Grantham
Scrivelsby Court
Sedgebrook Manor
South Ormsby
Springfields, Spalding
Stoke Rochford House
Sudbrooke Holme
Summer Castle, Fillingham
Tattershall Castle
Thornton Hall, Ulceby
Thorpe Hall, Louth
Uffington House
Walmsgate Hall, Louth
Well Vale, Spilsby
Willingham House, Market Rasen
Witham Hall, Witham on the Hill
Wootton Lodge

(GREATER) LONDON

Abney Park Cemetery, Stoke Newington
Adam and Eve Tea Gardens, Camden
Addington Place, Croydon
Addiscombe Farm, Croydon
Addiscombe Place, Croydon
Addison Lodge, Holland Park
Adon Mount, Dulwich
Albro House Farm, Ilford
Aldbury Place, Blackheath
Aldesbrook Manor, Newham
Alexander Palace, Haringey
Apollo Gardens, Lambeth
Arnos Grove, Southgate
Arundel House
Asgill House, Richmond
Ashurst House, Hornsey
Aubrey House, Kensington
Aviary, Southall
Bagnigge Wells, Camden
Bangors Park, Uxbridge
Barley Mow, Islington
Barn Elms, Barnes

Barrowpoint Hill, Harrow
Barwell Court, Surbiton
Baynard's Castle Palace
Bayswater Tea Gardens, Westminster
Beaufort House, Chelsea
Beaver Hall, Southgate
Beckenham, Bromley
Beddington, Sutton
Bedford Lodge, Campden Hill
Beechwood, Highgate
Belmount, Mill Hill
Belsize House, Lambeth
Belvedere House, Bexley
Belvedere Tea Gardens, Islington
Bentley Priory, Stanmore
Bermondsey Spa Gardens, Southwark
Bickley, Bromley
Black Queen Coffee House, Hackney
Blendon Hall, Bexley
Bloomsbury Square, Holborn
Boston Manor, Brentford
Bower House, Havering
Bowes Manor, Southgate
Bramblebury, Plumstead
Bristol House, Roehampton
Brittens, Hornchurch
Bromley College
Brompton Botanic Garden, Kensington
Brompton Cemetery, Kensington
Brondesbury, Willesden
Broome House, Fulham
Bruce Castle, Tottenham
Buccleuch House, Richmond
Buckingham House, St James Park
Buckingham Palace
Burlington House, Piccadilly
Bush Hill Park, Edmonton
Bushey Villa, Teddington
Cadogan Place, Chelsea
Caen Wood Towers, Highgate
Camberwell (J.C. Lettsom), Southwark
Cambridge House, Twickenham
Camden Place, Chislehurst
Campsbourne Lodge, Hornsey
Cannizaro Park, Wimbledon
Canonbury House Tea Gardens, Islington
Canons Park, Edgware
Cardigan House, Richmond
Carlton Hall, Ealing
Carlton House, St James's
Carlyle House, Chelsea
Carshalton House, Sutton
Carshalton Park, Sutton
Casina, Dulwich
Castle Hill, Ealing
Castle Inn Tea Gardens, Islington
Cedars, Harrow Weald
Cedars, Isleworth
Cedars, Lewisham
Charlton House, Greenwich
Charterhouse, Finsbury
Chase Side, Enfield
Cheam, Sutton
Chelsea. Physic Garden
Chelsea. Royal Hospital
Chelsea House
Chesfield, Hampton Wick
Chestnuts, Camberwell
Chiswick House, Hounslow

County Index

Clare Lawn, East Sheen
Claylands, Kennington
Cleveland House, Clapham
Colehill Cottage, Fulham
Colehill House, Fulham
Colesseum, Regent's Park
Colney Hatch, Barnet
Combe-down-side, Croydon
Coombe Court, Kingston
Coombe House, Croydon
Coombe Warren, Kingston
Copenhagen House, Islington
Copped Hall, Totteridge
Copse Hill, Wimbledon
Corridor House, Tottenham
Cranford Park, Hounslow
Craven Cottage, Fulham
Crayford Workhouse, Bexley
Cremorne, Chelsea
Cromwell's Gardens, Brompton
Cumberland Tea Gardens, Vauxhall
Cuper's Gardens, Lambeth
Dagnams, Havering
Danson, Bexley
Danvers House, Chelsea
Dawley, Uxbridge
Devonhurst, Chiswick
Devonshire House, Piccadilly
Dobney's Bowling Green, Islington
Dover House, Roehampton
Dowley Court, Uxbridge
Downhills, Hornsey
Downshire House, Roehampton
Drayton Green, Ealing
Drayton House, Uxbridge
Dudley Lodge, Harrow on the Hill
Dunedin, Streatham
Dyrham Park, Barnet
Eagle House, Clapham Common
Eagle Tavern, Islington
Ealing Park
Ealing Place
East Combe, Blackheath
East End House, Fulham
Eden Park, Beckenham
Elmer Lodge, Beckenham
Eltham (J. Sherard), Woolwich
Eltham Palace, Woolwich
Ely Place, Holborn
Enfield (J. Mellish)
Enfield Mills
Enfield Palace
English Grotto, Clerkenwell
Erskine House, Hampstead
Essex House, Westminster
Fairlawn, Wimbledon
Falkland Park, Norwood
Ferry House, Isleworth
Finch's Grotto Gardens, Southwark
Firs, Lewisham
Fitzroy Farm, Highgate
Flambards, Harrow
Flora Tea Gardens, Lambeth
Foots Cray Place
Fortis Green, Muswell Hill
Foxbury, Chislehurst
Frognal, Bromley
Fulham. Bishop's Park
Fulham Palace
Garrick's Villa, Hampton

Gaynes, Upminster
Gidea Hall, Romford
Golders Hill, Hampstead
Gordon House, Isleworth
Gough Park, Enfield
Grange, Highbury
Grange, Southgate
Grange, Sutton
Greenwich Hospital
Greenwich Palace
Grove, Harrow
Grove, Highgate
Grove, Lambeth
Grove, Twickenham
Grove End Road, St Johns Wood
Grove Hill, Camberwell
Grove House, Isleworth
Grove Lodge, Fulham
Grovelands, Enfield
Gunnersbury Park, Hounslow
Gwynns, Woodford
Hackbridge, Sutton
Hackney (Sir T. Cooke)
Hackney Theological Seminary
Haling House, Croydon
Hampstead Wells
Ham Frith Farm, Newham
Ham House, Richmond
Hampton. Bushey Park
Hampton Court House
Hampton Court Palace
Hanover Lodge, Regent's Park
Hanwell Park, Ealing
Hanworth Park, Hounslow
Hare Hall, Havering
Harefield Grove, Hillingdon
Harefield Park, Hillingdon
Haringey House, Hornsey
Harrow Manor House
Harts, Woodford
Havering Park, Romford
Hayes Place
Heath House, Hampstead
Hendon Hall, Barnet
Hendon House, Barnet
Hendon Place, Barnet
Hendon Rectory, Barnet
Hermes House, Islington
Hermitage, Fulham
Higham House, Walthamstow
Highams, Redbridge
Highbury Barn, Islington
Highgate Cemetery
Hill, Hampstead
Hill House, Bromley
Hill House, Streatham
Hillingdon Court, Uxbridge
Hillingdon House, Uxbridge
Hilingdon Place, Uxbridge
Hogarth House, Chiswick
Holcombe House, Hendon
Holland House, Kensington
Holme, Regent's Park
Holt, Harrow Weald
Holwood, Bromley
Hurlingham House, Fulham
Isleworth House, Hounslow
Islington. Albert Park
Islington Spa, Clerkenwell
Ivies, Enfield

Ivy House, Hampstead
Jenny's Whim, Pimlico
Keat's House, Hampstead
Kelmscott House, Hammersmith
Kelsey Manor, Bromley
Kennington, Lambeth
Kensal Green Cemetery
Kentish Town (W. Stukeley), Camden
Kenwood, Hampstead
Kew (Sir H. Capel), Richmond
Kew. Royal Botanic Gardens
Kilburn Wells, Hampstead
Kingsbury, Brent
Kingswood, Sydenham
Kneller Hall, Whitton
Knights Hill, Dulwich
Knott's Green, Leyton
Kymnel Manor, Chislehurst
Lacy House, Isleworth
Lake House, Wanstead
Lambeth (Capt. Foster)
Lambeth (Tradescants)
Lambeth. Archbishop's Park
Lambeth. Brackwell Park
Lambeth. Jubilee Gardens
Lambeth. Myatt's Fields
Lambeth. Ruskin Park
Lambeth. Streatham Memorial Garden
Lambeth. Vauxhall Park
Lambeth Palace
Langley Park, Beckenham
Langtons, Hornchurch
Lee Grove, Lewisham
Leighton Court, Streatham
Leighton House, Kensington
Leyton Grange, Waltham Forest
Lime Grove, Putney
Limes, Muswell Hill
Lion House, Stamford Hill
Little Grove, East Barnet
Littleberries, Hendon
London: Parks, squares and open places
  see under LONDON in main sequence
London Botanic Garden (W. Curtis)
London Botanic Garden (W. Salisbury)
London Spa, Clerkenwell
'Lord Cobham's Head', Islington
Loxford Hall, Ilford
Manresa House, Roehampton
Mansion House, Highgate
Marble Hall, Vauxhall
Marble Hill House, Twickenham
Marlborough House, Pall Mall
Marshalls, Romford
Marylebone Gardens
Merton Place
Minchenden House, Southgate
Mitcham Grove
Montagu House, Camden
Moselle Villa, Tottenham
Mote Mount, Mill Hill
Mount Clare, Roehampton
Mount Grove, Hampstead
Moyer House, Leyton
Mulberry Garden, Clerkenwell
Myddelton House, Enfield
New Georgia, Hampstead
New Globe Gardens, Mile End Road
New Park, Petersham
New Wells, Clerkenwell

Newlands, Harrow
Newstead, Wimbledon
Nonsuch, Cheam
Norbiton Place, Kingston
North Cheam Park
North Cray Place, Bexley
Norwood Cemetery
Nunhead Cemetery, Southwark
Oak Lodge, Kensington
Oakery, Beckenham
Observatory, Campden Hill
Old Meadows, West Drayton
Old Park House, Enfield
Orleans House, Twickenham
Osterley Park
Paddington House (J. Symmons)
Pancras Wells, Camden
Park Hill, Streatham
Park House, Hammersmith
Parkstead House, Roehampton
Pavilion, Isleworth
Peckham (P. Collinson), Southwark
Peckham (Mr Thomas), Southwark
Pinner Hill House, Harrow
Plaistow House, Bromley
Point Pleasant, Richmond
Pope's Villa, Twickenham
Poulett Lodge, Twickenham
Prospect House, Woodford
Purser's Cross, Fulham
Pyrgo Park, Havering
Radnor House, Twickenham
Ragman's Castle, Twickenham
Rainham Hall
Ranelagh Gardens, Chelsea
Ranelagh House, Chelsea
Ravensworth House, Walham Green
Redlees, Isleworth
Regent's Lodge, Regent's Park
Regent's Park (Marquess of Hertford)
Restoration Spring Gardens, Southwark
Richmond (Sir M. Decker)
Richmond (R. Dodsley)
Richmond Gardens
Richmond Palace
Richmond Park
Riversdale (Mr Drummond), Twickenham
Roehampton Grove
Roehampton House
Roehampton Park
Roehampton Priory
Rosedale House, Richmond
Rosslyn House, Hampstead
Rotherhithe, Southwark
Royal Hort. Soc. Chiswick
Royal Hort. Soc. South Kensington
Royal Hort. Soc. Turnham Green
Russell Square, Bloomsbury
Sadler's Wells, Islington
St Catherine's Lodge, Regent's Park
St Chad's Well, Camden
St Helena Gardens, Rotherhithe
St James's Palace
St Margaret's, Twickenham
St Mary Church, Lambeth
St Serf's House, Roehampton
Sanderstead Court, Croydon
Sayes Court, Deptford
Selsdon, Croydon

Sheen, Richmond
Sheen. Palace
Sheen Lodge, Richmond
Sheffield House, Kensington
Shirley House, Croydon
Shirley Vicarage, Croydon
Shrewsbury House, Greenwich
Sir John Oldcastle Tavern, Camden
Somerset House, Strand
South Lodge, Enfield
Southgate Grove, Enfield
Southgate House, Enfield
Southgate Lodge, Enfield
Southwood, Bickley
Southwood Hall, Highgate
Spa Fields Pantheon, Clerkenwell
Spaniards Inn, Hampstead
Spedan Tower, Hampstead
Spring Garden, Stepney
Spring Gardens, Charing Cross
Spring Gardens, Vauxhall
Spring Grove, Hounslow
Stafford House, Stanmore
Star and Garter Tavern, Westminster
Stewards Park, Romford
Stoke Newington (T. Gudgeon)
Stonard House, Stamford Hill
Strawberry Hill, Twickenham
Streatham, Lambeth
Strombole House, Chelsea
Stubbers, North Ockendon
Sudbrooke Cottage, Ham
Sundridge Park, Bromley
Surbiton Place
Surrey Zoological Gardens, Southwark
Swakeleys, Uxbridge
Syon Hill, Hounslow
Syon House, Hounslow
Teddington Grove, Twickenham
Telegraph Cottage, Kingston Hill
Temple of Flora, Lambeth
Tewkesbury Lodge, Forest Hill
Thorndon Lodge, Camden
Thrale Place, Streatham
Totteridge Park, Barnet
Tower of London
Trent Park, Barnet
Twickenham (T. Hudson)
Twickenham (I. Swainson)
Twickenham Meadows
Twickenham Park
Twyford Abbey, Ealing
Upton House, Stratford
Vale Mascal, Bexley
Valentines, Ilford
Vauxhall Gardens, Lambeth
Village Place, Beckenham
Waddon House, Croydon
Walham Green (J. Ord), Fulham
Wallwood House, Leytonstone
Walpole House, Chiswick
Walthamstow House, Waltham Forest
Wanstead Grove
Wanstead House
Warren House, Hayes
Warren House, Kingston
Warren House, Stanmore
Wembley, Harrow
West Drayton Manor, Hillingdon
West Farm, Barnet

West Hill, Wandsworth
Westcombe, Greenwich
Westminster Abbey Gardens
Westminster Palace
Westminster Physic Garden
White Conduit House, Islington
White House, Haringey
White Lodge, Richmond Park
White Webbs, Enfield
Whitechapel Botanical Garden
Whitehall Palace, Westminster
Whitton Place, Twickenham
Wicken Park, Croydon
Wickham Court, West Wickham
Wilderness, Croydon
Wilsley House, Cranbrook
Wimbledon House
Wimbledon Park
Winns, Walthamstow
Witanhurst, Highgate
Wood Hall, Sydenham
Wood House, Wanstead
Woodford Hall
Woodlands, Blackheath
Woodlands, Streatham
Woodside, Whetstone
Worcester Park, Sutton

(GREATER) MANCHESTER

Abney Hall, Cheadle
Agecroft Hall
Altrincham. Stamford Park
Ashfield House, Standish
Atherton Hall
Birch Hall, Bolton
Bramall Hall, Stockport
Brockhurst, Didsbury
Chadderton Hall
Cheadle. Bruntwood Park
Croft House, Ashton-under-Lyne
Didsbury Lodge
Dunham Massey Hall, Altrincham
Greenthorne, Bolton
Haigh Hall
Hall-i'-th'-Wood, Bolton
Heather Bank House, Cheadle
Heaton Park, Manchester
Hyde Hall, Denton
Irlam Hall
Longford Hall, Stretford
Manchester. Botanic Garden
Manchester. Victoria Park
Manley Hall, Manchester
Marple Hall
Oaklands House, Manchester
Oldham. Alexandra Park
Ordsall Hall, Manchester
Ravenhurst, Bolton
Rochdale. Falinge Park
Royton Hall
Shaw Hall, Eccles
Smithills Hall, Bolton
Stakehill House, Castleton
Standish Hall, Wigan
Stockport. Lyme Park
Summerfield, Bowdon
Towers, Didsbury
Trafford Park, Manchester

County Index

West Bank House, Heaton Mersey
Worsley Hall

MERSEYSIDE

Allerton Beeches, Liverpool
Allerton Tower, Liverpool
Bidston Priory, Birkenhead
Birkenhead. Public Park
Bromborough Hall, Bebington
Camp Hill, Liverpool
Charlwood House, Liverpool
Childwall Hall, Liverpool
Church Town Botanical Garden, Southport
Cleveley, Allerton
Croxteth, Prescot
Dawpool, Thurstaston
Dry Grange, Liverpool
Eccleston Hall, St Helens
Hale Hall, Speke
Handstyle House, Liverpool
Holmefield, Aigburth
Ince Blundell Hall
Knowsley Hall
Lee Hall, Gateacre
Liscard Hall, Birkenhead
Liverpool. Botanic Gardens
Liverpool. Princes Park
Liverpool. Sefton Park
Liverpool. Stanley Park
Meols Hall
Mosley Hill, Aigburth
Norris Green
Priory, Bidston
Roby Hall
Seaforth House
Southport. Hesketh Park
Speke Hall
Thornton Manor, Thornton Hough
Vinery House, Allerton
Wavertree Hall, Liverpool
Windle Hall, St Helens
Woolton Hall, Liverpool

NORFOLK

Baber (Bawburgh ?)
Barningham Hall, Holt
Barwick House, Fakenham
Bayfield Hall, Holt
Beeston
Bixley Park, Norwich
Blickling Hall, Aylsham
Bolwick Hall, Aylsham
Booton Hall, Aylsham
Bracondale Lodge, Norwich
Breccles Hall, Breckles
Bressingham Hall, Diss
Brooke Hall, Loddon
Brooke House, Loddon
Buckenham House
Burlingham Hall, Acle
Carrow Abbey
Carrow House
Catton Hall, Norwich
Colney Hall
Costessey Park
Crimplesham Hall, Downham Market
Cromer Hall
Denton House
Dereham
Didlington Hall, Northwold
Ditchingham Hall
Ditchingham House
Docking
Earlham Hall, Norwich
Earsham, Bungay
Easton Lodge
Elmham Park
Felbrigg Hall, Cromer
Felthorpe Park
Gillingham Hall
Gunthorpe Hall
Gunton
Hanworth Hall
Harford Hall
Haverland Park, Norwich
Hedenham Hall
Heydon, Aylsham
Hillington Hall
Holkham Hall
Home Place, Holt
Honing Hall
Honingham Hall
Horsford Hall
Houghton Hall
Hoveton Hall, Hoveton St Peter
Hoveton House, Hoveton St John
Hunstanton Hall
Intwood Hall
Kelling Place, Holt
Ken Hill, Snettisham
Keswick Hall
Ketteringham Park
Kimberley Hall
Kirby Cane Hall
Kirby Hall, Kirby Bedon
Langley Grange, Loddon
Langley Park
Larch Wood, Beachamwell
Letheringsett Hall
Letton Park
Lynford Hall
Lyng Rectory
Melton Constable
Melton Park
Mill House, Corpusty
Morton Hall
Narford Hall
Northrepps
Ormesby House
Overstrand Hall
Oxburgh Hall
Oxnead Hall
Pleasaunce, Overstrand
Plumstead Hall
Quidenham Park
Rackheath Park
Raveningham Hall
Raynham Hall, Fakenham
Riddlesworth Hall
Salhouse Hall
Salle Park, Sall
Sandringham
Scottow Park
Seeting Hall
Sennowe Park, Fakenham
Shadwell Park, Rushford
Sheringham Hall, Upper Sheringham
Shotesham Park
Somerton Hall
Spixworth Park
Sprowston Park
Stanfield Hall, Wymondham
Stratton Park
Stratton Strawless, Norwich
Sustead Old Hall, Sustead
Talbot Manor, Fincham
Taverham Hall
Thickthorn Hall, Hethersett
Thursford Hall
Tofts Hall, West Tofts
Tunstead Old House
Walsingham Abbey
Westacre High House, Swaffham
West Harling Hall
Westwick Park, North Walsham
Witchingham Hall, Reepham
Witton Park, North Walsham
Wiveton Hall
Wolterton Park, Aylsham
Wood Hall, Hilgay
Woodbastwick Hall, Norwich
Worstead House
Wroxham Hall
Wroxham House

NORTHAMPTONSHIRE

Abington Abbey, Northampton
Alderton
Aldwincle
Althorp
Apethorne Hall, Wansford
Arthingworth
Ashley
Astrop
Aynhoe Park
Barnwell Manor
Barton Seagrave
Biggin Hall, Oundle
Blakesley Hall, Woodend
Blatherwycke
Boughton, Kettering
Bradden House
Brigstock
Brixworth Hall, Northampton
Broxkhall, Daventry
Broughton House
Bulwick Hall, Oundle
Canons Ashby
Carham Hall
Carlton House
Castle Ashby
Catesby
Collyweston
Coton Manor
Cotterstock Hall, Oundle
Cottesbrooke Hall, Brixwroth
Courteenhall, Northampton
Dallington House, Northampton
Deene Park, Rockingham
Delapré Abbey, Northampton
Dingley Hall, Market Harborough
Dodford
Dover House, Northampton

County Index

Dower House, Northampton
Drayton House, Kettering
East Haddon Hall
Easton Maudit
Easton Neston, Towcester
Easton-on-the-Hill
Eastwood
Ecton Hall
Edgcote
Eydon Hall
Eyebury
Farmingwoods, Oundle
Fawsley Hall
Finedon Hall
Flore House
Fotheringhay
Friars Well, Aynho
Gayton
Geddington
Glendon Hall, Kettering
Grafton Regis
Grafton Underwood
Great Doddington
Great Oakley Hall, Kettering
Great Purston, Newbottle
Greatworth
Greens Norton
Guilsborough Grange
Halse, Brackley
Handley, Towcester
Hardwick
Harlestone Park
Harrington Hall
Harringworth
Harrowden Hall
Hartwell
Haselbech Hall
Helmdon
Hemington
Higham Ferrers
Holdenby House
Horton House
Kelmarsh Hall
King's Cliffe
Kirby Hall, Gretton
Lamport Hall
Laxton Hall
Lilford Hall
Lyvedon New Bield, Oundle
Maidwell Hall
Marholm
Moor-End
Moulton
Naseby Woolleys
Newnham Hall
Newton, Little Newton
Norton Hall, Daventry
Overstone Hall
Paulerspury
Plumpton Park
Potterspury
Preston Deanery
Redwell, Wellingborough
Rockingham Castle
Rushton Hall
Shipley
Shuthanger
Silverstone
Southwick Hall
Steane Park

Stoke Albany
Stoke Park, Stoke Bruerne
Stowe Nine Churches
Strixton
Sulby, Market Harborough
Sulgrave Manor
Thornhaugh
Thorpe Hall, Peterborough
Thorpe Mandeville Manor
Torpel
Wakefield Lodge, Potterspury
Wakerley, Luffenham
Walcott House, Stamford
Walgrave
Watford Court
Weldon
Welton Place
Whittlebury
Wicken Park
Woodford
Yardley Hastings

NORTHUMBERLAND

Alnwick Castle
Angerton Hall, Morpeth
Aydon Castle
Beaufront Castle, Hexham
Belford
Belsay Castle, Morpeth
Blagdon, Seaton Burn
Callaly Castle
Capheaton
Carham Hall
Chesterholme Cottage
Chesters, Humshaugh
Chillingham Castle
Chipchase Castle, Bellingham
Coupland Castle, Wooler
Cragside, Rothbury
Cresswell House
Dilston Castle
Eglingham Hall
Eslington Hall, Whittingham
Etal Manor
Featherstone Castle
Ford Castle
Goosewells, Belford
Herterton House, Cambo
Hesleyside, Bellingham
Holeyn Hall, Wylam
Howick Hall
Kilbryde, Corbridge
Kirkharle
Lilburn Tower
Lindisfarne Castle, Holy Island
Longhurst
Meldon Hall
Milbourne Hall
Newton Hall, Stocksfield
Nunnykirk, Morpeth
Oakwood, Wylam
Rothley
Sandhoe, Hexham
Seaton Delaval, Blyth
Wallington Hall, Cambo
West Bitchfield
Whalton Manor
Whitfield Hall
Widdrington Castle

NOTTINGHAMSHIRE

Annesley, Mansfield
Averham Park, Newark
Babworth, East Retford
Beauvale, Basford
Berry Hill, Mansfield
Bestwood Lodge, Nottingham
Blyth, Worksop
Bulcote Manor
Bulwell Hall
Bunny Hall
Caunton Manor
Clifton Hall, Nottingham
Clipstone Park
Clumber Park, Worksop
Colwick Hall
Edwinstowe Hall
Flintham Hall
Grove Hall
Haughton, Tuxford
Headon Hall
Hodsock Priory, Blyth
Holme Pierrepont Hall, Nottingham
Kelham Hall
Kingston Hall, Kingston on Soar
Newdigate House, Nottingham
Newstead Abbey
Nottingham (Marshal Tallard)
Nottingham. Colwick Park
Nottingham. University
Nuthall Temple, Nottingham
Osberton, Worksop
Owthorpe
Papplewick Hall
Pierrepont House, Nottingham
Rufford Abbey, Ollerton
Serlby Hall, Blyth
Shireoaks Hall
Stanford Hall
Tabramhill Gardens, Nottingham
Thoresby Park, Ollerton
Thrumpton Hall
Wallingwells, Worksop
Wansley Park, Brinsley
Welbeck Abbey, Worksop
West Retford House
Wilford Hall
Winthorpe Hall
Wiseton Hall
Wollaton Hall
Worksop Manor

OXFORDSHIRE

Adderbury
Adwell House, Tetsworth
Ambrosden, Islip
Appleton Manor
Ardington House, Wantage
Ashbury Manor
Ashdown House, Lambourn
Aston Rowant House
Baldon House, Oxford
Bampton Manor
Barton Abbey, Steeple Aston
Beckett, Shrivenham
Bicester House
Blackfriars, Oxford

County Index

Blenheim Palace, Woodstock
Britwell Salome
Brook Cottage, Alkerton
Broughton Castle, Banbury
Bruern Abbey, Churchill
Buckland House, Faringdon
Burford Priory
Buscot House, Faringdon
Castle House, Deddington
Chastleton House, Chipping Norton
Checkendon Court
Chislehampton House, Abingdon
Coach House, Little Haseley
Cogges Manor Farm
Cokethorpe Park, Witney
Coleshill
Compton Beauchamp
Cornbury Park, Charlbury
Cornwell Manor, Kingham
Court Farm, Little Haseley
Cowley House, Oxford
Crowsley Park, Rotherfield
Culham Manor
Cumnor Place
Ditchley Park, Woodstock
Dornford
Enstone
Epwell Mill, Banbury
Ewelme Down
Eynsham Hall
Faringdon House
Finmere Rectory
Friar Park, Henley-on-Thames
Garsington Manor
Glympton Park
Great Tews
Greenlands, Henley-on-Thames
Greys Court, Henley-on-Thames
Ham, Wantage
Hamels, Oxford
Hanwell
Hardwick House, Whitchurch
Haseley Court, Little Haseley
Headington Hill Hall
Heythrop, Chipping Norton
Hinton Waldrist
Home Close, Sibford
Hook End Farm, Checkendon
Hook Norton Manor
Islip Rectory
Jarn Mound Gardens, Oxford
Kelmscott Manor, Kelmscott
Kiddington
Kidlington
Kingston House, Kingston Bagpuize
Kingston Lisle Park, Wantage
Kirtlington Park
Lime Close, Drayton
Lockinge, Wantage
Manor House, Bampton
Manor House, Clifton Hampden
Manor House, Milton
Manor House, Sutton Courtenay
Mapledurham House
Marndhill, Ardington
Marsh Baldon House
Middleton Park, Middleton Stoney
Mill House, Sutton Courtenay
Milton Manor, Milton
Mongewell, Wallingford

Nuneham Park, Nuneham Courtenay
Old Forge, Henley-on-Thames
Old School, Langford
Oxford. Botanic Garden
Oxford. All Souls College
Oxford. Balliol College
Oxford. Brasenose College
Oxford. Christ Church College
Oxford. Corpus Christi College
Oxford. Exeter College
Oxford. Gloucester Hall
Oxford. Jesus College
Oxford. Keble College
Oxford. Lady Margaret Hall
Oxford. Lincoln College
Oxford. Magdalen College
Oxford. Merton College
Oxford. New College
Oxford. Oriel College
Oxford. Pembroke college
Oxford. Queen's College
Oxford. St Catherine's College
Oxford. St Hilda's College
Oxford. St Hugh's College
Oxford. St John's College
Oxford. Somerville College
Oxford. Trinity College
Oxford. University College
Oxford. Wadham College
Oxford. Worcester College
Paradise, Oxford
Park Place, Henley-on-Thames
Pusey House, Faringdon
Radley
Rest Hill Farm, Over Worton
Rousham House
Rycote, Thame
St Nicholas, Wallingford
Sandford Park, Sandford-on-Thames
Sarsden Glebe
Shiplake Court
Shipton Court, Shipton-under-Wychwood
Shirburn Castle
Shotover House, Oxford
Stanton Harcourt, Witney
Stonor Park
Studley Priory
Swerford. Old Rectory
Swinbrook House
Thame. Pearce Memorial Garden
Thame Park
Troy, Ewelme
Troy Farm, Somerton
Tusmore House
Tythrop House, Thame
Wallingford
Water Eaton Manor
Waterstock Manor
Watlington Park
Weald Manor, Bampton
Weston Manor
Westwell Manor
Wheatfield Manor
Whichford House, Chipping Norton
Whitefield, Tetsworth
Wilcote House, Finstock
Wilcote Manor, Finstock
Wood Croft, Boars Hill
Woodperry, Oxford

Woodstock Park
Wroxton Abbey, Banbury
Wytham Abbey
Yarnton Manor
Yeldhall Manor, Henley-on-Thames
Yewdon Manor, Henley-on-Thames

SHROPSHIRE

Acton Burnell
Acton Reynald
Adcote
Aldenham Park, Bridgnorth
Altingham Hall, Shrewsbury
Apley Park, Bridgnorth
Ashford Court, Ashford Carbonel
Astley Abbotts House, Bridgnorth
Attingham Park
Beamish, Albrighton
Beckbury Hall, Shifnal
Benthall Hall, Broseley
Berwick, Shrewsbury
Boscobel House, Shifnal
Broncroct Castle, Craven Arms
Buntingsdale, Market Drayton
Burford House, Tenbury Wells
Burwarton Howe, Ditton Priors
Cainham Court, Ludlow
Clovelley Hall, Whitchurch
Condover Hall
Court of Hill, Tenbury
Dairy House, Ludstone
Davenport House, Bridgnorth
Downton Hall, Ludlow
Dudmaston, Bridgnorth
Dunval Hall, Bridgnorth
Eyton on Severn, Much Wenlock
Ferney Hall, Ludlow
Gatacre, Six Ashes
Golding Manor, Shrewsbury
Habberley Hall, Shrewsbury
Halston, Oswestry
Hardwick Hall, Shrewsbury
Hardwicke Grange, Shrewsbury
Hatton Grange, Shifnal
Hawkstone Park, Wem
Henley Hall, Tasley
High Ercall
Hodnef Hall
Lilleshall Hall, Newport
Limeburners, Ironbridge
Linley Hall
Lodge, Ludlow
Longford Hall
Longnor Hall
Lower Hall, Worfield
Ludstone Hall, Claverley
Lythe, Ellesmere
Madeley Court
Maer Hall
Magnolias, Merrington
Mawley Hall, Cleobury Mortimer
Millichope Park, Munslow
Morleys, Wallsbank
Morville Hall
Oakly Park, Ludlow
Old Bell House, Ludford
Ofeley Park, Ellesmere
Peplow Hall, Hodnet

298

County Index

Pitchford Hall
Plaish Hall
Plowden Hall
Parkington, Oswestry
Sansaw Hall, Clive
Shavington Hall, Market Drayton
Shrewsbury. Quarry Park
Sibdon Castle
Stanley Hall, Bridgnorth
Stokesay Castle
Stokesay Court
Sundorne Castle, Shrewsbury
Sweeney Hall, Oswestry
Tedsmore Hall, Oswestry
Tong Castle
Upper Shelderton House, Clungunford
Walcot Hall
Wenlock Abbey, Much Wenlock
Whitehall, Shrewsbury
Whitton Court
Willey, Bridgnorth

SOMERSET

Abbey House, Glastonbury
Bales's Mead, Porlock
Barford House, Bridgwater
Barley Wood, Wrington
Barrington Court, Ilminster
Barwick Park, Yeovil
Bruton Abbey
Brympton D'Everly, Yeovil
Burton Pynsent, Langport
Butleigh Court
Cadbury House
Cadbury Manor
Camerton Court
Castle Farm, Ilchester
Chantry, Whatley
Clapton Court, Crewkerne
Coker Court, East Coker
Cothay Manor, Greenham
Cothelstone, Taunton
Cranmore Hall, Wells
Crowcombe Court, Watchet
Crowcombe Rectory, Watchet
Dillington House, Ilminster
Dunster Castle
Earnshill, Langport
East Lambrook Manor
Ellicombe, Williton
Enmore Castle, Bridgwater
Fairfield, Bridgwater
Farleigh House
Gaulden Manor, Tolland
Glastonbury Abbey
Glastonbury. Abbot's Lodgings
Goathurst, Enmore
Hadspen House, Castle Cary
Halswell, Goathurst
Hardington, Frome
Hatch Court, Hatch Beauchamp
Hestercombe, Taunton
Hill House, Langport
Hinton House, Hinton St George
Inwood House, Stalbridge
Kingweston
Low Ham

Lytes Cary, Ilchester
Manor House, Mells
Marlands, Sampford Arundel
Marston House, Marston Bigott
Mells Park
Midelney Manor, Langport
Milton Lodge, Wells
Montacute House
Nettlecombe Court
Newton Surmaville, Yeovil
Nynehead Court
Orchard Portman
Orchadleigh Park, Frome
Pilton Manor
Poundisford Lodge, Taunton
Poundisford Park, Taunton
Redlynch, Wincanton
Rimpton, Yeovil
St Audries, Watchet
Sandhill Park, Bishop's Lydeard
Selwood Cottage, Frome
Shapwick
South Hill House, Mendips
Southill, Wanstrow
Ston Easton Park
Stowell Hill, Templecombe
Tintinhull House, Yeovil
Underway, Porlock
Ven House, Milborne Port
Wayford Manor
Wells. Bishop's Palace
West Coker, Yeovil
Yarlington Lodge, Wincanton

STAFFORDSHIRE

Aldershaw, Lichfield
Alton Towers
Alveston
Aqualate Hall
Armitage Park
Ashcombe Park, Leek
Aston Hall, Stone
Ball Haye
Barlaston Hall, Stone
Basford Hall, Leek
Beaudesert, Lichfield
Beauhurst Hall
Bellamour House
Belmont
Biddulph Grange
Bishton Hall, Rugeley
Blithfield Hall, Abbots Bromley
Broughton Hall, Eccleshall
Burton on Trent Abbey
Canwell Hall, Tamworth
Caverswall
Chartley, Stafford
Darlaston Hall
Drayton Manor, Drayton Bassett
Eccleshall Castle
Elford Hall
Elmhurst Hall, Congleton
Enfield Hall
Enville Hall
Etruria, Stoke-on-Trent
Fisherwick
Freeford, Lichfield
Hamstead Mount

Hanch Hall, Lichfield
Hawkesyard Park, Armitage
Heath House, Tean
Hilton Park, Essington
Himley Hall
Hoar Cross Hall, Burton upon Trent
Ilam Hall
Ingestre Hall
Ingestre Rectory
Keele Hall
King's Bromley, Lichfield
Knypersley Hall
Lisways Hall, Lichfield
Little Aston Hall, Lichfield
Little Onn Hall, Church Eaton
Little Wyrley Hall
Loxley Hall
Madeley Manor
Manley Hall, Lichfield
Maples Hayes, Lichfield
Meaford Hall, Meaford
Milford Hall, Baswich
Moat Bank, Lichfield
Moss House, Shenstone
Okeover Hall
Oldershaw, Lichfield
Packington Hall, Lichfield
Patshull, Wolverhampton
Prestwood
Rangemore Hall
Rolleston Hall
Sandon Hall
Shawms, Stafford
Shenstone
Shenstone Court
Shugborough, Stafford
Smethwick Grove
Spring Vale, Stone
Stretton Hall
Sugnall, Eccleshall
Swinfen, Lichfield
Swynnerton Park
Teddesley, Penkridge
Tixall
Trentham Park
Tutbury Castle
Weston Park, Weston under Lizard
Westwood House, Leek
Whitmore Hall, Whitmore
Willoughbridge, Elds Wood
Wolseley Hall, Rugeley
Woodseat, Uttoxeter
Wootton Hall
Wootton Lodge
Wrottesley, Wolverhampton

SUFFOLK

Ampton Hall
Ashe High House, Wickham Market
Ashman's Hall, Beccles
Aspall Hall, Debenham
Bacton Hall
Barton Hall, Bury St Edmunds
Bawdsey
Benacre Hall, Southwold
Benhall Lodge, Saxmundham
Benton End, Hadleigh
Brampton Hall

County Index

Branches Park near Newmarket
Brightwell, Ipswich
Broke Hall, Ipswich
Brome Hall, Eye
Bury St Edmunds Abbey
Butley Priory
Campsea Ash
Chandos Lodge, Eye
Chequers, Boxford
Christchurch Manor, Ipswich
Clare Priory
Cockfield Hall
Coldham Hall, Bury St Edmunds
Cottage Farm, Little Blakenham
Crowfield, Needham Market
Crow's Hall, Debenham
Culford, Bury St Edmunds
Dalham Hall, Higham
Drinkstone Park, Stowmarket
East Bergholt Place
Easton Park
Elvedon, Thetford
Erwarton Hall
Euston Hall
Finborough Hall
Flixton Hall
Fornham, Bury St Edmunds
Giffords Hall, Nayland
Gipping Hall, Stowmarket
Glemham Hall
Glevering Hall, Easton
Grey Friars, Dunwich
Hardwick House, Bury St Edmunds
Harkstead, Ipswich
Haughley Park
Hawstead, Bury St Edmunds
Helmingham Hall
Hengrave Hall
Henham Hall
Henham Old Hall
Henstead, Beccles
Heveningham Hall
Hintlesham Hall
Holbecks, Hadleigh
Hurts Hall, Saxmundham
Ickworth, Bury St Edmunds
Ipswich (W.B. Coyte)
Kentwell Hall, Sudbury
Leaden Hall, Leavenheath
Lime Kiln, Claydon
Little Blakenham
Little Glemham
Little Haugh Hall, Norton
Livermere Park
Magnolia House, Yoxford
Marlesford Hall
Melford Hall, Long Melford
Moulton Paddocks
Nacton
Nether Hall, Bury St Edmunds
Nowton Court
Oakley Park, Eye
Old Hall, East Bergholt
Old Hall, Shadingfield
Old Rectory, Orford
Orwell Park
Otley Hall
Parham Old Hall
Plashwood, Stowmarket
Plumpton House, Whepstead

Redgrave Hall
Regal Lodge, Kentford
Rendlesham Hall
Rougham Hall
Rushbrooke Hall
St Peter's Home, Woolverstone
Saxham Hall, Great Saxham
Seckford Hall, Woodbridge
Shrubland Park, Coddenham
Somerleyton Hall
Sotterley Hall
South Bank, Ipswich
Sproughton Chantry, Ipswich
Sternfield House, Saxmundham
Stoke College, Stoke by Clare
Stone Hall, Euston
Stowlangtoft Hall
Sudbourne Hall
Tendring Hall, Stoke-by-Nayland
Warren Towers, Newmarket
West Wood, Walberswick
Wherstead Park
Wingfield Castle
Witnesham Hall
Woolverstone Park, Ipswich
Worlingham Hall

SURREY

Abinger Hall
Adair Place, Englefield Green
Addlestone Lodge, Chertsey
Albury House
Albury Park
Alderbrook Park, Cranleigh
Aldworth, Haslemere
Apps Court, Walton-on-Thames
Ardenrun, Blindley Heath
Ashley Park, Walton-on-Thames
Ashtead Park, Epsom
Badger's Rake, Hascombe
Bagshot Park, Ascot
Bank Grove, Kingston
Betchworth Castle, Reigate
Betchworth House, Reigate
Botleys, Chertsey
Boyle Farm, Thames Ditton
Bradeston Brook House, Shalford
Briar Cottage, Horsell
Bridge House, Weybridge
Bron-y-De, Churt
Buckland, Reigate
Burford Lodge, Dorking
Burwood House, Cobham
Burwood Park, Wilton
Bury Hill, Dorking
Busbridge, Godalming
Busbridge Wood, Hascombe
Byfleet (J. Spence)
Castle Hill, Englefield Green
Charles Hill Court, Tilford
Cherkley Court, Leatherhead
Chertsey Abbey
Chilworth Manor, Guildford
Chinthurst Hill, Bramley
Chobham Place
Chussex, Walton Heath
Clandon Park, Guildford
Claremont, Esher

Clive House, Esher
Cobham Park
Cooksbridge, Fernhurst
Cooper's Hill, Englefield Green
Coverwood, Ewhurst
Crooksbury House, Farnham
Crowhurst Place, Edenbridge
Deepdene, Dorking
Dell, Egham
Denbies, Dorking
Denbry House, Haslemere
Derry's Wood, Wonersh
Dormey House, Walton Heath
Down Lodge, Epsom
Downside, Leatherhead
Drynham, Walton-on-Thames
Duneevan, Walton-on-Thames
Durdans, Epsom
Eashing Park, Godalming
East Horsley Towers
Eastwick Park, Leatherhead
Effingham House, Leatherhead
Elvills, Englefield Green
Ember Court, Thames Ditton
Enton Lodge, Witley
Epsom (J. Diston)
Epsom. New Inn Lane
Esher Place
Ewell Castle
Ewell Grove
Eyot House, Weybridge
Farnham Castle
Feathercombe, Hambledon
Fetcham Park
Fir Grange, Weybridge
Fisher's Hill, Woking
Foldsdown, Thursley
Fort Belvedere, Virginia Water
Fox Hill, Chertsey
Frog's Island, Walton Heath
Fulbrook House, Elstead
Gatton Park, Reigate
Glenhurst, Esher
Goddards, Abinger Common
Grange, Farnham
Grayswood Hill, Haslemere
Great Fosters, Egham
Great Tangley Manor, Guildford
Grove, Epsom
Guildford Castle
Ham House, Weybridge
Hampton Lodge, Seale
Hartsfield, Betchworth
Hascombe Court
Hatch, Churt
Hatchford Park, Cobham
Hatchlands, East Clandon
Hazelhatch, Shere
Headley Court, Epsom
Heath House, Headley
Heatherbank, Weybridge
Heights, Witley
Hethersett, Seale
High Ashurst, Mickleham
High Trees, Redhill
Highmount, Guildford
Hillfield Gardens, Reigate
Hindhead Court, Haslemere
Hitherbury, Guildford
Holmesdale House, Reigate

Home Place, Limpsfield
Hurtside, Molesey
Hurtwood, Holmbury St Mary
Hut, Godalming
Imber Court, Thames Ditton
Joldwynds, Gomshall
Keffolds, Haslemere
Kempton Park, Kingston
King's House Garden, Burhill
Kingswood Lodge, Egham
Kingswood Warren
Knowle, Cranley
Laleham
Lascombe, Puttenham
Lea, Godalming
Leigh Place, Godstone
Leith Hill Place, Dorking
Lennoxwood, Windlesham
Lightwater Manor, Bagshot
Limpsfield
Little Holme, Guildford
Little Tangley, Wonersh
Littleton, Staines
Long View, Reigate
Laseley, Guildford
Lyne, Newdigate
Lythe Hill, Haslemere
Manor House, Stoke D'Abernon
Marden Park, Caterham
Merrow Grange
Mickleham Hall
Millmead, Bramley
Millwater, Ripley
Milton Court, Dorking
Moor Park, Farnham
Mount Felix, Walton-on-Thames
Munstead Oaks, Godalming
Munstead Orchard, Godalming
Munstead Place, Godalming
Munstead Wood, Godalming
Mynthurst, Reigate
New Chapel House, Lingfield
New Place, Haslemere
Norbury Place, Dorking
Nork, Binstead
Oaks, Woodmansterne
Oatlands, Weybridge
Ockham Mill, Ripley
Ockham Park, Ripley
Orchards, Godalming
Ottershaw Park
Ouborough, Godstone
Oxenford Grange, Peper Harow
Painshill, Cobham
Painshill Cottage
Pasturewood House, Holmbury St Mary
Pendell Court, Redhill
Peper Harow, Godalming
Pierrepont, Farnham
Pinehanger, Farnham
Pinewood House, Woking
Pixholme Court, Dorking
Podenhale, Wentworth
Polesden Lacey, Great Bookham
Poyle Park, Farnham
Priory, Reigate
Pyrford Court
Quadrangle, Munstead
Ramster, Chiddingfold
Randalls Park, Leatherhead

Red House, Effingham
Red House, Godalming
Redford, Ockley
Ridgemead, Englefield Green
Rivernook, Staines
Rookery, Dorking
Rook's Nest, Dorking
Ropes, Haslemere
Royal Horticultural Society Gardens, Wisley
Ruckmans, Oakwood Hill
Ruxley Lodge, Esher
St Ann's Hill, Chertsey
St George's Hill, Weybridge
Sandhills, Bletchingley
Sandhouse, Witley
Shabden Park, Redhill
Shalford House, Guildford
Shepperton
Slyfield Manor, Leatherhead
Stilemans, Godalming
Stoke Park, Guildford
Stroud House, Haslemere
Sullingstead, Hascombe
Sunbury House
Sunbury Place
Sunbury Villa
Sutton Place, Guildford
Tandridge Court, Godstone
Tangley Manor, Guildford
Thames Ditton (Sir T. Heathcote)
Thorncroft, Leatherhead
Tigbourne Court, Witley
Tillingbourne, Dorking
Titsey Place
Trevereux, Limpfield
Try Hill, Chertsey
Upper Gatton Park
Valewood, Haslemere
Valewood Farm, Lurgashall
Vann, Hambledon
Walton House, Walton-on-Thames
Warling Dean, Esher
Warren Lodge, Thursley
Waverley Abbey, Farnham
West Hall, Byfleet
West Horsley Place, Leatherhead
Westbrook, Godalming
Westwoods, Windlesham
Wiggie, Redhill
Wigmore Park, Dorking
Windlesham Moor
Windlesham Park
Windycroft, Godalming
Winkworth Arboretum, Godalming
Winkworth Farm, Hascombe
Witley Park
Wo Yuen, Milford
Woburn Farm, Addlestone
Woburn Place, Addlestone
Wonersh Park, Guildford
Wonham House, Godstone
Wood End, Witley
Woodcote Park, Epsom
Woodhatch, Reigate
Woolpits, Shere
Wotton House, Dorking

SUSSEX, EAST

Albourne Place, Brighton
Ashburnham Place, Battle
Barleys, Lewes
Bateman's, Burwash
Battle Abbey
Bayham Abbey
Beauport, Battle
Bentley, Halland
Bohemia Park, Hastings
Brickwall, Northiam
Brightling, Battle
Brighton. Athenaeum and Oriental Gardens
Brighton. Brown's Gardens
Brighton. German Spa
Brighton. Hollingbury Park
Brighton. Ireland's Royal Brighton Gardens
Brighton. Kemp Town Gardens
Brighton. Preston Park
Brighton. Promenade Grove
Brighton. Queen's Park
Brighton. Royal Pavilion
Brighton. Steine
Brighton. Victoria Gardens
Buckhurst Park, Withyham
Buxted Park
Charleston Manor, Seaford
Chelwood Manor
Cobblers, Crowborough
Compton Place, Eastbourne
Court Lodge, Groombridge
Crowhurst, Battle
Eridge Castle, Frant
Firle Place
Firle Vicarage
Folkington
Glynde Place
Glyndebourne
Grange, Rottingdean
Great Dixter, Northiam
Great Wigsell, Robertsbridge
Heathfield Park
Heron's Ghyll, Uckfield
Herstmonceux Castle
Highlands, Ticehurst
Holly Hill, Forest Row
Hoo, Willingdon
Horsted Place
Houndsell Place, Wadhurst
Houndstall House, Mark Cross
Hove. Athaeum
Hove. Brunswick Square
Hove. Chalybeate Spring
Iridge Place, Etchingham
Laines, Plumpton
Lamb House, Rye
Leyswood, Crowborough
Lower Sandhill, Halland
Manor House, Hove
Michelham Priory, Hailsham
Normanhurst, Battle
Old Lodge, Nutley
Old Vicarage, Firle
Oldlands Hall, Uckfield
Ote Hall, Wivelsfield
Penns in the Rocks, Groombridge
Plumpton Place

County Index

Possingworth. Waldron
Rotherfield Hall
Saxonbury Lodge, Tunbridge Wells
Sharnden, Mayfield
Sheffield Park, Uckfield
Shepherd's Hill, Uckfield
Shernfold Park, Frant
Stanmer Park, Brighton
Swanborough Manor, Lewes
Twitts Ghyl, Mayfield
Uckfield House, Uckfield
Whiligh, Etchingham
White House on the Cliff, Roedean
Willingham House, Ringmer
Windmill Hill, Wartling
Wootton Manor, Polegate
Wych Cross Place, Forest Row

SUSSEX, WEST

Aldingbourne House, Chichester
Arundel Castle
Ashdown, East Grinstead
Barton St Mary, East Grinstead
Beach House, Worthing
Beechwood, Lavington
Beedingwood, Beeding
Bignor Park, Petworth
Birch Grove House, Haywards Heath
Blackdown House, Haslemere
Borde Hill, Cuckfield
Bowhill, Chichester
Brambletye, East Grinstead
Brockhurst, East Grinstead
Burton Park, Petworth
Chestham Park, Henfield
Chidmere House, Chidham
Chithurst
Coates Manor, Fittleworth
Comptons Brow, Horsham
Cooke's House, West Burton
Coolhurst, Horsham
Cowdray Park, Midhurst
Cuckfield Park
Cuckfield Place
Dale Park, Arundel
Danny, Hurstpierpoint
Denmans, Chichester
Denne Park, Horsham
Ditton Place, Balcombe
Duckyls, East Grinstead
Dulany Cottage, Patching
Dutton Homestalls, East Grinstead
Eartham House, Chichester
Felbridge Place, East Grinstead
Fiddlers Copse, Plaistow
Field Place, Horsham
Finches, Lindfield
Fishbourne, Chichester
Ghyll Manor, Rusper
Goodwood, Chichester
Gravetye Manor, East Grinstead
Great Surries, Ashurstwood
Halnaker Park, Chichester
Handcross Park, Cuckfield
Heaselands, Haywards Heath
Henfield (W. Borrer)
Hickstead Place, Twineham
High Beeches, Crawley

Highdown, Goring
Hills
Holmbush, Beeding
Home House, Worthing
Homestall, East Grinstead
Hyde near Handcross
Imberhorne Park, East Grinstead
Kidbrooke Park, East Grinstead
Knepp Castle, Horsham
Lavington Park
Leonardslee, Horsham
Little Green, Compton
Little Thakeham, Pulborough
Manor House, Earnley
Manor of Dean, Tillington
Michel Grove, Arundel
Midhurst. King Edward VII Sanitorium
Mill House, Fittleworth
Monkton House, Singleton
Moonhill, Cuckfield
Mount, Ifield
Muntham Court, Findon
Newtimber Place
Nymans, Handcross
Oakwood, Funtington
Ockenden, Cuckfield
Offington Park, Worthing
Old Buckhurst House, East Grinstead
Old Place, Lindfield
Old Surrey Hall, East Grinstead
Paddockhurst, Worth
Parham Park
Pax Hill, Lindfield
Petworth House
Racton Tower, Chichester
Rowfant, East Grinstead
Rymans, Chichester
St Roche's Arboretum, West Dean
Sandgate Lodge, Sullington
Sedgwick Park, Horsham
Sennicots, Funtington
Shermanbury Park
Shillinglee Park, Fisherstreet
Slaugham Place
Slindon House
South Lodge, Horsham
Standen, East Grinstead
Stansted Park, Chichester
Stonelands, East Grinstead
Sunte House, Haywards Heath
Sutton End, Petworth
Swiss Gardens, New Shoreham
Telegraph House, Compton
Tilgate House, Crawley
Treemans, Horsted Keynes
Uppark, South Harting
Valewood Farm, Lurgashall
Wakehurst Place, Ardingly
Warnham Court
West Burton, Arundel
West Dean, Chichester
West Grinstead Park
Wiston Park
Woolbeding House
Worth Park
Worthing (J. Bateman)

TYNE AND WEAR

Anderson's Place, Newcastle upon Tyne
Ashburne House, Newcastle upon Tyne
Axwell Park, Blaydon
Barmston
Benwell Hall
Benwell Tower
Cheesburn Grange, Newcastle upon Tyne
Gibside, Rowlands Gill
Hylton Castle
Jesmond Dene
Newcastle upon Tyne (Sir W. Blackett)
Newcastle upon Tyne. Jesmond Cemetery
Newton Hall, Newcastle upon Tyne
Oakwood, Newcastle upon Tyne
Ravensworth Castle, Gateshead
South Shields. Harton Cemetery

WARWICKSHIRE

Admington Hall, Shipston on Stour
Alveston, Stratford-on-Avon
Arbury Hall, Nuneaton
Arlescote, Kineton
Armscote Manor, Ettington
Ashorne House
Astrop House, Frankton
Baddesley Clinton Hall
Badgers Cottage, Idlicote
Barford Hill
Barrels, Henley-in-Arden
Barton House
Beach Lawn, Leamington
Bickmarsh Hall, Bidford-on-Avon
Billesley Manor, Alcester
Bilton Hall, Rugby
Bithe Hall
Bradley House, Leamington
Budbrooke House, Warwick
Charlecote Park, Stratford-on-Avon
Cliff, Tamworth
Clifford Manor, Clifford Chambers
Clopton House, Stratford-on-Avon
Compton Verney
Compton Wynyates, Tysoe
Coughton Court, Alcester
Dunchurch Lodge, Rugby
Edgehill
Ettington Park
Farnborough Hall
Firs, Warwick
Foxcote, Shipston
Guy's Cliff, Warwick
Hams Hall, Coleshill
Haseley Manor
Hatton House
Hermitage, Priors Marston
Honiley, Warwick
Honington Hall
Ilmington Manor
Kenilworth Castle
Kissing Tree House, Alveston
Leicester Grange, Nuneaton
Lillington Manor, Leamington
Little Compton
Lower Eatington Hall, Shipston

County Index

Maxstoke Castle, Maxstoke
Merevale Hall, Meravale
Mill Garden, Warwick
Moreton Paddox, Moreton Morrell
Moxhull Hall, Coleshill
New Place, Stratford-on-Avon
Newnham Paddox, Rugby
Offchurch Bury
Old Rectory, Oxhill
Old Rectory, Whichford
Packington Hall
Priory, Leamington
Priory, Warwick
Radway Grange
Ragley Hall, Alcester
St Loe's, Henley-in-Arden
Salford Hall, Salford Priors
Savage's House, Bishops Tachbrook
Sherbourne Park
Shuckburgh Hall, Daventry
Snitterfield House
Stoneleigh Abbey
Studley Castle
Tysoe manor
Umberslade Hall, Henley-in-Arden
Upper Billesley, Stratford-on-Avon
Upton House, Edge Hill
Walton Hall, Stratford-on-Avon
Warwick Castle
Warwick Priory
Welcombe, Stratford-on-Avon
Weston, Kineton
Wootton Court, Warwick
Wootton Wawen Hall
Wroxall Abbey, Warwick

WEST MIDLANDS

Anstey Hall, Coventry
Aston Hall, Birmingham
Bankside, Sutton Coldfield
Barr Hall
Baskerville House, Birmingham
Bescot Hall, Walsall
Birmingham. Botanical Garden
Castle Bromwich Hall
Chillington Hall, Wolverhampton
Clent Hall, Stourbridge
Combe Abbey, Coventry
Court House, Birmingham
Coventry. London Road Cemetery
Davids, Northfield
Edgbaston, Birmingham
Fernwood, Birmingham
Four Oaks, Sutton Coldfield
Grimshaw Hall, Knowle
Hamstead, Birmingham
Highbury, Birmingham
Hillside, Four Oaks
Leasowes, Halesowen
Malvern Hall, Solihull
Moseley Hall, Birmingham
Moseley Old Hall, Wolverhampton
New Hall, Sutton Coldfield
Newbold Revel, Coventry
Old Swinford Castle
Oxley Manor, Wolverhampton
Packwood House, Hockley Heath
Penn Hall, Wolverhampton
Perry Hall, Sutton Coldfield
Sandwell Park, West Bromwich
Soho Manufactuary, Birmingham
Swallow Hayes, Wolverhampton
Uplands, Birmingham
Warley, Birmingham
Wergs Hall, Wolverhampton
Wightwick Manor, Wolverhampton
Woodgate, Sutton Coldfield

WILTSHIRE

Amesbury Abbey
Ashcombe, Tisbury
Avebury Manor
Basset Down House, Wootton Bassett
Belcombe Court, Bradford-on-Avon
Bemerton Rectory
Benacre Manor, Melksham
Berwick St John (Mr Foot)
Biddesden House, Ludgershall
Biddestone Manor, Chippenham
Bishop's Palace, Salisbury
Bishopstone House
Bolehyde Manor, Chippenham
Bowden Hill, Lacock
Bowood, Calne
boyton House, Heytesbury
Bridge House, Chilton Foliat
Broadleas, Potterne
Bulbridge House, Wilton
Castle Combe
Charlton Park, Malmesbury
Chisenbury Priory
Chute Lodge, Chute Forest
Clarendon Park, Salisbury
Clouds, Salisbury
Clyffe Hall, Market Lavington
Codford Manor
Cole Park, Malmesbury
Compton Park, Compton Chamberlayne
Conock Manor
Corsham Court
Corsley House
Courts. Holt
Devizes Castle
Dinton
Draycot House, Chippenham
Easton Grey House
Erlestoke Park, Devizes
Eyre's Folly, Whiteparish
Fonthill Abbey
Fonthill House
Frankleigh, Bradford-on-Avon
Fyfield Manor, Pewsey
Great Chalfield Manor
Hall, Bradford-on-Avon
Hampworth Lodge, Salisbury
Hartham Park, Chippenham
Hatch House, Hindon
Hazelbury Manor, Box
Heale House, Woodford
Heywood, Westbury
Hillbarn House, Great Bedwyn
Hungerdown House, Seagry
Iford Manor
Keevil Manor
Kellaways, Chippenham
Kingston House, Bradford-on-Avon
Lacock Abbey
Lake House, Wilsford
Larmer Gardens, Tollard Royal
Little Durnford, Wilton
Little Ridge, Tisbury
Littlecote Park, Hungerford
Longford Castle, Odstock
Longleat, Warminster
Lydiard, Lydiard Tregoze
Maiden Bradley House
Malmesbury House, Salisbury
Marlborough House, Preshute
Moot, Downton
Netheravon, Amesbury
New Park, Devizes
Newhouse, Downton
Notton Lodge, Lacock
Nunton House
Oare House
Ramsbury Manor
Reddish House, Broad Chalke
Richardson, Winterbourne Bassett
Rood Ashton, Trowbridge
Sevenhampton Place
Sheldon manor, Chippenham
Shute House, Donhead St Mary
South Wraxhall Manor
Spye Park, Calne
Standlynch Manor
Stanton Fitzwarren, Swindon
Stockton House
Stoke Park, Seend
Stourhead, Stourton
Tottenham Park, Marlborough
Trafalgar House, Salisbury
Upper Upham House
Urchfont Manor
Wardour Castle
Well House
Westrop House, Highworth
Westwood Manor House
Wilbury House, Newton Toney
Wilcot Manor
Wilsford Manor
Wilton House

YORKSHIRE, NORTH

Aldby Park, York
Arncliffe Hall, Northallerton
Ashton Hall
Aske Hall, Richmond
Baldersby Park, Ripon
Bear Park, Wensleydale
Bell Hall, Naburn
Belvedere, Harrogate
Beningbrough Hall, York
Bewerley House, Pateley Bridge
Birdsall
Bishopsbarns, York
Bishopsthorpe, York
Bolton Abbey, Ilkley
Bramley Grange, Ripon
Brough Hall, Richmond
Broughton Hall, Skipton
Carlton Towers
Carr Head, Skipton
Castle Howard, Malton
Clint Hall
Coghill, Harrogate

303

County Index

Constable Burton Hall, Leyburn
Cope Hewick
Crathorne Hall, Yarm
Danby Hall, Middleham
Denton Park
Duncombe Park, Hemsley
Easby Hall
Ebberston Hall
Elleron Lodge, Pickering
Elmcourt, Harrogate
Escrick Park
Eshton Hall
Farfield Hall, Bolton Abbey
Farnley Hall
Forcett Park
Fulford Hall
Gilling Castle
Gledstone Hall, Skipton
Goldsborough Hall
Grimston Park
Hackfall, Ripon
Hackness Hall
Halnaby Hall, Darlington
Halton Place
Harlow Car Gardens, Harrogate
Harlsey Hall, Northallerton
Harlsey Manor, Northallerton
Hazelwood Castle, Stutton
Heslington Hall, York
Hornby Castle
Hovingham Hall
Howsham Hall
Hutton Hall
Hutton Bonville Hall
Ingleborough (R. Farrer)
Ingleby Manor
Kepwick Hall, Thirsk
Kexby
Kildale Hall
Kildwick Hall
King's Manor, York
Kiplin Hall, Scorton
Kirkby Fleetham
Knapton
Lazenby Hall, Northallerton
Malsis Hall, Glusburn
Middlethorpe Hall, York
Middleton Lodge, Middleton Tyas
Mill Hill, Brandsby
Moreby Hall, Stillingfleet
Moulton Hall, Middleton Tyas
Moulton Manor, Middleton Tyas
Mulgrave Castle, Whitby
Naburn Hall
Nawton Tower
Newburgh Priory, Coxwold
Newby Hall
North Bierley Hall
North Grimston
Norton Conyers, Ripon
Nun Monkton Priory
Nunnington Hall
Otterington Hall
Otton Hall, Tadcaster
Parcevall Hall, Appletreewick
Peasholm Glen, Scarborough
Potholm, Eskdale
Ribston Hall
Rievault Terrace, Hemsley
Ripley Castle

Rounton Grange
Rudding Park, Harrogate
St Nicholas, Richmond
Sand Hutton Hall
Scampston Hall
Sedbury Hall, Gilling West
Sharrow Hall
Sheriff Hutton
Skipton Castle
Sleightholmedale Lodge, Fadmoor
Smeaton Manor, Northallerton
Sorrel Sykes Farm, Aysgarth
Stanwick Park, Richmond
Stonely Woods, Fadmoor
Stourton, Knaresborough
Studley Royal, Ripon
Sutton Park
Swarcliffe Hall, Ripley
Swinton Park, Masham
Thicket Priory, York
Thimbleby Hall
Thirkleby, Thirsk
Thornton Watlass, Bedale
Thorp Perrow, Firby
Upsall Castle
Valley Gardens, Harrogate
Welburn Hall
Whitby. Botanic Garden
Whixley
Wood End, Thirsk
Wycliffe Hall, Richmond
Wykeham Abbey
York. Treasurer's House
York. University

YORKSHIRE, SOUTH

Banks Hall, Barnsley
Banner Cross, Sheffield
Barnsley. Locke Park
Beauchief, Sheffield
Bessacre Manor
Bridge House, Sheffield
Brodsworth Hall, Doncaster
Cannon Hall, Barnsley
Carbrook Hall, Sheffield
Cusworth Hall, Doncaster
Darfield Rectory
Endcliffe Hall, Sheffield
Firbeck Hall
Hickleton
Hooton Roberts, Rotherham
Kiveton
Norwood Hall, Sheffield
Oakes Park, Norton
Oakholme, Sheffield
Owston Park
Ravenfield, Rotherham
Roche Abbey, Rotherham
Round Green House, Darfield
Sandbeck Park, Tickhill
Sheffield. Botanical Gardens
Shirecliffe Hall, Sheffield
Sprotborough Hall
Tankersley Park, Barnsley
Thornbury, Sheffield
Thrybergh Park, Rotherham
Thundercliffe Grange, Rotherham
Thurcroft, Rotherham

Totley Hall
Wadworth Hall
Warmsworth Hall
Wentworth Castle, Stainborough
Wentworth Woodhouse
Wheatley, Doncaster
Wortley Hall

YORKSHIRE, WEST

Allangate, Halifax
Armley (Gotts Park), Leeds
Arthington Hall
Badsworth Hall, Pontefract
Barratt's Botanic Garden, Wakefield
Bellevue, Halifax
Bermerside, Halifax
Bierley Hall, Oakenshaw
Bolton Royd, Bradford
Bowling Hall, Bradford
Bradford. Lister Park
Bradford. Oakworth Park
Bramham Park, Wetherby
Bretton Hall
Byram Hall, Ferrybridge
Chapel Allerton (R.A. Salisbury)
Chevet Park, Wakefield
Cliffe Castle, Keighley
Darrington
Denby Grange, Kirkheaton
Dungarth, Huddersfield
East Riddlesden Hall, Keighley
Elmet Hall, Leeds
Esholt Hall, Esholt
Ferniehurst, Shipley
Fixby Hall, Huddersfield
Gawthorpe, Leeds
Gledhow Hall, Leeds
Golden Acre Park, Leeds
Great Horton House, Bradford
Harewood House
Hawksworth, Otley
Heath Hall, Wakefield
Heathcote, Ilkley
Heaton Mount
High Fearnley, Bradford
Hollies, Leeds
Kettlethorpe Hall, Wakefield
Kippax Park
Kirkless Hall, Huddersfield
Knottfield House, Calverley
Ledston Hall
Leeds. Botanical Gardens
Ling Beeches, Scarcroft
Lotherton Hall, Aberford
Lupset Hall, Wakefield
Methley Hall
Milnerfield, Bingley
Milnes Bridge House, Huddersfield
Myddelton Lodge, Ilkley
Newton Green Hall, Leeds
Nostell Priory, Wakefield
Oakworth House, Keighley
Old Hall, Heath
Oulton Hall
Pierremount, Bradford
Pye Nest, Halifax
Roundhay Park, Leeds
Royds Hall, Bradford

County Index

Ryshworth Hall, Bingley
St Ives, Bingley
Seacroft Hall, Leeds
Shibden Hall, Halifax
Spofforth, Wetherby
Stapleton Park, Pontefract
Swillington Hall, Leeds
Temple Newsam, Leeds
Tong Hall
Uplands, Ben Rhydding
Walton Hall, Wakefield
Well Head Gardens, Halifax
Weston Hall, Otley
Whitley Beaumont, Upper Whitley
Woodleigh Hall, Rawdon
Woodsome Hall, Huddersfield
Woolley Hall
York Gate, Adel

Scotland

BORDERS

Abbey St Bathans, Duns
Abbotsford, Melrose
Arbigland
Ayton Castle
Barns, Manor
Belchester House, Eccles
Bemersyde, St Boswells
Birken Shaw
Blackadder House, Chirnside
Bowhill, Selkirk
Bridgelands, Selkirk
Broughton Place
Bughtrig, Coldstream
Chiefswood, Melrose
Cleuchheat House, Minto
Crailing Hall, Jedburgh
Dawyck, Stobo
Dryburgh Abbey, Melrose
Duns Castle
Easter Weens, Bonchester Bridge
Eden House, Ednam
Floors Castle, Kelso
Glen, Innerleithen
Glenburn Hall, Jedburgh
Grange, Lamancha
Haining, Selkirk
Haystoun, Peebles
Hirsel, Coldstream
Holmes, St Boswells
Houndwood House, Reston
Kailzie, Peebles
Kirklands, Ancrum
Lamanch, Newlands
Lambden, Greenlaw
Lochside, Yetholm
Mainhouse, Kelso
Manderston, Duns
Marchmont, Duns
Mellerstain, Gordon
Mertoun, St Boswells
Monteviot, Jedburgh
Neidpath Castle, Peebles
Netherbyres, Eyemouth
New Posso

Old Melrose
Paxton House
Philiphaugh, Selkirk
Priorwood, Melrose
Rawflat, Ancrum
Shortacres, Crailing
Sunderland Hall, Selkirk
Thirlestane Castle, Selkirk
Traquair House
Whim, Lamancha
Whitchester, Duns

CENTRAL

Airth Castle
Airthrey Castle
Argaty, Doune
Arngibbon, Port of Menteith
Aucheneck House, Killearn
Auchmar, Drymen
Bantaskin, Falkirk
Blair Drummon, Doune
Blairhoyle, Thornhill
Buchanan Castle, Drymen
Callander Lodge
Carnock, Stirling
Carron House
Cauldhame, Dunblane
Cowane's Hospital, Stirling
Culbuie, Bucklyvie
Deoran, Stirling
Dollarbeg, Dollar
Doune
Duchray Castle, Aberfoyle
Dunmore, Stirling
Duntreath Castle, Strathblane
Gargunnock House
Gartincaber, Doune
Gateside, Drymen
Harviestoun Castle, Dollar
Keir House, Dunblane
Kinnaird House, Larbert
Kippendavie, Dunblane
Larbert House
Leckie, Gargunnock
Montague Cottage, Blairlogie
Oakbank, Kippen
Old Ballikinrain, Balfron
Powfoulis, Airth
Rednock, Port of Menteith
Sauchieburn House, Stirling
Schaw Park, Alloa
Sheriffmuir, Dunblane
South Bantaskine, Falkirk
Stirling Castle
Touch, Cambushbarron

DUMFRIES AND GALLOWAY

Airds of Parton
Arbigland, Kirkbean
Ardwell House
Balgray, Lockerbie
Balmae
Bargaly, Newton-Stewart
Barjarg Tower, Thornhill
Barnbarroch, Wigtown
Barnhourie Mill

Brooklands, Crocketford
Broomholm, Langholm
Broughton House, Kirkcudbright
Cally, Gatehouse of Fleet
Castle Kennedy, Stranraer
Castle Stewart, Newton Stewart
Castledykes, Dumfries
Castlehill, Kirkmahoe
Castlemilk, Lockerbie
Closeburn Hall
Comlongon Castle, Ruthwell
Corsewall
Cowhill Tower, Holywood
Craigdarroch, Moniaive
Dalawoodie
Dalswinton House
Drumlanrig Castle, Thornhill
Drumpark, Dunscore
Duncow, Dumfries
Elmbank, Dumfries
Friars Carse, Dumfries
Galloway House, Garliestown
Grove, Dumfries
Hannayfield
Hensol, Mossdale
Jardine Hall, Lockerbie
Kenmure Castle, New Galloway
Kirkconnell, Dumfries
Kirkdale House, Creetown
Langholm Cottage
Lochinch, Castle Kennedy
Lochnaw Castle
Lochryan
Logan, Ardwell
Mabie, Dumfries
Maxwelton House, Moniaive
Maybo, Dumfries
Mochrum Park, Penninghame
Monreith, Whithorn
Munches, Dalbeattie
Newtonairds, Dumfries
Old Place of Mochrum
Penninghame House
Queensbery House, Drumlanrig
Raehills, Lockerbie
Roughhills, Colvend
St Mary's Isle, Kirkcudbright
St Peter's, Dalbeattie
Senwick House, Borgue
Shambellie, Dumfries
Shennanton Hall, Kirkcowan
Southwick House, Caulkerbush
Steadstone
Stewartry, Threave
Terregles, Dumfries
Threave Gardens
Walton Park, Castle Douglas

FIFE

Aberdour Castle, Aberdour
Balbirnie House, Markinch
Balcarres, Colinsburgh
Balcaskie, Pittenweem
Balcormo, Carnbee
Balfour House, Markinch
Barham, Cupar
Birkhill, Balmerino
Cambo, Crail

County Index

Castle Hill, Culross Abbey
Chapel, Kingskettle
Culross Abbey
Cunnoquhie, Monimail
Dalgairn House, Cupar
Denbrae, St Andrews
Donisbristle
Dunfermline. Pittencrieft Park
Falkland Palace
Fernie Castle
Fordell, Inverkeithing
Gibliston, Colinsburgh
Grangemuir, Pittenweem
Hill of Tarvit, Cupar
Hillside House, Ceres
Hilton House, Cupar
Inchrye, Newburgh
Kellie Castle, Pittenweem
Kilconquhar House
Lathallan, Colinsburgh
Leven
Melville House, Ladybank
Mount Melville, St Andrews
Myres Castle, Auchtermuchty
Naughton House, Balmerino
Raith House, Kirkaldy
Rankeilour, Cupar
St Adrians, Crail
St Andrews Priory
St Andrews University. Botanic Garden
St Clairtown, Kirkaldy
St Fort, Leuchars
Strathtyrum, St Andrews
Tayfield, Newport-on-Tay
Tulliallan
Valleyfield, Culross
Wemyss Castle, East Wemyss

GRAMPIAN

Aberdeen. Duthie Park
Aboyne Castle
Altyre, Forres
Arbuthnott House, Inverbervie
Balbithan House, Kintore
Balmoral Castle
Barra Castle, Old Meldrum
Bellenden, Aberdeen
Birkhall, Ballater
Blackhills, Elgin
Brackley, Ballater
Brodie Castle, Forres
Candacraig, Strathdon
Castle Forbes, Whitehouse
Castle Fraser, Monymusk
Coulmony House, Ardclach
Craigievar Castle, Lumphanon
Craigston Castle, Turriff
Crathes Castle, Banchory
Cullen House
Dalvey House, Forres
Darnaway Castle, Forres
Douneside House, Tarland
Drum, Aberdeen
Duff House, Banff
Dunecht House
Ellon Castle
Esslemont, Ellon
Fasque, Fettercairn

Fettercairn House
Fyvie Castle, Turriff
Glen Tana, Aboyne
Glenbervie, Drumlithie
Glenrothes, Rothes
Glentanar, Aboyne
Gordon Castle, Fochabars
Haddo House, Ellon
Inchmarlo, Banchory
Innes House, Elgin
Keith Hall, Inverurie
Kildrummy Castle
Kincardine Castle, Fettercairn
Kincardine O'Neil
Kincorth House, Forres
Kinrara
Leith Hall, Huntly
Lickleyhead Castle, Insch
Manse of Fyvie
Mar Lodge, Castleton
Milton Brodie, Forres
Monymusk House
Newton House, Alves
Newton House, Insch
Old Manse of Marnoch, Banff
Philorth House
Pitfour House
Pitmedden House
Pluscarden Abbey, Elgin
Quarry Gardens, Bellie
Raeden House
Skene House
Slains Castle
Thornton Castle, Laurencekirk
Tillypronie, Aboyne
Towie Barclay, Turriff
Warthill, Rayne
Williamston House, Insch

HIGHLAND

Arabela
Ardross Castle
Ardtornish
Armadale House, Skye
Beaufort, Beauly
Belladrum, Beauly
Brackla House, Cawdor
Brahan, Conon Bridge
Castle Grant, Grantown
Castle of Mey, Thurso
Cawdor Castle
Corrour
Culloden House, Inverness
Drumdevan House, Inverness
Dundonnell House, Ullapool
Dunrobin Castle
Eilean Aigas
Eilean Darach, Dundonnell
Geanies, Fearn
Inverewe, Poolewe
Kilcoy Castle, Muir of Ord
Kildonan, Helmsdale
Kilravock Castle, Nairn
Kinloch Hourn
Kyle House, Kyleakin
Mountgerald, Kiltearn
Nead-an-Eoin, Plockton
Relic

Skibo Castle, Dornoch
Stonefield, Tarbet
Tournaig, Poolewe

LOTHIAN

Addistoun House, Ratho
Amisfield House, Haddington
Archerfield, N. Berwick
Arniston, Gorebridge
Baberton, Edinburgh
Belhaven, Dunbar
Biel, Prestonkirk
Binns, Linlithgow
Bonnytonn House, Linlithgow
Borthwick Castle
Broxmouth Park, Dunbar
Cannongate House, Edinburgh
Canonmills Cottage, Edinburgh
Carberry Tower, Musselburgh
Carlowrie, Kirkliston
Champfleurie House, Linlithgow
Coalstoun, Haddington
Cockenzie House
Colinton House, Edinburgh
Craigie Hall
Dalhousie Castle, Edinburgh
Dalkeith Palace, Edinburgh
Dalmahoy, Ratho
Dalmeny, Edinburgh
Duddingston House, Edinburgh
Dundas Castle, Queensferry
Dunglass, Cockburnspath
Easter Duddingston Lodge
Edinburgh. Horticultural Society
Edinburgh. Princes St Gardens
Edinburgh. Royal Botanic Garden
Elvinston, Gladsmuir
Gosford, Aberlady
Granton House, Edinburgh
Grey Walls, Gullane
Hanley, Edinburgh
Hatton House, Ratho
Hawthornden Castle, Lasswade
Holyrood Palace, Edinburgh
Hopetoun House, South Queensferry
Inveralmond House, Cramond
Inveresk Lodge, Musselburgh
Inverleith, Edinburgh
Keir, Edinburgh
Lauriston Castle, Edinburgh
Lennoxlove, Haddington
Linlithgow Palace
Luffness, Aberlady
Malleny House, Balerno
Mavisbank, Loanhead
Melville House, Lasswade
Middleton House, Edinburgh
Millburn Tower, Edinburgh
Morton Hall, Edinburgh
Muirhouse, Edinburgh
Murieston House, Mid Calder
New Hailes, Edinburgh
Newbattle Abbey
Newhall, Penicuit
Newliston, Kirkliston
Niddrie Marischad, Edinburgh
North Merchiston, Edinburgh
Oxenfoord Castle, Dalkeith

County Index

Penicuik House
Pinkie House, Musselburgh
Preston Hall, Dalkeith
Prestonfield, Edinburgh
Ravelston, Edinburgh
Saint Mary's Pleasance
Salisbury Green, Edinburgh
Saughton House, Edinburgh
Smeaton-Hepburn
Stevenson House, Haddington
Trinity Grove, Edinburgh
Tyninghame, Linton
Wardie Lodge, Edinburgh
Westerlea, Edinburgh
Whitburgh, Crichton
Whitehouse, Baruton
Whittingehame House, East Linton
Winton House, Pencaitland
Woodhouselee, Roslin
Yester House

ORKNEY

Happy Valley, Bigswell

STRATHCLYDE

Abington
Achamore House, Isle of Gigha
Achnacloich, Loch Etive
Afton Lodge, Tarbolton
Allanton, Wishaw
Alloway
An Cala, Easdale
Ardanaiseig, Taynuilt
Ardchattan Priory, Loch Etive
Arddarroch, Garelochhead
Ardencraig, Rothesay
Ardgowan House, Inverkip
Ardkinglas, Inveraray
Ardoch, Cardross
Arduaine, Loch Melfort
Argyle House
Ascog Hall, Isle of Bute
Auchincruive, Ayr
Auchinraith, Bothwell
Balkail House, Glenluce
Ballimore, Loch Fyne
Balloch Castle
Ballochmyle House, Pinwherry
Bargany, Girvan
Barguillean, Taynuilt
Barncluith, Hamilton
Barskimming, Mauchine
Benmore, Dunoon
Biggar
Blairquhan, Straiton
Blochairn, Glasgow
Blythswood, Renfrew
Bothwell Castle
Brodick Castle, Isle of Arran
Cadzow Castle
Cameron, Loch Lomond
Camis Eskan, Helensburgh
Caprington Castle, Kilmarnock
Carnell, Hurlford
Carstairs, Lanark

Castle Levan, Gourock
Castle Semple, Lochwinnoch
Castle Toward, Rothesay
Chatelherault, Hamilton
Cleddans, Airdrie
College, Kirkoswald
Colonsay House
Coltness, Wishaw
Colzium, Kilsyth
Corehouse, Lanark
Crarae, Loch Fyne
Crosbie Tower
Crosslee Cottage
Culzean Castle, Maybole
Cumbernauld House
Dalmore, Helensburgh
Dalquharran Castle, Dailly
Dalzell House
Drum-na-Vullin, Lochgilphead
Drumpellier House, Coatbridge
Dunsyre
Earnock, Hamilton
Eglinton Castle, Irvine
Ericht Bank, Kirn
Erskine House
Ferguslie House, Paisley
Finlaystone, Langbank
Finnart, Arddarroch
Formakin, Bishopton
Garnkirk House, Glasgow
Garscube, Maryhill
Gartshore, Kirkintilloch
Garvald House, Dolphinton
Glasgow. Botanic Garden
Glasgow. Cemetery
Glasgow. Queen's Park
Glasgow. Tollcross Park
Glenapp Castle, Ballantrae
Glenarn, Rhu
Glenfeochan, Oban
Glenfinart, Helensburgh
Glenoran, Helensburgh
Greenbank, Glasgow
Hamilton Palace
Huntfield, Biggar
Inveraray Castle
Jordanhill House, Glasgow
Kelburne Castle, Largs
Kilarden, Rosneath
Kilkerran, Maybole
Kilmahew Castle, Cardross
Kilmory Castle, Lochgilphead
Kilnside, Paisley
Kings Inch, Paisley
Kinlochruel, Colintraive
Kirkbridge, Crosshill
Lansdown Park, Helensburgh
Lee Place, Lanark
Loudoun Castle
Luss, Dunbarton
Milton Lockhart, Carluke
Mount Stuart, Isle of Bute
Netherplace, Mauchline
Ormidale, Tighnabruaich
Pinmore, Girvan
Pollok, Barrhead
Poltalloch, Lochgilphead
Redlands, Glasgow
Roseneath, Helensburgh
Ross Priory, Balloch

Rossdhu, Luss
Skeldon House, Dalrymple
Stonypath, Dunsyre
Strone House, Cairndow
Torosay Castle, Mull
Towerville, Helensburgh
Westmount, Glasgow
Wishaw, Motherwell
Woodhall, Holytown
Woodside, Paisley

TAYSIDE

Abercairny, Crieff
Aberuchill Castle, Comrie
Airlie Castle, Kirriemuir
Annat
Annfield
Ardvorlich House, Loch Earn
Ascreavie, Kingoldrum
Balmanno Castle
Balmuir House, Dundee
Balthayock, Perth
Belmont Castle
Birnam, Dunkeld
Blair Castle
Blairadam, Kinross
Bolfracks, Aberfeldy
Bonskeid, Pitlochry
Braco Castle
Branklyn, Perth
Brechin Castle
Brigton, Forfar
Carie, Fortingall
Castle Huntley, Dundee
Castle Menzies, Aberfeldy
Castleroy, Broughty Ferry
Cloquhat, Bridge of Cally
Cluniemore, Pitlochry
Cluny House, Aberfeldy
Cortachy Castle
Craigantaggart, Dunkeld
Croft Cappanach, Pitlochry
Culdees Castle, Crieff
Dalguise, Dunkeld
Devonhall, Ochil Hills
Drumkilbo, Meigle
Drummond Castle, Crieff
Drummonie House, Bridge of Farn
Dukeld, Blair Atholl
Dunbarney, Perth
Dunira, Comrie
Dunkeld House
Dunninald
Dupplin Castle, Perth
Edzell Castle
Errol Park
Fingask Castle, Errol
Gask, Perth
Glamis Castle, Forfar
Glendoick House
Glenearn, Bridge of Earn
Glenoick, Glencarse
Grandtully Castle, Aberfeldy
Guthrie Castle, Forfar
Hermitage, Dunkeld
House of Pitmuies, Friokheim
House of Urrard, Killiecrankie
Inchyra House, Glencarse

County Index

Invermay, Forteviot
Keillour Castle, Methven
Keithock, Brechin
Kilgraston, Bridge of Earn
Kinfauns Castle, Perth
Kinnaird Castle, Brechin
Kinross House
Lawers
Laws, Kingennie
Lindertis, Kirriemuir
Lingwood, Scone
Marlee House, Kinloch
Meggernie, Killin
Megginch Castle, Errol
Methven Castle
Millearne, Auchterarder
Moncrieffe House, Perth
Monzie Castle
Murthly Castle
Ochtertyre, Crieff
Orchill House, Ardoch
Panmure House, Carnoustie
Rossie Castle, Montrose
Rossie Priory, Inchture
Roundlewood, Crieff
Scone Palace
Scone Pinetum
Stobhall, Perth
Stracathro House, Brechin
Strathallan Castle, Crieff
Taymouth Castle, Aberfeldy
Tealing
Tower of Lethendy, Meikleour

Wales

CLWYD

Bettisfield
Bodelwyddan Castle, St Asaph
Bodrhyddan, Rhuddlan
Broadlane House, Hawarden
Brynkinalt, Chirk
Chirk Castle, Wrexham
Downing, Holywell
Dyffryn Aled, Denbigh
Erddig, Wrexham
Flagstaff, Wrexham
Garthewin, Llanfair Talhaiarn
Greenfield Hall, Holywell
Gresford Cottage, Denbigh
Gwersyllt House
Gwysaney Hall, Mold
Gyrn, Mostyn
Harwarden Castle
Kelsterton
Kinmel
Leeswood, Mold
Llanerch House, Denbigh
Llangedwyn
Llewenny Hall, Denbigh
Mostyn Hall
Nant-y-Glyn, Colwyn Bay
Pengwern Place, St Asaph
Rhual, Mold
Rug, Corwen
Ruthin Castle

Trevalyn Hall, Wrexham
Trevor Hall, Llangollen
Whitehurst, Chirk
Wynnstay, Ruabon

DYFED

Aberystwyth University College
Carrog, Aberystwyth
Dynevor Castle, Llandeilo
Glanbran, Llandovery
Gogerddan, Aberystwyth
Hafod
Middleton Hall, Llanarthney
Nant-Eos, Aberystwyth
Orielton, Pembroke
Pantglas, Llandeilo
Picton Castle, Haverfordwest
Plas Penglais, Aberystwyth
Slebech Park
Stackpole Court
Trawscoed, Aberystwyth

MID GLAMORGAN

Ruperra, Caerphilly
Tythegston Court

SOUTH GLAMORGAN

Cardiff. Public Parks
Cardiff Castle
Cefn Mabley, Cardiff
Cefn-on, Cardiff
Dimland Castle, Cowbridge
Duffryn, Cardiff
Dulwich House, Cardiff
Dunraven Castle, Cowbridge
Ely Court, Cardiff
Fonmon Castle
Friar's House, Barry
Llanblethian, Cowbridge
Llantrithyd Place
St Donat's Castle
St Fagan's Castle
Wenvoe Castle

WEST GLAMORGAN

Gnoll, Neath
Grange, Swansea
Margam Park, Port Talbot
Penllergaer
Penrice Castle
Singleton Abbey, Swansea

GWENT

Bedwellty Park, Tredegar
Bryn Glas, Newport
Clytha Park, Abergavenny
Hendre, Monmouth
High Glanau, Trellech
Llanarth Court
Llandilo

Llangibby
Llanover Court
Llantarnam Abbey
Llanvihangel Court
Llanwern House, Newport
Maesruddud, Newport
Mathern Palace
Mounton House, Chepstow
Pantygoitre, Usk
Piercefield, Chepstow
Pontypool Park
St Pierre, Chepstow
Shirenewton Hall, Chepstow
Tredegar House, Newport
Troy House, Newport
Wyndcliffe Court, Chepstow
Yew Tree, Lydart

GWYNEDD

Baron Hill, Anglesey
Bodnant, Talycafn
Bodorgan, Anglesey
Bodysgallan, Llandudno
Bryn Bras Castle, Llanrug
Bryn-y-Neuadd, Llanfairfechan
Emral Hall, Bangor
Gilfach, Conway
Glan-y-Mawddach, Barmouth
Gloddaeth, Conway
Gwydir Castle, Llanrwst
Hafodunos, Llanrwst
Hendregadredd, Tremadoc
Henllys, Llanfaes
Llanbedrog, Pwllheli
Madryn, Pwllheli
Maenan Hall, Eglwys Fach
Penrhyn Castle, Bangor
Plas, Tan-y-Bwlch
Plas Brondanw, Tremadoc
Plas Coch, Llanfair
Plas Newydd, Llanfairpwll
Plas-yn-Rhin, Pwllheli
Portmerion, Penrhyndeudraeth
Rhianfa, Anglesey
Sunny Hill, Llandudno

POWYS

Boultibrook, Presteigne
Brynhyfryd
Cefnaes Hall, Rhayader
Craig-Nos Castle, Brecon
Glanusk, Crickhowell
Gregynog, Newtown
Hall, Leighton
Hay Castle
Lymore, Montgomery
Maesllwch Castle
Pennoyre, Brecon
Penpont, Brecon
Powis Castle, Welshpool
Stanage Park, Knighton
Treberfydd, Brecon

County Index

Channel Islands

Beau-Séjour, Guernsey
Beaulieu, Guernsey
Belmont Lodge, Guernsey
Caches, Guernsey
Candie Gardens, Guernsey
Domaine des Vaux, Jersey
Government House, Guernsey
Havelet, Guernsey
La Colline, Jersey
La Moye Manor, Jersey
Le Clos de Chemin, Jersey
Les Vaux, Jersey
Manor House of St Helena, Guernsey
Montville, Guernsey
Radier Manor, Jersey
Rozel Manor, Jersey
Samares Manor, Jersey
Sausmarez Manor, Guernsey
Trinity Manor, Jersey
Vauxbelets, Guernsey

Isle of Man

Ballamodar, Patrick
Bishopscourt
Castle Mona, Dougas
Castletown
Nunnery of St Bridget, Douglas
Rushen Abbey

Ireland

COUNTRY ANTRIM

Antrim Castle
Belfast. Botanic Garden
Bush, Antrim
Castle Dobbs, Carrickfergus
Cranmore, Belfast
Glenarm Castle
Joymount, Carrickfergus
Lissanoure Castle, Lough Guile
Shane's Castle, Antrim
Springfield, Lisburn

COUNTY ARMAGH

Argory, Verner's Bridge
Derrymore, Bessbrook
Tynan Abbey

COUNTY DOWN

Ballyalolly House
Ballywalter Park
Castle Ward, Downpatrick
Castlewellan, Newcastle
Clandeboye, Belfast
Donaghadee
Dromore
Grey Abbey House
Guincho, Helen's Bay
Hillsborough
Kilwarlin
Moira
Mount Stewart, Newtownards
Portaferry House
Quintin Castle
Rostrevor
Rowallane, Saintfield
Seaforde, Clough
Stormont Castle
Tollymore Park, Newcastle
Woburn House, Mill Isle

COUNTY FERMANAGH

Belleisle, Enniskillen
Castle Caldwell, Belleek
Castle Coole, Enniskillen
Crom Castle, Lisnaskea
Florence Court, Enniskillen
Fort Hill, Enniskillen
Tempo Manor

COUNTY LONDONDERRY

Bellarena, Londonderry
Coleraine (G.L. Wilson)
Downhill, Londonderry
Drenagh, Limivady
Springhill, Moneymore

COUNTY TYRONE

Aughentaine, Fivemiletown
Baronscourt, Newton-Stewart
Caledon
Drum Manor, Cookstown
Killymoon Castle

COUNTY MONAGHAN

Castle Blayney
Dartrey, Cootehill
Dawson's Grove
Gola House, Monaghan
Loughfea, Carrickmacross
Rossmore Park, Monaghan

COUNTY CARLOW

Borris
Fenagh

COUNTY CAVAN

Coote Hill
Farnham Lodge
Hollywell Lodge

COUNTY CLARE

Dromoland, Newmarket
Mount Ievers, Six-mile-Bridge

COUNTY CORK

Anne's Grove, Castletownroche
Ard Cairn
Ardnagashel, Bantry Bay
Ashbourne, Glounthane
Ballyheigue Castle
Bantry House
Bear Forest
Belgrove, Cobh
Burton House
Castle Freke, Clonakilty
Castlecor, Mallow
Cork. Botanical Garden
Doneraile
Fota Island, Cork
Garinish Island, Glengariff
Hollybrook House, Skibbereens
Lisselane, Clonakilty
Oakville, Clonmel
Tivoli
Vernon Mount

COUNTY DONEGAL

Carrablagh, Portsalon
Glenveagh Castle
Kildrum
Marble Hill, Dunfanaghy
Mulroy House, Milford
St Columb's, Church Hill

COUNTY DUBLIN

Alexandra College, Dublin
Aras an Auchtarain
Balygort, Balbriggan
Breckdenstown
Cedar Mount, Dundrum
Clontra, Dublin
Delville, Glasnevin
Dublin. National Botanic Gardens
Dublin. Phoenix Park
Dublin. Physic Garden
Dublin. Trinity College
Fern Hill
Hampton, Balbriggan
Howth Castle, Dublin
Kilbogget, Killiney
Knockmaroon Lodge, Dublin
Lambay Castle
Lucan House
Luttrellstown
Malahide Castle
Marino, Dublin
Montrose, Dublin
Mount Henry, Dalkey
Mount Merrion
Nutley, Booterstown
Phoenix Park Lodge, Dublin
Rathgar, Dublin
Rockville, Dublin

County Index

St Anne's, Clontarf
St Enda, Fathfarnham
Sandymount Castle, Dublin
Santry Court
Stillorgan, Dublin
Sutton House, Howth
Temple Hill, Blackrock
Templeogue, Dublin
Woodside, Howth

COUNTY GALWAY

Ballynahinch, Clifden
Castlegar, Galway
Coole Park
Garbally, Ballinasloe
Kylemore Castle
Lisnabrucka House, Clifden
Mount Bellew, Ballinasloe
St Cleran's, Loughrea
Thoor Ballylee

COUNTY KERRY

Ardtully
Bourne Vincent Park
Derreen, Kenmare
Flesk Castle, Killarney
Garinish Island, Parknasilla
Glanleam, Valentia Island
Kenmare House
Killarney House
Miltown House, Castlemaine
Muckross Abbey
Rossdohan Island

COUNTY KILDARE

Belan, Athy
Bishop's Court, Naas
Brannockstoun, Kilcudden
Carton, Maynooth
Castletown, Celbridge
Coolayna, Carbury
Curragh Grange
Harristown, Naas
Kildangan
Lyons, Celbridge
Mullaboden, Naas
Oldtown, Naas
Palmerstown House, Naas
St Wolstans, Celbridge
Straffan House
Tully, Kildare

COUNTY KILKENNY

Bessborough, Carrick
Gowran Castle, Kilkenny
Kilkenny Castle
Mount Juliet, Thomastown
Woodstock, Inistioge

COUNTY LAOIS

Abbeyleix
Ballyfinn
Blandsfort, Abbeyleix
Brockley Park
Emo Court, Portarlington
Gracefield Lodge, Athy
Heywood, Ballinakill
Knapton, Abbeyleix
Stradbally

COUNTY LIMERICK

Adare Manor
Ardanoir, Foynes
Bulgaden, Kilmallock
Glenstal Castle, Limerick
Glin Castle
Grange
Mount Shannon, Limerick

COUNTY LONGFORD

Castle Forbes, Longford
Edgeworthstown
Rathcline, Lanesborough

COUNTY LOUTH

Beaulieu, Drogheda
Castle Bellingham
Dundalk Archepiscopal Palace
Dundalk House
Oriel Temple, Collon
Townley Hall, Drogheda

COUNTY MAYO

Ballinrobe
Castle MacGarrett, Claremorris
Cill-Alaithe
Neale, Cong
Westport House

COUNTY MEATH

Ardbraccan
Balrath, Duleek
Beauparc, Navan
Bellinter, Navan
Dunsany Castle
Gormanstown Castle
Hamwood, Dunboyne
Headfort House, Kells
Loughcrew, Oldcastle
Slane Castle
Tullynally Castle

COUNTY OFFALY

Birr Castle
Charleville Forest
Gloster, Recess
Mountwilson House, Edenderry

COUNTY ROSCOMMON

Lough Key Forest Park
Rockingham, Boyle

COUNTY SLIGO

Hazelwood, Sligo
Lissadell, Sligo
Markree Castle, Collooney

COUNTY TIPPERARY

Ardsallagh, Fethard
Barne House, Clonmel
Greenfields
Thomastown

COUNTY WATERFORD

Ballysaggartmore, Lismore
Castle Richard, Lismore
Curraghmore, Portlaw
Dromana, Cappoquin
Lismore Castle
Mount Congreve, Waterford
Whitfield Court, Waterford

COUNTY WESTMEATH

Belvedere, Mullingar
Killua Castle
Ladiston, Mullingar
Middleton, Castleton
Moydrum Castle, Athlone
Pakenham Hall, Castlepollard

COUNTY WEXFORD

Ballynastrach, Gorey
Castleboro, Enniscorthy
Johnstown Castle, Wexford
Ramsfort, Gorey

COUNTY WICKLOW

Avondale, Rathdrum
Bellevue, Greystones
Blessington, Maas
Castle Howard, Rathdrum
Coollatin Park
Dargle Cottage, Enniskerry
Dunganstown Castle, Wicklow
Glenart Castle, Arklow
Glencormac
Craigueconna, Bray

Humewood, Baltinglass
Kilmacurragh, Rathdrum
Kilruddery, Bray
Luggala, Roundwood
Mount Kennedy, Newtown Mount Kennedy
Mount Usher, Ashford
Mucklagh, Aughrim
Old Conna Hill, Bray
Powerscourt
Russborough, Blessington
St Valery, Bray
Saunders Grove, Baltinglass
Shelton Abbey, Arklow

Appendix

The Wedgwood dinner service for Catherine the Great of Russia

In 1773 the Wedgwood factory undertook a most ambitious commission of producing for Catherine the Great of Russia a table and dessert service of 952 pieces all of which were to be decorated with different English scenes, mainly country seats. Existing paintings and engravings were used while other views were provided by a team of landscape painters. Thomas Bentley, Josiah Wedgwood's partner, compiled a manuscript list of almost the entire service which was reprinted in a monograph by G.C. Williamson, published in 1909, entitled *Imperial Russian dinner service*.

It is interesting to consider the choice of places to embellish all the dishes, plates, cups and saucers. Apart from Kew Gardens and Windsor Castle, no royal estates are included because both Wedgwood and Bentley remembered too late to seek royal permission. Stowe, as one would expect, was the country house most frequently depicted on the service. Enville was also popular but not so its equally famous neighbours: Hagley is represented on only two pieces while The Leasowes is entirely overlooked. Hampstead and Richmond were the two most popular towns in the London region. There was a marked preference for castles, especially those in a ruinous state. English estates were the main source for material; Scotland and Wales received token representation and Ireland not at all.

I have rearranged Bentley's haphazard list in the following alphabetical order of places, giving his catalogue numbers after each entry. A number of the place names are difficult to identify. Those qualified by (?) are possibly correct. I was unable to confirm the accuracy of those indicated by (!).

ENGLAND

Acton Burnell, Shropshire   *872*
Aire Castle, Norfolk (!)   *439*
Alderton Church, Suffolk   *440*
Allington Castle, Kent   *751*
Alnwick Castle, Northumberland   *462, 644, 699*
Althorp, Northants   *950*
Alton Towers, Staffs   *66, 574*
Anchor Church (Caves), Derbyshire   *281*
Appleby Castle, Cumbria   *23, 1265*
Arundel Castle, W. Sussex   *392*
Arwerton Hall (!), Suffolk
Ashby de la Zouch Castle, Leics   *276, 391, 463*
Audley End, Essex   *1272*
Avon, River   Near Bristol   *369, 748*
Aysgarth Bridge, N. Yorks   *1109*

Bamburgh Castle, Northumberland   *1274*
Barlaston, Staffs   *996*
Barlings Abbey, Lincs   *400*
Barnstaple, Devon   Castle Hill *912*
Battle Abbey, E. Sussex   *395, 420, 754*
Beaudesert, Staffs   *1066, 1107–08*
Bedford Bridge, Beds   *374, 772*
Beeston Castle, Cheshire   *40, 337, 666, 878*
Belton House, Lincs   *131*
Berkeley Castle, Glos   *358*
Berry Pomeroy Castle, Devon   *416*
Beverstone Castle, Glos   *29*
Birstall Abbey, W. Yorks   *227*
Bindon Abbey, Dorset   *655, 1056*
Binham Priory, Norfolk   *51*
Bishops Waltham Palace, Hants   *654, 841*
Blenheim Park, Oxfordshire   *962, 965, 971*

313

Appendix

Bodiam Castle, E. Sussex *25*
Bolingbroke House, Fulham (?), London *238*
Bolsover Castle, Derbyshire *1141, 1181*
Bolton Abbey, N. Yorks *73, 773*
Bolton Castle, N. Yorks *488*
Booth's Hall, Cheshire *326, 620, 621, 899, 908, 1076*
Bothal Castle, Northumberland *53, 431, 690*; chapel *828*
Boxgrove Priory, W. Sussex *480*
Bradenstoke Priory, Wilts *406*
Bradgate Park, Leics *312, 314–16, 459, 875*
Brampton Bryan Castle, Hereford & Worcs *354*
Brinkburn Priory, Northumberland *760*
Bristol, Avon   Mineral springs *159, 577*; Rocks of St. Vincent *160*
Bronsil (?) Castle, Hereford & Worcs *27*
Brough Castle, Cumbria *22*
Brougham Castle, Cumbria *397*
Broughton Castle, Cumbria *419*
Broughton Church, Northants *478*
Brownsea Island, Dorset *1059*
Bryanston, Dorset *983*
Buccleuch House, Richmond, London *527, 702*
Buildwas Abbey, Shropshire *476*
Burghley House, Cambs *1069–70*
Butley Abbey, Suffolk *456*
Butterton Castle, Staffs *489*
Byland Abbey, N. Yorks *88, 512*
Bywell Bay, Northumberland *807, 887–88*
Camborne, Cornwall *697*
Came, Dorset *1054–55, 1077*
Canterbury, Kent   Castle *263, 821*; city walls *696*; western gate *813*
Carclew, Cornwall *916*
Carisbrooke Castle, Isle of Wight *270, 479, 653, 779*
Carlisle Castle, Cumbria *523*
Carn Brea, Cornwall *689, 790, 809*
Castle Howard, N. Yorks *991, 1113, 1160, 1192*; temple *1090, 1114*
Castle Rising, Norfolk *342*
Castleton, Derbyshire *149*; Castle *13*; cavern *146*
Chatsworth, Derbyshire *662*
Chee Tor, Derbyshire *234*
Chelsea, London   Royal Hospital *237*; Thames *686, 860*
Chelsea Farm, Chelsea, London *688*
Chester, Cheshire   Castle *41, 448, 942, 1259*; Watergate *1175*
Chettle (?), Dorset *1016*
Chicksands Priory, Beds *1000*
Chideock (?) Castle, Dorset *19*
Chilham Castle, Kent *843*
Chillingham Castle, Northumberland *466*

Chipping Norton, Oxfordshire *1194*
Chiswick, London *955, 1115, 1241, 1243*; Thames *739*
Chiswick House, London *966*; bridge *181*; canal *292*; gardens *581*; orangery *179, 180*; temples *1121–22, 1127–28*
Cirencester House, Glos   King Alfred's Hall *85–86, 222, 509, 590*
Claremont, Surrey *201–02*; lake *178*
Cleeve Abbey, Somerset *639*
Cliveden, Bucks *405, 1158*
Clun Castle, Shropshire *91*
Coalbrookdale, Shropshire *147–48, 150–51, 157, 508*
Cockermouth Castle, Cumbria *17*
Codnor Castle, Derbyshire *415, 815*
Colchester Castle, Essex *360*
Combe Bank, Kent *104–05, 293*
Conisbrough Castle, S. Yorks *225*
Constable Burton, N. Yorks *1018, 1058*
Cooling (?) Castle, Kent *370, 635, 785, 794*
Corfe Castle, Dorset *417, 426, 634*
Cottam (?), Humberside *1024*
Coverham Abbey, N. Yorks *750, 1100*
Cowes Castle, Isle of Wight *455*
Crowland Abbey, Lincs *79*
Croydon, Archbishop's Palace, London *1171*
Dacre Castle, Cumbria *64*
Dale Abbey, Derbyshire *469, 866*
Dartford Priory, Kent *670*
Dartmouth Castle, Devon *60*
Davington Priory, Kent *810*
Deene, Northants *804*
Derwent Water, Cumbria *218, 536, 658–60, 835, 889*
Ditchley Park, Oxfordshire *230–31*
Donnington Castle, Berks *48, 375*
Dove Dale, Derbyshire *166, 296, 517*
Dover, Kent   Town and castle *283, 832, 851*; castle church *380*
Dunster Castle, Somerset *1180*
Dunstanburgh Castle, Northumberland *54, 267, 576*
Durham City *1004*
Eastby Abbey, N. Yorks *70, 598, 1280*
Ecclestone Abbey, Co. Durham *537*
Egremont Castle, Cumbria *18, 1258*
Elizabeth's Castle, Jersey, Channel Islands *941*
Ennerdale Water, Cumbria *219*
Enville Church, Staffs *328–29, 682*
Enville Hall, Staffs *709, 759, 891, 898, 953*; cascade *749*; Gothic gateway *310, 880*; menagerie *915*; rotunda *710, 1074*; ruin *700*; Sheepwalk *468, 683*; Shepherds' Bridge *465*; Shepherds Lodge *874*; vase on terrace *327, 331*
Enys, Cornwall *774*

Erith, London 743, 931
Esher Place, Surrey 3–4, 121, 630
Estivale House, Cliveden, Bucks 102–03
Eton College, Berks 501, 679
Etruria Hall, Staffs 1129
Exton Park, Leics 132–33
Eynsham Abbey, Oxfordshire 10
Farleigh (?) Castle, Avon 637, 1102, 1253
Farnham Castle, Surrey 262, 449
Farnly Castle, Hunts (!) 363
Faversham Abbey, Kent 1167, 1279
Fleet House, Dorset 1060
Folkestone, Kent 923
Foots Cray Place, London 108, 122–23, 570
Forkley Hall, Lincs (!) 65
Fountains Abbey, N. Yorks 1063
Fowey Castle, Cornwall 38, 575
Framlingham Castle, Suffolk 396, 441
Furness Abbey, Cumbria 1270
Gatton, Surrey 1101, 1112, 1159; temple 1111
Glastonbury, Somerset Abbey and/or village 362, 665, 825, 1278; Abbots kitchen 844; ruin 1249
Godstow Abbey, Oxfordshire 641, 778
Goodrich Castle, Hereford & Worcs 269
Gravesend, Kent 937
Great Malvern Abbey, Hereford & Worcs 384
Great Marlow Manor, Bucks 155
Groby Park, Leics 451
Guildford Castle, Surrey 473
Guisborough Priory, Cleveland 1138
Guiting Grange, Glos 1105
Hackfall, N. Yorks 970, 1025
Haddon Hall, Derbyshire 106–07
Hadleigh Castle, Essex 36, 762, 796
Hagley, Hereford & Worcs 145, 1154
Hall Barn, Bucks 229, 505; gardens 137–38
Halling House, Kent 546
Hammersmith, London 944, 1123–24
Hamoaze and Plymouth Docks, Devon 223–24, 603
Hampstead, London 492–98, 622–25, 627–29, 833, 855–56, 862, 884, 949, 956, 958–59
Harleyford, Bucks 236, 511
Harewood, W. Yorks 1064
Harsley Castle, N. Yorks 87, 89, 408
Hastings Castle, E. Sussex 693, 1094
Hawes Water, Cumbria 487, 993
Herstmonceux Castle, E. Sussex 388, 418
Highgate, London 499, 626, 812, 823, 858–59, 1116
Holdenby Palace, Northants 457, 642
Holkham, Norfolk Lake 1190–91
Holland House, Kensington, London 952
Holy Island. Castle and Monastery, Northumberland 55, 587
Hoppin-Mill-Weir, Derbyshire 173, 992

Hopton Castle, Shropshire 12
Hornby Castle, Lancs 335
Hurst Castle, Hants 28
Ingestre Hall, Staffs 703, 914, 1008, 1023; pond 1010; rotunda 913
Irwell, River. Aquaduct near Manchester 516
Jarrow Monastery, Co. Durham 378
Jervaulx Abbey, N. Yorks 795
Keele Hall, Staffs 324, 618; summerhouse 427
Kendal Castle, Cumbria 348
Kenilworth Castle, Warwickshire 126–27, 474, 808
Kensington Palace, London 306, 770
Kew. Royal Gardens, London 9, 401, 539–42, 559–61, 608–09, 715, 718, 720, 725, 840; Kew Palace 524; lake and island 92–93, 240–41, 286; menagerie 291; Mosque 144; Temple of Bellona 733; Temple of Eolus 731
Kew Bridge, London 742
Kingwood Colliery, Bristol, Avon 1205
Kirkham Priory, N. Yorks 209, 586, 589
Kirkstall Abbey, W. Yorks 78, 526, 1170
Kirkstead Abbey, Lincs 75
Kits Coty House, Kent 820
Knaresborough, N. Yorks Castle 162, 383; petrifying springs 161, 411
Knowsley Hall, Merseyside 771
Lambeth Palace, London 656, 672
Lancaster Castle, Northants (!) 1184
Latimer Abbey, Bucks 1187
Launceston Castle, Cornwall 39, 490
Leeds Castle, Kent 258–59
Leicester Abbey, Leics 264, 277
Levant Castle, Norfolk (!) 50
Lewes, E. Sussex Castle and/or Priory 394, 885; St. James's Hospital 776
Leybourne Castle, Kent 673, 852
Lima Castle, Kent (!) 1104
Lincoln Castle, Lincs 61, 308
Lindsey House, Chelsea, London 681
Looe, Cornwall 822, 834
London, Fulham Bridge 895
London, Mall 664
London, St. James's Park 691; Horse Guards 1011
London, St. Pancras Church 831
London Bridge 864
London Hospital, Whitechapel, London 818
Longford Castle, Wilts 1132
Louth, Lincs 1081; Abbey 211
Ludgershall Castle, Wilts 372
Ludlow Church, Shropshire 1092
Lulworth, Dorset Castle 982; Cove 1020
Lumley Castle, Co. Durham 471
Lyme Park, Cheshire 164
Lymm Church, Cheshire 321, 538, 556

Appendix

Maidenhead, Berks   423; Bridge *1009*
Maidstone, St. Mary's College, Kent   *853, 892*
Matlock, Derbyshire   Baths *172*; cascade *302*; High Tor *152–53, 305*; Lovers' Walk *297*
Mettingham Castle, Suffolk   *390, 422*
Middleham Castle, N. Yorks   *481, 1282*
Milborne St. Andrew, Dorset   *1061, 1083–84*
Milton Abbey, Dorset   *1067*
Minster Monastery, Kent   *753*
Monsal Dale, Derbyshire   *175–76, 504*
Moor Park, Surrey   *1065*
Moor Tower, Lincs   *74*
Morpeth Castle, Northumberland   *379*
Mount Edgcumbe, Cornwall   *193–95, 199, 203, 242, 251, 299, 549–50, 568*
Mount Grace Priory, N. Yorks   *518*
Netley Abbey, Hants   *640, 886, 890*
New Park, Petersham, London   *988*
Newark Abbey, Surrey   *482*
Newstead Abbey, Notts   *235, 403*
Norham Castle, Northumberland   *398*
Northumberland House, Trafalgar Square, London   *1003*
Norwich Castle, Norfolk   *364*
Nottingham Castle, Notts   *307*
Nunney Castle, Somerset   *141*
Nutley Abbey, Bucks   *806*
Oakham Castle, Leics   *893*
Oatlands, Surrey   *8, 119, 410, 553*; gardens *139, 245, 600*; Walton Bridge *140*
Odiham Castle, Hants   *445*
Okehampton Castle, Devon   *467, 797*
Orford Castle, Suffolk   *371*
Orleans House Twickenham, London   *125, 279*
Ostenhanger House, Kent   *698*
Oxford   *940*; Castle *788, 842, 868*; Christ Church College *1156*
Painshill, Surrey   Gardens *304, 435*; islands in gardens *142–43, 599*
Pendragon Castle, Cumbria   *344*
Penkridge, Staffs   *704*
Penrith Castle, Cumbria   *15*
Pilburgh Priory, Suffolk (!)   *437*
Plymouth, Devon   *799*
Pontefract, W. Yorks   'Castle *43*; church *814*
Portchester Castle, Hants   *355, 436*
Portsmouth, Hants   *680, 765*; Castle *764*
Powderham, Devon   *414*
Prescot Glassworks, Merseyside   *766–67*
Prior Park, Bath, Avon   *676*
Prudhoe Castle, Northumberland   *389, 393*
Purfleet, Essex   *936, 945*
Putney, London   *943, 1254*
Ranelagh, Chelsea, London   *685, 857*
Reading Abbey, Berks   *352, 906*
Reynard's Hall, Dovedale, Derbyshire   *830, 863*

Rhostherne Mere, Cheshire   *951*
Richmond, London   *433–34, 677–78, 735, 930, 1012, 1032, 1123–25, 1232, 1236*; Old Palace *428, 824, 836*
Richmond, N. Yorks   Castle *83–84, 675, 1068*; bridge *1277*
Rickmansworth Paper Mills, Herts   *1096*
Rillington, N. Yorks   *1087*
Roche Abbey, S. Yorks   *71, 695, 761*
Rochester Castle, Kent   *278, 432*
Rockingham Castle, Northants   *1183*
Rose Castle, Cumbria   *865*
Rothesay Castle, Strathclyde   *1037*
Royal Exchange, London   *1269*
St Albans Abbey, Herts   *1185*
St Augustine's Abbey, Canterbury, Kent   *668, 1099*
St Botolph's Priory, Colchester, Essex   *667*
St Briavels Castle, Glos   *30*
St Catherine's Hill, Guildford, Surrey   *376*
St Denys Priory, Hants   *1182*
St James's Palace, London   *1268*
St Just, Cornwall   *701*
St Levan, Cornwall   *883*
St Martin's Priory, Dover, Kent   *1176*
St Mary's Abbey, York, N. Yorks   *513*
St Marylebone, London   *948*
St Mawes Castle, Cornwall   *37*
St Michael's Mount, Cornwall   *643*
St Osyth Priory, Essex   *1150*
St Radigund's Abbey, Kent   *782, 903*
Saltwood Castle, Kent   *336, 507, 1281*
Sandal Castle, W. Yorks   *605*
Sandford Castle, Dorset   *20, 447*
Sandwell, Totnes, Devon   *1148*
Scilly Isles, Cornwall   *763, 882, 905, 909–10*
Sawley Abbey, N. Yorks   *519, 597*
Scarborough, N. Yorks   *228*
Shap Abbey, Cumbria   *1039*
Shepperton, Surrey   *934, 964*
Sherborne Castle, Dorset   *252, 461, 525, 1262*
Sheriff Hutton Castle, N. Yorks   *77, 535, 551*
Shobdon Court, Hereford & Worcs   *803, 924, 1142, 1202*; church *1143–45*
Shrewsbury, Shropshire   *876*; Castle *345*
Shugborough, Staffs   *740–41, 979, 1005, 1014–15, 1026, 1028–30, 1078–80*; temple *1088*
Silchester, Hants   *271*
Sithney, Cornwall   *846*
Somerset House, London   *1179*
Somerton Castle, Lincs   *72*
Southwell Palace, Notts   *68*
Stafford Castle, Staffs   *705*
Stainfield, Lincs   *1082*
Stanton Harcourt, Oxfordshire   *484, 792*
Steeple, Oxfordshire   *744–45*

Stogursey Castle, Somerset 90
Stonehenge, Wilts 1140
Stourhead, Wilts 578, 1103, 1165; bridge 1276; temples 1089, 1240, 1275
Stowe, Bucks Elysian Fields 187, 485; gardens 184–85, 188, 205, 208, 212, 214–16, 244, 289–90, 295, 510, 548, 552, 557, 567, 591–93, 610–11, 719, 723, 1117–19; George I's statue 515; grotto 206, 284; House 989; island, lake, Temple of Venus 189; Lord Cohham's column 183; Nelson's Seat 248, 506; pavilions 186, 288; pond 182, 309; temples 529, 545, 960, 1120
Stratford-upon-Avon, Warwickshire 1072; church 1098
Studley Royal, N. Yorks 502, 661, 663, 967–69, 972–73, 975–76, 980, 1073
Sudeley Castle, Glos 356
Sunbury, Surrey 933, 963
Swynnerton Park, Staffs 381, 1149
Syon House, Hounslow, London 647–48
Tabley House, Cheshire 325, 332–33, 651, 780, 1006, 1017
Tamworth Castle, Staffs 24
Tattershall Castle, Lincs 361, 464, 582, 585, 594
Tatton Park, Cheshire 319–20, 758
Teddesley Park, Staffs 706
Tees, River 171
Thetford Priory, Norfolk 265
Thirlmere, Cumbria 247
Thornbury Castle, Avon 357, 845
Thorpe Cloud, Derbyshire 174, 280
Tintagel Castle, Cornwall 261
Tichfield House, Hants 684, 755
Tiverton Castle, Devon 470
Tonbridge Castle, Kent 255–57
Torksey, Lincs 1071
Trelowarren, Cornwall 839, 904
Trematon Castle, Cornwall 819, 867, 881
Trent, River Near Church of Anchor 169–70
Trentham Park, Staffs 317–18, 614–15, 756, 873, 901
Trewithian, Cornwall 775
Tutbury Castle, Staffs 11
Tynemouth, Tyne & Wear Castle 128, 210, 300, 694, 1273; Monastery 52
Ullswater, Cumbria 995
Wadebridge, Cornwall 850
Waltham Abbey, Essex 1136
Wandsworth, London 734
Wardour Castle, Wilts 385
Warfield, Berks Garden 402, 728
Warkworth, Northumberland Castle 268, 1139; Hermitage 671, 1001
Warwick Castle, Warwickshire 669, 816, 1152
Welbeck, Notts 1106
Wenlock Abbey, Shropshire 869–70

Wentworth Woodhouse, S. Yorks 1147
West Acre Priory, Norfolk 649
West Malling Abbey, Kent 477
West Wycombe Park, Bucks Cascade 217; gardens 1, 111, 118, 191, 547, 554, 606; House 124, 990; lake 6, 112, 285; Walton Bridge and Temple of Venus 97
Westenhanger House, Kent 752
Westminster Abbey, London 738
Westminster Bridge, London 1163
Westminster Hall, London 1267
Weston, Warwickshire 1110
Wetheral Cells, Cumbria 1040
Wetton Mill, Derbyshire River Manifold 165, 294
White Horse Hill, Berks 838
Whitmore, Staffs 781
Whitton Place, Twickenham, London 109–10, 503; canal and Gothic tower 646
Widdrington Castle, Northumberland 486
Wigmore Castle, Hereford & Worcs 26
Wilton Castle, Hereford & Worcs 1195
Wilton House, Wilts 98–100, 580, 726
Wimborne St Giles, Dorset Gardens 604, 747
Wimpole Hall, Cambs 1198, 1201; gardens 113, 1207–08; pavilion 1200; ruin 1199
Winchelsea, E. Sussex Castle 341, 483; church 1174; Monastery of Grey Friars 421
Wincheap Castle (?), Canterbury 1173
Windermere, Cumbria 246, 413, 530
Windsor, Berks Cascade 135, 204, 631; Castle 1031; gardens 233; Great Park 562; grotto 136, 204; lake 558, 617; Lodge 96, 220, 232, 460; Moat Island 7, 115; stables 95; Virginia Water 134, 196, 404
Wingfield Castle, Suffolk 446
Winnington Bridge, Cheshire 616
Winster, Derbyshire 687
Woburn Farm, Surrey 116, 239, 520, 543–44, 607, 717; gardens 250; temple 721
Wolveton, Dorset 981
Worksop Abbey, Notts 76, 387
Worsley Bridge, Greater Manchester 1130
Wotton, Surrey Bridge over Thames 777
Wrekin, Shropshire 708
Wrest Park, Beds 1196–97, 1204, 1209, 1211
Wroxton, Oxfordshire Chinese pagoda 1210
York, N. Yorks 555; Abbey of St. Mary 67

SCOTLAND

Ailsa Craig, Strathclyde 1048
Blair, Tayside 491, 565, 714, 1035, 1169
Braemar Castle, Grampian 566, 584, 722
Caerlaverock Castle, Dumfries & Galloway 1036

Appendix

Dalkeith, Lothian *1155*
Dunkeld Cathedral, Tayside *974*
Duntulm Castle, Highland *1053*
Dupplin Castle, Tayside *1050–51*
Edinburgh Castle, Lothian *1034*
Elgin, Grampian *1049*
Freswick Castle, Highland *716*
Inverness, Highland *533, 583*
Inveraray, Strathclyde *1033*; Castle *1041*
Iona Cathedral, Strathclyde *1013*; General view *1052*
Jura, Strathclyde *1043–44*
Kilchurn Castle, Strathclyde *1062*
Lincluden Abbey, Dumfries & Galloway *999*
Loch Leven Castle, Tayside *1042*
Melrose Abbey, Borders *1137, 1271*
Shaw Park, Dumfries (?) *1162*
Staffa, Strathclyde *1019, 1022, 1027*
Stirling Castle, Central *730, 732*
Tantallon Castle, Lothian *1046*
Taymouth, Tayside *1047*
Urquhart Castle, Highland *532, 595*

WALES

Anglesey, Gwynedd *805, 907*
Beaumaris Castle, Gwynedd *353, 386, 827*
Brecon Castle, Powys *351, 450*
Briton Ferry, W. Glamorgan *425*
Bronllys (?) Castle, Powys *349*
Cader Idris, Gwynedd *994*
Caergwrle Castle, Clwyd *399*
Caernarvon Castle, Gwynedd *330, 534, 601, 724, 1234*
Caerphilly Castle, Mid Glamorgan *63, 1168, 1227*
Caldicott Castle, Gwent *368*
Cardiff Castle, S. Glamorgan *272*
Carew Castle, Dyfed *56*
Carmarthen Town and Castle, Dyfed *47, 346*
Chepstow Castle, Gwent *837, 1134*
Cilgerran Castle, Dyfed *338, 579, 614*
Conway Castle, Gwynedd *313, 442, 939*
Coyty Castle, Mid Glamorgan *32*
Crickhowell Castle, Powys *350*
Denbigh Castle, Clwyd *14*
Dinefwr Castle (?), Dyfed *44, 602*
Downing, Clwyd *1045*
Flint Castle, Clwyd *34*
Green Castle, Dyfed (!) *46*
Grosmont Castle, Gwent *430*
Harlech Castle, Gwynedd *343*
Haverfordwest, Dyfed *921*; Priory *452*
Hawarden Castle, Clwyd *35, 454*
Holt Castle, Clwyd *62*
Holyhead. Collegiate Church, Gwynedd *438*
Kidwelly, Dyfed *922*
Llansteffan Castle, Dyfed *45, 569*
Manorbier Castle, Dyfed *266*
Mumbles Castle, W. Glamorgan *1133*
Narberth Castle, Dyfed *58*
Neath, W. Glamorgan   Abbey *1131*; Castle *274*
Newport Castle, Dyfed *59*
Newport Castle, Gwent *443*
Pembroke Castle, Dyfed *57, 531, 563*
Penmaenmawr Waterfall, Gwynedd *1135*
Penrice Castle, W. Glamorgan *31, 573*
Raglan Castle, Gwent *366*
Rhuddlan Castle, Clwyd *33, 429, 938, 1233*
Ruthin Castle, Clwyd *21*
St Donats Castle, S. Glamorgan *359, 1172*
St Winifred's Well, Holywell, Clwyd *1178*
Skenfrith Castle, Gwent *453*
Snowdon, Gwynedd *613*
Starflour Abbey, Dyfed (!) *458*
Swansea Castle, W. Glamorgan *1177*
Tintern Abbey, Gwent *657, 783*
Usk Castle, Gwent *367*
White Castle, Gwent *340*